D0620054

The CD, that originally accompanied this book, has been replaced with downloadable materials. This material can be found by following these steps:

1. Go to http://www.informit.com/title/Your book's ISBN here

   Example: http://www.informit.com/title/1234567890

2. Click on the "Download" tab and follow instructions.

SQL Server 2005 Practical Troubleshooting

The Database Engine

Edited by Ken Henderson

SQL Server 2005 Practical Troubleshooting

Many of the designations used by manufacturers and sellers to distinguish their products are claimed as trademarks. Where those designations appear in this book, and the publisher was aware of a trademark claim, the designations have been printed with initial capital letters or in all capitals.

The authors and publisher have taken care in the preparation of this book, but make no expressed or implied warranty of any kind and assume no responsibility for errors or omissions. No liability is assumed for incidental or consequential damages in connection with or arising out of the use of the information or programs contained herein.

The publisher offers excellent discounts on this book when ordered in quantity for bulk purchases or special sales, which may include electronic versions and/or custom covers and content particular to your business, training goals, marketing focus, and branding interests. For more information, please contact:

> U.S. Corporate and Government Sales
> (800) 382-3419
> corpsales@pearsontechgroup.com

For sales outside the United States please contact:

> International Sales
> international@pearsoned.com

This Book Is Safari Enabled
The Safari® Enabled icon on the cover of your favorite technology book means the book is available through Safari Bookshelf. When you buy this book, you get free access to the online edition for 45 days. Safari Bookshelf is an electronic reference library that lets you easily search thousands of technical books, find code samples, download chapters, and access technical information whenever and wherever you need it.

To gain 45-day Safari Enabled access to this book:

- Go to http://www.awprofessional.com/safarienabled

- Complete the brief registration form

- Enter the coupon code 7FQ5-LMBQ-PHY2-R4PJ-5XB3

If you have difficulty registering on Safari Bookshelf or accessing the online edition, please e-mail customer-service@safaribooksonline.com.

Visit us on the Web: www.informit.com/aw

Library of Congress Cataloging-in-Publication Data

Henderson, Ken.
SQL server 2005 practical troubleshooting : the database engine / Ken Henderson.

    p. cm.
ISBN 0-321-44774-3 (pbk. : alk. paper) 1. SQL server. 2. Client/server computing. 3. Database management. I. Title.

QA76.9.C55H455 2007
004'.36—dc22

                    2006028971

ISBN 0-321-44774-3
This product is printed digitally on demand.
First printing, December 2006

This book is dedicated to all the people around the world who use SQL Server. Your loyalty, feedback, and enthusiasm have helped shape a product we can all be proud of.

Contents

About the Authors

The authoring team is a mix of developers from the SQL Server development team and support professionals from Microsoft's Customer Support Services organization. Seven developers from the SQL Server development team and three support professionals from Microsoft CSS contributed to this book.

SQL Server Development Team

August Hill has been a developer for more than 30 years. For the past six years he has been a member of the SQL Server Service Broker team. He's made a number of contributions to the product in the area of supportability. When he's not developing software he can be found playing guitar or tasting Washington wines. He can be reached at august.hill@microsoft.com.

Cesar Galindo-Legaria is the manager of the Query Optimizer group in SQL Server. He received a Ph.D. in computer science (databases) from Harvard University in 1992. After working for a graphics company in the Boston area, he went back to databases, doing post-doctoral visits in European research centers. In 1995 he joined Microsoft to work on a new relational query processor, first shipped with SQL Server 7.0, which introduced a fully cost-based query optimizer, a rich set of execution algorithms, and a number of auto-administration features. He has been working on query processing for SQL Server ever since. He holds several patents on query processing and optimization, and has published a number of research papers in that area.

Ken Henderson has been a developer for more than 25 years. He has worked with SQL Server since 1990 and has built software for a number of firms throughout his career, including H&R Block, the Central Intelligence Agency, the U.S. Navy, the U.S. Air Force, Borland International, JP Morgan, and various others. He joined Microsoft in 2001 and is currently a developer in the Manageability Platform group within the SQL Server development team. He is the creator of SQL Server 2005's SQLDiag facility and spends his days working on SQL Server management tools and related technologies. He is the author of eight books on a variety of computing topics, including the popular *Guru's Guide* series of SQL Server books available from Addison-Wesley. He lives with his family in the Dallas area and may be reached via email at khen@khen.com.

Sameer Tejani, originally from Arusha, Tanzania, has spent the past 10 years working at Microsoft in the SQL Server group. His work has exposed him to different areas of the SQL Server Engine, including the T-SQL execution framework, Open Data Services (ODS), connection management, User Mode Scheduler (UMS), and other areas. He **is** solely responsible for the infamous "non-yielding scheduler" error messages that support professionals have come to abhor! He is currently a software development lead in the SQL Server Security team. In his spare time, Sameer enjoys being outdoors and going on long bike rides. He lives with his wife Farhat in the Seattle area.

Santeri Voutilainen, better known as Santtu, has been a software design engineer in SQL Server storage engine team since 1999. He has worked closely on page allocation, latches, and the lock manager. A graduate of Harvard University, he is in the final stages of a master's degree in computer science from the University of Washington. Although he calls Seattle home, Santeri was born in Finland and spent most of his young life in Nepal. He is an avid traveler and outdoorsman and spends his free time exploring the Pacific Northwest with his wife and one-year-old son. Santtu can be reached at sql-santtu@vode.net.

Slava Oks is a software architect for the Storage Engine and Infrastructure team in SQL Server. He has been with Microsoft for more than nine years. During the SQL Server 2005 development, project he worked on architecture and implementation of SQLOS. He's made a number of contributions to the product in the area of performance, scalability, supportability, and testability. He is also the author of a popular SQL Server's blog located at blogs.msdn.com/slavao. When he's not developing software he can be found playing sports or having fun with friends and family.

Wei Xiao worked on the design of the SQL Server Storage Engine in Microsoft from 1996 to April 2006. His main areas of focus are access methods, concurrency control, space management, logging, and recovery. He also worked on SQL Server performance monitoring and troubleshooting. He has spoken at several industry conferences, including Microsoft Tech Ed and SQL PASS. He is currently working on a Microsoft internal data storage project.

Microsoft Customer Support Services

Bart Duncan has worked with SQL Server and related technologies for about 10 years. He is currently an escalation engineer in the SQL Server product support group. Bart lives in Dallas, Texas, where he is fortunate to share a home with his wonderful wife, Dr. Andrea Freeman Duncan.

Bob Ward is a senior escalation engineer in Microsoft Customer Service and Support (CSS) based in the Microsoft Regional Support Center in Irving, Texas. He has worked with Microsoft for 13 years and has now supported every release of Microsoft SQL Server from 1.1 for OS/2 to SQL Server 2005. His background in the computer industry spans 20 years and includes database development projects with companies like General Dynamics, Harris Hospital, and American Airlines. Bob graduated with a bachelor's degree in computer science from Baylor University in 1986. He currently lives in North Richland Hills, Texas, with his wife Ginger and two sons, Troy and Ryan. Bob spends his spare time coaching youth sports, cheering for the local professional sports teams, and sharpening his golf game for a dream of playing on the PGA Legends Tour.

Cindy Gross has been a member of the Texas Microsoft PSS support team for SQL Server and Analysis Services since 2000. Cindy has taken on many roles during this time, including support engineer, content lead, and Yukon readiness lead. Before joining Microsoft, Cindy was a SQL Server DBA for seven years, working on SQL Server versions 1.11 and later. She is an avid reader of science fiction and fantasy, with a special love for books starring women as fighters. Her favorite non-technical author is Sheri S. Tepper. Cindy spends many weekends racing her dirt bike—currently a 2004 Honda CRF250X. You may contact Cindy from her website http://cindygross.spaces.live.com/.

Preface

I originally conceived this book as a means of getting Microsoft support engineers to write down the many things they had learned from supporting SQL Server over the years. When I joined Microsoft, I was surprised to learn that much of the practical knowledge related to supporting the product (what those in epistemology refer to as "domain knowledge") that had been acquired by the support people was not written down anywhere. It was often communicated verbally and passed down from person to person via oral traditions.

This, of course, led to people not knowing how to do their jobs unless someone was kind enough to show them the way. It was also extremely error prone. And it led to some of the most important knowledge about supporting the product being concentrated among just a handful of individuals—which worked out nicely for them, but not so well for the rest of the support group.

I had been a fulltime software developer for over twenty years before joining Microsoft. Much to my surprise, I discovered that the upper ranks of the support organization consisted mostly of people who had at one time been developers themselves. Often, they had something in the neighborhood of three to five years of experience as developers before becoming support engineers. As a career developer, it was difficult for me to imagine finding support work truly fulfilling on a long-term basis. Support work, it seemed to me, was something akin to the janitor's job of the software development world. Someone had to clean up after all those messy developers, and that task often fell to the support staff. Although I knew it was important work, I could not personally envision being really happy pursuing support work as a career. Nevertheless, here were several former developers who evidently were. This mystified me.

I began to think about how to level the playing field and make the knowledge possessed by the upper echelon of the support group available to everyone. It seemed to me that the deep understanding of how to support the product, the domain knowledge so prized by the folks on Mount Olympus, should be available to everyone in the organization. Everyone who supported the product should have equal access to it.

My initial thought was that I would document how to troubleshoot the product in the book I was working on at the time, *The Guru's Guide to SQL Server Architecture and Internals*. However, it soon became evident to me that developing software or understanding it from a developer's perspective differs substantially from troubleshooting it. They are really two different disciplines. Although some overlap certainly exists, there is enough that is specific to troubleshooting the product that it warrants exploration and coverage of its own.

When I finally finished my architecture book, I returned to this idea of somehow documenting the many low-level details and insights the support group had learned from years of troubleshooting the product—details not so much about how the product worked, but about how to solve tough problems relating to it. I began to discuss the idea with some of the support engineers to gauge their interest in it. I suggested that we do a multi-author project wherein they could codify their hard-won troubleshooting knowledge in print—not only for their fellow support engineers, but also for their customers. Many had never been published before, and I felt that potentially seeing their words in print might motivate some of them to finally put down in writing what had thus far only been divulged to a select few within the company.

Responses ranged from tepid to enthusiastic, depending on the support engineer. After running down the roster of who was and was not interested in working on the project, it became obvious that I needed more authors to round out the book. There simply were not enough in the support organization who were willing and able to join the project.

I could have gone outside the support group to Microsoft Consulting Services or completely outside the company to MVPs and the like, but I really wanted to limit the author corps to those who had seen the SQL Server source code. There is no substitute for having access to the source code and being able to step through it under a debugger. By studying the product's source, you can come to understand the SQL Server technology at a depth and to a degree that would otherwise be impossible.

So, still in need of additional authors, I decided to extend an invitation to some of the top developers on the product team. Although completely distinct from the support group within Microsoft and focused on developing products, not supporting them, I knew many of these people personally and knew that they had spent a fair amount of their time debugging and troubleshooting complex problems with the product, particularly the parts they had built. You cannot write complex code without having to debug it occasionally, and I felt confident that they would augment the book's coverage of practical troubleshooting in novel and interesting ways.

The response from my colleagues in the product group was roundly enthusiastic, and several of the top developers from the SQL Server team agreed to join the project. I was able to enlist the talents of the very people who wrote the code to talk about how to troubleshoot both complex and commonplace problems with it. You will not find this in any other book, and I am excited to have been a part of making it available to you.

My architecture book tells you how SQL Server works. This book tells you what to do when something goes wrong with it. The former is generally applicable, regardless of what you might be doing with the server. The latter is, hopefully, an edge case (because the product does not break that often), but is something that can make the difference between a SQL Server application meeting customer needs and it going down in flames. Hopefully, you won't have problems with SQL Server. If you do, this book is a good place to begin your troubleshooting expedition.

My thanks go out to my fellow developers on the SQL Server product team who wrote portions of this book: August Hill, Cesar Galindo-Legaria, Sameer Tejani, Santeri (Santtu) Voutilainen, Slava Oks, and Wei Xiao. I also want to thank the support engineers who lent their voices to the project: Bart Duncan, Bob Ward, and Cindy Gross. These people all have their own unique ways of thinking (and writing!), but you could not ask for a better cast of characters to accompany you as you tackle the practicalities of SQL Server 2005 troubleshooting.

Ken Henderson
August 21, 2006

Acknowledgments

Cindy Gross: I would like to thank Ken Henderson for inviting me to participate in the creation of this book. It's been a wonderful experience! To everyone on the PSS SQL Server Data Services team, I appreciate the way you all helped me learn the ropes of clustering. Of course, I couldn't have done any of this without the support of my husband, Pat Burroughs. Pat is always supportive despite the long work hours and phone conversations full of strange acronyms. Last but not least, thanks to our cat Golgothan for chewing through power cords and inspiring the purchase of a new laptop; and thanks to our other cat Serendipity for letting us scratch her back a dozen times a day.

Santeri Voutilainen: I would like to thank Ken Henderson for corralling the chapters of this book; my wife for her love, encouragement, and gentle nudges to start writing; and my son for bringing me joy in a way only a happy one-year-old can.

Bob Ward: I want to personally thank Ken Henderson for coming up with this idea, helping to sell it to Addison-Wesley, and for his incredible patience in reminding all of us over and over when our chapters were due.

I also want to thank my family. First, my parents Don and Annette Gibaud for being an example of responsibility and doing what is right in this world. Second, to my wife, Ginger, and sons, Troy and Ryan. Thank you for putting up with those late nights so I could finish my work on this book. I'm not sure how I would function properly without you Ginger. I just thank the Lord that he brought someone in my life that would put up with me every day. I remain yours for life. And to my two boys, Troy and Ryan, my pride and joy. Forgive me for all of those times I've dragged you outside to improve your pitching mechanics or basketball shooting technique. I just want to see you succeed in something you both seem to enjoy so much. Just remember, I'm a problem solver and it is hard for me to take that hat off sometimes. May God bless you both and remain your source of guidance, strength, and encouragement.

Bart Duncan: Much of what I know about the topic I covered in this book was originally the property of one or more of my coworkers at Microsoft who happened to be generous enough to share their time and knowledge with me. I feel lucky to work on a team that has a surplus of brilliant people who are passionate about what they do. One of these people, Ken Henderson, deserves specific recognition for coming up with the idea behind this book, for finding the people with the right domain knowledge to participate in the project, and for his cat herding skills, which often came in handy as we moved haltingly toward the finish line.

Of course, I cannot express enough gratitude to my wife Andi; my parents Wendell and Lin Alyn Duncan; my brother Lane; and my sons, Walker and Texas Ranger, who have supported and encouraged me over the years in more ways than I can count.

Waiting and Blocking Issues

By Santeri Voutilainen

I will start this chapter on blocking by talking about waiting. Why would I start a chapter on blocking with waiting? Well, the two are very much related, and they are often treated as synonyms. Because they are so related, the SQL Server concepts and tools related to each are intermingled; therefore, it is important to distinguish one from the other.

Conceptually, *waiting* usually refers to an idle state in which a task is waiting for something to occur before continuing execution. This "something" might be the acquisition of a synchronization resource, the arrival of a new command batch, or some other event. Although this description is generally accurate, there is an important caveat: Not all tasks identified as waiting within SQL Server are in fact idle. This is because the waiting classification is sometimes used to indicate that the task is executing a particular type of code. This code is often outside the direct control of SQL Server. In effect, the SQL Server task is waiting for the completion of the external code.

Wait Types

All waits within SQL Server are categorized into wait types. The current wait type for a task is set based on the reason for the wait. Each wait type is given a name that describes, to some extent, the location, component, resource, or reason for the wait.

Although some of the names can be somewhat cryptic (I cover some of these later), others are self-explanatory. The list of wait types is available from the sys.dm_os_wait_stats dynamic management view (DMV). By default, the output from this DMV is not the full list. For SQL Server 2005, the SQL Server product team opted not to include some wait types that fall under one of the following three categories:

- Wait types that are never used in SQL Server 2005; note that some wait types not excluded are also never used.

- Wait types that can occur only at times when they do not affect user activity, such as during initial server startup and shutdown, and are not visible to users.

- Wait types that are innocuous but have caused concern among users because of their high occurrence or duration.

Unfortunately, the omission of these wait types can also lead to concern because the last category of excluded wait types does appear in other sources of waits—namely, the sys.dm_os_waiting_tasks DMV. The complete list of wait types is available by enabling trace flag 8001. The only effect of this trace flag is to force sys.dm_os_wait_stats to display all wait types.

```
dbcc traceon (8001, -1)
```

NOTE

This trace flag is undocumented, and, like all undocumented features, it is unsupported, so you use it at your own risk.

The list of wait types can be divided into four basic categories: Resource, Timer/Queue, IO, and External. The Resource waits category is by far the largest. It covers waits for resources such as synchronization objects, events, and CPU. The Timer/Queue wait category includes waits where the task is waiting for the expiration of a timer before proceeding or when a task is waiting for new items in a queue to process. The IO category contains most wait types related to IO operations. Both network and disk IO are included. The External waits category covers the cases mentioned earlier, where the task is executing certain types of code, often external to SQL Server, such as extended stored procedures.

The list of tasks currently in the waiting state is available from sys.dm_os_waiting_tasks. With regard to waiting, this DMV includes information identifying the waiting tasks, the duration of the wait, the wait type, and, in some cases, additional information about what is being waited for. The DMV also includes blocking-specific information—namely, the identity of the process blocking the continued execution of the task, when the identity is known. It is also the root source of blocking information, so knowing how to distinguish blocking from plain waiting using this DMV is important.

Blocking is distinguished from waiting in that the wait is not voluntary; instead, it is forced on the waiting worker by another task preventing worker's task from proceeding. This occurs when the tasks attempt simultaneous access of a shared resource.[1] This definition is generally considered to exclude the wait types in the External and Timer/Queue categories from indicating that the waiting task is blocking, even though the definition does not strictly exclude the External category. Nevertheless, short sections on both External and Timer/Queue waits are included toward the end of the chapter.

Troubleshooting Blocking

There are three general steps to investigate and deal with blocking:

1. Identify that blocking occurred.

2. Identify the cause of the blocking.

3. Eliminate the cause of the blocking.

This chapter focuses mostly on the first two steps. Because blocking can occur in a variety of components, and the causes can be specific to those components, the solutions often are component-specific, too. Rather than include detailed information on these components in this chapter, I make references to the documentation for those components. However, I have included causes and solutions for some of the more common blocking types.

Note that many of the examples and the discussion assume SQL Server 2005 SP1 (or later). This is particularly the case for the sys.dm_os_waiting_tasks DMV. Several changes and fixes for this DMV were included in SP1. The SQL Server 2005 RTM behavior would have significant differences compared to what is described next.

Identifying Blocking

Identifying Blocking Using *sys.dm_os_waiting_tasks*

In SQL Server 2005, the sys.dm_os_waiting_tasks DMV is the fundamental repository for blocking information within the server. Before discussing how it can be used to detect the existence of blocking, we cover some of its more important columns.

sys.dm_os_waiting_tasks contains three groups of columns: those that identify the waiter, those that identify the blocker (if applicable), and those that provide information about the wait.

---

1 *In general, this requires the existence of two tasks. However, it is possible for a task to block itself. In reality, this occurs rarely and generally results in a deadlock. Its existence can affect scripts used to monitor or investigate blocking.*

The columns that identify the waiting task are the waiting_task_address, session_id, and exec_context_id columns. The waiting_task_address contains the internal memory address of the object that represents the task. This uniquely identifies a task within SQL Server. The session_id represents the user session with which the task is currently associated. The association of a task with a session lasts only for the duration of the task, generally a batch. The blocking task is identified by the blocking_task_address, blocking_session_id, and blocking_exec_context_id. These have the same semantics as the columns identifying the waiting task.

The relationship between the task address and session id columns should be noted. Only sessions that are currently executing a statement within SQL Server have an associated task. However, a task need not be associated with a session ID: this occurs with various system tasks. Because all waiting in SQL Server is done by tasks, it is not possible for a session that is not currently associated with a task to be waiting or blocked. Therefore, the waiting_task_address is never null, but the session_id and exec_context_id columns may be null if the task is not associated with a session. On the flip side, a task can be blocked by either an active task or an inactive session. This occurs if the resource involved in the wait can be held by a session across tasks (that is, across batches). In SQL Server 2005, the only type of resource that can cause blocking and that is held across batches are locks. Note that although some other resources such as memory associated with a session are held across batches, these do not cause direct blocking but are rather represented through proxy waits such as the LOWFAIL_MEMMGR_QUEUE wait type. Locks are held by transactions, and because it is possible for a transaction to contain multiple batches, it is thus possible for locks to be held by a session that has a transaction active while performing operations on the client side and thus would not have an associated task within the server.

The identity of the blocking task is not always known. In these cases, the columns identifying the blocking task are null. This is rather common because blocker information is not available for most wait types—either because it does not make sense for the particular wait type or because the information is not tracked (due to, for example, performance concerns).

As its name implies, the wait_type column contains the current wait type for the waiting task. Similarly, the wait_duration_ms column contains the duration of the current wait. The resource_address column provides the memory address of the resource on which the task is waiting. This is mainly useful as an identifier to differentiate blocking on different instances of a resource when the wait type names are the same. The resource_description column can also provide differentiating information in such cases, but it is only populated with useful information by a handful of wait types—all lock and latch wait types, the CXPACKET and THREADPOOL wait types.

The simplest method for detecting blocking using sys.dm_os_waiting_tasks is simply to run the T-SQL query select * from sys.dm_os_waiting_tasks and treat any row in the output as signifying blocking. This, however, is not very useful, because there will almost always be at least a handful of task wait states from the categories that can generally be excluded from blocking investigations. For example, the deadlock monitor thread usually is listed as waiting with a wait type of REQUEST_FOR_DEADLOCK_SEARCH, which merely indicates that it is pausing between deadlock detection events and is not blocked by anything. The one time this category of waits should not be ignored is if the tasks in these waits are blocking others, which is almost never the case except with the WAITFOR wait type.

Although it is possible to memorize the set of excludable wait types and mentally exclude them from the result set, this is generally not efficient. A view built on top of sys.dm_os_waiting_tasks can help.

The amalgam.innocuous_wait_types view available on the accompanying CD produces a list of innocuous wait types that usually can be ignored. The amalgam.dm_os_waiting_tasks_filtered view uses the helper view to filter out these innocuous waits:

```
create view amalgam.dm_os_waiting_tasks_filtered
as
select *
from sys.dm_os_waiting_tasks
where wait_type not in (
    select *
    from amalgam.innocuous_wait_types)
go
```

Any rows left in the filtered rowset represent tasks that are truly blocked. This set can be further analyzed and narrowed based on the severity, cause, and nature of the blocking. You learn more about this analysis in the sections dealing with identifying the cause of blocking.

Why Not Use sysprocesses or sys.dm_exec_requests?

In previous versions of SQL Server, the DMV of choice for investigating waiting and blocking was sysprocesses. Although this DMV exists in SQL Server 2005, it has been deprecated and replaced by a set of new DMVs. The new DMV that contains the waiting and blocking information from sysprocesses is sys.dm_exec_requests. Although both of these DMVs contain information that you can use to investigate blocking and waiting, there are good reasons not to use them.

The main reason you should not use these views is that they do not provide the level of detailed information that is available from sys.dm_os_waiting_tasks. Sysprocesses and sys.dm_exec_requests display session-level information. This means that they do not contain system processes that are not associated with session IDs. Their session basis also makes it harder to handle parallel queries where multiple tasks are executing under the same session ID. sys.dm_exec_requests displays just one entry for each session. Because of this, sys.dm_exec_requests is not usable when investigating blocking involving parallel queries, because it displays only the blocked/waiting status of the parent task, not the child tasks.

The session-level focus also affects the display of blocker information. Both sysprocesses and sys.dm_os_waiting_tasks display only the session ID of the blocking task rather than the specific task in case of parallel queries.

Finally, the resource descriptions for sysprocesses and sys.dm_exec_requests are not as complete as those in sys.dm_os_waiting_tasks, which provides the most complete set of resource descriptions available. Further, the resource_address column in sys.dm_os_waiting_tasks can be used to differentiate between multiple resources that do not have resource descriptions. With the other two DMVs, these multiple resources could not be distinguished from each other.

Although sys.dm_exec_requests should not be used as the primary source of blocking information, it does contain information that is useful when you're investigating certain types of blocking, so it should not be ignored.

Statistically Identifying Blocking

Sys.dm_os_waiting_task, although a useful resource, is not the only resource for detecting blocking. Statistical information on waiting and blocking is available from several sources. This information can at times prove more useful than current wait and blocking data from sys.dm_os_waiting_tasks because the statistical information can differentiate between occasional and frequent, and short and long waits. Frequent long blocking is generally of much more concern than occasional short blocking.

sys.dm_os_wait_stats
In addition to providing a list of wait types, as mentioned in the first section, sys.dm_os_wait_stats provides statistics for each wait type. The information provided includes the number of times a wait with a given wait type has occurred, the total duration of those waits, and the maximum wait time for a single wait.

A single query over this DMV can be used to identify wait types with long average waits. Keep in mind that no significance should be assigned to the absolute wait counts returned by a single snapshot of the view, because these counts are cumulative since the last reset, which might have occurred some time ago. The wait counts are interesting when measured over a known time span. The deltas between two snapshots indicate the severity of blocking during that interval. These snapshots can be generated manually by running a query over the DMV twice and calculating the difference, or, more conveniently, using the SQLDiag tool that ships with SQL Server 2005.

```
-- Create temporary tables to store the initial
-- and final snapshots
--
create table #StatsInitial (
     wait_type sysname,
     waiting_tasks_count bigint,
     wait_time_ms bigint,
     signal_wait_time_ms bigint);
create table #StatsFinal (
          wait_type sysname,
          waiting_tasks_count bigint,
```

```
        wait_time_ms bigint,
        signal_wait_time_ms bigint);
-- Create indexes for join performance
--
create index idxInitialWaitType
        on #StatsInitial (wait_type);
create index idxFinalWaitType
        on #StatsFinal (wait_type);

-- Create an initial snapshot
--
insert into #StatsInitial
select wait_type,
        waiting_tasks_count,
        wait_time_ms,
        signal_wait_time_ms
from amalgam.dm_os_wait_stats_filtered;

  -- Wait for a ten second delay
  -- This delay can be adjusted to suit your needs
  -- and preferences
  --
waitfor delay '00:00:10';

  -- Create the final snapshot
  --
insert into #StatsFinal
select wait_type,
        waiting_tasks_count,
        wait_time_ms,
        signal_wait_time_ms
from amalgam.dm_os_wait_stats_filtered;

-- Report any wait types that had waits during
-- the wait delay, and the number and duration
-- of the waits
--
select f.wait_type,
        f.waiting_tasks_count - i.waiting_tasks_count
            as wait_tasks_count_delta,
        f.wait_time_ms - i.wait_time_ms
            as wait_time_ms_delta,
        f.signal_wait_time_ms - i.signal_wait_time_ms
            as signal_wait_time_delta
        from #StatsFinal f join #StatsInitial i
        on f.wait_type = i.wait_type
 where f.waiting_tasks_count - i.waiting_tasks_count > 0
order by f.waiting_tasks_count - i.waiting_tasks_count
desc;

-- Finally drop the tables
--
drop table #StatsInitial;
drop table #StatsFinal;
go
```

Note that, as written, the preceding queries exclude the innocuous wait types by referencing the `amalgam.dm_os_wait_stats_filtered` view.

Note that although it is possible to simplify this process by clearing the stats and then running the query, this approach has several drawbacks, including the loss of historical statistics, and the negative effect it can have on other tools that are also using the DMV for wait statistics, including some ISV monitoring tools:

```
dbcc sqlperf ('sys.dm_os_wait_stats', CLEAR)
waitfor delay '00:00:10';
select *
from amalgam.dm_os_wait_stats_filtered;
```

When determining the severity of blocking based on these statistics, it is important to keep in mind that these are aggregated statistics for all waits of each type. For many waits, this might not point to a single resource. Prime examples of this are latch and lock waits. The page latch count waits cover all pages in all databases, files, and objects. The same is true for lock waits.

Similarly, comparing overall wait counts is not as important as the rate of waits (waits per second) or the average duration of the waits. A few long waits generally indicate a localized issue, whereas many short or medium-length waits are more indicative of hot spotting or throughput bottlenecks.

Performance Counters

You can also use performance monitor counters to detect blocking. Some of the information provided by the performance counters mirrors the information available from `sys.dm_os_wait_stats`, but other counters provide information data that is available only from performance monitor counters.

Although the easiest way of monitoring SQL Server performance counters is via the SQLDiag tool, SQL Server's counters are also available in rowset form through the `sys.dm_os_performance_counters` DMV. The data in this DMV is the raw data reflected in the performance counters, so some of it requires some processing in order to be useful.

The Wait Statistics group accumulates counters for various types of waits. The Process blocked counter in the General Statistics group is a useful one that you can use to track the number of blocked processes without needing to query `sys.dm_os_waiting_tasks`.

Notification-Based Detection

SQL Server 2005 includes a built-in proactive method of blocking notification. This is the Blocked Process Report event, which can be captured in a trace and that can be used to trigger code to deal with the blocking or notify operators. This event is triggered when a wait exceeds the specified threshold. The usefulness of this event for monitoring general blocking is somewhat limited by the fact that it only detects blocking on resources that support deadlock detection. Resources that support deadlock detection are listed in Table 1-1 along with the corresponding wait types.

TABLE 1-1　Resources that support deadlock detection

Deadlock-Detectable Resource	Corresponding Wait Types
Locks	LCK_M_*
Worker threads	Any deadlock detectable resource wait types, but generally lock waits
Memory	RESOURCE_SEMAPHORE
Parallel query execution	CXPACKET, EXCHANGE, EXECSYNC
	Multiple active result set (MARS) resources TRANSACTION_MUTEX, MSQL_DQ, MSQL_XP, ASYNC_NETWORK_IO
CLR resources	SQLCLR_APPDOMAIN, CLR_MONITOR, CLR_RWLOCK_READER, CLR_RWLOCK_WRITER

The blocking threshold trigger is set using the `blocked process threshold` option of the sp_configure command. Note that this is an advanced option, so the `show advanced options` option must first be enabled. When the specified blocking threshold duration is crossed, the event is produced. As with other events, you can configure this event to produce an alert or run diagnostic scripts:

```
sp_configure 'show advanced options', 1;
go
reconfigure;
go
sp_configure 'blocked process threshold',
     <threshold-in-seconds>;
go
reconfigure;
```

The event includes a blocking graph similar to that produced for deadlocks. When the event fires because of blocking on a lock resource, identifying information for the lock resource is included in the event columns.

Using the Blocked Process Threshold event is particularly useful to capture unexpectedly long waits on lock and MARS resources. The threshold value should be established after having achieved an acceptable level of blocking by tuning the application and SQL Server. Under these conditions, this event provides a lightweight blocking monitoring mechanism for these types of blocking.

Identifying the Cause of Blocking

After blocking has been discovered, the next step is to identify the cause. The root cause is often specific to a particular wait type, but several shared concepts and operations help determine the root cause.

Current Statements and Plans

Although the name of the wait type and the wait description can help identify the component and resource in which blocking is occurring, the current statements for both the blocked and blocking tasks are useful to have for gathering more information. The current statement for both sessions is available from the sys.dm_exec_requests DMV. This works only for sessions that are currently executing. It is not possible, using DMVs, to find the text of the last batch for a session, although you can use DBCC INPUTBUFFER in many circumstances. sys.dm_exec_sessions does, however, contain the time the last batch was issued. You can use this to determine a minimum duration since the earliest possible start of blocking. Some blocking, especially lock-based blocking, is often affected by the query plans chosen. The current query plan is also available from sys.dm_exec_requests. The amalgam.current_statements_and_plans view included on the CD accompanying this book hides some of the messy details.

For monitoring purposes, it is useful to note that the source of the current statement text, sys.dm_exec_requests.sql_handle, is a durable handle within an instance of SQL Server. This means that the same sql_handle value is always used for the same batch on a particular instance of SQL Server. Note, however, that to retrieve the actual text corresponding to the sql_handle, the batch must be in cache. For dynamic SQL, the sql_handle can even be compared across SQL Server instances. For objects, such as stored procedures and functions, the sql_handle is derived from the database and object IDs, so it varies across instances.

A word of caution is in order regarding the current statement and query plan for the blocking tasks. A blocking task's current statement may not be the actual cause of the blocking. Given that some locks are held longer than a single statement, this is particularly the case with locks where the lock that is causing the blocking could have been acquired by any statement in the blocking task's transaction, not just the current statement.

Blocking Patterns

The output of sys.dm_os_waiting_tasks may exhibit several blocking patterns. These are relatively easy to identity, and their classification can be useful in determining which blocking issues to investigate first.

The first pattern is that of a single long wait. This is characterized by one task (or a small number of tasks) waiting on a unique wait type and resource for a long time. This type of blocking might not have a significant effect on the server's throughput, but it can dramatically increase the response time for the blocked query. Externally the response time delay could have more-significant effects. The following query lists waits that have lasted longer than ten seconds. The threshold level is relative and should be adjusted to the tolerances of each individual system. You can further adjust it to specific levels based on the wait type or some other qualifier:

```
select *
from amalgam.dm_os_waiting_tasks_filtered
```

```
-- adjust the following threshold as appropriate
where wait_duration_ms > 10000
order by wait_duration_ms desc
```

The next pattern is a large number of direct waits for a single resource. There is no extended blocking chain in this case—each task is blocked by the same single task. This blocking may start having an effect on the server throughput, because fewer workers are available to process the remainder of the workload. Response time is also affected for all queries. This pattern is often a hot spot, and because all contention is on a single resource, this type of blocking is generally relatively easy to resolve.

The third pattern is a large number of single waits on different resources. These can be much harder to handle than the previous categories, because there is no clear target to investigate. One option is to do short investigations of each of these waits. This might uncover a common trait between them. When this category is coupled with short wait times, it may be better to use statistical approaches to determining the cause of the blocking.

The final pattern is a blocking chain with multiple levels of blocking. Each level may have different types of waits as well as categories of blocking. This pattern is effectively a combination of the preceding three categories, and, as such, each level of blocking can be investigated separately.

Blocking Chains

As mentioned earlier, not all blocking is created equal. Some forms of blocking affect throughput or response times more than others. One measure of this is the number of other tasks blocked by a given blocking task. Some of these tasks are directly blocked by the head blockers; others are blocked indirectly. Indirect blocking is blocking where task T2 is blocked by T1 and T3 is blocked by T2, so T3 is indirectly blocked by T1 because it cannot proceed until T2 can proceed, which cannot occur until T1 unblocks T2.

Finding head blockers is deceptively simple: Just find all blocking tasks that are not blocked themselves. The task is made slightly more complex by the fact that not all waits have blocking information. Thus, if task T2 is blocked by T1, which itself is waiting but has no identified blocker, who should be marked as the head blocker? In order not to lose sight of this type of blocking chain, it is useful to consider tasks that are blocking others but do not have an identified blocker themselves as head blockers. This is especially the case for voluntary waits such as WAITFOR queries where there truly is no blocker:

```
create view amalgam.head_blockers
as
select blocking_task_address
as head_blocker_task_address,
        blocking_session_id
as head_blocker_session_id
from sys.dm_os_waiting_tasks
where blocking_task_address is not null OR
        blocking_session_id is not null
except
select waiting_task_address, session_id
```

```
from sys.dm_os_waiting_tasks
where blocking_task_address is not null OR
      blocking_session_id is not null
go
```

Note two important aspects about this query. First, it qualifies a task/session as a head blocker if it is blocking some task and it itself does not have an identified blocker—in fact, it may not even exist in the DMV as a waiter. Second, not all waiting tasks without an identified blocker are head blockers. This is the case for wait types that do not provide the ability to determine the blocker, in which case the head blocker may be waiting for a resource, but the identity of the blocker cannot be determined.

You can use the list of head blockers to calculate the number of direct and indirect blockers. This measure is one factor to consider when deciding which blocking chains to tackle first. You can use the amalgam.blocking_chain view to calculate the direct blocking counts for any blocker, and indirect blocking counts for head blockers. The view uses a recursive common table expression (CTE). The indirect count relies on the fact that at every level of the blocking chain, the head blocker information is maintained. Because of the possibility that any given snapshot of sys.dm_os_waiting_tasks may contain blocking chain cycles, the maxrecursion option should always be specified. This option could not be included as part of the view because option clauses are not allowed in views. Blocking chain cycles may exist due to three reasons:

- A deadlock exists, but the deadlock monitor has not yet detected it.

- A deadlock exists, but it cannot be detected, because it involves resources that do not participate in deadlock detection but populate the blocking information. This is the case, for example, with latches.

- No deadlock exists, but it appears as if one does exist (due to timing conditions when sys.dm_os_waiting_tasks was materialized).

```
-- Count of directly blocked tasks per blocker
--
select blocking_task_address,
     blocking_session_id,
     count(*) as directly_blocked_tasks
from amalgam.blocking_chain
group by blocking_task_address, blocking_session_id
option (maxrecursion 128)

-- Count of indirectly blocked tasks for each
-- head blocker
--
select head_blocker_task_address,
     head_blocker_session_id,
     count(*) as indirectly_blocked_tasks
from amalgam.blocking_chain
group by head_blocker_task_address,
     head_blocker_session_id
option (maxrecursion 128)
```

Resource Type Specifics

Beyond the common tools covered previously, much of the details of determining the cause of blocking and resolving it are specific to each wait type. Next, we'll cover some of the more common wait types.

Latches

Latches are short-term synchronization objects. Although originally used mainly for synchronization of physical access to database pages, their use in SQL Server as a general synchronization primitive has become widespread. SQL Server 2005 has more than 120 distinct usages of latches. Certain types of latches are a common source of blocking and, unfortunately, latch blocking is often hard to investigate and resolve (because of the scarcity of diagnostic information available for them). Fortunately, SQL Server 2005 provides much more information than was available in previous releases.

Latch waits are divided into two main groups: page latch waits and nonpage latch waits. Each of these groups can be subdivided into two subgroups. The main groups are the PAGELATCH and PAGEIOLATCH, and TRANMARKLATCH and LATCH wait base wait types, often referred to as page and nonpage latches, respectively. The TRANMARKLATCH group can be treated as any other nonpage latch even though it has the special status of having its own wait types.

In addition to these groups, different wait types exist for the latch mode being requested. The modes for each of these are NL, KP, SH, UP, EX, and DT. (Lock modes are defined in the Books Online topic sys.dm_os_wait_stats.) The actual wait type is formed by appending one of the modes to the group name (for example, LATCH_EX). Of the six modes, three are much more common the others. Waits for the NL, KP, and DT modes are rarely, if ever, seen. The NL mode is in fact never used. Although KP use is common, it only conflicts with DT, which is rarely used, so waits of either are quite rare.

Blocking Information

Blocking task information for latch waits is provided under certain circumstances. This information is not available for all latch waits because latches track information for only certain types of owners so as to remain lightweight. The blocking task information is known when a latch is held in UP, EX, or DT modes. The common factor with these modes is that a latch can be held in only one of these modes at a time and by only a single task, whereas KP and SH latches can be held by multiple tasks simultaneously. It is important to note that the available blocking information is not a factor of the mode specified in the wait type but rather a factor of the mode in which the latch is held. The mode specified in the wait type indicates the requested mode, not the blocking mode. If a latch is held in one of the preceding modes, all waiters for that latch are marked as blocked by the task that owns the latch in one of the preceding modes. Note that the blocking task information may change during a single uninterrupted wait. An example of this is the case in which the latch is held in both SH and UP modes and a task requests it in EX mode.

Although both the SH and UP modes are held by their respective tasks, the EX request is reported as blocked by the owner of the UP mode. When the UP mode is released while the SH is still held, the blocking information for EX reverts to unknown, because the owner of the SH mode is not available.

Grant Order

There are a few important aspects to the latch grant order. For the most part, latches are granted in first-in-first-out (FIFO) order, and any new requests need to wait if there are any other waiters—even if the requested mode is compatible with the granted modes. This is done to avoid starvation of the waiting task. Two exceptions apply to these rules. The first is that KP requests never need to wait to be granted unless the current mode is DT. The second is that when granting waiting requests after a release of a latch, all compatible requests are granted, regardless of their position in the list of waiters. An example illustrates this behavior: If a latch is held in UP mode, the first waiter also wants an UP mode latch, the second waiter wants an EX mode latch, and the following three want SH, EX, and SH, respectively. When the UP mode is released, not only is the first UP waiter granted, but the two SH requests are granted, too, even through they arrived after the first EX request. This does not cause starvation, because no grants are made unless the first waiter can be granted.

Latch Wait Time

The wait time displayed in sys.dm_os_waiting_tasks, and the averages derived from sys.dm_os_wait_stats, for latch waits is misleading. The wait time used in these locations is how long the task has been idle waiting for the latch. Latch waits, however, wake up every five minutes to check for signs of a problem with the latch. This check resets the wait time, so no latch wait ever shows having a wait time longer than five minutes. It is important to note that this does not mean that the logical duration for a latch wait never exceeds five minutes; it just means that this total duration is made up of units of at most five minutes. Although the full logical wait time for an individual latch wait is not available from a DMV, full logical average and maximum durations are available from the sys.dm_os_latch_stats DMV.

Latches were intended to be held for only short durations, and this is usually the case. However, in severely overburdened systems and in a few other rare cases, it is possible that a latch can take an extended amount of time to acquire—it cannot be acquired within five minutes. When this occurs, SQL Server writes a warning message in the error log. This warning is commonly referred to as a latch timeout warning. For nonpage latches, this is a purely informative message. Noncritical page latch waits abort with an 845 exception if the latch request is no closer to being granted than it was at the start of the five-minute duration.

Page Latches

Page latches are used to provide synchronization on physical access to individual database pages that are stored in the buffer pool. Access to on-disk database pages is controlled by the buffer pool; thus, page latches effectively provide access to the on-disk pages.

Resource Description

The resource description in the `resource_description` column of
`sys.dm_os_waiting_tasks` for all page latches is `<dbid>:<file-id>:<page-in-file>`. The
`<dbid>` is the database ID for the database to which the page belongs. The `<file-id>` is
the ID of the file within the database. This corresponds to the `file_id` column in the
`sys.database_files` catalog view. `<page-in-file>` corresponds to the `<page-in-file>`th
page in the file.

PAGELATCH **Versus** *PAGEIOLATCH*

The difference between the two wait type subgroups for page latches is minor. For a given
page ID, waits for a latch may use a wait type for either subgroup. The choice is determined by whether an IO operation is outstanding on the page at the time the latch wait
starts. The wait time is updated only every five minutes during a latch wait, corresponding to the timeout check described earlier.

Latch Mode Usage

To read a database page, at least an `SH` latch is required. Writes to a page generally require
an `EX` latch; exceptions to this rule are internal allocation system pages and versioning
pages in tempdb that require only `UP` mode latches.

Causes of Blocking on Page Latches

There are four main causes of page latch blocking:

- IO subsystem performance

- Contention on internal allocation system tables

- Contention on catalog pages

- Contention on data pages

The first cause manifests itself as `PAGEIOLATCH` waits. This is an indication that the IO subsystem cannot keep up with the IO load. This may be caused by a malfunctioning IO subsystem or excessive, and possibly unnecessary, load on the IO subsystem. When observing
the `PAGEIOLATCH` waits, the first thing to check is the duration of the waits. Very long
waits are signs of a malfunctioning IO subsystem; short durations are more likely to be a
sign of high IO load. In the middle are the troublesome ones that do not clearly belong in
either camp. SQL Server defines a long IO as one taking more than 15 seconds. If such an
IO is encountered, a message is written to the error log. Note that this error message
occurs only once every five minutes for a given file. The message includes a count of the
lengthy IOs seen for file in question during the past five minutes:

```
SQL Server has encountered 1 occurrence(s) of I/O requests taking longer than 15
seconds to complete on file [D:\SQL\DATA\tempdb.mdf] in database [tempdb] (2). The
OS file handle is 0x00000638. The offset of the latest long I/O is:
0x000000ffd00000
```

You can use the sys.dm_io_pending_io_requests DMV to determine where a pending IO is held up. The io_pending column indicates whether the operating system has marked the IO as completed. For long IOs, the next step is to examine where the IO is stuck. If the io_pending value is 1, the operating system has not completed the IO. These cases require investigating the operating system and/or IO subsystem for the cause of the delayed IO. Note that the duration of PAGEIOLATCH waits should not be used as a direct measure of IO duration; this also applies to wait statistics. This is because these latch waits start when someone attempts to wait for the completion of the IO, *not* when the IO was originally issued. Similarly, at the completion of the IO, the latch wait does not end until the latch has been granted. This could be some time after the completion of the physical IO, because there could have been multiple requests for the latch, and later requests would have to wait for earlier requests to be granted first. For similar reasons, the wait count counters for these waits do not indicate the number of IOs that were waited on, because multiple waiters can wait for the same IO to complete.

Many short IO waits are most likely caused by an overloaded IO subsystem. This requires investigation of what is causing the IO overload. One possible cause is lack of memory relative to the size of the application's working set of database pages. Not all pages accessed by an application need to be in memory, but if a significant fraction of the most often used pages do not fit in the buffer pool, they are likely to be constantly read from disk. A related cause is excessive and unnecessary IO activity from SQL Server, such as that caused by table scans on large tables when the query could benefit from an index to avoid the scan. These scans can cause unnecessary thrashing in the buffer pool, which is characteristic of the insufficient memory case. Therefore, it is important to rule out unnecessary buffer pool thrashing due to less-than-ideal access patterns before determining whether more memory is required. The sys.dm_exec_query_stats and sys.dm_db_index_operational_stats DMVs can be of help with this. The former contains counters for both logical and physical reads and for logical writes.[2] The latter contains counters for PAGEIOLATCH waits and wait times on a per-index basis. These stats can point toward queries and plans that perform a lot of IO and therefore might be worth investigation as to whether all that IO really needs to be generated. Similarly, indexes with heavy IO loads can be identified:

```
select sql_handle, plan_handle,
       total_physical_reads, last_physical_reads,
       min_physical_reads, max_physical_reads,
       total_logical_writes, last_logical_writes,
       min_logical_writes, max_logical_writes,
       total_logical_reads, last_logical_reads,
       min_logical_reads, max_logical_reads
from sys.dm_exec_query_stats
select database_id, object_id,
index_id, partition_number,
       page_io_latch_wait_count,
```

---

2 Queries never directly cause physical IO in SQL Server; therefore, physical IO counters are not included. All physical data page IOs are issued by the buffer pool as part of managing the set of cached pages.

```
page_io_latch_wait_in_ms
from sys.dm_db_index_operational_stats (null, null,
   null, null)
```

The remaining causes do not require IO activity; rather, they are caused by high concurrent activity on specific pages. Differentiating among the three requires determining which category the page ID falls under. The internal allocation system pages are the easiest to determine; the others need a bit more work.

The internal allocation system pages are at fixed intervals in each file, so they can be identified using simple calculations on the page-in-file portion of the page ID. The set of pages are the PFS, GAM, and SGAM pages. The first PFS page is always page-in-file ID 1; after that, it is always a multiple of 8088. The GAM and SGAM pages are page-in-file IDs 2 and 3, and thereafter occur every 511,232 pages, which is approximately 4GB worth of disk space per file.

Another alternative for identifying these pages is the latch mode requests. As mentioned earlier, for page latches, the UP mode is used almost exclusively for these internal allocation system pages. Thus, PAGELATCH_UP and PAGEIOLATCH_UP waits can be assumed to be for these internal system pages. These pages are used for tracking the allocation status of pages with each file. Contention on them reflects lack of file parallelism in a file group. Thus, contention on these pages can be reduced by adding more files to the file group. This is especially the case in tempdb. You can read more about tempdb-specific troubleshooting in Chapter 9, "Tempdb Issues."

As mentioned previously, distinguishing between the remaining two causes requires knowing the object to which a page belongs. Although there is no documented way to determine this link, you can use the undocumented DBCC PAGE command for this purpose. As with all undocumented commands, Microsoft does not provide support for usage of this command. Use it at your own risk. That said, DBCC PAGE is widely used. As its name implies, it provides information regarding a database page. Its can write its output in either text or rowset format. The former is more convenient to read, whereas the latter is easier to process programmatically. For the purposes of determining the object associated with a page, you can use the following snippet. It returns four rows, one each for the object ID, index and partition number, and allocation unit ID. An allocation unit is a set of related pages tracked as a unit. It corresponds to the set of pages tracked by a single IAM chain.

```
declare @dbccpage table (
     ParentObject sysname,
     Object sysname,
     Field sysname,
     VALUE sysname)
insert into @dbccpage
     exec ('dbcc page (<dbid>, <file-id>,
               <page-in-file>) with tableresults')
select Field, VALUE
from @dbccpage
where Field like 'Metadata:%'
```

Although contention on catalog table pages is not common in most databases, it does sometimes occur and is a sign of a high volume of DDL operations, because these operations modify catalog tables. This is most common in tempdb, where heavy usage of short-lived temp tables or table variables results in heavy catalog table activity. Contrary to popular belief, table variables are not fully in memory but have the same storage semantics as temp tables. As with contention on internal system allocation pages, resolution for catalog table page contention is discussed in Chapter 9. The key concept is to reduce the number of DDL operations by changing temp table and table-variable usage patterns so that either the tables are cachable or the usages are removed or reduced.

This leaves just user table latch contention. This contention occurs because of simultaneous access attempts on index or data pages in a table. The contention is generally on one or more hot pages. Hot pages are pages that are frequently accessed within conflicting modes, such as a combination of read and write access or multiple concurrent write accesses. Although multiple concurrent read accesess also make a page hot, they do not cause blocking, because read accesses require only SH latches, which are compatible with each other. This means that select queries by themselves do not cause page latch blocking, so the contention is caused by data modifications—by insert, update, and delete operations on the pages.

The resolution for this contention requires examining the reasons for the simultaneous access. This requires examining the table and index schema and data modification patterns. One common cause is concurrent insert activity into an index where inserts are adjacent, or nearly adjacent. Examples of these are identity columns as the first key of an index, or a datetime column that is populated by the current time. Because the rows are adjacent in the index, they are likely to be placed on the same page. Concurrent inserts to the same page are serialized by the required EX latch on the page. This might result in significant contention on the page latch if there are many concurrent inserts. This contention can be further exacerbated by another factor: page splits.

Page splits occur when a new row is inserted onto a page that is already full and the content of the existing page is split into two pages. During splits, latches are held on the page that is being split, the existing next page in the index, and the parent page in the index tree for the duration of the split. The latches are held in EX mode, thus blocking even read access to the pages. A split needs to allocate a new page and thus is not necessarily an instant operation. Attempts to access any of these pages during the split become blocked.

One solution to the insert point contention problem is to reorder the index keys so that the insert activity is distributed across multiple regions in the index. For an index of any significant size, this also distributes the activity across multiple pages. Of course, any changes to the order of index keys may result in application performance degradation, because the index might no longer be useful for the types of queries used in the application. If the contention is on a clustered index, in certain circumstances another option is to replace the clustered index with a heap (that is, to drop the clustered index). This might help as SQL Server automatically distributes heap inserts across multiple pages. Removal of the clustered index might also hurt application performance and should be done only after you have considered the trade-offs between clustered indexes and heaps.

Choosing Which Page Latch Contention to Focus On

It is unlikely that a few isolated page latch waits for a particular table will warrant extensive examination of the table and index schemas or access patterns—it would probably not be cost-effective, and some contention is bound to happen in any busy system. A better approach is to gather statistics based on the table/index affected by the page latch waits. Although this can be accomplished using sys.dm_os_waiting_tasks and DBCC PAGE, it is not a trivial task. Part of the reason for this is that, for programmatic processing, the DBCC PAGE output needs to be stored in a temporary table or table variable. More important, the page ID in object and index ID lookups needs to be performed at the time of the sys.dm_os_waiting_tasks query, because the pages could become reallocated to some other object if the lookup is delayed. Fortunately, the sys.dm_db_index_operational_stats DMV insulates you from many of the details. It contains several columns of interest, particularly page_latch_wait_count and page_latch_wait_in_ms. You can use deltas of these statistics to find indexes that are experiencing significant latch wait times or counts and focus the investigation on those indexes.

Nonpage Latches

In addition to being used for physical access control on database pages, latches are used for a variety of other synchronization needs within SQL Server. In fact, there are more than 100 unique nonpage latch usages. It is not possible to discuss all of these here, nor would it provide much useful information, because some are used extremely rarely. Therefore, I discuss some of the more common ones and provide general guidance for the rest. Although TRANMARK latches have unique wait type status within this group, that is only for backward compatibility, and they can be treated as any other nonpage latch.

Latch Classes

The different types of nonpage latches can be distinguished by their latch class. The latch class is an identifier attached to each latch that indicates is usage scenario. It can be used to group latches used for different purposes. The full list of latch classes is available from sys.dm_os_latch_stats. This DMV also provides statistical information similar to sys.dm_os_wait_stats for each of the latch classes. It is worth noting that latch classes apply to page latches, too; they are the BUFFER latch class. Because of their distinct and important usage, however, page latches are treated uniquely. The names of the latch classes were designed to provide some ability to infer the purpose of the latch or when it may be acquired. The names are generally in two or three parts: component, optional subcomponent, and usage within the component.

Resource Description

The resource description for nonpage latches provides arguably less information than page latches. The format for TRANMARK latches is a GUID. The GUID is the transaction UOW (unit of work) identifier for the owning task's current transaction at the time of the latch acquire. Latches are transactional, so this GUID just provides guidance as to which task acquired and holds the latch. This can be mapped to the transaction_uow column in the sys.dm_tran_active_transactions DMV. For all other nonpage latches, the convention is <latch-class-name> (<memory-address-for-the-latch>). This allows grouping latch waits by latch class as well as identifier and by which waits are on different instances of latches of the same class using the memory address. For example, each in-memory data structure that represents a database file contains a latch, of class FCB, so the address allows for determining whether the FCB latch contention is all on a single file or multiple files. The next logical step is to map this FCB latch to a database and file ID. Unfortunately, there is no way to do that mapping currently, but hopefully it will be considered in a future release of SQL Server.

Latch Class Descriptions
The next sections contain short descriptions of a handful of the latch classes on which latch contention is commonly seen. It is not a comprehensive list. For those that are not listed, the following generic latch investigation steps can be used:

1. Check the latch class description in Books Online, if available.

2. Examine the latch class for indications of what components or what type of statements may acquire the latch.

3. Examine the blocked task's current statement for more hints regarding the latch usage.

4. Use the suffix of the wait type to determine the mode for the blocked request. This will help identify whether the latch is being acquired for shared access—in which case, it must currently be held for exclusive access. An exclusive request implies that the blocked task's current session needs to do some update, and this can provide further info regarding resolving the blocking.

FCB, FCB_REPLICA, FGCB_ADD_REMOVE, FILE_MANAGER, FILEGROUP_MANAGER
These latch classes are all related to various aspects of database file management. FCB stands for File Control Block. The FCB latch is used to synchronize standard database files, whereas the FCB_REPLICA latch class is used by objects that represent the sparse files used for database snapshots.

The FGCB_ADD_REMOVE class is used to synchronize files within a file group. (FGCB stands for File Group Control Block.) It is acquired in SH mode during operations such as selecting a file from which to allocate. Operations such as adding or removing a file from the file group need to acquire it in EX mode. File grow operations also need to acquire the latch in EX mode. A file grow operation thus blocks not only other file grow operations but possibly other allocations, too. Because the latch is held for the duration of the operation, large file grow operations can cause a lot of blocking. For data files, SQL Server 2005 can make use of the Windows ability to instantly initialize a file to a given size, thus improving file growth performance dramatically. These performance optimizations cannot, however, be used for log files or on older versions of Windows. In these cases, the duration of the file grow operation is dependent on the size of the file grow and the amount of other IO activity.

ALLOC_EXTENT_CACHE and ALLOC_FREESPACE_CACHE

These classes are used to synchronize access to caches of extents and pages with available spaces. The extent cache is used by all HoBts, whereas the freespace cache is used by only heaps and lobs. Contention on these caches can occur during extremely high concurrent insert, update, and delete operations on an index or heap where the operations require new space within a page or a new page to be allocated. This contention is not affected by IO performance. If contention is significant, a possible solution is to partition the table so that the insert/update/delete operations are spread across the partitions. This helps because these caches are specific to a single HoBt, and partitions are implemented using multiple HoBts.

APPEND_ONLY_STORAGE_* and VERSIONING_*

These groups of latch classes are related to row versioning. The APPEND_ONLY_STORAGE group of latch classes is used for synchronization by append-only storage units. These are special allocation structures that exist only in tempdb and are heavily used by row versioning to store previous versions of rows. The VERSIONING group is used for state transitions and transaction management.

ACCESS_METHODS_*

This group of latches is used by the Access Methods component of SQL Server. This component handles the access paths to reach data; for example, it navigates the index and heap structures to reach the appropriate rows based on the query predicates.

Individual classes worth mentioning within this group are HOBT_COUNT, which is used to synchronize updates to row and page counters, and DATASET_PARENT, KEY_RANGE_GENERATOR, and SCAN_RANGE_GENERATOR, which are specific to parallel plans. Cache-only HoBts represent HoBts that do not appear in the system catalog, such as work tables, and thus are not persisted across SQL Server restarts.

TRACE_*

Classes within the trace group are used during SQL Server tracing, such as through Profiler. Contention caused by waits on these latches can be reduced by reducing or disabling trace activity.

LOG_MANAGER

With this class, it is important to note that it is not used for basic transaction log operations and thus does not affect mainline log throughput. It is, however, used to synchronize log file grow operations. Thus, an option for resolving contention on this latch class is to size the log file appropriately upfront or monitor log file usage and manually grow the file during slow periods.

TRANSACTION_*, MSQL_TRANSACTION_MANAGER, NESTING_TRANSACTION_FULL, NESTING_TRANSACTION_READONLY

Within this group of latch classes that are used during various transaction-related operations, the TRANSACTION_DISTRIBUTED_MARK latch is unique. It is used when placing markers in the transaction logs to allow for recovery to a named point. There is only one transaction mark latch in any instance of SQL Server 2005. This latch rarely, if ever, encounters contention, and thus there is no need for an extensive description. The source of any contention is also clear, because this latch is used by only a single operation. The other latch classes in this group are used in various transaction contents.

Locks

Blocking on lock resources is perhaps one of the most common causes of blocking. Although much information is available for investigating lock blocking, the process is made tricky by the fact that locks are one of the resources that can be held across batches. This is an important aspect to remember when investigating lock blocking and one that I cannot emphasize enough: *Locks held by a transaction may not have been acquired by the current statement within the transaction.* Waits on locks use one of the LCK_M_* wait types. The suffix of the wait type name is the lock mode requested by the blocked process.

Lock Resource Definition

Locks are acquired on lock resources. A lock resource is just a set of values that identifies the resource. Although these resources are divided into 11 groups based on the logical object being locked, no physical connection exists between the lock and the object. Therefore, it is possible to acquire a lock on an object that does not exist. This is important to keep in mind when attempting to query for additional information on a certain lock resource. The list of groups is available in Books Online under the sys.dm_tran_locks topic. In addition to the lock resource type, lock resources contain database ID and resource-type-dependent information. The size of the type-dependent data is limited, so some resource types cannot store full uniquely identifying information for a particular resource. This means that it is possible to have false collisions between locks for different resources of the same type. It is, however, impossible to have false collisions for locks in different databases or of different resource types, because that information is uniquely available for all lock resources. Some lock resource types also have subtypes. It is important to note that the type-subtype pairs do not form a hierarchy and specifically do not use multigranular locking. Subtypes only further scope the lock resource and are used for resources that are related to the main type.

A lock resource is described in readable form in the resource description of the sys.dm_os_waiting_tasks DMV and sys.dm_tran_locks. Note that the formats of the resource descriptions in these DMVs are new to SQL Server 2005. These new formats are described for each resource type in the section for that resource type.

Lock Grant/Blocking Order

It is often useful to know the order in which locks are granted, because this can help you understand why certain blocking occurs. This order also affects lock blocking chains, because it determines which tasks appear first in the blocking chain. Lock requests can be in one of three different states: granted, converting, or waiting. Requests in the GRANT state have been granted. (That is, the lock is held in that mode.) Requests in the CONVERT and WAIT states have not yet been granted. In both cases, the requestor is waiting for the lock to be granted. The difference between the two states is that in CONVERT, the requestor already holds a lock with a weaker mode on the resource, whereas in WAIT, it owns no lock on the resource. Conversion happens, for example, if a transaction first reads a row, resulting in an S lock, and then proceeds to update the row, which requires an X lock. Note that the update must happen before the S lock is released for conversion to occur. A conversion attempt simply converts (or upgrades) the existing grant mode; it does not result in a new entry in sys.dm_tran_locks when the conversion has been granted. In the following example, the first sp_getapplock acquires an S application lock on the resource amalgam-demo-lock, and the second converts it to an X:

```
begin tran
exec sp_getapplock 'amalgam-demo-lock', 'Shared'
select *
from sys.dm_tran_locks
where request_session_id = @@spid
exec sp_getapplock 'amalgam-demo-lock', 'Exclusive'
select *
from sys.dm_tran_locks
where request_session_id = @@spid
rollback
```

The order of blocking chains on a single lock resource is as follows:

- If a waiter is not the first waiter with state WAIT, it is always considered blocked by the first waiter with state WAIT. This because it cannot be granted before the first waiter is granted.

- If a waiter is the first waiter with state WAIT and at least one waiter has state CONVERT, the waiter is considered blocked by the conversion requests. This is because conversion requests have priority over nonconversion requests, so the waiter cannot be granted until the converter has been granted.

- If a waiter is the first waiter with state WAIT and no waiters have state CONVERT, it is considered blocked by all granted requests with incompatible lock modes.

- A waiter with state CONVERT is considered blocked by all granted requests with incompatible lock modes.

Note that if a waiter is considered blocked by multiple other tasks or sessions, sys.dm_os_waiting_tasks displays each of the blockers in a separate row. This is different from what sys.dm_exec_requests or the deprecated sysprocesses show; they show only the first blocker.

Locks are granted in a relaxed first-in, first-out (FIFO) fashion. Although the order is not strict FIFO, it preserves desirable properties such as avoiding starvation and works to reduce unnecessary deadlocks and blocking. New lock requests where the requestor does not yet own a lock on the resource become blocked if the requested mode is incompatible with the union of granted requests and the modes of pending requests. A conversion request becomes blocked only if the requested mode is incompatible with the union of all granted modes, excluding the mode in which the conversion request itself was originally granted. A couple exceptions apply to these rules; these exceptions involve internal transactions that are marked as compatible with some other transaction. Requests by transactions that are compatible with another transaction exclude the modes held by the transactions with which they are compatible from the unions just described. The exclusion for compatible transactions means that it is possible to see what look like conflicting locks on the same resource (for example, two X locks held by different transactions).

The FIFO grant algorithm was significantly relaxed in SQL Server 2005 compared to SQL Server 2000. This relaxation affected requests that are compatible with all held modes and all pending modes. In these cases, the new lock could be granted immediately by passing any pending requests. Because it is compatible with all pending requests, the newly requested mode would not result in starvation. In SQL Server 2000, the new request would not be granted, because, under its stricter FIFO implementation, new requests could not be granted until all previously made requests had been granted. In the following example, connections 1 and 3 would be granted when run against SQL Server 2005 in the specified order. In SQL Server 2000, only connection 1 would be granted:

```
/* Conn 1 */
begin tran
exec sp_getapplock 'amalgam-demo', 'IntentExclusive'
/* Conn 2 */
begin tran
exec sp_getapplock 'amalgam-demo', 'Shared'
/* Conn 3 */
begin tran
exec sp_getapplock 'amalgam-demo', 'IntentShared'
```

When Was a Lock Acquired?

As mentioned previously, locks may have been acquired by statements prior to the current statement, so the question of determining when a lock was acquired is a common one. Unfortunately, there is no guaranteed way to determine which statement acquired a lock, or even when a lock was acquired. It is sometimes possible to rule out the current statement as the acquirer. You can do this by comparing the wait time for the task that is blocked on the lock and the start time of the owner's last batch. If the lock owner's current batch has been running for a shorter time than the waiter has been waiting, the lock could not have been acquired by the owner's current statement. Here's an example:

```
select *,
case
when getdate () >
DateAdd (ms, wt.wait_duration_ms,
                          es.last_request_start_time)
        then 'yes'
        else 'unknown'
    end as blockers_past_statement_acquired_resource from
```

```
amalgam.dm_os_waiting_tasks_filtered wt left join
sys.dm_exec_sessions es
on es.session_id = blocking_session_id
```

Although this can be used to rule out the current statement, it does not help identify the specific previous statement that acquired the lock. The only way to reliably determine which statement acquired a lock is to examine all the statements executed within the owner's current transaction and analyze them to determine which one(s) would have needed to access the locked resource. This process is complicated by the fact that a transaction may have started earlier than the application developer planned. This can occur, for example, if a previous transaction was not terminated correctly. A simple case of this occurs when the application contains a bug that causes it to erroneously neglect to terminate a transaction. However, a more subtle cause occurs when a statement or batch is aborted and the application assumes the transaction has also been aborted, but, in fact, the error wasn't severe enough to abort the transaction. This is commonly caused by the client sending an abort request to the server. The transaction-related DMVs can be used to help detect cases such as these where a transaction has been active longer than expected. The following query, for example, shows the open transaction count and transaction name and start times for every session with an active transaction. Both the open transaction count and the transaction name can be of use in determining that a transaction has not been terminated properly. The open transaction count is incremented with each begin transaction, so a value greater than expected for the application's current location is a hint of a possible problem. Even clearer is a transaction name mismatch. This is, in fact, a good reason to use named transactions in applications. Here's a sample query:

```
select er.session_id, er.request_id,
    er.open_transaction_count, er.transaction_id,
    at.name, at.transaction_begin_time
from sys.dm_exec_requests er join
    sys.dm_tran_active_transactions at
    on er.transaction_id = at.transaction_id
```

When attempting to match a lock with a statement in a transaction, it is useful to know what lock mode the lock is held in by the owner. A simple way to do this is to look at the mode attribute in the sys.dm_os_waiting_tasks.resource_description. This mode corresponds to the sum of all granted lock modes on the resource. When there are multiple blockers, this value is the same for each of them, even if they acquired different lock modes.

Another technique is to get each owner's individual granted lock mode from sys.dm_tran_locks. To do this, the resource description attributes need to be mapped to lock resource identification information in sys.dm_tran_locks. The resource identification columns are all the columns with the resource_ prefix. As a unit, these columns uniquely describe a lock resource:

```
select request_mode
from sys.dm_tran_locks
```

```
where request_session_id = <blocker-session-id> and
request_execution_context =
<blocker-execution-context> and
resource_database_id =
<resource-dbid> and
resource_type =
<resource-type> and
resource_subtype =
<resource-subtype> and
resource_lock_partition =
<resource-lock-partition> and
resource_associated_entity_id =
<resource-associated-entity-id> and
resource_description =
<resource-other-desc-as-in-tran-locks>
```

Armed with the blocker's lock mode, it is easier to identify the statement that might have acquired the lock. Share-type lock modes may be acquired by any statement. Even DML statements may acquire such locks as part of subqueries or to qualify rows. Exclusive-type lock modes are usually acquired only by DML queries, although regular queries can also acquire them when a locking hint such as XLOCK is specified. SCH_M locks are acquired only for DDL operations that include table truncations. Even queries running under the read uncommitted isolation level or with NOLOCK hints acquire some locks. Specifically, they can acquire metadata locks while compiling the query and SCH_S locks on the objects used. The SCH_S locks are required even under these isolation-level requirements to block DDL operations for the duration of the query. Otherwise, the object could be dropped while the query is executing. Key range locks are acquired only by statements executed under the SERIALIZABLE ISOLATION level. This can help identify the statements responsible for acquiring the locks, because most applications do not make heavy use of this isolation level. Note that the HOLDLOCK locking hint is equivalent to the SERIALIZABLE ISOLATION level.

Although most locks are transaction scoped and are released when the transaction terminates, it is possible to hold locks across transaction boundaries. In these cases, the locks are owned by some other entity. The owning entity is available from the sys.dm_tran_locks.request_owner_type. Cursors and sessions are examples of such entities. For locks held by sessions, the scope of investigation expands to the start of the owner's session. Fortunately, only a limited number of lock types can be acquired at the session level; of those, only two are ever held across transaction boundaries—database and application locks. It is easy to identify which statements would have acquired these locks. Session-level database locks are acquired only by USE statements. Session-level application locks can only be acquired using the sp_getapplock stored procedure. Remember, however, that the sp_getapplock call could be made from another stored procedure. The statements responsible for acquiring the locks held by a cursor are also relatively easy to determine, because they could only have been acquired during cursor operations (for example, FETCH).

Although there is no way to accurately determine, in every case, which statement acquired a particular lock after the fact, it is possible in test environments with a little forethought. You can do this by capturing the Lock Acquire trace events along with Statement Start and End trace events. Note that this can produce an extremely large quantity of trace output and will likely cause performance degradation for the statement and the server, so the Lock trace event should not be used in production systems. Also note that the specific locks acquired depends on several factors, including the query plan and other concurrent operations. Query plans affect the locks acquired, because different plans may examine more or fewer lockable resources while producing the result set. Concurrent access can also result in the acquisition of different or varying numbers of locks. One example of a runtime behavior difference is an optimization used during read committed isolation-level queries that safely skips the acquisition of row locks if there have been no modifications to the page since the start of the transaction. When tracing multiple statements within a transaction, you can also use the Lock Release trace event to exclude locks that are released at the end of a statement.

When using lock tracing, it is advisable to filter the trace output based on the session ID for the connection on which the statement(s) of interest will be executed. This is because even on a relatively idle server, background system tasks acquire locks and cause trace output. Similarly, the trace should be started after the connection has been established so as not to populate the trace with events for locks acquired during the login phase. Also, ideally the statement will have been compiled and cached prior to the traced execution, because this further helps limit the amount of output to examine.

Lock Resource Descriptions
The next sections cover a selection of lock resources commonly seen in blocking situations. It is not a complete list, but the sys.dm_tran_locks topic in Books Online has good descriptions of the remaining resources.

Object
The objectlock resource is used for locking database objects. These objects can be tables, stored procedures, views, triggers, or any other object with an object ID as listed in the sys.all_objects catalog table. Object locks appear in blocking mainly in two flavors— object-level locks on tables that cause blocking and blocking on the COMPILE subresource.

The first step is to determine the identity of the object on which blocking is occurring. The format of the resource description in sys.dm_os_waiting_tasks for object locks is as follows:

```
objectlock
lockPartition=<lock-partition-id>
objid=<object-id>
subresource=<sub-resource-name>
dbid=<database-id>
id=lock<lock-memory-address>
mode=<sum-of-all-granted-owners>
associatedObjectId=<associated-object-id>
```

The non-self-explanatory fields are explained next. The `<sub-resource-name>` indicates the subresource used for this lock. A value of `FULL` indicates that the full resource is used, not the subresource. The `<associated-object-id>` is in fact the object ID, and it corresponds to the `resource_associate_entity_id` column in `sys.dm_tran_locks`.

The name of the object can be retrieved using the `OBJECT_NAME` function. Note that this function operates on the current database, so it must be used from the appropriate database for it to return accurate results, because the same object IDs likely refer to different objects in different databases:

```
SELECT OBJECT_NAME (<object-id>)
```

Alternatively, you can use the `sys.all_objects` catalog. This has the benefit of displaying the type of object too:

```
SELECT name, object_id, schema_id, type_desc
FROM sys.all_objects
WHERE object_id = <object-id>
```

Because of the use of multigranular locking in SQL Server, most statements need only an intent lock at the table level. (Refer to the Books Online topic "Lock Modes" for more information on intent and nonintent locks.) Because all intent locks are compatible with each other, under most circumstances blocking does not occur at the table level. Blocking occurs only if a statement requires a nonintent lock and conflicting locks are held by other transactions, or if the table is already held in a nonintent mode when an intent mode request is made. In both cases, avoiding the nonintent mode lock is the best option for resolving the blocking.

Three nonintent modes are responsible for most table lock blocking. The first are the SCH_M lock mode, the strongest possible mode, which is used for schema modifications. S and X locks may be caused by lock escalation, locking hints, the query plan or relevant statistics operations, or index options.

Index options can result in table-level locks if both page and row locking are disabled on an index. You can use the `INDEXPROPERTY` function to determine whether this is the case. Note that because an object lock covers an entire table, including all indexes, a single index with both page and row locking disabled will affect access to the entire table if the index is accessed.

A locking strategy is calculated for a query when it starts. This calculation determines what locking granularity the query should use. This calculation may determine that even with the decreased concurrency, it would be beneficial for the query to acquire a single table lock rather than thousands or millions of page and row locks. Note that these calculations are biased against table-level granularity because of potential negative concurrency effects. In certain cases, however, a table lock is the best option. Fortunately, a table-level granularity choice is only a best-effect choice—if the nonintent lock cannot be acquired instantly, the query backs off to page- or row-level locking. However, if there is no conflict at the start of the query, the table-level lock is granted. Often, these table-level granularity choices are caused by nonideal or out-of-date table statistics that skew the calculations in the table granularity direction. That said, it is of course certainly possible that the query plan is valid and a table lock is a good choice, in which case locking hints can be used to avoid the table-level lock if the query results in blocking. Either a page or row locking hint can be used.

A related cause of table-level locks are heaps (tables without clustered indexes) and the SERIALIZABLE ISOLATION level. Under the SERIALIZABLE ISOLATION level, any scan of a heap requires a table-level lock for maintaining isolation-level characteristics. These locks can be avoided either by not using the SERIALIZABLE ISOLATION level or by querying a heap through a secondary index rather than directly. Such a query acquires the appropriate locks on the index, and the access to the heap goes directly to the appropriate page and row, thus not requiring a table-level lock.

On the flip side, locking hints can also cause table-level locks. This is the case if the TABLOCK or TABLOCKX hints are used. These instruct query execution to acquire either an S or an X lock on the table, respectively. As opposed to table locks that are suggested by granularity calculations, table lock requests based on locking hints wait until the lock can be granted and thus are much more likely to cause blocking.

The final factor that can result in table-level locking is lock escalation. Lock escalation is the process of a statement escalating from using page or row-level locking granularity to table lock granularity based on a system observation that the statement is acquiring a large number of locks on the table. The trigger point for lock escalation is when a single query has acquired at least 5,000 locks on a single partition. Note that for self joins, each "instance" of a partition is counted separately. When lock escalation occurs, previously acquired page and row locks for the table in question are released after a table-level lock has been acquired. The intent of this is twofold: reduce the memory requirements of large queries (each lock takes about 96 bytes of memory) and slightly increase performance by avoiding the execution of the locking code completely. The attempt to escalate is best-effort; that is, if the table-level lock cannot be acquired, lock escalation is skipped. In certain types of workloads, it is fairly common for lock escalation to occur. Although the only way to determine whether lock escalation has occurred in a particular query is to run a trace that includes the Lock: Escalation event, it is possible to determine statistically which tables are likely to experience lock escalation based on their query patterns. This is done using the index_lock_promotion_attempt_count and index_lock_promotion_count columns in sys.dm_db_index_operational_stats. Lock promotion is a synonym for lock escalation. These counts tell you how many times lock escalation has been attempted and how many times it has succeeded. It is important to note that the attempt count is based on the number of times the lock manager suggests that escalation might be needed. This occurs even before the 5,000-lock-per-partition threshold is reached, so the attempt count should not be viewed as indicating that queries on this index have acquired 5,000 locks on the index but failed to acquire the table lock. A more accurate description is that the attempts count reflects the number of times the index has been used in a query where the transaction has acquired increments of 1,250 locks—the count is incremented every time a multiple of 1,250 locks is reached.

Even though it often has a bad reputation, lock escalation is not always a bad thing. The server supports lock escalation for a very good reason—to minimize the resources used to manage concurrency. However, when lock escalation affects concurrency negatively, it can be avoided either by modifying queries so that they do not acquire so many locks or by disabling lock escalation. Lock escalation can be disabled instance-wide by enabling trace flag 1211 or 1224. The difference between the two is that 1211 disables lock escalation across the board, whereas 1224 disables it only until the lock manager is under memory pressure. Lock escalation can also be prevented on a table-by-table basis with a little extra work. This involves making sure that an intent-exclusive lock is always held on the table. Because both S and X locks are incompatible with an IX lock, lock escalation would always fail. One way to guarantee this is to always start a process at SQL Server startup that connects to the server and within a transaction acquires a lock on the table using an update or delete statement that does not affect any rows. This connection would then need to remain idle. The connection cannot terminate, because that would release the lock. This approach is not always convenient, but it has been used successfully and is useful when lock escalation is desired on some tables but is causing blocking on others. A query like this would work, for example:

```
BEGIN TRAN
DELETE FROM <table-name> WHERE 1=0
```

Object Compile Locks

The COMPILE subresource of an object lock is used to synchronize compiles. Blocking on this resource indicates that multiple tasks are concurrently attempting to compile the same object. Usually, it is a stored procedure. After the object in question has been identified, the next step is to determine why the object is being compiled concurrently by multiple tasks. When the number of such compiles or recompiles has been reduced, the contention on the compile lock is alleviated.

Page, Key, and Row Locks

I have grouped these three resources because they share common traits and are closely related. As their names imply, these resources are used to lock database pages, index keys, and heap rows. Note that key locks are never acquired on heaps, and row locks are never acquired on indexes.

The resource description formats for these resources are as follows:

```
Page: pagelock
fileid=<file-id>
pageid=<page-in-file>
dbid=<database-id>
id=lock<memory-address-for-lock>
mode=<sum-of-all-granted-owners>
associatedObjectId=<associated-entity-id>
Row: ridlock
```

```
fileid=<file-id>
pageid=<page-in-file>
dbid=<database-id>
id=lock<memory-address-for-lock>
mode=<sum-of-all-granted-owners>
associatedObjectId=<associated-entity-id>
Key: keylock
hobtid=<hobt-id>
dbid=<database-id>
id=lock<memory-address-for-lock>
mode=<sum-of-all-granted-owners>
associatedObjectId=<associated-entity-id>
```

The dbid tag indicates the database for the resource. The id tag contains the in-memory address of the lock resource data structure; this is the structure shared among locks on a given resource. The resource_address column for locks contains the address of the lock owner structure, which is a per-lock owner structure. The mode tag contains the combined mode of all granted locks for this resource. For page and row locks, the file and pageid tags provide the page identity for the resource. For these two resources, the associatedObjectId tag contains the hobtid.

For key locks, the hobtid and associatedObjectId tags contain the same value—the HoBt ID of the HoBt in which the key exists. This can be mapped to a table, index, and partition using the sys.partitions catalog view:

```
select object_name (object_id), object_id, index_id,
     partition_number, hobt_id
from sys.partitions
where hobt_id = <hobtid>
```

Unfortunately, the "Row and Key" resource description in sys.dm_os_waiting_tasks leaves out two crucial pieces of information. This is regrettable considering that the DMV is otherwise an excellent and improved source of blocking information. The missing pieces are the slot ID for row locks and the key column hash for key resources. Each of these distinguishes a particular row or key resource from other resources on the same page or HoBt, respectively. Fortunately, it is relatively simple to get this information from other sources. The two options are the sys.dm_tran_locks and sys.dm_exec_requests DMVs. The sys.dm_tran_locks option is more reliable but is more expensive when a very large number of locks are held in the system. Conversely, the sys.dm_exec_requests option may be faster but is less accurate because it includes only the resource description for the main worker during parallel queries. Therefore, the key resource information would not be available if a parallel worker is blocked on the key lock.

The sys.dm_tran_locks option makes use of the sys.dm_os_waiting_tasks.resource_address column, which can be used to join with sys.dm_tran_locks.lock_owner_address to find the row corresponding to the pending lock request. The missing information is contained in the sys.dm_tran_locks.resource_description column and can be included in addition to the standard sys.dm_os_waiting_tasks columns. This additional information is included in the amal-gam.dm_waiting_tasks_filtered2 view:

```
select wt.*,
l.resource_description as
      addition_resource_description
from sys.dm_os_waiting_tasks wt left join
sys.dm_tran_locks l
      on wt.resource_address = l.lock_owner_address
```

Alternatively, the join can instead be with sys.dm_exec_requests:

```
select wt.*,
      er.wait_resource as
additional_resource_description
from amalgam.dm_os_waiting_tasks_filtered wt left join
      sys.dm_exec_requests er
      on wt.waiting_task_address = er.task_address
```

The extra information this makes available for row locks is the slot ID. The slot ID is the ordinal of the row slot on a page in which the row has been placed. Note that the extra column displays the full row ID—that is, <file-id>:<page-in-file>:<slot-id>. For key resources, the extra information is the hash of the index key values for the index row.

A common difficulty with page, row ID, and key resources is that they cannot be easily mapped to the actual row or rows that they cover. The difficulty with page resources is the page resource is a physical resource, which means the set of rows it covers can change. In fact, the page can be repurposed for another HoBt when it is no longer needed by the current HoBt. The result is that page resources have no permanent relationship to rows in a table except as the current storage for the rows. The same is the case for rows that are identified by a page ID and slot ID on the page. Page and Row ID resources can become associated with a different HoBt when a page becomes empty and is deallocated. At this point, it can be reallocated to some other object. The HoBt ID that is provided for page and row resources is extra information that is not always available. This is because it needs to be provided at the time the lock is acquired, and in some cases the code acquir-ing the lock knows only the page ID. As opposed to page and row resources, key resources are logical and are always specific to a particular HoBt, and the HoBt ID is an integral part of the resource identifier; a different HoBt ID changes the identity of the resource. Although key resources can always be matched to a HoBt, they cannot be easily matched to a particular index key, because the index keys are represented by a hash value in the key resource identifier. This hash is not reversible, and the system does not maintain a mapping of hash values to keys.

Although there is no built-in mapping, there are two ways to determine which rows exist on a given page and which rows correspond to a particular row or key resource. For row ID resources, there is also a third option. The first is common to pages, row, and key resources. It uses the fact that cursors can hold locks on the current page and key/row position. Therefore, if a cursor is used to scan an entire index, it is possible to definitively match the row values with the resource identifiers of the resources currently locked by the cursor and then compare these resource identifiers with those that are being searched. Here's an example:

```
declare @key1 keytype1
declare @key2 keytype2
...
declare @page_resource_description nvarchar(512)
declare @row_resource_description nvarchar(512)
-- some page resource of the form
-- '<file-id>:<page-in-file''
select @page_resource_description = ''
-- some row resource of the form
-- '<file-if>:<page-in-file>:<slot-id>'
-- or a key resource hash of the form
-- '(<hash-value>)'
select @row_resource_description = ''
declare find_lock_cursor cursor
scroll dynamic scroll_locks
for
      select <keyname1>, <keyname2>, ...
      from <table-name>
            with (index = <index-id>)
open find_lock_cursor
fetch next from find_lock_cursor
into @key1, @key2, ...
while @@fetch_status = 0
begin
      if (exists (
            select *
            from sys.dm_tran_locks
            where request_session_id = @@spid and
                  resource_database_id =
db_id (<target-database>) and
                  resource_associated_entity_id =
                        <hobtid-of-interest> and
                  (resource_description =
                        @page_resource_description or
                   resource_description =
                        @row_resource_description) and
                  request_owner_type = 'CURSOR'))
      begin
            select @key1, @key2, ...
      end
      fetch next from find_lock_cursor
      into @key1, @key2, ...
end
close find_lock_cursor
deallocate find_lock_cursor
go
```

There are several keys to making this method work. First, the HoBt ID corresponding to the page, row, or key needs to be known. This information is generally available from the resource descriptor in `sys.dm_os_waiting_tasks`; if not, you can use one of the alternative methods. The HoBt ID then needs to be mapped to a table and an index. The table name is needed for the `FROM` clause and the latter for the index hint. This hint needs to be used because the lock resources are specific to an index partition. Although including nonkey columns in the projection does not break the algorithm, it can make the search slower, because the index covers the query, and therefore the extra columns need to be retrieved from the base table.

Although the sample code does not demonstrate this, it is possible to terminate the loop early after all matching rows have been found. The termination case for row IDs and keys is obvious: only one row can match the lock resource, so, after that row has been seen, there is no need to continue searching. For pages, the termination case relies on the fact that the index is scanned in order, which means the same page is not visited twice during the scan. Therefore, if a matching page resource has been seen and the current page resource no longer matches, all rows on the page have been seen.

Note that it is theoretically possible to have multiple distinct index keys that hash to the same value. This is rare. The size of the hash is 6 bytes, which mathematically means that only in a HoBt with more than 2^{48} unique keys is such a collision guaranteed to occur. It is, however, theoretically possible to have such a false collision with just two keys. If a hash collision is suspected, the termination condition of the search can be removed to search the entire index. An output with more than two rows indicates that a collision has occurred. The effect of a collision is that attempts to lock two rows with distinct keys will conflict. Again, this false conflict is extremely rare, and other causes of blocking should be investigated before focusing on this remote possibility.

It is possible that the scan will not find any qualifying rows. This does not mean the process is broken, but rather that the row/key/page no longer exists in the HoBt. This occurs if the row has been deleted or moved or the page has been deallocated. It is also not possible to use this method while the blocking being investigated is occurring, because it relies on the ability to acquire locks on rows and pages in the index.

The second option for row and key resources is to use the `%%lockres%%` virtual column. This column contains the key hash or the row ID for index keys and heap rows, respectively. As with the cursor, an index hint is required, because `%%lockres%%` displays values for the index used. Note that this results in a full table scan unless a predicate is provided. Also, in contrast to the cursor method, this scan cannot be terminated early. The content of the virtual column matches the content of the `sys.dm_tran_locks.resource_description` column for key and row ID resources. You can use this method even when blocking is occurring by specifying the `NOLOCK` locking hint. The virtual column can produce the resource identifiers without needing to acquire the locks.

The other alternative for finding all rows on a page, and the third option for row IDs, is to use `DBCC PAGE`, which can be instructed to display the rows on the page:

```
dbcc page (1, 1, 19, 3) with tableresults
```

When using DBCC PAGE, it is important to verify that the page still belongs to the expected HoBt. This can be done by verifying the HoBt ID from the output by comparing the object, index, and partition IDs or names. The rows on the page are output in slot ID order. The Field column contains the column names, and the Value column contains the column's content. You can also use this method when blocking exists.

Range Locks

When using SERIALIZABLE ISOLATION level, it is important to understand the behavior of range locks. Range locks apply only to KEY locks. In SQL Server, key range locks are implemented as a special lock mode. Each range lock mode consists of two lock modes: a range mode and a specific key mode. The range mode covers the range from the key resource on which the lock is placed to the next lesser key value in the index. This range portion is exclusive of both key resources. The key portion covers the key on which the lock is placed. Thus, the combined mode is inclusive of the high key value and exclusive of the low key value. To lock the range from the highest index key to infinity, a special key resource is used. This key resource contains a hash value of FFFFFFFFFFFF and represents the infinity key. Any operations on key values that would exist between two existing keys coordinate with key range locking by attempting to acquire a lock on the next greater existing key. This design means that the range of key values covered by a key range lock depends on the existing keys in the index, and the number of key range locks required to lock a specific range depends on the number of existing keys within that range. Note that a key value considered existing for key range locking need not be visible to queries—keys that have been logically but not physically deleted from the index, such as ghosted records, qualify.

The key range behavior can lead to confusing situations where it appears an operation should not succeed but actually becomes blocked because of range locking. The rules for acquiring range locks are explained next.

When a predicate defines exactly one matching key, no range locks are acquired. This is because if there can be only one key with the specified values, the index must be unique, and any attempt to insert another matching key would violate the uniqueness predicate.

When a predicate may match multiple keys, range locks must be acquired for all ranges that could match the predicate. Range locks must obviously be acquired on existing keys that match the criteria. These range locks cover the range from the matching key to the next lower key. In addition, a lock must be acquired on the first key higher than the last matching key. This range lock is required to cover the range above the last existing key that currently qualifies.

The need to lock the next higher key may unexpectedly block attempts to access that range. For example, a query such as

```
select * from demo_table where a <= 4
```

would not intuitively require a lock on a key value of 10. But if only rows with a = 3 and a = 10 exist, to block inserts of keys with a = 4, the range from 3 to 10 must be locked. Therefore, take care not to miss this type of query when attempting to match locks to statements that may have acquired them.

External Wait Types

As mentioned at the beginning of this chapter, external wait types do not always indicate that the task is idle; instead, they are often used to indicate that SQL Server is executing code that may be outside its direct control. A prime example of this is an extended stored procedure call. Extended stored procedures can be written by users or third parties, and SQL Server does not have direct control over what they do. Therefore, to provide better task state information, the task is marked, for the duration of the call, as waiting for the external code to complete. This design allows for the side benefit of providing statistics on the duration of these calls—the total wait time and wait counter in sys.dm_os_waits_stats can be used to determine the average duration of these calls. Four wait types fall under this category:

- MSQL_DQ. This indicates that the task is executing a distributed query. The execution of the distributed query is outside of SQL Server's control, so the task is marked as waiting for the completion of the distributed query. Further investigation of these waits requires determining the destination of the distributed query and applying the tools available on the remote side. The destination can often be determined by examining the current statement, because it will likely be using a linked server or an ad-hoc method such as OPENROWSET or OPENDATASOURCE.

- MSQL_XP. This wait type occurs when a task is executing an extended stored procedure (XP). SQL Server does not have control over an XP even though it is executing within the SQL Server process. Investigation of these waits requires investigating the execution of the extended stored procedure code—the vendor may have provided diagnostic tools for the XP. If such tools are not available and the source code of the XP is not available and the documentation does not provide other troubleshooting information, contacting the vendor may be the only option.

- MSSEARCH. Full-text operations use this wait type to indicate that the task is processing such an operation.

- OLEDB. As its name implies, this wait type is used during calls to the Microsoft SQL Native Client OLEDB provider. It is also used during synchronization of certain full-text operations. Internally in SQL Server, DMVs are implemented as special OLEDB calls, and therefore any task executing a DMV-based query appears to be waiting with this wait type.

Timer and Queue Wait Types

The wait types that fall under this category do not indicate blocking. They are used by tasks for two main purposes: waiting for timers to expire before performing some periodic operation or to delay or throttle execution, and waiting for work packets for processing on a queue. Both are used almost exclusively by background system processes. Similarly, while idle with these wait types, tasks hardly ever hold any other resources on which other tasks could become blocked. Because of the nature of how these wait types are used, their associated wait times and counts can be extremely large. These high values can cause concern at first sight; however, they are perfectly normal:

- **BAD_PAGE_PROCESS.** This is used by a background bad page detection process to throttle its execution when running continuously for more than five seconds.

- **BROKER_TRANSMITTER.** When the service broker message transmitter has no messages to be processed, it waits on a queue for more work.

- **CHECKPOINT_QUEUE.** The database checkpoint task operates on a periodic basis. Instead of spawning a new task at every checkpoint interval, SQL Server uses a dedicated task that uses this wait type to indicate that it is waiting for the next interval, or for a new explicit checkpoint request.

- **DBMIRROR_EVENTS_QUEUE.** The database mirroring component uses this wait type when its work queue is empty.

- **LAZYWRITER_SLEEP.** This wait type is used by the background lazywriter tasks when they are suspended between work intervals. Lazywriter tasks write dirty data pages back to disk in a lazy manner; in other words, they attempt to not flood the disk subsystem with a large number of IOs.

- **ONDEMAND_TASK_QUEUE.** Long wait times on this wait type simply indicate that there have been no high-priority on-demand system tasks to execute. Although some background tasks, such as the deadlock monitor and checkpoint, have dedicated tasks, others share a pool of worker threads. These tasks are divided into high and low priority. The scheduler for these tasks uses this wait type when waiting for high-priority requests to arrive.

- **REQUEST_FOR_DEADLOCK_SEARCH.** The deadlock monitor is another background task that operates on a periodic basis and has a dedicated worker thread. In addition to period deadlock searches, other tasks can explicitly request a deadlock search. The deadlock monitor uses this wait type while waiting for the timer to expire or for explicit requests to arrive.

- **WAITFOR.** This is the one timer wait type that can occur while the task holds resources that could block other tasks. This is because this wait type is used for the WAITFOR T-SQL statement and thus is user-controlled. Any resources held by the connection when it executes a WAITFOR statement are held for the duration of the statement. Especially when a WAITFOR is executed within the context of a transaction, there is a risk that such resources are held.

- **LOGMGR_QUEUE.** The log write background thread waits on its work packet queue when it has no current work to do.

- **KSOURCE_WAKEUP.** When SQL Server is running as a service, a task is dedicated for responding to requests from the Service Control Manager. While waiting for such requests, the task is marked with this wait type.

- **SQLTRACE_BUFFER_FLUSH.** A dedicated worker is used for flushing trace buffers. This worker runs periodically, and between executions it idles with this wait type.

- **BROKER_EVENTHANDLER.** The Service Broker main event handler waits on its event queue using this wait type. The documentation for this wait type is somewhat misleading in Books Online, because it claims the duration should not last long; but in fact on an idle system or a system that does not use the Service Broker, this value is large by design.

- **DBMIRRORING_CMD.** As its name implies, database mirroring uses this wait type for a command queue.

IO Wait Types

There are several IO-related wait types. These wait types do not occur because of regular database page IO operations, because those are covered by the PAGEIOLATCH set of wait types. These other IO-related wait types apply to various other IO operations, such as log IOs, and can be either disk or network IO operations.

The LOGBUFFER and WRITELOG wait types are related to transaction logging. The latter occurs when tasks are waiting for a log flush to complete. This occurs most often during transaction commits where it is needed to maintain durability of transactions. Long wait times for this wait type generally indicate that the log disk cannot support the log volume being produced. Resolving these waits requires investigating the cause for the log disk performance problems. A common cause is having the transaction log on a shared drive. This limits the maximum performance levels, especially when the disk is used for random-access IO, such as data files. Log files are written sequentially and thus perform best when the underlying disk also can write sequentially. For highly active databases, it might be necessary to have a dedicated disk for the log. The cause of LOGBUFFER waits is similar; it occurs when no buffers are available in which to write a log record. There are a limited number of these buffers, and their unavailability indicates that the existing ones have not yet been written to the log file, allowing them to be reused.

DISKIO_SUSPEND and REQUEST_DISPENSER_PAUSE are related to external backups that freeze system IO for a moment while making a backup of the database files or drives.

Database snapshots store old copies of database pages in sparse files. Access to these pages can result in IO, which is reported with the FCB_REPLICA_READ, FCB_REPLICA_WRITE, and REPLICA_WRITES wait types. The first two indicate that multiple tasks are attempting to access the same pages in the database snapshots. The latter one occurs when a nonsnapshot statement needs to push out old copies of pages before updating the current version.

A long ASYNC_NETWORK_IO wait type is often caused by the client not processing results from the server. This causes the network buffers to fill. The server cannot send more data to the client, so the task executing the batch needs to pause while waiting for the ability to continue sending results. The fix is to change the client so that it does not leave a partially fetched result set open.

Other IO-related wait types are `ASYNC_IO_COMPLETION`, `DBMIRROR_SEND`, `IMPPROV_IOWAIT`, `IO_COMPLETION`, `SOAP_READ`, and `SOAP_WRITE`. Note that `BACKUPIO` and `IO_AUDIT_MUTEX` are not related to IO performance.

Other Wait Types

- `CMEMTHREAD`. This wait type occurs during synchronization of access to shared memory objects. This wait type was somewhat common in SQL Server 2000 during heavy query cache insert/delete activity because the memory for all cached query plans came from the same memory object. This has been improved in SQL Server 2005, but it can still occur. More information on memory-related investigations is available in Chapter 3, "Memory Issues."

- Parallel query wait types. Several wait types related to parallel queries are worth identifying. The `CXPACKET` wait type occurs when the parallel workers synchronize on a query processor exchange operator to transmit data between each other. It can indicate an imbalance in the work being performed by the tasks, and lowering the degree of parallelism may help alleviate the problem. The `EXCHANGE` and `EXECSYNC` wait types have similar causes. `QUERY_EXECUTION_INDEX_SORT_EVENT_OPEN` occurs during parallel index build operations.

- `MISCELLANEOUS`. Although common in past versions of SQL Server, this wait type should be less common in SQL Server 2005. As the name suggests, it indicates that a task is waiting for some miscellaneous reason. In SQL Server 2005, most of these unusual cases have been converted to more descriptive wait types, but several are still grouped under the `MISCELLANEOUS` wait type. Of these, two are worth mentioning. The first is synchronization for the `NEWSEQUENTIALID` built-in function. The other is synchronization of `CLR` assembly loads. Because these usages get clumped with each other in the `MISCELLANEOUS` bucket, it is not possible to differentiate between them without examining the statements being executed by the sessions.

- `THREADPOOL`. This wait type occurs when there are more concurrent work requests than there are workers to execute these requests. The waiting requests cannot be processed until a currently executing request completes. Depending on the expected usage levels of a system, this might indicate that the Max Workers configuration setting is too low. Whether this is the case depends on whether the currently executing requests are completing in the expected duration. Unusually long delays during the execution of requests can cause the worker pool to run out. If this is not the case, you can resolve `THREADPOOL` waits by increasing the Max Workers setting. However, if current statements are taking longer than average (for example, when some other blocking is causing long waits), increasing the Max Workers setting is likely to bring only temporary, if any, relief. This is because although more requests can be executed with the increased worker pool, it is likely that these requests will also execute slowly or become blocked and thus deplete the worker pool. Therefore, the key to dealing with `THREADPOOL` waits is to investigate and eliminate any other blocking that might be occurring.

Waits on THREADPOOL can be quite overwhelming in sys.dm_os_waiting_tasks because SQL Server SP1 considers all currently executing tasks as blocking the waiting request. This results in a large amount of output. The majority of this output can be ignored in favor of noting that a request is waiting for a worker to become available.

- SOS_SCHEDULER_YIELD. SQL Server uses cooperative scheduling. Under this scheduling model, workers are not arbitrarily interrupted by the system but are instead allowed to execute until they are forced to enter a wait state due to the unavailability of a resource or they yield voluntarily to allow other workers to execute. When a worker voluntarily yields to another worker, the yielding worker becomes idle and is effectively waiting for its turn to execute. The wait type used for this voluntary wait is the SOS_SCHEDULER_YIELD wait type, which indicates that the task yielded the scheduler and is waiting for access again. This is an expected wait type and should not be of concern; it simply indicates that the task is being a good cooperative player.

  Waits with this wait type populate the blocking task columns with the identity of the task that is currently executing on the scheduler. Until that task yields the scheduler, the blocked task will not be able to run.

A BIT OF TRIVIA

The wait type documentation in Books Online lists quite a few wait types as "Internal Only." This means that these wait types are not used in SQL Server 2005.

Deadlocks

Up to this point, I have not made much mention of deadlocks even though deadlocks are considered by many to be the ultimate in blocking. This has been intentional. In the final analysis, deadlocks are just cases of blocking that form a blocking chain with a cycle. This means that nearly everything that has been covered thus far is applicable to determining the cause and finding a resolution to deadlocks. This may sound a bit simplistic, and in certain respects it is, because deadlock avoidance may require more extensive modification than blocking avoidance. An example of this is reordering access to resources so that they are accessed in the same order so as to prevent deadlocks. However, both blocking and deadlocks can be lessened by holding resources for shorter durations, but neither is completely eliminated, because an increase in the workload could cause the blocking and deadlocking to become more prevalent.

The new deadlock output in SQL Server 2005 is far superior to the output available in previous versions. Collecting the new output does require changes to existing deadlock graph collection scripts, because it is enabled by a new trace flag. This trace flag is 1222. As with the old trace flag, the output is sent to the error log. This output can also be captured in traces, and the Profiler tool can display the deadlock graph in graphical format, which can also be saved as an XML file for more detailed analysis.

Among the improvements in the SQL Server 2005 deadlock output are the inclusion of session state, the start time of the current statement, and the transaction isolation level. Object IDs are also resolved to names when possible. The current statements of each participant are now more detailed, because they include a T-SQL call stack that shows the stored procedures and other objects in the current execution location. In addition, the SQL handle is available, so it can be used to query DMVs related to queries such as `sys.dm_exec_sql_text` and `sys.dm_exec_query_stats`.

Monitoring Blocking

The preceding sections have focused first on detecting that blocking is occurring and second on identifying the cause and possible resolutions. They have been geared more toward interactive investigations. However, it is generally not possible to dedicate a database operator to continuous active monitoring of a system. It would also not be efficient. This calls for a way to monitor blocking where alerts can be raised when blocking is encountered or the proper information gets collected automatically. To achieve this, many of the scripts from earlier sections, and some additional ones, can be rolled into a collection that can be run via SQLDiag to monitor blocking and collect the appropriate data. I have included here several script snippets and explanations as to why I would include them in a monitoring script. These can be used to build monitoring stored procedures such as `sp_blocker_pssNNN` used by SQLDiag and also available from the Microsoft website. As mentioned previously, SQLDiag is now included as part of SQL Server. This tool can collect many of the data points included here out of the box and can be extended to include custom scripts. The level of monitoring can be customized based on specific needs and the availability of CPU cycles to execute the scripts. This is an important concern because some of these script snippets can be somewhat expensive to run or might produce a lot of output that must then be analyzed.

Wait Statistics

It's always useful to collect wait statistics. These are low-impact queries. Filtering out the innocuous wait types and any zero statistics greatly reduces the output and makes it easier to review. Here's a sample query:

```
select *
from amalgam.dm_os_wait_stats_filtered
select *
from sys.dm_os_latch_stats
where waiting_requests_count <> 0
```

Current Wait Information

Various queries can be run against sys.dm_os_waiting_tasks to collect information on current waiters. The cheapest option is to just include the entire contents of sys.dm_os_waiting_tasks, or amalgam.dm_os_waiting_tasks_filtered, like this:

```
select * from sys.dm_os_waiting_tasks
select * from amalgam.dm_os_waiting_tasks_filtered
select * from amalgam.dm_os_waiting_tasks_filtered2
```

A slightly enhanced version includes the current statements and plans for the waiting tasks:

```
select
     amalgam.current_statement (
          st.dbid, st.objectid, st.encrypted,
st.text,
          er.statement_start_offset,
          er.statement_end_offset)
          as current_statement,
          qp.query_plan,
     wt.*
from amalgam.dm_os_waiting_tasks_filtered wt
     left join sys.dm_exec_requests er
          on wt.waiting_task_address = er.task_address
     outer apply
sys.dm_exec_sql_text (er.sql_handle) st
          outer apply
sys.dm_exec_query_plan (er.plan_handle) qp
```

And a further enhancement includes the blocking task's current statement and plan. Remember: Locks might have been acquired by a statement other than the current statement:

```
select
     amalgam.current_statement (
          st.dbid, st.objectid, st.encrypted,
st.text,
          er.statement_start_offset,
          er.statement_end_offset)
     as waiters_current_statement,
          qp.query_plan,
     amalgam.current_statement (
          stb.dbid, stb.objectid, stb.encrypted,
          stb.text,
          erb.statement_start_offset,
          erb.statement_end_offset)
     as blockers_current_statement,
          qp.query_plan,
     wt.*
from amalgam.dm_os_waiting_tasks_filtered wt
```

```
        left join sys.dm_exec_requests er
            on wt.waiting_task_address = er.task_address
        outer apply
sys.dm_exec_sql_text (er.sql_handle) st
            outer apply
sys.dm_exec_query_plan (er.plan_handle) qp
        left join sys.dm_exec_requests erb
            on wt.blocking_task_address =
                    erb.task_address
        outer apply
sys.dm_exec_sql_text (erb.sql_handle) stb
            outer apply
sys.dm_exec_query_plan (erb.plan_handle) qpb
```

These, however, require manual analysis of potentially verbose output. This can be eased by analyzing some of the information at the time of collection.

Often, it is useful to find the hottest resources or wait types. The following queries find all resources and wait types with at least five waiters:

```
select resource_description,
        additional_resource_description,
        count(*)
from amalgam.dm_os_waiting_tasks_filtered2
where resource_description is not null
group by resource_description, additional_resource_description
having count (*) > 5
select wait_type, count(*)
from amalgam.dm_os_waiting_tasks_filtered
group by wait_type
having count (*) > 5
```

Long waiters are generally of more concern than short-duration waiters, so it might be useful to call them out; let's see all waiters that have been waiting more than 10 seconds:

```
select *
from amalgam.dm_os_waiting_tasks_filtered
where wait_duration_ms > 10000
order by wait_duration_ms desc
```

The blocking chain also has some interesting information available (for example, head blockers that are blocking a large number of other tasks, and the chains themselves):

```
select head_blocker_task_address,
        head_blocker_session_id,
        count(*)
from amalgam.blocking_chain
group by head_blocker_task_address,
        head_blocker_session_id
having count(*) > 10
```

```
order by count(*) desc
option (maxrecursion 128)
select *
from amalgam.blocking_chain
option (maxrecursion 128)
```

The index operational statistics are also useful to have when looking for tables with high latch or lock waits:

```
select top 20 *
from sys.dm_db_index_operational_stats (
null, null, null, null)
order by page_latch_wait_count +
     page_io_latch_wait_count desc
select top 20 *
from sys.dm_exec_query_stats
order by
     (total_physical_reads +
total_logical_reads +
total_logical_writes) /
     execution_count desc
```

These are a sampling of queries that can prove useful in monitoring and then investigating blocking. Again, much of this can be easily collected using SQL Server's SQLDiag tool. Obviously, the more information that is available, the easier it is to investigate, but the costlier it is to monitor. The balance depends largely on the extra load that the system can handle without adversely affecting throughput and response times of actual application work.

Conclusion

Blocking is one of those issues that can touch many aspects of SQL Server. Although investigating blocking benefits from an understanding of how SQL Server works, it is also a good way to learn even more about the server. Of course, the immediate need to resolve blocking is often more important than learning more about the server. The intent of this chapter was to provide you with the tools and knowledge you need to face those situations when the phone is ringing off the hook on Monday morning because system performance has dropped through the floor due to heavy blocking.

And, remember that the locks in blocking you see might not have been acquired in the blocker's current statement. Look at the previous statements in the transaction; it might be immediately obvious why the locks are being held.

Other Resources

Quite a few resources deal with SQL Server blocking. Here is a sampling of some resources:

- Microsoft SQL Server Books Online. The descriptions of wait types and latch types are improving with every web release. The DMV documentation is also worth looking at.

- SQL Server Storage Engine Blog (http://blogs.msdn.com/sqlserverstorageengine/default.aspx)

- MSDN blogs in general (http://blogs.msdn.com—search for SQL and Blocking)

- *The Guru's Guide to SQL Server Architecture and Internals*, by Ken Henderson

Data Corruption and Recovery Issues

By Bob Ward

All the troubleshooting concepts discussed in this chapter relate to one common goal: protection and recovery of your most important asset—*your data*!

What is the key to recovering your data? The answer is simple. Restore from a valid backup. But you bought this book to find out "tips and tricks" for data recovery, and all I have told you is to restore from backup. Is that all? Well, not just that, but I am telling you that restoring from your backup is absolutely the most reliable and consistent method to recover your data. Why? BACKUP/RESTORE is SQL Server's primary mechanism for recovering your data in the most reliable and consistent fashion.

I have supported customers for every SQL Server version Microsoft has shipped over a 13-year period and have seen many customers contact technical support without the ability to restore a valid backup. SQL Server has such excellent tools to back up your data (and many ISVs have built products using our VDI API) that there really is no reason not to have a valid backup. It simply takes a well-thought-out strategy and the right hardware to ensure you have a backup to meet your recovery needs. The point I make here is that I will present many advanced features and techniques to recover your data; but in some cases, these would not be needed if you have the proper backups. But what if, despite your best efforts, you cannot restore from a backup? You've come to the right place. Although in some situations I discuss restoring from a backup as the best (and perhaps only) solution to a problem, I present other options specifically designed into SQL Server 2005.

Now let's take a look at how this chapter is organized so you can decide how best to read through this material. I have organized the chapter into three main sections that discuss building your knowledge, data recovery troubleshooting scenarios, and exercises.

If you want to *build your knowledge* in the area of data recovery, focus on this first section. I fill in some gaps from the product documentation on specific *storage internal topics* such as new allocation structure terminology. Second, I make sure you are educated on important *SQL Server 2005 enhancements* in the areas of backup/restore and DBCC CHECKDB. Third, I provide some tips and suggestions for *best practices* to avoid data recovery problems focusing on backup/restore, DBCC CHECKDB, and the system that supports SQL Server, the operating system, and the hardware. I said I wouldn't talk much about disaster recovery strategies, but I can't help it. One of my jobs at Microsoft is to educate and think of ways for customers to avoid calling technical support, which means thinking of ways to prevent problems. So I spend some time on best practices so that you can avoid using advanced techniques to recover your data.

The next section is all about *troubleshooting*, the main reason you purchased this book. Troubleshooting is all about solving problems. Problems can usually be categorized into various *scenarios*. Therefore, this section is organized into various scenarios that you might encounter, including failures to access, backup, restore, or check consistency on your data. If you want to learn about how to solve problems for specific scenarios, you should read this section. But as with all good books, many types of great technical tips and internal information are woven into this chapter. To teach you about troubleshooting data recovery, I first go over scenarios that require you to recover system databases. I then review how to troubleshoot situations when your user database is inaccessible (for example, your user database is marked SUSPECT). As mentioned previously, BACKUP/RESTORE is critical to data recovery. But what if it fails? Well, we talk about how to handle some of these situations. The last two subsections focus on database consistency. First, I review certain types of database consistency runtime errors. These are errors that can occur during execution of the most basic T-SQL queries (such as SELECT, INSERT, UPDATE, or DELETE) after the database has been successfully opened. Some of these scenarios may require you to use DBCC CHECKDB. So, I teach you what to do when DBCC CHECKDB reports errors. This is one of the most important tools in your *data recovery toolkit*, so it is important to understand more about how it works, proper usage, and what to do when it reports errors.

Fundamentals

Anyone who is good at solving problems will tell you it is important to know something about "how things work." Therefore, in this section, I help build your knowledge of important internal information for SQL Server 2005 related to the general topic of data recovery. But first, I recommend you review the following sections of SQL Server Books Online. Fundamental information in these sections provides a foundation for what I discuss:

> Database Engine Manageability Enhancements
>
> Database Engine Availability Enhancements
>
> Understanding Databases
>
> Database Snapshots
>
> Partitioned Tables and Indexes
>
> Understanding and Managing Transaction Logs
>
> Backing Up and Restoring Databases
>
> Using a Dedicated Administrator Connection
>
> Physical Database Architecture
>
> ALTER DATABASE (Transact-SQL)
>
> BACKUP (Transact-SQL)
>
> DBCC CHECKDB (Transact-SQL)
>
> System Views (Transact-SQL)

SQL Server 2005 Storage Internals

Database and File States

In SQL Server 2000, the state (or status) of the database was at best hard to understand. You had to decode special bits in the sysdatabases table, and the behavior of when statuses changed was not consistent. SQL Server 2005 does a nice job of cleaning this up. First, a descriptive state of the database can be found in the sys.databases catalog view (in a column called state). Second, the meaning and behavior of database states are easy to understand and consistent. For example, when you force a database offline with ALTER DATABASE SET OFFLINE, the database goes to the OFFLINE state. This was not always the case in SQL 2000.

To understand what these database states mean and how a database can move into each state, look at Figure 2-1.

This does not represent every possible scenario for state change for a database, but it covers the most common scenarios. A database is typically started during server startup, when it is first created, or when it is attached. When this occurs, the state of the database is temporarily changed to RECOVERING. If there is a resource problem with the database (such as a failure to open the database files), the state is changed to

RECOVERY_PENDING. This state is persisted, so after the resource problem has been corrected, the user must use ALTER DATABASE SET ONLINE to start it again.

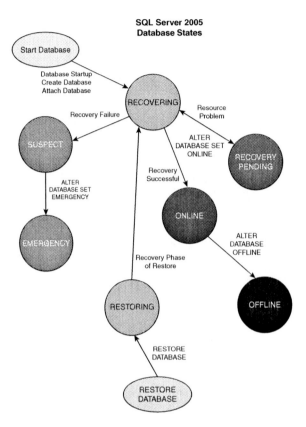

Figure 2-1
Status of the database

If no resource issues exist, the engine tries to run recovery on the database. If recovery is successful, the database state changes to ONLINE and is persisted. If recovery fails, the database state is changed to SUSPECT but is not persisted. This is a change from previous versions when the SUSPECT state was persisted. This caused customers and PSS headaches, because if the server was restarted, the ERRORLOG did not contain the original reason for the recovery failure. Now SUSPECT is temporary, so if the server is restarted, recovery runs again at database startup. Therefore, the cause for a recovery failure can be investigated from the ERRORLOG.

When the database is ONLINE, you can take if offline (which closes the database and the database file handles along with it) by running ALTER DATABASE <dbname> SET OFFLINE. This syntax changes the state to OFFLINE, which is persisted. At any persisted state, you can use ALTER DATABASE <dbname> SET EMERGENCY to change the database state to EMERGENCY, which is then persisted. This is another nice change from SQL Server 2000, where changing to EMERGENCY state required an update to the sysdatabases table setting specific bits. This was error-prone, so putting this syntax into ALTER DATABASE made perfect sense. As the name implies, setting the database state to EMERGENCY makes sense only when you cannot access the database, such as when it is marked SUSPECT. We discuss later in the chapter why it sometimes makes sense to use EMERGENCY.

It is also important to mention the states that occur when you restore a database. When you restore a database and the database is created as part of loading it from the backup, the database state starts out as RESTORING. When all the database pages have been restored, the state is changed to RECOVERING as the database is recovered. Then the process is the same as normal database startup.

Database files also have states.

Resource Database

A major change for SQL Server 2005 is the resource database. In previous versions of SQL Server 2000, all *executable* system objects were stored in the master database. By executable, I mean any object not used to store data such as stored procedures, views, functions, and triggers. If you look at a typical SQL Server 2000 master database, you will find approximately 1,200 objects. With SQL Server 2005, there are now only about 70. So where are these objects now stored? In a database called the resource database. The actual name of this database is mssqlsystemresource, but there is a twist. You cannot directly access this database. (In other words, you won't see this in Management Studio, and you get an error if you try to execute 'use mssqlsystemresource') So how do you get a list of objects in this database and execute them?

SQL Server 2005 introduces a new ownership concept called schemas. One special reserved schema is called sys. By using the sys schema, you can reference any system object that is physically stored in the resource database in the context of your database. For example, we discuss in the next section a view called sys.objects. The view definition for objects is stored in the resource database, but you can reference it in a select statement in your database like this: 'select * from sys.objects'. So when you use the sys schema name for an object, the engine looks for the definition of the object in the resource database.

Why was this change made in SQL Server 2005? There are many reasons, but here is my perspective.

System executable objects are like code from Microsoft, so they are now stored in a protected, read-only database much in a manner similar to a dynamic link library (DLL). The files for this database are not actual DLL executable code. They are two files, mssqlsystemresource.mdf and mssqlsystemresource.ldf, installed by default in the same directory as the master database files.

These system objects are now in a self-contained location. It is now simple to identify all of them and simpler to replace them. Changes to these objects come in the form of a new database and log file. Copy in a new version of these files for upgrades to these objects. I address versioning and servicing of this database later when I talk about system database recovery.

Referencing a system object is now done in a consistent and clear approach. No more special rules such as "If the name starts with sp_, first check the master database." You just use the sys schema name to reference a system executable object.

Catalog Views and Base System Tables

Around the same time the resource database was created, the system tables were also redesigned. SQL Server has always been a design where the storage of metadata and the interfaces to view them are the same. SQL Server 7.0 did implement INFORMATION_SCHEMA views for ANSI compliance, but most users directly accessed system tables such as sysobjects and sysindexes. But the access is wide open for administrators with the right access. You can query, insert, delete, or update these tables directly. Great for enthusiasts and certain PSS engineers trying to solve some advanced problem, but a nightmare for those trying to ensure consistency of the database. I've seen the root cause of some fairly complex customer case be the result of a mistake made by a customer trying to touch an obscure system table column value.

The sheer scope and number of new features for SQL Server 2005 would require major modifications to a 10-year-old system table architecture. An entirely new system table design was needed to support new features (such as partitions). At the same time, the design of these tables and the interfaces used to access and modify data within them needed to be decoupled. The challenge was to prevent users from "shooting themselves in the foot" while providing a comprehensive metadata interface so that users would have access to everything they need. The result was catalog views. The catalog of the database is all the metadata storage within any database. Approximately 200 views were created and stored in the resource database for users to query the database catalog. Furthermore, support for some operations that formerly required direct system table modification was added to the Transact-SQL language. For example, to put the database in emergency mode, you now use ALTER DATABASE instead of directly changing a system table.

This last point is important, because it highlights a restriction that was put in place as part of this change for catalog views and system tables. Users cannot directly read or change system tables. Your first reaction may be anger or frustration. Why is Microsoft taking away something from me? The intention is not to take anything away from you. The intention is to help you keep a consistent database, provide you with the best interface to view the catalog, and to help avoid backward-compatibility problems should system tables change in future releases. In fact, to help with backward compatibility with SQL Server 2000 users, the "old" system tables such as sysobjects exist in SQL Server 2005 as catalog views.

To help put this together, let's take a look at a few queries using catalog views to get metadata information about the database.

If I want to find out all objects physically stored in my database that I have access to, I run the following query:

```
select * from sys.objects
```

If you were a system administrator and you ran this query in the old pubs sample database (installed on SQL Server 2005), you would get the following results:

```
name
object_id   principal_id schema_id   parent_object_id type type_desc
create_date          modify_date          is_ms_shipped is_published is_schema_
published
----------------------------------------------------------------------------------
---------------------------------------------- ----------- ------------ ---------- --
-------------- ---- ------------------------------------------------------------
----------------------- ----------------------- ------------- ------------ --------
----------
CK_ _publisher_ _pub_i_ _023D5A04
37575172 NULL      1        5575058      C  CHECK_CONSTRAINT
2006-02-22 07:01:47.827 2006-02-22 07:01:47.827 0        0          0
CK_ _jobs_ _min_lvl_ _1920BF5C
421576540 NULL     1        373576369    C  CHECK_CONSTRAINT
2006-02-22 07:01:47.873 2006-02-22 07:01:47.873 0        0          0
CK_ _jobs_ _max_lvl_ _1A14E395
437576597 NULL     1        373576369    C  CHECK_CONSTRAINT
2006-02-22 07:01:47.873 2006-02-22 07:01:47.873 0        0          0
CK_emp_id
533576939 NULL     1        501576825    C  CHECK_CONSTRAINT
2006-02-22 07:01:47.873 2006-02-22 07:01:47.873 0        0          0
CK_ _authors_ _au_id_ _7D78A4E7
2105058535 NULL    1        2073058421   C  CHECK_CONSTRAINT
2006-02-22 07:01:47.780 2006-02-22 07:01:47.780 0        0          0
CK_ _authors_ _zip_ _7F60ED59
2137058649 NULL    1        2073058421   C  CHECK_CONSTRAINT
2006-02-22 07:01:47.780 2006-02-22 07:01:47.780 0        0          0
DF_ _authors_ _phone_ _7E6CC920
2121058592 NULL    1        2073058421   D  DEFAULT_CONSTRAINT
2006-02-22 07:01:47.780 2006-02-22 07:01:47.780 0        0          0
DF_ _employee_ _hire_d_ _25869641
629577281 NULL     1        501576825    D  DEFAULT_CONSTRAINT
2006-02-22 07:01:47.890 2006-02-22 07:01:47.890 0        0          0
DF_ _employee_ _job_id_ _20C1E124
549576996 NULL     1        501576825    D  DEFAULT_CONSTRAINT
2006-02-22 07:01:47.873 2006-02-22 07:01:47.873 0        0          0
DF_ _employee_ _job_lv_ _22AA2996
581577110 NULL     1        501576825    D  DEFAULT_CONSTRAINT
2006-02-22 07:01:47.890 2006-02-22 07:01:47.890 0        0          0
DF_ _employee_ _pub_id_ _239E4DCF
597577167 NULL     1        501576825    D  DEFAULT_CONSTRAINT
2006-02-22 07:01:47.890 2006-02-22 07:01:47.890 0        0          0
DF_ _jobs_ _job_desc_ _182C9B23
405576483 NULL     1        373576369    D  DEFAULT_CONSTRAINT
2006-02-22 07:01:47.873 2006-02-22 07:01:47.873 0        0          0
DF_ _publisher_ _count_ _03317E3D
53575229 NULL      1        5575058      D  DEFAULT_CONSTRAINT
2006-02-22 07:01:47.827 2006-02-22 07:01:47.827 0        0          0
DF_ _titles_ _type_ _060DEAE8
101575400 NULL     1        69575286     D  DEFAULT_CONSTRAINT
2006-02-22 07:01:47.840 2006-02-22 07:01:47.840 0        0          0
DF_ _titles_ _pubdate_ _07F6335A
133575514 NULL     1        69575286     D  DEFAULT_CONSTRAINT
2006-02-22 07:01:47.840 2006-02-22 07:01:47.840 0        0          0
```

```
FK_ _titles_ _pub_id_ _07020F21
117575457  NULL     1       69575286    F  FOREIGN_KEY_CONSTRAINT
2006-02-22 07:01:47.840 2006-02-22 07:01:47.840 0      0      0
FK_ _titleauth_ _au_id_ _0AD2A005
181575685  NULL     1       149575571   F  FOREIGN_KEY_CONSTRAINT
2006-02-22 07:01:47.840 2006-02-22 07:01:47.840 0      0      0
FK_ _titleauth_ _title_ _0BC6C43E
197575742  NULL     1       149575571   F  FOREIGN_KEY_CONSTRAINT
2006-02-22 07:01:47.840 2006-02-22 07:01:47.840 0      0      0
FK_ _sales_ _stor_id_ _108B795B
277576027  NULL     1       245575913   F  FOREIGN_KEY_CONSTRAINT
2006-02-22 07:01:47.857 2006-02-22 07:01:47.857 0      0      0
FK_ _sales_ _title_id_ _117F9D94
293576084  NULL     1       245575913   F  FOREIGN_KEY_CONSTRAINT
2006-02-22 07:01:47.857 2006-02-22 07:01:47.857 0      0      0
FK_ _roysched_ _title_ __1367E606
325576198  NULL     1       309576141   F  FOREIGN_KEY_CONSTRAINT
2006-02-22 07:01:47.857 2006-02-22 07:01:47.857 0      0      0
FK_ _discounts_ _stor_ __15502E78
357576312  NULL     1       341576255   F  FOREIGN_KEY_CONSTRAINT
2006-02-22 07:01:47.857 2006-02-22 07:01:47.857 0      0      0
FK_ _employee_ _pub_id_ _24927208
613577224  NULL     1       501576825   F  FOREIGN_KEY_CONSTRAINT
2006-02-22 07:01:47.890 2006-02-22 07:01:47.890 0      0      0
FK_ _employee_ _job_id_ _21B6055D
565577053  NULL     1       501576825   F  FOREIGN_KEY_CONSTRAINT
2006-02-22 07:01:47.890 2006-02-22 07:01:47.890 0      0      0
FK_ _pub_info_ _pub_id_ _1CF15040
485576768  NULL     1       453576654   F  FOREIGN_KEY_CONSTRAINT
2006-02-22 07:01:47.873 2006-02-22 07:01:47.873 0      0      0
queue_messages_1977058079
1993058136 NULL     4       1977058079  IT  INTERNAL_TABLE
2005-10-14 01:36:25.360 2005-10-14 01:36:25.380 1      0      0
queue_messages_2009058193
2025058250 NULL     4       2009058193  IT  INTERNAL_TABLE
2005-10-14 01:36:25.377 2005-10-14 01:36:25.383 1      0      0
queue_messages_2041058307
2057058364 NULL     4       2041058307  IT  INTERNAL_TABLE
2005-10-14 01:36:25.377 2005-10-14 01:36:25.383 1      0      0
byroyalty
677577452  NULL     1       0           P  SQL_STORED_PROCEDURE
2006-02-22 07:01:50.450 2006-02-22 07:01:50.450 0      0      0
reptq1
693577509  NULL     1       0           P  SQL_STORED_PROCEDURE
2006-02-22 07:01:50.483 2006-02-22 07:01:50.483 0      0      0
reptq2
709577566  NULL     1       0           P  SQL_STORED_PROCEDURE
2006-02-22 07:01:50.483 2006-02-22 07:01:50.483 0      0      0
reptq3
725577623  NULL     1       0           P  SQL_STORED_PROCEDURE
2006-02-22 07:01:50.483 2006-02-22 07:01:50.483 0      0      0
UPKCL_auidind
2089058478 NULL     1       2073058421  PK  PRIMARY_KEY_CONSTRAINT
2006-02-22 07:01:47.780 2006-02-22 07:01:47.780 0      0      0
```

```
UPKCL_pubinfo
469576711  NULL     1      453576654   PK  PRIMARY_KEY_CONSTRAINT
2006-02-22 07:01:47.873 2006-02-22 07:01:47.873 0       0       0
PK_emp_id
517576882  NULL     1      501576825   PK  PRIMARY_KEY_CONSTRAINT
2006-02-22 07:01:47.873 2006-02-22 07:01:47.873 0       0       0
PK_ _jobs_ _173876EA
389576426  NULL     1      373576369   PK  PRIMARY_KEY_CONSTRAINT
2006-02-22 07:01:47.857 2006-02-22 07:01:47.857 0       0       0
UPKCL_taind
165575628  NULL     1      149575571   PK  PRIMARY_KEY_CONSTRAINT
2006-02-22 07:01:47.840 2006-02-22 07:01:47.840 0       0       0
UPKCL_sales
261575970  NULL     1      245575913   PK  PRIMARY_KEY_CONSTRAINT
2006-02-22 07:01:47.857 2006-02-22 07:01:47.857 0       0       0
UPK_storeid
229575856  NULL     1      213575799   PK  PRIMARY_KEY_CONSTRAINT
2006-02-22 07:01:47.840 2006-02-22 07:01:47.840 0       0       0
UPKCL_pubind
21575115  NULL     1      5575058   PK  PRIMARY_KEY_CONSTRAINT
2006-02-22 07:01:47.827 2006-02-22 07:01:47.827 0       0       0
UPKCL_titleidind
85575343  NULL     1      69575286   PK  PRIMARY_KEY_CONSTRAINT
2006-02-22 07:01:47.840 2006-02-22 07:01:47.840 0       0       0
sysrowsetcolumns
4       NULL     4      0        S  SYSTEM_TABLE
2005-10-14 01:36:15.923 2005-10-14 01:36:15.923 1       0       0
sysrowsets
5       NULL     4      0        S  SYSTEM_TABLE
2005-10-14 01:36:15.910 2005-10-14 01:36:15.910 1       0       0
sysallocunits
7       NULL     4      0        S  SYSTEM_TABLE
2005-10-14 01:36:15.910 2005-10-14 01:36:15.910 1       0       0
sysfiles1
8       NULL     4      0        S  SYSTEM_TABLE
2003-04-08 09:13:38.093 2003-04-08 09:13:38.093 1       0       0
syshobtcolumns
13       NULL     4      0        S  SYSTEM_TABLE
2005-10-14 01:36:15.940 2005-10-14 01:36:15.940 1       0       0
syshobts
15       NULL     4      0        S  SYSTEM_TABLE
2005-10-14 01:36:15.923 2005-10-14 01:36:15.923 1       0       0
sysftinds
25       NULL     4      0        S  SYSTEM_TABLE
2005-10-14 01:36:17.063 2005-10-14 01:36:17.063 1       0       0
sysserefs
26       NULL     4      0        S  SYSTEM_TABLE
2005-10-14 01:36:15.940 2005-10-14 01:36:15.940 1       0       0
sysowners
27       NULL     4      0        S  SYSTEM_TABLE
2005-10-14 01:36:17.050 2005-10-14 01:36:17.050 1       0       0
sysprivs
29       NULL     4      0        S  SYSTEM_TABLE
2005-10-14 01:36:15.877 2005-10-14 01:36:15.877 1       0       0
```

```
sysschobjs
34      NULL      4        0          S  SYSTEM_TABLE
2005-10-14 01:36:15.987 2005-10-14 01:36:15.987 1          0        0
syscolpars
41      NULL      4        0          S  SYSTEM_TABLE
2005-10-14 01:36:17.017 2005-10-14 01:36:17.017 1          0        0
sysnsobjs
44      NULL      4        0          S  SYSTEM_TABLE
2005-10-14 01:36:16.000 2005-10-14 01:36:16.000 1          0        0
syscerts
46      NULL      4        0          S  SYSTEM_TABLE
2005-10-14 01:36:25.173 2005-10-14 01:36:25.193 1          0        0
sysxprops
49      NULL      4        0          S  SYSTEM_TABLE
2005-10-14 01:36:18.063 2005-10-14 01:36:18.063 1          0        0
sysscalartypes
50      NULL      4        0          S  SYSTEM_TABLE
2005-10-14 01:36:15.847 2005-10-14 01:36:15.847 1          0        0
systypedsubobjs
51      NULL      4        0          S  SYSTEM_TABLE
2005-10-14 01:36:17.033 2005-10-14 01:36:17.033 1          0        0
sysidxstats
54      NULL      4        0          S  SYSTEM_TABLE
2005-10-14 01:36:17.033 2005-10-14 01:36:17.033 1          0        0
sysiscols
55      NULL      4        0          S  SYSTEM_TABLE
2005-10-14 01:36:17.050 2005-10-14 01:36:17.050 1          0        0
sysbinobjs
58      NULL      4        0          S  SYSTEM_TABLE
2005-10-14 01:36:22.110 2005-10-14 01:36:22.123 1          0        0
sysobjvalues
60      NULL      4        0          S  SYSTEM_TABLE
2005-10-14 01:36:15.970 2005-10-14 01:36:15.970 1          0        0
sysclsobjs
64      NULL      4        0          S  SYSTEM_TABLE
2005-10-14 01:36:16.000 2005-10-14 01:36:16.000 1          0        0
sysrowsetrefs
65      NULL      4        0          S  SYSTEM_TABLE
2005-10-14 01:36:17.050 2005-10-14 01:36:17.050 1          0        0
sysremsvcbinds
67      NULL      4        0          S  SYSTEM_TABLE
2005-10-14 01:36:24.127 2005-10-14 01:36:24.143 1          0        0
sysxmitqueue
68      NULL      4        0          S  SYSTEM_TABLE
2005-10-14 01:36:24.143 2005-10-14 01:36:24.153 1          0        0
sysrts
69      NULL      4        0          S  SYSTEM_TABLE
2005-10-14 01:36:24.143 2005-10-14 01:36:24.160 1          0        0
sysconvgroup
71      NULL      4        0          S  SYSTEM_TABLE
2005-10-14 01:36:24.127 2005-10-14 01:36:24.147 1          0        0
sysdesend
72      NULL      4        0          S  SYSTEM_TABLE
2005-10-14 01:36:24.160 2005-10-14 01:36:25.160 1          0        0
```

```
sysdercv
73      NULL    4       0         S  SYSTEM_TABLE
2005-10-14 01:36:25.157 2005-10-14 01:36:25.167 1       0       0
syssingleobjrefs
74      NULL    4       0         S  SYSTEM_TABLE
2005-10-14 01:36:15.860 2005-10-14 01:36:15.860 1       0       0
sysmultiobjrefs
75      NULL    4       0         S  SYSTEM_TABLE
2005-10-14 01:36:15.877 2005-10-14 01:36:15.877 1       0       0
sysdbfiles
76      NULL    4       0         S  SYSTEM_TABLE
2005-10-14 01:36:15.953 2005-10-14 01:36:15.953 1       0       0
sysguidrefs
78      NULL    4       0         S  SYSTEM_TABLE
2005-10-14 01:36:23.110 2005-10-14 01:36:23.123 1       0       0
sysqnames
90      NULL    4       0         S  SYSTEM_TABLE
2005-10-14 01:36:23.110 2005-10-14 01:36:23.127 1       0       0
sysxmlcomponent
91      NULL    4       0         S  SYSTEM_TABLE
2005-10-14 01:36:23.127 2005-10-14 01:36:23.140 1       0       0
sysxmlfacet
92      NULL    4       0         S  SYSTEM_TABLE
2005-10-14 01:36:23.127 2005-10-14 01:36:23.137 1       0       0
sysxmlplacement
93      NULL    4       0         S  SYSTEM_TABLE
2005-10-14 01:36:23.127 2005-10-14 01:36:24.137 1       0       0
sysobjkeycrypts
94      NULL    4       0         S  SYSTEM_TABLE
2005-10-14 01:36:25.157 2005-10-14 01:36:25.177 1       0       0
sysasymkeys
95      NULL    4       0         S  SYSTEM_TABLE
2005-10-14 01:36:25.173 2005-10-14 01:36:25.193 1       0       0
syssqlguides
96      NULL    4       0         S  SYSTEM_TABLE
2005-10-14 01:36:25.190 2005-10-14 01:36:25.207 1       0       0
sysbinsubobjs
97      NULL    4       0         S  SYSTEM_TABLE
2005-10-14 01:36:22.110 2005-10-14 01:36:23.120 1       0       0
ServiceBrokerQueue
2041058307 NULL    1       0         SQ  SERVICE_QUEUE
2005-10-14 01:36:25.377 2005-10-14 01:36:25.377 1       0       0
QueryNotificationErrorsQueue
1977058079 NULL    1       0         SQ  SERVICE_QUEUE
2005-10-14 01:36:25.360 2005-10-14 01:36:25.360 1       0       0
EventNotificationErrorsQueue
2009058193 NULL    1       0         SQ  SERVICE_QUEUE
2005-10-14 01:36:25.377 2005-10-14 01:36:25.377 1       0       0
employee_insupd
645577338 NULL    1       501576825    TR  SQL_TRIGGER
2006-02-22 07:01:47.903 2006-02-22 07:01:47.903 0       0       0
authors
2073058421 NULL    1       0         U  USER_TABLE
2006-02-22 07:01:47.717 2006-02-22 07:01:49.997 0       0       0
publishers
```

```
5575058   NULL      1        0           U   USER_TABLE
2006-02-22 07:01:47.793 2006-02-22 07:01:47.890 0       0       0
titles
69575286  NULL      1        0           U   USER_TABLE
2006-02-22 07:01:47.840 2006-02-22 07:01:50.153 0       0       0
titleauthor
149575571 NULL      1        0           U   USER_TABLE
2006-02-22 07:01:47.840 2006-02-22 07:01:50.263 0       0       0
sales
245575913 NULL      1        0           U   USER_TABLE
2006-02-22 07:01:47.857 2006-02-22 07:01:50.090 0       0       0
stores
213575799 NULL      1        0           U   USER_TABLE
2006-02-22 07:01:47.840 2006-02-22 07:01:47.860 0       0       0
roysched
309576141 NULL      1        0           U   USER_TABLE
2006-02-22 07:01:47.857 2006-02-22 07:01:50.343 0       0       0
pub_info
453576654 NULL      1        0           U   USER_TABLE
2006-02-22 07:01:47.873 2006-02-22 07:01:47.877 0       0       0
jobs
373576369 NULL      1        0           U   USER_TABLE
2006-02-22 07:01:47.857 2006-02-22 07:01:47.890 0       0       0
discounts
341576255 NULL      1        0           U   USER_TABLE
2006-02-22 07:01:47.857 2006-02-22 07:01:47.860 0       0       0
employee
501576825 NULL      1        0           U   USER_TABLE
2006-02-22 07:01:47.873 2006-02-22 07:01:49.903 0       0       0
titleview
661577395 NULL      1        0           V   VIEW
2006-02-22 07:01:50.373 2006-02-22 07:01:50.373 0          0          0
```

Notice all the rows with this type of SYSTEM_TABLE. But earlier I said you cannot read system tables. This is true, but you can see a list of all of them. These system tables are the base system tables stored in your database. Earlier beta releases did not expose these table names in this view, but the decision was made to show them primarily because the object ID values were showing up in error messages and users were confused when they tried to figure out what table was associated with the message.

If you tried to query one of these tables like this:

```
select * from sysschobjs
```

you would get the following error:

```
Msg 208, Level 16, State 1, Line 1
Invalid object name 'sysschobjs'.
```

What about the executable system objects stored in the `resource` database? If I cannot actually access the `resource` database directly, how do I see a list of these object? Well, SQL Server includes a catalog view just for this purpose:

```
select * from sys.system_objects
name
object_id  principal_id schema_id  parent_object_id type type_desc
create_date          modify_date          is_ms_shipped is_published is_schema_published
--------------------------------------------------------------------------------
-------------------------------------------- ----------- ------------ ----------- --
--------------- ---- ---------------------------------------------------------------
---------------------------- ------------------------ ------------- ------------- ---------
----------
fn_cColvEntries_80
-61545096  NULL    4      0              FN   SQL_SCALAR_FUNCTION
2006-02-17 14:43:52.820 2006-02-17 14:43:52.820 1         0           0
fn_fIsColTracked
-242919846 NULL    4      0              FN   SQL_SCALAR_FUNCTION
2006-02-17 14:43:53.040 2006-02-17 14:43:53.040 1         0           0
fn_GetCurrentPrincipal
-986367695 NULL    4      0              FN   SQL_SCALAR_FUNCTION
2006-02-17 14:43:46.130 2006-02-17 14:43:46.130 1         0           0
fn_GetRowsetIdFromRowDump
-633331936 NULL    4      0              FN   SQL_SCALAR_FUNCTION
2006-02-17 14:41:07.853 2006-02-17 14:41:07.853 1         0           0
fn_IsBitSetInBitmask
-92987834  NULL    4      0              FN   SQL_SCALAR_FUNCTION
2006-02-17 14:44:11.087 2006-02-17 14:44:11.087 1         0           0
fn_isrolemember
-977642094 NULL    4      0              FN   SQL_SCALAR_FUNCTION
2006-02-17 14:44:15.147 2006-02-17 14:44:15.147 1         0           0
.
.
.
sp_help
-784136858 NULL    4      0              P   SQL_STORED_PROCEDURE
2006-02-17 14:41:29.803 2006-02-17 14:41:29.803 1         0           0
sp_help_agent_default
-930237674 NULL    4      0              P   SQL_STORED_PROCEDURE
2006-02-17 14:46:15.130 2006-02-17 14:46:15.130 1         0           0
sp_help_agent_parameter
-244913556 NULL    4      0              P   SQL_STORED_PROCEDURE
2006-02-17 14:46:16.443 2006-02-17 14:46:16.443 1         0           0
sp_help_agent_profile
-463476349 NULL    4      0              P   SQL_STORED_PROCEDURE
2006-02-17 14:46:14.913 2006-02-17 14:46:14.913 1         0           0
sp_help_datatype_mapping
-721021307 NULL    4      0              P   SQL_STORED_PROCEDURE
2006-02-17 14:46:22.350 2006-02-17 14:46:22.350 1         0           0
.
.
.
indexes
-397    NULL    4      0              V   VIEW
2006-02-17 14:38:43.433 2006-02-17 14:38:43.433 1         0           0
```

```
internal_tables
-468     NULL     4      0        V  VIEW
2006-02-17 14:38:42.340 2006-02-17 14:38:42.340 1       0      0
KEY_COLUMN_USAGE
-784887024 NULL     3      0        V  VIEW
2006-02-17 14:43:25.880 2006-02-17 14:43:25.880 1       0      0
key_constraints
-406     NULL     4      0        V  VIEW
2006-02-17 14:38:46.057 2006-02-17 14:38:46.057 1       0      0
key_encryptions
-465     NULL     4      0        V  VIEW
2006-02-17 14:39:26.200 2006-02-17 14:39:26.200 1       0      0
linked_logins
-222     NULL     4      0        V  VIEW
2006-02-17 14:39:17.120 2006-02-17 14:39:17.120 1       0      0
login_token
-77438453 NULL     4      0        V  VIEW
2006-02-17 14:39:49.777 2006-02-17 14:39:49.777 1       0      0
master_files
-216     NULL     4      0        V  VIEW
2006-02-17 14:39:11.870 2006-02-17 14:39:11.870 1       0      0
master_key_passwords
-243     NULL     4      0        V  VIEW
2006-02-17 14:39:14.167 2006-02-17 14:39:14.167 1       0      0
message_type_xml_schema_collection_usages
-478     NULL     4      0        V  VIEW
2006-02-17 14:38:59.730 2006-02-17 14:38:59.730 1       0      0
messages
-225     NULL     4      0        V  VIEW
2006-02-17 14:38:57.980 2006-02-17 14:38:57.980 1       0      0
module_assembly_usages
-484     NULL     4      0        V  VIEW
2006-02-17 14:38:51.307 2006-02-17 14:38:51.307 1       0      0
numbered_procedure_parameters
-419     NULL     4      0        V  VIEW
2006-02-17 14:38:52.510 2006-02-17 14:38:52.510 1       0      0
numbered_procedures
-418     NULL     4      0        V  VIEW
2006-02-17 14:38:52.183 2006-02-17 14:38:52.183 1       0      0
objects
-385     NULL     4      0        V  VIEW
2006-02-17 14:38:36.870 2006-02-17 14:38:36.870 1       0      0
.
.
.
sysindexes
-134     NULL     4      0        V  VIEW
2006-02-17 14:39:33.090 2006-02-17 14:39:33.090 1       0      0
sysindexkeys
-135     NULL     4      0        V  VIEW
2006-02-17 14:39:33.417 2006-02-17 14:39:33.417 1       0      0
syslanguages
-194     NULL     4      0        V  VIEW
2006-02-17 14:39:26.853 2006-02-17 14:39:26.853 1       0      0
```

```
syslockinfo
-204    NULL     4      0       V  VIEW
2006-02-17 14:41:00.633 2006-02-17 14:41:00.633 1      0        0
syslogins
-205    NULL     4      0       V  VIEW
2006-02-17 14:39:37.463 2006-02-17 14:39:37.463 1      0        0
sysmembers
-141    NULL     4      0       V  VIEW
2006-02-17 14:39:34.400 2006-02-17 14:39:34.400 1      0        0
sysmessages
-206    NULL     4      0       V  VIEW
2006-02-17 14:39:38.777 2006-02-17 14:39:38.777 1      0        0
sysobjects
-105    NULL     4      0       V  VIEW
2006-02-17 14:38:39.823 2006-02-17 14:38:39.823 1      0        0
.
.
.
xp_adsirequest
-60872162  NULL     4      0         X  EXTENDED_STORED_PROCEDURE
2006-02-17 14:53:06.237 2006-02-17 14:53:06.237 1      0        0
xp_availablemedia
-196500590 NULL     4      0         X  EXTENDED_STORED_PROCEDURE
2006-02-17 14:53:06.033 2006-02-17 14:53:06.033 1      0        0
xp_cleanupwebtask
-113576977 NULL     4      0         X  EXTENDED_STORED_PROCEDURE
2006-02-17 14:53:20.300 2006-02-17 14:53:20.300 1      0        0
xp_cmdshell
-1008137134 NULL     4      0        X  EXTENDED_STORED_PROCEDURE
2006-02-17 14:41:25.383 2006-02-17 14:41:25.383 1      0        0
```

This is not a complete list, because more than 1,700 system objects are accessible via the sys schema. You will see in this list some familiar names that used to be stored in the master database in SQL Server 2000, such as sp_help. You will also see new names such as views called indexes, master_files, and objects. Notice that names like sysindexes and sysobjects have a type VIEW. Also, you can see at the end of this list that Microsoft internal extended stored procedures are stored in the resource database.

Notice something interesting about the object_id of these names. They are listed as values < 0. Whenever you see an object_id listed as < 0, you know it is a system object that comes from the resource database.

I reference many of the catalog views in the remaining sections of this chapter. SQL Server Books Online has a complete reference of all the views, including the descripton of the column definitions.

One specific catalog view that I should mention is sys.system_sql_modules. In the early versions of the beta, there was no method to see the text of any system object. Based on user input during the beta, the SQL Server development team chose to expose the definitions of these objects with sys.system_sql_modules. The following syntax:

```
select * from sys.system_sql_modules where object_id = object_id('sys.sysobjects')
```

shows you the definition of the sysobjects catalog view. If you run this query, you will see it references the sys.sysschobjs base system table. Be careful relying on the results of this view. The SQL Server development team exposed this information so that you can see how views, procedures, and so on were built. But you cannot change the text, and the development team certainly could change these over time as they fix bugs, enhance performance, or change the design of base system tables. To help give you a quick start on catalog views, Table 2-1 shows a comparison of what catalog view to use based on the SQL 2000 equivalent system table.

TABLE 2-1   What catalog view to use based on the SQL 2000 equivalent system table

SQL Server 2000 System Table	SQL Server 2005 Catalog View
sysobjects	sys.objects
sysindexes	sys.indexes+sys.partitions +sys.allocation_units
syscolumns	sys.columns
syscomments	sys.sql_modules
sysdatabases	sys.databases
sysfiles	sys.database_files
sysaltfiles	sys.master_files

Let me make one final comment about base system tables, catalog views, and the resource database. Base system tables exist in every database and store all the metadata. All the catalog views and executable system objects (sometimes called just system objects in Books Online) are not stored in your database. The definition of these objects exists only in the resource database. The resource database is a *database*, so it has base system tables. Think of it this way. When you create a view in your database, SQL Server stores the definition of this view in base system tables in your database. The resource database is simply preloaded with a bunch of views, procedures, and so forth. No *user tables* exist in the resource database.

Allocation Structures

The internal structures used to organize allocation for SQL Server 2005 have not changed dramatically. Concepts such as GAM, IAM, SGAM, and PFS all still exist to internally track and organize allocation of pages and extents.

There are some differences at a higher level of allocation. The first difference is support for partitions. SQL Server 2000 enables you to place tables or indexes on specific disks by using filegroups. SQL Server 2005 expands this capability to place horizontal slices of tables or indexes on specific disks using partitions. Partitions allow you to specify that a particular range of values within a table or index is stored on specific filegroups. Every table or index has at least one partition, as can be seen by querying the sys.partitions catalog view. Each partition can have up to three different allocation units. An allocation unit is equivalent to an IAM chain. In SQL Server 2000, a table could have two different IAM chains: one for the data and one for TEXT/IMAGE data. SQL Server 2005 supports three different IAM chains for an object: data, LOB (TEXT/IMAGE), and SLOB. A Small Large Binary Object (SLOB) is also referred to as row overflow data. SQL Server 2005 enables you to store data in a row that is larger than the SQL Server page size (8KB). This is done by supporting a different IAM chain to store this extended row data.

Figure 2-2 shows the allocation structure objects and corresponding catalog views.

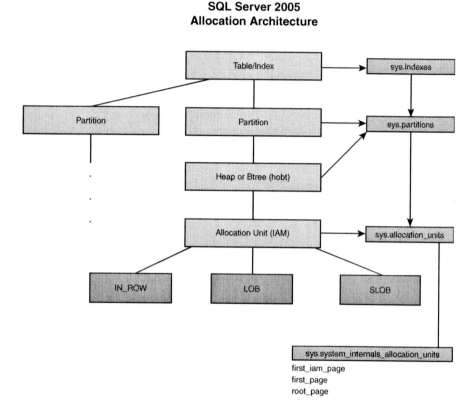

FIGURE 2-2   Allocation structure objects and corresponding catalog views

Let's take a look at a few of the catalog views that describe allocation structures. Let's create a table and index using the following query:

```
create table test_table (col1 int primary key clustered, col2 int,
col3 text, col4 varchar(5000) not null, col5 varchar(5000) not null)
go
create index test_idx on test_table (col2)
go
insert into test_table values (1, 1, 'this is text', 'this is test', 'this is
test')
go
```

To see the organization of allocation for this table and index, first look at the
sys.partitions catalog view:

```
select * from sys.partitions where object_id = object_id('test_table')
partition_id      object_id  index_id  partition_number hobt_id              rows
------------------ ---------- --------- ---------------- -------------------- -
-----
72057594038583296  2137058649 1         1                72057594038583296   1
72057594038648832  2137058649 2         1                72057594038648832   1
```

As you can see, the table and nonclustered index each have one partition. Notice the second column from the right, hobt_id. Hobt stands for heap or b-tree. Each partition is
made up of exactly one heap or b-tree index. Notice the value of hobt_id is the same as
partition_id. Why is the column needed? Very early designs of SQL Server 2005
included the ability for a heap or b-tree to store rows from multiple partitions. In other
words, a partition could have its data spread across multiple allocation units of the same
type. The final version of SQL Server 2005 doesn't contain this capability, but the base
system tables still support this concept. (This is why you see in the list of tables the name
syshobts.) In SQL Server 2005, a partition and hobt are basically equivalent, which is
why the ID for both is the same. You can see a reflection of this design in the page header
of a database page. The following is part of the output for DBCC PAGE for a page in a table
I created in the master database:

```
PAGE HEADER:
Page @0x0386A000
m_pageId = (1:509)          m_headerVersion = 1          m_type = 1
m_typeFlagBits = 0x4          m_level = 0              m_flagBits = 0xe200
m_objId (AllocUnitId.idObj) = 87    m_indexId (AllocUnitId.idInd) = 256
Metadata: AllocUnitId = 72057594043629568
Metadata: PartitionId = 72057594038779904              Metadata: IndexId = 1
Metadata: ObjectId = 1291151645    m_prevPage = (0:0)      m_nextPage = (0:0)
pminlen = 12              m_slotCnt = 1          m_freeCnt = 8017
m_freeData = 173            m_reservedCnt = 0          m_lsn = (2006:16:1)
m_xactReserved = 0          m_xdesId = (0:0)          m_ghostRecCnt = 0
m_tornBits = -1570474108
```

Instead of storing the object_id and index_id values as SQL Server did in previous versions, it stores the allocation_unit_id as seen in the sys.allocation_units catalog
view. DBCC PAGE decodes the allocation_unit id value such that it includes the
object_id and index_id from the system catalog metadata. You can see this from the
areas I highlighted that start with the word *metadata*.

Let's now look at the allocation units for the table and index using the
sys.allocation_units catalog view:

```
-- The table has a text column and possible row overflow ---- data so there
should be 3 rows for the clustered index --- and 1 row for the ncl index
select object_name(pt.object_id), pt.index_id, au.* from sys.allocation_units au
```

```
join sys.partitions pt
on au.container_id = pt.partition_id
and pt.object_id = object_id('test_table')
order by container_id
name
index_id  allocation_unit_id  type type_desc
container_id      data_space_id total_pages      used_pages         data_pages
-----------------------------------------------------------------------------------------
------------------------------------------------ ----------- -------------------- ---- -
------------------------------------------------------------- --------------------
------------ -------------------- -------------------- --------------------
test_table
1       72057594042843136  1   IN_ROW_DATA
72057594038583296  1       2           2             1
test_table
1       72057594042908672  3   ROW_OVERFLOW_DATA
72057594038583296  1       0           0             0
test_table
1       72057594042974208  2   LOB_DATA
72057594038583296  1       2           2             0
test_table
2       72057594043039744  1   IN_ROW_DATA
72057594038648832  1       2           2             1
```

Notice that index_id = 1 (the clustered index for test_table) has three types: IN_ROW_DATA (the actual data rows), ROW_OVERFLOW_DATA (this is the SLOB because we created the table with variable-length character columns that exceed 8KB), and LOB_DATA (the TEXT/IMAGE data). index_id = 2, the nonclustered index, has one allocation unit. Notice in the preceding query the column to join back to sys.partitions is container_id. Because of what I described with hobts, you could join to either partition_id or hobt_id. If you are a veteran SQL Server support engineer like me, you might see that something is missing from sys.allocation_units. What about first, root, and first_IAM? Initially, the SQL Server development team did not think anyone needed to see these columns. Feedback to Microsoft was that it would be valuable to still see these values. So, late in the beta cycle, the sys.system_internals_allocation_units catalog view was created. Let's run the preceding query again, this time changing it to use this view:

```
-- IAM information is only found in this internal catalog --- view. This view
may change so could
-- break your application if you rely on the result set
select object_name(pt.object_id) as name, pt.index_id, sau.* from
sys.system_internals_allocation_units sau
join sys.partitions pt
on sau.container_id = pt.partition_id
and pt.object_id = object_id('test_table')
order by container_id
go
name                                                                    index_id
allocation_unit_id  type type_desc                         container_id
filegroup_id total_pages      used_pages      data_pages      first_page
root_page    first_iam_page
```

```
----------------------------------------------------------------------------
----------------------------------------------------  ----------  --------------------  ----  -
----------------------------------------------------------------  --------------------
------------  --------------------  --------------------  --------------------  --------
------  --------------  --------------
test_table                                                                      1
72057594042843136   1   IN_ROW_DATA                        72057594038583296   1
2          2              1              0x9A0000000100  0x9A0000000100  0x9B0000000100
test_table                                                                      1
72057594042908672   3   ROW_OVERFLOW_DATA                  72057594038583296   1
0          0              0              0x000000000000  0x000000000000  0x000000000000
test_table                                                                      1
72057594042974208   2   LOB_DATA                           72057594038583296   1
2          2              0              0x980000000100  0x980000000100  0x990000000100
test_table                                                                      2
72057594043039744   1   IN_ROW_DATA                        72057594038648832
1          2          2              1              0x9C0000000100  0x9C0000000100
0x9D0000000100
```

Now the same page numbers in hex as you could find from sysindexes in SQL Server 2000 are available. Be careful with the usage of this view. As mentioned in the documentation, it might change over time, depending on changes to the architecture for allocation.

Database Checksum

One of the challenges in PSS for customer cases involving database corruption is to pinpoint whether the problem is specifically caused by a hardware or system problem. SQL Server 2005 adds checksum capabilities for database pages and log blocks. This is an important feature to determine how a database page might have become damaged. Here is how it works.

If you enable a database for checksum (it is on by default, or you enable it with ALTER DATABASE), right before the engine writes a page to disk, it calculates a checksum value based on the bits on the page and writes this value into the page header. When the page is read back from disk, SQL Server calculates the checksum value based on bits on the page (excluding the checksum itself in the header) and compares that to the checksum value in the page header. If they do not match, SQL Server knows the page must have been altered after it submitted it to be written to disk. The server doesn't know who altered it, but the path of IO from the operating system to the disk is subject to scrutiny.

Fast Recovery

A number of customer cases come into PSS in which the customer is struggling because the database is not accessible because of the length of database recovery on startup. Database recovery has three basic phases: analysis, redo, and undo. The final phase, undo, typically takes the longest and is the source of pain. SQL Server 2005 takes a step forward in database availability by allowing access to the database during the undo phase of recovery. How is this accomplished? The engine during recovery acquires locks during the redo phase and holds these locks for any uncommitted transaction. When the undo phase begins, recovery is in effect a "user" who is running transactions to undo operations that need to be rolled back. Because locks are acquired to perform this operation, transaction consistency can be maintained. Users can now access the database and run standard transactions. The caveat is that users may get blocked by a system session that is running recovery (because it is holding locks while processing undo). Users who need to access data not related to any transactions being rolled back by recovery will not be affected. The restrictions on this feature are as follows:

- It is supported only for Enterprise Edition.

- It works only for databases set up for full recovery.

- It works only for crash recovery. (In other words, it does not work when restoring a database.)

Deferred Transactions

Another important enhancement to database recovery is the concept of deferred transactions. Consider this scenario. Your system has an unexpected crash and reboots. SQL Server restarts and now has to run recovery on all databases. Because of a problem with your disk system, one of the database pages needed by recovery is damaged. Because the database is enabled for checksum, recovery detects a checksum error. In SQL Server 2000, a damaged page detected during recovery would result in an instant SUSPECT database. The entire database would be inaccessible, and the only method to recover reliably would be to restore the entire database from backup. SQL Server addresses this with a clever solution. In situations where damage to a single page is detected during recovery, the page is marked with a special bit called *RestorePending* so that it cannot be accessed. Furthermore, the transaction associated with the page is "deferred" if it is an active transaction that must be rolled back. What this means is that locks associated with the transaction are held after redo and are not released after undo. In fact, undo for the transaction is skipped.

So at the time recovery is complete, the database is still online, the page that is damaged is not accessible, and any locks associated with an associated uncommitted transaction are held. But the database status remains ONLINE and not SUSPECT. So, users can access the database but will encounter an error when accessing the page. Also, if the transaction associated with the page is deferred, a user could be blocked. (The locks are held by session_id = -3.) Resolution to the problem could then be to just restore the damaged page. More on the details behind this when I talk about recovering an inaccessible database.

Deferred transactions are supported for both crash and restore recovery, but this does not work for recovery when a database is attached.

Read-Only Compressed Databases

A frequent question I see about databases is whether you can use NTFS compression for the database and log files. The largest concern is consistency, because the server cannot guarantee sector-aligned writes. However, a read-only database has no consistency concern. Therefore, the SQL Server development team decided to allow a read-only database to be stored on NTFS compressed files. SQL Server 2000 did not prevent you from creating a read-write database on an NTFS compressed volume, even though this is not a supported configuration. However, in SQL Server 2005, if you shut down SQL Server, compress the files of a read-write database, and then try to restart SQL Server, you see the following errors in the ERRORLOG:

```
2006-03-18 22:49:14.87 spid15s    Starting up database 'pubs'.
2006-03-18 22:49:15.01 spid15s    Error: 5118, Severity: 16, State: 1.
2006-03-18 22:49:15.01 spid15s    The file  "C:\Program Files\Microsoft SQL
Server\MSSQL.1\MSSQL\DATA\pubs.mdf" is compressed but does not reside in a
read-only database or filegroup. The file must be decompressed.
```

As the message implies, it is also possible to mark a filegroup as read-only and compress the files just for that filegroup even though the rest of the database is read-write.

SQL Server 2005 Enhancements

I have discussed several storage internal concepts, including several enhancements for SQL Server 2005 based on customer and PSS experience with data recovery in SQL Server 2000 and previous versions.

A discussion of new enhancements for SQL Server 2005 data recovery would not be complete without talking about BACKUP/RESTORE and DBCC CHECKDB.

BACKUP Enhancements

The most noteworthy enhancement to BACKUP is verification. If you execute the T-SQL BACKUP command using the WITH CHECKSUM option, two things happen:

- As each database page is read from the database file from disk, the server verifies the checksum value in the page header if it exists. If it fails, the server raises an error and stops the backup.

- The server calculates a checksum value for all the bits from all pages in the backup and writes this in the backup media. This is called the backup checksum.

These both serve important purposes. By verifying the checksum on pages before the server writes them to the backup, you can prevent the server writing bad pages in your backup. Second, by writing a checksum value for the entire backup stream, the server can verify using RESTORE whether any bits in the backup media itself were damaged after backup writes were submitted to the target media. It is important to know that no new checksum value is written during BACKUP. So, if the database page did not contain a checksum value, a new one is not calculated and then written to the page before it is written to the backup media. But this page is still used as part of calculating the backup checksum.

If you do encounter an error when using WITH CHECKSUM because of a damaged page, you can choose to ignore any error using the WITH CONTINUE_AFTER_ERROR option. The best course of action is to resolve the checksum problem before taking the backup; in an emergency situation to ensure the rest of the database is backed up, however, you might consider using this option.

One other nice addition for SQL Server 2005 BACKUP is full-text data. Previously, to back up your full-text data, you had to manually back up the full-text catalog files associated with the database. Now if your database has full-text data, SQL Server automatically includes the full-text catalog information into the backup information associated with the database. You can even just back up the full-text catalog on it own using the T-SQL BACKUP command. (Refer to the Books Online reference for BACKUP for the proper syntax.)

RESTORE Enhancements

Until SQL Server 2005, the RESTORE VERIFYONLY command was not all that useful. This is because this option did not really verify much of what was contained in the backup set. That has changed for SQL Server 2005 in two ways:

- If the backup media contains a backup checksum, by default the server verifies it. The server also verifies any checksum that exists on a given page in the backup.

- Even if the backup does not contain any checksum, the server verifies that the page ID in the page header is valid.

The same verification occurs by default for the standard RESTORE command, not just with VERIFYONLY. But VERIFYONLY is now a useful command in your arsenal. With checksums, it becomes a quick solution to verifying the integrity of the backup media. (Remember, however, this doesn't mean the backup will actually restore successfully, because recovery could still fail.)

Another option for the RESTORE command that will be useful in emergency situations is CONTINUE_AFTER_ERROR. Before this option was added and a customer encountered a corrupt backup, there was no way to know whether a single page was damaged or whether the entire backup was bad.

If you encounter an error with RESTORE (such as failure verifying checksum) on SQL Server 2005, you can use the CONTINUE_AFTER_ERROR option. The engine just ignores all errors and loads all pages in the database as they exist in the backup. You can then decide how to fix any remaining errors (for example, using DBCC CHECKDB with repair options). This is not an option you want to use on a regular basis. If you do, it means you have problems with your backups. However, it might come in handy on some late night when you do have bad backups but want to extract as much as you can from them.

The last important enhancement for RESTORE is the page-level restore. A PAGE option has been added to the RESTORE command to specify page numbers (maximum of 1,000). The addition of this option is yet another to help increase database availability. Consider a case where you encounter a checksum error on a single page for a 10TB database. If you want to restore just this page, you can from the latest full backup and restore subsequent log backups to make the transactions affecting the page consistent. And with Enterprise Edition, you can do all of this online, allowing other users to access unaffected areas of the database. Of course, the speed of the RESTORE alone is improved, because the server only has to write one or more pages from the backup to the database. (It still takes time to find and read the page from the backup.) I fully expect customers to take advantage of this option, especially those who call PSS and want us to help with some type of advanced recovery because they cannot afford the downtime of a full restore. There is an exercise at the end of chapter you can use to see how to use page-level restore after encountering a damaged page.

DBCC CHECKDB Enhancements

Another area of significant investment for SQL Server 2005 is DBCC CHECKDB. A former PSS colleague of mine, Ryan Stonecipher, now owns this code. He worked with Paul Randal, who used to own it, to incorporate feedback from customers and PSS throughout the beta. The result is some of the following feature enhancements.

DATA_PURITY

DBCC CHECKDB can verify all types of things. But in previous releases of SQL Server, one thing it did not verify was the validity of values within certain data types (such as date/time). The SQL Server development team actually added an undocumented trace flag in SQL Server 2000 to check this because a few customers reported databases with invalid datetime or decimal data within the column values. This led to some strange problems including what appeared to be incorrect results. So, the development team decided in SQL Server 2005 to just add an option to check datetime and decimal columns for valid ranges of values as specified for that type.

For a new SQL Server 2005 database, DATA_PURITY checks are on by default (unless you use the WITH PHYSICAL_ONLY option). For an upgraded database, you must use WITH DATA_PURITY one time, and then it is implied from that point forward.

Progress Reporting

One common question for users of DBCC CHECKDB is a bit like your kids asking you in the car, "When do we get there?" Customers call PSS after DBCC CHECKDB has been running for an hour and say, "When will it be done?" So, the SQL Server development team added progress reporting capabilities for CHECKDB. A user can query the percent_complete and command columns of the sys.dm_exec_requests dynamic management view to see the current progress of CHECKDB. The command column displays a set of predefined values that describe the phase of execution of CHECKDB. (For example, DBCC SYS CHECK means CHECKDB is checking the consistency of system tables. The percent_complete column marks the progress within this phase.) SQL Server Books Online has a complete description of the phases and whether progress is reported for that phase.

"Last Known Good"

One of the questions I have asked customers when investigating a case involving database corruption is this: "When was the last time DBCC CHECKDB reported no errors for this database?" If the customer did not save all CHECKDB results or if the ERRORLOG files have wrapped, there is no way to answer this question. SQL Server 2005 saves in the database information about the last time a DBCC CHECKDB was run without errors on the database.

Anytime the database is started, the information about the "last known good" clean DBCC is reported in the ERRORLOG like the following:

```
2005-09-22 11:56:48.42 Server    Database mirroring has been enabled on this
instance of SQL Server.
2005-09-22 11:56:48.42 spid5s    Starting up database 'master'.
2005-09-22 11:56:48.73 spid5s    Recovery is writing a checkpoint in database
'master' (1). This is an informational message only. No user action is required.
2005-09-22 11:56:48.84 spid5s    CHECKDB for database 'master' finished without
errors on 2005-09-22 11:31:45.990 (local time). This is an informational
message only; no user action is required.
```

As you can see in this message, a CHECKDB was deemed to be "good." This information is updated every time a CHECKDB completes without errors for a specific database.

In addition to saving and recording the last clean CHECKDB, the SQL Server development team also enhanced the report in the ERRORLOG for each CHECKDB execution. The server now includes a duration value, so you can see how long it typically takes to run CHECKDB for your database. Here is an example of this ERRORLOG output:

```
2006-03-19 19:35:40.15 spid51   DBCC CHECKDB (troy) executed by NORTHAMERICA
\bobward found 0 errors and repaired 0 errors. Elapsed time: 0 hours 0 minutes 2
seconds.
```

Online Uses Database Snapshot

In SQL Server 2000, *online* DBCC CHECKDB reads the transaction log to check the consistency of the database. By online, I mean that the database is in MULTI_USER mode. Although this technique works, in some cases this might cause false CHECKDB errors. Therefore, in SQL Server 2005, CHECKDB takes advantage of the new snapshot database feature. An online CHECKDB now creates a database snapshot of the current database and uses the snapshot to check database consistency. This now makes online CHECKDB extremely simple. Just run the consistency check on the snapshot and you are guaranteed a consistent set of pages at the point in time CHECKDB was run. If a snapshot cannot be created (for example, because the databases are stored on the FAT file system), the table locks are used to ensure consistency.

Enhanced *CHECKCATALOG* Integrated

Any veteran SQL Server support engineer knows that DBCC CHECKCATALOG is not really worth running. In SQL Server 2000 and previous versions, only a few system tables were actually included in this check. Furthermore, the number of times an actual system table referential integrity occurs is few. Along with the new system table architecture, the SQL Server development team decided to actually implement a full catalog consistency check and include it by default when DBCC CHECKDB runs. DBCC CHECKCATALOG can still be run independently, but it is a quick operation as part of the overall CHECKDB execution.

Emergency Mode Repair

In SQL Server 2000, if the database is marked SUSPECT and you do not have a backup to restore, your options are pretty limited. One option some customers have chosen is to call Microsoft PSS to see whether they can help repair the database. This procedure involves some advanced undocumented commands that could end up resulting in a rebuild of the transaction log. This procedure can result in a CHECKDB with no errors, but logical consistency is now compromised. This request has come in so often that the SQL Server development team decided to include a recovery feature in the product so that customers could perform this operation themselves.

Data Recovery Best Practices

Before I dig into troubleshooting scenarios for various types of database recovery problems, let me share with you perspective on best practices for you to use to avoid problems. This section is not a complete study of disaster recovery strategies, but I give you some information you might find helpful based on my experience with data recovery customer cases.

BACKUP/RESTORE Best Practices

Your database is only as good as your last backup.

If you have a great backup strategy, more power to you. If you have any doubts, read on. You would be surprised how many customers call Microsoft PSS and have not backed up their database (or don't have a recent backup). If I had responsibility for any database being used in a business, my number one priority would be the safety and security of that data, which includes disaster recovery situations. I have many non-computer-savvy friends who I talk to about the files on their computer. They ask me how often they should back them up. I always tell them, "Your data is only as good as your most recent backup." As good as computer hardware is today, I've seen too many situations where someone didn't have a recent backup and lost data. It just takes one time of losing key data to learn to have timely and good backups. Don't let yourself run into that situation. You could run for years without ever needing a backup, but when you really need it, you will be so thankful that you spent careful time and consideration ensuring your backups are recent and up-to-date based on your needs and requirements.

Use the BACKUP CHECKSUM feature.

I personally would take any hit in backup performance that you may encounter when using the WITH CHECKSUM option of BACKUP. There is simply no better method in the database engine to detect whether the pages written to the backup are valid and to verify that the backup medium has not been damaged or altered after it is written. This feature actually makes RESTORE VERIFYONLY a viable option to determine whether you have a reasonable chance of restoring the database.

RESTORE is the only guaranteed method to verify backups.

Even with the checksum feature, if you want a guarantee that a backup can be verified, the only way is to restore it. This is because even if you use the WITH CHECKSUM feature, other problems could occur. For example, what if there is some logical problem with transaction log records so that when recovery runs during restore, a failure occurs? If the log record is physically correct but some logical problem exists that prevents redoing that log record within the engine, restoring the backup is the only way to find out.

As part of my advice on restore, I think it is important to test your disaster recovery strategy. For example, how long does it take to restore your backups at any given day or time of day? If your business requires the database to be back and available within 30 minutes during the day Monday through Friday, but with your current disaster recovery strategy, it would take 4 hours to restore your backups on Thursday at 2 p.m., clearly you have a problem. You may need to seek high-availability solutions such as database mirroring or log shipping.

Avoid network drive backups.

Customers seem to encounter more problems than not when backing up their databases or logs to a network drive. I've seen everything from damaged backups to network errors during the backup to Windows errors due to insufficient kernel resources when customers back up large databases to network drives. Using a storage area network (SAN) system seems to be fairly reliable, but I personally don't recommend you back up your database to a network mapped drive on another server on your network. If you have to store your backups on another server and you don't have a SAN system, I recommend you try to back up the database to a local drive, use a program or utility to compress the file (they usually put a checksum on the file as part of this), and then copy this file over the network to the remote server. If the compression utility supports checksum features, such as a cyclic redundancy check (CRC), when you uncompress you can at least safely know the bytes were copied to the remote server. Another alternative is to use a vendor backup solution that uses SQL Server VDI to stream the backup remotely to another computer.

Don't forget about page-level restore.

Remember when making key decision about restoring a database that you have a new feature to reduce the time to restore a backup sequence called page-level restore. Of course, to use this feature you need to know what page to restore, but in some cases, you may have damage to a single page for a multiterabyte database. If you have Enterprise Edition, why not then restore just the damaged page using database and log backups while users are online in the database? It could save you a lot of time and grief. I highly recommend you test this feature and understand exactly how it works before you rely on this possible strategy. An exercise at the end of this chapter helps you understand what is required to use this feature.

Back up system databases.

Don't forget the importance of your system databases. The failure to open these databases at startup can result in a failure to start SQL Server. If you can't restore from a backup, you could be looking at a longer recovery process to rebuild the system databases, attach user databases, re-create user logins, and so on. Because `tempdb` is re-created at each server startup, you (of course) don't back this up, but `model` is important because you may add objects in `model` for new databases, and `tempdb` requires `model` to be available to be created at server startup. I have an entire section of this chapter on recovery of system databases, and I think you will see that having a valid backup to restore makes your life easier.

Database and Transaction Log Best Practices

Don't delete your transaction log.

I hope one thing you get out of this chapter is how important your transaction log is to the logical consistency of your database. So, just because database recovery is taking a long time or the log is getting really big, don't think that simply shutting down SQL Server and deleting the log is a good idea. As with other scenarios, this is not uncommon for customers calling Microsoft PSS. They delete the log file and then call us wondering what to do because the database cannot be started.

If recovery is taking a long time, and you think it is stuck or will never recover, it is possible Microsoft PSS may have to help you rebuild the log, but consider contacting PSS first. You might just choose to restore from a backup, but if the backup is good, that is a much better alternative than just deleting your log.

The one scenario in which you can safely delete the log is if the database is detached and shut down cleanly and the recovery mode is `SIMPLE`. In this case, the log has nothing in it for recovery purposes, so you could delete it. Personally, I would use this method. I would simply shrink the log file using `DBCC SHRINKFILE`. Remember, if you choose to do this, you have to detach the database first.

Always detach before attaching a database.

The proper method to attach a database requires that you detach it first. Don't just shut down SQL Server, copy the database and log files to another computer, and then attach them. If you need to copy the database, use `BACKUP/RESTORE` or the Copy Database Wizard in Management Studio.

The process of detaching cleanly shuts down the database. Furthermore, if the database is suspect, detach fails in SQL Server 2005 (SQL Server 2000 didn't do this), preventing you from getting into a situation where you can't attach.

Moving the `resource` database.

If you need to move the resource database, there is a documented method to do this in SQL Server 2005 Books Online. However, you must move the database to the exact same drive and directory as the master database. Failure to do this will result in problems when trying to install a service pack or hotfix package.

Don't ignore runtime errors.

If you encounter any error related to a database that indicates possible consistency problems, don't ignore these or take care of them "when you have time." Take these seriously and put them on your high-priority list of things to do. The read retry feature is nice in

SQL Server 2005, but it means some underlying problem might exist with your disk system. A successful read retry one day could be a checksum failure the next. If you have any doubts or questions about these errors related to a possible database consistency problem and I don't have the information in this chapter, consult with experts such as MVPs in the SQL Server newsgroups, or contact Microsoft PSS.

DBCC CHECKDB Best Practices

Just use DBCC CHECKDB.

In SQL Server 2005, DBCC CHECKDB does it all. No need to run CHECKALLOC or CHECKCATALOG separately in SQL Server 2005. CHECKDB does it all. You may choose to use CHECKTABLE on individual tables, but if CHECKDB runs in a reasonable time frame, I recommend you check the entire database. You can also consider the WITH PHYSICAL_ONLY option to perform a reasonable minimum check for the database and reduce the time of overall execution.

Don't just run REPAIR.

I talk more about restoring a backup versus repair in the section on CHECKDB errors, but I'll say briefly here that I recommend that you not just blindly run CHECKDB with the REPAIR_ALLOW_DATA_LOSS option. Just because DBCC CHECKDB doesn't report errors after repair doesn't mean you don't have issues to deal with. Repair may de-allocate a page containing data rows, which now means you have logical inconsistency of your data. If you have to use repair because you can't restore a database, try to keep information about errors in CHECKDB and either a backup of the damaged database or a copy of the damaged page(s) before using repair. This is the only way to learn about the possible cause of the damage to the database.

Use RESTORE **rather than emergency mode** REPAIR.

Emergency mode repair is a great feature (especially for PSS). It makes the process to repair and rebuild a log simple and easy to use. But the key to its usage is the term *emergency*. The SQL Server development team put in this feature for situations that you simply didn't account for in your disaster recovery strategy. But don't rely on this feature. I hope you never have to use this in your usage and administration of SQL Server, but it is nice to know the feature exists should it be needed.

You can't overuse CHECKDB.

So how often should you use CHECKDB? Well, I would say first that you can't run this too often. It might affect performance because of its resource usage, but you won't burn up your hard drive by using this command every day. Having said that, you probably should use this command only on some type of regular, but minimal, basis. There is no single formula for how often to run this command, but here is my opinion of some checkpoints for when CHECKDB should be run:

- Whenever you see a critical error in the ERRORLOG, especially ones I've documented as runtime consistency problems.
- Before and after any SQL Server service pack or hotfix installations.

- Before and after any major database application upgrades.

- Before and after any Windows operating system service pack or hotfix installations or upgrade.

- Before and after any hardware or system maintenance such as drivers, firmware updates, new hardware installation, or replacement of hardware components.

- On a regular basis that makes you comfortable with the consistency of your database. (This may be daily, weekly, or monthly. I wouldn't go any longer than one month to use CHECKDB unless you have something like a read-only database you can easily re-create at any time.)

CHECKDB **on backup servers is not a guarantee.**

If you choose to restore backups to another server to keep an updated copy of your database available, be careful if regular DBCC CHECKDB on the backup server reports no errors. The primary server could have problems unique to that machine that are not carried into a restore on the backup server. Now if you restore a full database backup and immediately run CHECKDB on that restored backup, it is reasonable to assume the primary databases based on that backup are clean.

Data Recovery Troubleshooting Scenarios

I've organized the various type of data recovery scenarios I want to teach you how to troubleshoot into system database recovery, user database inaccessible, BACKUP/RESTORE failures, runtime consistency errors, and CHECKDB errors. Each section is self-contained so that you can focus on the area you are most interested in.

System Database Recovery

In most cases, recovering your database is your primary concern, because it contains the data that supports your application and business. However, understanding how to recover system databases can be important even though it occurs less often. This is because in most cases, a problem with a system database can mean SQL Server cannot start. The exception in this chapter is the MSDB database, but this too can be critical if you rely on it for its capability to run SQLAgent jobs.

Recovering Master

There are two possible scenarios where SQL Server cannot access any database including master or your user database:

- A resource problem opening database or log files.

- Recovery fails, causing the database to become SUSPECT.

A resource problem means that the engine encountered an error when trying to open a database or log file.

Scenario 1: Failure to Open the Master Database File (master.mdf)

Let's consider this scenario first. The master database is a unique database because it is the single database used to bootstrap the execution of the engine. Server-wide information is only stored in the master database, such as the registration of all other databases, login accounts, configuration values, error messages, and linked server information.

When the engine first starts, it must first open the master database to read the server-wide configuration information. At this point, if the master database file (`master.mdf`) cannot be opened, SQL Server does not start. The `ERRORLOG` would look something like this:

```
2006-01-28 11:07:37.06 Server    Microsoft SQL Server 2005 - 9.00.1399.06
(Intel X86)
        Oct 14 2005 00:33:37
        Copyright (c) 1988-2005 Microsoft Corporation
        Developer Edition on Windows NT 5.1 (Build 2600: Service Pack 2)
2006-01-28 11:07:37.06 Server    (c) 2005 Microsoft Corporation.
2006-01-28 11:07:37.06 Server    All rights reserved.
2006-01-28 11:07:37.06 Server    Server process ID is 4036.
2006-01-28 11:07:37.06 Server    Logging SQL Server messages in file 'C:\Program
Files\Microsoft SQL Server\MSSQL.1\MSSQL\LOG\ERRORLOG'.
2006-01-28 11:07:37.06 Server    This instance of SQL Server last reported using a
process ID of 2952 at 1/26/2006 5:04:21 PM (local) 1/26/2006 11:04:21 PM (UTC).
This is an informational message only; no user action is required.
2006-01-28 11:07:37.06 Server    Registry startup parameters:
2006-01-28 11:07:37.06 Server        -d C:\Program Files\Microsoft SQL
Server\MSSQL.1\MSSQL\DATA\master.mdf2
2006-01-28 11:07:37.06 Server        -e C:\Program Files\Microsoft SQL
Server\MSSQL.1\MSSQL\LOG\ERRORLOG
2006-01-28 11:07:37.06 Server        -l C:\Program Files\Microsoft SQL
Server\MSSQL.1\MSSQL\DATA\mastlog.ldf
2006-01-28 11:07:37.07 Server    Error: 17113, Severity: 16, State: 1.
2006-01-28 11:07:37.07 Server    Error 2(The system cannot find the file
specified.) occurred while opening file 'C:\Program Files\Microsoft SQL
Server\MSSQL.1\MSSQL\DATA\master.mdf2' to obtain configuration information at
startup. An invalid startup option might have caused the error. Verify your
startup options, and correct or remove them if necessary.
```

You can see that `Msg 17113` indicates a problem trying to read the configuration information from the master database file.

Troubleshooting Steps

Look at the error information right after the 17113 message. In this case, it says this:

```
2006-01-28 11:07:37.07 Server    Error 2(The system cannot find the file specified.)
occurred while opening file 'C:\Program Files\Microsoft SQL
Server\MSSQL.1\MSSQL\DATA\master.mdf2'
```

Error 2 is the Windows error returned from the Windows API `CreateFile` call. The text description follows the error number.

Determine the cause of the Windows error. In this case, error 2 means that the filename SQL Server passed to `CreateFile` does not exist. This means the path is wrong or the file does not exit. Check the full name of the path in the message. The standard name for the master database file is `master.mdf`, not `master.mdf2`.

If this is true, why does the engine think the name is `master.mdf2`? Because the master database is the bootstrap database, the engine has to get the location of the master database files from a source other than a database. It uses program parameters to do this. `-d` is used to specify the location of the master database file, and `-l` for the master transaction log file. Because SQL Server is normally run as a service, it must get the default startup parameter values from the registry.

Rather than edit the registry directly, use the SQL Server Configuration Manager. This is a good time to point out that any startup parameter setting or service configuration option (such as the startup account for SQL Server) should be done using the SQL Configuration Manager. Figure 2-3 shows what the interface looks like to change startup parameters for SQL Server.

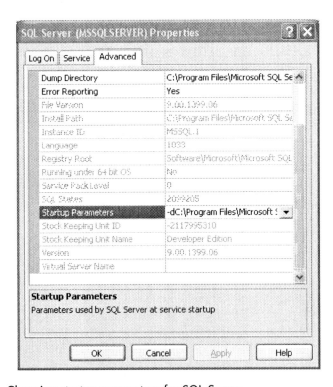

FIGURE 2-3   Changing startup parameters for SQL Server

One tip when using this dialog box. The Startup Parameters is a single text field. To add a new parameter, you need to add it to the end of the parameters delimited by a semicolon.

Even though a failure to open the transaction log file can be resolved using the same technique, the errors reported in the ERRORLOG are slightly different:

```
2006-02-04 17:25:15.37 spid5s    Error: 17207, Severity: 16, State: 1.
2006-02-04 17:25:15.37 spid5s    FCB::Open: Operating system error 2(The system
cannot find the file specified.) occurred while creating or opening file
'C:\Program Files\Microsoft SQL Server\MSSQL.1\MSSQL\DATA\mastlog.ldf2'. Diagnose
and correct the operating system error, and retry the operation.
2006-02-04 17:25:15.40 spid5s    Error: 17204, Severity: 16, State: 1.
2006-02-04 17:25:15.40 spid5s    FCB::Open failed: Could not open file C:\Program
Files\Microsoft SQL Server\MSSQL.1\MSSQL\DATA\mastlog.ldf2 for file number 2. OS
error: 2(The system cannot find the file specified.).
2006-02-04 17:25:15.48 spid5s    Error: 5120, Severity: 16, State: 101.
2006-02-04 17:25:15.48 spid5s    Unable to open the physical file "C:\Program
Files\Microsoft SQL Server\MSSQL.1\MSSQL\DATA\mastlog.ldf2". Operating system
error 2: "2(The system cannot find the file specified.)".
```

Scenario 2: Master Database Recovery Failure

Like any user database, if recovery fails, the database is marked SUSPECT. However, one major difference is that the server shuts down when it detects that recovery has failed. Consider a situation where SQL Server attempts to start but fails. You look at the ERRORLOG and see the following:

```
2006-03-19 22:35:02.14 Server    Microsoft SQL Server 2005 - 9.00.1399.06
(Intel X86)
       Oct 14 2005 00:33:37
       Copyright (c) 1988-2005 Microsoft Corporation
       Developer Edition on Windows NT 5.1 (Build 2600: Service Pack 2)
2006-03-19 22:35:02.14 Server    (c) 2005 Microsoft Corporation.
2006-03-19 22:35:02.14 Server    All rights reserved.
2006-03-19 22:35:02.14 Server    Server process ID is 2040.
2006-03-19 22:35:02.14 Server    Logging SQL Server messages in file 'C:\Program
Files\Microsoft SQL Server\MSSQL.1\MSSQL\LOG\ERRORLOG'.
2006-03-19 22:35:02.15 Server    This instance of SQL Server last reported using a
process ID of 3628 at 3/19/2006 10:32:33 PM (local) 3/20/2006 4:32:33 AM (UTC).
This is an informational message only; no user action is required.
2006-03-19 22:35:02.15 Server    Registry startup parameters:
2006-03-19 22:35:02.15 Server        -d C:\Program Files\Microsoft SQL
Server\MSSQL.1\MSSQL\DATA\master.mdf
2006-03-19 22:35:02.15 Server        -e C:\Program Files\Microsoft SQL
Server\MSSQL.1\MSSQL\LOG\ERRORLOG
2006-03-19 22:35:02.15 Server        -l C:\Program Files\Microsoft SQL
Server\MSSQL.1\MSSQL\DATA\mastlog.ldf
2006-03-19 22:35:02.18 Server    SQL Server is starting at normal priority base
(=7). This is an informational message only. No user action is required.
2006-03-19 22:35:02.18 Server    Detected 1 CPUs. This is an informational message;
no user action is required.
2006-03-19 22:35:02.56 Server    Using dynamic lock allocation. Initial allocation
of 2500 Lock blocks and 5000 Lock Owner blocks per node. This is an informational
message only. No user action is required.
2006-03-19 22:35:02.56 Server    Attempting to initialize Microsoft Distributed
```

Transaction Coordinator (MS DTC). This is an informational message only. No user
action is required.
2006-03-19 22:35:02.59 Server   The Microsoft Distributed Transaction Coordinator
(MS DTC) service could not be contacted. If you would like distributed transaction
functionality, please start this service.
2006-03-19 22:35:02.59 Server   Database Mirroring Transport is disabled in the
endpoint configuration.
2006-03-19 22:35:02.59 spid5s   Starting up database 'master'.
2006-03-19 22:35:04.34 spid5s   Error: 824, Severity: 24, State: 2.
2006-03-19 22:35:04.34 spid5s   SQL Server detected a logical consistency-based I/O
error: incorrect pageid (expected 1:506; actual 39321:-1717986919). It occurred
during a read of page (1:506) in database ID 1 at offset 0x000000003f4000 in file
'C:\Program Files\Microsoft SQL Server\MSSQL.1\MSSQL\DATA\master.mdf'. Additional
messages in the SQL Server error log or system event log may provide more detail.
This is a severe error condition that threatens database integrity and must be
corrected immediately. Complete a full database consistency check (DBCC CHECKDB).
This error can be caused by many factors; for more information, see SQL Server
Books Online.
2006-03-19 22:35:04.34 spid6s   Error: 922, Severity: 14, State: 1.
2006-03-19 22:35:04.34 spid6s   Database 'master' is being recovered. Waiting until
recovery is finished.
2006-03-19 22:35:04.34 spid6s   System Task System Task produced an error that was
not handled. Major: 9, Minor: 22, Severity:14, State:1
2006-03-19 22:35:04.34 spid5s   Error: 3313, Severity: 21, State: 2.
2006-03-19 22:35:04.34 spid5s   During redoing of a logged operation in database
'master', an error occurred at log record ID (2017:314:13). Typically, the specific
failure is previously logged as an error in the Windows Event Log service. Restore
the database from a full backup, or repair the database.
2006-03-19 22:35:04.34 spid5s   Cannot recover the master database. SQL Server
is unable to run. Restore master from a full backup, repair it, or rebuild
it. For more information about how to rebuild the master database, see SQL
Server Books Online.

Troubleshooting Steps

First, read the errors from the bottom up. You can see that the problem is a recovery problem for master, the error was during the redo of a log operation, and that the cause of
that problem is an 824 error on the database page. The 824 error in this case is due to an
incorrect page ID on page 1:506.

Because deferred transactions don't apply to the master database, your choices are the
following:

- Restore a backup of the master database.

- Rebuild it using the setup program that comes with the installation medium.

Let's address how to restore a backup in this situation. You always have to start SQL Server
in single user mode (using the -m startup parameter) to restore master, but in this case,
SQL Server cannot be started because of the master recovery failure. Well, a nice trace flag
helps you in this situation, trace flag 3607. Trace flag 3607 tells the engine to open just
the master database, but don't run recovery on it. It is only to be used in this type of
emergency situation, when master database recovery fails.

So the steps are as follows:

1. Start SQL Server with -m and -T3607 as startup parameters using the SQL Server Configuration Manager.

2. Restore your backup of the master database.

   You see a message indicating SQL Server is being shut down:

   ```
   Processed 360 pages for database 'master', file 'master' on file 1.
   Processed 2 pages for database 'master', file 'mastlog' on file 1.
   The master database has been successfully restored. Shutting down SQL Server.
   SQL Server is terminating this process.
   ```

   SQL Server shuts down by design whenever you restore master. It is important to pay attention to the message to the client, because the ERRORLOG will not show a reason why SQL Server was shut down in this situation.

3. Remove the -m and -T3607 startup parameters and restart SQL Server.

So if you don't happen to have a backup of the master database, your only choice is to rebuild it. After you rebuild it, you lose any previous information in master. Unfortunately, trace flag 3607 is only helpful to restore master. When you use this trace flag, any attempt to access an object in master results in the following error:

```
Msg 904, Level 16, State 1, Line 1
Database 32767 cannot be autostarted during server shutdown or startup.
```

Putting master in emergency mode won't help either, because it is not allowed for the master database.

So now that you are faced with the prospect of rebuiding master, how do you go about it? The first step is to find the installation media or source for your install (perhaps a net-work drive). Why? Because the method to rebuild the master database is contained within the SQL Server Setup program that only comes with the installation media. The steps to use setup to rebuild master are actually well documented in SQL Server Books Online in the section "Rebuilding System Databases, Rebuilding the Registry," so I don't list them here. An important point for you to keep in mind is that after rebuilding master, you must reapply any service packs or hotfixes you have previously installed, because they might have updated catalog information or the resource database.

The third scenario that I didn't call out specifically is simply a need to restore master because of a corruption problem or perhaps a change made that you want undone (for example, dropping some important logins). If the master database is fully available and ONLINE, all you need to do is RESTORE your backup.

Recovering Model

Just like the master database, if the model database cannot be started, SQL Server will not start successfully. If the problem was due to a problem with opening the model database file, the ERRORLOG shows entries such as the following:

```
2006-03-19 23:52:11.06 spid9s    Error: 17207, Severity: 16, State: 1.
2006-03-19 23:52:11.06 spid9s    FCB::Open: Operating system error 2(The system
cannot find the file specified.) occurred while creating or opening file
'C:\Program Files\Microsoft SQL Server\MSSQL.1\MSSQL\DATA\model.mdf'. Diagnose and
correct the operating system error, and retry the operation.
2006-03-19 23:52:11.06 Server    Server is listening on [ 127.0.0.1 <ipv4> 1434].
2006-03-19 23:52:11.06 spid9s    Error: 17204, Severity: 16, State: 1.
2006-03-19 23:52:11.06 spid9s    FCB::Open failed: Could not open file C:\Program
Files\Microsoft SQL Server\MSSQL.1\MSSQL\DATA\model.mdf for file number 1. OS
error: 2(The system cannot find the file specified.).
2006-03-19 23:52:11.06 Server    Dedicated admin connection support was established
for listening locally on port 1434.
2006-03-19 23:52:11.06 spid9s    Error: 5120, Severity: 16, State: 101.
2006-03-19 23:52:11.06 spid9s    Unable to open the physical file "C:\Program
Files\Microsoft SQL Server\MSSQL.1\MSSQL\DATA\model.mdf". Operating system error 2:
"2(The system cannot find the file specified.)".
2006-03-19 23:52:11.12 spid9s    Error: 945, Severity: 14, State: 2.
2006-03-19 23:52:11.12 spid9s    Database 'model' cannot be opened due to
inaccessible files or insufficient memory or disk space. See the SQL Server
errorlog for details.
2006-03-19 23:52:11.14 spid9s    Could not create tempdb. You may not have
enough disk space available. Free additional disk space by deleting other
files on the tempdb drive and then restart SQL Server. Check for additional
errors in the event log that may indicate why the tempdb files could not be
initialized.
```

This is similar to the situation with the master database; just the error numbers have changed. In this case, error 5120 contains the Windows error to explain why the model database file could not be opened. In the preceding scenario, it is Windows error 2, which means the file could not be found. Troubleshoot the same way as master, except the location for where the engine believes the file should exist is stored in the master database rather than in the registry. If I encountered this error, I would check to see whether the file existed in the path. If it did not, I would see if the model.mdf file existed anywhere on the drive. If I found it, I could copy it to the path as listed in the message or change the location where the engine should look for the file.

How do I do this if the engine will not start? Here are the steps:

1. Add the startup parameter -T3608 to start SQL Server. This tells the engine to not start any database except master.

2. Use ALTER DATABASE and the MODIFY FILE option to change the path of the model database file to its correct path.

3. Shut down and restart SQL Server without -T3608 so that all system and user databases can recover.

A more obscure scenario would be for recovery to fail for the model database. I say this because the model database is not changed very often by customers. Customers who do want to add objects to the model database so that every new database will have them usually do this infrequently. But should recovery fail for the model database, you need to use trace flag 3608 again to start the server so that you can restore model from a backup. This was not possible in SQL Server 2000, because the engine would attempt to use tempdb during the RESTORE command. Because tempdb first requires model to be started, the RESTORE command would fail. Now that restriction is removed, and RESTORE should work with trace flag 3608. What about that cool feature I told you about called emergency mode repair with CHECKDB? Is that possible for model? Does it make sense? First of all, it doesn't make sense. You don't want to create new databases based on a possible logically inconsistent model database. But it really doesn't matter anyway, because ALTER DATABASE SET EMERGENCY is not allowed on the model database. (For that matter, it isn't allowed on any system database.)

Recovering MSDB

The msdb database is considered a system database even though it is not required to start SQL Server. One reason that you can consider it a system database is that if you rebuild the master database with setup, you are in effect rebuilding all system databases, including model, MSDB, and the resource database. Furthermore, MSDB (in case you were wondering, MSDB stands for Microsoft System Database) is used to store important information such as backup/restore history and SQL Server Agent jobs. In fact, the SQL Server Agent service will not start if the MSDB database is not available.

The scenarios for problems accessing MSDB are the same as master and model. Either you can encounter a resource problem (such as problems opening the database/log files), or recovery could fail, causing the database to become SUSPECT.

Because MSDB is more like a user database than model, you can use more-conventional techniques to recover it. For example, because SQL Server can start if a problem exists with MSDB, you don't need any special trace flags to restore a backup of MSDB. If the MSDB database becomes SUSPECT, you can just restore from a backup. If you don't have a backup available, you must rebuild the system databases using the same technique as you would rebuild master or model. In previous versions, you could get away with manually running the instmsdb.sql script in the INSTALL directory of SQL Server. Unfortunately, this technique is no longer that simple (the gyrations to make it work are pretty complex, and I don't think they are reliable), so the safest bet is to rebuild system databases.

If the MSDB database or log files cannot be opened, the database state appears as RECOVERY_PENDING, as described in the "Storage Internals" section. The errors you will see in the ERRORLOG look much like the scenario with model:

```
2006-03-20 18:58:47.71 spid12s    Error: 17207, Severity: 16, State: 1.
2006-03-20 18:58:47.71 spid12s    FCB::Open: Operating system error 2(The system
cannot find the file specified.) occurred while creating or opening file
'c:\program files\microsoft sql server\mssql.1\mssql\data\msdbdata.mdf'. Diagnose
and correct the operating system error, and retry the operation.
```

```
2006-03-20 18:58:47.71 spid12s    Error: 17204, Severity: 16, State: 1.
2006-03-20 18:58:47.71 spid12s    FCB::Open failed: Could not open file c:\program
files\microsoft sql server\mssql.1\mssql\data\msdbdata.mdf for file number 1. OS
error: 2(The system cannot find the file specified.).
2006-03-20 18:58:47.73 spid12s    Error: 5120, Severity: 16, State: 101.
2006-03-20 18:58:47.73 spid12s    Unable to open the physical file "c:\program
files\microsoft sql server\mssql.1\mssql\data\msdbdata.mdf". Operating system
error 2: "2(The system cannot find the file specified.)".
```

In fact, as you will see in the next section on user databases, these errors look the same as
if a user database files could not be opened. The difference between this scenario and the
model database is that the server is still up and running. You can then try to resolve the
problem (perhaps by getting the msdbdata.mdf file in its right location) and simply execute ALTER DATABASE msdb SET ONLINE to start it up. By the way, don't get nervous when
doing this in SQL Server Management Studio. If you attempt to connect to Object
Explorer for the server in this state, you will get the error shown in Figure 2-4.

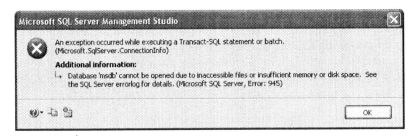

FIGURE 2-4   Error message from attempting to connect to Object Explorer for the server

After you click OK, you won't see anything under the server name from Object Explorer.
This is because Object Explorer tries to execute a stored procedure in the msdb database to
show properties for SQL Server Agent after it connects. If this fails, it just doesn't show
you anything. That's okay. Get MSDB back online, and then right-click the server instance
listed. Select Disconnect, which removes the server instance from the screen. Now you
can select the Connect drop-down option and reconnect to Object Explorer.

Recovering the Resource Database

You recall the resource database is read-only and "hidden." This means you can't reference this in commands such as ALTER DATABASE. So the techniques to recover from problems with it are different than even other system databases. For example, there is no way
to BACKUP the resource database online. But because you can't modify it, there is no need
to. The only way to back up the resource database is to back up the files themselves.

This scenario is very much the model database, because the server cannot start if it cannot
open the resource database. In fact, the errors are identical to what you see in this situation for model. So look at the Windows error and resolve this to restart SQL Server. There
is one big difference from the model situation. Even if you want to start SQL Server with
-T3608 to avoid starting the resource database, you really cannot do anything. What I
mean is that you can't query any catalog view, because they require the resource database.

Furthermore, as I've said, T-SQL commands can't reference the resource database by name. Given this information, the only way to encounter a problem opening the resource database files is something occurring external to SQL Server (for example, someone going into the DATA directory and renaming the mssqlsystemresource.mdf file).

The other scenario could simply be damage to the resource database caused by some external factor (perhaps the portion of the disk containing this database was damaged). Because there is no way to BACKUP the database or RESTORE it, the only method to recover is to copy the resource database files themselves from the proper source. What is the proper source? This is where you have to manage these files a bit. For the RTM version of SQL Server 2005, no problem. These files are on the installation media. You may not have this lying around, which is why I recommend you copy them to some backup source you can get to easily. For any hotfixes or service packs you apply, you should also keep this copy of the files handy to replace.

When you start applying hotfixes or future service packs, you may ask, "How do I know if I've got the correct version to copy?" There is a method to find out the version of the resource database. Remember I told you to think of the resource database as DLL. The problem with versions is that the resource database files are not DLLs, so there is no way with Windows to put in a version value in the property of these files. So, the SQL Server development team built in the version to the resource database and provided you a way to query it:

```
select ServerProperty('ResourceVersion')
```

For the RTM version of SQL Server, this returns the following result:

```
-------------------------------------------
9.00.1399
```

So how do I know whether this is the "right" version of the resource database? This version matches the engine's build number. And the query to find out the build number is the following:

```
select ServerProperty('ProductVersion')
```

For the original shipping version of SQL Server 2005 (known internally as the RTM version), this returns the following:

```
-------------------------------------------
9.00.1399.06
```

You can ignore the .06 on this version for comparison's sake. This is just an internal number used as part of the final builds for SQL Server 2005 RTM. So if you run these two queries and you receive the same results for the first three numbers separated by the decimal, you have the correct resource database. If they don't match, you have a problem and need to find the correct version. This is why I recommend whenever you apply a hotfix or service pack, you take the resource database files copied to the DATA directory and keep them tucked away in a safe place. What would happen if these two versions differ? For SQL Server 2005 RTM, maybe nothing. The true answer is the behavior of catalog views and system objects in the engine is unpredictable. For future versions of the engine (hint: perhaps in the first service pack of SQL Server 2005), an error may be produced in the ERRORLOG, and the engine might not start.

Failure to Create *tempdb*

As with previous versions of SQL Server, tempdb is created from scratch each time SQL Server is started. This means recovery is not run for tempdb. This does not mean there won't be problems creating tempdb at server startup. One such problem I've seen as reported by customers is not having enough disk space to create the tempdb files. By default, tempdb is created with a single 8MB database file and 512KB transaction log file. So no matter how large tempdb grows, when SQL Server is restarted, it is re-created with these default sizes. However, you can change these default sizes using ALTER DATABASE or SQL Server Management Studio. In fact, for performance reasons, I highly recommend you not rely on autogrowth of these files and change tempdb to a size that meets the needs of your application. (Unfortunately, I do not get into a recommendation here, but there is a section in Books Online called "Capacity Planning for tempdb.")

Reinstalling the Operating System

One other possible scenario to mention about system databases is reusing them if you have to reinstall the operating system. Consider the scenario where for whatever reason you decide to reinstall the Windows operating system. This will also require you to reinstall SQL Server. But if the drive containing the system database files and your user database files is valid and intact, why should you have to rebuild the system databases? In SQL Server 2000, this was exactly what you had to do. In SQL Server 2005, the setup program is smart enough to detect existing system databases.

When you run the setup for SQL Server, you can specify a path for the DATA directory where system databases will reside. Simply point that DATA directory to the same path where the valid system databases exist. If you do this, you see the dialog box from setup, as shown in Figure 2-5.

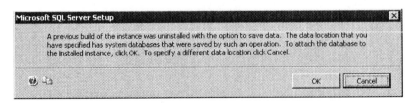

FIGURE 2-5   Dialog box from setup

Just click OK and setup will use your existing system databases. When setup is done, you should be at the same state as you were before reinstalling the operating system (unless you had applied hotfixes or service packs, because they must be reapplied after this).

User Database Inaccessible

Let's shift focus now and talk about scenarios where you may have problems accessing your database. The scenarios are similar to some of the system database situations, but other options are available for recovery, because SQL Server can start even if your database cannot.

Database Marked *RECOVERY_PENDING*

Remember the database state diagram I explained earlier in the chapter. If there is any problem opening the database or transaction log files for a database, the database state is changed to RECOVERY_PENDING. In this scenario, if you attempt to access the database, you get the following error:

```
use pubs
go
Msg 945, Level 14, State 2, Line 1
Database 'pubs' cannot be opened due to inaccessible files or insufficient
memory or disk space. See the SQL Server errorlog for details.
```

Much like the case with MSDB, the ERRORLOG shows errors like these:

```
2006-03-23 14:26:05.99 spid18s    Error: 17207, Severity: 16, State: 1.
2006-03-23 14:26:05.99 spid18s    FCB::Open: Operating system error 2(The system
cannot find the file specified.) occurred while creating or opening file
'C:\Program Files\Microsoft SQL Server\MSSQL.1\MSSQL\DATA\pubs.mdf'. Diagnose and
correct the operating system error, and retry the operation.
2006-03-23 14:26:06.10 spid18s    Error: 17204, Severity: 16, State: 1.
2006-03-23 14:26:06.10 spid18s    FCB::Open failed: Could not open file C:\Program
Files\Microsoft SQL Server\MSSQL.1\MSSQL\DATA\pubs.mdf for file number 1. OS error:
2(The system cannot find the file specified.).
2006-03-23 14:26:06.21 spid18s    Error: 5120, Severity: 16, State: 101.
2006-03-23 14:26:06.21 spid18s    Unable to open the physical file "C:\Program
Files\Microsoft SQL Server\MSSQL.1\MSSQL\DATA\pubs.mdf". Operating system
error 2: "2(The system cannot find the file specified.)".
```

Unfortunately in this case, Management Studio does not give you any clue in Object Explorer that the database may have a problem (see Figure 2-6).

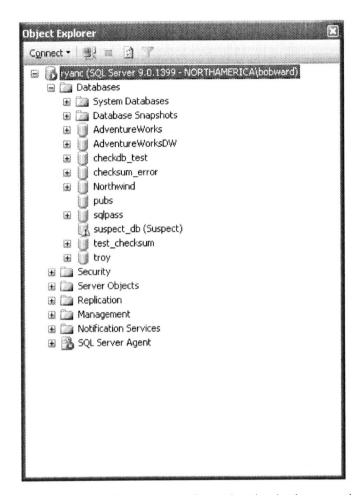

FIGURE 2-6   Management Studio does not indicate that the database may have a problem.

You can see, though, that next to the pubs database icon there is no plus sign (+) to examine objects in that database. This is a clue that there may be an issue with pubs. If you run into this situation, try to right-click the database icon and select Properties. This forces Management Studio to try and access the database (trying to obtain metadata about the state of files in the database).

In this particular scenario, you get a dialog box with any errors encountered trying to access properties for the database (in this case, Msg 945), as shown in Figure 2-7.

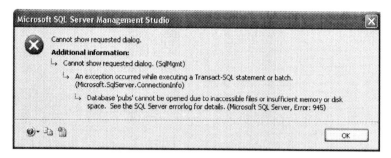

FIGURE 2-7 Dialog box with errors encountered while trying to access properties for the database

If you query the sys.databases catalog view, you can see the pubs database status of RECOVERY_PENDING:

```
select state_desc, name from sys.databases where name = 'pubs'
go

state_desc                                                      name
--------------------------------------------------------------- -----------------------
-----
RECOVERY_PENDING                                                pubs
```

If the transaction log file is not available, the database state is marked RECOVERY_PENDING, but errors reported in the ERRORLOG are slightly different:

```
2006-03-23 14:47:12.81 spid13s    Error: 17207, Severity: 16, State: 1.
2006-03-23 14:47:12.81 spid13s    FileMgr::StartLogFiles: Operating system error
2(The system cannot find the file specified.) occurred while creating or opening
file 'C:\Program Files\Microsoft SQL Server\MSSQL.1\MSSQL\DATA\pubs_log.LDF'.
Diagnose and correct the operating system error, and retry the operation.
2006-03-23 14:47:12.81 spid13s    File activation failure. The physical file
name "C:\Program Files\Microsoft SQL Server\MSSQL.1\MSSQL\DATA\pubs_log.LDF"
may be incorrect.
```

There is an interesting exception to this scenario when the transaction log file cannot be opened and the database uses a recovery mode of SIMPLE. If the database was shut down "cleanly," which means no recovery is required for the database on startup and the database recovery mode is SIMPLE, it is a safe operation for SQL Server to rebuild the transaction log. Why?

- A SIMPLE recovery has no log backups, so media recovery is not an issue.

- If there is no recovery to run on the database, no consistency is lost by rebuilding the log.

In this situation, on database startup, you will see some failures in the ERRORLOG but also a message indicating the transaction log is being rebuilt:

```
2006-03-23 14:42:59.28 spid13s    Error: 17207, Severity: 16, State: 1.
2006-03-23 14:42:59.28 spid13s    FileMgr::StartLogFiles: Operating system error
2(The system cannot find the file specified.) occurred while creating or opening
file 'C:\Program Files\Microsoft SQL Server\MSSQL.1\MSSQL\DATA\pubs_log.LDF'.
Diagnose and correct the operating system error, and retry the operation.
2006-03-23 14:42:59.36 spid13s    File activation failure. The physical file name
"C:\Program Files\Microsoft SQL Server\MSSQL.1\MSSQL\DATA\pubs_log.LDF" may be
incorrect.
2006-03-23 14:42:59.68 spid12s    Starting up database 'troy'.
2006-03-23 14:43:00.23 spid15s    CHECKDB for database 'test_checksum' finished
without errors on 2005-09-22 11:31:57.547 (local time). This is an informational
message only; no user action is required.
2006-03-23 14:43:01.06 spid12s    CHECKDB for database 'troy' finished without
errors on 2006-03-19 19:36:09.937 (local time). This is an informational message
only; no user action is required.
2006-03-23 14:43:01.17 spid13s    New log file 'C:\Program Files\Microsoft SQL
Server\MSSQL.1\MSSQL\DATA\pubs_log.LDF' was created.
2006-03-23 14:43:01.17 spid13s    New log file 'C:\Program Files\Microsoft SQL
Server\MSSQL.1\MSSQL\DATA\pubs_log.LDF' was created.
```

As I discuss later in this section, this comes in handy for attaching SIMPLE model databases with a single transaction log file. You don't even need the transaction log file to attach, because it is perfectly safe for SQL Server to rebuild one for you. Unfortunately, the log is rebuilt to a default size of 1MB, so you need to resize this to your needs.

Troubleshooting Steps

If the cause for RECOVERY_PENDING is inability to open the database files, the steps are simple, exactly as they were for MSDB:

1. Correct the problem that caused the file open failure.

2. Run ALTER DATABASE <dbname> SET ONLINE.

3. If ALTER DATABASE doesn't report any errors, you know that the database started successfully. You can also see your actions allowed the database to start in the ERRORLOG:

```
2006-03-23 15:07:44.18 spid51    Setting database option ONLINE to ON for
database pubs.
2006-03-23 15:07:44.25 spid51    Starting up database 'pubs'.
```

If no errors exist in the ERRORLOG after the "Starting up" message, the database should now be ONLINE (which you can also confirm by looking at sys.databases).

There is an interesting situation involving a failure to open a database or log file I want you to know about because it is tricky to troubleshoot. Look at the following ERRORLOG entries and notice the OS Error description for why the file cannot be opened:

```
2006-03-23 15:15:25.71 spid15s    Error: 17207, Severity: 16, State: 1.
2006-03-23 15:15:25.71 spid15s    FCB::Open: Operating system error 32(The process
cannot access the file because it is being used by another process.) occurred while
creating or opening file 'C:\Program Files\Microsoft SQL
Server\MSSQL.1\MSSQL\DATA\pubs.mdf'. Diagnose and correct the operating system
error, and retry the operation.
2006-03-23 15:15:25.71 spid15s    Error: 17204, Severity: 16, State: 1.
2006-03-23 15:15:25.71 spid15s    FCB::Open failed: Could not open file C:\Program
Files\Microsoft SQL Server\MSSQL.1\MSSQL\DATA\pubs.mdf for file number 1. OS error:
32(The process cannot access the file because it is being used by another
process.).
2006-03-23 15:15:25.71 spid15s    Error: 5120, Severity: 16, State: 101.
2006-03-23 15:15:25.71 spid15s    Unable to open the physical file "C:\Program
Files\Microsoft SQL Server\MSSQL.1\MSSQL\DATA\pubs.mdf". Operating system
error 32: "32(The process cannot access the file because it is being used by
another process.)".
```

How can this situation occur? Why would SQL Server not be able to open a file because another program had it open? How do I find what program is doing this? There is a nice utility on the web called Process Explorer (which you can download from www.sysinternals.com).

To find which program has this open, launch Process Explorer and select the Find, Find Handle menu option. Type in the name of the file in the SQL error, and the program will tell you exactly what process has your database file handle open (see Figure 2-8).

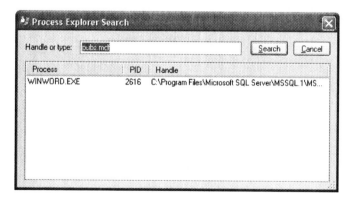

FIGURE 2-8   What process your database file handle opened

In this case, someone has accidentally opened the file using Microsoft Word. Well, okay, it was me deliberately doing this to demonstrate the problem.

The same troubleshooting steps I've provided for database files apply to transaction log files. But what if you cannot resolve the problem with accessing the transaction log file? Do you have any other options? You do, but there are limits on how successful they will be.

In this situation, you can change the database state to EMERGENCY using ALTER DATABASE
<dbname> SET EMERGENCY. At this point, you can access the database to query your data.
But only SELECT statements to read data. You will encounter the following error if you try
to modify the database:

```
Msg 3908, Level 16, State 1, Line 1
Could not run BEGIN TRANSACTION in database 'pubs' because the database is in
bypass recovery mode.
```

You can run some diagnostics like DBCC CHECKDB. However, you may get errors from this
command, because the transaction log file was not available and recovery could not run.
Recovery may be necessary to bring the database into a consistent state. So, your options
are to copy all the data from your database to a new one or to use emergency mode
repair. I covered this in the earlier section on enhancements to DBCC CHECKDB for SQL
Server 2005.

Here are the steps to use CHECKDB in this situation (assuming the preceding example,
where the pubs transaction log file could not be opened):

1. ALTER DATABASE pubs SET EMERGENCY.

2. ALTER DATABASE pubs SET SINGLE_USER.

3. DBCC CHECKDB (pubs, REPAIR_ALLOW_DATA_LOSS).

4. CHECKDB returns the following messages:

```
File activation failure. The physical file name "C:\Program Files\Microsoft
SQL Server\MSSQL.1\MSSQL\DATA\pubs_log.LDF" may be incorrect.
Warning: The log for database 'pubs' has been rebuilt. Transactional consistency
has been lost. The RESTORE chain was broken, and the server no longer has context
on the previous log files, so you will need to know what they were. You should run
DBCC CHECKDB to validate physical consistency. The database has been put in dbo-
only mode. When you are ready to make the database available for use, you will need
to reset database options and delete any extra log files.
DBCC results for 'pubs'.
Service Broker Msg 9675, State 1: Message Types analyzed: 14.
Service Broker Msg 9676, State 1: Service Contracts analyzed: 6.
Service Broker Msg 9667, State 1: Services analyzed: 3.
Service Broker Msg 9668, State 1: Service Queues analyzed: 3.
Service Broker Msg 9669, State 1: Conversation Endpoints analyzed: 0.
Service Broker Msg 9674, State 1: Conversation Groups analyzed: 0.
Service Broker Msg 9670, State 1: Remote Service Bindings analyzed: 0.
DBCC results for 'sys.sysrowsetcolumns'.
There are 626 rows in 6 pages for object "sys.sysrowsetcolumns".
DBCC results for 'sys.sysrowsets'.
There are 97 rows in 1 pages for object "sys.sysrowsets".
DBCC results for 'sysallocunits'.
There are 110 rows in 2 pages for object "sysallocunits".
DBCC results for 'sys.sysfiles1'.
There are 2 rows in 1 pages for object "sys.sysfiles1".
DBCC results for 'sys.syshobtcolumns'.
```

There are 626 rows in 6 pages for object "sys.syshobtcolumns".
DBCC results for 'sys.syshobts'.
There are 97 rows in 1 pages for object "sys.syshobts".
DBCC results for 'sys.sysftinds'.
There are 0 rows in 0 pages for object "sys.sysftinds".
DBCC results for 'sys.sysserefs'.
There are 110 rows in 1 pages for object "sys.sysserefs".
DBCC results for 'sys.sysowners'.
There are 14 rows in 1 pages for object "sys.sysowners".
DBCC results for 'sys.sysprivs'.
There are 123 rows in 1 pages for object "sys.sysprivs".
DBCC results for 'sys.sysschobjs'.
There are 99 rows in 2 pages for object "sys.sysschobjs".
DBCC results for 'sys.syscolpars'.
There are 497 rows in 9 pages for object "sys.syscolpars".
DBCC results for 'sys.sysnsobjs'.
There are 1 rows in 1 pages for object "sys.sysnsobjs".
DBCC results for 'sys.syscerts'.
There are 0 rows in 0 pages for object "sys.syscerts".
DBCC results for 'sys.sysxprops'.
There are 0 rows in 0 pages for object "sys.sysxprops".
DBCC results for 'sys.sysscalartypes'.
There are 30 rows in 1 pages for object "sys.sysscalartypes".
DBCC results for 'sys.systypedsubobjs'.
There are 0 rows in 0 pages for object "sys.systypedsubobjs".
DBCC results for 'sys.sysidxstats'.
There are 127 rows in 2 pages for object "sys.sysidxstats".
DBCC results for 'sys.sysiscols'.
There are 244 rows in 1 pages for object "sys.sysiscols".
DBCC results for 'sys.sysbinobjs'.
There are 23 rows in 1 pages for object "sys.sysbinobjs".
DBCC results for 'sys.sysobjvalues'.
There are 147 rows in 22 pages for object "sys.sysobjvalues".
DBCC results for 'sys.sysclsobjs'.
There are 14 rows in 1 pages for object "sys.sysclsobjs".
DBCC results for 'sys.sysrowsetrefs'.
There are 0 rows in 0 pages for object "sys.sysrowsetrefs".
DBCC results for 'sys.sysremsvcbinds'.
There are 0 rows in 0 pages for object "sys.sysremsvcbinds".
DBCC results for 'sys.sysxmitqueue'.
There are 0 rows in 0 pages for object "sys.sysxmitqueue".
DBCC results for 'sys.sysrts'.
There are 1 rows in 1 pages for object "sys.sysrts".
DBCC results for 'sys.sysconvgroup'.
There are 0 rows in 0 pages for object "sys.sysconvgroup".
DBCC results for 'sys.sysdesend'.
There are 0 rows in 0 pages for object "sys.sysdesend".
DBCC results for 'sys.sysdercv'.
There are 0 rows in 0 pages for object "sys.sysdercv".
DBCC results for 'sys.syssingleobjrefs'.
There are 163 rows in 1 pages for object "sys.syssingleobjrefs".
DBCC results for 'sys.sysmultiobjrefs'.
There are 133 rows in 1 pages for object "sys.sysmultiobjrefs".
DBCC results for 'sys.sysdbfiles'.
There are 2 rows in 1 pages for object "sys.sysdbfiles".

```
DBCC results for 'sys.sysguidrefs'.
There are 0 rows in 0 pages for object "sys.sysguidrefs".
DBCC results for 'sys.sysqnames'.
There are 91 rows in 1 pages for object "sys.sysqnames".
DBCC results for 'sys.sysxmlcomponent'.
There are 93 rows in 1 pages for object "sys.sysxmlcomponent".
DBCC results for 'sys.sysxmlfacet'.
There are 97 rows in 1 pages for object "sys.sysxmlfacet".
DBCC results for 'sys.sysxmlplacement'.
There are 17 rows in 1 pages for object "sys.sysxmlplacement".
DBCC results for 'sys.sysobjkeycrypts'.
There are 0 rows in 0 pages for object "sys.sysobjkeycrypts".
DBCC results for 'sys.sysasymkeys'.
There are 0 rows in 0 pages for object "sys.sysasymkeys".
DBCC results for 'sys.syssqlguides'.
There are 0 rows in 0 pages for object "sys.syssqlguides".
DBCC results for 'sys.sysbinsubobjs'.
There are 0 rows in 0 pages for object "sys.sysbinsubobjs".
DBCC results for 'publishers'.
There are 8 rows in 1 pages for object "publishers".
DBCC results for 'titles'.
There are 18 rows in 1 pages for object "titles".
DBCC results for 'titleauthor'.
There are 25 rows in 1 pages for object "titleauthor".
DBCC results for 'stores'.
There are 6 rows in 1 pages for object "stores".
DBCC results for 'sales'.
There are 21 rows in 1 pages for object "sales".
DBCC results for 'roysched'.
There are 86 rows in 1 pages for object "roysched".
DBCC results for 'discounts'.
There are 3 rows in 1 pages for object "discounts".
DBCC results for 'jobs'.
There are 14 rows in 1 pages for object "jobs".
DBCC results for 'pub_info'.
There are 8 rows in 1 pages for object "pub_info".
DBCC results for 'employee'.
There are 43 rows in 1 pages for object "employee".
DBCC results for 'x'.
There are 0 rows in 0 pages for object "x".
DBCC results for 'sys.queue_messages_1977058079'.
There are 0 rows in 0 pages for object "sys.queue_messages_1977058079".
DBCC results for 'sys.queue_messages_2009058193'.
There are 0 rows in 0 pages for object "sys.queue_messages_2009058193".
DBCC results for 'sys.queue_messages_2041058307'.
There are 0 rows in 0 pages for object "sys.queue_messages_2041058307".
DBCC results for 'authors'.
There are 23 rows in 1 pages for object "authors".
CHECKDB found 0 allocation errors and 0 consistency errors in database 'pubs'.
DBCC execution completed. If DBCC printed error messages, contact your system
administrator.
```

Pay special attention to the following message in this chain:

```
Warning: The log for database 'pubs' has been rebuilt. Transactional consistency
has been lost. The RESTORE chain was broken, and the server no longer has context
on the previous log files, so you will need to know what they were. You should run
DBCC CHECKDB to validate physical consistency. The database has been put in dbo-
only mode. When you are ready to make the database available for use, you will need
to reset database options and delete any extra log files.
```

What does this message mean? Well, it has a bunch of warnings, so let me summarize them for you:

- Transactional consistency

    Even though DBCC CHECKDB reports no errors, it doesn't mean that the database is logically consistent. What I mean is that since the log was rebuilt there could have been modifications to the database that need to be redone or undone during recovery for transactions to be consistent.

    Consider the following scenario. Your application credits a customer account for $10,000. The rows on the database page are updated to reflect a credit to the customer's account. Let's say the user of the application is not done with this customer, so by design the transaction for this operation is still active. But, because of memory pressure in the engine, this page is flushed to disk. To ensure consistency, SQL Server also flushes the log records associated with the transaction to disk. But the user realizes he made a mistake and clicks the Cancel button. This causes the application to roll back the transaction. In memory, the page and log records are changed. Within the next few minutes, a serious problem occurs on the server, and it crashes and reboots. SQL Server is robust to crash recovery. Even though the database page on disk shows a credit for $10,000, the transaction log never shows this transaction was committed. So when recovery runs, the modification undone. But what if the engine encountered an error opening the transaction log file and you choose to use emergency mode repair? Recovery never ran, so a credit exists for $10,000 for this customer account. Who would be able to find this problem? Could this really occur? The timing might be difficult, but who would want to take this risk? This is why the SQL Server development team put the text in this message and is why Microsoft PSS always has a serious conversation with customers who want to rebuild their transaction log.

- RESTORE chain broken

    Because we rebuild the transaction log, your backup log chain sequence is broken. You cannot rely on these backups, and you need to take a full backup of the database to restart a new backup sequence.

- Database options

    The database is left in SINGLE_USER mode and is changed to the SIMPLE recovery model.

The SQL Server development team put emergency mode repair in the product for customers to use, but only, as the name implies, for emergency situations. The development team also put in this message so that it would be clear to you that the server cannot vouch for the transactional consistency of your database. Just to make sure you understand that you or another DBA performed this operation, the server writes the following messages to the ERRORLOG:

```
2006-03-23 15:37:48.01 spid51   Warning: The log for database 'pubs' has been
rebuilt. Transactional consistency has been lost. The RESTORE chain was
broken, and the server no longer has context on the previous log files, so
you will need to know what they were. You should run DBCC CHECKDB to validate
physical consistency. The database has been put in dbo-only mode. When you are
ready to make the database available for use, you will need to reset database
options and delete any extra log files.
2006-03-23 15:37:48.01 spid51   Warning: The log for database 'pubs' has been
rebuilt. Transactional consistency has been lost. The RESTORE chain was broken, and
the server no longer has context on the previous log files, so you will need to
know what they were. You should run DBCC CHECKDB to validate physical consistency.
The database has been put in dbo-only mode. When you are ready to make the database
available for use, you will need to reset database options and delete any extra log
files.
2006-03-23 15:37:48.57 spid51   EMERGENCY MODE DBCC CHECKDB (pubs,
repair_allow_data_loss) executed by NORTHAMERICA\bobward found 0 errors and
repaired 0 errors. Elapsed time: 0 hours 0 minutes 0 seconds.
```

Handling Deferred Transactions

As discussed in the "Storage Internals" section, when recovery fails for a user database but the cause of the recovery is damage to a database page, SQL Server may not mark the database SUSPECT. Instead, the engine marks a bit on the damaged page in the header (set to a status called RestorePending). If the transaction associated with the operation that encountered the damaged page is still active after redo, all locks are held that are part of the transaction, and undo for the transaction is skipped (or deferred). The good news is that the database is still ONLINE and not SUSPECT. Only users who need to access this page or access data associated with any deferred transaction are affected.

How do you know whether recovery had to defer transactions but not mark the database SUSPECT?

- You see evidence in the ERRORLOG.

- You encounter an error when accessing a page that is marked RestorePending.

- You are blocked by session_id = -3.

The choices and steps for recovering a deferred transaction are simple:

- Restore a backup. But in this case, because only a single page is damaged, you could use online page restore to keep the rest of the database online and affect only the deferred transaction.

- If you don't have a backup to use, you can repair the page (but lose the data on it) by using DBCC CHECKDB and the REPAIR_ALLOW_DATA_LOSS option.

The steps for using page-level restore are documented in Books Online in the section "Performing Page Restores." Although I won't add anything about these steps in this section, there is an exercise in the end of this chapter to walk you through using this feature during a data recovery scenario.

Finding the root cause for a deferred transaction is not complicated, because the cause is damage to the database page, as outlined in the ERRORLOG (for example, a checksum error on a page). Therefore, you must investigate the cause of this problem just like you would for any checksum failure. As I mentioned earlier in this chapter, the cause of a checksum page error is not SQL Server but a problem in the IO path.

Database Marked *SUSPECT*

Suppose recovery fails and one of the conditions for a deferred transaction doesn't qualify or the failure is not associated with a single database page (for example, damage to the transaction log is detected). In this situation, the engine changes the database state to SUSPECT.

The following is an example of an ERRORLOG entry for a database marked SUSPECT:

```
2006-03-26 22:14:10.98 spid13s    Error: 824, Severity: 24, State: 4.
2006-03-26 22:14:10.98 spid13s    SQL Server detected a logical consistency-based
I/O error: (bad checksum). It occurred during a read of page (0:-1) in database ID
8 at offset 0x00000000013800 in file 'C:\Program Files\Microsoft SQL
Server\MSSQL.1\MSSQL\DATA\suspect_db_log.LDF'. Additional messages in the SQL
Server error log or system event log may provide more detail. This is a severe
error condition that threatens database integrity and must be corrected
immediately. Complete a full database consistency check (DBCC CHECKDB). This error
can be caused by many factors; for more information, see SQL Server Books Online.
2006-03-26 22:14:11.43 spid13s    Error: 3414, Severity: 21, State: 1.
2006-03-26 22:14:11.43 spid13s    An error occurred during recovery, preventing
the database 'suspect_db' (database ID 8) from restarting. Diagnose the
recovery errors and fix them, or restore from a known good backup. If errors
are not corrected or expected, contact Technical Support.
```

Any attempt to access the database results in the following error:

```
Msg 926, Level 14, State 1, Line 1
Database 'suspect_db' cannot be opened. It has been marked SUSPECT by
recovery. See the SQL Server errorlog for more information.
```

Fortunately, Management Studio gives us a visual clue to the status of the database (see Figure 2-9).

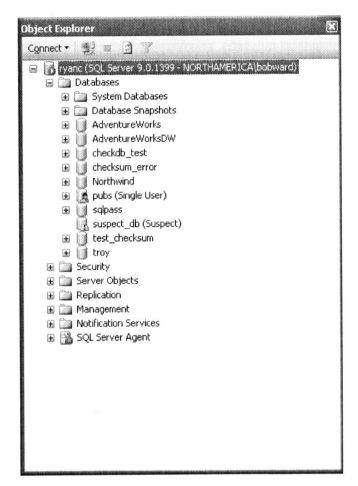

FIGURE 2-9   Management Studio gives a visual clue to the status of the database

As in the case of a deferred transaction, your options to recover are similar:

- You can restore from a backup. Page-level restore is not an option here, because the problem is not specific to a database page.

- Use DBCC CHECKDB for emergency mode repair. I outlined how this works when I discussed the scenario of the transaction log being unavailable.

- If emergency mode repair does not work, you could change the database state to EMERGENCY and try to copy as much data as possible.

Remember that the SUSPECT state for a database is temporary. This means to find the original cause for why the database was marked SUSPECT, you can either restart SQL Server or you can try to change the database state to ONLINE. Consider the example of the database suspect_db. If I try to change the database state to ONLINE, I get the following messages:

```
Msg 926, Level 14, State 1, Line 1
Database 'suspect_db' cannot be opened. It has been marked SUSPECT by recovery. See
the SQL Server errorlog for more information.
Msg 5069, Level 16, State 1, Line 1
ALTER DATABASE statement failed.
Msg 824, Level 24, State 4, Line 1
SQL Server detected a logical consistency-based I/O error: (bad checksum). It
occurred during a read of page (0:-1) in database ID 8 at offset 0x00000000013800
in file 'C:\Program Files\Microsoft SQL
Server\MSSQL.1\MSSQL\DATA\suspect_db_log.LDF'. Additional messages in the SQL
Server error log or system event log may provide more detail. This is a severe
error condition that threatens database integrity and must be corrected
immediately. Complete a full database consistency check (DBCC CHECKDB). This error
can be caused by many factors; for more information, see SQL Server Books Online.
Msg 3414, Level 21, State 1, Line 1
An error occurred during recovery, preventing the database 'suspect_db'
(database ID 8) from restarting. Diagnose the recovery errors and fix them, or
restore from a known good backup. If errors are not corrected or expected,
contact Technical Support.
```

The first message after 5069 is the root cause of the SUSPECT failure, which in this example is a checksum failure (Msg 824) when reading the transaction log. (Yes, the transaction log uses checksum technology, too, to detect IO consistency.)

Attach Database Failures

It is possible to encounter different types of errors when attaching a database. First, let me eliminate one consideration that could occur in previous versions of SQL Server. You can't detach a database whose state is SUSPECT. Attempting to do this results in the following error:

```
Msg 3707, Level 16, State 2, Line 1
Cannot detach a suspect database. It must be repaired or dropped.
```

Although this may be true, you could technically do something you are not supposed to do. You could shut down SQL Server and still use the files from a SUSPECT database to attach to another server. In this case, the attach fails because the database was SUSPECT. Of course, you are supposed to *always* detach a database before you attach it. I've just now showed you an example of why it is important to do this.

Most problems I see with attaching databases have to do with missing some of the files associated with the database. If the database was detached properly (which means it was cleanly shut down) and the database has only one transaction log file, all you need to attach the database are the database files. The log will be rebuilt safely as I've described earlier when the log file is not available at startup (even for a database using FULL recovery). But if you do not have all the transaction log files as they existed for the original database, the server returns the following error:

```
File activation failure. The physical file name "C:\Program Files\Microsoft
SQL Server\MSSQL.1\MSSQL\DATA\test_attach_log2.ldf" may be incorrect.
The log was not rebuilt because there is more than one log file.
Msg 1813, Level 16, State 2, Line 1
Could not open new database 'test_attach'. CREATE DATABASE is aborted
```

In SQL Server 2000, you had no options at this point. SQL Server 2005 offers a new
option to FOR ATTACH_REBUILD_LOG. This option still requires the database to be detached
properly, but it lets you rebuild the log if you don't have all transaction log files.

BACKUP/RESTORE Failures

Because BACKUP and RESTORE are your most important tools to recover your data, I think
it's important to briefly discuss some scenarios where these commands can fail and how
to handle them.

BACKUP Failures

The T-SQL BACKUP command can fail for various reasons, some of them simpler to solve
than others. For example, if you try to use BACKUP LOG and the database is using SIMPLE
recovery, you will encounter the following error:

```
Msg 4208, Level 16, State 1, Line 1
The statement BACKUP LOG is not allowed while the recovery model is SIMPLE. Use
BACKUP DATABASE or change the recovery model using ALTER DATABASE.
Msg 3013, Level 16, State 1, Line 1
BACKUP LOG is terminating abnormally.
```

This error is descriptive and tells you exactly the problem. Other errors or problems are
not as intuitive and simple to resolve, so I focus on those in this section.

Media Failures

One of the most common issues I've seen in technical support regarding backup is a failure writing to the target media. Target media is the destination for the backup stream,
such as a disk file(s) or tape.

Tape failures were more common with previous releases of SQL Server because tape was
the most common format for backing up large databases. I don't see as many of these
cases anymore, but when they do occur, the cause of the failure is almost always a problem with the tape drive, the tape, or device drivers associated with the tape drive. I've
seen this time and time again. Here is a sample ERRORLOG showing a failure writing to the
tape that doesn't appear very intuitive.

```
spid324   BackupMedium::ReportIoError: write failure on backup device '\\.\tape0'.
Operating system error 1117(The request could not be performed because of an I/O
device error.).
```

The steps to resolve a problem such as this or other tape errors is to focus on the tape drive, tape, or device drivers. Try a different tape or a different tape drive. Make sure the device drivers for the tape drive are up-to-date. One common misconception for troubleshooting a problem with writing to tape is that if the Windows NTBACKUP program works, the problem must be SQL Server. Although it is a good idea to see whether you can back up a file using NTBACKUP to the tape drive, if it works but you still encounter an error with SQL Server, the problem could still be the tape system. This is because SQL Server uses Windows API calls that NTBACKUP doesn't when writing to the tape.

Before I talk about some common issues when writing to a disk drive, one simple troubleshooting step to help in many backup cases is to simplify what you are backing up. For example, if you are struggling to back up a 30GB database, try backing up just a small database, such as the sample AdventureWorks database. If you cannot back up even a small sample database, there is a good chance you should focus on the target media, whether it is a tape system, local disk, SAN, or network drive. If a small database sample works, but your database does not, it could still be the target media system, but there is a little more evidence that it could be a SQL Server problem. This is good information to give to a technical support engineer should you decide to contact Microsoft for assistance.

Let's talk about a few more common scenarios that you could encounter today—failures writing to a local disk, SAN, or network drive. As with tape, the cause of these problems is almost always something to do with the target media, current operating system environment, or target operating system environment. Let's take a look at two possible scenarios you may encounter where the solution to the problem is not obvious.

```
2005-05-02 09:15:28.05 spid69 BackupMedium::ReportIoError: write failure on backup
device 'G:\MSSQL\Backups\caamdb.BAK'. Operating system error 64(The specified
network name is no longer available.).
```

In this situation, the error is indicative of a network problem. The error has nothing to do with SQL Server. You should troubleshoot this problem as though there was a network I/O issue communicating with whatever disk is mapped to the G: drive. This may even be a SAN drive.

```
BackupMedium::ReportIoError: read failure on backup device
'\\FFGPS\D$\MSSQL\BACKUP\FSPRD_DB.BAK'. Operating system error
1450(Insufficient system resources exist to complete the requested service.).
```

In this situation, the error is coming from Windows when writing the backup file. I've especially seen this situation when backing up to a network drive. I've also seen this problem with the use of the /3GB switch in boot.ini because there is not enough nonpaged pool memory for Windows to handle the I/O associated with the backup. Your choices are 1) Don't back up to a networked drive, 2) Remove the use of /3GB, 3) Tune nonpaged pool according to the guidelines in Knowledge Base article 304101.

CHECKSUM Failures

I discussed earlier in the chapter a new feature for SQL Server 2005 called backup check-sum. When the WITH CHECKSUM option is specified for the BACKUP command, the engine verifies the checksum for any pages it reads from the database file that previously had a checksum calculated for it. If any page fails this verification check, BACKUP fails with the following error:

```
Msg 3043, Level 16, State 1, Line 1
BACKUP 'test_checksum' detected an error on page (1:177) in file 'C:\Program
Files\Microsoft SQL Server\MSSQL.1\MSSQL\DATA\test_checksum.mdf'.
Msg 3013, Level 16, State 1, Line 1
BACKUP DATABASE is terminating abnormally.
```

The ERRORLOG shows the following information:

```
2006-08-25 14:18:21.49 Backup      Error: 3043, Severity: 16, State: 1.
2006-08-25 14:18:21.49 Backup      BACKUP 'test_checksum' detected an error on page
(1:177) in file 'C:\Program Files\Microsoft SQL
Server\MSSQL.1\MSSQL\DATA\test_checksum.mdf'.
2006-08-25 14:18:21.52 Backup      Error: 3041, Severity: 16, State: 1.
2006-08-25 14:18:21.52 Backup      BACKUP failed to complete the command
BACKUP DATABASE test_checksum. Check the backup application log for detailed
messages.
```

Your choices here are simple:

- Correct the checksum problem.

- Remember the cause of the problem is something within the disk system, so be sure to check all is well here first. I say this because if you choose to repair the database to correct the problem, but the disk still has problems, you will continue to run into other inconsistency issues. To repair the current problem, you can choose to restore from a backup (remember page-level backup restore is a possible option) or you can use DBCC CHECKDB to repair the page (which will result in data loss as the page will be de-allocated to "fix" it).

- Ignore the error and continue the BACKUP.

Let's say you just want to go ahead and back up the database ignoring this error, knowing it will be a bad page. You have an option with BACKUP called CONTINUE_AFTER_ERROR that will let you do just that. If you use this option, you will get the following warning after the BACKUP completes:

```
Processed 208 pages for database 'test_checksum', file 'test_checksum' on
file 1.
Processed 1 pages for database 'test_checksum', file 'test_checksum_log' on file 1.
BACKUP WITH CONTINUE_AFTER_ERROR successfully generated a backup of the damaged
database. Refer to the SQL Server error log for information about the errors that
were encountered.
BACKUP DATABASE successfully processed 209 pages in 1.879 seconds (0.910
MB/sec).
```

The ERRORLOG will contain the following information:

```
2006-08-25 14:20:30.83 Backup        Error: 3043, Severity: 16, State: 1.
2006-08-25 14:20:30.83 Backup        BACKUP 'test_checksum' detected an error on page
(1:177) in file 'C:\Program Files\Microsoft SQL
Server\MSSQL.1\MSSQL\DATA\test_checksum.mdf'.
2006-08-25 14:20:31.03 Backup        Database backed up. Database:
test_checksum, creation date(time): 2006/02/22(11:35:35), pages dumped: 219,
first LSN: 22:16:26, last LSN: 22:28:1, number of dump devices: 1, device
information: (FILE=1, TYPE=DISK: {'c:\test_checksum.bak'}). This is an
informational message only. No user action is required.
```

Why would you consider this option? One reason may be that you want to back up the database in its current state before trying to repair it and correct the damaged page. I'm not saying repair will cause problems for you so you must back up your current database, but I've met careful DBAs who want to back up the current state of the database before trying any fairly major modification operation. The only way for you to do this is to use the CONTINUE_AFTER_ERROR option.

One point of clarification about the WITH CHECKSUM option for BACKUP. The BACKUP command itself does not verify any data after writing it to disk. In other words, BACKUP doesn't verify checksums, write the backup stream checksum, and then go back and verify everything. What it does is verify database page checksums as it reads pages from the database file, write these pages to the backup media, and then write a backup checksum value based on all data written to the media. You can do this yourself by immediately executing RESTORE WITH VERIFYONLY right after the BACKUP.

If you use Management Studio to back up a database, you are presented with an Options dialog box where you can select to use checksum and verify the integrity of the database (see Figure 2-10).

FIGURE 2-10   Option to use checksum and verify the integrity of the database

Look at the options in the Reliability section of the dialog box. If you select these options and use the Script menu at the top of the dialog box (this is a nice feature in Management Studio where you can generate scripts based on options picked in a dialog box for different types of tasks), the resulting T-SQL script will look like this:

```
BACKUP DATABASE [pubs] TO DISK = N'c:\pubs.bak' WITH NOFORMAT, NOINIT, NAME =
N'pubs-Full Database Backup', SKIP, NOREWIND, NOUNLOAD, STATS = 10, CHECKSUM
GO
declare @backupSetId as int
select @backupSetId = position from msdb..backupset where database_name=N'pubs' and
backup_set_id=(select max(backup_set_id) from msdb..backupset where
database_name=N'pubs' )
if @backupSetId is null begin raiserror(N'Verify failed. Backup information for
database ''pubs'' not found.', 16, 1) end
RESTORE VERIFYONLY FROM DISK = N'c:\pubs.bak' WITH FILE = @backupSetId, NOUNLOAD,
NOREWIND
GO
```

This is effectively what Management Studio (through SMO) will use to back up the database with checksum and then verify the backup when it is complete.

Performance Problems: Memory

One possible scenario you may encounter will not show up as an error message. The issue is performance problems with your BACKUP. Perhaps you have seen this before and were not sure as to the cause. We have had customers contact technical support and say that their backups are slowing down and in some cases taking twice as long. In some situations, this degradation has occurred over time. Let's explore how to recognize this behavior and what you can do to resolve it.

When customers have contacted us and complained about backup performance, we quickly noticed in most cases Performance Monitor would show a significant drop in backup throughput via the following counter: Physical Disk/Avg Disk Bytes Per Transfer. We observed this for the disk drive where the customer was writing backup. We noticed that this value on that drive was something much lower than we expected. For a normal SQL Server disk backup, this number should be close to 1MB. This is because we knew internally in SQL Server that the backup code will write out buffers of ~1MB in size to the target disk. The numbers we observed were more like 64KB. What this means is that the SQL engine is writing out a large number of small disk writes versus a smaller number of larger writes. This is not efficient for writing out to a disk drive (assuming no bottlenecks exist).

After some investigation, we discovered the problem. The SQL Server backup code calculates what will be its buffer size (called MAXTRANSERSIZE) based on the number of files for the database/log and the number of target disk drives. (Remember you can back up to multiple disk files at the same time, called a stripe dump.) The backup code then takes the total number of buffers and tries to allocate memory for them at a default size of 960KB. If any of these memory allocations fail, the code *downgrades* its MAXTRANSFERSIZE to 64KB. In SQL Server 2005 (and in SQL Server 2000 SP4), if you observe the following message in the ERRORLOG:

```
2005-12-02 02:00:21.93 spid100  Downgrading backup buffers from 960K to 64K
```

you know that the default MAXTRANSERSIZE could not work. As with any memory problem, the issue is not having enough free memory for these allocations. But here is the twist to this problem. The issue is not having enough contiguous memory to allocate a 960KB block. Furthermore, the memory for the backup buffers doesn't come from the SQL Server buffer pool. This comes from the remaining virtual address space after the buffer pool reserves its memory. This is a precious resource for systems with 2GB+ of physical memory, because the buffer pool consumes most of the virtual address space. This means there are two resolutions to this problem:

- Free up more virtual address space or find out why it is fragmented.

- Use the new MAXTRANSFERSIZE for a lower default setting than 960KB.

RESTORE Failures

Like BACKUP, there are various reasons for restore failing, but two that are the most complex are as follows:

- A consistency problem with the backup media

- A failure during recovery

The second scenario should be investigated just like the scenarios I've already described for deferred transactions and a SUSPECT database. This is because the problems are the same. One is a failure during crash recovery (when the database comes online), and the other is a failure of recovery during media recovery (when the database is being restored).

The first case is the one for us to focus on. This is where database and backup checksums can make the process of determining the cause of a restore failure so valuable. Remember we talked about how restore verifies database page checksums and the backup stream checksum if they exist in the backup.

As we talked about for verifying the integrity of a backup, you can use RESTORE WITH VERIFYONLY. If this fails with the following error, you know the backup media was altered after it was written. You can't tell from this message whether the problem was with a damaged page, but you know the backup media itself was altered and the checksum is now different than when it was written.

```
Msg 3189, Level 16, State 1, Line 1
Damage to the backup set was detected.
Msg 3013, Level 16, State 1, Line 1
VERIFY DATABASE is terminating abnormally.
```

If you run the actual RESTORE DATABASE command and the damage was to a database page that has checksum values on it, you can see this type of error:

```
Msg 3183, Level 16, State 1, Line 1
RESTORE detected an error on page (1:177) in database "test_checksum" as read from
the backup set.
Msg 3013, Level 16, State 1, Line 1
RESTORE DATABASE is terminating abnormally.
```

In either case, a problem was detected with the integrity of the backup. In the case of an error with a database page checksum in the backup, the error could be due to the use of CONTINUE_AFTER_ERROR with BACKUP, or it could be that the page was damaged after the backup was written. Remember this key point about checksum. As with a standard database page checksum, the intention is for SQL Server to detect that data was modified *after* SQL Server wrote it to disk. So if you get one of the preceding two errors (assuming you didn't use BACKUP WITH CONTINUE_AFTER_ERROR) you must focus your root cause analysis of the disk system used to store the backup media.

You can always restore a different backup should you encounter these errors. But if that is not an option, you do have another choice. One of the difficult problems we had in technical support when we determined that a customer's backup was damaged was to determine the severity of the problem. In other words, if the RESTORE fails when restoring the fifth page in the backup, it stops. How can we determine whether the rest of the backup is good? In some extremely urgent cases, I even had to resort to a debugger to "skip" errors during the restore to see how badly it was damaged. SQL Server 2005 introduces a new option for RESTORE called CONTINUE_AFTER_ERROR. If you use this option, RESTORE ignores any error and proceeds to copy all data from the backup media. This way you can try to recover as much data as you possibly can. At this point, you can use DBCC CHECKDB WITH REPAIR_ALLOW_DATA_LOSS to de-allocate the damaged page(s). The damaged page from the backup was lost anyway, but now you can use the rest of the database that is still valid. One key point when using CHECKDB here: You must use the WITH TABLOCK option, too, because online repair will not provide consistent results after you have used CONTINUE_AFTER_ERROR.

Database Consistency Errors

At this point, we have covered three major areas of data recovery: issues with accessing system databases, problems accessing user databases, and backup/restore failures. Now let's talk about detecting database consistency problems during the normal database operation. I classify database consistency detection (errors) into two types:

- Runtime error, errors detected by the engine during standard usage of the database (SELECT, UPDATE, background thread such as lazywrite, and so on)

- Errors detected by DBCC CHECKDB

Handling Database Consistency Runtime Errors

The SQL Server engine contains code to perform some validation of the data (and transaction) log as you execute commands such as SELECT, INSERT, and so on against a database. The following is not a complete list of these errors, but these are the ones I anticipate you may encounter the most.

Msg 823 and 824

The SQL Server engine has two methods to report problems reading database pages (and transaction log blocks):

- If the Windows API calls return an error when reading the page, Msg 823 is raised.

- If the Windows API call is successful, the engine performs a series of logical checks on the page (based on database options configured). If any of these checks fails, an Msg 824 is raised.

The following is an example of a Msg 823 error:

```
2005-09-07 10:51:05.16 spid18s    Error: 823, Severity: 24, State: 6.
2005-09-07 10:51:05.16 spid18s    The operating system returned
error 1117(The request could not be performed because of an I/O device error.)
to SQL Server during a read at offset 0000000000000000 in
file 'E:\EdgeTachyonDatabaseFiles\EdgePerfTachyonDB.mdf'.
```

Additional messages in the SQL Server error log and system event log may provide more detail. This is a severe system-level error condition that threatens database integrity and must be corrected immediately. Complete a full database consistency check (DBCC CHECKDB). This error can be caused by many factors; for more information, see SQL Server Books Online.

As you can see from the message, the SQL Server development team included the Windows error returned from the Windows API call to read the page from disk. Almost every 823 error is caused by a system problem. In this case, SQL Server reports only the error the operating system reported when reading from the file. Look at preceding the example. The text of the message even indicates there is a problem with a disk storage device. The one exception to this guideline that I've seen is error 6, "Invalid handle." In this situation, it is possible SQL Server passed an invalid file handle to the Windows API call, so this should be investigated with technical support.

If the Windows API call to read the page is successful, the following logical checks are applied in this order:

1. Is the page torn (torn page detection)?

2. Did a checksum fail when reading the page (checksum error)?

3. Is the pageid on the page different from the page we expected to read from disk (bad pageid)?

The following is an example of a Msg 824 due to a database checksum validation check failure:

```
2006-08-25 14:38:39.34 spid53      Error: 824, Severity: 24, State: 2.
2006-08-25 14:38:39.34 spid53      SQL Server detected a logical consistency-
based I/O error: incorrect checksum (expected: 0x6cbf615; actual: 0x6dacdc1).
It occurred during a read of page (1:177) in database ID 13 at offset
0x00000000162000 in file 'C:\Program Files\Microsoft SQL
Server\MSSQL.1\MSSQL\DATA\test_checksum.mdf'.  Additional messages in the SQL
Server error log or system event log may provide more detail. This is a
severe error condition that threatens database integrity and must be corrected
immediately. Complete a full database consistency check (DBCC CHECKDB). This
error can be caused by many factors; for more information, see SQL Server
Books Online.
```

Should you see an 824 error in the ERRORLOG, take immediate action, because this means the engine has detected a consistency problem in the database. The damage may be isolated to the page reported in the log, but it could go beyond that. Therefore, I recommend you run DBCC CHECKDB on the database as soon as possible. But which database? The server cannot provide you database context for this error, but it does provide you the filename associated with the physical filename it was reading for this page. If you can't recognize the database associated with the filename in the error, take the filename from the message and use it in the catalog view query:

```
select * from master.sys.master_files where physical_name = '<filename>'
```

At minimum, I expect DBCC CHECKDB to report an error for the page associated with Msg 824. At this point, if only a single page is damaged, you could restore from a backup (remember page-level restore here), or you can repair the database WITH REPAIR_ALLOW_DATA_LOSS. If more errors exist, your options may be more limited, or your data loss may be more severe. The point is, don't ignore 824 errors. It could be the tip of the iceberg of larger damage to your database.

Msg 825 (Read Retry)

While investigating a series of Exchange storage consistency problems, the Exchange development team discovered that if they were to retry failed read operations from disk, in some cases the second, third, or even fourth read attempt would succeed. So, instead of taking a beating from their customers for Exchange store corruption, they decided to add in logic to retry database read failures.

The SQL Server development team decided to adopt this same strategy for SQL Server 2005. Any read failure (823 or 824) will first be retried up to four times by the SQL Engine, before reporting the failure. If at any point the read succeeds, the following message is written to the ERRORLOG:

```
2005-04-27 16:06:35.98 spid346 A read of the file
'f:\mssql\mssql.1\mssql\data\stressdb2.ndf'
at offset 0x00000000302000 succeeded after failing 1 time(s) with error:
incorrect pageid (expected 4:385; actual 0:0).
Additional messages in the SQL Server error log and system event log may provide
more detail. This error condition threatens database integrity and must be
corrected. Complete a full database consistency check (DBCC CHECKDB).
This error can be caused by many factors; for more information, see SQL Server
Books Online.
```

Remember that because the retry succeeded, the user will not see any error. The only difference will be a slight delay in performance (which may or may not truly be seen by the application user). But this does not mean you do not need to address this problem. Think of this message the same as you would an 823 or 824 error, but perhaps at a slightly less-urgent pace. The engine avoided a failure, but this doesn't mean this retry will work all the time. Some disk system issue caused at least one read to fail and therefore should be investigated.

Msg 5242 and 5243 (RecBase Error)

The SQL Server engine also has logical checks to detect consistency problems for a row within a database page. In previous versions of SQL Server, this check would result in an assertion (a fatal error that results in a stack dump) with the expression containing the word RecBase. RecBase is the name of a class used to logically read the elements of a row on a page. See Microsoft Knowledge Base article 828337 for more information.

In SQL Server 2005, two errors were introduced to report all row consistency errors detected while reading a row as part of a standard SELECT, UPDATE, and so on, Msg 5242 and 5243. The following is an example of an ERRORLOG containing a Msg 5242 error (with some sections omitted for brevity):

```
2006-02-18 19:33:09.40 spid51    ex_raise2: Exception raised, major=52,
minor=42, state=1, severity=22, attempting to create symptom dump
2006-02-18 19:33:09.58 spid51    Using 'dbghelp.dll' version '4.0.5'
2006-02-18 19:33:09.59 spid51    **Dump thread - spid = 51, PSS = 0x048B9278,
EC = 0x048B9280
2006-02-18 19:33:09.59 spid51    *
2006-02-18 19:33:09.59 spid51    * User initiated stack dump. This is not a server
exception dump.
2006-02-18 19:33:09.59 spid51    *
2006-02-18 19:33:09.61 spid51    ***Stack Dump being sent to C:\Program
Files\Microsoft SQL Server\MSSQL.1\MSSQL\LOG\SQLDump0001.txt
2006-02-18 19:33:09.61 spid51    *
***********************************************************************
2006-02-18 19:33:09.61 spid51    *
2006-02-18 19:33:09.61 spid51    * BEGIN STACK DUMP:
2006-02-18 19:33:09.61 spid51    *   02/18/06 19:33:09 spid 51
2006-02-18 19:33:09.61 spid51    *
2006-02-18 19:33:09.61 spid51    * ex_raise2: Exception raised, major=52, minor=42,
state=1, severity=22
2006-02-18 19:33:09.61 spid51    *
***********************************************************************
2006-02-18 19:33:09.61 spid51    * ------------------------------------------------
----------------------------
2006-02-18 19:33:09.61 spid51    * Short Stack Dump
2006-02-18 19:33:09.62 spid51    77E55DEA Module(kernel32+00015DEA)
2006-02-18 19:33:09.62 spid51    02172CE4 Module(sqlservr+01172CE4)
2006-02-18 19:33:09.62 spid51    02176BA0 Module(sqlservr+01176BA0)
2006-02-18 19:33:09.62 spid51    0217674D Module(sqlservr+0117674D)
2006-02-18 19:33:09.62 spid51    01597EA2 Module(sqlservr+00597EA2)
2006-02-18 19:33:09.62 spid51    01095FFE Module(sqlservr+00095FFE)
2006-02-18 19:33:09.62 spid51    02389FB0 Module(sqlservr+01389FB0)
2006-02-18 19:33:09.62 spid51    0158E526 Module(sqlservr+0058E526)
2006-02-18 19:33:09.62 spid51    0100C833 Module(sqlservr+0000C833)
2006-02-18 19:33:09.62 spid51    0100BF0F Module(sqlservr+0000BF0F)
2006-02-18 19:33:09.62 spid51    010106EB Module(sqlservr+000106EB)
2006-02-18 19:33:09.62 spid51    01010B3A Module(sqlservr+00010B3A)
2006-02-18 19:33:09.62 spid51    01010932 Module(sqlservr+00010932)
2006-02-18 19:33:09.62 spid51    010C0E2B Module(sqlservr+000C0E2B)
2006-02-18 19:33:09.62 spid51    01210454 Module(sqlservr+00210454)
2006-02-18 19:33:09.62 spid51    013F65A8 Module(sqlservr+003F65A8)
2006-02-18 19:33:09.62 spid51    013B3E42 Module(sqlservr+003B3E42)
2006-02-18 19:33:09.62 spid51    013B35EC Module(sqlservr+003B35EC)
2006-02-18 19:33:09.62 spid51    012101C2 Module(sqlservr+002101C2)
2006-02-18 19:33:09.62 spid51    01188FC9 Module(sqlservr+00188FC9)
2006-02-18 19:33:09.62 spid51    01189021 Module(sqlservr+00189021)
2006-02-18 19:33:09.62 spid51    01330A25 Module(sqlservr+00330A25)
2006-02-18 19:33:09.62 spid51    01330421 Module(sqlservr+00330421)
2006-02-18 19:33:09.62 spid51    01332C55 Module(sqlservr+00332C55)
2006-02-18 19:33:09.62 spid51    0100889F Module(sqlservr+0000889F)
2006-02-18 19:33:09.62 spid51    010089C5 Module(sqlservr+000089C5)
2006-02-18 19:33:09.62 spid51    010086E7 Module(sqlservr+000086E7)
2006-02-18 19:33:09.62 spid51    010D764A Module(sqlservr+000D764A)
2006-02-18 19:33:09.62 spid51    010D7B71 Module(sqlservr+000D7B71)
2006-02-18 19:33:09.62 spid51    010D746E Module(sqlservr+000D746E)
```

```
2006-02-18 19:33:09.62 spid51    010D83F0 Module(sqlservr+000D83F0)
2006-02-18 19:33:09.62 spid51    781329AA Module(MSVCR80+000029AA)
2006-02-18 19:33:09.64 spid51    78132A36 Module(MSVCR80+00002A36)
2006-02-18 19:33:09.65 spid51    * ------------------------------------------------
------------------------------
2006-02-18 19:33:09.65 spid51    Stack Signature for the dump is 0xE09D5555
2006-02-18 19:33:10.48 spid51    External dump process return code 0x20000001.
External dump process returned no errors.

2006-02-18 19:33:10.58 spid51    Error: 5242, Severity: 22, State: 1.
2006-02-18 19:33:10.58 spid51    An inconsistency was detected during an
internal operation in database 'master'(ID:1) on page (1:306). Please contact
technical support. Reference number 3.
```

The error message says to contact technical support (I sure hate when our errors say that), but in reality you need to first run a DBCC CHECKDB in the database listed in the message. If it returns errors indicating row damage, you need to address those problems as a true database corruption problem. If CHECKDB does not report errors, it may be a good idea to contact technical support. Have the stack dump and ERRORLOG available for them to review.

Msg 605

Msg 605 is a legacy carryover from the original SYBASE code for SQL Server. In fact, it was pretty much the only way to know about a database consistency problem aside from DBCC CHECKDB. This error check still remains in the SQL Server 2005 code. You should treat this error much like the row-level consistency errors 5242 and 5243. If CHECKDB reports errors, treat the problem as database corruption. If not, consider contacting technical support if the errors occur frequently. It could indicate some problem in the SQL Server code that should be addressed.

Access Violations

For performance reasons, the SQL Server development team cannot put in validation checks for every bit on the database page at every place in the engine code. Therefore, it is possible the engine will run into an access violation because of database corruption. How can you recognize this case? Well, because an access violation could occur at so many different places due to corruption, there is one stack dump signature I could show you to say the problem is corruption. My advice is that if you are getting access violations frequently, you should always ensure DBCC CHECKDB is run for all databases before pursuing the cause of the access violation as a SQL Server bug.

Failed Rollback

Another example is online rollback recovery. If the rollback of a user transaction fails, this is a critical problem. So, the engine reacts by taking the user database offline and restarting it. This allows recovery to run on the database with the hopeful effect of rolling back the transaction that couldn't roll back online. This technique actually is quite successful, because in some cases the online rollback failure is an interim problem that won't reoccur when the transactions are rolled back from the log on disk. Again, in this situation, SQL Server attempts to isolate the failure. Only the database associated with the failed rollback is affected. The rest of the engine remains intact, and other databases are not affected. As with any reliability feature, there are always exceptions. Any failure to roll back a transaction in `tempdb` results in a server shutdown because there is no method to run recovery on `tempdb`, and it is a critical shared resource for all users.

Handling *DBCC CHECKDB* Errors

I've recommended that you run DBCC CHECKDB if you encounter some of the errors described here. You may also decide to run DBCC CHECKDB at any point in time to check the consistency of your database. I presented earlier in the chapter some nice enhancements to CHECKDB to help provide more consistency checks (for example, DATA_PURITY and CHECKCATALOG). Let's talk about a strategy to address errors that you can encounter with DBCC CHECKDB. In this section, I do not go over every error that CHECKDB can report. I talk later about how you can look for information on the web about each of the errors (documented by the authors of DBCC CHECKDB, Ryan Stonecipher and Paul Randal).

Look at Summaries and Recommendation First

When you run DBCC CHECKDB and it reports errors, I recommend you do two things first:

- Look at what I call the summary messages.

- Look at the recommendation messages.

Let's look at some example output that contains errors so that I can show you what I mean:

```
DBCC results for 'checkdb_test'.
Service Broker Msg 9675, State 1: Message Types analyzed: 14.
Service Broker Msg 9676, State 1: Service Contracts analyzed: 6.
Service Broker Msg 9667, State 1: Services analyzed: 3.
Service Broker Msg 9668, State 1: Service Queues analyzed: 3.
Service Broker Msg 9669, State 1: Conversation Endpoints analyzed: 0.
Service Broker Msg 9674, State 1: Conversation Groups analyzed: 0.
Service Broker Msg 9670, State 1: Remote Service Bindings analyzed: 0.
Msg 8909, Level 16, State 1, Line 1
Table error: Object ID 0, index ID -1, partition ID 0, alloc unit ID 0 (type
Unknown), page ID (1:153) contains an incorrect page ID in its page header. The
PageId in the page header = (0:0).
Msg 8909, Level 16, State 1, Line 1
Table error: Object ID 0, index ID -1, partition ID 0, alloc unit ID 0 (type
Unknown), page ID (1:154) contains an incorrect page ID in its page header. The
PageId in the page header = (0:0).
Msg 8909, Level 16, State 1, Line 1
Table error: Object ID 0, index ID -1, partition ID 0, alloc unit ID 0 (type
Unknown), page ID (1:155) contains an incorrect page ID in its page header. The
PageId in the page header = (0:0).
Msg 8909, Level 16, State 1, Line 1
Table error: Object ID 0, index ID -1, partition ID 0, alloc unit ID 0 (type
Unknown), page ID (1:156) contains an incorrect page ID in its page header. The
PageId in the page header = (0:0).
Msg 8909, Level 16, State 1, Line 1
Table error: Object ID 0, index ID -1, partition ID 0, alloc unit ID 0 (type
```

Unknown), page ID (1:157) contains an incorrect page ID in its page header. The
PageId in the page header = (0:0).
Msg 8909, Level 16, State 1, Line 1
Table error: Object ID 0, index ID -1, partition ID 0, alloc unit ID 0 (type
Unknown), page ID (1:158) contains an incorrect page ID in its page header. The
PageId in the page header = (0:0).
CHECKDB found 0 allocation errors and 6 consistency errors not associated with any
single object.
DBCC results for 'sys.sysrowsetcolumns'.
There are 544 rows in 5 pages for object "sys.sysrowsetcolumns".
DBCC results for 'sys.sysrowsets'.
There are 81 rows in 1 pages for object "sys.sysrowsets".
DBCC results for 'sysallocunits'.
There are 92 rows in 1 pages for object "sysallocunits".
DBCC results for 'sys.sysfiles1'.
There are 2 rows in 1 pages for object "sys.sysfiles1".
DBCC results for 'sys.syshobtcolumns'.
There are 544 rows in 5 pages for object "sys.syshobtcolumns".
DBCC results for 'sys.syshobts'.
There are 81 rows in 1 pages for object "sys.syshobts".
DBCC results for 'sys.sysftinds'.
There are 0 rows in 0 pages for object "sys.sysftinds".
DBCC results for 'sys.sysserefs'.
There are 92 rows in 1 pages for object "sys.sysserefs".
DBCC results for 'sys.sysowners'.
There are 14 rows in 1 pages for object "sys.sysowners".
DBCC results for 'sys.sysprivs'.
There are 120 rows in 1 pages for object "sys.sysprivs".
DBCC results for 'sys.sysschobjs'.
There are 50 rows in 1 pages for object "sys.sysschobjs".
DBCC results for 'sys.syscolpars'.
There are 423 rows in 7 pages for object "sys.syscolpars".
DBCC results for 'sys.sysnsobjs'.
There are 1 rows in 1 pages for object "sys.sysnsobjs".
DBCC results for 'sys.syscerts'.
There are 0 rows in 0 pages for object "sys.syscerts".
DBCC results for 'sys.sysxprops'.
There are 0 rows in 0 pages for object "sys.sysxprops".
DBCC results for 'sys.sysscalartypes'.
There are 27 rows in 1 pages for object "sys.sysscalartypes".
DBCC results for 'sys.systypedsubobjs'.
There are 0 rows in 0 pages for object "sys.systypedsubobjs".
DBCC results for 'sys.sysidxstats'.
There are 106 rows in 1 pages for object "sys.sysidxstats".
DBCC results for 'sys.sysiscols'.
There are 218 rows in 1 pages for object "sys.sysiscols".
DBCC results for 'sys.sysbinobjs'.
There are 23 rows in 1 pages for object "sys.sysbinobjs".
DBCC results for 'sys.sysobjvalues'.
There are 104 rows in 16 pages for object "sys.sysobjvalues".
DBCC results for 'sys.sysclsobjs'.
There are 14 rows in 1 pages for object "sys.sysclsobjs".
DBCC results for 'sys.sysrowsetrefs'.
There are 0 rows in 0 pages for object "sys.sysrowsetrefs".

```
DBCC results for 'sys.sysremsvcbinds'.
There are 0 rows in 0 pages for object "sys.sysremsvcbinds".
DBCC results for 'sys.sysxmitqueue'.
There are 0 rows in 0 pages for object "sys.sysxmitqueue".
DBCC results for 'sys.sysrts'.
There are 1 rows in 1 pages for object "sys.sysrts".
DBCC results for 'sys.sysconvgroup'.
There are 0 rows in 0 pages for object "sys.sysconvgroup".
DBCC results for 'sys.sysdesend'.
There are 0 rows in 0 pages for object "sys.sysdesend".
DBCC results for 'sys.sysdercv'.
There are 0 rows in 0 pages for object "sys.sysdercv".
DBCC results for 'sys.syssingleobjrefs'.
There are 133 rows in 1 pages for object "sys.syssingleobjrefs".
DBCC results for 'sys.sysmultiobjrefs'.
There are 102 rows in 1 pages for object "sys.sysmultiobjrefs".
DBCC results for 'sys.sysdbfiles'.
There are 2 rows in 1 pages for object "sys.sysdbfiles".
DBCC results for 'sys.sysguidrefs'.
There are 0 rows in 0 pages for object "sys.sysguidrefs".
DBCC results for 'sys.sysqnames'.
There are 91 rows in 1 pages for object "sys.sysqnames".
DBCC results for 'sys.sysxmlcomponent'.
There are 93 rows in 1 pages for object "sys.sysxmlcomponent".
DBCC results for 'sys.sysxmlfacet'.
There are 97 rows in 1 pages for object "sys.sysxmlfacet".
DBCC results for 'sys.sysxmlplacement'.
There are 17 rows in 1 pages for object "sys.sysxmlplacement".
DBCC results for 'sys.sysobjkeycrypts'.
There are 0 rows in 0 pages for object "sys.sysobjkeycrypts".
DBCC results for 'sys.sysasymkeys'.
There are 0 rows in 0 pages for object "sys.sysasymkeys".
DBCC results for 'sys.syssqlguides'.
There are 0 rows in 0 pages for object "sys.syssqlguides".
DBCC results for 'sys.sysbinsubobjs'.
There are 0 rows in 0 pages for object "sys.sysbinsubobjs".
DBCC results for 'sys.queue_messages_1977058079'.
There are 0 rows in 0 pages for object "sys.queue_messages_1977058079".
DBCC results for 'sys.queue_messages_2009058193'.
There are 0 rows in 0 pages for object "sys.queue_messages_2009058193".
DBCC results for 'sys.queue_messages_2041058307'.
There are 0 rows in 0 pages for object "sys.queue_messages_2041058307".
DBCC results for 'table1'.
Msg 8928, Level 16, State 1, Line 1
Object ID 2073058421, index ID 0, partition ID 72057594038321152, alloc unit ID
72057594042318848 (type In-row data): Page (1:153) could not be processed. See
other errors for details.
Msg 8928, Level 16, State 1, Line 1
Object ID 2073058421, index ID 0, partition ID 72057594038321152, alloc unit ID
72057594042318848 (type In-row data): Page (1:154) could not be processed. See
other errors for details.
Msg 8928, Level 16, State 1, Line 1
Object ID 2073058421, index ID 0, partition ID 72057594038321152, alloc unit ID
72057594042318848 (type In-row data): Page (1:155) could not be processed. See
```

other errors for details.
Msg 8928, Level 16, State 1, Line 1
Object ID 2073058421, index ID 0, partition ID 72057594038321152, alloc unit ID 72057594042318848 (type In-row data): Page (1:156) could not be processed. See other errors for details.
Msg 8928, Level 16, State 1, Line 1
Object ID 2073058421, index ID 0, partition ID 72057594038321152, alloc unit ID 72057594042318848 (type In-row data): Page (1:157) could not be processed. See other errors for details.
Msg 8928, Level 16, State 1, Line 1
Object ID 2073058421, index ID 0, partition ID 72057594038321152, alloc unit ID 72057594042318848 (type In-row data): Page (1:158) could not be processed. See other errors for details.
There are 88 rows in 44 pages for object "table1".
CHECKDB found 0 allocation errors and 6 consistency errors in table 'table1' (object ID 2073058421).
DBCC results for 'table2'.
Msg 2511, Level 16, State 1, Line 1
Table error: Object ID 2089058478, index ID 2, partition ID 72057594038452224, alloc unit ID 72057594042449920 (type In-row data). Keys out of order on page (1:210), slots 157 and 158.
There are 1000 rows in 3 pages for object "table2".
CHECKDB found 0 allocation errors and 1 consistency errors in table 'table2' (object ID 2089058478).
CHECKDB found 0 allocation errors and 13 consistency errors in database 'checkdb_test'.
repair_allow_data_loss is the minimum repair level for the errors found by DBCC CHECKDB (checkdb_test).
DBCC execution completed. If DBCC printed error messages, contact your system administrator.

Go to the bottom of the output and look at the summary and recommendation messages for the database:

CHECKDB found 0 allocation errors and 13 consistency errors in database 'checkdb_test'.
repair_allow_data_loss is the minimum repair level for the errors found by DBCC CHECKDB (checkdb_test).

You know from this message that 13 errors related to the consistency of pages or indexes have been detected (as opposed to allocation errors that are specific to problems with allocation structures found by the CHECKALLOC phase). You also know that in order to repair *all* 13 errors, you must use the REPAIR_ALLOW_DATA_LOSS repair option. You could just move forward with this recommendation and check the results. However, if you want to know what the repair recommendation is for each table found to have problems, you could check each one. Which tables do I check? Look at the summary messages for each table:

CHECKDB found 0 allocation errors and 6 consistency errors not associated with any single object.
CHECKDB found 0 allocation errors and 6 consistency errors in table 'table1' (object ID 2073058421).

```
CHECKDB found 0 allocation errors and 1 consistency errors in table 'table2'
(object ID 2089058478).
```

First, you should know that CHECKDB won't produce this summary message for a table unless it detects problems with that table. Second, notice the first summary message says "not associated with any single object." This message indicates that CHECKDB found errors associated with pages that don't appear to belong to a known table.

In this situation, what is happening is that CHECKDB is in a way "double-reporting" errors, but that is to your advantage in this situation. Let's look at the errors "not associated with any single object."

```
Msg 8909, Level 16, State 1, Line 1
Table error: Object ID 0, index ID -1, partition ID 0, alloc unit ID 0 (type
Unknown), page ID (1:153) contains an incorrect page ID in its page header.
The PageId in the page header = (0:0).
```

This message indicates a problem with the page ID as found on the page header. The page ID was expected to be 153, but on the page it was found to be 0:0. The routine that detects this problem is used throughout the CHECKDB code to read a page. In this routine, the table associated with the page is found by looking up the allocation unit ID on the page header. As you can see from the error message, that value is 0, and therefore CHECKDB doesn't know what table this page belongs to.

Now look at the errors associated with table1:

```
Msg 8928, Level 16, State 1, Line 1
Object ID 2073058421, index ID 0, partition ID 72057594038321152, alloc unit
ID 72057594042318848 (type In-row data): Page (1:153) could not be processed.
See other errors for details.
```

If you look closely, you will notice this error is for the same page as the one I just talked about for 8909. In fact, all the pages in errors 8909 and 8928 are the same. Why does the server report two different errors for the same page? I just mentioned that the 8909 error is reported in a general routine to read a page. This routine is self-contained and so relies on finding the object from the allocation unit id on the page. The code that raises the 8928 error is part of a routine that is checking "facts" about pages associated with an index. (In this case, it was actually just a heap for table1.) This code already "knows" what index it was checking (table1) and knows what page it was trying to read, so it can accurately report that it had a problem reading a page and what table it thought the page was associated with. You will notice this error says, "See other errors for details." What this message is saying is this: "I've detected a problem with this page, but there should be another error describing the actual problem." In this case, the other error is 8909, but it is not associated with table1 for the reasons I just described. Perhaps by now you can guess the problem in this scenario with some of these pages. A quick glance at page 1:153 using DBCC PAGE would tell you. (I didn't include the entire output because it is not important for this situation.)

```
dbcc traceon(3604)
go
dbcc page(10, 1, 153, 2)
```

```
go
DBCC execution completed. If DBCC printed error messages, contact your system
administrator.
PAGE: (0:0)

BUFFER:

BUF @0x02BF096C
bpage = 0x05052000          bhash = 0x00000000          bpageno = (1:153)
bdbid = 10                  breferences = 1             bUse1 = 50447
bstat = 0xc00809            blog = 0x32159              bnext = 0x00000000
PAGE HEADER:

Page @0x05052000
m_pageId = (0:0)            m_headerVersion = 0          m_type = 0
m_typeFlagBits = 0x0        m_level = 0                  m_flagBits = 0x0

m_objId (AllocUnitId.idObj) = 0    m_indexId (AllocUnitId.idInd) = 0   Metadata:
AllocUnitId = 0
Metadata: PartitionId = 0        Metadata: IndexId = -1        Metadata: ObjectId = 0
m_prevPage = (0:0)          m_nextPage = (0:0)          pminlen = 0
m_slotCnt = 0               m_freeCnt = 0               m_freeData = 0
m_reservedCnt = 0           m_lsn = (0:0:0)             m_xactReserved = 0
m_xdesId = (0:0)            m_ghostRecCnt = 0           m_tornBits = 0
Allocation Status
GAM (1:2) = ALLOCATED          SGAM (1:3) = NOT ALLOCATED
PFS (1:1) = 0x64 MIXED_EXT ALLOCATED 100_PCT_FULL                  DIFF (1:6) = CHANGED
ML (1:7) = NOT MIN_LOGGED
DATA:

Memory Dump @0x44C7C000
44C7C000:   00000000 00000000 00000000 00000000 †................
44C7C010:   00000000 00000000 00000000 00000000 †................
44C7C020:   00000000 00000000 00000000 00000000 †................
44C7C030:   00000000 00000000 00000000 00000000 †................
44C7C040:   00000000 00000000 00000000 00000000 †................
44C7C050:   00000000 00000000 00000000 00000000 †................
44C7C060:   1000a80f 02000000 4d595441 42202020 †........MYTAB
44C7C070:   20202020 20202020 20202020 20202020 †
44C7C080:   20202020 20202020 20202020 20202020 †
44C7C090:   20202020 20202020 20202020 20202020 †
44C7C0A0:   20202020 20202020 20202020 20202020 †
44C7C0B0:   20202020 20202020 20202020 20202020 †
44C7C0C0:   20202020 20202020 20202020 20202020 †
44C7C0D0:    20202020 20202020 20202020 20202020 †

44C7C0E0:    20202020 20202020 20202020 20202020 †
```

The first 96 bytes of any page is the page header. I think you can easily see that just about the entire header has all values of 0. If in this situation the page ID were the only problem with the page, Msg 8909 would have correctly shown up as a problem for table1. So, in this example, you can see that of the 13 errors, six of them are reported more than once. In reality, therefore, only seven pages have problems from this database.

Let's take a look at the errors for table2:

```
Msg 2511, Level 16, State 1, Line 1
Table error: Object ID 2089058478, index ID 2, partition ID 72057594038452224,
alloc unit ID 72057594042449920 (type In-row data). Keys out of order on page
(1:210), slots 157 and 158.
```

In this case, there is only one error, and as you can see it is associated with a nonclustered index (index ID 2). You saw that the 8928 errors were associated with data pages (index ID 0). Can you guess what the recommended repair level for table2 would be? Because the output may not always be this simple, let's use DBCC CHECKTABLE on each table to know for sure.

Here are the results for CHECKTABLE for table1:

```
Msg 8909, Level 16, State 1, Line 1
Table error: Object ID 0, index ID -1, partition ID 0, alloc unit ID 0 (type
Unknown), page ID (1:153) contains an incorrect page ID in its page header. The
PageId in the page header = (0:0).
Msg 8909, Level 16, State 1, Line 1
Table error: Object ID 0, index ID -1, partition ID 0, alloc unit ID 0 (type
Unknown), page ID (1:154) contains an incorrect page ID in its page header. The
PageId in the page header = (0:0).
Msg 8909, Level 16, State 1, Line 1
Table error: Object ID 0, index ID -1, partition ID 0, alloc unit ID 0 (type
Unknown), page ID (1:155) contains an incorrect page ID in its page header. The
PageId in the page header = (0:0).
Msg 8909, Level 16, State 1, Line 1
Table error: Object ID 0, index ID -1, partition ID 0, alloc unit ID 0 (type
Unknown), page ID (1:156) contains an incorrect page ID in its page header. The
PageId in the page header = (0:0).
Msg 8909, Level 16, State 1, Line 1
Table error: Object ID 0, index ID -1, partition ID 0, alloc unit ID 0 (type
Unknown), page ID (1:157) contains an incorrect page ID in its page header. The
PageId in the page header = (0:0).
Msg 8909, Level 16, State 1, Line 1
Table error: Object ID 0, index ID -1, partition ID 0, alloc unit ID 0 (type
Unknown), page ID (1:158) contains an incorrect page ID in its page header. The
PageId in the page header = (0:0).
CHECKTABLE found 0 allocation errors and 6 consistency errors not associated with
any single object.
DBCC results for 'table1'.
Msg 8928, Level 16, State 1, Line 1
Object ID 2073058421, index ID 0, partition ID 72057594038321152, alloc unit ID
72057594042318848 (type In-row data): Page (1:153) could not be processed. See
other errors for details.
Msg 8928, Level 16, State 1, Line 1
Object ID 2073058421, index ID 0, partition ID 72057594038321152, alloc unit ID
72057594042318848 (type In-row data): Page (1:154) could not be processed. See
other errors for details.
Msg 8928, Level 16, State 1, Line 1
Object ID 2073058421, index ID 0, partition ID 72057594038321152, alloc unit ID
72057594042318848 (type In-row data): Page (1:155) could not be processed. See
other errors for details.
```

```
Msg 8928, Level 16, State 1, Line 1
Object ID 2073058421, index ID 0, partition ID 72057594038321152, alloc unit ID
72057594042318848 (type In-row data): Page (1:156) could not be processed. See
other errors for details.
Msg 8928, Level 16, State 1, Line 1
Object ID 2073058421, index ID 0, partition ID 72057594038321152, alloc unit ID
72057594042318848 (type In-row data): Page (1:157) could not be processed. See
other errors for details.
Msg 8928, Level 16, State 1, Line 1
Object ID 2073058421, index ID 0, partition ID 72057594038321152, alloc unit ID
72057594042318848 (type In-row data): Page (1:158) could not be processed. See
other errors for details.
There are 88 rows in 44 pages for object "table1".
CHECKTABLE found 0 allocation errors and 6 consistency errors in table 'table1'
(object ID 2073058421).
repair_allow_data_loss is the minimum repair level for the errors found by
DBCC CHECKTABLE (checkdb_test.dbo.table1).

DBCC execution completed. If DBCC printed error messages, contact your system
administrator.
```

Notice the repair recommendation is still REPAIR_ALLOW_DATA_LOSS. Because these six pages are all data pages, a repair will actually result in lost data, because the pages will be de-allocated.

Here are the results of CHECKTABLE for table2:

```
DBCC results for 'table2'.
Msg 2511, Level 16, State 1, Line 1
Table error: Object ID 2089058478, index ID 2, partition ID 72057594038452224,
alloc unit ID 72057594042449920 (type In-row data). Keys out of order on page
(1:210), slots 157 and 158.
There are 1000 rows in 3 pages for object "table2".
CHECKTABLE found 0 allocation errors and 1 consistency errors in table
'table2' (object ID 2089058478).
repair_rebuild is the minimum repair level for the errors found by DBCC
CHECKTABLE (checkdb_test.dbo.table2).

DBCC execution completed. If DBCC printed error messages, contact your system
administrator.
```

You can see that the repair recommendation is REPAIR_REBUILD, which means a rebuild of an index will correct any errors, and no data loss should occur.

Let's see what the output of CHECKDB looks like in this situation (because CHECKDB will report messages on what actions it took to repair any error it can fix):

```
DBCC results for 'checkdb_test'.
Service Broker Msg 9675, State 1: Message Types analyzed: 14.
Service Broker Msg 9676, State 1: Service Contracts analyzed: 6.
Service Broker Msg 9667, State 1: Services analyzed: 3.
Service Broker Msg 9668, State 1: Service Queues analyzed: 3.
Service Broker Msg 9669, State 1: Conversation Endpoints analyzed: 0.
Service Broker Msg 9674, State 1: Conversation Groups analyzed: 0.
```

Service Broker Msg 9670, State 1: Remote Service Bindings analyzed: 0.
Msg 8909, Level 16, State 1, Line 1
Table error: Object ID 0, index ID -1, partition ID 0, alloc unit ID 0 (type
Unknown), page ID (1:153) contains an incorrect page ID in its page header. The
PageId in the page header = (0:0).
    The error has been repaired.
Msg 8909, Level 16, State 1, Line 1
Table error: Object ID 0, index ID -1, partition ID 0, alloc unit ID 0 (type
Unknown), page ID (1:154) contains an incorrect page ID in its page header. The
PageId in the page header = (0:0).
    The error has been repaired.
Msg 8909, Level 16, State 1, Line 1
Table error: Object ID 0, index ID -1, partition ID 0, alloc unit ID 0 (type
Unknown), page ID (1:155) contains an incorrect page ID in its page header. The
PageId in the page header = (0:0).
    The error has been repaired.
Msg 8909, Level 16, State 1, Line 1
Table error: Object ID 0, index ID -1, partition ID 0, alloc unit ID 0 (type
Unknown), page ID (1:156) contains an incorrect page ID in its page header. The
PageId in the page header = (0:0).
    The error has been repaired.
Msg 8909, Level 16, State 1, Line 1
Table error: Object ID 0, index ID -1, partition ID 0, alloc unit ID 0 (type
Unknown), page ID (1:157) contains an incorrect page ID in its page header. The
PageId in the page header = (0:0).
    The error has been repaired.
Msg 8909, Level 16, State 1, Line 1
Table error: Object ID 0, index ID -1, partition ID 0, alloc unit ID 0 (type
Unknown), page ID (1:158) contains an incorrect page ID in its page header. The
PageId in the page header = (0:0).
    The error has been repaired.
CHECKDB found 0 allocation errors and 6 consistency errors not associated with any
single object.
CHECKDB fixed 0 allocation errors and 6 consistency errors not associated with any
single object.
DBCC results for 'sys.sysrowsetcolumns'.
There are 544 rows in 5 pages for object "sys.sysrowsetcolumns".
DBCC results for 'sys.sysrowsets'.
There are 81 rows in 1 pages for object "sys.sysrowsets".
DBCC results for 'sysallocunits'.
There are 92 rows in 1 pages for object "sysallocunits".
DBCC results for 'sys.sysfiles1'.
There are 2 rows in 1 pages for object "sys.sysfiles1".
DBCC results for 'sys.syshobtcolumns'.
There are 544 rows in 5 pages for object "sys.syshobtcolumns".
DBCC results for 'sys.syshobts'.
There are 81 rows in 1 pages for object "sys.syshobts".
DBCC results for 'sys.sysftinds'.
There are 0 rows in 0 pages for object "sys.sysftinds".
DBCC results for 'sys.sysserefs'.
There are 92 rows in 1 pages for object "sys.sysserefs".
DBCC results for 'sys.sysowners'.
There are 14 rows in 1 pages for object "sys.sysowners".
DBCC results for 'sys.sysprivs'.

```
There are 120 rows in 1 pages for object "sys.sysprivs".
DBCC results for 'sys.sysschobjs'.
There are 50 rows in 1 pages for object "sys.sysschobjs".
DBCC results for 'sys.syscolpars'.
There are 423 rows in 7 pages for object "sys.syscolpars".
DBCC results for 'sys.sysnsobjs'.
There are 1 rows in 1 pages for object "sys.sysnsobjs".
DBCC results for 'sys.syscerts'.
There are 0 rows in 0 pages for object "sys.syscerts".
DBCC results for 'sys.sysxprops'.
There are 0 rows in 0 pages for object "sys.sysxprops".
DBCC results for 'sys.sysscalartypes'.
There are 27 rows in 1 pages for object "sys.sysscalartypes".
DBCC results for 'sys.systypedsubobjs'.
There are 0 rows in 0 pages for object "sys.systypedsubobjs".
DBCC results for 'sys.sysidxstats'.
There are 116 rows in 2 pages for object "sys.sysidxstats".
DBCC results for 'sys.sysiscols'.
There are 228 rows in 1 pages for object "sys.sysiscols".
DBCC results for 'sys.sysbinobjs'.
There are 23 rows in 1 pages for object "sys.sysbinobjs".
DBCC results for 'sys.sysobjvalues'.
There are 114 rows in 17 pages for object "sys.sysobjvalues".
DBCC results for 'sys.sysclsobjs'.
There are 14 rows in 1 pages for object "sys.sysclsobjs".
DBCC results for 'sys.sysrowsetrefs'.
There are 0 rows in 0 pages for object "sys.sysrowsetrefs".
DBCC results for 'sys.sysremsvcbinds'.
There are 0 rows in 0 pages for object "sys.sysremsvcbinds".
DBCC results for 'sys.sysxmitqueue'.
There are 0 rows in 0 pages for object "sys.sysxmitqueue".
DBCC results for 'sys.sysrts'.
There are 1 rows in 1 pages for object "sys.sysrts".
DBCC results for 'sys.sysconvgroup'.
There are 0 rows in 0 pages for object "sys.sysconvgroup".
DBCC results for 'sys.sysdesend'.
There are 0 rows in 0 pages for object "sys.sysdesend".
DBCC results for 'sys.sysdercv'.
There are 0 rows in 0 pages for object "sys.sysdercv".
DBCC results for 'sys.syssingleobjrefs'.
There are 133 rows in 1 pages for object "sys.syssingleobjrefs".
DBCC results for 'sys.sysmultiobjrefs'.
There are 102 rows in 1 pages for object "sys.sysmultiobjrefs".
DBCC results for 'sys.sysdbfiles'.
There are 2 rows in 1 pages for object "sys.sysdbfiles".
DBCC results for 'sys.sysguidrefs'.
There are 0 rows in 0 pages for object "sys.sysguidrefs".
DBCC results for 'sys.sysqnames'.
There are 91 rows in 1 pages for object "sys.sysqnames".
DBCC results for 'sys.sysxmlcomponent'.
There are 93 rows in 1 pages for object "sys.sysxmlcomponent".
DBCC results for 'sys.sysxmlfacet'.
There are 97 rows in 1 pages for object "sys.sysxmlfacet".
DBCC results for 'sys.sysxmlplacement'.
```

There are 17 rows in 1 pages for object "sys.sysxmlplacement".
DBCC results for 'sys.sysobjkeycrypts'.
There are 0 rows in 0 pages for object "sys.sysobjkeycrypts".
DBCC results for 'sys.sysasymkeys'.
There are 0 rows in 0 pages for object "sys.sysasymkeys".
DBCC results for 'sys.syssqlguides'.
There are 0 rows in 0 pages for object "sys.syssqlguides".
DBCC results for 'sys.sysbinsubobjs'.
There are 0 rows in 0 pages for object "sys.sysbinsubobjs".
DBCC results for 'sys.queue_messages_1977058079'.
There are 0 rows in 0 pages for object "sys.queue_messages_1977058079".
DBCC results for 'sys.queue_messages_2009058193'.
There are 0 rows in 0 pages for object "sys.queue_messages_2009058193".
DBCC results for 'sys.queue_messages_2041058307'.
There are 0 rows in 0 pages for object "sys.queue_messages_2041058307".
DBCC results for 'table1'.
Repair: The page (1:153) has been deallocated from object ID 2073058421, index ID
0, partition ID 72057594038321152, alloc unit ID 72057594042318848 (type In-row
data).
Repair: The page (1:154) has been deallocated from object ID 2073058421, index ID
0, partition ID 72057594038321152, alloc unit ID 72057594042318848 (type In-row
data).
Repair: The page (1:155) has been deallocated from object ID 2073058421, index ID
0, partition ID 72057594038321152, alloc unit ID 72057594042318848 (type In-row
data).
Repair: The page (1:156) has been deallocated from object ID 2073058421, index ID
0, partition ID 72057594038321152, alloc unit ID 72057594042318848 (type In-row
data).
Repair: The page (1:157) has been deallocated from object ID 2073058421, index ID
0, partition ID 72057594038321152, alloc unit ID 72057594042318848 (type In-row
data).
Repair: The page (1:158) has been deallocated from object ID 2073058421, index ID
0, partition ID 72057594038321152, alloc unit ID 72057594042318848 (type In-row
data).
Msg 8928, Level 16, State 1, Line 1
Object ID 2073058421, index ID 0, partition ID 72057594038321152, alloc unit ID
72057594042318848 (type In-row data): Page (1:153) could not be processed. See
other errors for details.
    The error has been repaired.
Msg 8928, Level 16, State 1, Line 1
Object ID 2073058421, index ID 0, partition ID 72057594038321152, alloc unit ID
72057594042318848 (type In-row data): Page (1:154) could not be processed. See
other errors for details.
    The error has been repaired.
Msg 8928, Level 16, State 1, Line 1
Object ID 2073058421, index ID 0, partition ID 72057594038321152, alloc unit ID
72057594042318848 (type In-row data): Page (1:155) could not be processed. See
other errors for details.
    The error has been repaired.
Msg 8928, Level 16, State 1, Line 1
Object ID 2073058421, index ID 0, partition ID 72057594038321152, alloc unit ID
72057594042318848 (type In-row data): Page (1:156) could not be processed. See
other errors for details.
    The error has been repaired.

```
Msg 8928, Level 16, State 1, Line 1
Object ID 2073058421, index ID 0, partition ID 72057594038321152, alloc unit ID
72057594042318848 (type In-row data): Page (1:157) could not be processed. See
other errors for details.
        The error has been repaired.
Msg 8928, Level 16, State 1, Line 1
Object ID 2073058421, index ID 0, partition ID 72057594038321152, alloc unit ID
72057594042318848 (type In-row data): Page (1:158) could not be processed. See
other errors for details.
        The error has been repaired.
There are 88 rows in 44 pages for object "table1".
CHECKDB found 0 allocation errors and 6 consistency errors in table 'table1'
(object ID 2073058421).
CHECKDB fixed 0 allocation errors and 6 consistency errors in table 'table1'
(object ID 2073058421).
DBCC results for 'table2'.
Repair: The Nonclustered index successfully rebuilt for the object "dbo.table2,
PK_ _table2_ _7D78A4E7" in database "checkdb_test".
Msg 8945, Level 16, State 1, Line 1
Table error: Object ID 2089058478, index ID 2 will be rebuilt.
        The error has been repaired.
Msg 2511, Level 16, State 1, Line 1
Table error: Object ID 2089058478, index ID 2, partition ID 72057594038452224,
alloc unit ID 72057594042449920 (type In-row data). Keys out of order on page
(1:210), slots 157 and 158.
        The error has been repaired.
There are 1000 rows in 3 pages for object "table2".
CHECKDB found 0 allocation errors and 1 consistency errors in table 'table2'
(object ID 2089058478).
CHECKDB fixed 0 allocation errors and 1 consistency errors in table 'table2'
(object ID 2089058478).
CHECKDB found 0 allocation errors and 13 consistency errors in database
'checkdb_test'.
CHECKDB fixed 0 allocation errors and 13 consistency errors in database
'checkdb_test'.
DBCC execution completed. If DBCC printed error messages, contact your system
administrator.
```

In this case, I've highlighted the important messages that are added as part of repair:

```
Repair: The page (1:153) has been deallocated from object ID 2073058421, index ID
0, partition ID 72057594038321152, alloc unit ID 72057594042318848 (type In-row
data).
Repair: The page (1:154) has been deallocated from object ID 2073058421, index ID
0, partition ID 72057594038321152, alloc unit ID 72057594042318848 (type In-row
data).
Repair: The page (1:155) has been deallocated from object ID 2073058421, index ID
0, partition ID 72057594038321152, alloc unit ID 72057594042318848 (type In-row
data).
Repair: The page (1:156) has been deallocated from object ID 2073058421, index ID
0, partition ID 72057594038321152, alloc unit ID 72057594042318848 (type In-row
data).
```

```
Repair: The page (1:157) has been deallocated from object ID 2073058421, index
ID 0, partition ID 72057594038321152, alloc unit ID 72057594042318848 (type
In-row data).
Repair: The page (1:158) has been deallocated from object ID 2073058421, index
ID 0, partition ID 72057594038321152, alloc unit ID 72057594042318848 (type
In-row data).
```

You can see from these messages that the method to repair these pages is to de-allocate them. There is no method to retrieve any data that could have been on these pages:

```
Repair: The Nonclustered index successfully rebuilt for the object "dbo.table2,
PK_ _table2_ _7D78A4E7" in database "checkdb_test".
Msg 8945, Level 16, State 1, Line 1
Table error: Object ID 2089058478, index ID 2 will be rebuilt.
```

This is the error for table2. You can see that the only method needed to repair the table is to rebuild the nonclustered index:

```
CHECKDB found 0 allocation errors and 13 consistency errors in database
'checkdb_test'.
CHECKDB fixed 0 allocation errors and 13 consistency errors in database
'checkdb_test'.
```

This is the most important message to look for. Was the repair successful? If the number of messages *fixed* is less than those *found,* the repair couldn't fix all the problems.

Repair Versus Restore

How do you know whether you should restore from a database backup or use repair? One consideration is what I've described in the section "Best Practices": the primary feature for a recovery of data for the SQL Server product is RESTORE. Repair has been a great feature of DBCC CHECKDB, but you should use it only for emergency purposes. We talk shortly about what REPAIR_ALLOW_DATA_LOSS really means, but you should know that in most cases it does mean you will probably lose data. Here is the problem. Aside from knowing what table is affected by the data loss, you won't know what rows you lost. It is now your responsibility to understand what level of logical consistency you now have in your database.

If you have the proper backup strategy in place, you should almost never have to rely on repair. But the functionality is still there in case you need it. (Perhaps you couldn't predict that a disk that holds backups and is always reliable has an unexpected failure. Of course, I think you should have a plan for even this scenario.) You will find that if you call Microsoft PSS to talk about a situation where you have a damaged database and want to talk about whether repair will fix the problem, instead of just helping you run REPAIR, PSS will almost always talk to you about using a backup first.

What Does Each Error Mean?

Each error produced by DBCC CHECKDB is documented on the Events and Errors Message Center. Some of these errors that apply to both SQL Server 2000 and 2005 are documented under SQL Server 2000. Here is an example of the documentation of an error that can be encountered in CHECKDB:

Details

Product:	SQL Server
Event ID:	2531
Source:	MSSQLServer
Version:	9.00.1281.60
Symbolic Name:	DBCC_BTREE_SIBLING_LEVEL_MISMATCH
Message:	Table error: object ID %d, index ID %d, partition ID %l64d, alloc unit ID %l64d (type %.*ls) B-tree level mismatch, page %S_PGID. Level %d does not match level %d from the previous %S_PGID.

Explanation

Two pages are linked as immediate neighbors on a level of a B-tree. The level, LEVEL2, on the right page, P_ID2, does not match the level, LEVEL1, on the left page, P_ID1.

To determine which page is incorrect, examine the surrounding pages and the contents of the two pages in question. Also, look for MSSQLEngine_8931 errors, which indicate B-tree parent-child-level mismatches.

Possible Causes

This error can be caused by one of the following problems:

- A random page corruption.

- A bug in the B-tree manager.

- If LEVEL1 and LEVEL2 are 0 or 1 and the index is a clustered index, there might be a bug in the Access Methods code that determines page levels. In ssVersion2005, for a clustered index, page levels progress from 0, 1, 2 to X, but in ssVersion2000, for a clustered index, page levels progress from 0, 0, 1, 2 to X, where X is the maximum depth of the B-tree.

User Action

Run hardware diagnostics and correct any problems. Also examine the Microsoft Windows system and application logs and the SQL Server error log to see whether the error occurred as the result of hardware failure. Fix any hardware-related problems that are contained in the logs.

If you have persistent data corruption problems, try to swap out different hardware components to isolate the problem. Check to make sure that the system does not have write caching enabled on the disk controller. If you suspect write caching to be the problem, contact your hardware vendor.

Finally, you might find it useful to switch to a new hardware system. This switch may include reformatting the disk drives and reinstalling the operating system.

Results of Running Repair Options
Repair will rebuild the index.

This is the general format for each message:

- An explanation of what the error means with regard to what type of data is damaged

- Possible causes of the problem

- What actions you can take

- What repair will do to correct the problem

The actions to take seem general (check the hardware and so forth), but you will see when I talk about finding the root cause of corruption that these actions make sense for many errors detected by CHECKDB.

What Does *REPAIR_ALLOW_DATA_LOSS* Really Mean?

This repair option means that CHECKDB has detected at least one error that could result in data loss. I've already talked about how this may not apply to every error detected. This is why the repair recommendation message says the *minimum* repair level:

```
repair_allow_data_loss is the minimum repair level...
```

The method for repair to correct a problem recommended by REPAIR_ALLOW_DATA_LOSS usually is to de-allocate the page or groups of pages (extent) based on the error. In some scenarios, a data row could be deleted rather than the entire page, but they are limited (for example, if the LOB pages associated with the row are damaged and must be de-allocated). If any part of the structure of the data row itself is damaged, the entire page must be de-allocated.

I know of two situations in which the recommendation is REPAIR_ALLOW_DATA_LOSS but repair actually can correct the problem without a loss of data.

Damaged index page

If DBCC CHECKDB encounters an error such as a checksum failure for a nonclustered or nonleaf page of a clustered index, it recommends REPAIR_ALLOW_DATA_LOSS. This is because it cannot trust the allocation unit ID information on the page to know for sure it is a nonclustered index page. So it must de-allocate the page. However, the repair logic in this case also rebuilds the index so that the result is simply to rebuild the nonclustered index.

PFS free space error

You may encounter the following error when running DBCC CHECKDB:

```
Msg 8914, Level 16, State 1, Line 1
Incorrect PFS free space information for page (1:128) in object ID 60, index
ID 1, partition ID 281474980642816, alloc unit ID 71776119065149440 (type LOB
data). Expected value  0_PCT_FULL, actual value 100_PCT_FULL.
```

In this case, the CHECKDB code recommends REPAIR_ALLOW_DATA_LOSS but repair simply fixes the free space information in the PFS page with no data loss occurring as a result.

Root Cause Analysis Before Recovering

It is perfectly understandable for you in situations where CHECKDB reports an error to want to correct the problem as soon as possible, either by restoring from a backup or by using repair. However, if you want to have the ability to determine the possible root cause of the problem, I recommend you take the following steps:

1. Try to back up the damaged database, and keep it before restoring or repair.

   You may not have time to do this. That is understandable in production situations. But if you have the time and disk space, please take this step. If you contact Microsoft technical support, this is one of the things they will want you to do.

2. Take the time to investigate any possible hardware or system problems.

3. Use some of the techniques I describe later in this chapter for root cause analysis to check your system.

What if Repair Doesn't Work?

There are some errors that CHECKDB cannot fix:

- Critical system table damage
- PFS page damage
- Data purity errors

So what if you run repair and it doesn't fix all errors? In previous versions, I would tell you to just try it again. There were some situations where repair had to be run more than once to clean up all errors. Those have been corrected for SQL Server 2005. If repair simply can't fix all of your errors, your only choice is to copy all data possible from the database using BCP or SELECT and move it to another database.

Copying Data Versus Repair

Are there situations where you should consider trying to copy data using BCP or SELECT *before* you try to use repair? The only example I know of is where you may want to try and copy valid rows from a page where only a single row or a few rows are damaged. Because a damaged row would cause repair to de-allocate the page, you may want to see whether you can copy valid rows from the page except for these damaged rows. Of course, this makes sense only if these specific rows are that crucial to your business.

The only method to do this is to force the use of a nonclustered index to select specific rows (using the index hint in the SELECT statement) based on values using the index to obtain rows "around" the damaged row(s). This assumes the nonclustered index itself is intact. If you don't have a valid nonclustered index, you cannot create one in this situation. This technique can work because when the engine finds a specific row based on using the nonclustered index (assuming you have the right WHERE criteria), it can avoid scanning unnecessary rows. I've included an exercise at the end of this chapter for you to walk through an example of how to do this.

Find the Root Cause of Corruption: The Checklist

So, let's say you encounter errors from DBCC CHECKDB, but this is the first time you have ever seen it. You decide you don't want to invest much time in finding the cause. A restore of the database resolves the problem, it didn't take long, and you want to move on to other problems you need to solve. That may be fine, but what if at some point a few weeks you run CHECKDB and the same database has errors again? What if a different database is now damaged?

I've put together here a checklist of what I as a PSS engineer over the years use when a customer wants me to investigate the root cause of a database corruption problem as evidence of reoccurring errors from CHECKDB (or perhaps checksum errors on various pages).

As you read through this list, keep in mind one key fact about root cause of database corruption: *Almost all database corruption situations are caused by a problem with the underlying disk system* (drivers, controllers, firmware, disk, and so on). I'm not just telling you this because I work for Microsoft. I give you this observation based on my experience of seeing many customer reports of database corruption through the years of supporting SQL Server 7.0, 2000, and now 2005. As I go through this list, I indicate whether a particular piece of information you collect could point to a system problem or perhaps some other possible cause.

You should also know that in my experience many corruption problems go unsolved. Typically this is because

- There may not be an obvious sign of why the corruption occurred (for example, no system event log entry for a hardware problem).

- Many corruption problems do not reoccur.

- The diagnostics and time required to find the cause can be expensive.

Time will tell, but I'm hopeful that the database checksum feature for SQL Server 2005 will help improve the first reason. This is because a checksum error (Msg 824) would indicate some alteration to a database page had occurred since the engine wrote the page to disk.

As you read through this checklist, keep in mind that just about any information I discuss for data collection can be obtained using the SQLDIAG.EXE utility. This is the primary data collection tool to ensure all information is captured at a consistent point in time.

Keep Track of Problem Details and History

The root cause of any problem is always difficult if you don't have the right information and, in some cases, the history behind the problem. For reoccurring corruption problems, this is important.

Review ERRORLOG and Event Log

I hope you know how important it is to have the SQL ERRORLOG and System/Application event logs when working on problems of this magnitude. The typical information I look for when reviewing an ERRORLOG for this type of problem is as follows:

- "Last known good" for CHECKDB of databases

- Summary message on errors and repair

- Any stack dumps or critical errors (such as Msg 824)

- The use of any extended procedures or sp_OA COM objects (memory scribblers)

The event log is important, too. First, perhaps your ERRORLOG files have wrapped, but important past information in the event log has not been cleared.

Next, the System event log may contain information about possible disk, hardware, or Windows system problems. Table 2-2 contains a few common event log entries seen by PSS in the context of corruption cases, with pointers on content to read about each type of error.

TABLE 2-2   Event log entries seen by PSS

Source	Error	Notes
<any>	The device, \Device\Scsi\ cpqcissm1, did not respond within the timeout period.	See KB 259237 and 154690.
Disk	The driver detected a controller error on \Device\Harddisk4\DR4.	See KBs 259237 and 154690.
Disk	The device, \Device\Harddisk14\ DR14, is not ready for access yet.	See KB 259237.
SaveDump	The computer has rebooted from Bluescreen...a bugcheck. The bugcheck was: ...	Engage Windows Support.
Disk	An error was detected on device \Device\Harddisk3\DR3 during a paging operation.	This error indicates an I/O error during a hard page fault. Discussed in KBs 304415 and 305547.
ClusSvc	Cluster disk resource Disk J:: is corrupt. Running ChkDsk /F to repair problems.	KB 259237: "can be the result of SCSI host adapter configuration issues" or a malfunctioning device. Also see 311081 and 259237.
Ntfs	The file system structure on the disk is corrupt and unusable. Please run the chkdsk utility on the volume F:.	Note that there is at least one case (320866) where this error is erroneously raised.
Disk	Data was recovered using error correction code on device \Device\ Harddisk5\DR5.	
EventLog	The previous system shutdown at 9:45:36 AM on 9/5/2004 was unexpected.	Typically indicates a hard server cycle after a hang or a blue screen. Could also indicate something more mundane such as a power failure if the system isn't protected by UPS.
Ftdisk	{Lost Delayed-Write Data} The system was attempting to transfer file data from buffers to \Device\ HarddiskVolume4. The write operation failed, and only some of the data may have been written to the file.	Indicates a failed I/O request. Discussed in KBs 311081 and 304415. Could be anything from a firmware bug to faulty SCSI cables.

Perform Hardware Evaluation and Updates

As previously mentioned, many corruption cases turn out to be caused by fault disk systems. Yet for as many of these I've seen, I also find that many customers don't keep their disk hardware and system up-to-date. Some disk vendors provide basic diagnostics you can run regularly for the disk system, and many have updates for their drivers and firmware (much like Microsoft has for its software). So, include evaluation and updates for your disk system (plus all of your server hardware) as a regular part of your maintenance plan and strategy.

Install the Windows PAE Fix (KB 838765)

If you read anything in this section, pay attention to what I'm about to tell you. Any Windows 2000 or 2003 server using the physical addressing extensions (PAE) should make sure they have the necessary Windows fixes as described in Microsoft Knowledge Base article 8387765 applied. If you are running Windows 2003 Service Pack 1, you are covered. If not, read the article and get the fixes the article describes.

This problem in Windows can result in unpredictable behavior, including access violations and database corruption. The reason is that the bug can result in unexpected frames from Windows pages for other processes to be written on top of memory pages for the SQL Server process.

Note that on some systems, PAE is enabled even if you don't specify the /PAE switch in your boot.ini. My advice is to get the fixes for this problem installed on your server.

Run *CHKDSK.EXE*

This program is often forgotten when analyzing root cause of corruption problems. If the CHKDSK.EXE program from Windows shows damage to the NTFS file system for the drive where SQL Server database and log files exist, your search for a cause should stop there. Any damage to the file system could result in database or log corruption.

One common question for CHKDSK.EXE is "Can I run the repair option for SQL Server files?" The answer is yes, but you lose data if repair moves NTFS clusters where SQL Server data is stored. The actions to take before running CHKDSK repair depend on your available backups and the state of the disk system. If you believe the disk system is not a problem (perhaps you don't see any disk-related problems aside from NTFS errors in the event log) and you can restore from a backup, proceed with CHKDSK repair. If you cannot restore from a backup, however, you might want to consider copying data from the SQL database in question before you do anything else. This is because CHKDSK repair could move clusters of your SQL Server database file, and you might not know what is really damaged or available to copy. One thing you should not do is rely on DBCC CHECKDB repair when NTFS problems exist. This is the same advice I have provided for disk system problems. If the disk is damaged, running CHECKDB repair is not a wise decision. Why repair SQL Server pages based on a faulty disk system? Who knows whether repair will work or itself encounter corruption problems.

Evaluate *CHECKDB* Results

Saving the result of DBCC CHECKDB when errors are detected is the most important piece of information to analyze the possible root cause of corruption. If you don't know what errors were encountered, it is difficult to discuss the cause of corruption. My philosophy is that you should save *any* execution of DBCC CHECKDB whether it was successful or not. Keep the results of CHECKDB in the same LOG directory where ERRORLOG files are kept.

Inspect Damaged Databases

In some cases, just looking at the errors raised by DBCC CHECKDB is not enough to understand a possible root cause. It is important to look at the actual damage to a page to understand a possible cause. It may be important to also look at previous copies of the database (through older backups) to look for any special patterns of the damage.

This is one reason why it is important to back up a database before you repair it or at least dump the pages with DBCC PAGE.

Let's say you encounter a checksum error on a page like the following:

```
Msg 824, Level 24, State 2, Line 1
SQL Server detected a logical consistency-based I/O error: incorrect checksum
(expected: 0xc3e99060; actual: 0x78dc1f61). It occurred during a read of page
(1:152) in database ID 17 at offset 0x00000000130000 in file 'C:\Program
Files\Microsoft SQL Server\MSSQL.1\MSSQL\DATA\test.mdf'.  Additional messages
in the SQL Server error log or system event log may provide more detail. This
is a severe error condition that threatens database integrity and must be
corrected immediately. Complete a full database consistency check (DBCC
CHECKDB). This error can be caused by many factors; for more information, see
SQL Server Books Online.
```

Let's say you look at this page with DBCC PAGE and get the following output (I included only a portion of the page):

```
DBCC PAGE(17, 1, 152, 2)

DBCC execution completed. If DBCC printed error messages, contact your system
administrator.

PAGE: (1:152)


BUFFER:


BUF @0x02BEA7C0

bpage = 0x04DC0000              bhash = 0x00000000
bpageno = (1:152)
bdbid = 17                     breferences = 3
bUse1 = 25322
bstat = 0xc00809               blog = 0x999a2159
bnext = 0x00000000
```

```
PAGE HEADER:


Page @0x04DC0000

m_pageId = (1:152)                          m_headerVersion = 1
m_type = 1
m_typeFlagBits = 0x4                        m_level = 0
m_flagBits = 0x8200
m_objId (AllocUnitId.idObj) = 67      m_indexId (AllocUnitId.idInd) = 256
Metadata: AllocUnitId = 72057594042318848
Metadata: PartitionId = 72057594038321152
Metadata: IndexId = 0
Metadata: ObjectId = 2073058421      m_prevPage = (0:0)
m_nextPage = (0:0)
pminlen = 12                                m_slotCnt = 1
m_freeCnt = 8079
m_freeData = 111                            m_reservedCnt = 0
m_lsn = (37:79:3)
m_xactReserved = 0                          m_xdesId = (0:0)
m_ghostRecCnt = 0
m_tornBits = -1008103328


Allocation Status

GAM (1:2) = ALLOCATED               SGAM (1:3) = ALLOCATED
PFS (1:1) = 0x61 MIXED_EXT ALLOCATED   50_PCT_FULL
DIFF (1:6) = CHANGED
ML (1:7) = NOT MIN_LOGGED


DATA:


Memory Dump @0x4454C000

4454C000:   01010400 00820001 00000000 00000c00 †...............
4454C010:   00000000 00000100 43000000 8f1f6f00 †........C.....o.
4454C020:   98000000 01000000 25000000 4f000000 †........%...O...
4454C030:   03000000 00000000 00000000 6090e9c3 †............`...
4454C040:   00000000 00000000 00000000 00000000 †...............
4454C050:   00000000 00000000 00000000 00000000 †...............
4454C060:   10000c00 01000000 01000000 0200fc00 †...............
4454C070:   68656c6c 6f776f72 6c640000 00000000 †helloworld......
4454C080:   0000ba03 00000000 00000000 00000000 †...............
4454C090:   00000000 00000000 00000000 00000000 †...............
4454C0A0:   c0000080 00000000 00000000 00000000 †...............
4454D9A0:   00000000 00000000 00000000 00000000 †...............
4454D9B0:   00000000 00000000 00000000 00000000 †...............
4454D9C0:   00000000 00000000 00000000 00000000 †...............
4454D9D0:   00000000 00000000 00000000 00000000 †...............
4454D9E0:   00000000 00000000 00000000 00000000 †...............
```

Let's say you know that this page is for a table that shouldn't contain any character columns. Notice the "helloworld" string stored on the page. This may be a hint to you that *something* wrote incorrectly the string helloworld on a database page in memory and then the page was written to disk. Now it is damaged. I've seen this exact type of problem occur when a buggy extended stored procedure wrote strings on database pages, causing corruption.

Use the Database/Log "Replay" Technique

Suppose you don't see any common disk system type of errors in the event log, SQLIOSTRESS doesn't encounter any errors, and CHKDSK doesn't report any problems. Now what? Well, first you should know that the underlying cause could still be the disk system. I've seen situations where the event log has no errors, CHDDSK is clean, and SQLIOSTRESS running for hours showed no errors. Yet when the customer replaced the SCSI adapter or disk drive, the problem went away. I don't have scientific explanations for these situations except to say that some problems could be timing-related and specific to IO patterns from the use of SQL Server in production. Existing tools or utilities don't expose the problem.

Having said that, I've also been in situations in which I suspected SQL Server could be the cause due to symptoms such as the following:

- The errors from CHECKDB are always with the same table and perhaps are even the same type of errors (say row damage to an index).

- A "replay" of a clean database full backup and a series of transaction log backups show the errors from CHECKDB.

I've seen situations where the first point is true, but the problem was still system-driven just because the index or table was a hotspot and was used frequently. I've even seen the second point being a system problem just because of the nature of what was recorded in the transaction log.

Having said that, if you can take a full database backup and restore a series of transaction log backups to replay errors from CHECKDB, you should engage Microsoft PSS. Be careful here. You must first ensure that the full database backup is clean. In other words, if you just restored the database backup, CHECKDB should report no errors.

The reason this technique is important is that it indicates some transaction log record can be redone or undone and cause an error to occur with CHECKDB. If you replay a backup and transaction logs and you don't find any errors from CHECKDB, the problem must have occurred on the original database or log file and is not *baked* into a record from the transaction log.

One possible explanation at this point is that a database page was damaged when it was written to disk or after being written to disk. Database checksum is the primary technique to discover if a page was damaged after SQL Server wrote it to disk. Let's look at another alternative and methods to detect damage to a page *before* it is written to disk.

Use SQL Server IO Audits

I've described in this chapter the new database checksum feature for SQL Server 2005. Now I show you some more advanced techniques used to detect certain types of damage to pages in addition to checksum. It is important to know that the use of some of these features, usually by trace flags, can have performance implications for your server. Database checksum was designed into the product and tested for performance (which is why it is the default option for a database in 2005). My recommendation is that you consult with Microsoft PSS when considering these options.

Stale Read (Trace Flag 818)

A *stale read* occurs when SQL Server writes a modified page to disk but the disk system returns a previous version of the page (perhaps from hardware cache). A *lost write* occurs when SQL Server modifies a page and writes it to disk, but the disk system never stores this modification to disk, so the previous version is returned when reading the page from disk. These differences are subtle, and the symptoms of the problem can appear to be the same: A modification to disk appears to be lost. One primary difference is that a stale read can result in correct data after something like a system reboot occurs to clear the cache.

It is important to know that this situation would not be detected by a database checksum. This is because the page itself is valid based on the checksum value; the hardware is simply giving back an unexpected version of the page.

In SQL Server 2000, the SQL Server development team added logic to detect this problem if an error for a page was encountered such as Msg 823 or 605. If you enabled trace flag 818, the engine would keep track of the latest LSN value for a database page in memory. When an error was encountered, the engine would compare the LSN value on the read page to the last known modified LSN in its "list of LSN values." If they didn't match, an error like the following was written to the ERRORLOG:

```
SQL Server has detected an unreported OS/hardware level read or write
problem on Page (1:75007) of database 12
LSN returned (63361:16876:181), LSN expected (63361:16876:500)
Contact the hardware vendor and consider disabling caching mechanisms to
correct the problem
```

In SQL Server 2000 Service Pack 4 and SQL Server 2005, the SQL Server development team enhanced the design of this trace flag to perform the LSN check on every read of a page and to store the LSN list in a more efficient hash table design. This auditing is not only by default and requires the trace flag to be enabled at server startup time. Again, you should use this trace flag only if you are having difficulty tracking down the cause of the corruption problem.

Eliminate Possible Memory Scribbler Software

If you think the problem is a damaged database page before it is written to disk, seriously consider eliminating any software running in the SQL Server process space that could cause unexpected memory damage. This includes user-written extended stored procedures, COM objects loaded by sp_OA, and linked server providers. I'm not saying this because it is a safe thing to do. I'm telling you this because I've seen things like user-written extended stored procedures have bugs that overwrite SQL Server database pages leading to corruption as they are written to disk.

If you can't disable these custom objects and procedures, considering moving them out of the process space for SQL Server. The SQL Server documentation provides information on how to run COM objects out of process with sp_OA and linked servers out of process when configuring the linked server. An extended procedure would be run out of process on the primary SQL Server by installing it on another SQL Server and executing it from the primary as a SQL remote stored procedure call.

Relocate Files to an Alternative Location
The last item on the root cause checklist may sound too simple, but I put this here because I've seen it work before. If you have tried all these options and are still scratching your head for a possible cause, it could still be your disk system. I've had customers simply move their database (or a system database such as tempdb) to another disk drive or disk system (such as a SAN or off of a SAN), and the problem has disappeared. To be fair and accurate, the move of the files might have changed the timing of the problem, and it could still be SQL Server. In many of these cases, however, I've seen customers then replace the original disk controller or disk system, and the problem will permanently go away. Don't discount this simple technique when you are thinking of all of these trace flags and tools to use.

Memory Issues

By Slava Oks

Introduction to Windows Memory Management

In this section, I will briefly describe how the Windows memory manager works. These concepts are key to understanding how SQLOS and SQL Server manage memory. We will talk about the key aspects of the Windows virtual and physical memory management, as well as features that enable high-end servers—such as SQL Server—fine-grain control over their memory usage.

We look at memory as a set of common resources shared by applications, their components, and operating system. It is important to be very specific when talking about memory. In many cases, developers, users, and DBAs mistakenly refer to different memory resources and concepts using the generic term *memory*, disregarding the fact that there are several types of memory. These different types of memory can be classified as shown in Table 3-1. *External* and *Internal* refer to memory resources relative to a process.

TABLE 3-1   Different types of memory

	Internal	External
Virtual memory	Virtual address space, virtual address descriptors	Swap file, physical memory, RAM
Physical memory	Working set and private bytes AWE mechanisms, locked pages in memory, large pages	Physical memory (RAM)

Internal Virtual Memory—Virtual Address Space

The virtual address space (VAS) is a memory resource that is often overlooked when dealing with memory issues and in books describing the Windows memory manager. Even the Windows Task Manager lacks a distinct VAS counter per process. As it turns out, understanding how Windows interoperates with the VAS during a process is very important when dealing with memory.

Windows creates a separate VAS for each process when processing the CreateProcess API. After a process is created, developers allocate/free VAS regions by using VirtualAlloc/VirtualFree APIs. The VAS region can be bound to physical memory or not, depending on how it is used. The minimal size of the VAS region is 64KB. Moreover, all VAS regions are multiples of 64KB. Committing or binding of VAS regions to physical memory is done based on the system page size, which can be 4KB or 8KB, based on the processor architecture. (There are also large pages of 4MB and 16MB on x86 and IA64, but we will talk about them later.) For now, just keep in mind that any new allocation of VAS using VirtualAlloc or other APIs is always rounded up to a 64KB boundary, although binding to physical memory happens at system page granularity. This means that if you allocate and commit a new VAS region, Windows consumes an amount of physical memory equal to the requested amount rounded up to the next page and consumes the VAS of the process rounded up to the next 64KB boundary. For example, if you allocate 13KB of memory using the VirtualAlloc Win32 API, Windows allocates 64KB of VAS inside your process and commits 16KB of physical memory.

The bottom line is that you need to be very careful when using APIs that manipulate the VAS. Even if you don't use these APIs directly, SQL Server does. It's important to have a good understanding of how they operate so that you can understand how SQL Server works and so that you can more easily troubleshoot memory-related issues. For example, it is becoming increasingly more common on the x86 platform for processes to run out of VAS. In order for you to troubleshoot such cases, you have to know what VAS is and how it can be consumed. Also keep in mind that, despite what some might tell you, it's still possible to exhaust the VAS on 64-bit platforms. Even on 64-bit systems, VAS is not an unlimited resource. For example, VAS space on Windows 2003 SP1 is equal to 8TB of memory. It's quite possible to run out of a resource such as this if application data structures scale with that amount of physical memory installed on the machine.

As I've said, VAS is per-process. Everything that gets allocated, loaded, created, and mapped in a Windows process uses VAS. In order for components to use VAS, they make use of the VirtualAlloc family of Windows APIs. For every VAS region, Windows locates its corresponding virtual address descriptor (VAD) object, a structure that describes the region. Each VAD object fully describes each VAS region (its size, allocation, attributes, and protection). Internally, Windows maintains a VAD tree. The VAD tree enables Windows to efficiently provide VAS management. Conceptually, Windows manages a process's VAS the same way as anyone would manage a heap with an allocation block size of 64KB.

You can take a look at the process VAD tree using WinDbg's local kernel debugger commands. In addition, Windows provides the VirtualQuery* family of APIs to enable an application to walk its VAD tree if necessary. SQL Server implements the sys.dm_os_virtual_address_dump DMV using these APIs.

VAS Size

The VAS size of a Windows process on a 32-bit system is 4GB. Windows splits this 4GB VAS into two 2GB halves: the user mode space and the kernel mode space. All allocations by an application come from its user mode partition. Some applications need more than 2GB of space. For such applications, Windows provides a configuration mechanism—/3GB and /USERVA switches in a boot.ini file—to customize the VAS split between the user and kernel mode partitions. The configuration setting is global. Once applied, it affects all the processes on the machine that have been linked with a special flag (the LARGEADDRES-SAWARE flag), indicating that they support more than 2GB of user mode space.

The maximum size of the user portion of VAS on 32-bit Windows is 3GB. Setting the user mode partition to 3GB necessarily shrinks the kernel partition to 1GB. Depending on the load characteristics, such configuration might significantly affect performance and stability of the system as a whole. Due to these and other issues that I'll talk about later in this chapter, my usual recommendation is to avoid the use of the /3GB and /USERVA switches.

As I've said, on x86 platforms, VAS is limited to 3GB. On x64 platforms, 32-bit large address-aware applications receive a 4GB VAS without requiring any special boot switches. One thing to keep in mind is that some legacy applications and libraries were written with a maximum VAS of 3GB in mind and might perform address manipulation that is illegal with VAS sizes larger than 3GB. Such applications might be unstable in WOW mode on x64 Windows, so you must be careful to test them thoroughly before assuming that they'll simply work.

Although the VAS size can be changed for 32-bit applications, to really overcome VAS limitations, you're better off leveraging 64-bit Windows and native 64-bit applications.

Tracking VAS

The VAS is a key resource, and it is used by a lot of different components (such as libraries loaded into your process space), so the ability to track or account for its usage is very important. Table 3-2 lists a set of process entities that can consume user mode VAS.

TABLE 3-2 **Set of process entities that can consume user mode VAS**

Component	Description	Tools to Track	Example
Application code and static data	Application image and static data are mapped to VAS	`Vadump.exe` `Windbg.exe`	
DLL code and static data	DLLs, loaded libraries, and static data are mapped to VAS	`Vadump.exe` `Windbg.exe`	
Threads	Thread Environment Block (TEB) and thread stacks `Windbg.exe`	Perfmon, Task Manager,	Perfmon: Process\ Thread Count * Thread Stack Size Task Manager: Thread Count * Stack Size `Windbg.exe:!~`
Windows heaps	Process heaps and heaps created using the CreateHeap API	`Windbg.exe`	`Windbg.exe: !heap`
Memory-mapped files	Section objects, shared memory, and memory-mapped files created through the CreateFile Mapping family of APIs	`Windg.exe,` `vadump.exe`	`Windbg.exe: !vadump`
VirtualAlloc calls	Application-specific memory managers, application-direct calls to the VirtualAlloc family of APIs	`Vadump.exe` `Windbg.exe`	`Windbg.exe: !vadump`

You can get an idea of how much VAS is currently consumed inside a process by looking at perfmon's virtual bytes counter.

Unfortunately, Windows doesn't provide a simple way of tracking VAS usage by components. Several tools can be used to track VAS. One of them is VADUMP. VADUMP produces plenty of information regarding VAS usage. However, in many cases, it might be enough to understand complete VAS distribution. For the majority of VAS regions, VADUMP doesn't provide the developer with information regarding what component the VAS region belongs to. One way to get such information is to hijack VirtualAlloc/VirtualFree calls and then keep track of all VAS operations. This is exactly what the LeakDiag tool does. It leverages the detours library provided by Microsoft Research to hook VAS APIs. For every allocation, it remembers allocation information along with the stack. At any point in time, the information can be dumped into the file and analyzed. Leakdiag can be downloaded from ftp://ftp.microsoft.com/PSS/Tobols/Developer%20Support %20Tools/LeakDiag/.

NOTE

You might need to contact Microsoft Product Support Services in order to obtain permission to access this ftp site. See http://support.microsoft.com for more info.

External Virtual Memory

The Windows virtual memory mechanism consists of physical memory (RAM), a swap or paging file, and VAS. We covered VAS in the previous section. In this section, we will discuss RAM and the swap file. The sum of RAM size and max possible swap file size is the maximum amount of memory all processes on the system (including kernels) can commit, allocate, and use. It is very important to properly configure a system so that it has an adequate amount of RAM and swap file size to accommodate the expected load. Although it is possible for Windows to run without a swap file, it is not recommended because some crucial functionality, such as generating a kernel dump, might be missing.

After you configure a system to run with a swap file, make sure that the swap file is of proper size. Keep in mind that if a swap file is present, the Windows kernel will be using it for internal use as well. Therefore, it is possible that with plenty of RAM on the machine, Windows returns an out-of-memory error for the VirtualAlloc call if the system is out of swap files.

Windows provides a set of notification APIs, discussed in the next section. Applications can subscribe in order to find out the physical memory state, but there isn't a similar mechanism for the swap file. Server-side applications have to be careful when deciding whether to grow their memory usage. It is possible for Windows to broadcast high memory availability for physical memory, but at the same time to be low on the swap file.

You can track RAM and swap file availability by looking at the Task Manager's Performance pane or perfmon's Memory counters.

Internal Physical Memory

Most of the complex services and applications, in addition to Windows memory management, have their own internal memory manager. The goal of this type of internal memory manager is to distribute physical memory among large memory consumers inside a process. The complex internal memory managers take VAS management into account as well because on 32-bit platforms, VAS limitation might affect physical memory availability and distribution.

Internal memory managers use VirtualAlloc APIs to allocate large regions of VAS to bind them to physical memory, divide them into smaller pieces, and then service them to clients that need memory. Some of the clients can be more complex than others. For example, some memory manager clients can release memory back to the memory manager if the latter requests it.

Complex memory managers, along with memory distribution, attempt to perform more complex services such as working set management (the set of physical pages allocated to a given process and currently in use) and memory pressure avoidance. The extended functionality can sometimes interfere with the OS and hence should be carefully handcrafted. For example, one of the main functionalities of the Windows memory manager is to maintain optimal physical memory distribution across the processes. If one of the processes on a system overcommits its physical memory usage, Windows might swap the process to a swap file. If such an event occurs, the performance of the process can be degraded significantly. An internal memory manager might attempt to recognize such a situation, broadcast memory state to its clients and release, decommit, and process memory as necessary before Windows begins paging out the process. As you might expect, recognizing such an event and figuring out the amount of memory to be freed is not a trivial task.

Windows Support for Sophisticated Memory Managers
To assist internal memory managers of complex applications, Windows provides several services such as physical memory notification of APIs and direct allocation of physical pages, sometimes referred to as AWE, or the Locked Pages in Memory mechanism. The former service enables the process to monitor overall system memory state and properly react when the system is low on memory. The latter enables direct allocation of physical memory so that the OS can't take it away from a process without actually killing it. This service helps a process allocate physical memory and completely avoid the OS taking it away. In addition, the AWE mechanism allows a process to bind physical memory to any given region in VAS. This functionality can be used by the process memory manager to map physical memory to any given VAS region so that a process can use more physical memory than there is VAS, which is good for 32-bit installations. The use of the AWE mechanism has its drawbacks, however. If the process memory manager makes a mistake and doesn't release physical memory when the whole system is out of physical memory, it can affect stability of the whole system. Due to this problem, the mechanism should be used very carefully and should be well tested before it is put into production. For example, SQL Server's internal memory manager makes use of both memory notification and the AWE mechanism on 32-bit as well as 64-bit platforms.

In addition to the mechanisms discussed, Windows provides large-page support. As you know, every time a process needs to retrieve or store something from or to memory, it supplies a virtual address. A virtual address is an address of the process VAS region. Hardware translates a virtual address to a physical address. Because there potentially can be plenty of virtual addresses, the operation can be slow. To improve performance, hardware manufacturers introduced translation look-aside buffer (TLB). TLB performs caching of the most recent translations of a virtual address to a physical address. As you might expect, a TLB has limited size so that once it is fully populated, the system has to evict a least recently used entry in order to accommodate a new request. TLB performs translation at the system page boundary. Therefore, if the TLB size is 128 entries at most, it can keep the translation for 128 * page_size, which might be small considering the size of a single page and the number of pages a thread can touch. To minimize the effect of TLB size limitations, both CPU manufacturers and OS developers introduced support for different page sizes. For example, the Windows process on the IA64 can use pages of 8KB or 16MB, depending on its needs. Pages with large sizes are called large pages. On the AMD64, the size of large pages is 2MB, and on the x86 the size is 4MB. Due to the size of large pages, TLB can effectively provide translation of larger sets of VAS regions. On a system with a large amount of memory, it can be very beneficial to use large pages for hot and/or global data to minimize risks of TLB misses. An application's memory manager can make use of large pages. For example, the SQL Server memory manager allocates its lock manager using large pages. As with any technology, large pages have a drawback that you should be aware of: An OS can be very slow allocating large pages, so using large pages for global structures can significantly affect an application's start time. In addition, Windows doesn't have swapping support for large pages, so they are effectively locked pages and can't be reclaimed by Windows. If an application misuses large pages, it can halt the whole system.

External Physical Memory

The amount of external physical memory is defined by two main factors: the amount of actual RAM installed on the system, and system configuration. Table 3-3 represents the max amount of physical memory the system can use for a given configuration.

TABLE 3-3   Max amount of physical memory the system can use for a given configuration

Configuration	Max System Memory
32-bit default	4GB
32-bit with /PAE in boot.ini	64GB
32-bit with /PAE and /3GB in boot.ini	16GB
32-bit in WOW	128GB
X64	1TB
IA64	1TB

Max system memory also controls the maximum amount of physical memory that a given application can use. By leveraging the AWE mechanism, 32-bit applications can use a RAM amount larger than their VAS.

As we mentioned in previous chapters, you can track the amount of available system memory by looking at the Task Manager's Performance pane or perfmon's Memory counters.

Memory Pressure

In the previous section, we described types of memory resources that applications have to deal with. In this section, we analyze a state of the application or system when available memory is low. We characterize memory pressure as a state of the application or machine in which one of the memory resources corresponding to the VAS, the swap file, RAM, or internal physical memory managed by the application heap is decreasing and forces its corresponding memory managers to work harder and harder to produce new additional resources.

Since there are four major types of memory resources, there are four types of memory pressures that a system can be exposed to. To maximize its performance and reliability, a process might want to react to all of them. Each type of memory pressure can have its own side effect. For example, RAM pressure might cause a process and whole system to go into paging. In turn, heap pressure might cause OOM conditions and, eventually, the process may crash (but most likely won't affect the system). Table 3-4 attempts to characterize memory pressure and its corresponding resource type.

TABLE 3-4   Memory pressure and its corresponding resource type

	Internal Pressure	External Pressure
Virtual memory	VAS	Swap file + RAM
Physical memory	Process memory manager	RAM

External virtual memory pressure, or swap file pressure, is controlled by Windows. This type of memory pressure might drive the whole system into an out-of-virtual-memory condition. You might have seen a pop-up in the lower-right corner of the Windows taskbar indicating that the system is running low on virtual memory. Currently, Windows doesn't provide notification mechanisms for applications to detect this type of memory pressure. In order for applications to identify this, they need to monitor the size of the swap file. The majority of applications don't detect this type of pressure and, consequently, can drive themselves and the whole system into an out-of-memory condition without noticing it.

The external physical memory, or RAM pressure, rises when Windows runs low on free RAM and is about to start trimming existing working sets on the system. A process can monitor this type of pressure by leveraging memory resource notification with the API described at: http://msdn.microsoft.com/library/default.asp?url=/library/en-us/memory/base/querymemoryresourcenotification.asp. An application can have dedicated threads that monitor memory resource notifications. Keep in mind that these notifications are global (they are shared by all processes). A thread can wait on two types of memory resource notifications: high memory and low memory. Before Windows starts paging, it turns on low memory resource notification. The application threads that are waiting on such notification are awakened and given the opportunity to shrink the process's memory usage before the OS starts the process of paging. This is very useful for high-end services that have a better idea than the operating system about their memory usage and what needs to be shrunk. Once the physical memory state goes back to normal, Windows unsets the low memory resource notification. As you might expect, when Windows identifies that there is plenty of memory on the system, it turns on high memory resource notification. If neither of the memory resource notifications are set, it means that the system is in a stable state, and its processes should neither grow nor shrink.

Depending on its memory manager, or heap manager, there are several ways for a process to get into physical internal memory pressure. For example, external pressure might cause a process to start shrinking. This might trigger the process to release memory and cause the size of the internal heap to shrink. It turn, heap shrinkage might trigger internal memory pressure. The other possibility to get into this type of pressure is for an administrator to set process custom heap limits. After the amount of memory allocated from the heap gets closer to the configured setting, the process enters a condition of internal memory pressure. The application might attempt to recover from this type of pressure by shrinking internal caches and memory pools back to its heap. The heap might decide to hold on to the freed physical memory, depending on the state of external physical memory pressure.

VAS pressure is the most difficult one to detect and react to. VAS pressure can happen for two reasons. The first is VAS fragmentation, which happens when a process might have plenty of VAS regions but no VAS region of a given size is available. Currently, there is no easy way to detect the largest free VAS region. You can try to allocate a VAS region of a given size to identify VAS pressure state. Be careful, though—periodic attempts to allocate a VAS region of large size—say, 4MB—might cause VAS fragmentation. This happens if some component in the process keeps on allocating and caching VAS regions of smaller sizes. For example, if an application keeps on creating threads with stack sizes of 512KB and pools them, periodic allocation and the release of 4MB of memory might cause fragmentation. The second reason for VAS pressure is that the whole VAS can be consumed. In this case, any VAS allocation fails. High-end servers have to be able to deal with VAS pressure, especially on 32-bit platforms. Not recovering from VAS pressure might cause the first process to slow down and the actual process to terminate. When an application detects VAS pressure, it can react to it in the same way as to internal physical pressure by shrinking caches and memory pools. In addition, a process might decide to shrink thread pools, remove shared memory regions, unload DLLs, and so on.

To correctly handle all four types of memory pressure, you need to build a special infrastructure. As it turns out, this type of infrastructure is not trivial. Just consider different states your process can be in at the same time. For example, Windows might indicate that there is plenty of external RAM, enabling your process memory consumption to grow, but at the same time, your process can encounter internal heap pressure or VAS pressure.

There are several implementation caveats that you need to be aware of when implementing such an infrastructure. If your process is slow enough to react to external pressure, Windows pages out your process. Then it turns off the low memory resource and, consequently, turns on the high memory resource. In this case, you might see that high memory is on and start allocating more memory even though your process is paged out. This might cause your process to page against itself. It seems that when deciding to grow, you need to take your working set into account—but remember that neither AWE pages nor large pages are part of the working set, so you have to be really careful. The other caveat here is that when the system runs low on the paging file, Windows doesn't turn on the low memory resource even though it is about to return OOM for the next memory requests. In addition, keep in mind that your well-behaved application can be affected by bad ones that might completely disregard system memory state.

NUMA Support

The NUMA system can have two major configurations: pure NUMA and interleaved NUMA. Pure NUMA will appear to the operating system as a set of CPU nodes, sometimes called cells or pods, with local memory. Every node has its own memory. Remote memory is memory that is attached to other nodes. Depending on the hardware manufacturer, performance penalties to access remote memory are different and can be substantial. For an application to perform and scale well on NUMA, it has to minimize a number of remote accesses.

When the system is configured to use interleaved memory, it essentially appears as an SMP box. In this type of configuration, all memory is global, and every cache line is interleaved across different NUMA nodes. Interleaved configuration is suitable for systems that don't have NUMA optimizations. For example, SQL 2000 prior to SP4 doesn't have NUMA optimizations and most likely will perform better on interleaved systems.

When Windows starts up on pure NUMA hardware, it recognizes the system multinode configuration and boots accordingly. From our experience, we have noticed that during the start, the OS allocates memory mostly from a single node. Keep in mind that this depends on memory availability on the nodes, as well as the number of applications the OS has to start. This allocation pattern during the OS startup can be problematic for a NUMA-aware application because memory is not distributed evenly across the nodes and there is no way to find out memory distributions across the nodes. As the system continues to run, the problem becomes more severe—less and less free memory is available on the nodes. This can be due to memory-hungry applications or to System File Cache (SFC). Depending on the system configuration, it is possible for SFC to allocate a significant amount of memory. Moreover, on NUMA configurations, it is quite possible for SFC to unevenly use memory across nodes. If a NUMA-aware application only attempts to allocate local memory, it might become a victim of memory starvation on the nodes that collided with SFC or with other memory-hungry applications.

Windows exposes a set of APIs that allows applications to take advantage of NUMA. There are several API "gotchas" that every developer should be aware of:

A. There is no explicit way to allocate memory from the given node. A thread allocates memory from a given memory node by changing its affinity to the given node and then calling VirtualAlloc (if running with a swap file, you have to touch the virtual address before it gets bound to the physical page) or other low-level APIs that trigger physical page allocation. If the OS doesn't have memory on a given node, it serves the memory from the different node. It won't fail the allocation.

B. GetNumaAvailableMemoryNode can return 0 even though there can still be memory that the OS can serve from the node.

C. Windows serves memory in the following order: 1) from the node a thread is affinitized to, 2) from the node that has memory free, and 3) from any node—memory is freed from standby lists, working sets, and SFC.

The consequences of A and C are that NUMA-aware applications should have more special handling for remote memory. A and C might cause the OS to return memory in random order, such as remote, local, remote, and so on. Keep in mind that if an application decides not to cache remote memory, it might get in trouble, because when memory is freed, this memory gets put on the free list and is given away on the next allocation request.

The consequences of B are that applications can't reliably decide whether they can or can't allocate memory from the node. Case B usually occurs after the system runs for some time, especially when large applications are present.

SQLOS and SQL Server Memory Management

Up to this point, we have been talking about Windows memory management. Now the time has come to dive into SQL Server's memory management. SQL Server utilizes SQLOS services to manage its memory. SQLOS's memory manager consists of several components such as memory nodes, memory clerks, memory caches, memory objects, and a memory broker. Figure 3-1 depicts memory manager components and their relationship.

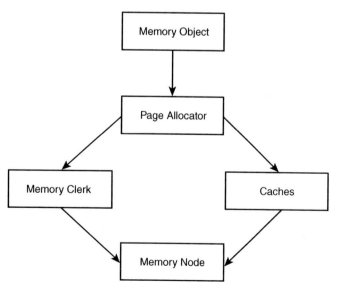

FIGURE 3-1   Memory manager components and their relationship

Memory Node

The SQLOS memory manager consists of a set of memory nodes. The actual number of nodes depends on the hardware configuration of the system SQLOS is running on. A memory node is not visible outside of the memory manager; it is inside to SQLOS. The major goal of a memory node is to provide locality of allocations. The memory node contains several basic memory allocators that are divided into three main types:

- A set of page allocators

- A virtual allocator leveraging Windows VirtualAlloc APIs

- A shared memory allocator that is fully based on Windows file-mapping APIs

The page allocators are the most commonly used allocators in the SQLOS memory manager. The reason they are called page allocators is because they allocate memory in multiples of the SQLOS page. A single-page size is 8KB, the same size as a database page in SQL Server. As you will learn later, this is not a coincidence.

There are four different types of page allocators:

- **Single.** Provide only one page at a time.

- **Multi.** Provide a set of contiguous 8KB pages.

- **Large.** Can be used to allocate large pages. SQLOS and SQL Server use large pages to minimize TLB misses when accessing hot data structures. Currently, large pages are supported only on IA64 or x64 hardware with at least 8GB of RAM.

- **Reserved.** Can be used to allocate a special set of pages reserved for an emergency (such as when SQL Server is low on memory).

Figure 3-2 shows the memory node and its allocators.

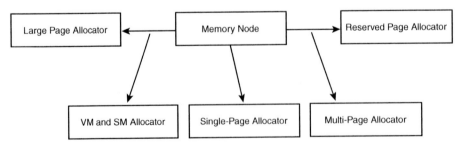

FIGURE 3-2 Memory node and its allocators

At this point, SQL Server doesn't have a dynamic management view (DMV) that will dump a set of all memory nodes and information about their allocators. However, dbcc memorystatus comes pretty close—it outputs information per scheduler nodes that are a proper subset of the memory nodes.

Please keep in mind that page allocators discussed here are different from the ones exposed in DMV, such as `sys.dm_os_memory_clerks` and `sys.dm_os_memory_objects`.

Memory Clerks

As we have already said, memory nodes are hidden from memory manager users. If a memory manager client needs to allocate memory, it first creates a memory clerk. There are four types of memory clerks:

- Generic memory

- Cache store

- User store

- Object store (also referred to as memory pool)

The latter three are a bit convoluted. Along with memory clerk functionality, they provide data caching and data pooling.

One can think of a memory clerk as a memory interface along with a bag of statistics. Memory clerks support the same type of allocators as memory nodes. In addition, they allow large memory consumers to hook into memory brokerage infrastructure. SQLOS provides several global memory clerks. SQLOS's middle and large memory consumers are encouraged to use their own clerk so that memory consumption can be understood by a given consumer. The memory clerk infrastructure enables us to track and control the amount of memory consumed by a memory component. Each scheduler node has a list of memory clerks that we can safely walk during runtime. SQL Server implements `sys.dm_os_memory_clerks` dmv to dump clerk information. This view outputs one row per memory clerk. Columns in this view represent allocators that the clerk user leverages to allocate memory. Also, combined clerk information can be derived from the dbcc `memorystatus` command.

Memory Objects

Memory clerks provide allocations on page boundary only, but what if you need allocations of smaller granularity? This type of functionality usually is provided by memory heaps. SQLOS's memory object is an actual heap. A memory object leverages a memory clerk to allocate its memory. SQLOS supports three types of memory objects:

- A **variable memory object** is a regular heap.

- An **incremental memory object** is a mark/shrink, arena, or zone heap. It comes in very handy during query compilation and execution. Both compilation and execution happen in two phases. The first phase is to grow memory usage, and the second is to shrink memory usage. If execution is self-contained, it doesn't need to perform any cleanup except for freeing actual memory. Mark/shrink heap significantly improves performance.

- A **memory object** is a fixed-size heap. As you can guess, components can use this type of heap when they need to allocate objects of a given size.

The smallest payload for a given memory object is 8KB. It is exactly the same as a SQLOS page size. It also means that a memory object can be created from a memory clerk leveraging a single-page allocator. (This is yet another very important point! Keep this in mind until we connect SQLOS memory manager and the buffer pool [BP].)

For tracking purposes, SQL Server exposes a DMV to output all memory objects in its process: sys.dm_os_memory_objects.

In both memory clerks and memory objects, DMVs expose a page allocator column. (In the memory manager diagram, we outlined a page allocator.) The reason we expose this column via DMVs is that, internally, the memory object uses the memory clerk's page allocator interface to allocate pages. This information can be used to join memory clerk and memory object DMVs. Use the page allocator column to join them.

Memory Caches

SQL Server 2005 memory management is different from SQL Server 2000 in that its elaborative caching framework is exposed by SQLOS. SQL 2000 has two major caches: data page cache, called buffer pool, and procedure cache, the cache of query plans. In SQL Server 2000, the buffer pool and procedure cache are very tightly coupled. For example, procedure cache relies on the buffer pool's eviction mechanism to control its size, even though both have separate costing policies. Having BP and procedure cache tied together has significantly simplified caching machinery in SQL Server 2000.

With the addition of new features and new requirements in SQL Server 2005, a number of caches we have to support have exploded. Tying all caches to the buffer pool has become not only problematic, but not even feasible. It has become obvious that we need to create a common caching framework, and SQLOS is the perfect solution.

Common Caching Framework

To cache different types of data, SQLOS implements a common caching framework. There are three types of cache mechanisms: cache store, user store, and object store. Each store has its own properties and hence its own usage. User store is a slightly awkward name for the cache, but after we describe its usage, it will make more sense to you.

Before we jump into further description of stores, let's discuss the difference between caches and pools. In SQLOS's world, cache is a mechanism to cache heterogeneous types of data with a given cost for each entry. Usually a given state is associated with an entry. A cache implements lifetime control of an entry and its visibility and provides some type of LRU policies. Depending on the type of data cached, each entry can be used by multiple clients at the same time. For example, the SQL Server procedure cache resides in SQLOS. A plan's lifetime, visibility, and cost are controlled by SQLOS's cache mechanism. Each plan can be used by multiple batches at the same time.

In SQLOS, pool is a mechanism for caching homogeneous data. In most cases, cached data has neither state nor cost associated with it. A pool has limited control over the lifetime of the entry and its visibility. After an entry is taken from the pool, it is actually removed from the pool, and the pool no longer has any control over the entry until the entry is pushed back to the pool. Only one client can use an entry at a time. An example of a pool is a pool of network buffers: no state, no cost, and all buffers are the same size. Keep in mind that SQL Server's buffer pool is a cache in SQLOS. Currently, it doesn't use any of SQLOS's caching mechanism.

Cache Store and User Store

Both cache and user stores are actual caches and are very similar. The cache store implements support for hash tables, and the user store requires cache developer users to leverage the framework to implement their own storage semantics—hence the name user store. Figure 3-3 shows how the cache store and user store are laid out.

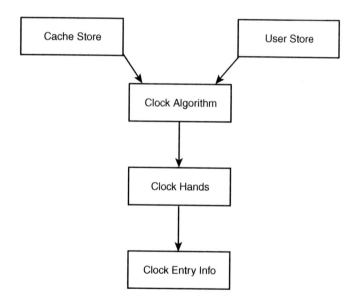

FIGURE 3-3   Layout of cache store and user store

Conceptually, there are two major controls in SQLOS caches: lifetime and visibility. Lifetime control provides lifetime management of an entry. Visibility control manages visibility of an entry. It is important to understand that an entry in a cache can exist but might not be visible. For example, if a cache is marked for single use only, an entry won't be visible after it is given away. In addition, an entry might be marked as dirty. It will continue to exist and live in the cache, but it won't be visible to any lookup.

The lifetime of entries is controlled by a store's mechanism. In a cache store, the lifetime is fully controlled by SQLOS's caching framework. In a user store, the entry's lifetime is only partially controlled by a store. Since the user store implements its own storage, it also participates in lifetime control. For both stores, the entry's visibility is controlled by the caching framework.

Lifetime of an entry is managed by an embedded reference count in Clock Entry Info. After this count goes to 0, an entry is destroyed. In a user store, only Clock Entry Info (but not the actual data) is destroyed.

Visibility of an entry is implemented by a pin count embedded in Clock Entry Info. Keep in mind that pin count and reference count are different mechanisms. Reference count manages lifetime, and pin count manages visibility. For an entry to be visible, its pin count needs to be visible and have a value larger than 0. It also needs to be non-dirty and not marked for single usage. A pin count of 1 means that the entry is visible and is currently not in use.

Hash Tables
The cache store mechanism implements its own storage—hash tables. A single cache store can have several hash tables. This is very useful when cache store users need support for different types of lookup. For example, SQL Server's procedure cache leverages this functionality to enable looking up procedures by name or by ID. The lookup process in different hash tables is independent of each other and doesn't conflict with clock hand movement, described next.

Clock Algorithm
SQLOS's caching framework implements LRU policy to control visibility and lifetime of entries in the cache. It simulates LRU by implementing a clock algorithm. A clock algorithm object is embedded both in cache and user stores. It currently contains two clock hands—internal and external. An external clock hand is moved by the resource monitor (RM) when the whole process gets into memory pressure, as discussed next.

The internal clock hand is used to control the size of a cache relative to other caches. You can think of the internal clock hand as a way to put a max cap on a single cache. If this mechanism didn't exist, it would be possible for a single cache to push the whole process into different types of memory pressure. For example, if you execute numerous ad hoc queries, they can be cached. Without an internal clock hand, that could force the whole SQL Server procedure list into internal physical memory pressure. To avoid this type of situation, the internal clock hand starts moving after the framework predicts that the procedure cache's max cap is reached.

The clock hand's movement doesn't interfere with store usage. Every time the clock hand steps on a not-in-use entry, it decreases cost by some amount. If the entry is not in use and its cost is zero, the clock hand makes the entry invisible and then attempts to remove it from the cache. The removal process can fail if another clock hand is currently working on the same entry. After both clock hands move away from the entry, it is removed.

In the future, it is possible that we can add more clock hands so that we can get better control over a single cache or group of caches.

Object Store

An object store is a simple memory pool of objects of a given size. It is used to cache homogeneous types of data. Currently, it doesn't have any costing associated with its entries. It implements max cap to control its size relative to other caches. In addition, on every memory pressure notification sent by the resource monitor, the object store removes the preconfigured number of entries. It is possible to implement more sophisticated algorithms in the future. For now, we will keep things as simple as possible.

Tracking Caches and Pools

SQL Server 2005 DMVs enable you to observe cache behaviors in action. Following is a list of tables you can use to get information you need:

- **sys.dm_os_memory_cache_counters** provides you with summary information for every store—amount of memory used, number of entries, number of entries in use, and so on. You can use this view to find cache memory usage and number of entries in a cache.

- **sys.dm_os_memory_cache_hash_tables** provides you with information about the cache store's hash tables—max, min, average bucket length, and so on. This view is useful to find out distribution of entries per bucket for each cache table in the cache store.

- **sys.m_os_memory_cache_clock_hands** provides you with information about clock hands for every cache and user store—hand is running, number of rounds, amount of entries removed, and so on. This view is useful to find out the current state of clock hands, as well as the clock hand moving history.

These tables are very useful in understanding, monitoring, and tuning behavior of a single store, and SQL Server overall. For example, if you observe permanent hands' movement, you might improve server performance by finding ways to stop them.

So far, we have described how SQLOS's memory manager is structured inside. Now it is time to start talking about how all this fits into SQL Server.

Buffer Pool

In this section, we bind SQLOS and SQL Server memory managers and the buffer pool and show how they form one cohesive memory manager unit.

The buffer pool's internal behavior differs on 32-bit and 64-bit systems and also depends on AWE or locked pages in enabled memory. Conceptually, however, regardless of system configuration, the BP consists of two major parts: a fixed, 8KB memory manager and the database page's cache. The main task of the memory manager is to allocate VAS regions of a size depending on system configuration, map them to NUMA nodes, and then bind them to physical memory allocated from the bound node. Allocated memory is then broken into 8KB buffers and put on per-node free lists. From the free lists, the 8KB buffer can be served to the SQLOS memory manager or to the BP's data page cache.

The buffer pool's memory manager populates free lists on demand or when it notices they become too short. Depending on internal memory requirements and external memory state, it calculates its target—the amount of physical memory it estimates it should allocate before it can get the system into physical memory pressure. To keep the system out of physical memory pressure, the BP's memory manager recalculates the target constantly. Keep in mind that target memory shouldn't exceed max memory.[1] If such a situation arises, all large memory consumers—including the BP's data cache—must shrink their memory usage.

As we have already mentioned, the BP is NUMA-aware. perfmon exposes a BufferNode counter for every NUMA node on the system. You can find a complete description of the counter in SQL Server Books Online. Max and min server memory settings affect buffer pool size only. On NUMA systems, these settings are divided equally across the nodes, so it is important to configure the system in a homogeneous way such that all nodes have equal amounts of memory.

The SQLOS memory manager leverages the BP's memory manager. Figure 3-4 shows where both of them meet.

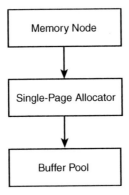

FIGURE 3-4 Where the SQLOS memory manager and the BP's memory manager meet

The SQLOS memory manager can be dynamically configured to use a specific single-page allocator. This is exactly what SQL Server does during startup—it configures the buffer pool to be SQLOS's single-page allocator. From that point on, all dynamic single-page allocations are provided by the buffer pool. For example, remember that the memory object's payload is 8KB. When a component creates a memory object, the allocation is served by SQLOS's single-page allocator, which leverages the BP's memory manager.

---

[1] Remember that SQL Server has two memory settings that you can control using sp_configure. They are max and min server memory. These two settings really control the size of the SQL Server's BP. They do not control the overall amount of physical memory consumed by SQL Server. In reality, we can't control the amount of physical memory consumed by the SQL Server process because external components could be loaded into the server's process, such as COM objects or third-party DLLs.

When describing the memory manager, we mentioned that every large component has its own memory clerk. The buffer pool is not an exception—it has its own memory clerk as well. However, to avoid any circular dependencies, the buffer pool never uses any type of page allocator from SQLOS. It only leverages virtual memory and AWE SQLOS's interfaces. (See Figure 3-5.)

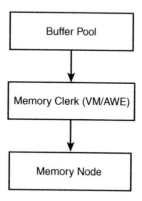

FIGURE 3-5   The buffer pool

All of SQL Server's components are optimized for 8KB allocations so that they can allocate memory through SQLOS's single-page allocator and, consequently, through the buffer pool. However, there are cases when a component requires large buffers. If this happens, allocation is satisfied either by the memory node's multipage allocator or by its virtual allocator. As you might guess, memory is allocated outside of the buffer pool in this case.

The Buffer Pool's AWE and Locked Pages Mechanisms
When talking about the SQLOS memory manager and the buffer pool, the discussion would be incomplete without a description of how AWE and locked pages in memory fit in.

On 32-bit systems, AWE mode should be used to enable SQL Server to manipulate with more than 3GB of physical memory. Remember that this amount is naturally limited on x86 platforms by a max VAS size of 3GB. Windows and CPU manufacturers provide ways to overcome such a limitation. When configured in this mode, the BP's memory manager allocates physical pages directly from the OS by leveraging AWE APIs. After pages are allocated, the memory manager maps into SQL Server's process to put them on free lists. The buffer pool's data cache is AWE-aware and can leverage AWE mapping and unmapping functionality. When a data page is bound to the BP memory manager's free page, its VAS region can be reused by another page as long as no one is using the page. Next time, the page can be mapped to a different place in VAS as long as no one keeps a direct reference to its previous VAS address. This means that the BP's data cache can load the database into physical memory even when the amount of physical memory significantly exceeds VAS size and map and unmap database pages on demand. The key here is that the BP's cache components can't hold page references, called latches, for a long time. If this happens, the cache won't be able to remap pages and will run out of VAS. It is important to note that only the BP cache can perform such mapping. The rest of the components, such as procedure cache and query execution, are query compilation/AWE-unaware, and their max memory usage is limited by VAS size.

You might want to consider using locked pages in memory on 64-bit systems. You can enable them the same way you enable AWE mechanisms on an x86 system but without running the sp_configure statement to turn on the AWE setting. Using locked pages in memory enables SQL Server to avoid paging because the pages are allocated through special mechanisms. Windows can't use its paging infrastructure to page them out. Avoiding external paging might bring better stability into your environment.

Both AWE and locked pages in memory have to be used very carefully. If system configuration is misused, it can cause system instability and even crashes.

SQLOS Responds to Memory Pressure
When configuring SQL Server, it is very important to understand how it reacts to memory pressure. We have already explained four types of memory pressure. In this section, we will drill down on how SQLOS and, consequently, SQL Server react to them.

SQLOS implements a complete framework to enable a process to handle three types of memory pressure out of four. SQLOS doesn't handle external memory pressure imposed by a swap file. In the heart of SQLOS's memory pressure framework lies the resource monitor task. RM monitors the state of the external and internal memory indicators. When one of them changes, RM observes the state of all indicators, recalculates notification to be sent, and sends if necessary. (See Figure 3-6.)

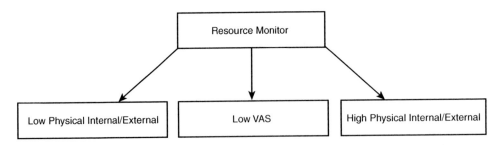

FIGURE 3-6   The resource monitor task

Resource Monitor and Memory Clerks
SQLOS has two types of nodes: memory and CPU. Memory nodes provide locality of allocations, and CPU nodes, covered in Chapter 8, "SQLOS and Scheduling Issues," provide locality of scheduling. Currently, every CPU node has its own RM. The reason for this is to be able to react to memory pressure on a given node. Depending on machine configuration, multiple RM tasks could be running at the same time.

As we have already discussed, large memory consumers leverage memory clerks to allocate memory. One more important task of memory clerks is to process memory pressure notifications from the RM. A memory consumer can subscribe its memory clerk to receive memory pressure notifications and react to them accordingly.

Every CPU node has a list of memory clerks, as shown in Figure 3-7. First, the RM calculates notification it needs to send. Then it goes through the list and broadcasts notification to each memory clerk one by one. During the broadcast, SQLOS caches receive notification as well, because they are memory clerks.

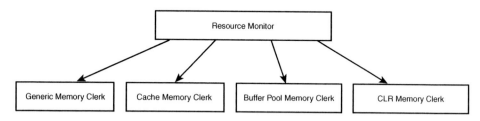

FIGURE 3-7   CPU node's list of memory clerks

From the RM's scheduling point of view, there are a few important points you should be aware of:

- The RM runs on its own scheduler, called a hidden scheduler.

- The RM runs in nonpreemptive mode.

- The DAC node doesn't have its own RM.

Several memory clerks can respond to memory pressure. We already talked about caches. In addition, every CPU node leverages its clerk to trim worker and system thread pools. Full text leverages its memory clerk to shrink shared memory buffers. CLR uses its clerk to trigger GC. The buffer pool leverages its clerk to respond to external and VAS memory pressure.

External Memory Pressure: Resource Monitor and Buffer Pool
From a SQLOS perspective, the buffer pool is a single-page allocator, extensively used by the memory manager. External physical memory pressure is signaled by Windows. The RM wakes up and broadcasts corresponding notification to memory clerks. Upon receiving notification, the BP recalculates its target commit—the amount of physical memory the BP is allowed to consume. Keep in mind that the target commit can't be lower than the configuration parameter specified through the sp_configure min server memory and can't be higher than the max server memory. If the new target commit is lower than the currently committed buffers, the buffer pool starts shrinking until external physical memory pressure disappears. During this process, the buffer pool tries to decommit or—in the case of AWE mechanism usage—tries to free physical memory back to the OS.

There are other ways for internal physical pressure to appear. The administrator can introduce it by dynamically changing the max server memory setting through the sp_configure command. In addition, if most of the BP is used by SQLOS's single-page allocator, SQLOS's memory broker, described later, might trigger internal memory pressure.

Internal Memory Pressure: Buffer Pool and Resource Monitor

Shrinkage of the BP might cause internal memory pressure. The BP notifies the RM indicator corresponding to internal memory pressure. As you learned earlier, the RM translates the indicator's signal and state of the other indicators into notifications it broadcasts. The BP has its own memory clerk to get notifications about VAS and external physical memory pressure. However, the BP memory clerk ignores internal physical memory pressure since it is initiated by the BP itself.

VAS Memory Pressure

So far, we have discussed how SQLOS and, consequently, SQL Server handle physical external and internal memory pressure. Handling VAS pressure is harder because in Windows, it is difficult to recognize it. There are two ways the RM gets notified about VAS pressure. The first way is for the memory node to notify the RM. When the memory node's virtual or shared memory interfaces fail to allocate a region of 4MB or below (the RM doesn't get notified if the size of a region is above 4MB), the memory node turns on the RM's VAS low indicator. There also is a proactive way: When the RM is running, it probes VAS for a 4MB size region. If such a region no longer exists, the RM itself turns on the VAS low signal and starts broadcasting corresponding notification. VAS pressure notification is sent to all memory clerks so they have the opportunity to shrink. For example, the CPU node shrinks its threads, the CLR might unload appdomains not currently in use, and network libs shrinks their network buffers.

When configured to use AWE mechanisms, the BP is capable of reacting to VAS pressure. When it receives VAS low notification, it enumerates its 4MB VAS regions and freezes them if it can.

Memory Broker

The Memory Broker's responsibility is to distribute memory across large memory consumers based on their demands. The Memory Broker is a SQLOS component but is tightly integrated with the buffer pool. Furthermore, the Memory Broker only takes into consideration memory that is managed by the buffer pool's memory manager. The Memory Broker monitors the buffer pool's memory demand and consumption by large memory consumers. Based on the collected information, it calculates "optimal" memory distribution for each consumer and broadcasts the information to the consumers. Each consumer uses the information to adapt its memory usage accordingly.

SQL Server 2005 has four major memory consumers: the BP's data cache, the query execution engine (sometimes referred to as workspace memory), caches, and the compilation engine. In SQL Server 2005, only the latter three are monitored by the Memory Broker.

You can monitor the Memory Broker's current, predicted, and suggested distributions by querying the Memory Broker's ring buffer:

```
select * from sys.dm_os_ring_buffer
where
ring_buffer_type = 'RING_BUFFER_MEMORY_BROKER'
```

Keep in mind that the Memory Broker's ring buffer is updated only when the Memory Broker wants the behavior of a given component to change: shrink, grow, or stay stable.

You can use dbcc memorystatus to find out the last Memory Broker notification.

Troubleshooting

In this section, I'll talk about how to troubleshoot memory-related errors and issues. Now that you have some understanding of how SQL Server manages memory, you can use this knowledge to solve difficult memory-related problems.

Performance Degradation and Instability Due to Memory Pressure

The reason we spent a significant amount of time on different types of memory resources and their corresponding memory pressures is because memory pressure can significantly degrade performance and also the stability of SQL Server. For example, if SQL Server doesn't react to external physical memory pressure in a timely manner, Windows pages out SQL Server out, which causes significant performance degradation. Moreover, SQL Server might never be able to recover from this state.

Recognizing and treating memory pressure before it translates into an out-of-memory condition or other types of instability issues is very important. In the following section, we show how to recognize and treat memory pressure.

Recognizing VAS Pressure

As you've learned so far, VAS pressure can be caused by two things:

- Fragmentation
- Imposed VAS limits

You can recognize VAS fragmentation by taking advantage of sys.dm_os_virtual_dump and a customized view built on top of it. Following is the view definition:

```
CREATE VIEW vasummary AS
select
 Size = VaDump.Size,
 Reserved =  sum(case (convert (INT,VaDump.Base) ^ 0) when 0 then 0 else 1
end),
 Free = sum(case (convert (INT,VaDump.Base) ^ 0x0) when 0 then 1 else 0 end)
from
```

```
(
--- combine all allocation according with allocation base, don't take into
--- account allocations with zero region_allocation_base_address
---
select CONVERT (varbinary,sum(region_size_in_bytes)) AS Size,
  region_allocation_base_address AS Base
from sys.dm_os_virtual_address_dump
  where region_allocation_base_address <> 0x0
  group by region_allocation_base_address
UNION
(
--- we shouldn't be grouping allocations with zero allocation base
--- just get them as is
---
select CONVERT (varbinary,region_size_in_bytes),
region_allocation_base_address
  from sys.dm_os_virtual_address_dump
    where region_allocation_base_address = 0x0)
)
as VaDump
group by Size
```

Now we can use this view to understand VAS region distribution by size and consequently fragmentation:

```
--- Get vasummary information: A number of VAS regions of a given size inside
of SQL Server reserved or freed
select * from vasummary
```

Size	Reserved	Free
0x0000000000001000	75	1
0x0000000000002000	2	1
0x0000000000003000	3	0
0x0000000000004000	2	1
0x0000000000005000	3	0
0x0000000000006000	4	1
0x0000000000007000	1	1
0x0000000000008000	3	1
0x0000000000009000	2	1
0x000000000000A000	1	1
0x000000000000B000	1	1
0x000000000000C000	1	1
0x000000000000D000	0	1
0x000000000000E000	0	1
0x000000000000F000	1	1
0x0000000000010000	96	1
0x0000000000011000	10	1
0x0000000000012000	2	1
0x0000000000013000	2	0
0x0000000000014000	1	1
0x0000000000015000	2	0
0x0000000000016000	1	0

0x0000000000017000	2	1
0x0000000000019000	1	0
0x000000000001A000	2	1
0x000000000001B000	1	0
0x000000000001E000	11	1
0x0000000000020000	1	0
0x0000000000022000	1	0
0x0000000000024000	2	0
0x0000000000026000	1	0
0x0000000000027000	2	1
0x0000000000028000	1	0
0x0000000000029000	2	1
0x000000000002B000	1	0
0x000000000002E000	1	0
0x000000000002F000	1	0
0x0000000000030000	2	0
0x0000000000031000	4	0
0x0000000000033000	1	0
0x0000000000034000	1	0
0x0000000000035000	0	1
0x0000000000037000	0	1
0x0000000000038000	0	1
0x0000000000039000	0	1
0x000000000003C000	0	1
0x000000000003D000	1	1
0x0000000000040000	15	0
0x0000000000041000	2	0
0x0000000000045000	2	0
0x0000000000048000	1	0
0x000000000004A000	1	0
0x000000000004B000	0	1
0x000000000004F000	0	1
0x0000000000050000	3	0
0x0000000000052000	1	0
0x0000000000055000	1	0
0x0000000000058000	2	0
0x0000000000059000	1	0
0x000000000005A000	1	0
0x0000000000061000	1	0
0x000000000006D000	0	1
0x0000000000078000	1	0
0x0000000000080000	52	1
0x0000000000083000	1	0
0x0000000000087000	1	0
0x000000000008B000	0	1
0x000000000008C000	1	0
0x0000000000090000	1	0
0x0000000000092000	1	0
0x0000000000093000	1	0
0x0000000000097000	1	0
0x000000000009B000	1	0
0x000000000009C000	1	0
0x000000000009F000	1	0

0x00000000000A9000	0	1
0x00000000000C0000	1	0
0x00000000000C4000	1	0
0x00000000000C6000	1	0
0x00000000000C8000	1	0
0x00000000000D1000	0	1
0x00000000000D4000	0	1
0x00000000000FE000	0	1
0x0000000000100000	8	0
0x0000000000102000	1	0
0x0000000000103000	2	0
0x0000000000116000	0	1
0x0000000000118000	1	0
0x0000000000134000	1	0
0x0000000000189000	0	1
0x000000000018C000	0	1
0x0000000000191000	1	0
0x00000000001A9000	0	1
0x00000000001B5000	0	1
0x00000000001C6000	0	1
0x00000000001D0000	4	0
0x0000000000200000	1	0
0x000000000021E000	1	0
0x0000000000258000	1	0
0x0000000000268000	0	1
0x0000000000270000	1	0
0x00000000002AA000	0	1
0x00000000002C5000	1	0
0x0000000000300000	1	0
0x000000000035D000	0	1
0x00000000003CB000	0	1
0x00000000003E6000	0	1
0x00000000007F0000	0	1
0x0000000000803000	1	0
0x00000000009E3000	1	0
0x0000000000B12000	0	1
0x0000000000B2B000	0	1
0x0000000000B4A000	0	1
0x0000000000E30000	1	0
0x0000000000E35000	0	1
0x0000000001237000	0	1
0x00000000018A6000	0	1
0x000000000198B000	0	1
0x00000000019D2000	0	1
0x0000000001E87000	0	1
0x0000000002408000	0	1
0x00000000024DF000	0	1
0x0000000002571000	0	1
0x000000000261D000	0	1
0x000000000291F000	0	1
0x0000000002E7C000	0	1
0x0000000002E9E000	1	0

```
0x0000000002FBB000                                              0          1
0x0000000003663000                                              0          1
0x00000000051DA000                                              0          1
0x0000000006E38000                                              0          1
0x0000000007310000                                              0          1
0x00000000099BC000                                              0          1
0x000000001302D000                                              0          1
0x00000000234DB000                                              0          1
0x000000003F450000                                              1          0
```

Using this view, we can find out the size of the largest block:

```
--- Retrieve max available block
---
select max(size) from vasummary where Free <> 0
----------------------------------------------------------------
0x00000000234DB000
```

In addition, we can find out the amount of VAS that is actually free. If the first value keeps on decreasing over a period of time and gets closer and closer to 4MB but the amount of free VAS doesn't drop, it means that SQL Server is getting into VAS pressure due to fragmentation. You will be able to identify the size that caused the fragmentation by sorting output from the vasummary view in the Reserved column.

```
--- Find out size that contributes to VAS fragmentation
---
select * from vasummary order by Reserved desc
```

You might recognize several sizes that contribute to the fragmentation. Thread stacks and sometimes Windows heaps are recognizable. The SQL Server stack size on an x86 is 512KB (0x80000), on an x64, it is 2MB (0x200000), and on an IA64, it is 4MB (0x400000). For example, from the preceding output, you can see that there are approximately 52 threads (a number of regions with size of 0x80000).

If you identified the threads to be the issue, you can decrease the number of threads SQL Server uses by changing the max server thread option through the sp_configure command. Be careful when you change this setting, though. If the number of threads is too low, the server might get into a thread deadlock situation—not enough threads to run a particular load.

OS heaps usually grow in multiples of 1MB, so if you notice that there is an excess of 1MB blocks, it might be due to the number of OS heaps. Keep in mind that SQL Server hardly makes use of OS heaps, so if the number of heaps does grow, it means you need to take a closer look at the libraries, such as COM's, or the set of XPs you are loading into SQL Server address space. If there is a leak in the OS heap, it appears as a number of 1MB, 2MB, or 4MB blocks of Reserved regions. Therefore, if you see over time that the number of 1MB through 4MB regions is growing, it might be coming from a heap leak. As we have already mentioned, you would have to look into the external libraries in order to pinpoint the leak. In general, if you suspect you are having a heap leak, your best bet is to attempt to reproduce the problem offline and analyze it using Windows debugging tools that you can freely download from http://www.microsoft.com.

Using this view, you can also identify the misuse of a VirtualAlloc API if the number of regions with a size below 64KB continues to increase. Especially when the size of the allocations is 4KB, this indicates that a component is misusing VirtualAlloc and should be changed. A common fix would be to change the component to use an allocator other than VirtualAlloc.

The other case for SQL Server to get into the VAS pressure is when the amount of free VAS drops. You can recognize it by monitoring output from the following query:

```
select sum(size*Free) from vasummary where Free <> 0
-----------
1974444032
```

SQL Server does react to VAS pressure. However, it is very important to try to avoid VAS pressure as much as you can, especially on a production server. If you monitor the resource monitor's ring buffer, you will see a broadcast of VAS pressure. Following is an example:

```
<Record id = "91"
    type ="RING_BUFFER_RESOURCE_MONITOR"
    time = "2039969266">
    <ResourceMonitor>
        <Notification>RESOURCE_MEMVIRTUAL_LOW</Notification>
        <Indicators>7</Indicators>
        <NodeId>0</NodeId>
    </ResourceMonitor>
    <MemoryNode d="0">
        <ReservedMemory>2995148</ReservedMemory>
        <CommittedMemory>175128</CommittedMemory>
        <SharedMemory>0</SharedMemory>
        <AWEMemory>0</AWEMemory>
        <SinglePagesMemory>5696</SinglePagesMemory>
        <MultiplePagesMemory>27968</MultiplePagesMemory>
        <CachedMemory>241672</CachedMemory>
    </MemoryNode>
    <MemoryRecord>
        <MemoryUtilization>100</MemoryUtilization>
        <TotalPhysicalMemory>1047524</TotalPhysicalMemory>
        <AvailablePhysicalMemory>260312</AvailablePhysicalMemory>
        <TotalPageFile>2577508</TotalPageFile>
        <AvailablePageFile>1437196</AvailablePageFile>
        <TotalVirtualAddressSpace>3145600</TotalVirtualAddressSpace>
        <AvailableVirtualAddressSpace>23772</AvailableVirtualAddressSpace>
<AvailableExtendedVirtualAddressSpace>0</AvailableExtendedVirtualAddressSpace>
    </MemoryRecord>
</Record>
```

When this message is broadcast, large components that can make use of VAS will attempt to decrease their VAS usage. This set of components includes the buffer pool, CLR, Full Text, thread pool, caches, and others. Since the buffer pool can react to VAS by shrinking its size, VAS pressure can possibly translate to internal physical memory pressure. This is yet another reason to avoid getting SQL Server into VAS pressure.

If you notice that your SQL Server installation gets into VAS pressure, you have several options to address the issue. We list them in preferred order:

- Move SQL Server to a 64-bit system.

- Run a 32-bit version in WOW mode on a 64-bit system.

- Enable AWE mode through sp_configure. In this mode, the buffer pool can respond to VAS pressure and possibly give you some relief.

- Change /3GB or /Userva settings as discussed in the previous sections. You have to be careful when applying these settings. They will affect the amount of physical memory SQL Server can use, as well as introduce overall system instability.

- Minimize usage of external components. External components such as COM, XPs, and CLR can cause severe VAS pressure, especially on 32-bit systems.

Recognizing External Physical Memory Pressure

As you've learned so far, external memory pressure can be caused by

- The number of applications running on the system

- A single application, SQL Server, running on the system

As with VAS pressure, it is best practice to prevent the server from getting into external physical memory pressure. You can take preventive measures by monitoring the amount of available physical memory on the system. If the amount of available physical memory keeps dropping over time and drops below 100MB, it is possible you will get into the pressure. You can monitor available system memory using the Memory.Available MBBytes perfmon counter.

After you recognize the pressure, you need to find out what application is causing it. The Task Manager has a Mem Usage column that you can use to find out the amount of physical memory used by each process. It is possible that by using this information, you won't be able to attribute all of the system physical memory. It can happen when one of the applications uses AWE or locked pages in memory mechanisms to allocate memory. In such cases, you will have to find out those applications and use custom methods to retrieve the amount of memory they allocate through these mechanisms. Luckily, only a few applications actually use such mechanisms to allocate memory. SQL Server is one of them. You can use the following command to find out how much memory SQL Server allocates using the AWE mechanism:

```
dbcc memorystatus

Memory Manager                       KB
-----------------------------   --------------------
VM Reserved                          1085260
VM Committed                         60680
AWE Allocated                        0
Reserved Memory                      1024
Reserved Memory In Use               0
```

If applications different from SQL Server cause external physical pressure, you don't have much choice but to either stop those applications or move them to a box other than SQL Server.

If the physical pressure is caused by SQL Server, you have several options to minimize or avoid it altogether:

- Put more RAM into the system. Keep in mind that if you have the /3GB switch turned on in 32-bit systems, the system won't be able to use an amount of memory larger than 16GB. In addition, when running in WOW mode, the max amount of memory that the 32-bit version of SQL Server can use is still 64GB, even though the system itself is capable of using 128GB.

- Change the "max server memory" configuration value to an amount such that the number of available bytes stays above 100MB. Keep in mind that on systems with an amount of memory between 16GB and 32GB, you will probably want to keep the amount of available memory higher than 1GB. On systems with larger amounts of memory, keep an extra 1GB per every 32GB. This recommendation is just a guesstimate—the actual values might vary depending on your installations. Remember that in SQL Server 2005, changing max server memory is a dynamic procedure and doesn't require a server restart.

- Decrease SQL Server memory load by

  - Minimizing the use of external components. External components such as COM, XPs, and CLR can be a legitimate cause of external memory pressure.

  - Minimizing the use of a multipage allocator. A multipage allocator allocates memory outside of a buffer pool and, strangely enough, can be an actual cause of external memory pressure. You can identify the multipage usage by using the following query. A common cause of bad multipage usage is a network buffer configuration size larger than 4KB. If this is the case, SNI memory clerk will come on top of this query.

```
select  top (10) type, multi_pages_kb from sys.dm_os_memory_clerks order by
multi_pages_kb desc

type
multi_pages_kb
--------------------------------------------------------------- -------------------
MEMORYCLERK_SOSNODE                                              25304
MEMORYCLERK_SOSNODE                                              3784
MEMORYCLERK_SQLGENERAL                                           1744
MEMORYCLERK_SQLBUFFERPOOL                                        256
MEMORYCLERK_SQLSERVICEBROKER                                     192
MEMORYCLERK_SQLSTORENG                                           176
MEMORYCLERK_SQLOPTIMIZER                                         72
MEMORYCLERK_SNI                                                  16
MEMORYCLERK_SNI                                                  16
CACHESTORE_STACKFRAMES                                           8
```

As with VAS pressure, it is very important to avoid getting the system into external physical memory pressure. Memory consumers such as the buffer pool, CLR, Full Text, and others react to pressure through resource monitor notification. Since the buffer pool reacts to this pressure by decreasing its target, external physical pressure might translate into internal physical pressure.

As we noted earlier, external memory pressure can degrade SQL Server performance as well as introduce instability. To find out if strange behavior is due to this type of pressure, you have to analyze resource monitor ring buffer records. To deduce an encounter of external physical pressure, you have to observe several records. The pressure indication is a drop in available physical memory followed by RESOURCE_MEMPHYSICAL_LOW. For example:

```
<Record id = "86" type ="RING_BUFFER_RESOURCE_MONITOR" time "2039966617">
    <ResourceMonitor>
        <Notification>RESOURCE_MEMPHYSICAL_LOW</Notification>
        <Indicators>2</Indicators>
        <NodeId>0</NodeId>
    </ResourceMonitor>
    <MemoryNodeId="0">
        <ReservedMemory>2996876</ReservedMemory>
        <CommittedMemory>175236</CommittedMemory>
        <SharedMemory>0</SharedMemory>
        <AWEMemory>0</AWEMemory>
        <SinglePagesMemory>5672</SinglePagesMemory>
        <MultiplePagesMemory>27968</MultiplePagesMemory>
        <CachedMemory>241872</CachedMemory></MemoryNode>
    <MemoryRecord><MemoryUtilization>100</MemoryUtilization>
        <TotalPhysicalMemory>1047524</TotalPhysicalMemory>
        <AvailablePhysicalMemory>50272</AvailablePhysicalMemory>
        <TotalPageFile>2577508</TotalPageFile>
        <AvailablePageFile>1437668</AvailablePageFile>
        <TotalVirtualAddressSpace>3145600</TotalVirtualAddressSpace>
```

```
        <AvailableVirtualAddressSpace>22556</AvailableVirtualAddressSpace>

<AvailableExtendedVirtualAddressSpace>0</AvailableExtendedVirtualAddressSpace>
        </MemoryRecord>
</Record>
```

When SQL Server doesn't use either an AWE mechanism or locked pages in memory, it is
possible for Windows, under heavy physical memory pressure, to page out of SQL Server
before the resource monitor and buffer pool have a chance to react. In such cases, SQL
Server performance can be degraded significantly. You can find out whether the server has
ever encountered such a scenario from the resource monitor's ring buffer. If there is a
record with memory utilization below 70%, most likely the server did encounter degraded
performance due to being paged out.

```
<Record id = "97" type ="RING_BUFFER_RESOURCE_MONITOR" time  "2039977680">
        <ResourceMonitor>
                <Notification>RESOURCE_MEMPHYSICAL_HIGH</Notification>
                <Indicators>1</Indicators>
                <NodeId>0</NodeId>
        </ResourceMonitor>
        <MemoryNode id="0">
                <ReservedMemory>1080140</ReservedMemory>
                <CommittedMemory>55440</CommittedMemory>
                <SharedMemory>0</SharedMemory>
                <AWEMemory>0</AWEMemory>
                <SinglePagesMemory>5768</SinglePagesMemory>
                <MultiplePagesMemory>27968</MultiplePagesMemory>
                <CachedMemory>2392</CachedMemory>
        </MemoryNode>
        <MemoryRecord>
                <MemoryUtilization>100</MemoryUtilization>
                <TotalPhysicalMemory>1047524</TotalPhysicalMemory>
                <AvailablePhysicalMemory>380380</AvailablePhysicalMemory>
                <TotalPageFile>2577508</TotalPageFile>
                <AvailablePageFile>1559796</AvailablePageFile>
                <TotalVirtualAddressSpace>3145600</TotalVirtualAddressSpace>
                <AvailableVirtualAddressSpace>1939292</AvailableVirtualAddressSpace>

<AvailableExtendedVirtualAddressSpace>0</AvailableExtendedVirtualAddressSpace>
        </MemoryRecord>
</Record>


<Record id = "98" type ="RING_BUFFER_RESOURCE_MONITOR" time="2045457609">
        <ResourceMonitor>
                <Notification>RESOURCE_MEMPHYSICAL_LOW</Notification>
                <Indicators>2</Indicators>
                <NodeId>0</NodeId></ResourceMonitor>
        <MemoryNode id="0"><ReservedMemory>1080140</ReservedMemory>
                <CommittedMemory>55952</CommittedMemory>
                <SharedMemory>0</SharedMemory>
                <AWEMemory>0</AWEMemory>
                <SinglePagesMemory>6000</SinglePagesMemory>
```

```
            <MultiplePagesMemory>27968</MultiplePagesMemory>
            <CachedMemory>2600</CachedMemory>
    </MemoryNode>
    <MemoryRecord>
            <MemoryUtilization>4</MemoryUtilization>
            <TotalPhysicalMemory>1047524</TotalPhysicalMemory>
            <AvailablePhysicalMemory>382972</AvailablePhysicalMemory>
            <TotalPageFile>2577508</TotalPageFile>
            <AvailablePageFile>1572236</AvailablePageFile>
            <TotalVirtualAddressSpace>3145600</TotalVirtualAddressSpace>
            <AvailableVirtualAddressSpace>1938268</AvailableVirtualAddressSpace>

<AvailableExtendedVirtualAddressSpace>0</AvailableExtendedVirtualAddressSpace>

    </MemoryRecord>
</Record>
```

From the preceding example, notice that record 97 indicates that memory utilization is at 100%, meaning that the majority of SQL Server committed memory is resident and is part of SQL Server's working set. Record 98 shows memory utilization to be at 4%, which indicates that Windows fully paged out of SQL Server to disk. You can observe this behavior if you start SQL Server from the command line with the -c option and then minimize the SQL Server console window. When the console is minimized, Windows pages out of the corresponding process, and hence, SQL Server's memory utilization is low.

When running 32-bit SQL Server in AWE mode, Windows can't page out of memory allocated through the AWE mechanism. In this mode, SQL Server 2005 (compared to SQL Server 2000) is capable of responding to external physical memory pressure dynamically. This means that when pressure is encountered, SQL Server 2005 sets its new target accordingly and starts shrinking its memory usage without OS interference. Running SQL Server in AWE mode makes response behavior to memory pressure predictable.

Windows can page out of SQL Server on 64-bit hardware as well. If this happens, the effects are much more disastrous. After the 64-bit version of SQL Server is paged out, it is almost impossible to recover and, in many cases, this requires restarting the server. To avoid such behavior, we strongly recommend you use locked pages in memory on 64-bit platforms. In order to do this, you have to enable the account under which SQL Server is running to have the Locked Pages in Memory privilege enabled. You don't have to enable the AWE Enabled option through sp_configure. After the privilege is turned on, SQL Server automatically makes use of locked pages in memory.

Recognizing Internal Physical Memory Pressure
Internal physical memory pressure can be caused by VAS or external physical memory pressure, a decrease in max server memory settings by DBA, or the internal demand for buffer pool pages. As you remember, for SQL Server, internal physical memory is defined by a number of pages in the buffer pool. The buffer pool can be used either by database pages or by memory consumers for dynamic memory allocations. When demand for the buffer pool pages grows, the buffer pool and hence SQL Server can get into internal physical memory pressure.

However, as with other types of memory pressure, it is better to avoid internal physical memory pressure. Running SQL Server all the time in a state of internal physical pressure will affect the performance and should be avoided.

You can recognize the possibility of getting into internal memory pressure by either identifying the possibility of VAS or external physical memory, or by monitoring the buffer pool statistics such as stolen, hash, and free buffers. You can monitor this by leveraging perfmon counters: sys.sysperfinfo or dbcc memorystatus.

```
select * from sys.sysperfinfo where
        object_name = 'SQLServer:Buffer Manager' AND
        (counter_name = 'Target pages' OR
        counter_name = 'Total pages' OR
        counter_name = 'Dtabase pages' OR
        counter_name = 'Stolen pages' OR
        counter_name = 'Free pages')

dbcc memorystatus
```

```
Buffer Distribution             Buffers
-----------------------------   -----------
Stolen                          428
Free                            77
Cached                          572
Database (clean)                2181
Database (dirty)                38
I/O                             0
Latched                         0

(7 row(s) affected)

Buffer Counts                   Buffers
-----------------------------   --------------------
Committed                       3296
Target                          62142
Hashed                          2219
Stolen Potential                122097
External Reservation            0
Min Free                        128
Visible                         62142
Available Paging Fil            260165
```

If you notice that the amount of stolen pages doesn't stabilize over time, it is possible that the server will eventually get into internal physical memory pressure.

In SQL Server 2005, stolen pages are primarily used for three major purposes: query compilation, query execution, and caching. As we have already discussed, the Memory Broker is responsible for adjusting memory distribution among these three usages. When running low on a number of available buffers, the buffer pool notifies the Memory Broker. The Memory Broker then performs distribution recalculation and lets the resource monitor know whether to broadcast memory pressure. It is also possible for the Memory Broker to trigger internal memory pressure even when the number of stolen pages stays close to constant. This can happen when the Memory Broker decides to change memory distribution among three major memory consumers.

To identify whether SQL Server has encountered internal memory pressure, look at the Memory Broker's ring buffer. If you notice records indicating shrinkage notification to one of the three components, SQL Server has encountered internal physical memory pressure. It is normal for the server to periodically get into internal physical memory pressure, so you shouldn't worry too much when the Memory Broker's ring buffer is not empty. However, you do want to avoid the state in which a shrink operation with a long duration is the last notification in the buffer—that is, you don't see stable memory or a growth notification following it.

```
<Record id = "88" type ="RING_BUFFER_MEMORY_BROKER" time "122294508">
    <MemoryBroker>
        <DeltaTime>109</DeltaTime>
        <Broker>MEMORYBROKER_FOR_CACHE</Broker>
        <Notification>SHRINK</Notification>
        <MemoryRatio>96</MemoryRatio>
        <NewTarget>33334</NewTarget>
        <Overall>66798</Overall>
        <Rate>-11665</Rate>
        <CurrentlyPredicted>34540</CurrentlyPredicted>
        <CurrentlyAllocated>46205</CurrentlyAllocated>
        <PreviouslyAllocated>43646</PreviouslyAllocated>
    </MemoryBroker>
</Record>
```

Recognizing Swap File Memory Pressure

Swap file memory pressure can be due to overcommitted memory on the machine. It is usually observed on 64-bit systems when

- The Locked Pages in Memory privilege is used

- Swap file size is small

You can detect possible swap file pressure by monitoring the amount of available swap files either through the system performance counter or by using the dbcc memorystatus command:

```
Buffer Counts                       Buffers
------------------------------      --------------------
Committed                           1024
Target                              60226
Hashed                              157
Stolen Potential                    122364
External Reservation                0
Min Free                            128
Visible                             60226
Available Paging File               259715
```

SQL Server 2005 doesn't dynamically detect swap file pressure, so if it's encountered, SQL Server gets into an out-of-memory state right away. If you see a Failure to Perform VirtualAlloc call in ERRORLOG or an out-of-memory ring buffer on a 64-bit version of SQL Server, you have encountered swap file pressure. It this happens on a 32-bit version, you still have to confirm if you didn't run out of VAS.

```
select * from sys.dm_os_ring_buffers where
ring_buffer_type ='RING_BUFFER_OOM'
```

Effects of Memory Pressure

Effects of memory pressure can be very dramatic. You might observe them in multiple places. For example, when encountering performance or stability issues, it is very important to check SQL Server for possible existence of any type of memory pressure. Following is a list of issues that can be caused by memory pressure:

- Significant increase in query execution time

- Unexpected change in a number of compilations or recompilations

- Unexpected changes in a number of active compiles

- Unexpected increase in a query compilation time

- Unexpected drop in a number of active queries

- Unexpected increase/drop in CPU utilization

- Long waits on execution semaphore

- Long waits on memory allocations

- Memory state dump in ERRORLOG

Platform-Specific Memory-Related Issues

Microsoft recently published a white paper (http://download.microsoft.com/download/1/3/4/134644fd-05ad-4ee8-8b5a-0aed1c18a31e/TShootPerfProbs.doc) that has great insights into some of the memory issues you might encounter, such as actual out-of-memory errors.

In this section, we will examine two major platforms—32-bit and 64-bit—their specific configuration and possible memory problems you might encounter, and how to deal with them.

32-Bit Version of SQL Server 2005

This platform has several interesting memory configuration specifics, including physical memory, VAS, boot.ini, server, and system configuration parameters. Table 3-5 shows interesting configuration parameters, issues they might cause, and possible ways of resolving them.

TABLE 3-5 **Configuration parameters, issues they might cause, and possible ways of resolving them**

Configuration	Issues	Resolution
Physical Memory: < 2GB	External physical memory pressure Internal physical memory pressure	Add more physical memory. Enable SQL Server to use AWE mechanisms to allocate more memory.
Physical Memory: Up to 4GB	VAS memory pressure	Move to 64-bit platform. Move to WOW mode. Configure VAS to be 3GB.
Physical Memory: Up to 16GB	Can't use more than 4GB of physical memory	Configure system and boot.ini to run in PAE mode.
Physical Memory: Between 16GB and 64GB	Can't use more than 16GB of physical memory	Remove /3GB settings from boot.ini.
`sp_configure`: Max server threads above 1024	External physical memory pressure VAS memory pressure	Consider changing this setting to a lower number.
`sp_configure`: AWE enabled	Can't use more than 4GB of physical memory External physical memory pressure VAS memory pressure	Make sure that boot.ini is configured correctly. Give SQL Server's execution account privilege to lock pages in memory. Consider the max server memory setting to keep the system happy.
`sp_configure`: CLR enabled	External physical memory pressure Internal physical memory pressure VAS memory pressure	Add more physical memory. Enable SQL Server to use AWE mechanisms to allocate more memory. Move to 64-bit platform. Move to WOW mode. Configure VAS to be 3GB. Disable CLR.
`sp_configure`: Max degree of parallelism > 4	External physical memory pressure Internal physical memory pressure VAS memory pressure	Configure DOP below 4.

TABLE 3-5   **Continued**

Configuration	Issues	Resolution
`sp_configure`: Network packet size > 4092	External physical memory pressure VAS memory pressure	Configure network packet size to be 4092.
`sp_configure`: Max server memory is default value	External physical memory pressure	Configure max server memory so that the amount of physical memory on the system is always above 100MB.
`sp_configure`: Min server memory is larger than default value	SQL Server's memory consumption doesn't increase right away	Apply load that will force SQL Server to grab more memory. For example, large DB scan and index build/rebuild over large DB.
`Boot.ini`: /PAE	SQL Server can't use more than 16GB of physical memory	Remove /3GB `boot.ini` parameter. Grant SQL Server account permission to lock pages in memory.
`Boot.ini`: /3GB	SQL Server and the whole machine become unresponsive SQL Server AVs	Either remove /3GB parameter or experiment with /USERVA. Remove usage of external DLLs.

64-Bit Version of SQL Server 2005

The same as 32-bit, this platform has several interesting memory configuration parameters. Although the majority of the parameters are the same, the set of issues you might encounter could be different. Table 3-6 lists a set of issues and possible resolutions for every configuration parameter.

TABLE 3-6 Set of issues and possible resolutions for every configuration parameter

Configuration	Issues	Resolution
Physical Memory: < 8GB	External physical memory pressure Internal physical memory pressure	Add more physical memory
sp_configure: Max server threads above 1024	External physical memory pressure External virtual memory pressure (swap file memory pressure)	Consider changing this setting to a lower number. Make sure that the size of a swap file is at least ■ On an IA64, 2 * (4MB * number of threads) ■ On an x64, 2 * (2MB * number of threads) where 4MB and 2MB are thread stack sizes on an IA64 and an x64, respectively.
sp_configure: AWE enabled	Nothing happens	This setting doesn't have any effect on a 64-bit platform. Most likely, it will be removed in the next release. If you want to use locked pages in memory, make sure that you grant the SQL Server account a corresponding permission.
sp_configure: CLR enabled	External physical memory pressure	Add more physical memory. Enable SQL Server to use locked pages. Disable CLR.
sp_configure: Max degree parallelism>4	External physical memory pressure Internal physical memory pressure VAS out-of-memory issues	Configure DOP below 4. Decrease the max server memory setting to a value that makes available physical memory about 1GB per 16GB. Increase the size of the swap file as recommended for max server thread settings.

TABLE 3-6 Continued

Configuration	Issues	Resolution
sp_configure: Network packet size > 8000	External physical memory pressure VAS out of memory issues Possible performance degradations	Configure the network packet size to be 4092. Increase the size of the swap file. Decrease the max server thread settings.
sp_configure: Max server memory is default value	External physical memory pressure	Configure max server memory so that the amount of physical memory on the system is always above 1GB per every 16GB, and max value is about 5GB. Grant the Lock Pages in Memory privilege to the SQL Server account to avoid OS paging. After SQL Server gets into paging, it will be hard to recover.
sp_configure: Min server memory is larger than default value	SQL Server's memory consumption doesn't increase right away	Apply load that will force SQL Server to grab more memory. For example, large DB scan and index build/rebuild over large DB.
Locked Pages in Memory privilege	SQL Server doesn't make use of locked pages System becomes unresponsive SQL Server start time is slower All tools show that SQL Server doesn't use much physical memory	Make sure you reboot the machine after you grant the privilege to the SQL Server account. Make sure that you keep the proper amount of available free memory on the machine by correctly configuring max server memory settings. If the privilege is enabled, SQL Server attempts to use large pages for some of the hot data structures. In some cases, allocation of large pages can be slower. Currently, Windows doesn't have a counter that shows memory allocated through the Locked Pages in Memory mechanism.

Platform-Agnostic Memory-Related Issues

Some of the memory-related problems are common to all configurations. Table 3-7 lists problems, possible ways of uncovering them, and resolution.

TABLE 3-7   Problems, possible ways of uncovering them, and resolution

Problem	Ways of Uncovering	Resolution

Performance of SQL Server degrades over time due to severe memory usage increase by one of the memory consumers	`-- Find out top 10 memory consumers`
	`select top(10)`
	`type,`
	`single_pages_kb`
	`from sys.dm_os_memory_clerks`
	`order by 2 desc`
	
	`-- Find out top 10 memory`
	`objects heaps`
	`select`
	`type,pages_allocated_count`
	`from sys.dm_os_memory_objects`
	`where page_allocator_address in`
	`(select top(10)`
	`        page_allocator_address`
	`        from sys.dm_os_memory_clerks`
	`        order by single_pages_kb desc)`
	`order by pages_allocated_count desc`
		If the top entry is a cache store, user store, or object store, you can try to use dbcc freesystemcache.
		
		Decrease SQL Server load.
		
		Increase amount of physical memory SQL Server can use.
		
		Decrease usage of specific functionality. For example, if you find out that CLR's memory clerk is a culprit, try to decrease/stop CLR usage.
		
		Use types/names to map them to your knowledge domain. Use the information to pinpoint the problem.
		
		If you identify specific memory objects in which size keeps on growing and you don't have a way of stopping the growth, contact Microsoft support for assistance.

TABLE 3-7   Continued

Problem	Ways of Uncovering	Resolution
| Performance of SQL Server degrades due to severe memory usage increase in area outside of the buffer pool, creating multipage allocations | ```
-- Find out top 10 memory consumers
select top(10)
type,
multi_pages_kb
from sys.dm_os_memory_clerks
order by 2 desc

-- Find out top 10 memory
objects
select
type,pages_allocated_count
from sys.dm_os_memory_objects
where page_allocator_address in
(select top(10)
        page_allocator_address
        from sys.dm_os_memory_clerks
        order by multi_pages_kb desc)
order by pages_allocated_count desc
``` | If the top entry is a cache store, user store, or object store, you can try to use dbcc freesystemcache. Decrease SQL Server load. Increase amount of physical memory SQL Server can use. Decrease usage of specific functionality. For example, if you find out that CLR's memory clerk is a culprit, try to decrease/stop CLR usage. Use types/names to map them to your knowledge domain. Use the information to pinpoint the problem. If you identify specific memory objects in which size keeps on growing and you don't have a way of stopping the growth, contact Microsoft support for assistance. |
| SQL Server can't grow its memory usage due to large amount of memory used by file system cache | File system cache size is relatively large | Make sure machine is configured to optimize its memory usage for programs, not system cache. Identify applications that consume file system cache and either find ways to control their usage of the cache or move them to a different machine. |
```

Problem	Ways of Uncovering	Resolution

SQL Server performance degrades significantly due to SQL Server procedure cache (Object Plans, SQL Plans) suddenly dropping in size and hence causing a lot of new compilations	Perfmon counters, sys.dm_os_memory_clerks, or sys.dm_os_memory_cache_counters Use history from Memory Broker ring buffer to find out actual memory distribution that caused procedure cache to drop its memory usage
	
	`--- Get information about`
	`--- memory broker's ring`
	`--- buffer`
	`---`
	
	`select * from`
	`sys.dm_os_ring_buffers where`
	`ring_buffer_type`
	`='RING_BUFFER_MEMORY_BROKER'`
		Identify large query that required a lot of compilation or execution memory so that Memory Broker had to perform memory redistribution across query executions, query compilations, and caches.

NUMA-Specific Memory-Related Issues

There are some memory-related issues that you can see only on NUMA machines. Table 3-8 shows the set of problems, ways of uncovering them, and resolution.

TABLE 3-8   Problems, possible ways of uncovering them, and resolution

Problem	Ways of Uncovering	Resolution
NUMA nodes have memory cells of different sizes	Review hardware configuration of your system	Make sure that memory cells attached to each node are of equal size. Properly configure the max server memory setting.
SQL Server doesn't grow its memory usage close to the max server memory setting	Perfmon counter `BufferManager.Totalpages` stays lower than max server memory setting `dbcc memorystatus` 'Buffer counts:Committed' stays lower than max server memory setting	Remember that the max server memory setting is equally divided across all nodes SQL Server is running on. Load data on all nodes by connecting to each node and performing either an index build or a table scan. Make sure that for every node, you are operating with different tables.
BufferNode perfmon counters show that memory usage is not balanced	Monitor BufferNode perfmon counters for each node	Try to rebalance the load by rebalancing connections. Load data on all nodes by connecting to each node and performing either an index build or a table scan. Make sure that for every node, you are operating with different tables.

Problem	Ways of Uncovering	Resolution
`BufferNode.Foreign` pages is very high for some nodes	Monitor BufferNode perfmon counters for each node	Configure SQL Server so that min server memory = max server memory. (This is necessary only if you want to avoid the issue in the future. Be careful—this setting can put the system in external memory pressure.) Enable the Lock Pages in Memory privilege. Load data on all nodes by connecting to each node and performing either an index build or a table scan. Make sure that for every node, you are operating with different tables.

Procedure Cache Issues

By Bart Duncan

IN THIS CHAPTER

- Procedure Cache Architecture
- Common Cache-Related Problems and Solutions
- Conclusion

The SQL Server query optimizer grows more intelligent—and more complex—with each release. Query compilation has become more expensive as the query optimizer increases in complexity, and it has become more common to see application workloads that spend a great deal of time in query compilation. The primary purpose of the procedure cache is to cache query plans and allow for their reuse, minimizing compile time and improving the server's performance. An application that makes efficient use of the procedure cache minimizes both the amount of CPU time spent in unnecessary query compilation and the amount of memory consumed by cached plans. Keeping the procedure cache small also frees up memory for data cache, which can reduce a server's I/O burden.

For some workloads, minimizing query compilation can be a big deal, not just a matter of single-digit cost savings. As evidence of this, an ERP software vendor that Microsoft worked with when designing SQL Server 2005 found that ensuring reuse of their ad hoc query plans allowed them to support more than twice as many users per server. The procedure cache is what made those performance gains possible. Not every application will present that kind of opportunity, but if your application is not already written in a way that promotes plan reuse in the right places, some significant gains could be awaiting it.

On the other hand, inefficient use of the procedure cache can cause everything from out-of-memory errors to excessive CPU use to poor query plans. Later in the chapter, I'll go into detail about some of the more common procedure cache issues that you might encounter. First, though, it's important to understand how the procedure cache works.

Many of the general concepts presented in this chapter apply to SQL Server 7.0 and SQL Server 2000 as well as SQL Server 2005, but the technical details and examples of trouble-shooting queries are based on SQL Server 2005.

Procedure Cache Architecture

In this section, I'll explore SQL Server's procedure cache architecture so that the trouble-shooting methods I'll talk about later will make sense. A good understanding of procedure cache fundamentals is essential to being able to troubleshoot procedure caching issues.

Types of Cached Objects

Several different types of objects can be stored in the procedure cache:

- **Compiled plans.** When the query optimizer finishes compiling a query plan, the principal output is a *compiled plan*. A compiled plan is the SQL Server equivalent of MSIL in the .NET world. It's a set of instructions that describes exactly how SQL Server will implement a query. If you submit a T-SQL query for execution, all you have supplied is a set of logical instructions. There may be thousands of different ways that SQL Server could execute the query. The compiled plan for this query, though, would tell SQL Server exactly which physical query operators to use. For example, the compiled plan would specify whether to use an index seek, an index scan, or a table scan to retrieve rows from each table. A compiled plan represents a collection of all the query plans for a single T-SQL batch or stored procedure. Compiled plans are reentrant, which is to say that if multiple users are simultaneously executing the same stored procedure, they can all share a single compiled plan.

- **Execution contexts.** While executing a compiled plan, SQL Server has to keep track of information about the state of execution. The execution context tracks a particular execution's parameter and local variable values, which statement in the plan is currently being executed, and object IDs for any temp objects created during execution. This information is unique to a particular user, and that means it can't be stored in a compiled plan that might be shared by multiple users. It is instead stored in an *execution context* (also called an *executable plan*), which can be used by only a single user at a time. If two users are executing the same stored procedure at the same time, each user has his or her own execution context, but the two users may share a single compiled plan. Execution contexts cannot be shared simultaneously, but once one user is done with an execution context, it can be reused by the next user to execute the same query. For this reason, execution contexts are cached.

Every execution context is linked to a particular compiled plan. Execution contexts are much cheaper to create than compiled plans, so under memory pressure they are always aged out of cache before compiled plans.

- **Cursors.** Cursors track the execution state of server-side cursors, including the cursor's current location within a resultset. Cursors have the same relationship to a compiled plan as execution contexts; every cursor is tied to a particular compiled plan. Like execution contexts, cursors can be used by only one connection at a time, but the compiled plan that the cursor is linked to can be concurrently used by multiple connections.

- **Algebrizer trees.** The query optimizer does not directly act on raw query text; it needs a more structured input. The Algebrizer's job is to produce an *algebrizer tree*, which represents the logical structure of a query. As part of this process, the Algebrizer performs tasks like resolving table, column, and variable names to particular objects in the database. It also determines the data types of any expressions in the query. In SQL Server 2000, what I call an algebrizer tree may also be referred to as a *normalized tree* or a *parse tree*. Because algebrizer trees are used only during query compilation, they are usually not cached. After all, what's the point of caching an algebrizer tree once you have a compiled plan that you can reuse for any subsequent executions? Algebrizer trees for views, defaults, and constraints, however, are an exception to this rule. They are cached because a view may be referenced by many different queries. Caching the view's algebrizer tree prevents SQL Server from repeatedly having to parse and algebrize the view every time another query is compiled that references the view.

NOTE

You may also see a few cache entries labeled "Extended Proc." This represents a small cached object that tracks metadata for an extended stored procedure. These cache objects are very cheap to create, and the amount of memory they use is very small. We won't spend much more time talking about them.

All of these objects are closely related. When you send a query to SQL Server, the batch is parsed and fed into the Algebrizer, which spits out an algebrizer tree. The algebrizer tree is handed off to the query optimizer, which uses it to produce a compiled plan. Finally, in order to execute the compiled plan, an execution context must be created to track runtime state.

As I mentioned, the reason that view algebrizer trees are cached is to reduce the cost of compilation. The caching of compiled plans and execution contexts, on the other hand, has an even more ambitious goal: to eliminate the need for compilation whenever possible.

Let's explore what you might see if you could peek into the SQL Server procedure cache while the server was processing a couple of typical query workloads. First, let's suppose you had a high-volume, well-tuned OLTP workload with a lot of users and a small number of distinct queries that were frequently reused. Compiled plans can be shared, so each of these few queries will need only a single compiled plan. When a lot of users are executing those same few queries, though, there will be cases where multiple people are simultaneously executing the same query. They will all need their own execution context. So, you might expect to find a high ratio of execution contexts to compiled plans in the procedure cache.

Now consider a SQL Server instance used to support ad hoc reporting. Such a workload might feature a relatively small number of users, a large number of unique queries, and a low rate of plan reuse. You might initially find that there were just as many cached compiled plans as execution contexts. When the procedure cache ran into memory pressure, the relative cheap execution contexts would be the first things that the procedure cache tossed away. Therefore, with this workload, it wouldn't be surprising to find a low ratio of execution contexts to compiled plans.

You can see cached compiled plans and parse trees on your own SQL Server 2005 instance by querying the `sys.dm_exec_cached_plans` dynamic management view (DMV). The procedure cache can grow fairly large, so the following query includes a TOP clause to limit the number of rows that will be retrieved.

```
SELECT TOP 1000 usecounts, size_in_bytes, cacheobjtype, objtype, plan_handle
FROM sys.dm_exec_cached_plans
```

The `plan_handle` column is a binary value that is used to identify a particular cached compiled plan or parse tree. You can pass the `plan_handle` value to other DMVs and dynamic management functions (DMFs) to get additional information about the plan. Want to see the SQL text of the top 10 most frequently reused stored procedures in your plan cache? Try this query:

```
SELECT TOP 10 usecounts, size_in_bytes, cacheobjtype, objtype,
    REPLACE (REPLACE ([text], CHAR(13), ' '), CHAR(10), ' ') AS sql_text
FROM sys.dm_exec_cached_plans AS p
CROSS APPLY sys.dm_exec_sql_text (p.plan_handle)
WHERE p.objtype = 'Proc' AND cacheobjtype = 'Compiled Plan'
ORDER BY usecounts DESC
```

The procedure cache also keeps track of useful statistics for each cached plan. Suppose you wanted to see the amount of CPU or the number of reads and writes that each of these procedures has consumed since it was inserted into cache. The `sys.dm_exec_query_stats` DMV exposes these statistics. The statistics are tracked separately for each query in a procedure or a batch, so the following query rolls up the statistics to the stored procedure level with a GROUP BY:

```
SELECT TOP 10 usecounts, size_in_bytes, cacheobjtype,
  SUM (total_worker_time / 1000) AS total_cpu_time_in_ms,
  SUM (total_physical_reads) AS total_physical_reads,
  SUM (total_logical_reads) AS total_logical_reads,
  SUM (total_logical_writes) AS total_logical_writes,
  REPLACE (REPLACE ([text], CHAR(13), ' '), CHAR(10), ' ') AS sql_text
FROM sys.dm_exec_cached_plans AS p
INNER JOIN sys.dm_exec_query_stats stat ON p.plan_handle = stat.plan_handle
CROSS APPLY sys.dm_exec_sql_text (p.plan_handle)
WHERE p.objtype = 'Proc' AND cacheobjtype = 'Compiled Plan'
GROUP BY usecounts, size_in_bytes, cacheobjtype, [text]
ORDER BY usecounts DESC
```

The sys.dm_exec_cached_plans DMV doesn't show cached execution contexts; to see cached execution contexts, pass a plan handle to sys.dm_exec_cached_plan_dependent_objects. Due to a bug in the RTM release of SQL Server 2005, you should avoid using any query that references the dm_exec_cached_plan_dependent_objects DMF on a production server until you have applied Service Pack 1 or later.

CAUTION

Some of the hands-on exercises in this chapter are designed to simulate a problem so that you can learn how to recognize and troubleshoot the problem when you encounter it in the future. The scripts may also make use of commands like DBCC FREEPROCCACHE that can have an effect on a production server, so it is recommended that you work through the hands-on exercises on a test server.

Exercise: Compiled Plans and Execution Contexts

1. Run DBCC FREEPROCCACHE. This clears the procedure cache of any cached plans that are not currently in use.

2. Create the following procedure:

```
CREATE PROCEDURE usp_wait AS
WAITFOR DELAY '0:0:20'
SELECT * FROM master.dbo.sysprocesses
GO
```

3. Open two new query windows and run the following query simultaneously from the two windows:

```
exec usp_wait
```

4. After the two executions of the procedure complete, run the following query. This shows the cached execution contexts and compiled plan for the usp_wait stored procedure:

```
SELECT p.usecounts, p.cacheobjtype COLLATE database_default,

    LEFT (text, 30) AS sql
FROM sys.dm_exec_cached_plans AS p
CROSS APPLY sys.dm_exec_sql_text (p.plan_handle) AS sql
WHERE p.objtype = 'Proc' AND sql.[text] LIKE '%usp_wait%'
UNION ALL
SELECT pdo.usecounts, pdo.cacheobjtype COLLATE database_default,
    LEFT (text, 30) AS sql
FROM sys.dm_exec_cached_plans AS p
CROSS APPLY sys.dm_exec_cached_plan_dependent_objects (p.plan_handle) AS
pdo
CROSS APPLY sys.dm_exec_sql_text (p.plan_handle) AS sql
WHERE p.objtype = 'Proc' AND sql.[text] LIKE '%usp_wait%'
```

Note that there are now two "Executable plans" (execution contexts) for the batch you ran in step 4, and just one compiled plan. The usecounts value for the compiled plan should be 2, and the use count for each of the execution contexts should be 1.

Following is a query that will output the entire contents of your procedure cache, providing the type and SQL text of each object in the cache along with execution statistics and the number of cursors and execution contexts associated with each compiled plan.

```
SELECT
    cacheobjtype, usecounts, size_in_kb, dbname,
    SUM (total_worker_time/1000) AS tot_cpu_time_in_ms,
    SUM (total_physical_reads) AS tot_phys_reads,
    SUM (total_logical_reads) AS tot_log_reads,
    SUM (total_logical_writes) AS tot_log_writes,
    [Executable Plan] AS ec_count, [Cursor] AS cursors,
    sql_text
FROM (
    SELECT
        p.cacheobjtype + ' (' + p.objtype + ')' AS cacheobjtype,
        p.usecounts, p.size_in_bytes / 1024 AS size_in_kb,
        CASE WHEN pa.value=32767 THEN 'ResourceDb'
        ELSE ISNULL (DB_NAME (CAST (pa.value AS int)), CONVERT (sysname,
pa.value))
        END as dbname,
```

```
      pdo.cacheobjtype AS pdo_cacheobjtype,
      stat.total_worker_time, stat.total_physical_reads,
  stat.total_logical_writes,
      stat.total_logical_reads, stat.total_elapsed_time,
      sql.text AS sql_text
    FROM sys.dm_exec_cached_plans p
    OUTER APPLY sys.dm_exec_plan_attributes (p.plan_handle) pa
    INNER JOIN sys.dm_exec_query_stats stat ON p.plan_handle = stat.plan_handle
    OUTER APPLY sys.dm_exec_cached_plan_dependent_objects (p.plan_handle) AS pdo
    OUTER APPLY sys.dm_exec_sql_text (p.plan_handle) AS sql
    WHERE pa.attribute = 'dbid'
) t1
PIVOT (
    COUNT(pdo_cacheobjtype) FOR pdo_cacheobjtype IN ([Executable Plan],
[Cursor])
) AS pvt2
GROUP BY cacheobjtype, usecounts, size_in_kb, dbname,
    [Executable Plan], [Cursor], sql_text
```

NOTE

On SQL Server 2000, you can get a similar view of the procedure cache by querying the syscacheobjects system table. However, some of the more useful statistics, such as the cumulative amount of CPU time used by each plan, are available only on SQL Server 2005.

Structure of the Procedure Cache

The procedure cache is built on top of a caching infrastructure that exposes objects called *cachestores*. A cachestore provides a common set of memory allocation interfaces that are reused for many different memory consumers inside SQL Server. The use of a shared framework allows the various caches in SQL Server to respond to memory pressure in a fairer and more consistent way than would otherwise be possible.

The procedure cache is split into several cachestores. The object cachestore is used to cache compiled plans and related objects for stored procedures, functions, and triggers. The SQL cachestore holds plans for ad hoc and prepared queries. Other cachestores hold algebrizer trees and extended stored procedure objects; these are usually dwarfed by the SQL and object cachestores.

Within each cachestore is a hash table that allows for efficient plan lookup. Each plan is assigned a hash value, and this value determines which bucket within the hash table will hold the plan. Multiple plans may reside in the same hash bucket, but SQL Server limits the number of entries in each cachestore in an attempt to prevent excessive plan lookup times caused by long hash chain lengths. The SQL and object cachestores are each permitted to grow to approximately 160,000 entries on 64-bit servers, and approximately 40,000 entries on most 32-bit servers. (Desktop servers with a buffer pool smaller than 64MB have fewer buckets than this.)

The cachestore holds a hash table, and the hash table is divided into buckets. Each bucket holds zero or more cached compiled plans. Each compiled plan may contain cached execution contexts and cached cursors.

Procedure Cache and Memory

When there is a need to reclaim memory that is being used by cached plans, a thread begins examining the contents of the cache, looking for cached objects that can be freed to make room for new items. The cached objects are examined in sequence, and when the end of the cache is reached, the scan begins again at the beginning. This circular search is sometimes referred to as a *clock sweep*.

SQL Server 2000

In SQL Server 2000, when a compiled plan or execution context is first stored in the procedure cache, its cost is set to an initial value that is related to how expensive it was to compile the plan. The cost is a number that reflects the amount of CPU, disk, and memory used during compilation of the query. Each time the clock sweep passes the plan, its cost is decremented. Each time the plan is executed, its cost is restored to the initial compile cost. The plan is removed from the procedure cache if its cost ever reaches zero. In this way, infrequently used, cheaper plans are removed from cache before frequently used or expensive plans.

The maximum size of the procedure cache is 50% of the *visible buffer pool* (the portion of the buffer pool that excludes AWE memory) or 1GB, whichever value is lower. In SQL Server 2000, the thread that performs the clock sweep is called the *lazywriter* thread. The same thread is responsible for aging old cached data pages out of cache; SQL Server 2000 has a single unified cache for both cached data and cached query plans.

SQL Server 2005

In SQL Server 2005, the procedure cache responds to memory pressure in a slightly different way. One difference is that execution contexts are treated as a part of a compiled plan rather than being handled as separate cache objects. Every time the clock sweep passes a plan, the plan voluntarily releases half of the plan's cached execution contexts even if the plan itself will survive that sweep and stay in cache. The background thread that ages plans out of the cache in SQL Server 2005 is called the *resource monitor* thread.

Unlike SQL Server 2000, where all different cached objects were stored together in one cache, SQL Server 2005 has a different cachestore for each type of cached object (see Table 4-1).

TABLE 4-1   Cachestore for each type of cached object

Cachestore	Description
CACHESTORE_OBJCP	Stored procedures, functions, and triggers
CACHESTORE_SQLCP	Ad hoc and prepared queries
CACHESTORE_PHDR	View, default, and constraint algebrizer trees
CACHESTORE_XPROC	Extended stored procedures

You can see the current size of the various cachestores that make up the procedure cache by querying the sys.dm_os_memory_cache_counters DMV or by capturing the counters in the SQLServer:Plan Cache performance monitor object:

```
SELECT [name], type, single_pages_kb, multi_pages_kb, entries_count
FROM sys.dm_os_memory_cache_counters r
WHERE [type] IN
  ('CACHESTORE_OBJCP', 'CACHESTORE_SQLCP', 'CACHESTORE_PHDR',
'CACHESTORE_XPROC')
```

Sample output:

```
name            type                single_pages_kb  multi_pages_kb
entries_count
------------    ----------------    ---------------  ---------------  -------------
-
Object Plans    CACHESTORE_OBJCP    4086                  12               129
SQL Plans       CACHESTORE_SQLCP    3984480             6960             39453
```

As you can see, the memory used by each cachestore is broken down by single-page allocations and multi-page allocations. The single-page allocations come from the buffer pool. Multi-page allocations must be drawn from non-buffer pool memory, which is typically a smaller region than the buffer pool.

NOTE

A SQLServer:Plan Cache\Cache Pages performance monitor counter also reports the size of the procedure-cache cachestores. Unfortunately, the performance monitor counter records the amount of memory used by top-level cache objects (compiled plans and algebrizer trees), but fails to account for execution plans and other execution-related objects associated with each compiled plan. The query shown here provides a more complete view of the size of the procedure cache than this counter.

The SQL Server 2005 procedure cache shrinks in response to external memory pressure or internal size limits. *External memory pressure* occurs when the number of free buffers on the system drops below a minimum threshold and the procedure cache is asked to release memory to make room for other memory consumers. *Internal memory pressure* occurs when the size of the procedure cache reaches certain limits. The first internal trigger to release cached objects occurs if the number of objects in the cache exceeds approximately 40,000 objects on a 32-bit server, or approximately 160,000 objects on a 64-bit server. The second condition that can trigger movement of the internal clock hand is the amount of memory used by the procedure cache. The calculation of the cache size limits is not straightforward, so I've provided Table 4-2 with some approximate procedure cache size limits for various amounts of system memory. Approximate numbers are fine here because these are not hard size limits; the thresholds determine the point where the internal clock hand begins sweeping and removing plans, but you may notice that the size of the procedure cache occasionally grows beyond these limits for a brief period of time. There are separate and independent memory limits for single-page allocations and multi-page allocations within each cachestore.

TABLE 4-2   **Approximate procedure cache size limits for various amounts of system memory**

Memory	Internal Memory Pressure Threshold (Multi-Page Allocations)	Internal Memory Pressure Threshold (Single-Page Allocations)
1GB	375MB	500MB
2GB	750MB	1GB
4GB	1.5GB	2GB
8GB	3GB	5GB
16GB	5GB	8GB
32GB	9GB	14GB
64GB	18GB	26GB
128GB	26GB	38GB
256GB	42GB	62GB
512GB	74GB	110GB

These numbers are for a dedicated, single-instance SQL Server machine where SQL Server can use most of the memory on the server. If SQL Server is unable to use a significant portion of the memory on the server, you'll need to reduce the amount of memory accordingly. For example, if the `max server memory` sp_configure option is set to 16GB on a 64-bit server, you should reference the 16GB row in the table even if the server has 32GB of RAM. Also, on a 32-bit machine, the amount of memory that can be used for procedure cache is limited to a portion of the 2GB virtual address space (3GB if you are using the `/3GB BOOT.INI` switch). In other words, the approximate limits in the "2GB" row would be the upper limits on a 32-bit machine, even if the server had 16GB of memory.

You can see current internal and external clock hand state (SUSPENDED or RUNNING) and the amount of prior activity from each hand by querying the `sys.dm_os_memory_cache_clock_hands` DMV:

```
SELECT * FROM sys.dm_os_memory_cache_clock_hands
WHERE [type] IN
  ('CACHESTORE_OBJCP', 'CACHESTORE_SQLCP', 'CACHESTORE_PHDR',
'CACHESTORE_XPROC')
```

Some plans cannot be entirely removed from cache even if there is internal or external memory pressure. The most straightforward example of this is a plan that is currently being used. Other examples include explicitly prepared queries or cursors that have been prepared or opened but not yet closed. Still, SQL Server can free some of the cached memory for these items. For example, a cached plan for a prepared query can be removed from cache (if it is not currently being executed) because SQL Server retains the query's text when it is prepared. A new plan can always be compiled from the text when someone executes the prepared query.

Non-Cached Plans and Zero Cost Plans

Certain query plans are never inserted into the procedure cache. Of course, if a plan is never cached, it cannot be reused. Query plans used to create or update statistics, those used to execute DBCC commands, and plans used to create or rebuild indexes are some examples of plans that SQL Server does not cache. Dynamic SQL executed via EXEC(), or any stored procedure or query executed with RECOMPILE, is not cached. Any query that contains a string or binary literal larger than 8KB is not cached. There is also a set of plans called *zero cost plans* that may not be cached. Zero cost plans are plans that are extremely inexpensive to compile. If every such plan was cached, the cache could fill up very quickly with plans that were not very valuable. SQL Server 2000 never caches zero cost plans, but SQL Server 2005 makes some exceptions to this rule. For example, zero cost cursor fetch plans are cached because they are likely to be reused many times. Also, any batch that includes BEGIN TRAN, COMMIT TRAN, or a SET statement will be cached in an attempt to avoid repeated parsing of certain batches that are frequently executed by the SQL Server ODBC driver and OLEDB provider. Finally, any plan that undergoes full optimization is cached; this last rule encompasses nearly every SELECT, INSERT, UPDATE, or DELETE query. Any zero cost plan that SQL Server 2005 decides to cache is cached with an initial cost of zero, meaning that if no one has reused the plan it is immediately discarded the first time the clock sweep encounters it. However, if the plan is ever reused, its cost is incremented to 1—a value that is higher than the actual compile cost—in order to give the plan a chance to survive in the cache for as long as it continues to be frequently reused.

Plan Sharing

Plan sharing refers to the ability for different users to reuse the same compiled plan. The most common reason for a lack of plan sharing is a lack of schema-qualified table names (the dbo in dbo.MyTable is the schema). For example, consider the following query:

```
SELECT * FROM MyTable
```

If user Joe executes the query, the table reference MyTable could refer to table Joe.MyTable, owned by Joe. If user Dan executed the same query, the table reference could refer to a different table named Dan.MyTable. In other words, a table name without a schema reference is ambiguous. A query that contains schema-qualified table names (most tables are in the DBO schema) is safe for sharing by different users. This is indicated by a special user_id value of -2 in the sys.dm_exec_plan_attributes DMF.

If your application connects to the database with a different login for each end user, plan sharing can be an important consideration. Suppose that 100 logins are all executing the same set of parameterized queries without schema-qualified table names. You would have up to 100 copies of each query plan in cache. This means that your procedure cache will be up to 100 times larger than it could be, and the overall CPU cost paid for query compilation will be up to 100 times higher than it could be with schema-qualified queries.

This applies only to queries in ad hoc or prepared batches. Queries in stored procedures, triggers, or user-defined functions are unambiguous even without schema-qualification because tables referenced by a T-SQL object always resolve as if they were being referenced by the user who created the object. In other words, there is no performance or memory penalty for a lack of schema-qualification of tables referenced in T-SQL objects, though you may wish to qualify even queries in your stored procedures for the sake of consistency and clarity.

Recompilation

Pop quiz: If you have past experience with stored procedure recompilation, see whether you know the correct answer.

Why did Microsoft add stored procedure recompilation to SQL Server?

A. It helps ensure employment for starving SQL Server consultants.

B. It spurs DBAs to consume even more coffee, driving up our personal Starbucks stock holdings.

C. Recompilation generally improves performance and ensures correct query results.

Performance problems commonly associated with recompiles have earned stored procedure recompilation a bad reputation. Some DBAs and SQL Server developers might wish that there was a way to turn off recompilation, but anyone with this opinion is probably not aware of the benefits that recompilation provides. Consider that the SQL Server development team has invested a lot of effort in creating and refining the feature. Occasional appearances to the contrary, they didn't do it in order to harass DBAs.

I've spent the entire chapter up to this point extolling the many virtues of query plan reuse and explaining how to avoid unnecessary query compilation. Recompilation forces what might be a perfectly serviceable cached plan to be discarded, and a new plan to be compiled. If you're wondering how this could be a good thing, the reason is simple: Sometimes the cost of generating a new query plan is less than the cost of sticking with an old plan. The state of a typical database is constantly changing, and query plans have to adapt to those changes.

Here are a few scenarios where plan recompilation is a positive thing:

- The schema of a table referenced by the query plan has changed. For example, a dropped column or a modified column data type might have invalidated the current query plan.

- Statistics on a table referenced by the query have changed. Automatically updated statistics generally indicate that users have made many modifications to a table. Significant changes to table cardinality or data distribution mean that a different query plan might be more efficient.

- The batch has changed a plan-affecting SET option like ANSI_NULLS or CONCAT_NULL_YIELDS_NULL. Plan-affecting SET options can change the semantics of a query, which means that the old query plan must be discarded.

NOTE

In SQL Server, "recompile" and "compile" have slightly different meanings. In order for a query compilation event to be considered a recompile, SQL Server must be in the middle of executing a previously compiled plan when the decision is made to create a new plan. If the decision to generate a new plan is made prior to the start of query execution, that is considered a compile, not a recompile. It's a subtle distinction, but an important one to remember in order to interpret certain diagnostics correctly. For example, separate performance monitor counters track compiles/sec and recompiles/sec, and the approach you would take to reduce a high recompile rate is different from the approach you would take to address a high compile rate.

In SQL Server 2000, the unit of recompilation was the batch or stored procedure. If 1 of 50 queries in a stored procedure triggered a recompile, SQL Server 2000 would compile a new plan for all 50 queries. SQL Server 2005 improves on this situation with the introduction of statement-level recompilation. Statement-level recompilation helps reduce the cost of recompiles by allowing a single query to be recompiled independently of the other queries in a batch or stored procedure. This feature should significantly reduce the cost of recompilation in SQL Server 2005 relative to prior versions.

Parameterization

When a query is parameterized, the cached query plan can be repeatedly reused across multiple executions even if the parameter values change. If a query is not explicitly parameterized, in most cases the cached plan can only be reused for subsequent executions with the exact same parameter values. This means that each execution must pay the cost of query compilation. Whether or not a query is parameterized has traditionally been determined by the application developer. Here's some C# code that runs a query in a loop without parameterization:

```
static private bool RunQueriesNotParameterized()
{
    SqlCommand cmd = new SqlCommand();
    cmd.Connection = cn;

    for (int i = 0; i < QueryIterations; i++)
    {
        cmd.CommandText = @"
            SELECT *
            FROM Sales.SalesOrderHeader h
            LEFT OUTER JOIN Sales.SalesOrderDetail d ON h.SalesOrderID =
d.SalesOrderID
            LEFT OUTER JOIN Sales.vSalesPerson p ON h.SalesPersonID =
p.SalesPersonID
            LEFT OUTER JOIN Sales.vSalesPersonSalesByFiscalYears sfy
                ON sfy.SalesPersonID = h.SalesPersonID
            WHERE h.OrderDate BETWEEN '20040101' AND '20040110'
                AND h.SalesPersonID = " + i.ToString();
        cmd.ExecuteNonQuery();
    }
    return true;
}
```

Each execution of the query performs a lookup using a different SalesPersonID value. Notice that the search values are inline literals in the query; when you write code like this, any change to the query's search values ends up changing the text of the query. By default, the query text must *exactly* match a prior query's text for the prior query's plan to be reused. Coding in this way is likely to prevent plan reuse, which is another way of saying that the code will cause a new query compilation for every query execution.

So, how could you modify this function to explicitly parameterize the query? Here's one approach:

```
static private bool RunQueriesParameterized()
{
    SqlCommand cmd = new SqlCommand();
    cmd.Connection = cn;

    cmd.CommandText = @"
        SELECT *
        FROM Sales.SalesOrderHeader h
        LEFT OUTER JOIN Sales.SalesOrderDetail d ON h.SalesOrderID =
d.SalesOrderID
```

```
            LEFT OUTER JOIN Sales.vSalesPerson p ON h.SalesPersonID =
p.SalesPersonID
            LEFT OUTER JOIN Sales.vSalesPersonSalesByFiscalYears sfy
                ON sfy.SalesPersonID = h.SalesPersonID
            WHERE h.OrderDate BETWEEN @StartDate AND @EndDate
                AND h.SalesPersonID = @SalesPersonID";
    cmd.Parameters.Add("@StartDate", SqlDbType.DateTime);
    cmd.Parameters.Add("@EndDate", SqlDbType.DateTime);
    cmd.Parameters.Add("@SalesPersonID", SqlDbType.Int);

    for (int i = 0; i < QueryIterations; i++)
    {
        cmd.Parameters["@SalesPersonID"].Value = i;
        cmd.Parameters["@StartDate"].Value = DateTime.Parse("2004/01/01",
            CultureInfo.InvariantCulture);
        cmd.Parameters["@EndDate"].Value = DateTime.Parse("2004/01/10",
            CultureInfo.InvariantCulture);
        cmd.ExecuteNonQuery();
    }
    return true;
}
```

If you captured a Profiler trace of this code executing, you would see a series of RPC:Starting and RPC:Completed events, with event text that looked like this:

```
exec sp_executesql N'
    SELECT *
    FROM Sales.SalesOrderHeader h
    LEFT OUTER JOIN Sales.SalesOrderDetail d ON h.SalesOrderID =
d.SalesOrderID
    LEFT OUTER JOIN Sales.vSalesPerson p ON h.SalesPersonID = p.SalesPersonID
    LEFT OUTER JOIN Sales.vSalesPersonSalesByFiscalYears sfy
        ON sfy.SalesPersonID = h.SalesPersonID
    WHERE h.OrderDate BETWEEN @StartDate AND @EndDate
        AND h.SalesPersonID = @SalesPersonID',
  N'@StartDate datetime,@EndDate datetime,@SalesPersonID int',
    @StartDate='2004-01-01 00:00:00:000',
    @EndDate='2004-01-10 00:00:00:000',
    @SalesPersonID=7
```

Note that instead of inline literal values, there are now parameter placeholders in the body of the query. The values of the parameters are provided outside of the query text. In this way, the query text remains constant across multiple executions of the query, allowing a single plan to be reused even when the parameter values change.

There are various ways to explicitly parameterize a query; the options depend on the data access API that the program is using. For example, in ODBC, you would use SQLExecDirect or SQLPrepare/SQLExecute with ? as a placeholder for each parameter. In an ADO application, you would execute the query with a Command object after explicitly populating the Command object's Parameters collection. In a T-SQL application, you can use the sp_executesql stored procedure to explicitly parameterize a query. If there is ever any doubt, you can always capture a Profiler trace to determine whether a query is being executed as a parameterized query (an RPC:Starting event) with the parameters separated from the query text, or as a non-parameterized ad hoc query (a SQL:BatchStarting event) with constant parameter values inline in the query.

The preceding information describes *explicit parameterization*, which occurs when an application is written to explicitly separate query parameter values from the query text. Another type of parameterization allows for implicit parameterization of queries. Implicit parameterization comes in two flavors: forced and simple.

Forced Parameterization

Remember the brief anecdote I shared at the beginning of this chapter about the ERP software vendor that scaled to twice its previous maximum users per server simply by ensuring that its ad hoc query plans could be reused? That app had not been written to submit queries as explicitly parameterized queries, and the huge gains found were achieved by causing the app's queries to be parameterized so that query plans could be reused. One way to do this would have been to modify the application as described previously to explicitly parameterize every query. However, the results were achieved without making any changes to the application. Instead, the ISV took advantage of a powerful new feature in SQL Server 2005 called *forced parameterization*. Forced parameterization is a database-level option that is disabled by default but can be enabled by running an ALTER DATABASE command. After forced parameterization is enabled for a database, any query that arrives at the server while that database has context is implicitly parameterized. In other words, forced parameterization provides the benefits of query parameterization for free, without changing a single line of application source code.

Forced parameterization can automatically parameterize many queries, but not all of them. For example, literals in a SELECT's column list or certain query hints prevent forced parameterization from being able to parameterize a query. For a complete list of the exception cases, see the "Forced Parameterization" topic in SQL Server Books Online.

Forced parameterization also prevents queries from making use of indexes on views, so you should be cautious of enabling it on a production database without testing beforehand.

Simple Parameterization

If forced parameterization is not enabled for a database, SQL Server uses a different and much more limited form of implicit parameterization called *simple parameterization*. Simple parameterization only implicitly parameterizes queries that match a relatively small number of very simple and strictly defined templates. Adding even a modest amount of complexity to your query blocks simple parameterization from implicitly parameterizing your query. Next is a partial list of some of the things that prevent implicit parameterization within a database that is in simple parameterization mode.

NOTE

Autoparameterization in SQL Server 2000 is the same thing as simple parameterization. SQL Server 2000 doesn't support forced parameterization, so to get plan reuse through parameterization on SQL Server 2000, you need to modify your applications to explicitly parameterize frequently executed queries.

- References to more than one table

- IN clauses or OR expressions

- UPDATE SET @variable=...

- SELECT with UNION

- SELECT INTO

- Any query hint

- SELECT with DISTINCT

- TOP

- A DELETE or UPDATE with a FROM clause

- A reference to fulltext catalogs, linked server queries, or table variables

- Subqueries

- GROUP BY

- A predicate of the form Expression <> Constant

- References to most intrinsic functions

On top of this, the query optimizer gets to make a final call about whether it is "safe" to implicitly parameterize a query using simple parameterization. If SQL Server can determine that you might get one query plan with one set of parameter values and a different query plan with a different set of parameter values, the implicit parameterization attempt is deemed "unsafe" and the query is not parameterized. Simple parameterization applies only to queries that do not already have any explicitly defined parameters.

As you can see, simple parameterization is so limited in scope that you should assume that most of your query workload will not benefit from it.

How Cache Lookups Work

The method that is used to look things up in the procedure cache depends on the type of the object. The database ID and object ID of a stored procedure, for example, are used to look up stored procedure plans. For ad hoc and prepared queries, the text of the query is pushed through a hash function. The hash function returns an integer value that is then referred to as the "object ID" of the SQL compiled plan object. SQL Server 2000 hashed only the first 8KB of a query's text, but SQL Server 2005 hashes the entire query text. The object ID and database ID aren't the only properties that must match the user's current environment for a plan to be reused. Other properties like user ID and language settings may be required to match, as well; any property of the cached object that must match in order for a lookup to succeed is referred to as a *cache key*. The cache keys for a plan are combined by another hash function to determine the bucket in the procedure cache where the plan will be stored. You can see the bucket ID for each cached object in the sys.dm_exec_cached_plans DMV. It is possible for multiple objects to be stored in the same cache bucket; SQL Server examines each item in that bucket to determine whether it is a proper match for the object it is looking for.

The objects in the cache should be fairly evenly distributed over the hash buckets so that no single bucket grows to hold a disproportionate number of objects. If the number of objects in a given hash bucket grows too large, the iteration over the list of objects in that bucket on every cache lookup can start to take more time, and performance of the work-load can suffer. Ideally, the number of objects in a given bucket should be fewer than about 20; if the number of items in a "hot" bucket that contains a frequently used object grows beyond 100 or so, this may be cause for concern.

You can examine max and average chain length and overall cache hit ratios for the procedure cache cachestores by querying the sys.dm_os_memory_cache_hash_tables DMV:

```
SELECT * FROM sys.dm_os_memory_cache_hash_tables
WHERE [type] IN ('CACHESTORE_OBJCP', 'CACHESTORE_SQLCP', 'CACHESTORE_PHDR',
'CACHESTORE_XPROC')
```

If a cache lookup finds a compatible object in cache:

- The SQLServer:Plan Cache\Cache Hit Ratio performance monitor counter is adjusted upward to reflect the cache hit.

- The hits_count column in the sys.dm_os_memory_cache_hash_tables DMV is incremented by 1.

- An SP:CacheHit Profiler trace event is generated (only for stored procedure objects).

- The usecount property for the object is incremented. This property is exposed in sys.dm_exec_cached_plans.

If a cache lookup fails to find a compatible object in cache:

- The SQLServer:Plan Cache\Cache Hit Ratio performance monitor counter is adjusted downward to reflect the cache miss.

- The misses_count column in the sys.dm_os_memory_cache_hash_tables DMV is incremented by 1.

- The object is created and inserted into cache.

- An SP:CacheInsert event is generated (only for stored procedure objects).

- The SQLServer:SQL Statistics\SQL Compilations/sec performance monitor counter is incremented (for SQL or object Compiled Plans).

Cached Plan Reuse

The procedure cache is just a waste of memory if the plans in the cache are never reused. It is therefore important to ensure that query plans are reused whenever possible. A number of things are taken into account when determining whether a plan will be reused. First, recall that the "object ID" for a cached ad hoc query plan is determined by the hashed query text. One side effect of this is that the text of two ad hoc queries must exactly match in order for a cached ad hoc plan to be reused. Even tiny differences in white space or comments prevent plan reuse for ad hoc queries.

Different values for certain SET options can prevent plan reuse for ad hoc and prepared queries. SET options like CONCAT_NULL_YIELDS_NULL and ANSI_NULLS can change the semantics of a query. For example, you can get different results for the exact same query if you execute it first with ANSI_NULLS turned on, and then again with ANSI_NULLS turned off. To reuse a query plan, a connection must therefore have the same values for all plan-affecting SET options that were in effect when the query plan was compiled and cached.

Other connection-level settings like dateformat and language can affect the outcome of some queries, so the current values for these settings must also match those that were in effect when the query plan was compiled.

As you can see, sometimes fairly subtle differences can prevent plan reuse. If you see multiple plans in cache for what appears to be the same query, you can determine the key differences between them by comparing the sys.dm_exec_plan_attributes DMF output for the two plans. The plan attributes that must match in order for reuse to occur will have an is_cache_key column value of 1. Let's take a look at sample sys.dm_exec_plan_attributes output for a cached stored procedure plan:

```
select * from sys.dm_exec_plan_attributes
(<plan_handle_from_dm_exec_cached_plans>)

attribute                      value       is_cache_key
------------------------    ----------   ------------
set_options                    4347        1
objectid                       981578535   1
dbid                           2           1
dbid_execute                   2           1
user_id                        1           1
language_id                    0           1
date_format                    1           1
date_first                     7           1
status                         0           1
required_cursor_options        0           1
acceptable_cursor_options      0           1
```

```
inuse_exec_context        0           0
free_exec_context         1           0
hits_exec_context         0           0
misses_exec_context       0           0
removed_exec_context      0           0
inuse_cursors             0           0
free_cursors              0           0
hits_cursors              0           0
misses_cursors            0           0
removed_cursors           0           0
sql_handle                NULL        0
```

Note the attributes that are flagged as cache keys for the plan. If one of these properties does not match the state of the current connection, the plan cannot be reused, and a new plan must be compiled and inserted into the cache. This can cause the cache to fill up more quickly.

Flushing the Procedure Cache

The most common method of flushing the contents of the procedure cache is to run DBCC FREEPROCCACHE. In addition, ALTER DATABASE or DROP DATABASE commands, closing a database (for example, due to the autoclose database option), and changes to sp_configure options can all implicitly free all or portions of the procedure cache.

Common Cache-Related Problems and Solutions

We've just covered the architecture of the procedure cache in some detail. Now we'll see why this matters by looking at a variety of problems that you're likely to run into sooner or later as a SQL Server developer or administrator.

Using the Procedure Cache to Identify Expensive Queries

Exposing execution statistics for your queries is not the procedure cache's primary mission, but thanks to the sys.dm_exec_query_stats DMV, the procedure cache can be very handy for problem query identification. Here's a query that you can use to instantly retrieve your top 20 most expensive cached query plans in terms of cumulative CPU cost:

```
SELECT TOP 20
  LEFT (p.cacheobjtype + ' (' + p.objtype + ')', 35) AS cacheobjtype,
  p.usecounts,
  p.size_in_bytes / 1024 AS size_in_kb,
  stat.total_worker_time/1000 AS tot_cpu_ms,
  stat.total_elapsed_time/1000 AS tot_duration_ms,
  stat.total_physical_reads,
  stat.total_logical_writes,
  stat.total_logical_reads,
  LEFT (CASE
    WHEN pa.value=32767 THEN 'ResourceDb'
```

```
      ELSE ISNULL (DB_NAME (CONVERT (sysname, pa.value)), CONVERT (sysname,
pa.value))
    END, 40) AS dbname,
    sql.objectid,
    CONVERT (nvarchar(50), CASE
      WHEN sql.objectid IS NULL THEN NULL
      ELSE REPLACE (REPLACE (sql.[text],CHAR(13), ' '), CHAR(10), ' ')
    END) AS procname,
    REPLACE (REPLACE (SUBSTRING (sql.[text], stat.statement_start_offset/2 + 1,
        CASE WHEN stat.statement_end_offset = -1 THEN LEN (CONVERT
(nvarchar(max), sql.[text]))
        ELSE stat.statement_end_offset/2 - stat.statement_start_offset/2 + 1
END),
        CHAR(13), ' '), CHAR(10), ' ') AS stmt_text
FROM sys.dm_exec_cached_plans p
OUTER APPLY sys.dm_exec_plan_attributes (p.plan_handle) pa
INNER JOIN sys.dm_exec_query_stats stat ON p.plan_handle = stat.plan_handle
OUTER APPLY sys.dm_exec_sql_text (p.plan_handle) AS sql
WHERE pa.attribute = 'dbid'
ORDER BY tot_cpu_ms DESC
```

You can find the top queries by other measures, including total execution time, execution count, number of pages modified, or physical reads, just by modifying the ORDER BY clause.

In all versions of SQL Server prior to SQL Server 2005, to get this type of analysis of a workload, you would have to capture a possibly expensive and almost certainly large Profiler trace, load this trace into a table, and use either a set of homegrown queries or another tool to calculate the cumulative cost of all executions of a given stored procedure or query. However, I also don't want to give you the impression that the sys.dm_exec_query_stats DMV will be a complete replacement for this type of analysis in every case. Here are some sys.dm_exec_query_stats limitations that you should be conscious of:

- The sys.dm_exec_query_stats DMV provides a view of query plans in the procedure cache. As we saw earlier, though, not every query gets cached. For example, a DBCC DBREINDEX might be an extremely expensive operation, but the plan for this query will not be cached, and its execution statistics will therefore not be exposed in this DMV.

- A plan can be removed from cache at any time. The sys.dm_exec_query_stats DMV can only show statistics for plans that are still in cache.

- sys.dm_exec_query_stats only reflects the cost of query execution. Query compilation cost is not reflected in the CPU or other statistics.

- Any query that contains inline literals and is not explicitly or implicitly parameterized will not be reused. Every execution of this query with different parameter values will end up getting a new compiled plan. If a query does not see consistent plan reuse, the sys.dm_exec_query_stats DMV will not show the cumulative cost of that query in a single row. (The DMV exposes execution statistics on a per-statement-plan basis.) You can prevent this problem if you ensure plan reuse by enabling forced parameterization or by modifying the application to explicitly parameterize its queries.

Despite these limitations, sys.dm_exec_query_stats is a very handy and easy-to-use tool, and I encourage you to take full advantage of it whenever you have a need to identify the "expensive" queries in your application workload.

The first and second limitations mentioned previously could be effectively mitigated by combining a snapshot of the sys.dm_exec_query_stats DMV with a Profiler trace that included the Performance Statistics trace event. The Performance Statistics trace event is a new event in SQL Server 2005 that exposes the same query execution statistics that are exposed in sys.dm_exec_query_stats. SQL Server produces a Performance Statistics event every time a query plan is discarded. It would be possible to get a complete picture of the execution cost of every query that ran within a particular time window by combining the Performance Statistics data with a final sys.dm_exec_query_stats snapshot. Because the Performance Statistics event contains aggregate execution statistics for all executions of a plan, and because the event is not produced for every execution of a query, a trace consisting of this event would be much smaller and cheaper to capture than a trace of every SQL:BatchCompleted and RPC:Completed event.

Exercise: Using *sys.dm_exec_query_stats* to Identify Expensive Queries

1. Run DBCC FREEPROCCACHE. This clears the procedure cache of any cached plans that are not currently in use.

2. Run the ProcCache\dm_exec_query_stats\sample_workload.sql script via sqlcmd.exe. This runs a simulated application workload by executing a variety of different queries in the AdventureWorks database.

   Sqlcmd.exe -E -S *yoursqlserver* -i dm_exec_query_stats.sql > NUL

3. Run the following query to identify the most expensive query by cumulative CPU cost:

```
SELECT TOP 20
    LEFT (p.cacheobjtype + ' (' + p.objtype + ')', 35) AS cacheobjtype,
    p.usecounts,
    p.size_in_bytes / 1024 AS size_in_kb,
    stat.total_worker_time/1000 AS tot_cpu_ms,
    stat.total_elapsed_time/1000 AS tot_duration_ms,
    stat.total_physical_reads,
    stat.total_logical_writes,
    stat.total_logical_reads,
    LEFT (CASE
```

```
    WHEN pa.value=32767 THEN 'ResourceDb'
    ELSE ISNULL (DB_NAME (CONVERT (sysname, pa.value)), CONVERT
(sysname, pa.value))
  END, 40) AS dbname,
  sql.objectid,
  CONVERT (nvarchar(50), CASE
    WHEN sql.objectid IS NULL THEN NULL
    ELSE REPLACE (REPLACE (sql.[text],CHAR(13), ' '), CHAR(10), ' ')
  END) AS procname,
  REPLACE (REPLACE (SUBSTRING (sql.[text], stat.statement_start_offset/2
+ 1,
      CASE WHEN stat.statement_end_offset = -1 THEN LEN (CONVERT
(nvarchar(max), sql.[text]))
      ELSE stat.statement_end_offset/2 - stat.statement_start_offset/2 +
1 END),
    CHAR(13), ' '), CHAR(10), ' ') AS stmt_text
FROM sys.dm_exec_cached_plans p
OUTER APPLY sys.dm_exec_plan_attributes (p.plan_handle) pa
INNER JOIN sys.dm_exec_query_stats stat ON p.plan_handle =
stat.plan_handle
OUTER APPLY sys.dm_exec_sql_text (p.plan_handle) AS sql
WHERE pa.attribute = 'dbid'
ORDER BY tot_cpu_ms DESC
```

Note that some of the queries that used the most CPU actually didn't use very many CPU cycles per individual execution, but their cumulative CPU cost is high because they were so frequently executed. This is not unusual; it is often the case that the query that is using the most resources is a low-cost but high-volume query.

Parameter Sniffing

Earlier, I mentioned that simple parameterization is the default parameterization setting for databases despite the fact that simple parameterization applies to only the most straightforward queries. If simple parameterization is unable to parameterize even relatively simple queries, why did Microsoft decide to make simple parameterization the default setting for new databases? And why wouldn't you enable forced parameterization for all of your databases in order to maximize plan reuse and minimize the cache size and unnecessary query compilation?

The answer has to do with a behavior called *parameter sniffing*. In just a moment we'll look more closely at how parameter sniffing in concert with parameterization can cause problems. First, though, let's take a brief look at what parameter sniffing is and how it works.

Parameter sniffing is a performance optimization that allows SQL Server to optimize the query plan for the particular parameter values that were passed in for the initial compilation of the query. To better understand why this could be a useful feature, consider the TerritoryID values in the Sales.Customer table in the AdventureWorks database. Table 4-3 shows the various TerritoryID values and the number of rows that have each TerritoryID value.

TABLE 4-3   *TerritoryID* values and the number of rows that have each *TerritoryID* value

TerritoryID	Number of Customers
4	4581
9	3631
1	3433
10	1953
7	1850
8	1820
6	1685
5	97
3	71
2	64

As you can see, many of this company's customers can be found in TerritoryID 4. TerritoryID 2, on the other hand, has only a few dozen customers.

Run the following in the AdventureWorks database and look at their query plans that result from the two executions of the stored procedure:

```
CREATE PROCEDURE usp_paramsniffingtest @TerritoryID int AS
SELECT TerritoryID, CustomerID, CustomerType
FROM Sales.Customer
WHERE CustomerID > 25000 AND TerritoryID = @TerritoryID
GO
SET STATISTICS PROFILE ON
GO

DBCC FREEPROCCACHE
EXEC usp_paramsniffingtest @TerritoryID = 4
GO

DBCC FREEPROCCACHE
EXEC usp_paramsniffingtest @TerritoryID = 2
GO

SET STATISTICS PROFILE OFF
GO
```

The only difference between these two queries is the `TerritoryID` value. We won't get into the details of the query plans, but do note that the two plans are different. One of the plans is the fastest possible plan when `@TerritoryID` is 2, and the other plan is the fastest possible plan when `@TerritoryID` is 4. The query optimizer "sniffed" the compile-time parameter values and used that additional information to select the optimal plan. This sample runs `DBCC FREEPROCCACHE` to clear the procedure cache before both executions. Let's take a look at what happens if we skip the second `DBCC FREEPROCCACHE` so that the plan from the first execution gets reused:

```
SET STATISTICS PROFILE ON
GO

DBCC FREEPROCCACHE
EXEC usp_paramsniffingtest @TerritoryID = 4
GO

EXEC usp_paramsniffingtest @TerritoryID = 2
GO

SET STATISTICS PROFILE OFF
GO
```

If you look at the query plans this time, you should find that they are the same. The first execution caused a compilation that was optimized for an `@TerritoryID` value of 4. That plan was inserted into the procedure cache and was reused for subsequent executions, even though the subsequent executions passed in a different parameter value.

Parameter sniffing provides the query optimizer with the most detailed information possible so that the optimizer can select the fastest possible query plan for the current execution of a query. Most of the time, parameter sniffing results in much better query plans than you would get without it; sometimes, though, it can cause problems. Have you ever encountered a situation where a SQL Server instance's performance suddenly and inexplicably took a dive, without any significant change in schema, workload, or data? This could be caused by a number of different issues, but query plan variations caused by parameter sniffing are perhaps the most common cause of this phenomenon.

Performance Problems Caused by Parameter Sniffing

SQL Server has a certain amount of inherent tension between the procedure cache and the query optimizer. The procedure cache strives to ensure that plans are reused whenever possible, while the query optimizer wants to choose the most efficient plan for the current database conditions and parameter values. Choosing an optimal plan for the immediate conditions requires a new query compilation, but compilation works against the procedure cache's goal of plan reuse. In many cases, the rules built into SQL Server will strike a reasonable balance between these two competing needs. Occasionally, the procedure cache's zeal for providing plan reuse and the optimizer's capability to take certain details into account during query compilation interact in an unfortunate way.

This risk applies to two of the three forms of parameterization: explicit parameterization and forced parameterization. Simple parameterization is immune from parameter sniffing problems because it is conservative and refuses to parameterize queries that might get different plans for different parameter values.

Let's take a look at an example of a parameter sniffing performance problem:

```
DROP PROCEDURE usp_GetProductTransactionHistory
GO

CREATE PROCEDURE usp_GetProductTransactionHistory @ProductID int AS
DECLARE @starttime datetime, @elapsedms int
DBCC DROPCLEANBUFFERS
SET @starttime = GETDATE()

SELECT SUM (Quantity) AS Quantity, AVG (ActualCost) AS AvgCost
FROM Production.TransactionHistory
WHERE ProductID = @ProductID

SET @elapsedms = DATEDIFF (ms, @starttime, GETDATE())
PRINT 'Execution time: ' + CAST (@elapsedms AS varchar) + ' ms'
GO

DBCC FREEPROCCACHE
EXEC usp_GetProductTransactionHistory @ProductID=843 -- ParamA (1st)
EXEC usp_GetProductTransactionHistory @ProductID=870 -- ParamB (2nd)
GO

DBCC FREEPROCCACHE
EXEC usp_GetProductTransactionHistory @ProductID=870 -- ParamB (1st)
EXEC usp_GetProductTransactionHistory @ProductID=843 -- ParamA (2nd)
GO
```

Table 4-4 shows execution times I observed for the four stored procedure calls on my server.

TABLE 4-4   Execution times for the four stored procedure calls

Query	Execution Time
ParamA (1st)	30ms
ParamA (2nd)	377ms
ParamB (1st)	296ms
ParamB (2nd)	860ms

You can clearly see the dangers of parameter sniffing here. If an @ProductID of 843 is used to generate the plan, any subsequent execution with a parameter value of 870 will be two to three times slower than it could be. On the other hand, if an @ProductID value of 870 is used to compile the query plan, subsequent executions with a parameter value of 843 will be almost 10 times slower than they would have been had a different plan been selected! This is an example of a case where no single plan is the fastest plan for all possible parameter values. Whichever parameter gets through the door first gets to generate a plan that is tailored to that particular parameter value. Subsequent executions will reuse the cached plan, even if they have a different parameter value that might benefit more from a different query plan.

No matter which plan gets selected, someone will lose. Even worse, the current plan could get tossed out of cache at any time, and the DBA has no direct control over the lifetime of a plan in cache. Every time a plan gets removed from cache, there is the chance of a dramatic change in the query's typical execution time. The outcome depends on the luck of the draw, since SQL will optimize the new plan for whichever parameter happens to get passed to the procedure next.

Solving Parameter Sniffing Issues with *RECOMPILE*

How would you solve this problem? One solution is to ensure that everyone gets a new plan that is customized for his or her particular parameter values. You can do this by adding WITH RECOMPILE to the stored procedure definition or by adding a WITH (RECOMPILE) hint to the particular affected query. If you are on SQL 2005, the latter option is preferable because it avoids unnecessary compiles of other queries in the stored procedure. Try this, and note that both parameters now get their ideal plan on every execution:

```
DROP PROCEDURE usp_GetProductTransactionHistory
GO
CREATE PROCEDURE usp_GetProductTransactionHistory @ProductID int AS
DECLARE @starttime datetime, @elapsedms int
DBCC DROPCLEANBUFFERS
SET @starttime = GETDATE()

SELECT SUM (Quantity) AS Quantity, AVG (ActualCost) AS AvgCost
FROM Production.TransactionHistory
WHERE ProductID = @ProductID
OPTION (RECOMPILE)

SET @elapsedms = DATEDIFF (ms, @starttime, GETDATE())
PRINT 'Execution time: ' + CAST (@elapsedms AS varchar) + ' ms'
GO

DBCC FREEPROCCACHE
EXEC usp_GetProductTransactionHistory @ProductID=843 -- Param843 (1st)
EXEC usp_GetProductTransactionHistory @ProductID=870 -- Param870 (2nd)
GO
```

```
DBCC FREEPROCCACHE
EXEC usp_GetProductTransactionHistory @ProductID=870 -- Param870 (1st)
EXEC usp_GetProductTransactionHistory @ProductID=843 -- Param843 (2nd)
GO
```

TABLE 4-5   Sample execution times after the modification

Query	Execution Time
Param843 (1st)	31ms
Param843 (2nd)	36ms
Param870 (1st)	362ms
Param870 (2nd)	370ms

Yes, a RECOMPILE hint will prevent plan reuse, but remember that this is a case where plan reuse is the cause of the problem. Reuse of any single plan would guarantee that certain parameter values would suffer from a suboptimal plan. Check the compile time by running DBCC FREEPROCCACHE and SET STATISTICS TIME ON; if the compile time is small relative to the execution time, an OPTION (RECOMPILE) hint is a reasonable solution to this problem. In the example we just looked at, the compile time of the stored procedure is tiny (less than 10 milliseconds) relative to the execution time savings that the OPTION (RECOMPILE) hint provides.

There are three ways to tell SQL Server to recompile every execution of a query. The first is the OPTION (RECOMPILE) hint, which can be applied to individual queries in SQL 2005. An example of this hint is shown previously.

Similarly, you can use the WITH RECOMPILE hint to tell SQL Server 2000 or SQL Server 2005 to compile a new plan for every execution of a stored procedure. WITH RECOMPILE applies to every execution of a stored procedure. You can use the WITH RECOMPILE hint when executing a stored procedure:

```
EXEC usp_GetProductTransactionHistory @ProductID=843 WITH RECOMPILE
```

Or you can apply it as part of the stored procedure definition:

```
CREATE PROCEDURE usp_GetProductTransactionHistory @ProductID int WITH
RECOMPILE AS
...
```

Both of these hints cause SQL Server to generate a new plan and skip the insertion of that plan into the procedure cache. Executing a stored procedure with the WITH RECOMPILE hint will cause that execution to get its own plan, but will not remove a previously cached plan for that stored procedure from the cache.

The word *recompile* in these hints is a bit of a misnomer. The hints cause a new plan to be generated before query execution begins, which means that the operation that they trigger is a simple compile, not a recompile. You'll see this work reflected in the SQLServer:SQL Statistics\SQL Compilations/sec performance monitor counter, but not in SQLServer:SQL Statistics\SQL Re-Compilations/sec.

Solving Parameter Sniffing Issues with *OPTIMIZE FOR*

Suppose that our usp_GetProductTransactionHistory stored procedure was most commonly executed with ProductIDs that have a lot of transactions (like ProductID 870, which has over 4,000 rows in the TransactionHistory table). ProductIDs with very few transactions (like ProductID 843, with only a single TransactionHistory row) are only infrequently passed to the procedure. You may not care much about optimizing the execution for these infrequently used parameters. In situations like this where you know what type of parameter is the important one, you can use an OPTION (OPTIMIZE FOR) hint to tell SQL Server which parameter values you want it to use for plan selection. This doesn't have any effect on the runtime value of the parameter; it just provides a certain degree of plan stability by telling SQL to always choose the plan that would be best for your handpicked "typical" parameter values.

```
DROP PROCEDURE usp_GetProductTransactionHistory
GO
CREATE PROCEDURE usp_GetProductTransactionHistory @ProductID int AS
DECLARE @starttime datetime, @elapsedms int
DBCC DROPCLEANBUFFERS
SET @starttime = GETDATE()

SELECT SUM (Quantity) AS Quantity, AVG (ActualCost) AS AvgCost
FROM Production.TransactionHistory
WHERE ProductID = @ProductID
OPTION (OPTIMIZE FOR (@ProductID=870))

SET @elapsedms = DATEDIFF (ms, @starttime, GETDATE())
PRINT 'Execution time: ' + CAST (@elapsedms AS varchar) + ' ms'
GO

DBCC FREEPROCCACHE
EXEC usp_GetProductTransactionHistory @ProductID=843 -- Param843 (1st)
EXEC usp_GetProductTransactionHistory @ProductID=870 -- Param870 (2nd)
GO

DBCC FREEPROCCACHE
EXEC usp_GetProductTransactionHistory @ProductID=870 -- Param870 (1st)
EXEC usp_GetProductTransactionHistory @ProductID=843 -- Param843 (2nd)
GO
```

Once you make this change, you'll find that it no longer matters what parameter value is passed in for the initial execution of the stored procedure; the optimizer always selects the query plan that is ProductID 870's ideal plan. Occasional executions with much less frequent parameter values, like 843, will suffer, but this may be more than offset by the fact that the dominant type of parameter in your workload will never be hurt by reuse of a plan that was optimized for an atypical parameter value.

Replacing Parameters with Local Variables

You may have run into situations in the past where you found that the speed of a query changed significantly after you pulled it out of a stored procedure, replaced the parameters with local variables, and ran it as an ad hoc batch. If you've ever noticed this, you were seeing the effects of parameter sniffing in action. Perhaps inadvertently, you also discovered what may be the most common approach to parameter sniffing performance issues: defeating parameter sniffing by using local variables in queries instead of parameters. Here's an example showing how you could apply this technique to the usp_GetProductTransactionHistory stored procedure:

```
CREATE PROCEDURE usp_GetProductTransactionHistory @ProductID int AS
DECLARE @v_ProductID int
SET @v_ProductID = @ProductID

SELECT SUM (Quantity) AS Quantity, AVG (ActualCost) AS AvgCost
FROM Production.TransactionHistory
WHERE ProductID = @v_ProductID
GO
```

Note that the WHERE clause now references the local variable @v_ProductID instead of directly referencing the @ProductID value. The value of the local variable is not known at compilation time because it is not set until execution of the stored procedure begins. Using a local variable in a query forces the optimizer to use average column density to estimate the number of rows that will be returned by a filter. This effectively disables parameter sniffing for the query. The plan that is chosen may not be the ideal one (you are, after all, depriving the optimizer of important information that it would normally use when selecting a plan), but at least it will be consistent and will not vary from one parameter value to another.

Using local variables to defeat parameter sniffing is a fairly common trick, but the OPTION (RECOMPILE) and OPTION (OPTIMIZE FOR) hints that are available in SQL Server 2005 are generally more elegant and slightly less risky solutions.

> **NOTE**
>
> In SQL Server 2005, statement-level compilation allows for compilation of an individual statement in a stored procedure to be deferred until just before the first execution of the query. By then, the local variable's value would be known. Theoretically, SQL Server could take advantage of this to sniff local variable values in the same way that it sniffs parameters. However, because it was common to use local variables to defeat parameter sniffing in SQL Server 7.0 and SQL Server 2000, sniffing of local variables was not enabled in SQL Server 2005. It may be enabled in a future SQL Server release, though, which is a good reason to use one of the other options outlined in this chapter if you have a choice.

Plan Guides

Sometimes you may find that you want to apply a hint like OPTION (RECOMPILE) or OPTION (OPTIMIZE FOR) to a parameterized query, but it is not practical to modify the application that is submitting the query. In SQL Server 2005, you can tackle this situation with a plan guide. Let's assume you found that this query was falling victim to parameter sniffing–related performance problems:

```
EXEC sp_executesql
  N'SELECT SUM (Quantity) AS Quantity, AVG (ActualCost) AS AvgCost
    FROM Production.TransactionHistory
    WHERE ProductID = @ProductID',
  N'@ProductID int',
  @ProductID=843
```

To create a plan guide for this parameterized query, you pass the exact text of the parameterized query and the query hint you want to apply to it to sp_create_plan_guide:

```
EXEC sp_create_plan_guide N'MyPlanGuide1',
  @stmt=N'SELECT SUM (Quantity) AS Quantity, AVG (ActualCost) AS AvgCost
    FROM Production.TransactionHistory
    WHERE ProductID = @ProductID',
  @type=N'sql',
  @module_or_batch=NULL,
  @params=N'@ProductID int',
  @hints=N'OPTION (RECOMPILE)'
```

After the plan guide has been created, the OPTION (RECOMPILE) hint will be implicitly added to the query whenever it arrives. All of this can happen with zero changes to the application that runs the query. Plan guides allow you to instantly apply hints, force a particular query plan, or turn forced parameterization on and off for any query. They are a powerful new tool for Database Administrators in SQL Server 2005 that empower the DBA to solve a wide range of problems that previously would have required an application modification. I'll point out other opportunities to take advantage of plan guides as we discuss other problems.

Drop the plan guide when you are finished so that it doesn't affect subsequent exercises:

```
EXEC sp_control_plan_guide @operation=N'DROP', @name=N'MyPlanGuide1'
```

Modifying Parameter Values

Any novice programmer will quickly learn that it is smart to avoid unnecessary assumptions about user input. It may therefore seem helpful, even necessary, to "clean up" user-specified parameter values before using them. For example, it's common to see stored procedures that will replace a NULL parameter with some reasonable default value. Here's another example, showing the work of a thoughtful programmer who felt that it would be nice to ensure that a LIKE search string included wildcards:

```
CREATE PROCEDURE usp_SearchContactEmail @SearchSubstring nvarchar(100) AS
-- Add a trailing wildcard if the user didn't provide one
IF RIGHT(RTRIM(@SearchSubstring),1) != '%' SET @SearchSubstring =
@SearchSubstring + '%'
IF LEFT(LTRIM(@SearchSubstring),1) != '%' SET @SearchSubstring = '%' +
@SearchSubstring

SELECT * FROM Person.Contact WHERE EmailAddress LIKE @SearchSubstring

GO
```

Can you spot the danger in this stored procedure? Parameter sniffing uses the original parameter value when estimating the number of rows that will be returned by an operation. Consider what would happen if a user passed in a value of A for the @SearchString parameter. When compiling a plan for the final SELECT statement, SQL Server would substitute the value A for the @SearchSubstring parameter. There are no rows with an EmailAddress of exactly A, so SQL would estimate that at most a single row will be returned by the query. Based on this estimate, the optimizer would choose to use a plan based on an index seek. However, after the plan has been selected, the @SearchSubstring parameter is modified at execution time by adding leading and trailing wildcards. Instead of returning zero rows, the modified search string returns every row in the table! The most efficient plan to use in this case would have been a table scan, but you end up stuck with a much less efficient plan that was optimized for a value that could never be the actual runtime value of the parameter.

Now, I'm definitely not recommending that you just cross your fingers and hope that you never get an unexpected piece of input. Instead, you should try to defer compilation of any query that uses parameters until those parameters have taken on their final value. One way to do this would be to use sp_executesql to execute the query in a different scope:

```
CREATE PROCEDURE usp_SearchContactEmail @SearchSubstring nvarchar(100) AS
-- Add a trailing wildcard if the user didn't provide one
IF RIGHT(RTRIM(@SearchSubstring),1) != '%' SET @SearchSubstring =
@SearchSubstring + '%'
IF LEFT(LTRIM(@SearchSubstring),1) != '%' SET @SearchSubstring = '%' +
@SearchSubstring

EXEC sp_executesql
  N'SELECT * FROM Person.Contact WHERE EmailAddress LIKE @P1',
  N'@P1 nvarchar(100)', @P1 = @SearchSubstring

GO
```

You could also use the OPTION (RECOMPILE) hint that we discussed earlier:

```
SELECT * FROM Person.Contact WHERE EmailAddress LIKE @SearchSubstring
OPTION (RECOMPILE)
```

The OPTION (RECOMPILE) hint doesn't prevent parameter sniffing, but it does modify its behavior slightly by sniffing the parameter values as they are when the query is compiled, just prior to query execution.

Personally, I would lean toward the use of OPTION (RECOMPILE) for a query like this one. This is because the number of rows returned by different LIKE parameters can so vary so wildly. One parameter value will return no rows; the next will qualify every row in the table. This variability just begs for parameter sniffing problems, and makes it very unlikely that a single plan will be reasonable for all parameter values. Inequality predicates like WHERE column > @userprovidedparameter are also susceptible to parameter sniffing problems for the same reason. They also make good candidates for a carefully considered OPTION (RECOMPILE) hint.

Forced Parameterization and Parameter Sniffing

Forced parameterization may provide you with parameterization and plan reuse for free, but it carries with it all the parameter sniffing risks that come with explicit parameterization. Let's suppose you have determined that, overall, your workload benefits significantly from forced parameterization. During testing, though, you have identified a particular query that now suffers from occasional bad plan issues because you are sometimes reusing a plan that was optimized for an atypical parameter:

```
SELECT SUM (Quantity) AS Quantity, AVG (ActualCost) AS AvgCost
FROM Production.TransactionHistory
WHERE ProductID = 843
```

You have three options for handling this problem. You should already be familiar with two of them: Add an OPTION (RECOMPILE) or an OPTION (OPTIMIZE FOR) hint to the query. These hints can be applied directly (if you can modify the application), or via a plan guide. The third option is to use a *template plan guide* to disable forced parameterization for this particular query.

To create a template plan guide, you must first retrieve the standard parameterized form of the query from sp_get_query_template. SQL Server will match this to any instance of your query that arrives, regardless of the particular inline ProductID value. Then, an OPTION (PARAMETERIZATION SIMPLE) hint will disable forced parameterization for the query:

```
DECLARE @stmt nvarchar(max)
DECLARE @params nvarchar(max)
EXEC sp_get_query_template
  N'SELECT SUM (Quantity) AS Quantity, AVG (ActualCost) AS AvgCost
  FROM Production.TransactionHistory
  WHERE ProductID = 843',
  @stmt OUTPUT,
  @params OUTPUT
EXEC sp_create_plan_guide N'MyTemplatePlanGuide',
  @stmt,
  N'TEMPLATE',
  NULL,
```

```
@params,
N'OPTION(PARAMETERIZATION SIMPLE)'
```

Use `sp_control_plan_guide` to drop the plan guide:

```
EXEC sp_control_plan_guide @operation=N'DROP', @name=N'MyTemplatePlanGuide'
```

You can also use this technique in reverse. In other words, you can leave the database in simple parameterization mode, and use a template plan guide to apply an `OPTION (PARAMETERIZATION FORCED)` hint just to those particular queries that you have determined would benefit most from parameterization.

High Compile Time Due to Poor Plan Reuse

The less often SQL reuses a existing plan, the more often it will have to use CPU cycles compiling new query plans. A high enough rate of compilation can bring a server to its knees.

Detecting Excessive Compilation

Excessive compilation due to poor plan reuse usually manifests itself as high CPU utilization (as a rule of thumb, I look for utilization rates greater than 80% for a sustained period) across all the CPUs that the SQL Server instance is using. However, many other things can also cause high CPU utilization, so even if you are suffering from high CPU usage, you should check for one of the following conditions before concluding that you need to reduce unnecessary query compilation:

- Examine the "Object Plans" and "SQL Plans" instances of the SQLServer:Plan Cache\Cache Hit Ratio performance monitor counter. Ideally, the cache hit ratio should be fairly high (>80%). If it is considerably lower than this during problem periods and if you have a sustained query execution rate greater than about 20 queries/sec for decision support workloads, or 100 queries/sec for simple OLTP workloads, there is a possibility that you could lower your CPU usage by increasing your plan cache hit ratio. You can use the SQLServer:SQL Statistics\Batch Requests/sec performance monitor counter to determine your server's query execution rate.

- If you frequently see queries waiting with a `RESOURCE_SEMAPHORE_QUERY_COMPILE` waittype in `sys.dm_exec_requests`, this can also be an indication that improved plan reuse could help improve performance.

Here are the most effective ways to increase your plan reuse rate:

- Explicitly parameterize your queries.

- Turn on forced parameterization, either for individual high-volume queries (through template plan guides) or at the database level.

- If many different users in a database are all running the same queries, be sure that the tables referenced in those queries are schema-qualified.

- Apply the latest SQL Server 2005 service pack. An issue in the original release of SQL Server 2005 could cause certain parameterized queries to unnecessarily flood the procedure cache with large numbers of nearly identical plans.

You probably don't need to rewrite entire applications to significantly improve your overall plan reuse rate. With most workloads, a very small number of queries (fewer than 10 or 20) comprise the majority of the workload, as measured by query frequency. It is generally sufficient to achieve consistent plan reuse for your most frequently executed queries.

Let's take a look at an example of this problem and solve it using two of the approaches listed previously. The following exercises make use of an application named ParamDemo.exe, a simple .NET Framework 2.0 command line utility that is written in C#. The source code for the utility can be found on the CD in the ProcCache\Parameters folder. The utility runs the following fairly simple query a number of times and then reports total and average query duration.

```
SELECT *
FROM Sales.SalesOrderHeader h
LEFT OUTER JOIN Sales.SalesOrderDetail d ON h.SalesOrderID = d.SalesOrderID
LEFT OUTER JOIN Sales.vSalesPerson p ON h.SalesPersonID = p.SalesPersonID
LEFT OUTER JOIN Sales.vSalesPersonSalesByFiscalYears sfy ON sfy.SalesPersonID
= h.SalesPersonID
WHERE h.OrderDate BETWEEN '20040101' AND '20040110' AND h.SalesPersonID = 199
```

The utility runs the query without any parameterization if you pass -R0 on the command line. If you pass -R1, it executes the same query using explicit parameterization. Here are the two most important methods in the utility. The first runs the query with explicit parameterization; the second runs it without parameterization.

```
static private bool RunQueriesParameterized()
{
    SqlCommand cmd = new SqlCommand();
    cmd.Connection = cn;

    cmd.CommandText = @"
        SELECT *
        FROM Sales.SalesOrderHeader h
        LEFT OUTER JOIN Sales.SalesOrderDetail d
            ON h.SalesOrderID = d.SalesOrderID
        LEFT OUTER JOIN Sales.vSalesPerson p
            ON h.SalesPersonID = p.SalesPersonID
        LEFT OUTER JOIN Sales.vSalesPersonSalesByFiscalYears sfy
            ON sfy.SalesPersonID = h.SalesPersonID
        WHERE h.OrderDate BETWEEN @StartDate AND @EndDate
            AND h.SalesPersonID = @SalesPersonID";
    cmd.Parameters.Add("@StartDate", SqlDbType.DateTime);
    cmd.Parameters.Add("@EndDate", SqlDbType.DateTime);
    cmd.Parameters.Add("@SalesPersonID", SqlDbType.Int);
```

```
    Console.WriteLine("Running parameterized query {0} times with different
parameter values...",
        QueryIterations);
    long TickCount = Environment.TickCount;
    for (int i = 0; i < QueryIterations; i++)
    {
        cmd.Parameters["@SalesPersonID"].Value = i;
        cmd.Parameters["@StartDate"].Value = DateTime.Parse("2004/01/01",
CultureInfo.InvariantCulture);
        cmd.Parameters["@EndDate"].Value = DateTime.Parse("2004/01/10",
CultureInfo.InvariantCulture);
        cmd.ExecuteNonQuery();
    }
    TickCount = Environment.TickCount - TickCount;
    Console.WriteLine("\n      Query executions: {0}", QueryIterations);
    Console.WriteLine("  Total execution time: {0} ms", TickCount);
    Console.WriteLine("Average execution time: {0} ms", TickCount /
QueryIterations);

    return true;
}

static private bool RunQueriesNotParameterized()
{
    SqlCommand cmd = new SqlCommand();
    cmd.Connection = cn;

    Console.WriteLine("Running non-parameterized query {0} times with
different inline literal values...",
        QueryIterations);
    long TickCount = Environment.TickCount;
    for (int i = 0; i < QueryIterations; i++)
    {
        cmd.CommandText = @"
            SELECT *
            FROM Sales.SalesOrderHeader h
            LEFT OUTER JOIN Sales.SalesOrderDetail d
                ON h.SalesOrderID = d.SalesOrderID
            LEFT OUTER JOIN Sales.vSalesPerson p
                ON h.SalesPersonID = p.SalesPersonID
            LEFT OUTER JOIN Sales.vSalesPersonSalesByFiscalYears sfy
                ON sfy.SalesPersonID = h.SalesPersonID
            WHERE h.OrderDate BETWEEN '20040101' AND '20040110'
                AND h.SalesPersonID = " + i.ToString();
        cmd.ExecuteNonQuery();
    }
    TickCount = Environment.TickCount - TickCount;
    Console.WriteLine("\n      Query executions: {0}", QueryIterations);
    Console.WriteLine("  Total execution time: {0} ms", TickCount);
    Console.WriteLine("Average execution time: {0} ms", TickCount /
QueryIterations);

    return true;
}
```

Exercise: Improving Plan Reuse with Explicit Parameterization

1. Start Performance Monitor and add the SQLServer:Plan Cache(SQL Plans)\Cache Hit Ratio counter.

2. Run the `ProcCache\Parameters\ParamDemo.exe` utility using the following command line. This will execute a fairly simple query 200 times, without any form of parameterization. Note the amount of time that it takes to execute. On my server, it completed 200 executions of the query in about 15 seconds.

   ```
   paramdemo.exe -S yoursqlserver -R0
   ```

   Sample output:

   ```
   Connecting to SQL...
   Clearing procedure cache...
   Running non-parameterized query 200 times with different inline literal
   values...

        Query executions: 200
     Total execution time: 14828 ms
   Average execution time: 74 ms
   ```

3. Note the cache hit ratio reported by the Performance Monitor counter. It should be at or near 0, indicating a very low rate of plan reuse.

4. Execute the utility again, but this time tell `ParamDemo.exe` to explicitly parameterize the query (do this by passing the `-R1` command-line parameter):

   ```
   paramdemo.exe -S yoursqlserver -R1
   ```

   Sample output:

   ```
   Connecting to SQL...
   Clearing procedure cache...
   Running non-parameterized query 200 times with different inline literal
   values...

        Query executions: 200
     Total execution time: 145 ms
   Average execution time: 0 ms
   ```

5. Note the new cache hit ratio in Performance Monitor. It should be near 1.0, indicating a high rate of plan reuse.

As you can see, eliminating unnecessary compiles of this particular query increased the speed of the application by a factor of about 100. This is an extreme example of the dangers of poor plan reuse. It also highlights the potential performance benefits that could be seen if you manage to improve a compile-bound workload's plan cache hit ratio.

Exercise: Improving Plan Reuse with Forced Parameterization

The `ParamDemo.exe` application was written to support explicit parameterization of its queries, but suppose you're dealing with an application that can't be easily modified to explicitly parameterize its queries. Let's see whether we can approximate the perf benefits of explicit parameterization by taking advantage of the forced parameterization feature in SQL Server 2005:

1. Run the `ProcCache\Parameters\ParamDemo.exe` utility using the following command line. This will execute a query 200 times, without any form of parameterization. Note the amount of time that it takes to execute.

```
paramdemo.exe -S yoursqlserver -RO
```

Sample output:

```
Connecting to SQL...
Clearing procedure cache...
Running non-parameterized query 200 times with different inline literal
values...

        Query executions: 200
   Total execution time: 15735 ms
 Average execution time: 78 ms
```

2. Run the following command to enable forced parameterization in the AdventureWorks database:

```
ALTER DATABASE AdventureWorks SET PARAMETERIZATION FORCED
```

3. Now run `ParamDemo.exe` again. Use the exact same command line, including the `-RO` command-line parameter to tell the utility *not* to explicitly parameterize its queries:

```
paramdemo.exe -S yoursqlserver -RO
```

Sample output:

```
Connecting to SQL...
Clearing procedure cache...
Running non-parameterized query 200 times with different inline literal
values...

        Query executions: 200
   Total execution time: 187 ms
 Average execution time: 0 ms
```

4. Return the AdventureWorks database to Simple Parameterization mode:

```
ALTER DATABASE AdventureWorks SET PARAMETERIZATION SIMPLE
```

These are impressive results. Without modifying a single line of application code, forced parameterization delivered the same degree of plan reuse as explicit parameterization and nearly identical performance benefits.

As we saw earlier, parameterizing a query can expose it to parameter sniffing–related performance problems, so be careful about enabling forced parameterization without thorough testing. Also, don't forget that enabling forced parameterization will effectively disable use of any indexed views in your database. If you don't have the opportunity to test out the impact of forced parameterization, an alternative would be to identify the 5 or 10 most frequently executed queries that aren't explicitly parameterized, and create template plan guides to turn on forced parameterization just for those queries. This more surgical approach could provide nearly as large a benefit as explicit parameterization, with a much lower risk of parameter sniffing problems. However, it does require a bit more work than running a single ALTER DATABASE command.

High CPU Due to Excessive Cache Lookup Time

If you have a high CPU issue, the first task is to determine whether the CPU cycles are being spent on query execution (remember that you can use sys.dm_exec_query_stats to find the expensive query in many cases). If the CPU time is not being spent on query execution, the next most common cause is excessive query compilation, as we just discussed. If your plan cache hit ratio is high and you do not feel that query compile time is the cause of the problem, you can run this query to check to see whether an excessively long hash chain is slowing down cache lookups for one of your most frequently executed queries.

```
SELECT * FROM sys.dm_os_memory_cache_hash_tables
WHERE [type] IN ('CACHESTORE_OBJCP', 'CACHESTORE_SQLCP', 'CACHESTORE_PHDR',
'CACHESTORE_XPROC')
```

Check the buckets_max_length column to see whether you currently have buckets with more than a few dozen entries. Also, check the buckets_avg_scan_hit_length and buckets_avg_scan_miss_length columns to see whether the typical cache lookup has to pay the cost of examining more than 10 or 20 entries.

If you feel you are hitting this problem, query the sys.dm_exec_cached_plans DMV to find the buckets that are overpopulated. If the plans cached in these buckets are variations on the same query, use the techniques we have already discussed to try to get a single plan to be reused instead of having multiple plans in cache for different instances of the same query.

```
SELECT p.bucketid,
   p.cacheobjtype + ' (' + p.objtype + ')' AS cacheobjtype,
   sql.text AS sql_text, p.plan_handle
FROM sys.dm_exec_cached_plans p
OUTER APPLY sys.dm_exec_sql_text (p.plan_handle) AS sql
WHERE p.bucketid IN (
```

```
  SELECT bucketid
  FROM sys.dm_exec_cached_plans
  GROUP BY bucketid
  HAVING COUNT(*) > 30)
ORDER BY p.bucketid
```

Memory Pressure Caused by Procedure Cache

If the procedure cache grows large enough, it can deprive other caches in SQL Server of
memory that could be used to speed up critical operations. It is possible to get into a situation
where new plans are being inserted into the cache at a faster rate than the resource
monitor can remove them. You can tell whether this is the case by checking to see
whether the size of one of the procedure cache cachestores significantly exceeds the limits
described in the "Procedure Cache and Memory" section of this chapter. Brief periods
where these limits are exceeded are not abnormal; the cachestore size should stay above
these limits for an extended period of time.

The best solution to this problem is to prevent flooding of the procedure cache with low-value
plans that are rarely or never reused. For example, turn on forced parameterization
at the query level (via plan guides) or database level, or modify the application to explicitly
parameterize its high-volume queries.

Cached Object Leaks

Sometimes a coding error can result in a user application opening cursors and forgetting
to close them. If the cursor leak goes on long enough, eventually the procedure cache will
consume the entire SQL Server buffer pool and simple operations will begin to fail with
out-of-memory messages (error 701, for example). An out-of-memory condition can be
caused by many things, but you can rule the possibility of a cached object leak in or out
by running a query like this one:

```
SELECT [name], type, single_pages_kb, multi_pages_kb, entries_count
FROM sys.dm_os_memory_cache_counters r
WHERE [type] IN
  ('CACHESTORE_OBJCP', 'CACHESTORE_SQLCP', 'CACHESTORE_PHDR',
'CACHESTORE_XPROC')
```

Compare the output of this query to the approximate size limits discussed in the
"Procedure Cache and Memory" section earlier in this chapter. If the procedure cache has
grown much larger than its allowed limits, run the following query:

```
SELECT
  cacheobjtype, usecounts, size_in_kb, dbname,
  [Executable Plan] AS ec_count, [Cursor] AS cursors,
  sql_text
FROM (
  SELECT
    p.cacheobjtype + ' (' + p.objtype + ')' AS cacheobjtype,
    p.usecounts, p.size_in_bytes / 1024 AS size_in_kb,
```

```
        CASE WHEN pa.value=32767 THEN 'ResourceDb'
        ELSE ISNULL (DB_NAME (CAST (pa.value AS int)), CONVERT (sysname,
pa.value))
        END as dbname,
        pdo.cacheobjtype AS pdo_cacheobjtype,
        REPLACE (REPLACE (sql.text, CHAR(13), ' '), CHAR(10), ' ') AS sql_text
    FROM sys.dm_exec_cached_plans p
    OUTER APPLY sys.dm_exec_plan_attributes (p.plan_handle) pa
    OUTER APPLY sys.dm_exec_cached_plan_dependent_objects (p.plan_handle) AS pdo
    OUTER APPLY sys.dm_exec_sql_text (p.plan_handle) AS sql
    WHERE pa.attribute = 'dbid'
) t1
PIVOT (
    COUNT(pdo_cacheobjtype) FOR pdo_cacheobjtype IN ([Executable Plan],
[Cursor])
) AS pvt2
GROUP BY cacheobjtype, usecounts, size_in_kb, dbname,
    [Executable Plan], [Cursor], sql_text
ORDER BY size_in_kb DESC
```

This query orders the cache entries by their size, in kilobytes. Check the top of the list for any large objects that consume many megabytes of memory and could be individually responsible for the out-of-memory condition. If you find suspects of this sort, check the cursors column for the plan; if the cursor count is in the thousands, it is likely that you have a bug in your application that is causing the application to open cursors and fail to close them. Use the database name and query text associated with the compiled plan to track down the source of the leak.

Exercise: Identifying Cursor Leaks

This exercise will deliberately leak cursors. You should only run this on a test server.

1. Run this script to leak 10,000 cursors:

```
CREATE TABLE #cursoutput (i int)
GO
DECLARE @x int
DECLARE @P1 int
SET @x = 1
SET NOCOUNT ON
WHILE (@x < 10000)
BEGIN
    INSERT INTO #cursoutput EXEC sp_cursoropen @P1 OUTPUT, 'SELECT 1'
    SET @x = @x + 1
END
GO
```

2. Run the SELECT query listed earlier in this section. This source of the leak should be clearly visible in the output.

3. Log out of the query window where you ran queries in step 1. This should allow the leaked cursors to be freed.

Conclusion

The procedure cache exists to reduce or eliminate the cost of query compilation wherever possible. By doing this, it reduces the cost of each query execution and minimizes the cost of the increasingly intelligent query optimizer. Code that makes good use of the procedure cache can see significant performance gains.

SQL and object query plans are stored in separate cachestores that can respond to both external memory pressure (a low free buffer count) and internal memory pressure (cache size limits).

If you are a DBA, you need to know about the procedure cache so that you can recognize and fix caching-related problems. You also want to be able to take advantage of new procedure cache features that can be invaluable when troubleshooting general performance issues and other problems.

If you are a developer, you need to know how the procedure cache works so that you can develop code that ensures plan reuse in the appropriate places. Without this, as your transaction volume swells, your application will hit scalability limits that could have been avoided.

You should now know more about how to write an application that promotes healthy reuse of query plans and how to troubleshoot common problems like memory errors, high CPU due to excessive compilation, and long cache lookup times that can occur when an application is not written to encourage plan reuse. You should be able to recognize and avoid problems like parameter sniffing that can occur in those cases where parameterization is unsafe. And you should be familiar with some very useful tools—like the sys.dm_exec_query_stats DMV—that the cache provides you.

Query Processor Issues

By Cesar Galindo-Legaria

Core to the value proposition of modern databases is the ability to reason and manipulate data at a high level of abstraction. You don't have to think about and design the detailed layout of bytes in memory or on disk, but need only to think of your data as making up rows in a table that can grow and shrink. You don't have to design and implement data structures that allow you to navigate and access information as part of your application. Finally, when writing the logic of an application, you don't need to encode detailed access navigation patterns, but can express search conditions through very simple and very general predicates.

Query Processor Basics

The query processor fills the gap between your high-level searching and update operations and efficient execution plans. A query execution engine provides a spectrum of data manipulation algorithms that are effective for a variety of scenarios. A query optimizer analyzes the high-level data requests—queries or updates—and decides which of the various choices is appropriate at this point, based on the state of your data, its volume and distribution, and the available indices. Bottom line, the query processor provides applications flexibility, ease of use, and performance.

Compared to standard programming languages such as VB or C#, the gap between the SQL query abstraction and its execution is very large, as is the spectrum of choices for execution and the different performance behavior of each choice. The most efficient way of executing a particular query for some state of your database may be 100 times slower than another plan for the same query but a different database state. The argument goes both ways: Effective query optimization gives you dramatic performance improvements, and optimization failures can cause dramatic slowdowns.

In this chapter, we cover the basics of query processing and optimization, talk about how to diagnose and troubleshoot common issues, and go over some best practices to get efficient and reliable behavior out of the query processor.

Compilation-Execution Sequence

The basic execution model for SQL is on-demand compilation, but there are some quirks and details that need to be understood for efficient troubleshooting and application development. The *execution plan* for a query can be seen as the object code for some abstract machine and it has the following dependencies:

- The query text is the source code.

- The plan has a hard dependency on the metadata version. Metadata is expected to change as part of the regular maintenance of an application (for example, by the addition or removal of indices). These changes invalidate existing execution plans.

- The plan has a soft dependency on the database contents. Correctness of execution plans does not depend on the size of the tables involved, but efficiency does. So, a plan that was adequate for a particular database state may need to change if the data contents have changed sufficiently.

Figure 5-1 shows the logic of executing a SQL request.

The basic flow of execution for a request is the following:

- For query operations, client *requests* are basically the invocation of a stored procedure with particular parameter values, or the execution of a dynamic SQL batch.

- The system first checks the *plan cache* (also known as the *procedure cache*) to see if an execution plan exists for the request. The query identity is defined by its text (i.e., the name of the stored procedure or the SQL text), plus additional context information that affects the interpretation of the query text, such as some connection options.

- If no plan is found for the query, we *compile* the query to generate an execution for all queries in the stored procedure or in the dynamic SQL batch. Execution plans are placed in the cache.

- The plan identified for the request is *validated* for metadata and data statistics changes. If the plan is invalid, we discard it and *recompile* the query.

- Validated plans are then *executed* and results are returned to the client.

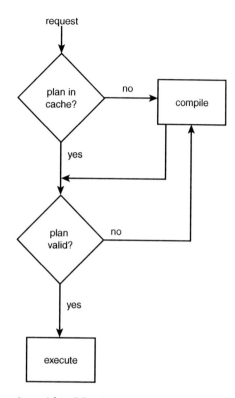

FIGURE 5-1   Request execution within SQL Server

The plan cache is a main memory structure and is never stored on disk. Under memory pressure, SQL Server will gradually discard its contents and repeated query requests may incur new compilation.

Execution Plans

The query execution engine implements a number of generic data manipulation and processing operations that are combined to construct query execution plans. These operations are called *iterators*. In general, they consume a stream of rows and output a stream of rows. The data flow is demand-driven—consumers requesting rows drive producers to do work. Some iterators such as sort are called *stop-and-go* because they need to read all the input rows before starting to produce any output; others such as filter are called *pipelined* because they work on one row at a time.

Iterators are combined in many different forms to implement execution plans, but it is convenient to think about two prototypical types of plans: *navigational* and *set-oriented*. Navigational plans touch only a few rows on conditions that are supported by indices, usually doing random disk I/Os. Set-oriented plans touch a large number of rows, exploit sequential I/O, and perform special data preparation steps such as sorting or partitioning to process data in bulk. Note that queries specify only a logical data request, but do not tell which type of plan to use. It is the task of the query optimizer to determine the plan.

The typical query execution tradeoff is captured by cost graphs, as shown in Figure 5-2.

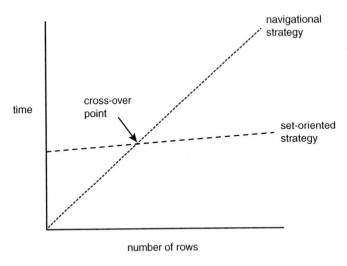

FIGURE 5-2   Cost graphs in query execution

Navigational strategies are very efficient to process a few rows, but the cost goes up quickly as the number of rows increases. Set-oriented strategies have a high up-front cost but a small incremental cost to produce more rows. The exact cross-over point and the maximum distance between the cost lines depend on the strategies under consideration. Later in this section, we go into more detail of the comparison between navigational index lookup join and set-oriented hash join.

Index Operations
Index access is one of the main tools for efficient execution of queries. The query processor exploits indices in three forms: to look up values qualifying a condition, to deliver a set of columns required in a query, and to deliver rows in sorted order.

Directly locating rows that match a condition can make a huge difference in the execution of queries because it avoids examination of every row in the table. For search purposes, the conceptual view of our B-tree structure is a list of rows, sorted by some columns, with a fast operation to find the first or last row for specific values of the sort columns and the ability to scan forwards or backwards from that point until a stopping condition. Index searches provide a navigational execution strategy for queries (i.e., find some rows in a particular table, and then find their matching rows in other tables).

Some simple conditions such as A = 5, B > 20, or C IN (3, 5, 7) have relatively straightforward translations for index searches. Others, such as D LIKE 'pre%', require a somewhat more elaborate translation. There are conditions that could be mapped to indexed searches but are currently not handled by the query optimizer (e.g., E / 12 > 100).

A very important issue to consider when designing or troubleshooting index issues is whether or not indices are *covering* for the columns required in a query. Secondary indices typically store only a subset of the columns available in the table. Such an index can quickly locate row identifiers qualifying some filter condition, but if the index doesn't contain all the columns necessary for the query, we need to retrieve them from the base table. Such an index is said to be non-covering for the query. Retrieving extra columns from the base table is effectively another index lookup operation, and it typically requires random I/Os. For this reason, when the number of rows qualified by the non-covering index is sufficiently large, the query optimizer will prefer a sequential scan of the base table.

Indices can also be used to provide the rows in sorted order. However, the comments about column coverage apply here as well, so a non-covering index is rarely used to provide sorted order.

Sorting and Hashing

Sorting and hashing can be seen as preprocessing data or constructing efficient access paths on-the-fly, in the context of certain queries. In particular, they optimize the process of finding matches, or equal values in large data sets. We may want to find the rows with equal values within a single table to compute grouping operations such as total number of orders per store or per customer. Or we may want to find the matching rows across two or more tables. These on-the-fly access paths are the basis for execution of ad hoc queries that have no pre-declared supporting indices. But even when there are indices available, sorting and hashing are further optimized to process a large number of rows at a time and exploit sequential I/O operations.

To see the differences between navigational and set-oriented strategies, consider execution of a join of two tables, customers and orders. Assume that we want to find all orders placed by a set of customers and an index on customerid exists in orders. These are some of the possible choices:

- **Index lookup into orders.** First, the navigational strategy is to do direct lookups in the customerid index and immediately find the qualifying orders. But, in general, these lookups will be scattered in random positions in the orders table, so a number of random I/Os will take place. Furthermore, each random I/O retrieves a page full of rows, yet only a few of those rows may be of interest. And each row lookup requires traversing the B-tree from the root. So, only the qualifying rows are accessed but the cost per row can be stiff.

- **Sort lookup keys.** An improvement over simple lookup is to sort the keys that will be looked up, which improves the locality of the operation. If multiple rows happen to be in the same disk page, they will be accessed consecutively so there is no need to load the same page multiple times into memory, regardless of the available buffer size. Also, if neighboring pages are required, they will also be requested consecutively, increasing disk access locality. The cost per qualifying orders row is reduced, but extra cost is incurred in sorting the lookup keys.

- **Hash join.** A third, completely set-oriented alternative is to build a hash table on the customers of interest, and then read the orders table sequentially and probe into the hash table. The cost per row is the lowest, both in I/O and CPU. Sequential I/O is much cheaper than random I/O, and hash tables are optimized for equality lookups and are cheaper in terms of CPU in comparison with B-tree traversal. However, using this strategy requires reading the entire orders table.

Choosing an execution strategy for a particular query is based on models that expand on the preceding ideas.

The package of sort-oriented operations is made up of sort itself, stream aggregation, and merge join. Stream aggregation takes an input table that is sorted on the grouping keys and identifies group breaks as it reads its input. It aggregates data for each group, if needed, and outputs one row per group. Merge join takes as input two tables sorted on the join key and progressively reads each side, outputting matching rows.

Stream aggregation and merge join are pipelined operations since they work one row at a time. They are often used on top of indices that provide the necessary sort order. As I've mentioned, sorting is a stop-and-go operation since it needs to read its entire input before starting to produce rows. In addition to preparing data for join or aggregation, it is used to increase data locality for index lookup values, and also to sort rows for final presentation.

Hashing operations implement joins and aggregation. The basic implementation pieces are construction and probing into main memory hash tables. To handle data volumes larger than main memory, all or part of the input rows can be saved to disk and processed in chunks.

Parallel Execution

Parallel query execution targets response time reduction by utilizing multiple CPUs to process a query. Executing a query in parallel requires data partitioning and coordination across threads, thus adding processing overhead, so the total amount of work carried out is higher than that of serial execution.

Parallelism is implemented in SQL Server using the exchange operator, which distributes its input data to multiple execution threads, either in a round-robin fashion or using a partitioning function on a set of columns.

Data flow within each thread remains demand-driven. However, data is pushed in batches across exchange operators. This modifies the flow dynamics, in particular when a result is not consumed in its entirety. In serial execution, the extent of processing is only that required to deliver the rows requested by the root or consuming operators. This allows some optimizations, such as inner hash join not reading any rows from its probe input if there are no rows in the build input and therefore the hash table is empty. In parallel execution, the machinery has some "stopping distance." Multiple parts of the execution plan are activated concurrently and start processing. When later operations decide they no longer need rows, they will close down part of the execution but some extra work may have been done already.

Parallel query execution targets set-oriented queries and its use does not pay off on navigational queries that look up a few rows in indices. The query processor has logic to automatically generate parallel queries on multi-processor machines, for queries that manipulate a large-enough number of rows.

Query Compilation and Plan Selection

The query compilation process is composed of the following main steps:

- The first step consists of parsing the statement text, and resolving names of objects such as tables and columns. It produces a tree representation of the statement based on logical data operators.

- The second step is the logical simplification/normalization step, where predicates are normalized, contradictions are detected, and redundant operations are removed. The output is a simplified logical operator tree representing the query.

- The final step is cost-based optimization, where an execution plan is selected based on available access paths, data volume, and distribution.

The first two steps depend only on the logical database schema and the text of the query, and are independent of the actual database contents. They can be understood as a linear sequence of transformations on the query representation.

The last step is a search process that follows a generate-and-test approach: A (potentially large) number of candidate execution plans are enumerated and their efficiency on the current contents of the database is estimated. The most attractive plan in terms of anticipated execution cost is picked. The search process can be computationally very expensive, so a number of heuristics are used to limit the optimization effort and yet consider the most promising execution plans.

Front-End and Logical Simplification

The front end deals with query syntax, name resolution, and view substitution. View definitions are expanded "in place" in the query that uses them and handed off for optimization. The execution plans considered are the same as if the view definition had been used directly, instead of a view reference.

Logical simplification performs a semantic analysis of the filter predicates and data operations to convert a query into a simpler form. No statistical information or cost models are used during this step, but only constraints declared in the schema. Following are the main optimizations that take place:

- Evaluate constant expressions.

- Push all filter operators down to be evaluated as early as possible.

- Convert subqueries into joins. Depending on the subquery, a regular inner join may not be appropriate to preserve the original semantics, so outerjoins and Group By operations are added when necessary.

- Identify and remove unnecessary joins and outerjoins (e.g., joins on foreign keys where columns of the referenced table are not required in the query).

- Convert outerjoins into joins, when later predicates reject the NULL-padded rows introduced by the join.

- Detect contradictions and eliminate provably empty subexpressions. Contradiction detection considers predicates explicitly written in the query as well as check constraints for the base tables.

One of the targets for the preceding features is to allow the use of views as a programming convenience or for access control, without incurring performance penalties. For example, it may be convenient to expose a view that provides the result of a foreign key join. Many different queries can use such a view, but the join will be executed only for those queries that need it.

Simplification also helps with automatically generated queries, which may include redundant or unnecessary constructs.

Cost-Based Optimization

Cost-based optimization is made up of two main components: generation of candidate plans and estimation of their anticipated execution cost. Unlike query parsing and simplification, selecting an appropriate execution plan depends entirely on the physical access paths available and on the data distribution in the database. A good plan for a particular state of the database contents may be bad for a different state.

SQL Server uses a generic tree transformation approach to generate candidate execution plans. It considers different execution orders and implementation algorithms for join, Group By, and union operations. Unlike competing database systems, the infrastructure for generation of alternatives is not focused on enumerating joins but is capable of dealing with arbitrary data manipulation operators.

Evaluation of candidate plans is itself divided into cardinality and cost estimation. Cardinality estimation is about determining how many rows need to be processed at each step in the query execution plan, while cost estimation is about determining the CPU and I/O expense as well as the elapsed time for each operation. The cost of individual operators is rolled up into a total cost for the entire plan.

Reliability of plan selection depends heavily on the accuracy of estimation for the execution cost, which is implemented through the following layers of functionality:

- Statistics on the database contents are captured in the form of histograms reflecting the distribution of values for a particular column. The number of distinct values for one or more columns is also collected and used for estimation.

- Cardinality estimation uses statistics to predict the number of rows that will be output by filter, join, or Group By operations. New statistics are derived for the results of each intermediate step to be used in estimation of later operations.

- Cost estimation uses a model of the various execution algorithms and plugs in the results of cardinality estimation to predict the CPU, I/O, and elapsed time of each operation in the execution plan. Plans are compared based on their elapsed time.

The starting point for reliable selection of execution plans is up-to-date statistics for all columns involved in comparison operations—filters, joins, or Group By. SQL Server's automatic statistics take care of this case for common cases. If missing statistics are found while compiling a query, they will be created before proceeding with optimization. Also, when validating execution plans, the system checks the amount of change on each table since the time stats were computed for compilation of the plan. If the table has changed enough, statistics are recomputed (and the query recompiled).

Special Optimizations and Scenarios

In this section, I'll talk about some of the special optimizations the query optimizer supports. It has been designed to accommodate a wide variety of scenarios that customers sometimes encounter.

Handling Very Large Queries

The number of feasible execution alternatives for a query can be enormous, and there is no known general and effective shortcut to arrive at the optimal plan. SQL Server implements a number of heuristics to deal with very large queries and adapt the compilation time automatically. But, in general, it is unfeasible to review the entire space of alternatives, and larger estimation errors are encountered with larger queries. The execution plan will start depending on the surface syntax of the query.

When is your query large enough to be a concern? This is a difficult question to answer, because it depends on the number of tables involved, the form of filter and join predicates, and the operations performed. If you are joining over 20 tables, chances are the optimizer is not reviewing the entire space but relying more on heuristics. On the higher end of the scale, we have seen applications that run regular queries dealing with over 100 tables. While it is possible to run such very large queries, you really are stretching the system in these cases and should be very careful going this far.

The current heuristics for large queries target finding a good execution order for a collection of joins. They look for clear "data reduction sequences" by starting with the smallest tables in the query or by the joins that achieve the largest filtering, and then continue joining with the other tables. Outerjoin execution is delayed after the joins. These heuristics work relatively well when the query contains only joins, especially if there is a join sequence that processes few rows and supporting indices exist.

In summary, you can expect the best results in terms of plan quality and reliability on smaller queries; good reliability on larger join-only queries; and less reliability and more dependence on the original query syntax on large queries that also involve non-join operators.

Computed Columns

There are a number of services of the database and the query processor that are centered on the notion of column. For example, you can create indices on particular columns of a table. But it is sometimes the case that queries need to filter not on a column but on the result of some scalar computation, on a scalar expression.

Computed columns allow you to name to scalar expressions in the column name space. After you have named an expression, you can use it in queries as if it were a regular column. In this sense, it can be seen as a lightweight version of views, which allow you to give a name to an arbitrary query computation.

In addition to convenience for query writing, computed columns allow the query processor to do a better job because it enables the creation of indices and (auto-) creation of statistics on such "virtual columns." If you have a filter on an expression and it has no corresponding computed column, very simple heuristics will be used to guess the number of qualifying rows, but no statistics will be used. This may lead to bad plans.

In terms of query processing, computed columns are most useful to have for expressions that will be compared to resolve the query—filtering conditions in the WHERE clause, grouping expressions in the GROUP BY clause, or sorting expressions in the ORDER BY clause. Expressions in the SELECT clause that are not compared but only returned to the client can also benefit from the use of covering, narrow indices, instead of reading the entire table. But the impact here is less, relative to the benefit obtained for cases that do require comparison, so in most common cases it is not worth defining computed columns for expression in the SELECT clause.

In SQL 2005, the query processor implements automatic matching of computed columns, which enables you to create and exploit computed columns without having to change your application. Computed column matching is based on identical comparison. So, a computed column of the form A + B + C will not match an expression of the form A + C + B.

Autoparameterization

Query compilation can take significant resources compared to query execution, especially for very simple and fast queries such as those that only process a few rows and are well supported by indices. Starting in 7.0, SQL Server introduced special support for automatic parameterization of simple queries. The basic idea is to create a single parameterized plan that is used for queries issued by the application that differ only on the constants provided.

It is not always appropriate to parameterize queries and reuse plans. Parameterization tradeoffs are discussed in detail in a separate section. So a very conservative policy is used for autoparameterization. It covers statements such as INSERT VALUES and simple queries retrieving rows by key. A safety analysis is performed based on the existing indices of a table. If a "best" index can be determined logically, independent of the actual parameter value and contents of the database, the parameterized plan is considered safe and reused for different queries.

SQL Server 2005 introduced more extensive server-side parameterization functionality, which needs to be turned on explicitly by users and is described in detail later, along with other control mechanisms. The automatic server parameterization based on safety analysis and available since SQL Sever 7.0 is now called SIMPLE parameterization, and it continues to be on all the time.

Autoparameterization can be very effective in reducing the CPU consumption for applications that issue simple statements dynamically. But it is also relatively fragile, in the sense that it depends on the existing indices of tables. Adding or removing indices can introduce cost-based choices that did not exist before, and cause some queries to not be autoparameterized anymore. Depending on the system load and frequency of those queries, this can result in performance degradation.

You can validate the use of autoparameterization by examining the contents of the plan cache, as described later in the diagnostics section.

It is always preferable that frequent, short-running queries be parameterized at the application level, because this leads to more predictable sharing of plans.

Partial Result Queries

In some situations, the entire result of a query or of parts of a query is not required. For example, you may have a condition of the form

```
EXISTS(SELECT * FROM TABLE)
```

In this case, you are not interested in returning all the rows of the table, but only want to know whether or not the table is empty. Another example is the use of the TOP clause, which allows limiting the number of rows returned. The following query returns the 10 customers with the highest balance from Washington:

```
SELECT TOP 10 *
FROM CUSTOMER
WHERE STATE = 'WASHINGTON'
ORDER BY BALANCE DESC
```

These scenarios are about retrieval of partial results. To implement this functionality, cost estimation considers the number of expected rows to read. The choice of a plan remains cost-based, and there are tradeoffs involved. Take the preceding query and assume table CUSTOMER has two indices: one on BALANCE and one on STATE. There are two possible plans to compute the query:

- Scan the index on BALANCE, which provides the desired Order By. Filter by STATE and stop after retrieving the desired 10 rows.

- Look up the qualifying rows using the STATE predicate, and then sort the results on BALANCE and return the first 10 rows.

Which of the two strategies is better to compute the query? A major factor in the answer is the selectivity of the filter predicate. On one extreme, assume that there are very few customers from Washington. In that case, we may scan a large part of the BALANCE index and reject many rows until we collect 10 rows from Washington. It would be more efficient to locate the few Washington state rows and then sort them. This strategy does most of the computation required to answer the entire query since it retrieved and sorted all qualifying rows, and then returned only the first 10.

On the other end of the spectrum, assume that most of your customers are in Washington. Reading the BALANCE index, you are likely to find 10 Washington customers quickly—assuming that they are randomly located within the BALANCE index. This is a partial-retrieval strategy that expects to limit the number of rows right at the source.

Estimation of partial-retrieval strategy needs to make assumptions regarding how many rows are needed in order to satisfy a certain number of qualifying rows. The system currently assumes uniformity in the input distribution. So, if your filter has 50% selectivity, one of every two input rows is expected to qualify.

Dynamic and *fast_forward* Cursors

Using a dynamic cursor to consume the result of a query imposes a number of constraints on execution plans for the query. The functionality for dynamic cursors that restrict execution plans can be summarized as follows:

- **Go dormant.** Dynamic cursors can be use to read a few rows, wait for an indefinitely long amount of time, and then read some more rows. Many cursors can be active in the server and read at a different pace. Between cursor fetch operations, the server makes the execution plan "go dormant," releasing server resources and storing only minimal information to be able to continue producing rows from the point where it was suspended.

- **Go forwards and backwards.** Dynamic cursors provide the ability to read the next N rows from the current point, as well as the previous N rows.

- **Return the most recent data.** The rows visible to a dynamic cursor are those committed at the time of the fetch operation, not at the time of cursor creation. Reading over the same cursor multiple times can return different results, reflecting the update activity on the underlying table.

As a result of the preceding requirements, execution plans for dynamic cursors contain no stop-and-go operators. They are based on streaming operations such as index seek, scan, and nested loops. The optimizer operates using the same cost-based principles and actual infrastructure, except that the space of alternatives is reduced because some of the execution algorithms are not allowed. Since you are effectively disabling the set-oriented computation strategies of the query processor, dynamic plans for some queries can be significantly slower than plans you get when you don't request dynamic cursor functionality. It depends on the volume of data to process, the existing indices, and the type of operations performed.

Requesting dynamic cursors with sorted output, through an Order By clause, also requires special care because sort is not allowed in dynamic plans. You need to have an index that supports the desired order. For this reason, you cannot tell syntactically by simply looking at a query whether or not a dynamic plan exists for it, and changes in the physical schema of a table may affect the cursors you are using on such table.

You need to be careful about the functionality associated with dynamic cursors and the plan restrictions that such functionality imposes. A more relaxed cursor type that reduces some of the plan restrictions and may be adequate for your application is fast_forward. This cursor has the ability to go dormant, but allows reading the result in forward direction only and does not guarantee that you see changes to the underlying table.

To implement a fast_forward cursor, the query optimizer makes a cost-based choice between two alternatives:

- A **dynamic plan**, with the restrictions and functionality described previously. It will expose the most recent changes to the base tables.

- An **unrestricted plan** that computes and stores the result at cursor open time. All resources used to compute the result are released after cursor open. Cursor fetches are served from the stored query result. The cursor results are determined at cursor open time and do not reflect later changes to the base tables.

fast_forward cursors are available in SQL Server 2000 and SQL Server 2005.

In SQL Server 2005, you should also consider the use of Multiple Active Result Sets (MARS) instead of cursors, which allow you to issue and consume the result of multiple queries through a single connection. You can find information on how to enable and use MARS in the references at the end of this chapter.

Common Issues

The query process of SQL Server implements reliable and efficient behavior for most customer scenarios, requiring little tuning and administration in comparison with competing products. However, in some situations, the default algorithms do not perform the way expected or required by applications. We next go over some of these problematic situations.

Compilation Time and Parameterization

An issue that is sometimes encountered in applications is long compilation times. There are distinct forms of this problem that we will examine in detail, but here is the main tradeoff: Do you want a more specific and potentially more efficient execution plan that is tailored to a specific query, parameter values, and database state? Or do you want a single generic plan that is used for different conditions? More specific plans will cost more in compilation time, but depending on the circumstances, this will pay off in query execution time.

In general, query compilation is an expensive process and, in some scenarios, can be a significant or even dominant part of the system utilization. If the workload consists of a fixed collection of queries executed for different parameter values, the main tool used to avoid the compilation overhead is parameterization. This way, a single "query template" is compiled and the same plan is used for the different parameter values.

Parameterization is a great too to avoid compilation, but its implications and limits need to be understood to apply it correctly. The drawback of parameterization is that the best execution plan may depend on the actual values of the parameters, especially when data is skewed and some parameter values require processing many more rows than others. In some cases, the performance difference can be very large and the best plan for some parameter values is very inefficient for other values, so avoiding compilation may result in slow execution for some values.

Compilation Time—OLTP

Query compilation can take a significant amount of time in some scenarios and this may be a problem for some applications. But what is meant by "the system is taking too long to compile?"

A scenario where we see long compilation times is with applications that issue queries touching a few rows and navigating via indices—that is, short-running queries in an OLTP system. Both compilation and execution for this class of queries are in the order of milliseconds, so you do see an immediate answer if you execute this query in isolation. However, compilation can take 10 times more work than execution for these kinds of queries, so if you are issuing a large number of requests and compiling every time, your CPU will spend most of its cycles compiling.

If high throughput is important for your application, you need to move compilation out of the critical execution path. And how do you do that? Through parameterization. The best way to approach a high-throughput OLTP system is using parameterized stored procedures. In addition to avoiding compilation, application logic is encoded and executed on the server, potentially avoiding roundtrips to the client.

A lightweight version of stored procedures is the use of sp_executesql to submit queries. You can think of sp_executesql as on-demand definition and invocation of temporary stored procedures. The first call to execute some parameterized query text compiles and generates an execution plan, and puts it in the procedure cache where it is available for later calls. The lifetime of this temporary stored procedure is as long as it remains in the procedure cache. Since the stored procedure definition never goes to metadata, there is no permanent object to maintain in the database.

Using stored procedures or sp_executesql require that the application be written in a particular form. What to do if the application is not using either of the preceding techniques and you cannot change the application code? You can force parameterization of queries on the server side. The result is comparable to having changed the application to use sp_executesql.

You can force parameterization of all statements received by the server through a database option (i.e., the "big hammer" approach). Change the database setting to force parameterization and you will see compilation vanish for queries that are identical except for literal constants. This is extremely easy to do, but there may be some queries in the application that you really don't want to parameterize. We come back to this point later, but the general idea is that the more information is made available to the query optimizer, the better the plans it can generate. So, this global setting needs to be used very carefully and, in my opinion, not very often.

SQL Server's plan guides facility provides a more "surgical" approach to controlling query optimization. Plan guides let you control exceptional problem queries at the server. In the context of parameterization, an exception can be set up from both sides—either you give a list of patterns for which you want query parameterization done, or request global parameterization and provide a query exception list. Providing an explicit list of patterns to parameterize requires more work to set up, but I see it as a safer and effective approach. Oftentimes, there are only a handful of critical templates for short-running queries in a given application. Targeting those templates for parameterization will provide most of the benefit of compilation reduction in a scoped and controlled way.

Parameter-Sensitive Queries
Query parameterization helps minimize compilation overhead and it is critical for a number of applications. However, a parameterized query provides less information to the query optimizer and requires the use of a more general plan. Generally, a more specific plan can be more efficient.

For example, suppose we have a query that looks up the orders shipped to a given state. If there is significant variability in how much is sold to different states, we might have a problem using a query parameterized on state, because some values may require a navigational plan and others a set-oriented plan. A similar situation occurs when the filter condition specifies an interval with parameterized end-points, which can potentially qualify anything from a single row to the entire table. These parameterized queries are compiled on first invocation and the plan generated is based on the first parameter values seen, which introduces some amount of non-determinism. Later memory pressure can cause the plan to be discarded from the cache and cause a new compilation, and potentially a different plan, next time the query is invoked.

The most general solution to the problem is to go the opposite way of parameterization—issue independent queries that specify the constants used through dynamic SQL. The tradeoff here is clear: You are incurring additional compilation overhead in return for a more specific plan, tuned to specific parameter values. For queries that take longer to execute, processing many rows on skewed data, this extra compilation overhead may very well be justifiable.

Instead of using dynamic SQL, you can force query recompilation on each execution with the RECOMPILE query hint. The results are comparable, but not identical. Dynamic SQL does reuse plans, if you happen to use the exact same query text, whereas RECOMPILE will preclude any plan reuse. RECOMPILE is a convenient option over dynamic SQL, in particular in stored procedures, for three main reasons: First, it avoids the complexity of assembling a correct and safe SQL string, when all you are doing is providing the value of some search constants. Second, it avoids security issues related to the fact that dynamic SQL is executed with permissions of the caller and not the stored procedure owner, which may require granting access to more data than you would like. Third, for existing applications, it can be used with plan guides to force recompilation of specific problem queries without the need to change the application code.

The simplest choice for parameter-sensitive plans is to recompile every time and, when possible, this is the preferred alternative that we have discussed so far. However, there are applications where this overhead is unacceptable, and a single plan for a "typical" parameter value is adequate for the full spectrum of query invocations. The tool to use in this case is the OPTIMIZE FOR hint, which lets you specify a parameter value to assume when compiling the query. The optimizer will still generate a plan that is correct for all parameter values, but it will estimate the number of rows to process based on the parameter value provided through OPTIMIZE FOR. This tool preserves the semantics of plan reuse, but removes the non-determinism caused by compilation or recompilation with a different parameter value. Like RECOMPILE, this query hint can be used "surgically" on specific problem queries without changing the application through the use of plan guides.

There is currently no automatic support in the product to keep multiple plans for the same query and pick one at execution time depending on the parameter values. You can implement this behavior in your application by having multiple instances of the same query and calling one of them based on the parameter values seen. For example, you could be directing some specific frequent values to one instance of the query and the rest of the values to a second instance, which use OPTIMIZE FOR to indicate to the optimizer the value to assume and generate different plans. You can have multiple copies of the same query under different stored procedure names and dispatch the call to one of them, based on the parameter value. The optimizer will use parameter sniffing and compile each of the stored procedure instances with different values as they get called. This technique should be used only when strictly necessary because the application code gets polluted with instance-specific information about frequent values, which makes it harder to maintain.

To deal with parameter-sensitive plans, some applications used to implement a "plan-priming step," which executes stored procedures for the first time with a set of typical parameter values before the real workload starts. This helps, but it is not a complete solution because if memory pressure forces some plans out of the cache, the next invocation will cause a compilation for whatever parameter values used at that time. SQL Server 2005 provides a much more reliable alternative with OPTIMIZE FOR and plan guides.

Queues and Volatile Tables

Using tables as queues presents a challenge to the standard mechanisms of the query processor. There are two main issues: First, when the system is started and the first queries are issued, queue tables may be empty, so there is no statistical information to make cost-based decisions for the stable state of the system. Second, since the queue table will be subject to continuous insert and delete operations, the standard statistics policies will trigger regathering of statistics and recompilation relatively frequently. This will cause unnecessary compilation overhead as well as the risk of plan regressions.

Turning off auto-statistics is not recommended, in general. But depending on the throughput requirements, this is a scenario where turning off auto-stats is sometimes necessary. Data changes will no longer trigger regathering of statistics and recompilation of queries. This reduces variability in the system, but it also eliminates a valuable source of information for the query optimizer.

With reduced statistical information, the optimizer can still exploit structural information, and you should make sure to provide as much as possible. The main forms of this information are constraints, unique indices, and generally a set of indices that matches well the query navigation expected in the application.

In some cases, for highly critical queries in the application, it may be appropriate to force specific execution plans through hints.

Compilation Time—Large and Complex Queries

High compilation time can also be seen when processing complex, potentially long-running queries, but the nature of the problem is different than that of the simple, navigational OLTP queries. One can divide compilation time in two aspects: First, there is the minimum overhead of going through the compilation process, parsing a query text, loading information about statistics and indices, and generating a plan. This is code-path overhead, which grows slowly (linearly) with the size of the query and, as discussed earlier, can be higher than executing simple OLTP queries. Second, there is the time required to enumerate and evaluate possible execution alternatives. This is the combinatorial overhead, which can grow very fast (exponentially) with the number of tables and complexity of the query. Thorough examination of feasible execution plans could take hours or even days for a query with two dozen tables.

The query optimizer implements a number of practical heuristics to deal with this combinatorial explosion, achieving a reasonable balance between compilation time and plan quality most of the time. However, these heuristics have limits and they cannot effectively handle all possible cases. It is important to keep in mind that simpler, smaller queries can be handled in a more reliable and efficient way.

What is a large and complex query, anyway? There are a few basic metrics for the actual optimization difficulty of a query in SQL Server:

- **Number of tables involved.** If only a few tables are involved, the query optimizer can and in some cases will consider all execution orders. Beyond a certain number of tables this is impossible, so only a subset of alternatives will be considered. The threshold for comprehensive versus reduced search is not fixed, but depends on the pattern of join predicates and the other complexity metrics listed here.

- **Complexity of data operations.** For optimization purposes, inner joins are easier than outerjoins, subqueries, or grouping/aggregate operations. To be clear, SQL Server does implement very efficient optimizations for the more difficult operators, but these optimizations are harder to identify and apply when queries are large. A query with a dozen tables and no aggregates is considerably simpler to handle than a query with the same dozen tables but three interspersed grouping operations.

- **Simple navigational access paths/clear restriction patterns.**

- **Complexity of filter conditions.**

If your large queries are processing only a handful or rows (as in OLTP scenarios), make sure you have the right indices available. This is likely to address compilation time issues. Do keep in mind that queries that contain multiple Group By operations incur additional expense and are harder to optimize. For those scenarios and also when you are processing a large volume of rows, you may need to split the computation into a sequence of statements, storing intermediate results from one step in a temporary table and consuming the result in the next step.

Cursors

You can have compilation time issues with dynamic cursors that join multiple tables and use an Order By clause. Since dynamic cursor plans do not allow sort operations, the query optimizer needs to find a proper execution order that will exploit existing indices to deliver rows in the requested order.

Sort orders that specify columns from multiple tables may be impossible to satisfy from base table indices. In these scenarios, the query optimizer will end up doing an exhaustive search of the space, only to determine that no plan can satisfy the requirement. At that point, the cursor promotion logic kicks in and a different type of cursor is generated. But by then, a considerable amount of CPU may have been spent.

In summary, the complexity of finding a dynamic cursor with Order By increases rapidly as you join more tables in your query.

Indexing

Efficient index utilization is one of the most important techniques that a query processor can use to execute queries. They are essential for OLTP queries, and are likely to have a major or even dominant role in practically any application.

Missing Indices

When looking into application performance issues, it is not uncommon to find that queries would execute much more efficiently if a particular index were added to the system. Adding this index typically results in reliable and efficient plans and resolves the performance problem.

It is difficult to anticipate all important indices at development or deployment time, and the need for some of them only surfaces after the database has grown sufficiently or when a particular pattern of ad hoc queries becomes common. Given the dramatic impact of having proper indices in the system, this area is one of the first you should examine when facing a performance problem, and perhaps one to be reviewed periodically.

In the diagnostics section, we review the SQL Server tools that give you information about index utilization, possible indices to add to your system, and index configuration recommendations.

A scenario that requires manual handling is indexing for predicates on scalar expressions, to the extent that a computed column needs to be defined. The issue of statistics for scalar expressions is discussed in detail later on. You can create an index to be used for filters on scalar expressions. To do so, you first create a computed column for the expression, and then an index. The two statements to create an index on expression T.A + T.B are the following:

```
ALTER TABLE MYTABLE ADD CC AS A+B
CREATE INDEX MYINDEX_CC ON MYTABLE(CC)
```

Prior to SQL Server 2005, you had to reference column CC directly in your query for the index to be used. This is no longer needed in SQL Server 2005, where scalar expression references will be matched and associated to column CC. Once a computed column is defined, the index diagnostic tools will also provide information relative to the use of the scalar expression/computed column in queries.

An index on computed column can also be used to satisfy Order By requests. For example, you may have common queries that request the output sorted on a different collation such as

```
SELECT ID, NAME
FROM T
ORDER BY NAME COLLATE ICELANDIC_CS_AS
```

The following two statements create an index to support the preceding query and avoid sorting during query execution:

```
ALTER TABLE MYTABLE ADD
CCNAME AS NAME COLLATE ICELANDIC_CS_AS
```

```
CREATE INDEX MYINDEX_CCNAME ON
     MYTABLE(CCNAME) INCLUDE(ID, NAME)
```

Notice that all columns required by the query are included in the index. The Order By query will be answered by scanning the index directly.

Expected Index Not Used

It sometimes happens that you have an index you think should be used to process a particular query, yet the plan does not use it. You can use index hints (described later in the "Control" section) to force the utilization of the index, but it is important for you to know the reasons why a particular index is not used.

Non-Covering Index

When an index can be used to locate rows qualifying a predicate, but it doesn't contain all columns required by the query, the base table needs to be accessed to retrieve the additional columns. This additional base table access was named "fetch" in the showplan of SQL 2000, but in SQL 2005 is shown as an index lookup operation.

Typically, accessing the base table for additional columns will require random I/O because rows appear in different order. Since random I/O is much more expensive than sequential I/O, the lookup must qualify relatively few rows for this strategy to be efficient. In practice, if the non-covering index qualifies more than 1% of the rows, chances are a sequential table scan will be more efficient. This 1% can serve as a rough rule of thumb, but the exact cross-over point is determined by the estimated cost of both alternatives, which depends on the size of the table and the indices.

For this reason, you could have a secondary index that can resolve your filter conditions, yet the execution plan uses a table scan. To address this situation, you can create a covering index (i.e., one that includes all the columns required by the query). In SQL Server 2005, you can create indices with included columns, in addition to the key columns. This is useful to create wide covering indices, while keeping few pages for the lookup structures of the index. For example, to create an index that supports seeking on T.A and also includes columns B, C, D, you use the following command:

```
CREATE INDEX MYINDEX ON T(A) INCLUDE(B, C, D)
```

A clustered index prior to SQL Server 2005 already behaved this way since the lookup structures contain only the clustering key, but the data pages contain all the columns. The index diagnostics tools described later deal with both key and included columns, calling them out explicitly.

Physical Index Correlation

Although, in general, fetching additional columns after a secondary index lookup requires random I/O, there are situations where the order of rows in the non-covering index is highly correlated with their order in the base table. When this physical correlation exists, the assumptions of the costing model for column retrieval don't hold. A non-covering index retrieving 10% of the rows may only need to touch 10% of the base table to fetch additional columns and therefore be much more efficient than a table scan.

The statistics available in SQL Server 2005 do not capture this physical correlation. You can tell that this is the problem if your filter could be resolved by a non-covering index; it qualifies over 1% of the table, but forcing a plan with the index results in a faster plan.

The most robust to address this problem is to create a covering index. Other than that, you need to force the use of the index. The specifics of how to do this are covered in the control section.

Cardinality and Cost Estimation

Proper cardinality and cost estimation are the basis for robust plan selection. Limitations in the estimation model may surface as unreliable plans and unpredictable query performance. Next we go over the most common issues in this area.

Complex Expressions

Cardinality estimation is based on statistics of data distribution in base tables. These statistics are very effective to estimate the number of rows satisfying common predicates, but they are of limited value when estimating complex operations. The situations where cardinality estimation has limited accuracy can be classified as follows:

- **Conditions on complex scalar operations.** For example, you may have a comparison of the form PRICE * (1 – DISCOUNT) > 1000. In general, you cannot make a reliable estimation of the result with statistics on the individual columns.

- **Conditions on UDFs.** These are a special case in point and their estimation is not supported natively by the query optimizer. As a simple rule of thumb, comparison of columns with constant expressions can be estimated very accurately, but comparisons that involve a scalar expression on columns are not estimated as well.

- **Lack of statistics on data source.** There are three cases in SQL Server 2005: Table variables do not support statistics; non-inlined TVFs do not support statistics; and some providers for distributed query do not provide statistics. In all these scenarios, the query optimizer assumes that these tables are small. If this assumption does not hold, or if the tables have skewed distributions, you may run into reliability issues.

- **Complex relational expressions.** These include operations like recursive query or window aggregates (both new in SQL Server 2005). It is very hard to estimate these results accurately, so you may see large errors in the estimation of the result of these constructs.

It is important to note that cardinality estimation problems typically don't affect the operations on which they happen (i.e., the particular filter or recursive query operation), but later choices. For example, underestimating the result of a lower filter may lead to the incorrect choice of a later navigational algorithm because only a few rows are expected, when a set-oriented strategy would have been more efficient. For this reason, when the problematic operation is the last step of the query, you are likely to see a good execution plan, even if the number of final rows or resulting data distributions have estimation errors.

The technique to deal with complex scalar expressions is to introduce computed columns, which is described in detail later. For complex relational expressions, you need to separate the query into multiple steps, storing intermediate results in temporary tables. This allows statistics to be gathered on the intermediate results, leading to more reliable plans.

TOP Queries

Queries that require partial retrieval of results, such as those that use the TOP clause, or EXISTS subqueries, have special costing support. This support is based on the notion of a rowgoal—that is, how many rows out are required from particular parts of the tree. The rowgoal is computed top-down, depending on the cardinality estimation and choice of algorithms.

For example, the rowgoal below a stop-and-go operator is always "all rows," regardless of how many rows are needed by the parent. This is because the operation needs to consume its entire input before returning any results. For a pipelined operation, the rowgoal for the input is computed based on the selectivity of the pipelined operation. So if 10 rows are needed on the result of a filter operation, then depending on the selectivity of the filter, we may estimate that 200 rows are needed below the filter.

The initial value of a rowgoal is based on the query itself (e.g., TOP 10 defines a rowgoal of 10 at the root of the query). From this root value, rowgoals for parts of the tree are computed. Uniformity of distribution is assumed to compute these rowgoals for the children of different operations. For example, if a filter qualifies 5% of the data, the estimation is that as we read the input stream, 1 in each 20 rows qualifies such filter. So, to satisfy a rowgoal of 10 on the result of the filter, we need about 200 rows from the input.

An issue encountered sometimes is the underestimation of rowgoals due to non-uniform sequences in the stream of rows. Going back to the preceding example, the worst case scenario is that the 5% of the data qualifying the predicate happens to occur at the very end of the stream. In that case, to obtain 10 rows out of the filter, we need to read 95% of the stream plus 10 rows. If the estimation led to the choice of a navigational plan, this "unfavorable" stream sequence may make the plan perform poorly due to a much larger volume of data to process.

The order of rows is not fixed by the logical contents of the database. For example, when an index or base table is scanned, but the result is not required in a particular order, the storage engine returns the pages in a convenient fashion that depends on physical page proximity and other operations. So the same query may process more or less rows, depending on the state of the system. This introduces an element of unpredictability in the performance of TOP queries.

As with other situations, building covering indices can help to improve the reliability of plan selection. If this is not possible, you probably need to use query hints, which are described later in the "Control" section.

Troubleshooting

The query processor philosophy regarding tuning and troubleshooting is the following: We target a default operation that works well for the broadest possible set of scenarios, requiring minimal configuration work. And we also provide the means to identify and correct exceptional problem queries.

We now go over the tools available in SQL Server to investigate and address query processing issues described earlier.

Diagnostics

Here, we separate the diagnostics tools for query processing in two classes. One is about extracting aggregate information from a system, such as which queries are taking the longest to execute. The other class is about working with a single query.

It is common in troubleshooting situations that you would first find the bottleneck of the system or somehow narrow down the problem. This part of the process is broader than query processing and we don't attempt to cover it here in its full generality. Other chapters of this book contain more information about the process of narrowing down problems.

Next, we review some of the systemwide tools that can help with query processing problems and then go into more details about the information available for single queries.

DMVs

SQL Server 2005 introduced a number of dynamic management views (DMVs). These views return internal system information in the form of tables and allow easy access and manipulation of important properties in the system.

sys.dm_exec_query_stats

For query processing, one of the most useful DMVs is sys.dm_exec_query_stats. It outputs aggregate information about queries that have been executing in the system. To access this information, you simply need to query the DMV. For example, the following query retrieves the number of executions, average CPU, I/O reads, and elapsed time of each plan currently in the plan cache. It also retrieves an identifier for the query and the plan:

```
SELECT SQL_HANDLE, PLAN_HANDLE, EXECUTION_COUNT,
    TOTAL_WORKER_TIME / EXECUTION_COUNT,
    TOTAL_PHYSICAL_READS / EXECUTION_COUNT,
    TOTAL_ELAPSED_TIME / EXECUTION_COUNT
FROM SYS.DM_EXEC_QUERY_STATS
```

You can use the full power of SQL to process the result. In particular, you can use ORDER BY and TOP to find out the most frequent queries, the longest running on average, or the queries consuming the most resources.

The handles output by this DMV are internal, transient IDs that can later be used to find the text of the queries and the execution plans. The function sys.dm_exec_sql_text serves to get the text from a handle. For example, this query returns the text of the top three most frequently executed queries:

```
SELECT FREQ.EXECUTION_COUNT, TXT.TEXT
FROM (SELECT TOP 3 SQL_HANDLE, EXECUTION_COUNT
          FROM SYS.DM_EXEC_QUERY_STATS
ORDER BY EXECUTION_COUNT DESC) AS FREQ
       CROSS APPLY SYS.DM_EXEC_SQL_TEXT(SQL_HANDLE) AS TXT
```

The cross-apply operation is a special type of join also introduced in SQL Server 2005, which allows invoking a table-valued function for each row on the left table—in the preceding case, FREQ.

sys.dm_exec_sql_text returns the entire batch. If the batch contains more than one query, you need to use columns statement_start_offset and statement_end_offset from sys.dm_exec_query_stats. You can use the following string computation:

```
SUBSTRING(TEXT, (STATEMENT_START_OFFSET / 2) + 1,
    ((CASE WHEN STATEMENT_END_OFFSET = -1
            THEN DATALENGTH(TEXT)
            ELSE STATEMENT_END_OFFSET
    - STATEMENT_START_OFFSET) / 2) + 1)
```

To get the execution plan used for the statement in the procedure case, you use function sys.dm_exec_query_plan. We can extend the preceding query so that in addition to the query text, you get the execution plan for the top three most frequently executed queries:

```
SELECT FREQ.EXECUTION_COUNT, TXT.TEXT, PLN.QUERY_PLAN
FROM (SELECT TOP 3 SQL_HANDLE, PLAN_HANDLE,
EXECUTION_COUNT
          FROM SYS.DM_EXEC_QUERY_STATS
ORDER BY EXECUTION_COUNT DESC) AS FREQ
       CROSS APPLY SYS.DM_EXEC_SQL_TEXT(SQL_HANDLE) AS TXT
       CROSS APPLY SYS.DM_EXEC_QUERY_PLAN(PLAN_HANDLE)
AS PLN
```

The column query_plan contains the execution plan in XML format, which we describe in more detail next.

sys.dm_exec_query_optimizer_info

This DMV tracks some internal optimizer counters. Two counters you may find useful in investigations are the number of optimizations and the average optimization time. You can extract the information using the following query:

```
SELECT *
FROM SYS.DM_EXEC_QUERY_OPTIMIZER_INFO
WHERE COUNTER IN ('OPTIMIZATIONS', 'ELAPSED TIME')
```

There is currently no generic mechanism to reset aggregation DMVs such as the above, so you would typically take two snapshots of the contents and compute differentials.

Execution Plans and Basic Query Performance Information

It is typical to investigate a query performance problem interactively in Management Studio (or the query analyzer in SQL Server 2000). Two basic commands to get performance information in this mode are

```
SET STATISTICS TIME ON
SET STATISTICS IO ON
```

`TIME ON` will return information about the compilation and execution of each query. Both elapse and CPU time are reported. `IO ON` will return information about how many logical and physical disk operations are done for each table in the query. These basic statistics can help you get a sense of what is taking the most time.

Beyond these simple statistics, a major tool for troubleshooting is to view execution plans. SQL Server 2005 provides several variants of showplan. The simplest for troubleshooting is to display the graphical showplan in Management Studio. This displays an operator tree with each execution iterator and additional information. The width of links between operators gives you an immediate indication of what part of the plan is processing the most rows. When viewing showplan information, it is convenient to show the property window (F4 key), which provides detailed information for every operator in the plan.

You can view an *estimated* execution plan, which does not require executing the query but does show the plan that will be used, along with additional information derived by the query optimizer. This information includes

- Execution iterator to use (e.g., table scan, index seek, hash aggregation, etc.)

- Expected number of rows output by each operator

- Estimated CPU and I/O cost for an operator and for the execution of the plan up to this operation (also called subtree cost)

- In table and index operations, information about non-clustered indices that would make this query execute more efficiently, if one is identified

- Value assumed for parameter values by the query optimizer to estimate number of rows to process

There are some simple rules and caveats for reading the graphical showplan that we enumerate next:

- Data flow is from right to left.

- For nested loop joins, the lower side is the "inner" and it is executed once for each row returned in the upper side, which is the "outer."

- For the inner side of a nested loop join, the cardinality and cost estimates are *per execution* of the outer side.

- The inner side of nested loop joins also shows the number of expected executions.

- For hash joins, the upper side is the "build," and it is read first to build a hash table. The lower side is the "probe," and each of its rows is used to look up into the hash table to find matches.

There are a few things you can check on the estimated plan. First, you can check for the use of proper indices and order of execution of the query. Through row counts, you can tell what part of the query plan is processing the largest number of rows and look into alternatives to reduce the volume of processing, if possible. You can also see the cost percentage of different operations and again look into alternatives to reduce those operations, when possible.

A common scenario is to find that a large part of the query cost is in scanning a large table, or retrieving additional columns for rows qualified through a non-covering index. Depending on the scenario, creating a covering index can help reduce the processing cost significantly.

All the information described so far is generated in the compilation process. You can also gather and display actual execution information for a plan, which is displayed in addition to that described earlier. In SQL Server 2005, the additional information provided is

- **Actual number of executions of the operation.** This is a counter of the number of execution of the inner side of nested loop joins, as well as the degree of parallelism. So, if a plan does not have nested loop operations but is executed in parallel, say with degree of parallelism four, you will see this counter with four executions.

- **Actual number of rows output by each operation.** This is the sum over all executions of the operation.

The main thing you are likely to check on the actual execution showplan is how well the estimated cardinality matches reality. When doing this, take into account that estimated row information is per execution, but actual row counts are over all executions of an operation. In the next section, we describe various plan control alternatives that can help resolve problems you find through showplan.

Something to watch when analyzing showplan information is non-key sargs in index lookup operations, which can make some important information less transparent. Here is the situation. Suppose you have an index on columns (A, B, C, D) and you have a predicate, say A = 5 and D = 7. Both predicates will be pushed to the storage engine, but they are used differently. In the information for the index lookup, you will see the predicates tagged differently as

```
SEEK: A = 5
WHERE: D = 7
```

SEEK predicates are used to navigate the access path and directly locate the qualifying rows, in this case A = 5. WHERE conditions are checked on those rows located by the SEEK predicate. When the WHERE condition is very selective but the SEEK condition is not, you will see in showplan that few rows are coming out of the index operation and may incorrectly think that this is an efficient access. A high estimated cost for the index operation, relative to the output rows, may alert you to this situation, which you can validate by querying on the SEEK condition only. The missing index information in showplan may also be set in this case.

Although the graphical form of showplan is the most comfortable for interactive troubleshooting, you may need the textual form of showplan. It can be used for storing, programmatic analysis, or plan forcing, which is described in detail later.

There are three different settings you can use to get the estimated (compilation only) showplan:

- **SET SHOWPLAN_TEXT ON.** After setting this option, running the query will only compile and return a rowset with one row per execution iterator. The tree is shown is displayed in preorder and fairly readable for small plans.

- **SET SHOWPLAN_ALL ON.** This is similar to the preceding but contains more columns with information such as cardinality estimation, costing, and output columns.

- **SET SHOWPLAN_XML ON.** With this option set, executing the query returns a single row with a single column with an XML value containing all the information about the estimated plan. This setting is new in SQL Server 2005. The information contained here is the basis for graphical showplan. This is also the format used for plan forcing.

You can use two settings to obtain actual execution showplan:

- **SET STATISTICS PROFILE ON.** With this setting, executing a query will return a second rowset after the regular query return set. This second rowset is similar to the output of SHOWPLAN_ALL above. It contains the compile time information plus additional columns on the actual number of executions and total rows processed, per execution iterator.

- **SET STATISTICS XML.** With this option set, the second rowset contains a single row with a single column with an XML value containing both compile-time and execution time information. This is new in SQL Server 2005 and it is used as the basis for graphical showplan in Management Studio. It can be used for plan forcing.

In SQL Server 2005, actual execution showplan does not include actual CPU utilization or elapsed time, per operator.

Indexing Information
Since indexing has such a critical role in the performance of your applications, SQL Server has included index analysis and recommendation tools for several releases. In SQL Server 2005, Index Tuning Wizard (ITW) has been renamed Data Tuning Advisor (DTA) in SQL Server 2005 and incorporates many efficiency and reliability improvements. In addition to recommending indices and indexed views, it now also covers recommendations for table partitioning. You can start DTA to analyze a query or workload directly from Management Studio.

SQL Server 2005 also includes additional tools for index statistics and analysis, which are described next.

Index Usage Stats
SQL Server 2005 collects continuous statistics about index utilization, so can tell the extent of use of your index set in your production system. This information is exposed through a DMV, which you can query as follows:

```
SELECT * FROM SYS.DM_DB_INDEX_USAGE_STATS
```

Each row of the output corresponds to an index in the system, identified through columns database_id, object_id, and index_id. Use catalog views to get symbolic names for each of those ids. Suppose you store the id numbers from a particular row in variables @DATABASE_ID, @OBJECT_ID, and @INDEX_ID. You can use the following query to get the database name:

```
SELECT NAME FROM SYS.DATABASES
WHERE DATABASE_ID = @DATABASE_ID
```

Keep in mind that object ids for tables are local to a particular database, so you need to query the catalog views of the particular database, either setting the appropriate default database or using three-part names. Index ids are local to a particular table. You can use the following queries to get the appropriate table and index names:

```
USE < DATABASE FOR @DATABASE_ID>
GO

SELECT NAME FROM SYS.TABLES
WHERE OBJECT_ID = @OBJECT_ID

SELECT NAME FROM SYS.INDEXES
WHERE OBJECT_ID = @OBJECT_ID
AND INDEX_ID = @INDEX_ID
```

In practice, you are probably focused on a particular database, so you would query index statistics and resolve names for such database only.

The statistics provided by sys.dm_db_index_usage_stats include read and write counts, as well as timestamps for last access or each category. The counters refer to the number of queries executed that access the index in some particular way.

This information can be helpful when examining the usefulness of a set of indices, perhaps created some time back on the system. Indices that have not been read for a long time but are being updated may be candidates for removal from the system.

Missing Index Info in XML Showplan

In the process of compiling queries, the query optimizer identifies and makes a note of "obvious" secondary indices that would make a query perform much better. This is a very lightweight process in comparison with the thorough workload analysis done by DTA. This missing index detection is on all the time and the information is available through XML Showplan.

Using graphical showplan in Management Studio, you can view missing index information in the property window. It is associated to the root of the tree, the leftmost node. The property name is MissingIndexes and it is an option, so it will be there only if one such index was identified for this query.

When you open this property, you see an "impact" field, which is a number between 0 and 100 giving a rough-estimate improvement, if a suitable index were available, with higher numbers corresponding to higher benefit. Drilling into the missing index, you have information about the database and table name, and the columns that need indexing. Columns are listed in three groups: equality, inequality, and include. The index key would be made up of equality columns, followed by inequality, and the include columns that are needed for the index to be covering.

In determining these missing indices, the query processor considers seek operations and secondary indices only. The use of indices to satisfy the Order By clause is not currently considered.

Since XML Showplan is the common representation of plans within the server, you can pick up this information from a number of places. For example, you can retrieve the plans for queries that are most frequently executed or that are consuming the most resources through sys.dm_exec_query_stats, as described earlier. You would find in those execution plans whether the system has identified an obvious index that would speed up your query.

Missing Index Stats

The information about missing indices described previously is aggregated by the system in a fashion similar to sys.dm_dv_index_usage_stats, and exposed through DMVs. There are three DMVs involved: One keeps the global aggregation of total benefit, another has the details of particular columns to index, and the third serves as a link. The following query displays aggregate information about the missing indices of your running queries:

```
SELECT * FROM
SYS.DM_DB_MISSING_INDEX_GROUP_STATS MIGS,
SYS. DM_DB_MISSING_INDEX_GROUPS MIG,
SYS. DM_DB_MISSING_INDEX_DETAILS MID
WHERE MIGS.GROUP_HANDLE = MIG.INDEX_GROUP_HANDLE
AND MIG.INDEX_HANDLE = MID.INDEX_HANDLE
ORDER BY
USER_SEEKS * AVG_TOTAL_USER_COST * AVG_USER_IMPACT
```

As with index usage stats, columns database_id and object_id identify a table. Information about the columns interesting for indexing is in equality_columns, inequality_columns, and included_columns. There are seek and scan counts—meaning the number of seek or scans that would have been done had an index been available. There are columns for utilization timestamp, as well as average query execution cost, and impact of the index.

Note that the information in these views tracks executing queries. If you only compile a query but do not execute it, missing index information is computed and made available in XML Showplan, but it does not affect the counters for missing index DMVs.

The aggregation and counting is simple and it does not attempt to combine or consolidate multiple indices. It gives you useful raw information about your running system that can aid you in tuning.

Control

Next, we review the various control mechanisms you can use to affect query processor behavior and correct problems. They are roughly listed in order of preference, from the simplest to use and maintain to the more intrusive and specialized.

Creation of Indices

Creating appropriate indices for your queries is one of the simplest, most general, and most powerful techniques to address performance problems. Whenever possible, this is the preferred troubleshooting method because it fits well with the overall approach of relational databases and it is the least intrusive on the logical design or maintenance of the application.

When a query filter selects only a small subset of the rows of a table, the appropriate index can be used to directly locate the desired rows and avoid large table scans. Do keep in mind that if the index is not covering (i.e., does not contain all the rows required by the query), an additional table access step is required to retrieve the additional columns. The ideal index provides both direct access to the rows qualifying the filter predicate as well as all the columns required by the query.

How to tell which index or indices are necessary? SQL Server provides tools to aid in identifying good indices for an application, which have been described earlier.

Manual Statistics

SQL Server uses automatic, default policies for creating and refreshing statistics on table columns that work well for most scenarios. However, in some situations, it is necessary to override the default policies and control statistics manually. We first go over the commands to see the statistics available in the system and then go over problem situations and how to address them.

To view the statistics available in a table, say CUSTOMER, you use the following command:

```
DBCC     HELPSTATS CUSTOMER
```

You will see automatically created statistics with system-created names. Now, each index also creates statistics, so for a complete list of the statistics on your table, you also need to enumerate your indices:

```
DBCC HELPINDEX CUSTOMER
```

You can view the statistics contents by specifying table and statistics name, which in the case of indices is the same as the index name:

```
DBCC SHOW_STATISTICS(CUSTOMER, C_KEY_CLUIDX)
```

This command tells you when the statistics were created, how many rows the table contained at the time, and how many of those rows were sampled in the statistics creation operation. It shows the histogram of values and information about the number of distinct values, or "density." The density is a number between 0 and 1 and is interpreted as follows. If the density for a column C is X, $Y = 1/X$ is the average number of duplicates for each value of column C. Distinct columns have a density of 1. If you have an equality condition of the form C = @PARAM and the value of @PARAM is unknown, the system will estimate that Y rows are selected. If you have GroupBy C, the estimation is the total number of rows in the table divided by Y. If your filter uses an actual constant, cardinality estimation is based on the histogram and not the density since it provides more accurate information.

Next are some situations when you may need to consider manual statistics:

- Filtering on the result of scalar expressions.

- Multi-column statistics are required on non-indexed columns.

- Auto-refresh policy frequency is inadequate, either too frequent or too infrequent.

- Default scan rate is inadequate, typically too small.

The first two are about statistics creation whereas the last two are about automatic statistics refresh.

Statistics on Computed Columns

Column statistics are not useful, in general, to estimate the selectivity of filters on the result of scalar expressions. For example, table PURCHASES may have a column for list PRICE and another for DISCOUNT. A query on discounted price may have a filter of the form

```
PRICE * (1 - DISCOUNT) > 1000
```

Attempting to estimate the number of rows qualifying this condition using column statistics on PRICE and DISCOUNT is likely to introduce large errors. The current code uses a standard "guess" of 30% selectivity on inequality comparisons with constructs that are not in the model, such as the preceding. Depending on your query, such estimation errors may lead to the choice of a very inefficient plan—in particular, they will affect the choice of operations that appear after the filter itself. To provide statistics to the query optimizer, you can define a computed column for the expression on which you want to filter. You do so on the table, as follows:

```
ALTER TABLE PURCHASES ADD
DISCOUNTED_PRICE AS PRICE * (1 - DISCOUNT)
```

In SQL Server 2005, the query optimizer will automatically detect the use of the computed column expression in queries and create statistics if necessary. So, all you need is to declare the above computed column to get appropriate cardinality estimation on the filter above.

In SQL Server 2000 and earlier releases, no automatic matching is available. After defining the computed column, you need to create statistics on it and also change the query to refer to the column explicitly, so it needs to become

```
DISCOUNTED_PRICE > 1000
```

Another example of computed columns is the use of bits in an integer column to encode properties, and test those properties through bitwise operations. For example, the following filter checks whether the second bit is set:

```
BITS ^ 0x02 <> 0
```

As with the earlier example, it is unfeasible to use standard column statistics to estimate this predicate. But you can create a computed column for BITS ^ 0x02 and have statistics available.

You could be encoding logical AND/OR through bitmap operations. For example, this predicate checks whether both bits 0x04 and 0x02 are set:

```
BITS ^ 0x06 = 0x06
```

Note that computed column matching is structural only and does not get into the semantics of operations. So, you will not get an estimate for the preceding expressions if you have computed columns on both BITS ^ 0x04 and BITS ^ 0x02. They don't match. You will get an estimation if you have a computed column on BITS ^ 0x06. Alternatively, you can use expressions that test the primitive bits and combine the results with SQL connectives, whose semantics are understood by the query processor. So, instead of checking against 0x06, you use

```
BITS ^ 0x04 <> 0 AND BITS ^ 0x02 <> 0
```

This way, statistics for each of the two parts will be used. They will be combined using the standard independence assumption. As long as the bits are independent, this is the preferred path since it bounds the number of statistics to create and makes for simpler rules to write your predicates.

Multi-Column Statistics

Multi-column statistics are helpful for the query optimizer when columns are correlated and they are processed together in queries. For example, if you have a database of cars and have columns for COMPANY and MODEL, rows will not include all possible combinations of values for the two columns. MODEL = 'CIVIC' can only go together with COMPANY = 'HONDA'. This information is not available through single-column statistics. Multi-column statistics help in this scenario. In the current SQL Server product, they consist of the number of distinct values for sets of columns. Creating statistics on columns (MODEL, COMPANY) computes the number of distinct values for columns (MODEL), and for (MODEL, COMPANY). In this case, you may have 60 distinct values for (MODEL), and the same 60 distinct values for (MODEL, COMPANY), even though you may have 10 values for COMPANY. This information will be used when estimating the result of Group By operations and filtering. For filtering, we will ignore a condition on COMPANY if you are already filtering on MODEL. This follows the "inclusion" assumption, which basically means we expect that you query on data that exists in the database. You create multi-column statistics as follows:

```
CREATE STATISTICS MYSTATISTICS ON CARS(MODEL, COMPANY)
```

Multi-column statistics are automatically crated on multi-column indices and cover all prefixes of the index. For an index on (A, B, C), you get a distinct count on (A), (A, B), and (A, B, C). Unlike single-column statistics, multi-column statistics are not automatically created, so you may need to create these if you have correlated columns and they are used together for grouping or filtering purposes in your queries. Once created, it will be refreshed automatically by the system.

Manual Statistics Refresh

You can use the UPDATE STATISTICS command to manually update statistics on a particular table or statistics within a table. You can provide a larger sampling size in the command, including a full scan of the table. It is a common practice for troubleshooting bad query plans to refresh statistics with full scan. The resulting better statistics often correct the problem. To refresh all statistics on table CUSTOMER with full scan, use the following:

```
UPDATES STATISTICS ON CUSTOMER WITH FULLSCAN
```

Depending on the pattern of data changes for your application, you may want to schedule statistics updates during your maintenance window. Once you know that the important statistics for your application are created, either automatically or manually, you can switch to manual updates. To do so, disable automatic statistics on the database with the following command:

```
ALTER DATABASE MYDATABASE
SET AUTO_UPDATE_STATISTICS OFF
```

Afterwards, you can rely on your (scheduled) statistics updates to refresh statistics. If your system has a periodic data load cycle, it may make sense for you to update statistics as part of your load cycle. This front-loads the statistics-gathering process and ensures that by the time you start using queries, there are no additional maintenance tasks left. To update statistics for tables that have changed since the last statistics were gathered, you can use the following stored procedure, which operates on all tables of the current database:

```
USE MYDATABASE
GO
EXEC SP_UPDATESTATS
```

For other applications that do change the data during regular operation, but you are certain that the data distributions are preserved, you may want to do manual statistics as well and avoid performance hiccups associated with the system deciding it's time to refresh statistics and compile your plans.

Turning off automatic statistics may be appropriate for some applications, but it does complicate maintenance of the application. Whenever possible, the recommended practice is to leave auto-statistics on.

Asynchronous Statistics

Asynchronous statistics refresh is a useful new setting available in SQL Server 2005, which may reduce the need to turn off automatic statistics in operational systems. By default, statistics staleness is checked during the plan validation process. The statistics version used when producing this plan is checked; if there are more recent statistics or the table has changed sufficiently, then statistics are gathered again and the query recompiled. This happens in synchronous fashion, so execution of the query will be blocked until the new statistics are gathered and the query is recompiled.

The asynchronous statistics option modifies the preceding scheme by detaching the statistics update operation from the plan validation and execution path. If the system determines that new statistics are needed, an update operation is scheduled, but plan is not blocked and simply proceeds to execution. After the update operation is complete, the resulting statistics will have a new version. Next time the dependent plan is validated for execution, the new statistics version will trigger a recompilation. To use asynchronous statistics refresh, use the following command:

```
   ALTER DATABASE MYDATABASE
SET AUTO_UPDATE_STATISTICS_ASYNC ON
```

The response time hiccup associated with recomputation of statistics is not completely eliminated, because plan recompilation still occurs synchronously, but it is greatly reduced because the work required for gathering statistics moves out of the critical execution path.

Query Hints—Controlling Query Plans

In cases where the default execution plans and policies are not appropriate, query hints allow you to exercise explicit control over the behavior of the system. The term *hint* is a misnomer since these are effectively directives to the query processor. Using hints can be compared to writing assembly language—it can get you better performance, but you give up in terms of flexibility and maintainability. Our expectation is for the default behavior to improve over successive releases and therefore reduce the need for hints.

Syntactically, hints appear in three forms:

- Locking and table hints, which appear in the middle of your otherwise declarative SQL statement

- Query hints through the separate OPTION clause in your statement

- Connection-setting hints

Next we review the most common hints.

Bypass Cost-Based Optimization for Joins

Some applications are interested in very simple and predictable execution strategies, navigating through predefined paths. The FORCEPLAN connection setting can be used in these cases. It is equivalent to using query hints FORCE ORDER along with LOOP JOIN, described later. This setting does not preclude query simplification, so things like predicate push-down and removal of redundant joins are still applied. This setting also reduces compilation time since the space of alternatives is dramatically reduced and the query is pretty much executed as written. Make sure that the proper indices exist to support the required join navigation if you use FORCEPLAN. For example, the following query navigates from CUSTOMER to ORDERS since that is how tables appear in the FROM clause.

```
SET FORCEPLAN ON

SELECT O_ORDERKEY
FROM CUSTOMER, ORDERS
WHERE C_CUSTKEY = O_CUSTKEY
AND C_NAME = 'ADAM SMITH'
```

Locking

You can override the default locking strategy by specifying an embedded locking hint. For example, this can be used for an ad hoc query that requires only an approximate, best-effort result, but does not want to block other executing transactions. For example:

```
SELECT COUNT(*)
FROM CUSTOMERS WITH (NOLOCK)
WHERE C_NATIONKEY = 5
```

Index Hint

This is also an embedded hint that directs the query process to use a particular index to access a table. If the specified index is not covering, the base table is accessed as well to retrieve any missing columns. Using index hints makes your queries dependent on the physical configuration of your database. The query will fail to compile if the index you specify does not exist for the table. Using the number "0" for the index forces the use of table scans. An example of index hint is the following:

```
SELECT *
FROM CUSTOMERS WITH (INDEX = C_NATIONKEY_IDX)
WHERE C_NATIONKEY = 5
```

Embedded Join Hint

Either hash, merge, or nested loop joins can be specified in the FROM clause of queries to force particular execution of algorithms. One caveat when using embedded join execution hints is that this also forces the join execution order for the whole query. For nested loop joins, the table on the left side is used as "outer" and each of its rows is used to process the right, "inner" side. For hash join, the left side is used to build a hash table, and then each row from the right side looks up for matches in this hash table. The following query will do a hash join between CUSTOMER and ORDERS:

```
    SELECT *
    FROM ORDERS INNER LOOP JOIN CUSTOMER
ON C_CUSTKEY = O_CUSTKEY
    WHEREcx
 O_ORDERDATE = '1-31-2006'
```

Algorithm Restriction

In the OPTION clause, you can also restrict the execution algorithms allowed for the query. For joins, the options are HASH JOIN, MERGE JOIN, and LOOP JOIN. To control the execution algorithm for Group By operations, you can use ORDER GROUP for sort-based distincting and aggregation and HASH GROUP for hash aggregation. For example, the following query forces the use of hash aggregation:

```
    SELECT O_CUSTKEY, COUNT(*)
FROM ORDERS
GROUP BY O_CUSTKEY
OPTION(HASH GROUP)
```

Forcing Execution Order

You can force the query optimizer to execute joins and Group By operations in the order specified in the SQL syntax. Tables separated by commas in the FROM clause will be joined left to right. You can also use parentheses to specify any desired execution order. Note that forcing execution order does not preclude simplification, so some joins could be dropped, if appropriate, and predicates will be pushed down. The next query forces a join from NATION to CUSTOMER to ORDERS.

```
SELECT *
FROM NATION, CUSTOMER, ORDERS
WHERE N_NATIONKEY = C_NATIONKEY
AND C_CUSTKEY = O_CUSTKEY
OPTION(FORCE ORDER)
```

Limiting Parallelism

The option clause can also specify the maximum degree of parallelism allowed for executing a query. For example, you can specify the use of no more than four concurrent threads on a machine with eight processors. It can also be used to disable parallelism entirely for a query. The query forces serial execution by specifying a maximum degree of parallelism of 1.

```
    SELECT O_CUSTKEY, COUNT(*)
FROM ORDERS
GROUP BY O_CUSTKEY
OPTION(MAXDOP 1)
```

Optimize for Partial Result Retrieval

In some scenarios, applications may want to look only at the first few rows of the result-set and then shut down the query. This query hint tells the query optimizer to generate a plan that optimizes retrieval of these first few rows. As other hints, this does not modify the query semantics, so the plan will produce the entire result if the application keeps pulling rows. This is in contrast to the use of TOP in the SELECT clause, which restricts the resultset and therefore it is part of the query semantics. For example, the next query generates a plan that is optimized for retrieval of the first 20 rows:

```
SELECT *
FROM ORDERS
WHERE O_CUSTKEY = 13681
ORDER BY O_ORDERDATE DESC
OPTION (FAST 20)
```

Optimize for a Particular Parameter Value

When a parameterized query is compiled, there is no guarantee about the actual values that will be used when executing the query. This happens all the time in stored procedures. But the actual parameter value may make a big difference in the number of rows to process, the cost of different alternatives and, ultimately, on the best plan for the query, when the data filtered has a skewed distribution. To estimate, the query optimizer looks at the parameter value used on the first compilation, if one is provided, or else assumes some average value. Depending on the application, these assumptions may not be right for later executions of the query. You can specify an expected parameter value to be used in evaluating candidate plans. As indicated earlier, there is no change in query semantics and the plan generated is valid for any parameter value. You would pick a typical frequent or infrequent value in the domain, depending on your expected utilization pattern. For example:

```
    SELECT *
FROM CUSTOMER JOIN ORDERS
ON C_CUSTKEY = O_CUSTKEY
WHERE C_NATIONKEY = @NATIONPARAM
OPTION(OPTIMIZE FOR (@NATIONPARAM = 5))
```

OPTIMIZE FOR is new in SQL 2005 and not available in earlier releases.

Recompile on Each Execution

If your data is skewed and you can afford to compile on each execution, instead of trying to provide a typical value, you can simply request no plan reuse. Each compilation will have the values of parameters available, and they will be used for plan evaluation and selection. The preceding query would then look as follows:

```
SELECT *
FROM CUSTOMER JOIN ORDERS
ON C_CUSTKEY = O_CUSTKEY
```

```
WHERE C_NATIONKEY = @NATIONPARAM
OPTION(RECOMPILE)
```

RECOMPILE is new in SQL 2005 and not available in earlier releases.

Query Hint Caveats

Using query hints is sometimes necessary but should be avoided when possible. It breaks the declarative, logical specification of queries and creates dependencies that may be a burden for future maintenance.

A simple example of this dependency is the use of index hints. Creation and removal of indices belong in the physical design space and affects only the performance of the system but not the correctness or functionality of the application—except if you are using index hints. Dropping an index can cause queries to fail to execute if they had references to this particular index.

Since hints restrict the search space of the optimizer, it is possible that the restricted space does not contain a valid execution plan. Compilation will then fail with a No Plan Found error. For example, hash joins can only support equality comparison joins, so the following query will fail to compile:

```
SELECT C2.C_NAME
FROM CUSTOMER C1, CUSTOMER C2
WHERE C1.C_BALANCE < C2.C_BALANCE
    AND C1.C_NAME = 'ADAM SMITH'
OPTION(HASH JOIN)
```

More complex scenarios can result from query simplification. For example, the following query will also fail to compile:

```
SELECT C_NAME, C_ORDERKEY
FROM CUSTOMER, ORDERS
WHERE C_CUSTKEY = O_CUSTKEY
AND C_CUSTKEY = 13681
```

The reason is that the filter on C_CUSTKEY = 13681 will be propagated to the other column as O_CUSTKEY = 13681 and the join condition disappears. The resulting cross product can only be implemented as nested loops join (and it wouldn't make any sense to implement the query using hash join, even if the join condition were preserved). Enhancements in query simplification can lead to other, similar situations.

So, use hints only when absolutely necessary, use the weakest form of hint you can, and keep in mind the maintenance implications.

Plan Guides—Granular Control Without App Changes

In general, adding query hints requires change to the application. But this may be inconvenient or impossible to do in some cases. It also breaks the logical design of the application, as discussed earlier. To address this problem, SQL 2005 introduced plan guides as a mechanism to associate hints to a query without changing the application. The general idea is to have an association table residing in the server, where an administrator can add control hints for specific queries issued by the application. This is illustrated in Figure 5-3.

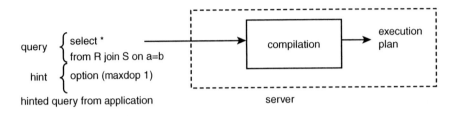

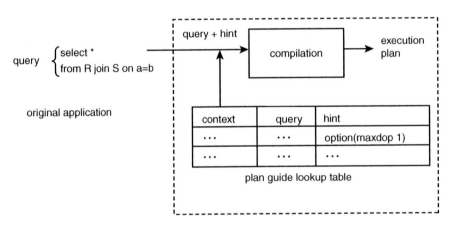

FIGURE 5-3   Association table residing in the server

At compilation time, queries are first looked up in the plan guide table. Any associated query hints are incorporated as if they had appeared in the query text itself. Query matching is done within a context, which can be the name of a particular stored procedure or trigger. If the application does not call stored procedures but sends query text to the server, then the context is the batch (i.e., the text with a series of statements that will be sent to the server as a single unit). If the batch contains a single statement, you don't need to provide the context explicitly.

To define plan guides, use procedure sp_create_plan_guide. To drop, enable, or disable, use sp_control_plan_guide. You can query view sys.plan_guides to see the contents of the association table. The following example creates a hint for a statement in a stored procedure, specifying that value 5 should be assumed for parameter value @NATIONPARAM:

```
    EXEC SP_CREATE_PLAN_GUIDE
@NAME = N'MyGuide',
@STMT = N' SELECT C_NAME, C_ADDRESS, O_SHIPDATE
FROM CUSTOMER JOIN ORDERS
```

```
ON C_CUSTKEY = O_CUSTKEY
WHERE C_NATIONKEY = @NATIONPARAM',
@TYPE = N'OBJECT',
@MODULE_OR_BATCH = N'MyStoredProcedure',
@PARAMS = NULL,
@HINTS = N'OPTION(OPTIMIZE FOR (@NATIONPARAM = 5))'
```

The incoming query text may itself have an OPTION clause. This is part of the statement and needs to be included in the query text to match the plan guide. In this case, the original OPTION clause is ignored and replaced by that provided by the plan guide. By specifying an empty hint in the plan guide, you are effectively removing the original query hint provided by the application.

Plan Forcing

Starting in SQL Server 2005, the USE PLAN query hint allows for very precise specification of a desired execution plan, beyond the expressive power of hints available in earlier releases. The target plan is specified using XML, with the same schema as that of XML Showplan. In fact, the expected usage is that you take XML Showplan generated by the database and use it as the argument of USE PLAN.

Like other hints, USE PLAN does not modify the semantics of the original query but affects only the choice of execution plan. The basic idea in implementing this hint is to shut down the cost estimation component of the optimizer, as the mechanism for plan selection, and replace it by a test against the target plan provided by USE PLAN. The plan generation component of the optimizer is used as in normal optimization, except for two modifications. First, the target plan is used to guide the search and avoid considering irrelevant plans. It is unfeasible to determine very efficiently (e.g., linearly, in the size of the query) how to generate the target plan from the original query, but our guidance mechanisms work well, in particular for join queries. Second, we relax some of the heuristics that are in place during normal optimization. For example, you can force a plan that uses cross products, even though they are not considered during normal optimization.

In summary, we do preserve the overall generate-and-test optimization algorithm and use the execution plan provided as a target to be found in the search space. If the target plan is not found, the compilation fails with a No Plan Found error. USE PLAN is not a compilation time reduction feature. Depending on the query and the contents of the database, forcing a plan can take more or less time than un-hinted optimization. On one hand, guidance toward the target plan can cut down on very large search spaces. On the other hand, XML Showplan is verbose and the time to parse it can be significant. For short-running queries, the heuristics based on cost can be more efficient than the guidance toward a desired plan.

We expect USE PLAN to be used in conjunction with plan guides to force particular execution plans for problematic queries in an application. Simply use the procedure sp_create_plan_guide as described previously with the hint

```
OPTION(USE PLAN '<ShowPlanXML ... /ShowPlanXML>')
```

The XML Showplan is passed as a string, so you need to make sure to escape any string quote inside of it. If you took the XML Showplan using cut-and-paste, it is sufficient to do a global replace of single quotes (') by two quotes ('') in an editor. You can do this editing in the query window of Management Studio.

In principle, it is possible to manually create an XML Showplan for a desired plan, but this representation is too large to make this practical. Instead, you would use the system to generate the XML Showplan you want, and use it on the problem query. This may appear as a circular argument since the assumption is that the system did not generate the plan you wanted in the first place. You can take your original query and make modifications on it (e.g., use embedded hints or change the predicates) to push the system into generating a different plan. You then take the resulting XML Showplan and force it on your original query.

You may also use an XML Showplan that was generated earlier or in a different system (e.g., captured by SQL Server Profiler).

There are a couple of important points regarding matching that you should keep in mind for a more effective utilization of the feature. Matching is based on the relational operations only, and access paths are matched by fully qualified name.

- Scalar operations are ignored for matching. So, for example, you can generate XML Showplan for a query that uses a predicate, say A = 15, and then force that plan on a different query that uses predicate A = 20, or predicate A = @X. You can even force a plan generated with predicates A = 15 and B = 20 on a query that uses only A = 15, or vice versa. This gives you some flexibility in generating the plan you want to force.

- Table and index names are fully qualified and must match fully, including database name, schema name, table name, and index name. For example, if you take XML Showplan from objects in some database DB1, they will fail on objects for database DB2. Since the matching is by name, you can simply edit the XML Showplan and correct the database name.

The combination of plan guides with the USE PLAN hint give you the ability to effectively "freeze" as many execution plans as you want, without the need to change the application. As with other hints, we recommend this to be used only when necessary and view it as a means to deal with exceptional cases.

USE PLAN has some limitations in SQL Server 2005. It does not handle insert, update, and delete statements. It does not handle remote queries and full-text queries. For cursor queries, it handles only static and fast-forward.

Server-Side Parameterization
It is possible to use plan guides not to target a specific query, but rather a template, in particular to force the use of a single parameterized plan for the various instances sent by the application. For example, suppose an application issues the following query to

retrieve the orders placed by particular customers, and it uses a different customer name on each invocation:

```
    SELECT O_ORDERKEY
    FROM CUSTOMER, ORDERS
    WHERE C_CUSTKEY = O_CUSTKEY
AND C_NAME = 'ADAM SMITH'
```

The application is effectively using a template. It could have used a stored procedure or sp_executeSQL to parameterize. But it didn't. You can configure the server to parameterize in this case. First, get the template for the query. You extract the template by providing one example invocation to sp_get_query_template as follows:

```
    DECLARE @TEMPLATE VARCHAR(MAX)
    DECLARE @PARAMETER VARCHAR(MAX)
    EXEC SP_GET_QUERY_TEMPLATE
        N'SELECT O_ORDERKEY
            FROM CUSTOMER, ORDERS
            WHERE C_CUSTKEY = O_CUSTKEY
AND C_NAME = ''ADAM SMITH'' ',
        @TEMPLATE,
        @PARAMETERS
```

Note that string constants in the query need to escape delimiting quotes (i.e., two consecutive single-quote characters) because you are passing the entire query string as an argument. For the preceding example, the results in @TEMPLATE and @PARAMETERS are the following:

```
    SELECT O_ORDERKEY
    FROM CUSTOMER, ORDERS
    WHERE C_CUSTKEY = O_CUSTKEY
AND C_NAME = @0

    @0 VARCHAR(8000)
```

Then a plan guide can be created on the template as follows, assuming @TEMPLATE and @PARAMETERS were set by sp_get_query_template:

```
    EXEC SP_CREATE_PLAN_GUIDE
@NAME = N'MyGuide',
@STMT = @TEMPLATE,
@TYPE = N'TEMPLATE',
@MODULE_OR_BATCH = NULL,
@PARAMS = @PARAMETERS,
@HINTS = N'OPTION(PARAMETERIZATION FORCED)'
```

You can force parameterization only for batches that contain a single statement.

Parameterization can also be forced globally, but this is a heavy-handed option that in my opinion should be used only in very rare cases. To do this, set a database option using the following:

```
ALTER DATABASE MYDATABASE SET PARAMETERIZATION FORCED
```

If MYDATABASE is the default database on a particular connection, all statements received though such connection will be parameterized. Plan guides can be used in this case to selectively exclude some queries to be parameterized, using the hint OPTION(PARAMETERIZATION SIMPLE).

Best Practices

Many problematic situations in applications can be avoided by following good development and testing practices. Looking into application issues over the past three releases of SQL Server, we have found a number of practices that, if taken into account during application development and deployment, can lead to better performance and reliability. Some of the top things we have found are listed next.

Use Set-Oriented Programming

One of the common issues we find in stored procedures is that developers implement their own joins at the application level. For example, they may use a cursor to enumerate all the rows for some tables, perhaps after filtering, and use each of the rows from this set in a second parameterized query.

This is effectively an implementation of nested loop joins. It is not a good database programming practice for several reasons. It is less efficient than the native nested loops iterator provided by the engine because it exercises a much deeper execution stack for each row. It gives no chance to the query optimizer to execute the query in a different order or with different execution algorithms. And it makes for more complex code that is more difficult to reason about and maintain.

This use of SQL may be the simplest to understand to a new database developer who is familiar with procedural languages, but it gives up on the higher-level, declarative power of the language. Try to avoid row-per-row manipulation in your application to the extent that you can. Push set-oriented, declarative processing to the database.

Provide Constraints and Statistics Information

The robustness and general quality of plans produced by the query optimizer depend heavily on the quality of information it has available. There are two main sources of information that you can provide:

- **Constraints.** Uniqueness constraints, foreign key constraints, and check constraints. Declare the constraints you expect your data to satisfy. The system can verify that these constraints hold and the query optimizer can generate better plans.

The query process can reason about declarative constraints, so use those when possible, instead of validating through a general stored procedure.

- **Statistics.** Run with the default auto-statistics whenever possible. If necessary, switch to manual maintenance. If you need to force plans, it is preferred that you do so explicitly rather than going with no statistics, because that leaves the system in an unreliable state.

Watch Complex Constructs

Earlier sections of this chapter have described query constructs that are harder to handle by the query optimizer. They can be summarized as follows:

- **Very large queries or constructs that increase the search space.** The issue here is that once the space gets sufficiently large, the system will rely more on heuristics and some alternatives will not be considered. In general, join optimization scales better than multiple Group By and subqueries.

- **Constructs for which it is hard to estimate the number of qualifying rows or the data distribution.** These include aggregations, scalar expressions, UDFs, and non-inlined Table-Valued functions.

In general, the preceding can reduce the reliability of plan selection, so be careful when you use those constructs. The following principles can be used to make processing more robust:

- Create computed columns for scalar expression that will be used to filter, as we described earlier.

- Errors in estimation of cardinality or data distribution tend to affect the choice of operators that come later. Therefore, if you need to use complex constructs, use them at the end of the query and not somewhere in the middle.

- Related to the preceding, split your query into multiple steps and store intermediate results in temporary tables.

We expect that future releases of SQL Server will improve the automatic handling of these scenarios.

Avoid Dynamic Language Features When Possible

SQL Server allows a number of dynamic language features that are convenient in some scenarios but have some overhead. Some of those are mentioned next.

- **Fully qualified names.** Tables in different schemas may have the same name. When no schema is specified, the table referenced depends on the user that executes the query. This complicates the logic for plan reuse and introduces additional processing overhead. If you don't expect to be using dynamic resolution of schema, then fully qualifying table references will give you better performance. Typically, this means referring to a table as DBO.TABLE instead of simply TABLE.

- **Temporary tables with changing schema.** You may have stored procedures that operate on temporary tables defined outside the stored procedure body. The temporary table is resolved dynamically at execution time, and it is possible to create different temporary tables, including changes in the schema. This is a more extreme case of the dynamic name resolution situation and it should also be avoided.

- **Dynamically generated SQL.** Many applications need to use dynamically generated SQL and the ability to do this is one of the strengths of relational databases to implement ad hoc queries. However, there are security risks in assembling SQL dynamically. Dynamic SQL issued from a stored procedure executes under the security context of the caller, not the owner of the stored procedure. This may require granting higher security privileges to callers. Also, parameter values carefully constructed by a malicious user can leak information or otherwise disrupt the system. The SQL Server hint OPTION(RECOMPILE) may help you avoid dynamic SQL in some cases.

- **Connection settings changes throughout your application.** In general, connection settings such as ANSI_NULLS or ARITH_ABORT affect the semantics and therefore the plans generated for SQL queries. Executing the same set of queries with different values of connection settings requires recompilation, increases overhead, and reduces plan reuse. Also, since connection settings are not statically scoped, a change you make inside a stored procedure remains active after leaving such stored procedure and affects other parts of the application. The preferred practice is to keep the default SQL Server settings and not change them dynamically in your application.

Further Reading

The following are papers or blogs from the SQL Server engineering team, where you can find additional information and ideas about performance debugging:

- SQL Server Engine Dev blog, http://blogs.msdn.com/sqltips.

- Ken Henderson's technical blog, http://blogs.msdn.com/khen1234.

- Arun Marathe, *Batch Compilation, Recompilation, and Plan Caching Issues in SQL Server 2005*, http://www.microsoft.com/technet/prodtechnol/sql/2005/recomp.mspx, July 2004.

- Burzin A. Patel, *Forcing Query Plans*, http://www.microsoft.com/technet/prodtechnol/sql/2005/frcqupln.mspx, November 2005.

- SQL Server QO Team blog, http://blogs.msdn.com/queryoptteam.

The following papers describe in more detail some query processing features of SQL Server:

- José A. Blakeley, Conor Cunningham, Nigel Ellis, Balaji Rathakrishnan, Ming-Chuan Wu, *Distributed/Heterogeneous Query Processing in Microsoft SQL Server*. ICDE 2005: 1001-1012.

- César A. Galindo-Legaria, Stefano Stefani, Florian Waas, *Query Processing for SQL Updates*. SIGMOD Conference 2004: 844-849.

- Eric N. Hanson, *Statistics Used by the Query Optimizer in SQL Server 2005*, http://www.microsoft.com/technet/prodtechnol/sql/2005/qrystats.mspx, April 2005.

- Eric N. Hanson, *Improving Performance with SQL Server 2005 Indexed Views*, http://www.microsoft.com/technet/prodtechnol/sql/2005/ipsql05iv.mspx, March 2005.

- Christian Kleinerman, *Multiple Active Result Sets (MARS) in SQL Server 2005*, http://msdn.microsoft.com/library/default.asp?url=/library/en-us/ dnsql90/html/MARSinSQL05.asp, June 2005.

The following papers present in more detail the principles behind query optimization and execution in SQL Server:

- César A. Galindo-Legaria, Milind Joshi, *Orthogonal Optimization of Subqueries and Aggregation*. SIGMOD Conference 2001: 571-581.

- Goetz Graefe, *Query Evaluation Techniques for Large Databases*. ACM Computing Surveys 25(2): 73-170 (1993).

- Arjan Pellenkoft, César A. Galindo-Legaria, Martin L. Kersten, *The Complexity of Transformation-Based Join Enumeration*. VLDB 1997: 306-315.

- Florian Waas, César A. Galindo-Legaria, *Counting, Enumerating, and Sampling of Execution Plans in a Cost-Based Query Optimizer*. SIGMOD Conference 2000: 499-509.

Server Crashes and Other Critical Failures

By Bob Ward

I don't think anyone can dispute that SQL Server has become a very reliable database management system. In the early days of my career as a support engineer, server-down problems were often the cause of bugs in the product. Today we certainly still have customers calling us because their SQL Server is down or their application is unavailable, but situations where the SQL Server software is at fault are much fewer than in years past.

Having said that, this book is all about troubleshooting problems and critical problems that can occur. Being a member of the technical support team, my life revolves around problem solving. My family sometimes gets frustrated with me because even the smallest of issues around the house turn into problem-solving exercises. This chapter is focused on scenarios I don't expect you to see often, but when they do occur, they can be serious and affect the stability and accessibility of SQL Server, which of course affects your application and business operations. The more you can learn about how to recognize and resolve these quickly, the less your business is affected, the quicker you can go home after being paged, and the happier your users will become.

Fundamentals

In order to understand how to analyze, diagnose, and resolve critical errors, I think it is important for you to understand some internal information about how certain parts of the SQL Server engine work. I'll first talk about internals related to the startup of the engine, the handling of errors, and the detection of possible server hang situations. I'll then review SQL Server 2005 enhancements that include important tools that will assist you in the diagnosis and recovery of critical errors.

> **NOTE**
> When I refer to the SQL Server engine or just engine, I mean the SQLSERVR.EXE program.

SQL Server 2005 Server Recovery Internals

I'll kick off this discussion of recovery internals with a brief tour of SQL Server engine startup parameters and events. Understanding what happens when the server starts is key to understanding how it works in general.

SQL Engine Startup

There is no more urgent problem to handle than the failure of the SQL Server service to start. To be clear on what I mean by "failure to start," I mean failure to *completely* start. Aside from disk damage to the sqlservr.exe image, the SQL Server engine will always attempt to start. It is the execution at engine startup that could cause it to prematurely stop after attempting to start.

Table 6-1 represents some of the parameters I use in the course of troubleshooting cases or running tests against the server engine:

TABLE 6-1   Parameters used for troubleshooting cases or running tests against the server engine

Parameter	Description
-c	Use this when starting from the command line. Skips code to interact with SCM.
-g	Reserves memory in the virtual address space for components like xprocs, COM objects, and other DLLs. The number provided is interpreted as Mb. The default is 256Mb.
-m	Start the server to allow only one user to log in at a time.
-n	Disables writing messages and errors in the Windows Event Log
-s	Name for a named instance. You must supply this parameter if you are starting a named instance from the command line. When you start a named instance as a service, the Service Control Manager passes in the -s parameter as specified in the registry key ImagePath for the service.

Parameter	Description
-T	The value after this parameter is used to set a global trace flag for the server. I use this because I don't want to forget to run DBCC TRACEON if the server is restarted.
-v	Used from the command line to display the version and ProcessID of the server engine.
-y	When supplied with an error number, causes the engine to generate a stack dump when that error is encountered.

Now let's break down the ERRORLOG using a SQL Server 2005 x86 edition running on Windows 2003 Server:

```
2006-08-27 22:27:57.23 Server        Microsoft SQL Server 2005 - 9.00.2047.00
(Intel X86)
        Apr 14 2006 01:12:25
        Copyright (c) 1988-2005 Microsoft Corporation
        Enterprise Edition on Windows NT 5.2 (Build 3790: Service Pack 1)

2006-08-27 22:27:57.23 Server        (c) 2005 Microsoft Corporation.
2006-08-27 22:27:57.23 Server        All rights reserved.
2006-08-27 22:27:57.23 Server        Server process ID is 5724.
2006-08-27 22:27:57.23 Server        Logging SQL Server messages in file
'C:\Program Files\Microsoft SQL Server\MSSQL.1\MSSQL\LOG\ERRORLOG'.
```

This represents the startup messages when the ERRORLOG is created. The build of SQL Server, the platform of SQL (in this case, x86), and the date the SQLSERVR.EXE was built are in the first two lines. Build 9.00.2047 represents SQL Server 2005 Service Pack 1. The line after the copyright message shows the package or SKU of SQL Server—in this case, the Enterprise Edition—and the version of Windows. Windows NT 5.2 is Windows 2003 Server (and, in this case, Windows 2003 Service Pack 1).

Next is the Windows ProcessID for SQLSERVR.EXE. This is obtained using the GetCurrentProcessID() API call and is the same value you will find in Task Manager. Next is the full path of the ERRORLOG file.

```
2006-08-27 22:27:57.23 Server        This instance of SQL Server last reported using
a process ID of 2844 at 8/27/2006 10:26:22 PM (local) 8/28/2006 3:26:22 AM (UTC).
This is an informational message only; no user action is required.
```

This line shows the previous ProcessID for this instance of SQL Server and the date and time it was shut down before this execution was started.

```
2006-08-27 22:27:57.23 Server        Registry startup parameters:
2006-08-27 22:27:57.23 Server         -d C:\Program Files\Microsoft SQL
Server\MSSQL.1\MSSQL\DATA\master.mdf
2006-08-27 22:27:57.25 Server         -e C:\Program Files\Microsoft SQL
```

```
Server\MSSQL.1\MSSQL\LOG\ERRORLOG
2006-08-27 22:27:57.25 Server         -l C:\Program Files\Microsoft SQL
Server\MSSQL.1\MSSQL\DATA\mastlog.ldf
```

Next, a new feature of SQL Server 2005 is to print the startup options as read from the registry and/or command line. This can be a very handy feature if a problem occurs due to an invalid startup parameter.

```
2006-08-27 22:27:57.28 Server       SQL Server is starting at normal priority
base (=7). This is an informational message only. No user action is required.
2006-08-27 22:27:57.28 Server       Detected 4 CPUs. This is an informational
message; no user action is required.
2006-08-27 22:27:57.73 Server       Using dynamic lock allocation.   Initial
allocation of 2500 Lock blocks and 5000 Lock Owner blocks per node.   This is
an informational message only.   No user action is required.
```

Next, the configuration values as stored in the master.mdf are read from the disk and loaded into memory. If an error occurs reading the master.mdf file, you would see that failure in the ERRORLOG. The previous messages are displayed after reading the configuration block. This is also where you would see a message showing the configured affinity mask for SQL Server. Note in this case that the engine detected four CPUs on the computer. This is the total CPUs as reported by Windows, so it accounts for multi-core and hyperthreaded CPUs (I pulled this ERRORLOG from a hyperthreaded enabled dual-CPU server).

The SQLOS subsystem is then initialized. You might not see any ERRORLOG entries as part of this process (you would, for example, if you had lightweight pooling or fiber mode enabled). In this process, SQLOS checks for fiber mode, enables its routines, and enables DAC. It is also where SQLOS creates the necessary schedulers on the server, which is the first time multiple threads are created. It is also at this point that initial memory allocation occurs for the server based on the configuration values, -g parameter, platform (32- or 64-bit), and amount of physical memory.

```
2006-08-27 22:27:57.92 Server       Attempting to initialize Microsoft
Distributed Transaction Coordinator (MS DTC). This is an informational message
only. No user action is required.
2006-08-27 22:28:00.22 Server       Attempting to recover in-doubt distributed
transactions involving Microsoft Distributed Transaction Coordinator (MS DTC).
This is an informational message only. No user action is required.
```

DTC transaction initialization is then started, including the attempt to recover any in-doubt DTC transactions. Failures won't cause the server to fail to start, but there could be delay here that would cause delay in overall server startup and database recovery.

Next, SNI (SQL Network Interface) is initialized. This doesn't mean that the code is executed to listen for network connections. But routines like WSAStartup for Windows sockets are called to prepare the server to listen for connections.

```
2006-08-27 22:28:00.23 Server       Database mirroring has been enabled on this
instance of SQL Server.
```

Next, the main background threads in the server start, including LazyWriter, LogWriter, Checkpoint, and Database Mirroring. The only evidence you see of this is shown in the previous message—Database Mirroring is enabled (you will not see this message unless you are running SQL Server 2005 SP1 or using trace flag 1400 for RTM).

```
2006-08-27 22:28:00.25 spid4s       Starting up database 'master'.
2006-08-27 22:28:00.33 spid4s       Recovery is writing a checkpoint in
database 'master' (1). This is an informational message only. No user
action is required.
2006-08-27 22:28:00.41 spid4s       CHECKDB for database 'master' finished
without errors on 2006-07-21 17:06:54.247 (local time). This is an
informational message only; no user action is required.
```

Now we are ready to start up the system databases and user databases. But processing is forked at this point. You can see from this ERRORLOG fragment that master is started. However, instead of the word "server" in the third column, there is a spid number. The "s" after the number means system spid (or session). The spid number in the ERRORLOG also indicates that processing is split at this point. The main thread that has been either processing or farming out all the work is still running, but it now waits for tempdb to be recovered. This new session to start up databases proceeds to recover system and user databases. After tempdb is recovered, it signals the main thread that connections can be allowed in the server.

```
2006-08-27 22:28:00.48 spid4s       SQL Trace ID 1 was started by login "sa".
2006-08-27 22:28:00.51 spid4s       Starting up database 'mssqlsystemresource'.
2006-08-27 22:28:00.56 spid4s       The resource database build version is
9.00.2047. This is an informational message only. No user action is required.
```

Next we start up the default trace in the engine (configurable via the "default trace enabled" sp_configure option), and the resource database is started. The build version message is new to SQL Server 2005 SP1.

```
2006-08-27 22:28:00.97 spid4s       Server name is 'RCWARD'. This is an
informational message only. No user action is required.
2006-08-27 22:28:00.97 spid9s       Starting up database 'model'.
2006-08-27 22:28:01.41 spid9s       Clearing tempdb database.
2006-08-27 22:28:02.20 spid9s       Starting up database 'tempdb'.
```

As you can see, model is started and then `tempdb` is created. Note the different spid number. This is because the work to start model and create `tempdb` is started from a different system session. The server name is displayed from the current system session that opened master. The system session that creates `tempdb` ends after that is completed, but the system session that opened master remains as the signal handler (this thread checks if the engine has been notified to shut down by SCM). You can see this system session by looking for a row in sys.dm_exec_requests where command = 'SIGNAL HANDLER'.

```
2006-08-27 22:28:02.22 Server        Server is listening on [ 'any' <ipv4>
1433].
2006-08-27 22:28:02.28 Server        Server local connection provider is ready
to accept connection on [ \\.\pipe\SQLLocal\MSSQLSERVER ].
2006-08-27 22:28:02.28 Server        Server local connection provider is ready
to accept connection on [ \\.\pipe\sql\query ].
2006-08-27 22:28:02.28 Server        Server is listening on [ 127.0.0.1 <ipv4>
1434].
2006-08-27 22:28:02.28 Server        Dedicated admin connection support was
established for listening locally on port 1434.
```

Now that `tempdb` has been created, it is time to let connections into the server (allowing connections into the server before this could prevent `tempdb` from starting, because all worker threads were consumed by incoming connections). This is done by the original main thread (hence the word "server" instead of a spid number). However, the system session that will become the signal handler is still running.

```
2006-08-27 22:28:02.61 spid12s       The Service Broker protocol transport is
disabled or not configured.
2006-08-27 22:28:02.61 spid12s       The Database Mirroring protocol transport
is disabled or not configured.
2006-08-27 22:28:02.64 spid12s       Service Broker manager has started.
2006-08-27 22:28:03.56 Server        SQL Server is now ready for client
connections. This is an informational message; no user action is required.
```

As part of letting connections in, the server starts protocols for Service Broker and Database Mirroring (if they are enabled) and starts the Service Broker Manager. It then announces that the server can accept connections (technically, by the time this message has printed, connections could be allowed).

```
2006-08-27 22:28:04.14 spid20s       Starting up database 'ReportServerTempDB'.
2006-08-27 22:28:04.14 spid21s       Starting up database 'AdventureWorksDW'.
2006-08-27 22:28:04.14 spid18s       Starting up database 'ReportServer'.
2006-08-27 22:28:04.14 spid23s       Starting up database 'pubs'.
2006-08-27 22:28:04.14 spid22s       Starting up database 'AdventureWorks'.
2006-08-27 22:28:04.14 spid19s       Starting up database 'msdb'.
2006-08-27 22:28:04.16 spid24s       Starting up database 'pubs2'.
2006-08-27 22:28:04.16 spid25s       Starting up database 'test'.
2006-08-27 22:28:06.14 spid25s       Analysis of database 'test' (14) is 100%
complete (approximately 0 seconds remain). This is an informational message
```

only. No user action is required.
2006-08-27 22:28:06.17 spid23s   Analysis of database 'pubs' (11) is 100%
complete (approximately 0 seconds remain). This is an informational message
only. No user action is required.
2006-08-27 22:28:08.03 spid4s   Recovery of any in-doubt distributed
transactions involving Microsoft Distributed Transaction Coordinator (MS
DTC) has completed. This is an informational message only. No user action is
required.
2006-08-27 22:28:08.03 spid4s   Recovery is complete. This is an
informational message only. No user action is required.

While this is being printed, the system session that opened master reads information in master about user databases and starts them. This involves opening each user database and running recovery on them. Notice the different spid numbers in the ERRORLOG for these databases. This step is skipped if trace flag 3607 or 3608 is enabled or if the –f startup parameter is used for SQLSERVR.EXE. The server, by default, throttles the maximum number of workers to recover user databases to 4 times the number of CPUs detected for SQL Server to run on, but it will not use any more than the number of databases to start up.

Finally, just before becoming the SIGNAL HANDLER, the system session that opened master launches any startup stored procedures. What happened to the original thread that called wmain?

SQL Server Error and Exception Handling
In this section, you'll learn how SQL Server handles errors and exceptions. Because SQL Server hosts third-party code, it must handle not only its own exceptions and errors, but also those of foreign code running in its process space.

SQL Server and Windows Exceptions
One of the most powerful features in the SQL Server engine is its robust handling of critical problems. The engine makes every attempt to isolate a critical error and affect only the minimal user or database. For example, if a thread inside the SQL Server engine encounters an EXCEPTION_ACCESS_VIOLATION, in most cases, the engine handles this exception, attempts to roll back any active transactions, clean up thread resources, notify the user of a fatal error, and return the thread to a pool of worker threads. I'll talk later in this chapter about situations where this cannot be done safely. But in most situations, the exception is handled, reported to the user, and logged. In the ideal case, only a single user is affected by the problem. That is the ideal situation. Later I'll discuss situations where it doesn't always work out this way.

Many commercial software products do not attempt to handle Windows exceptions in this fashion. The default behavior for these programs is to *crash* and allow the default debugger (usually the infamous Dr. Watson) for Windows to capture dump information about the exception. The developers of the SQL Server engine from the very first version on Windows NT decided to take advantage of Structured Exception Handling (SEH) to provide a more robust engine. As I said, in some situations, the engine gets into some unusual states due to this feature. For the most part, I would say that this feature has been a very big plus for the SQL Server engine. With the exceptions that I'll mention later in the chapter, most EXCEPTION_ACCESS_VIOLATION situations are bugs with the SQL Server product. Without this feature, I have no doubt the pain for customers and my job would involve many sleepless nights attempting to figure out the cause of an access violation because the entire server crashed. Instead, in some cases the opposite has occurred. Because the engine handles these exceptions by default, I've had to point out to some customers their system has encountered a few access violations. I'll show you later in the chapter exactly how to recognize these situations and what to do about them.

SQL Server Engine Errors

Windows exceptions are not the only error situations the engine will encounter during its execution. I will not attempt in this book to address how to handle every critical error situation (but I will talk about a few interesting ones later in the chapter), but let me talk some about how the SQL Server engine handles errors, resolve some myth and mystery about error logging and severity, and talk about some of the interesting diagnostics available to resolve situations involving errors.

First, all errors encountered in the SQL Server engine go through the same common code to "raise" an error. This has the advantage of allowing the engine developers to provide some common diagnostics to provide more information when any error is raised.

- All raised errors can be traced using the SQLTrace Exception event.

- For advanced diagnostics, you can enable the engine to produce a dump file for debugging purposes when a specific error number is raised.

What about the ERRORLOG and EventLog? Why do some errors get reported in these logs and others don't? Why do some errors get reported in just the ERRORLOG? All good questions. Sometimes all this seems like a bit of a mystery!

First, you can disable the writing of errors and messages to the Windows Event Log with the –n startup parameter (errors and messages are still written to the ERRORLOG). Second, there are some situations where the engine has no user application to return a message, such as a background process like LazyWriter. In these cases, it would only log the message in the ERRORLOG and/or Event Log. Third, some errors or messages are not localized to the language installed for SQL Server. These messages go only to the ERRORLOG. They sometimes come from system sessions, are typically rare messages to encounter, and sometimes contain verbose information about a problem.

SQL Server 2005 Enhancements

It is hard not to brag about the work my fellow support engineers and I did in getting SQL Server 2005 out the door. I know it took longer to release this product than customers would have liked. But I will say that it did give the SQL Server development team the time to put in some really neat supportability features. The jury is still out on what type of job the SQL Server development team did. In some cases, they put in these features with the anticipation for their need based on past experience and how the software was designed and developed. The proof will be in the experience of customers and PSS as we tackle new problems over the next few years with SQL Server 2005.

Dynamic Management Views (DMV)

Have you ever wondered about the magic behind `sysprocesses` and `syslockinfo` in SQL Server 2000? If you understand the engine, you know some of that magic. Anytime you reference `sysprocesses` or `syslockinfo` in a query, the engine creates a virtual table on-the-fly based on the current values of memory structures within the engine. This information can be very helpful in so many different situations. It's a way to actually query the state of the SQL Server engine at any given point in time using the T-SQL language. No debugger or special tool—just built right into the natural query language of the engine.

By the time SQL Server 2000 was developed, the SQL Server development team realized that being able to just diagnose the basic server processes (SPIDs) and locks was not enough. They did add a few other features to provide information based on memory structures in the form of functions such as `::fn_virtualfilestats` and `::fn_get_trace_info`. But the team knew it was possible to expose much more data that would help diagnose important execution information about the engine.

Thus was born the concept of dynamic management views (DMVs). These were originally referred to as virtual tables, which is the term used for `sysprocesses` and `syslockinfo` in previous versions. But someone aptly pointed out that *virtual tables* was actually a definition for a SQL view based on a true table. Other names were tossed around until DMV finally stuck. These really are virtual tables, because they are not actual tables. But they are special views because they are usually not based on a table either. They are instead derived from "dynamic" information stored within engine memory structures. The term "management" made sense because these views assist in the management of the server.

I won't use this section to list all the DMVs that the SQL Server development team built into the engine, but I will talk about how to use some of them as part of troubleshooting in the rest of this chapter. You can run a query to find all the DMVs by executing the following from any database context:

```
select * from sys.system_objects where name like 'dm_%'
```

This is all possible because the SQL Server development team ensured that any DMV they created had to start with the name dm_. No other system object defined in the resource database is created in this fashion. There is no special "type" for you to use to find these. You must rely on the naming convention. If you run this query on a SQL Server 2005 RTM server, you will get back 85 rows. But not every one of these is documented and intended for standard customer use. These are listed in the SQL Server Books Online. (Just pull up the Index and type **sys.dm_** and you will see all of them in order (79 of them, in fact). I'll actually cover one of them in this book because it contains some interesting information, `sys.dm_os_ring_buffers`. This wasn't originally documented because it wasn't expected that most customers would use it to manage their systems. Some of these are not views but rather functions such as `sys.dm_exec_sql_text`. To complicate the story, the server still has some functions based on memory structures that still use the fn_ naming convention, such as `fn_virtualfilestats`. This was done to avoid breaking any customers relying on these functions.

While this chapter is not a tutorial on how to use Dynamic Management Views, here are some of the more important DMVs I've been using to troubleshoot customer problems and dig into server behavior:

- `sys.dm_exec_sessions` and `sys.dm_exec_requests`. These two combine effectively as the replacement for sysprocesses.

- `sys.dm_exec_query_stats`. Current performance statistics for cached objects and queries.

- `sys.dm_os_wait_stats`. Find out where the waits are occurring in the engine. Replaces DBCC SQLPERF('WAITSTATS').

- `sys.dm_db_missing_index_details`. See what indexes could have helped performance of previous queries. A must to look at for any server that is having performance problems.

- `sys.dm_exec_sql_text`. A dynamic management function to get the text of a SQL query based on its SQL handle.

- `sys.dm_os_ring_buffers`. As stated, this one is not documented but might have some practice use for the advanced user.

TIP

To "join" the use of a function like sys.dm_exec_sql_text you need to use the CROSS APPLY operator. For example, here is a query to get the "input buffer" for sessions found in sys.dm_exec_requests:

```
select session_id, s2.text from sys.dm_exec_requests
cross apply sys.dm_exec_sql_text(sql_handle) s2
```

Don't run this query in the context of a database in a compatiblity mode < 90. It will fail because the APPLY operator is new to SQL Server 2005.

Dedicated Admin Connection (DAC)

In SQL Server 7.0 SP3 and SQL Server 2000 SP1, the SQL Server development team invented the concept of messages that would warn the user that SQL Server may be partially or fully hung. The most common of these messages is 17883. I'll also talk more about this message later in the chapter.

In the early days of Yukon design, the SQL Server development team began to think about a way of connecting to the server when it was in a hung state. Since the hung state meant that standard connections and queries couldn't be run from the normal worker pool of threads, a special type of connection would have to be established at startup and just "wait" for someone who really needed it. We talk more about the DAC elsewhere in this book, but let me give you some additional perspective on its design and use.

1. Even though it is called Dedicated Admin Connection, it is not something to be used by administrators for everyday work. It is *dedicated*, or *reserved*, for emergency purposes only.

2. Be careful if you try to connect to DAC with Management Studio by supplying a connection string of `admin:<instance name>`. This is because SMSS remembers the last name you used for a connection and by default uses this the next time you connect. You might notice this, click the OK button, and be using DAC when you did not intend to.

3. Only one is allowed per instance at a time. So if someone accidentally uses DAC and leaves the connection open, when you really need it for a hung server, you are out of luck.

4. It may be difficult to figure out who is using DAC if you want to kick them out and make sure they are not using it unnecessarily.

5. By default, DAC is allowed only on a local connection. You must enable it for a remote connection. This means that DAC is not on by default for a clustered instance. This may seem like a fairly limiting decision on our part, but if you think about it, it's not all that bad. Clustering by its nature is designed to fail over to another node if the current instance is not "online." A hung SQL Server will be considered offline after a period of time, so you may not have time to even connect with DAC.

I'll talk more later in this chapter about how to use DAC in a situation where a server may be hung.

Dump Enhancements

Later in the chapter, I'll talk about a stack dump and why you might encounter the terms *stack dump*, *user dump*, *mini-dump*, or *crash dump*. Your experience with "dumps" will be mostly to send them to PSS (I hope to change that for the future, and I'll explain why later). But the development team did make some enhancements with how the server generates dump files that has an impact on supporting the product:

- A "full" user dump file is a snapshot of all committed memory of a process. The format of this file is per the design of the Windows Debuggers (see the Debugging Tools for Windows documentation). For x86 computers, this is not that much of a problem since, at the most, the committed memory in the virtual address space will be 3GB. For IA64 and x64 machines with 32GB of RAM, this presents a new problem. Getting a full user dump file for a 32GB SQL Server could take a long time, and the process is suspended when the dump is taking place.

  The SQL Server development team worked with the team that develops the Microsoft debuggers and developed a method to dump only the memory in the process space that is normally required to troubleshoot a problem. So the server can now capture a "filtered" dump, which is the committed bytes of SQL Server minus the data/index pages of the buffer pool.

This is fine, because when a support engineer needs to look at a full user dump file, we usually don't need to look at all of the data and index pages. We typically just need much of the "overhead" memory structures that are not part of the normal buffer pool. (This same "debugging" feature is available in SQL Server 2000 Service Pack 4.)

■ We have the ability to configure the engine to create a dump file (mini, filtered, or full) to capture the exact context of the engine code when an error is encountered. More on how this can be helpful later in the chapter.

■ The server doesn't symbolize stack dumps in the ERRORLOG anymore. The server had done this ever since SQL Server 6.0. But the penalty has now become too high to do this. To completely create a symbolized stack dump in the ERRORLOG costs memory and CPU consumption. The SQL Server development team found that in many cases, a handled exception for one thread would result in a dump that caused so much resource consumption it was not worth the cost. I'll talk more about how there is still beneficial information in the ERRORLOG to help determine if the stack dump is due to a SQL Server problem.

Surface Area Configuration Manager

Common sense tells us that reducing SQL Server's attack surface is a wise move. Every day, hackers are looking to break into systems in new and unusual ways.

One of these areas of attacks was through extended stored procedures and the OLE Automation object (sometimes just called sp_OA). Unfortunately, some of these extended procedures (or xprocs) were ones that shipped with the product.

So, by default, the SQL Server development team decided to disable many of these extended procedures and the use of sp_OA objects out of the box after install. If you as an administrator think they need to be available to users, the Surface Area Configuration (SAC) Manager can be used to turn them on/off. These "features" are also available to configure directly with the sp_configure stored procedure. In fact, SAC simply runs sp_configure queries behind the scenes based on user input.

For example, xp_cmdshell has been a worry for many administrators in recent years. (It seemed like such a cool thing back in the SQL 4.21 days.) So by default, no one—not even administrators—can run this procedure. Any attempt to do so results in the following error:

```
Msg 15281, Level 16, State 1, Procedure xp_cmdshell, Line 1
SQL Server blocked access to procedure 'sys.xp_cmdshell' of component
'xp_cmdshell' because this component is turned off as part of the security
configuration for this server. A system administrator can enable the use of
'xp_cmdshell' by using sp_configure. For more information about enabling
'xp_cmdshell', see "Surface Area Configuration" in SQL Server Books Online.
```

I personally would be excited to see some of these extended procedures and especially sp_OA disabled by default. I'll show you some examples later of just how dangerous this can be. So be careful when you decide to enable some of the SAC features turned off by default.

Public Symbols

As Ken Henderson has pointed out in his books, if you really want to understand SQL Server at an expert level, learn how to use a debugger. I'm not saying you must learn how to interpret assembly code for a live process. Just learn the basics of how to bring up the debugger and especially how to load a dump file with the debugger.

Using a dump file is fairly useless without being able to resolve symbol names like functions and variables. In fact, one of the more frustrating debugging scenarios for me over the years is having an issue finding the right symbols to match the version of images (EXEs and DLLs) from a dump file.

Microsoft allows customers to access what are called *public* symbols. Public symbols contain only enough information for you to get valid "stack frames" with symbols of function names for any given thread. This can be helpful to you in certain situations, especially if you use extended stored procedures, `sp_OA COM` objects, or linked servers.

I'll show you an example later of how to use this to find out how a poorly written extended procedure can cause you problems.

The proper method to load symbols from the Microsoft public symbol server is via the symbol path: http://msdl.microsoft.com/download/symbols.

Critical Errors and Server Recovery Troubleshooting

Troubleshooting Server Startup Failures

In some situations, if the server engine encounters an error during startup, the result is a catastrophic server termination. In this section, I'll discuss the most common scenarios that cause a server startup failure and how you can resolve them.

One of the reasons for a startup failure for SQL Server is a failure to open or recover the system database's master, model, tempdb, or resource database. These scenarios are covered in detail in Chapter 2, "Data Corruption and Recovery Issues." In this section, I'll talk about two scenarios where SQL Server fails to start:

- Problems in starting the SQL Server service
- Failures in starting the server networking components

Service-Specific Problems

SQL Server is installed and normally run as a Windows Service. This means there are some scenarios to consider for startup failure that are specific to services versus startup failures within the `SQLSERVR.EXE` code.

How can you tell whether a startup problem is an issue specific to a service? Let's start by looking at the most common problem for service startup: a logon failure. Every service has properties, and one of them is the Log On account for the service. Anytime you run a program in Windows, the program typically runs under the context of the account logged in to Windows. So if you were to run SQLSERVR.EXE from the command prompt, it would run under the security context of you. But a service can be started automatically at Windows Startup, so you must configure what Windows Account will be used for its security context.

Take a look at the Properties screen in Figure 6-1 for the SQL Server service from the SQL Configuration Manager.

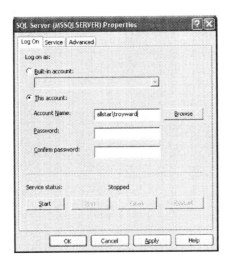

FIGURE 6-1   The SQL Configuration Manager

This first tab, Log On, is used to set up the security context account for the service. Any operation performed by the service is typically performed under this security context.

Let me take a second to talk about the use of SQL Configuration Manager. You absolutely *must* use SQL Configuration Manager to modify the properties of any of the installed services for SQL Server. Do not use the Services applet from Administrative Tools in Windows. This is because the SQL Configuration Manager performs additional operations to set the security context of SQL Server files and resources that are not done by the Windows Services applet. Consider the following situation: You decide you want the SQL Server service running under the Power User account called ryanward. So you use the Services applet to change the Log On account properties to this account. When you restart SQL Server, you may encounter the error shown in Figure 6-2.

FIGURE 6-2 Problems when changing the startup account

So your first thought is to check the SQL ERRORLOG file. But the ERRORLOG file is not updated for this startup sequence. So, your next stop is the EventLog (Application). You now see a series of 17058 errors (which happens to be the service-specific error in the dialog box) like the following:

```
initerrlog: Could not open error log file 'C:\Program Files\Microsoft SQL
Server\MSSQL.1\MSSQL\LOG\ERRORLOG'. Operating system error = 5(Access is denied.).
```

You can see the problem. The account ryanward does not have permissions to access the ERRORLOG file. This is because the SQL Server Configuration Manager modifies the NTFS security permissions for the installed SQL Server files to the Log On account you specify with the tool. The Services applet has no knowledge of what files are installed for the service, so it does not perform this operation.

Now back to a common problem for the Log On account for SQL Server even if you used the SQL Configuration Manager. Let's stay with the account ryanward that you now successfully have configured. What if, based on your corporate policy, you are forced to change the password for this account? You forgot you had SQL Server configured for this account, and one morning after restarting your computer, you get the error shown in Figure 6-3 when starting SQL Server from the SQL Configuration Manager.

FIGURE 6-3 An error when starting SQL Server

Unfortunately, this error doesn't tell you much, so you'll have to look at the EventLog:

```
The MSSQLSERVER service was unable to log on as .\ryanward with the currently
configured password due to the following error:
Logon failure: unknown user name or bad password.
```

To ensure that the service is configured properly, use the Services snap-in in Microsoft Management Console (MMC).

You can see this quicker if you just try to start the service from the command prompt with the net start command (see Figure 6-4).

FIGURE 6-4   Starting from the command prompt

When you encounter this problem, it is almost always a password problem, and you need to correct the password for the Log On account (remember to use SQL Configuration Manager).

There is something common about these two situations, and a big clue would be to determine if the problem is specific to starting as a service or starting the SQL Server engine. If a new ERRORLOG file is not created in the LOG directory, the problem has occurred as part of the Windows Service Control Manager (SCM) starting the SQL Server service. In this case, pay attention to any error you get from the application you use to start the service, and look at the System and Application Event Log. Any errors encountered by the Windows SCM would be logged in the System Event Log. The one interesting twist to this situation is if the Log On security account for the service cannot open the ERRORLOG file. (This is the situation I showed you earlier about what can happen if you don't use the SQL Configuration Manager.) In this case, the Windows SCM has successfully started the SQLSERVR.EXE program, but the program fails during startup when trying to create the ERRORLOG file. So there is no ERRORLOG, but in this situation, the SQL Server engine writes errors about accessing the ERRORLOG in the Windows Event Log.

Another method for you to narrow down a problem specific to starting as a service is to run SQLSERVR.EXE from the Windows command prompt. All the program parameters for SQLSERVR.EXE are documented in the SQL BOL. My standard process is to just run the program as shown in Figure 6-5.

The -c just means "I'm not running SQL as a service." There is no harm in leaving this off; it just delays startup as SQL Server figures out that it was not started as a service. Notice that the information that is displayed in the command window is the same as what you see in the ERRORLOG. This is not actually 100% accurate, because you can see more information in the console than in the ERRORLOG. There may be a few places in the SQL Server code where the engine dumps information to stdout, which shows up only if we run SQL Server from the command window. (The information goes to a hidden desktop you can't see when running as a service.) The first line of this output is an example of this:

```
2006-05-23 22:38:10.96 Server    Authentication mode is MIXED.
```

FIGURE 6-5   Running SQL Server as a console app

Anytime I've had a customer contact me and tell me that SQL Server won't start, I do the following:

1. I ask the customer what the ERRORLOG says.

2. If no new ERRORLOG was created, I start from the command prompt.

3. If this works, I check the Event Log to see possible causes.

What might be a reason that SQL Server can't start as a service but can from the command line? Well, if you run SQL Server from the command line, it is starting under your security context. The service may be configured to log on as a different account.

Server Network Cannot Start

You have a big problem if SQL Server cannot accept connections. One possible reason for this is that the software within the SQL Server engine that is "listening" on various network protocols fails to initialize, or start up.

Consider the following scenario. SQL Server is enabled to listen for connections over TCP/IP, Named Pipes, and local shared memory connections.

Let's say at server startup, SQL Server cannot properly "bind" to the default configured port 1433 for TCP/IP. Therefore, it cannot respond to any SQL connections from a client using TCP/IP. In this scenario, SQL Server shuts down the engine when it determines it cannot "listen" over TCP/IP. Let's say that you decide to configure SQL Server to listen on a default port other than 1433. Unfortunately, you pick a port that another program is already using. When you attempt to start SQL Server, it fails on startup. Remember our check from before? Well, a new ERRORLOG was created, so take a look at it and notice these errors at the end of the log file:

```
2006-05-24 20:54:32.40 Server         Error: 26023, Severity: 16, State: 1.
2006-05-24 20:54:32.40 Server         Server TCP provider failed to listen on
[ 'any' <ipv4> 6129]. Tcp port is already in use.
2006-05-24 20:54:32.40 Server         Error: 17182, Severity: 16, State: 1.
2006-05-24 20:54:32.40 Server         TDSSNIClient initialization failed with
error 0x2740, status code 0xa.
2006-05-24 20:54:32.40 Server         Error: 17182, Severity: 16, State: 1.
2006-05-24 20:54:32.40 Server         TDSSNIClient initialization failed with
error 0x2740, status code 0x1.
2006-05-24 20:54:32.40 Server         Error: 17826, Severity: 18, State: 3.
2006-05-24 20:54:32.40 Server         Could not start the network library
because of an internal error in the network library. To determine the cause,
review the errors immediately preceding this one in the error log.
2006-05-24 20:54:32.40 Server         Error: 17120, Severity: 16, State: 1.
2006-05-24 20:54:32.40 Server         SQL Server could not spawn FRunCM thread.
Check the SQL Server error log and the Windows event logs for information
about possible related problems.
```

This may seem like a lot to digest, but the errors are really in "levels" starting from the bottom up. The top or first error in the log is the true core problem. The error is actually very descriptive: Tcp port is already in use. I can even see in the message that the port I was using was already being used by someone else.

If I were to now run the following command from a Windows command prompt, I would see the information shown in Figure 6-6.

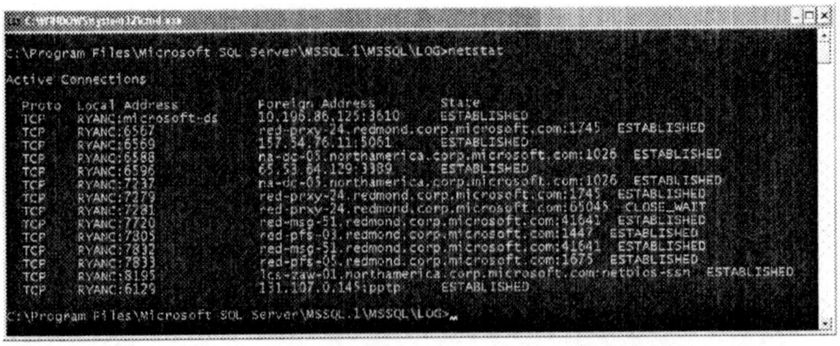

FIGURE 6-6   The Windows command prompt

You can see from the Local Address column that port 6129 is already in use (in this case, a PPTP session I'm using).

This is not likely the problem of why the server networking components could not start, but it is an example for you to see the symptoms. If you encounter this problem, you have two courses of action:

- Disable the network protocol that has the problem so you can start the server if you need to get it up and running.

- Unless the problem is really obvious, like the one I presented here, you need to work with your network administrator to determine the cause of the network provider problem.

In this situation, the top or "first" error is a key one to focus on. In this case, the error was

```
2006-05-24 20:54:32.40 Server      Error: 26023, Severity: 16, State: 1.
2006-05-24 20:54:32.40 Server      Server TCP provider failed to listen on
[ 'any' <ipv4> 6129]. Tcp port is already in use
```

This is a specific error number for the port-in-use problem. Other errors you might see in this situation are 26024 (general TCP failure), 26029 (general Named Pipes failure), or 26031 (general shared memory failure). Each of these messages includes more specific error information to indicate why the networking API associated with the protocol could not "listen" for connections.

Failed Hardware Check

The SQL OS system in SQL Server 2005 requires some specific CPU instructions in order for the SQL Server to start up. The SQL Server development team found during the beta that some CPUs didn't support this instruction. Unfortunately, the development team didn't get code changes before release checked in to the initial Setup Consistency Check to catch this. Therefore, as part of installing the product, SQL Server may attempt to start but will fail with the following error (the EventID in the Event Log is 17203):

```
SQL Server cannot start on this machine. The processor(s) (CPU) model does not
support all instructions needed for SQL Server to run. Refer to the System
Requirements section in BOL for further information.
```

This error results in the shutdown of the server engine. So what is the story behind this error? The SQL development team is always looking for methods to increase performance. Specific CPU chipsets expose an instruction to pre-fetch data in the local memory cache of the CPU. This can allow SQL Server to access specific memory buffers faster. The only problem is that your CPU must support this instruction. This should not be a problem for most modern computers. For x86 systems, if the computer is Pentium III class or higher, you should not run into any problems. For x64 and IA64, you should not see any issues. (None were seen during the beta.)

If you do encounter this problem, you should check whether the CPU on your computer supports the intrinsic _mm_prefetch (x86 and x64) or _ _lfetch (ia64). There is no workaround for this problem except to install SQL Server on a different computer. This is a requirement for SQL Server to start successfully.

Troubleshooting Server-Critical Errors

After SQL Server has successfully started and business is as usual, the server engine is pretty robust to errors. For the majority of customers I've worked with—for SQL Server 2000 and my current experience with SQL Server 2005—the error conditions they encounter do not result in what we support engineers call a server-down situation. However, these situations can happen and, when they do, you need to be able to react and get quick resolution to the issue.

In this section, I'll discuss three categories of critical errors:

- **Stack dumps.** These are situations that are considered "fatal" errors because the end result is a termination of the connection that initiated the request that led to the stack dump. (Hold on—I'm about to tell you what a stack dump is.) I'll focus on scenarios here where the SQL Server engine remains running.

- **Crashes.** These are situations where SQL Server has started and is running, but an exception leads to an expected termination of the server engine. In many cases, the crash is identified by a stack dump.

- **Other critical errors.** These are errors that are critical because they affect more than one user or connection. The symptoms are typically an error in the ERRORLOG but may not include a stack dump.

SQL Server Stack Dumps

I mentioned earlier in this chapter that SQL Server has used Structured Exception Handling since the first version of SQL Server on Windows NT back in 1993. In order to get the right diagnostic information to debug an exception that is handled, the SQL Server development team implemented the concept of a *stack dump*. This concept is actually nothing new. If you run a program on a Windows XP or 2003 Server and the program does not have Structured Exception Handling, it is considered an unhandled exception. But this doesn't mean you can't get information about the exception. "Wrapped" around your program's execution is a special exception handler that "catches" the exception and invokes the *default debugger*. This default debugger for a standard Windows installation is a program called Dr. Watson (drwtsn32.exe). This program is designed to attach to your process and capture information about the exception, including stack frames for all threads and information about the exception. So, in essence, you could call this a stack dump.

For SQL Server, the SQL Server development team knew that when they handled the exception, if they didn't provide some of the same information you could get from Dr. Watson or a debugger, PSS engineers would be left with no visible trace of what caused the exception. So the development team added code into the engine to *dump* information about the exception, including the stack frame of the thread that encountered the exception.

Perhaps you have seen something like this in SQL Server 2000 in your ERRORLOG and wondered what kind of error it was:

```
*Stack Dump being sent to S:\MSSQL$AXEVSQL01\log\SQLDump0082.txt
2006-04-19 16:17:44.79 spid144    Error: 0, Severity: 19, State: 0
2006-04-19 16:17:44.79 spid144    SqlDumpExceptionHandler: Process 144
generated
fatal exception c0000005 EXCEPTION_ACCESS_VIOLATION. SQL Server is terminating
this process..
```

```
*
**************************************************************************
*
* BEGIN STACK DUMP:
*    04/19/06 16:17:44 spid 144
*
*    Exception Address = 009898D1 (CDStream::operator= + 0003F734 Line
0+00000000)
*    Exception Code    = c0000005 EXCEPTION_ACCESS_VIOLATION
*    Access Violation occurred reading address 00000000
* Input Buffer 306 bytes -
*  SELECT   spid, blocked, hostprocess, hostname FROM master..sysprocesses
*       WHERE blocked > 1    and blocked <> spid     exec dba_reports..DBA_SQL
  Short Stack Dump
* 009898D1 Module(sqlservr+005898D1) (CDStream::operator=+0003F734)
* 0098C536 Module(sqlservr+0058C536) (CDStream::operator=+00042399)
* 0098D08B Module(sqlservr+0058D08B) (CDStream::operator=+00042EEE)
* 0098D144 Module(sqlservr+0058D144) (CDStream::operator=+00042FA7)
* 00534C25 Module(sqlservr+00134C25)
* 004298F7 Module(sqlservr+000298F7)
* 004DC401 Module(sqlservr+000DC401)
* 00535B53 Module(sqlservr+00135B53)
* 0043288B Module(sqlservr+0003288B)
* 0042F0D1 Module(sqlservr+0002F0D1)
* 0043990D Module(sqlservr+0003990D)
* 0043990D Module(sqlservr+0003990D)
* 0043990D Module(sqlservr+0003990D)
* 0040C369 Module(sqlservr+0000C369)
* 0040C285 Module(sqlservr+0000C285)
* 004384BB Module(sqlservr+000384BB)
* 00415D04 Module(sqlservr+00015D04)
* 00416214 Module(sqlservr+00016214)
* 00415F28 Module(sqlservr+00015F28)
* 0050BCEF Module(sqlservr+0010BCEF)
* 0050BB13 Module(sqlservr+0010BB13)
* 00415D04 Module(sqlservr+00015D04)
* 00416214 Module(sqlservr+00016214)
* 00415F28 Module(sqlservr+00015F28)
* 0049C32E Module(sqlservr+0009C32E)
* 0049C46A Module(sqlservr+0009C46A)
* 41075309 Module(ums+00005309) (ProcessWorkRequests+000002D9 Line
456+00000000)
* 41074978 Module(ums+00004978) (ThreadStartRoutine+00000098 Line
263+00000007)
* 7C34940F Module(MSVCR71+0000940F) (endthread+000000AA)
* 77E66063 Module(kernel32+00026063) (GetModuleFileNameA+000000EB)
* -------------------------------------------------------------------------
--
2006-04-19 16:17:48.76 spid144     Stack Signature for the dump is 0x8B25ABAA
2006-04-19 16:17:48.79 spid144     Error: 0, Severity: 19, State: 0
2006-04-19 16:17:48.79 spid144     language_exec: Process 144 generated an
access
violation. SQL Server is terminating this process..
```

For years, the engine produced the stack dump in the ERRORLOG (called the *short stack dump*) and a more comprehensive dump of information into a .TXT file in the LOG directory of the SQL Server installation. Starting in SQL Server 2000 Service Pack 3, the SQL Server development team realized that debugging efforts would be improved if they also produced a mini-dump file in the standard Windows Debugging dump file format. To accomplish this, they created a program called SQLDUMPER.EXE. The design was for the SQL Server engine to spawn the SQLDUMPER.EXE process and pass the appropriate information for SQLDUMPER.EXE to obtain a mini-dump file for the SQLSERVR.EXE process. SQLDUMPER.EXE was designed to be generic, though, so that it could be used for any program in the SQL Server box. (Analysis Services and Reporting Services use this, for example.) In fact, SQLDUMPER.EXE can be used with any Windows program. It uses the MiniDumpWriteDump API call from the Windows SDK. You can actually run SQLDUMPER.EXE yourself, specifying the ProcessID of any running Windows program to obtain a dump file of its current state. (See Microsoft Knowledge Base article 917825 for more information about the 2005 version of this program.)

The mini-dump files are stored in the LOG directory. In addition, all executions of SQLDUMPER.EXE are logged in a special text log file called SQLDUMPER_ERRORLOG.log. Not really much for you to interpret in here, except that you can get a quick feel for how many stack dumps were generated for a particular instance. For SQL Server 2005, anytime the engine produces a stack dump for an exception, four files are created in the LOG directory:

- The mini-dump file called SQLDump*nnnn*.mdmp

- A manifest file that is used by DW20.EXE and sent to the Microsoft servers to classify the dump called SQLDump*nnnn*.mft

- A text file (this is the "old full" stack dump) called SQLDump*nnnn*.txt

- The ERRORLOG file at the time of the exception called SQLDump*nnnn*.log

Certain other scenarios that cause a stack dump will not result in an error reported to Watson, and I'll cover those in this section. Furthermore, some dump files created for "hang" scenarios (as I will describe later in this chapter) use a naming convention of sqldmpr*nnn*.mdmp.

Moving forward with creating mini-dumps gave the development team some nice wins:

- It made it simpler to obtain a mini-dump file from a customer and load it in a debugger to look at the problem (like the stack frame for a thread that encountered an access violation).

- The server could bundle the mini-dump and ERRORLOG file into a cab file and push this to the Watson Error Reporting Server at Microsoft.

So, when you elect to participate in Error Reporting, behind the scenes SQLDUMPER.EXE takes the mini-dump file and calls a program named DW20.EXE. DW20.EXE is the one responsible for communicating with Microsoft to send the "error report." So what does

Microsoft do with these files? Despite your most suspicious thoughts, they don't go into the garbage can of network file servers. The product groups actually have servers and databases where they can run analyses on customer reports of these stack dump scenarios. So if you encountered an access violation one time and didn't feel like calling PSS, but you participated in Error Reporting, Microsoft would see that some user encountered the access violation. In fact, Microsoft has a method to see if many users encounter the same problem. If the mini-dump file provides enough information, the development team may even be able to craft a code fix for the next service pack to resolve the problem before you call to report it.

Windows Exceptions

Let's talk now about some scenarios where stack dumps are produced. The most common situation where the SQL Server engine produces a stack dump is a handled Windows exception. As I've mentioned, the SQL Server engine uses Structured Exception Handling in much of its code to catch Windows exceptions such as an Access Violation (AV). Let's see what the stack dump looks like for an AV for SQL Server 2005 in the ERRORLOG and see if any of this information may be helpful for you to resolve the problem. (I formatted this some to make it easier to read. Also note that this stack dump is from an x86 machine. The stack dump can look different on x64 and IA64 processors because they support 64-bit pointers and possibly different registers.)

```
2006-02-19 20:01:22.63 spid51   Using 'dbghelp.dll' version '4.0.5'
2006-02-19 20:01:22.73 spid51   ***Stack Dump being sent to C:\Program
Files\Microsoft SQL Server\MSSQL.1\MSSQL\LOG\SQLDump0118.txt
2006-02-19 20:01:22.73 spid51   SqlDumpExceptionHandler: Process 51 generated
fatal exception c0000005 EXCEPTION_ACCESS_VIOLATION. SQL Server is terminating
this process.
2006-02-19 20:01:22.73 spid51
*********************************************************************************
2006-02-19 20:01:22.73 spid51   *
2006-02-19 20:01:22.73 spid51   * BEGIN STACK DUMP:
2006-02-19 20:01:22.74 spid51   *   02/19/06 20:01:22 spid 51
2006-02-19 20:01:22.74 spid51   *
2006-02-19 20:01:22.74 spid51   *
2006-02-19 20:01:22.74 spid51   *   Exception Address = 0110B72B
Module(sqlservr+0010B72B)
2006-02-19 20:01:22.74 spid51   *   Exception Code    = c0000005
EXCEPTION_ACCESS_VIOLATION
2006-02-19 20:01:22.74 spid51   *   Access Violation occurred reading address
00000020
2006-02-19 20:01:22.74 spid51   *   Input Buffer 172 bytes -
2006-02-19 20:01:22.76 spid51   *     select * from V1  where foo > 'p' and
(customerid > 10 or
2006-02-19 20:01:22.76 spid51   *     orderid < 20)
2006-02-19 20:01:22.77 spid51   *
2006-02-19 20:01:22.77 spid51   *
2006-02-19 20:01:22.77 spid51   *  MODULE                              BASE
END       SIZE
2006-02-19 20:01:22.77 spid51   * sqlservr                          01000000
02BA7FFF   01ba8000
```

```
2006-02-19 20:01:22.77 spid51  * ntdll       7C900000  7C9AFFFF  000b0000
2006-02-19 20:01:22.77 spid51  * kernel32    7C800000  7C8F3FFF  000f4000
2006-02-19 20:01:22.77 spid51  * MSVCR80     78130000  781CAFFF  0009b000
2006-02-19 20:01:22.77 spid51  * msvcrt      77C10000  77C67FFF  00058000
2006-02-19 20:01:22.77 spid51  * MSVCP80     7C420000  7C4A6FFF  00087000
2006-02-19 20:01:22.77 spid51  * ADVAPI32    77DD0000  77E6AFFF  0009b000
2006-02-19 20:01:22.77 spid51  * RPCRT4      77E70000  77F00FFF  00091000
2006-02-19 20:01:22.77 spid51  * USER32      77D40000  77DCFFFF  00090000
2006-02-19 20:01:22.77 spid51  * GDI32       7F10000   77F56FFF  00047000
2006-02-19 20:01:22.77 spid51  * CRYPT32     77A80000  77B13FFF  00094000
2006-02-19 20:01:22.77 spid51  * MSASN1      77B20000  77B31FFF  00012000
2006-02-19 20:01:22.77 spid51  * Secur32     77FE0000  77FF0FFF  00011000
2006-02-19 20:01:22.77 spid51  * MSWSOCK     71A50000  71A8EFFF  0003f000
2006-02-19 20:01:22.77 spid51  * WS2_32      71AB0000  71AC6FFF  00017000
2006-02-19 20:01:22.77 spid51  * WS2HELP     71AA0000  71AA7FFF  00008000
2006-02-19 20:01:22.77 spid51  * USERENV     769C0000  76A72FFF  000b3000
2006-02-19 20:01:22.77 spid51  * opends60    333E0000  333E6FFF  00007000
2006-02-19 20:01:22.77 spid51  * NETAPI32    5B860000  5B8B3FFF  00054000
2006-02-19 20:01:22.77 spid51  * SHELL32     7C9C0000  7D1D4FFF  00815000
2006-02-19 20:01:22.77 spid51  * SHLWAPI     77F60000  77FD5FFF  00076000
2006-02-19 20:01:22.77 spid51  * comctl32    773D0000  774D1FFF  00102000
2006-02-19 20:01:22.77 spid51  * comctl32    5D090000  5D126FFF  00097000
2006-02-19 20:01:22.77 spid51  * psapi       76BF0000  76BFAFFF  0000b000
2006-02-19 20:01:22.77 spid51  * instapi     48060000  48069FFF  0000a000
2006-02-19 20:01:22.77 spid51  * sqlevn70    4F610000  4F7A0FFF  00191000
2006-02-19 20:01:22.77 spid51  * SQLOS       344D0000  344D4FFF  00005000
2006-02-19 20:01:22.77 spid51  * rsaenh      33940000  33967FFF  00028000
2006-02-19 20:01:22.77 spid51  * AUTHZ       776C0000  776D0FFF  00011000
2006-02-19 20:01:22.77 spid51  * MSCOREE     79000000  79044FFF  00045000
2006-02-19 20:01:22.77 spid51  * ole32       774E0000  7761CFFF  0013d000
2006-02-19 20:01:22.77 spid51  * msv1_0      77C70000  77C92FFF  00023000
2006-02-19 20:01:22.77 spid51  * iphlpapi    76D60000  76D78FFF  00019000
2006-02-19 20:01:22.77 spid51  * kerberos    71CF0000  71D3AFFF  0004b000
2006-02-19 20:01:22.77 spid51  * cryptdll    76790000  7679BFFF  0000c000
2006-02-19 20:01:22.77 spid51  * schannel    767F0000  76816FFF  00027000
2006-02-19 20:01:22.77 spid51  * COMRES      77050000  77114FFF  000c5000
2006-02-19 20:01:22.77 spid51  * XOLEHLP     58CA0000  58CA5FFF  00006000
2006-02-19 20:01:22.77 spid51  * MSDTCPRX    6E560000  6E5CBFFF  0006c000
2006-02-19 20:01:22.77 spid51  * MSVCP60     76080000  760E4FFF  00065000
2006-02-19 20:01:22.77 spid51  * MTXCLU      750F0000  75102FFF  00013000
2006-02-19 20:01:22.77 spid51  * VERSION     77C00000  77C07FFF  00008000
2006-02-19 20:01:22.77 spid51  * WSOCK32     71AD0000  71AD8FFF  00009000
2006-02-19 20:01:22.77 spid51  * CLUSAPI     76D10000  76D20FFF  00011000
2006-02-19 20:01:22.77 spid51  * OLEAUT32    77120000  771ABFFF  0008c000
2006-02-19 20:01:22.77 spid51  * RESUTILS    750B0000  750C1FFF  00012000
2006-02-19 20:01:22.77 spid51  * FwcWsp      55600000  5562DFFF  0002e000
2006-02-19 20:01:22.77 spid51  * DNSAPI      76F20000  76F46FFF  00027000
2006-02-19 20:01:22.77 spid51  * winrnr      76FB0000  76FB7FFF  00008000
2006-02-19 20:01:22.77 spid51  * WLDAP32     76F60000  76F8BFFF  0002c000
2006-02-19 20:01:22.77 spid51  * hnetcfg     662B0000  66307FFF  00058000
2006-02-19 20:01:22.77 spid51  * wshtcpip    71A90000  71A97FFF  00008000
2006-02-19 20:01:22.77 spid51  * rasadhlp    76FC0000  76FC5FFF  00006000
2006-02-19 20:01:22.77 spid51  * security    71F80000  71F83FFF  00004000
```

```
2006-02-19 20:01:22.77 spid51   * dssenh           68100000   68123FFF   00024000
2006-02-19 20:01:22.77 spid51   * msfte            49910000   49B67FFF   00258000
2006-02-19 20:01:22.77 spid51   * dbghelp          440F0000   44207FFF   00118000
2006-02-19 20:01:22.77 spid51   * WINTRUST         76C30000   76C5DFFF   0002e000
2006-02-19 20:01:22.77 spid51   * IMAGEHLP         76C90000   76CB7FFF   00028000
2006-02-19 20:01:22.77 spid51   * NTMARTA          77690000   776B0FFF   00021000
2006-02-19 20:01:22.77 spid51   * SAMLIB           71BF0000   71C02FFF   00013000
2006-02-19 20:01:22.77 spid51   * ntdsapi          767A0000   767B2FFF   00013000
2006-02-19 20:01:22.77 spid51   * xpsp2res         44610000   448D4FFF   002c5000
2006-02-19 20:01:22.77 spid51   * CLBCATQ          76FD0000   7704EFFF   0007f000
2006-02-19 20:01:22.77 spid51   * sqlncli          448E0000   44AFDFFF   0021e000
2006-02-19 20:01:22.77 spid51   * comdlg32         763B0000   763F8FFF   00049000
2006-02-19 20:01:22.77 spid51   * SQLNCLIR         00770000   007A2FFF   00033000
2006-02-19 20:01:22.77 spid51   * xpstar90         53C30000   53C74FFF   00045000
2006-02-19 20:01:22.77 spid51   * SQLSCM90         53AD0000   53AD8FFF   00009000
2006-02-19 20:01:22.77 spid51   * ODBC32           74320000   7435CFFF   0003d000
2006-02-19 20:01:22.77 spid51   * BatchParser90    520C0000   520DDFFF   0001e000
2006-02-19 20:01:22.77 spid51   * SQLSVC90         53B00000   53B19FFF   0001a000
2006-02-19 20:01:22.77 spid51   * SqlResourceLoader53AB0000  53AB5FFF   00006000
2006-02-19 20:01:22.77 spid51   * ATL80            7C630000   7C64AFFF   0001b000
2006-02-19 20:01:22.77 spid51   * odbcint          450E0000   450F6FFF   00017000
2006-02-19 20:01:22.77 spid51   * SQLSVC90         45100000   45102FFF   00003000
2006-02-19 20:01:22.77 spid51   * xpstar90         45110000   45135FFF   00026000
2006-02-19 20:01:22.77 spid51   * dbghelp          452A0000   453B7FFF   00118000
2006-02-19 20:01:22.77 spid51   *
2006-02-19 20:01:22.77 spid51   * Edi: 072FAE48: 010F2C58 00000003 0731A620
00000003 072FAE5C 07311AF8
2006-02-19 20:01:22.77 spid51   * Esi: 440ECDC4: 00000001 00000002 073106D0
0734E040 00000000 00000001
2006-02-19 20:01:22.77 spid51   * Eax: 06381840: 010F2CB8 00000004 0734E040
07310C70 06381830 07361010
2006-02-19 20:01:22.77 spid51   * Ebx: 00000000:
2006-02-19 20:01:22.77 spid51   * Ecx: 00000014:
2006-02-19 20:01:22.77 spid51   * Edx: 07310C70: 0110592C 00000000 00000000
0001FEFF 00000000 00000000
2006-02-19 20:01:22.77 spid51   * Eip: 0110B72B: 850C418B E1840FC0 E8000007
FFFFF67F 840FC085 000007D4
2006-02-19 20:01:22.77 spid51   * Ebp: 440ECC58: 440ECC88 0110B647 00000014
072AF758 00000000 00000002
2006-02-19 20:01:22.77 spid51   * SegCs:0000001B:
2006-02-19 20:01:22.77 spid51   * EFlags:00010202: 00500046 004E005F 005F004F
004F0048 00540053 0043005F
2006-02-19 20:01:22.77 spid51   * Esp: 440ECC4C: 072FAE48 00000000 00000001
440ECC88 0110B647 00000014
2006-02-19 20:01:22.77 spid51   * SegSs: 00000023:
2006-02-19 20:01:22.77 spid51
********************************************************************
2006-02-19 20:01:22.77 spid51   * ------------------------------------------
------------------
2006-02-19 20:01:22.77 spid51   * Short Stack Dump
2006-02-19 20:01:22.79 spid51   0110B72B Module(sqlservr+0010B72B)
2006-02-19 20:01:22.79 spid51   0110B647 Module(sqlservr+0010B647)
2006-02-19 20:01:22.79 spid51   01108F4C Module(sqlservr+00108F4C)
2006-02-19 20:01:22.79 spid51   0110BD80 Module(sqlservr+0010BD80)
```

```
2006-02-19 20:01:22.79 spid51    01160082 Module(sqlservr+00160082)
2006-02-19 20:01:22.79 spid51    011087AD Module(sqlservr+001087AD)
2006-02-19 20:01:22.79 spid51    011080C2 Module(sqlservr+001080C2)
2006-02-19 20:01:22.79 spid51    01105E6B Module(sqlservr+00105E6B)
2006-02-19 20:01:22.79 spid51    01105EF5 Module(sqlservr+00105EF5)
2006-02-19 20:01:22.79 spid51    01105EB1 Module(sqlservr+00105EB1)
2006-02-19 20:01:22.79 spid51    0135F338 Module(sqlservr+0035F338)
2006-02-19 20:01:22.80 spid51    0135ED54 Module(sqlservr+0035ED54)
2006-02-19 20:01:22.80 spid51    0125215D Module(sqlservr+0025215D)
2006-02-19 20:01:22.80 spid51    012540BC Module(sqlservr+002540BC)
2006-02-19 20:01:22.80 spid51    01253617 Module(sqlservr+00253617)
2006-02-19 20:01:22.80 spid51    01253CCA Module(sqlservr+00253CCA)
2006-02-19 20:01:22.80 spid51    01253DF8 Module(sqlservr+00253DF8)
2006-02-19 20:01:22.80 spid51    0125B712 Module(sqlservr+0025B712)
2006-02-19 20:01:22.80 spid51    0125B0B5 Module(sqlservr+0025B0B5)
2006-02-19 20:01:22.80 spid51    01320C83 Module(sqlservr+00320C83)
2006-02-19 20:01:22.80 spid51    0125B99F Module(sqlservr+0025B99F)
2006-02-19 20:01:22.80 spid51    0102C51D Module(sqlservr+0002C51D)
2006-02-19 20:01:22.80 spid51    010438E5 Module(sqlservr+000438E5)
2006-02-19 20:01:22.80 spid51    01041C35 Module(sqlservr+00041C35)
2006-02-19 20:01:22.80 spid51    0100889F Module(sqlservr+0000889F)
2006-02-19 20:01:22.80 spid51    010089C5 Module(sqlservr+000089C5)
2006-02-19 20:01:22.80 spid51    010086E7 Module(sqlservr+000086E7)
2006-02-19 20:01:22.80 spid51    010D764A Module(sqlservr+000D764A)
2006-02-19 20:01:22.80 spid51    010D7B71 Module(sqlservr+000D7B71)
2006-02-19 20:01:22.80 spid51    010D746E Module(sqlservr+000D746E)
2006-02-19 20:01:22.82 spid51    010D83F0 Module(sqlservr+000D83F0)
2006-02-19 20:01:22.82 spid51    781329AA Module(MSVCR80+000029AA)
2006-02-19 20:01:22.83 spid51    78132A36 Module(MSVCR80+00002A36)
2006-02-19 20:01:22.88 spid51    Stack Signature for the dump is 0x844218F0
2006-02-19 20:01:25.57 spid51    External dump process return code 0x20002001.
The error information has been submitted to Watson error reporting.
2006-02-19 20:01:25.60 Server   Error: 17310, Severity: 20, State: 1.
```

```
2006-02-19 20:01:25.60 Server   A user request from the session with SPID 51
generated a fatal exception. SQL Server is terminating this session. Contact
Product Support Services with the dump produced in the log directory.
```

This stack dump is from an actual bug with SQL Server 2005 RTM (yes, the development team fixed this in SP1). Let's break down the pieces of the stack dump and discover more about what all of this information means.

Stack Header
```
2006-02-19 20:01:22.63 spid51    Using 'dbghelp.dll' version '4.0.5'
```

```
2006-02-19 20:01:22.73 spid51    SqlDumpExceptionHandler: Process 51 generated
fatal exception c0000005 EXCEPTION_ACCESS_VIOLATION. SQL Server is terminating
this process.
```

The first line represents the version of the dbghelp.dll used by SQL Server to produce information about an exception. The DLL name is how I search for any stack dump in an ERRORLOG. Simply find all occurrences of Using 'dbghelp.dll' and you will find each stack dump (regardless of whether the dump is from an exception). dbghelp.dll is provided by the Windows Platform SDK, but SQL Server installs a version of it for its own use in the \BINN subdirectory of the SQL Server installation files. dbghelp.dll provides "debugging" functions for an application (this is the same DLL that SQLDUMPER.EXE uses to produce a mini-dump). You can read all about this in the MSDN documentation at http://msdn.microsoft.com/library/default.asp?url=/library/en-us/debug/base/about_dbghelp.asp. The versions of this DLL are a bit hard to keep up with. Any Windows installation comes with a version of this file in the SYSTEM32 subdirectory. The latest version of this DLL can be found by installing the Windows Debuggers. But the SQL Server development team knows specific functionality and fixes they need to ship a specific version to be used by the engine and SQLDUMPER.EXE:

```
2006-02-19 20:01:22.73 spid51   ***Stack Dump being sent to C:\Program
Files\Microsoft SQL Server\MSSQL.1\MSSQL\LOG\SQLDump0118.txt
```

This information allows you to link the stack dump in the ERRORLOG with the dump files I mentioned before that are written to the LOG directory. In this case, you would look for all files starting with SQLDump0118:

```
2006-02-19 20:01:22.73 spid51   SqlDumpExceptionHandler: Process 51 generated fatal
exception c0000005 EXCEPTION_ACCESS_VIOLATION. SQL Server is terminating this
process.
```

This line generally appears only for exceptions and shows up only in the ERRORLOG. It is a simple method to see from the very beginning that the stack dump is the result of an AV (c0000005 is the internal Windows error number for access violation, as defined in header file ntstatus.h from the Platform SDK). This message also gives you a clue that the session that encountered the exception will be terminated. I'll talk about implications of "termination" later in the breakdown of the stack dump.

```
2006-02-19 20:01:22.73 spid51
*********************************************************************
2006-02-19 20:01:22.73 spid51   *
2006-02-19 20:01:22.73 spid51   * BEGIN STACK DUMP:
2006-02-19 20:01:22.74 spid51   *    02/19/06 20:01:22 spid 51
2006-02-19 20:01:22.74 spid51   *
2006-02-19 20:01:22.74 spid51   *
2006-02-19 20:01:22.74 spid51   *    Exception Address = 0110B72B
Module(sqlservr+0010B72B)
2006-02-19 20:01:22.74 spid51   *    Exception Code    = c0000005
EXCEPTION_ACCESS_VIOLATION
2006-02-19 20:01:22.74 spid51   *    Access Violation occurred reading address
00000020
2006-02-19 20:01:22.74 spid51   *    Input Buffer 172 bytes -
2006-02-19 20:01:22.76 spid51   *      select * from V1  where foo > 'p' and
(customerid > 10 or
2006-02-19 20:01:22.76 spid51   *      orderid < 20)
2006-02-19 20:01:22.77 spid51   *

2006-02-19 20:01:22.77 spid51   *
```

This is known as the *stack dump header*. As you will see in this section, the format of the stack dump header varies some based on the reason for the stack dump. The date and time the stack was initiated (which is the same time the exception occurred) are displayed, along with the session_id. (Yes, the server still prints the word spid in the ERRORLOG. Why add more characters in the file?) This is responsible for producing the stack dump (in this case, session_id or spid 51 encountered the access violation). As you can see from the ERRORLOG entries, you can also figure out which session_id was responsible for the stack dump by looking at the spid number between the date time and the stack dump information. Why would the spid number in the second column of the ERRORLOG be different from the spid number the header? Well, normally, it should be the same. However, there are cases where a stack dump is produced for all sessions from a single error condition. In this case, several stack headers show sessions that don't correspond to the one that produced the dump. So the definitive method to determine what session_id encountered an event that caused a stack dump is the spid number in the second column next to the timestamp of the errorlog entry.

Next in the stack header is information about the exception that is directly extracted from a structure called the EXCEPTION_RECORD. Anytime a thread catches a Windows exception, key information can be found in the EXCEPTION_RECORD.

```
2006-02-19 20:01:22.74 spid51   *    Exception Address = 0110B72B
Module(sqlservr+0010B72B)
```

This is the instruction address SQLSERVR.EXE that caused the exception (in this case, an AV). A basic definition of an AV is an attempt to access a memory address that is not accessible to the program's virtual address space. The typical cause is that the memory address is not actually committed memory, but it could also be that the memory address is part of a region that is marked NO_ACCESS or READ_ONLY. The first 64KB of the virtual address space of any Windows process is automatically marked NO_ACCESS. This means any attempt by a thread to access a memory address of 0 -65536 results in an AV. This is specifically done in Windows to catch any NULL pointers in programs. Memory regions marked READ_ONLY cause an AV to occur if a thread attempts to write at a memory address in that region. This will become important later when I talk about "memory scribbler" scenarios.

The exception address is very important for you in making a quick determination about whether this problem may be a SQL Server issue. In previous versions of SQL Server, the server used dbghelp.dll to symbolize the exception address and specifically list the function name within the module. I mentioned earlier in the book why the server doesn't do this anymore (a simple problem of performance and too much overhead, plus the symbols are no longer included with the product). But the name of the module associated with the exception address instruction is still listed next to the module. So in this case, you can see that the instruction address where the exception occurred is SQLSERVR.EXE. So you know already that this problem is an issue within the SQL Server code and this is a candidate for you to possibly call Microsoft PSS (we will talk later about a checklist of what you can do before calling PSS).

So what if the module name is not SQLSERVR.EXE? It could still be a SQL Server bug or issue to contact Microsoft, but some may be instant candidates to investigate on your own. Consider this stack dump:

```
***********************************************************************
*
* BEGIN STACK DUMP:
*    09/07/04 11:56:00 spid 219
*
*    Exception Address = 185D73C2 (nttini + 000063A2 Line 0+00000000)
*    Exception Code    = c0000005 EXCEPTION_ACCESS_VIOLATION
*    Access Violation occurred reading address 00000578
*     s p _ e x e c u  0a 00 73 00 70 00 5f 00 65 00 78 00 65 00 63 00 75 00
*     t e     &        74 00 65 00 02 00 00 00 26 04 04 01 00 00 00
*
* Short Stack Dump
* 185D73C2 Module(orantcp9+000073C2) (nttini+000063A2)
* 117AD200 Module(msafd+0000D200) (StartWsdpService+0000718C)
* 77F9FF3B Module(ntdll+0001FF3B) (KiUserApcDispatcher+00000007)
* 4107144D Module(UMS+0000144D) (UmsThreadScheduler::Switch+0000004C)
* 41071906 Module(UMS+00001906)
(UmsThreadScheduler::SwitchNonPreemptive+0000003B)
* 00428648 Module(sqlservr+00028648) (write_data+0000029C)
* 0042876B Module(sqlservr+0002876B) (flush_buffer+000000DD)
* 006C78CE Module(sqlservr+002C78CE) (TSendRowClass<3,0>::TSendNVN+0000008F)
* 006C5A47 Module(sqlservr+002C5A47) (CValOdsRow::SetDataX+000001CB)
* 0040E5E7 Module(sqlservr+0000E5E7) (SetDataWithPop+0000001C)
* 0040EBFB Module(sqlservr+0000EBFB) (CEs::GeneralEval+00000088)
* 0041E13A Module(sqlservr+0001E13A) (CStmtQuery::ErsqExecuteQuery+000003D7)
* 0042CADB Module(sqlservr+0002CADB) (CStmtSelect::XretExecute+00000229)
* 0041B632 Module(sqlservr+0001B632) (CMsqlExecContext::ExecuteStmts+000003B9)
* 0041AC44 Module(sqlservr+0001AC44)  (CMsqlExecContext::Execute+00000205)
* 0041BB0C Module(sqlservr+0001BB0C) (CSQLSource::Execute+00000357)
* 005F422A Module(sqlservr+001F422A) (SpExecute+00000227)
* 005F5F0E Module(sqlservr+001F5F0E) (CSpecProc::ExecuteSpecial+00000264)
* 005F59E3 Module(sqlservr+001F59E3) (CXProc::Execute+000000A3)
* 005F7BEB Module(sqlservr+001F7BEB) (CSQLSource::Execute+000003C0)
* 0043A57F Module(sqlservr+0003A57F) (execrpc+00000507)
* 004397E1 Module(sqlservr+000397E1) (execute_rpc+00000019)
* 00428B21 Module(sqlservr+00028B21) (process_commands+00000232)
* 41072838 Module(UMS+00002838) (ProcessWorkRequests+00000272)
* 410725B3 Module(UMS+000025B3) (ThreadStartRoutine+00000098)
* 78008454 Module(MSVCRT+00008454) (endthread+000000C1)
* 7C57438B Module(KERNEL32+0000438B) (TlsSetValue+000000F0)
```

This is a dump from a problem in SQL Server 2000, so you see the function symbol names in the ERRORLOG. Look at the exception address. Next to it is nttini, which is the function name of the module that contains the exception address instruction. If you look down toward the short stack dump, you see the module names. The module name for nttinit is orantcp.dll. What I immediately do is find this DLL on my machine and use Windows Explorer to look at its properties. The properties of the DLL include a Company Name, and if you look at orantcp.dll, you will see the company is the ORACLE Corporation. In this case, you could certainly contact Microsoft PSS, but we would kindly point out that the access violation is with a DLL that Microsoft does not ship. If this particular exception occurred in 2005, the header would show the exception address as

```
2006-02-19 20:01:22.74 spid51   *    Exception Address = 185D73C2
Module(orantcp9+000073C2)
```

At the end of this section, I'll cover special types of scenarios you may encounter and how to handle them.

Let's get back to our breakdown of the stack dump. The next lines in the header provide the type of exception and the memory address that caused the exception (if an access violation):

```
2006-02-19 20:01:22.74 spid51   *    Exception Code    = c0000005
EXCEPTION_ACCESS_VIOLATION
2006-02-19 20:01:22.74 spid51   *    Access Violation occurred reading address
00000020
```

The exception code comes right from the EXCEPTION_RECORD. The next line would only be seen for an access violation but is very important for debugging purposes. In this particular case, I see that the AV occurred when reading memory address 00000020. Remember that the first 64KB is marked NO_ACCESS. In this case, my bet is a NULL pointer problem. I say this because of the address 0x20 in the dump. Probably the code was attempting to access a member of a class or structure that is at offset 0x20 within the structure, but the pointer that the code is using is NULL. When I talk more about the register output in the stack dump, we will try to prove/disprove my theory.

The next line in the stack dump is very important for purposes of diagnosing the problem:

```
2006-02-19 20:01:22.74 spid51   *    Input Buffer 172 bytes -
2006-02-19 20:01:22.76 spid51   *       select * from V1  where foo > 'p' and
(customerid > 10 or
2006-02-19 20:01:22.76 spid51   *       orderid < 20)
```

This is called the input buffer and represents the query executed by the session on behalf of the application that results in the condition for the stack dump. The input buffer is displayed only for a session that actually ran a query. So, for example, if an access violation was encountered by a "system session" like checkpoint, you would not see an input buffer. Why is the input buffer important? Because it may provide all the information you and PSS need to reproduce the problem. In this case, you might be able to find the appropriate database context for this query, run it, and reproduce the same access violation. You now have a reproduction for a problem that you could 1) validate whether a newer build of SQL Server could fix this like a service pack, and 2) significantly reduce the time for PSS to help you work around or obtain a fix for this problem. Now, let me be clear on one point. For the sake of your production system, I'm not suggesting that you immediately try to run the query in the input buffer. In fact, it is far better for you to attempt to run this on a test server that perhaps has the same database. There is a problem with this methodology. It is possible that the conditions that caused the problem to occur in production won't occur in test. However, I've seen many cases where this problem can be reproduced by simply running the query in the input buffer on a test server database. Other factors could affect the ability to reproduce the issue, such as the SET options or the transaction isolation level currently in effect for the session at the time of the exception. But let's say you want to give this a try. How do you know the database context for this query? Unfortunately, this is not information the server provides in any of the dump files produced as part of the stack dump. So your choices are

1. Find the object referenced in the query by searching the catalog views of each database. In this case, look for an object called V1 by searching sys.objects in each user database on your server.

2. Set up a SQLTrace to capture the next occurrence. The database context can be collected as a column for the events to capture queries in the SQLTrace.

3. Try to find the query listed in the input buffer by searching the application code.

The input buffer may contain a series of hexadecimal digits like in the previous SQL Server 2000 stack for the orantcp.dll problem:

```
*    s p _ e x e c u   0a 00 73 00 70 00 5f 00 65 00 78 00 65 00 63 00 75 00
*    t e       &         74 00 65 00 02 00 00 00 26 04 04 01 00 00 00
```

This type of input buffer is a SQL Remote Procedure Call (RPC). An RPC is used by an application to execute a stored procedure and bind parameters to it without executing a T-SQL string command. The name of the stored procedure is displayed on the left side of this dump output. If you encounter a situation like this, you must use SQLTrace to find out the parameters of procedure execution. In fact, in this example, the name of the stored procedure is sp_execute. sp_execute is a special procedure in the engine to execute prepared statements. So, in this case, you would need to have the previous sp_prepare procedure execution to know what statement was prepared.

The next section of the stack dump header is the module list (I omitted many of the entries for brevity):

```
2006-02-19 20:01:22.77 spid51   *   MODULE          BASE       END        SIZE
2006-02-19 20:01:22.77 spid51   *   sqlservr        01000000   02BA7FFF   01ba8000
2006-02-19 20:01:22.77 spid51   *   ntdll           7C900000   7C9AFFFF   000b0000
2006-02-19 20:01:22.77 spid51   *   kernel32        7C800000   7C8F3FFF   000f4000
2006-02-19 20:01:22.77 spid51   *   MSVCR80         78130000   781CAFFF   0009b000
2006-02-19 20:01:22.77 spid51   *   msvcrt          77C10000   77C67FFF   00058000
2006-02-19 20:01:22.77 spid51   *   MSVCP80         7C420000   7C4A6FFF   00087000
2006-02-19 20:01:22.77 spid51   *   ADVAPI32        77DD0000   77E6AFFF   0009b000
2006-02-19 20:01:22.77 spid51   *   SQLNCLIR        00770000   007A2FFF   00033000
2006-02-19 20:01:22.77 spid51   *   xpstar90        53C30000   53C74FFF   00045000
2006-02-19 20:01:22.77 spid51   *   SQLSCM90        53AD0000   53AD8FFF   00009000
2006-02-19 20:01:22.77 spid51   *   ODBC32          74320000   7435CFFF   0003d000
2006-02-19 20:01:22.77 spid51   *   BatchParser90   520C0000   520DDFFF   0001e000
2006-02-19 20:01:22.77 spid51   *   SQLSVC90        53B00000   53B19FFF   0001a000
```

```
2006-02-19 20:01:22.77 spid51   * SqlResourceLoader53AB0000   53AB5FFF   00006000
2006-02-19 20:01:22.77 spid51   * ATL80               7C630000   7C64AFFF   0001b000
2006-02-19 20:01:22.77 spid51   * odbcint             450E0000   450F6FFF   00017000
2006-02-19 20:01:22.77 spid51   * SQLSVC90            45100000   45102FFF   00003000
2006-02-19 20:01:22.77 spid51   * xpstar90            45110000   45135FFF   00026000
2006-02-19 20:01:22.77 spid51   * dbghelp             452A0000   453B7FFF   00118000
```

I find this module list invaluable because I can see all DLLs loaded in the SQL Server
process and their memory address range. Even though the module name associated with
the exception address is listed in the header, it might be helpful to know what other DLLs
are loaded. I'll explain later in this section why this could come in handy for something
like a heap corruption problem.

The next section is a dump of registers:

```
2006-02-19 20:01:22.77 spid51   * Edi: 072FAE48: 010F2C58 00000003 0731A620
00000003 072FAE5C 07311AF8
2006-02-19 20:01:22.77 spid51   * Esi: 440ECDC4: 00000001 00000002 073106D0
0734E040 00000000 00000001
2006-02-19 20:01:22.77 spid51   * Eax: 06381840: 010F2CB8 00000004 0734E040
07310C70 06381830 07361010
2006-02-19 20:01:22.77 spid51   * Ebx: 00000000:
2006-02-19 20:01:22.77 spid51   * Ecx: 00000014:
2006-02-19 20:01:22.77 spid51   * Edx: 07310C70: 0110592C 00000000 00000000
0001FEFF 00000000 00000000
2006-02-19 20:01:22.77 spid51   * Eip: 0110B72B: 850C418B E1840FC0 E8000007
FFFFF67F 840FC085 000007D4
2006-02-19 20:01:22.77 spid51   * Ebp: 440ECC58: 440ECC88 0110B647 00000014
072AF758 00000000 00000002
2006-02-19 20:01:22.77 spid51   * SegCs:0000001B:
2006-02-19 20:01:22.77 spid51   * EFlags:00010202: 00500046 004E005F 005F004F
004F0048 00540053 0043005F
2006-02-19 20:01:22.77 spid51   * Esp: 440ECC4C: 072FAE48 00000000 00000001
440ECC88 0110B647 00000014
2006-02-19 20:01:22.77 spid51   * SegSs: 00000023:
```

As I stated earlier, this stack dump is for an x86 machine. x64 looks similar except the
address looks different. IA64 looks completely different, because the register set is different for that chipset.

The format of this register dump is

```
<register>: <value>: <first 24 bytes of memory at the address of value>
```

So for the edi register,

```
Edi: 072FAE48: 010F2C58 00000003 0731A620 00000003 072FAE5C 07311AF8
```

The value of the register at the time of the exception was 010F2C58. The first 24 bytes starting at memory address 010F2C58 are

```
00000003 0731A620 00000003 072FAE5C 07311AF8
```

This is not data I expect you to really look at. But pay attention to registers that only have values but don't have the 24 bytes listed after them, like Ebx:

```
2006-02-19 20:01:22.77 spid51   * Ebx: 00000000:
```

When the server produces the stack dump, it tries to see if the value of the register is a valid memory address (it does this using the Windows VirtualQuery API). If the value is not a valid memory address, the server doesn't display any bytes on the right side. This is an easy method to see whether any registers might contain an invalid address. Of course, not all registers are used just for pointers, so it might be perfectly normal for it to contain a valid value that is not to be used as a memory address.

Short Stack Dump

The next section of the stack dump is called the *short stack dump*. This is because it is a dump of the stack frame at the context of the event that caused the stack dump (like an AV).

```
2006-02-19 20:01:22.77 spid51   * Short Stack Dump
2006-02-19 20:01:22.79 spid51   0110B72B Module(sqlservr+0010B72B)
2006-02-19 20:01:22.79 spid51   0110B647 Module(sqlservr+0010B647)
2006-02-19 20:01:22.79 spid51   01108F4C Module(sqlservr+00108F4C)
2006-02-19 20:01:22.79 spid51   0110BD80 Module(sqlservr+0010BD80)
2006-02-19 20:01:22.79 spid51   01160082 Module(sqlservr+00160082)
2006-02-19 20:01:22.79 spid51   011087AD Module(sqlservr+001087AD)
2006-02-19 20:01:22.79 spid51   011080C2 Module(sqlservr+001080C2)
2006-02-19 20:01:22.79 spid51   01105E6B Module(sqlservr+00105E6B)
2006-02-19 20:01:22.79 spid51   01105EF5 Module(sqlservr+00105EF5)
2006-02-19 20:01:22.79 spid51   01105EB1 Module(sqlservr+00105EB1)
2006-02-19 20:01:22.79 spid51   0135F338 Module(sqlservr+0035F338)
2006-02-19 20:01:22.80 spid51   0135ED54 Module(sqlservr+0035ED54)
2006-02-19 20:01:22.80 spid51   0125215D Module(sqlservr+0025215D)
2006-02-19 20:01:22.80 spid51   012540BC Module(sqlservr+002540BC)
2006-02-19 20:01:22.80 spid51   01253617 Module(sqlservr+00253617)
2006-02-19 20:01:22.80 spid51   01253CCA Module(sqlservr+00253CCA)
2006-02-19 20:01:22.80 spid51   01253DF8 Module(sqlservr+00253DF8)
2006-02-19 20:01:22.80 spid51   0125B712 Module(sqlservr+0025B712)
2006-02-19 20:01:22.80 spid51   0125B0B5 Module(sqlservr+0025B0B5)
2006-02-19 20:01:22.80 spid51   01320C83 Module(sqlservr+00320C83)
2006-02-19 20:01:22.80 spid51   0125B99F Module(sqlservr+0025B99F)
2006-02-19 20:01:22.80 spid51   0102C51D Module(sqlservr+0002C51D)
2006-02-19 20:01:22.80 spid51   010438E5 Module(sqlservr+000438E5)
2006-02-19 20:01:22.80 spid51   01041C35 Module(sqlservr+00041C35)
2006-02-19 20:01:22.80 spid51   0100889F Module(sqlservr+0000889F)
2006-02-19 20:01:22.80 spid51   010089C5 Module(sqlservr+000089C5)
2006-02-19 20:01:22.80 spid51   010086E7 Module(sqlservr+000086E7)
2006-02-19 20:01:22.80 spid51   010D764A Module(sqlservr+000D764A)
2006-02-19 20:01:22.80 spid51   010D7B71 Module(sqlservr+000D7B71)
2006-02-19 20:01:22.80 spid51   010D746E Module(sqlservr+000D746E)
2006-02-19 20:01:22.82 spid51   010D83F0 Module(sqlservr+000D83F0)
2006-02-19 20:01:22.82 spid51   781329AA Module(MSVCR80+000029AA)

2006-02-19 20:01:22.83 spid51   78132A36 Module(MSVCR80+00002A36)
```

As I said earlier, the server doesn't symbolize the function names from the stack frame anymore for performance reasons. The reason this is called the short stack dump is that a complete dump of the thread stack memory is included in both the mini-dump (the .mdmp file) and the full stack dump file (the .txt file).

In this particular situation, the module listing is not very helpful. If I wanted to see a symbolized version of the stack frames, I would use the mini-dump file with a debugger and symbols. The short stack dump could come in handy in recognizing certain "signatures" of exceptions, which I'll talk about shortly.

Stack Dump Conclusion

After the short stack dump is the conclusion of the dump with information about the stack dump:

```
2006-02-19 20:01:22.88 spid51   Stack Signature for the dump is 0x844218F0
2006-02-19 20:01:25.57 spid51   External dump process return code 0x20002001.
The error information has been submitted to Watson error reporting.
2006-02-19 20:01:25.60 Server   Error: 17310, Severity: 20, State: 1.
2006-02-19 20:01:25.60 Server   A user request from the session with SPID 51
generated a fatal exception. SQL Server is terminating this session. Contact
Product Support Services with the dump produced in the log directory.
```

The fist line is called a *stack hash* and is a value the server generated to uniquely identify the addresses of functions in the short stack dump. This information is sent to Watson error reporting to group stack dumps of the same problem. The next line is reported only if you have enabled ErrorReporting for SQL Server. The last line is just a message the engine prints to the ERRORLOG if an exception was caught as part of processing a batch from a user connection.

I mentioned earlier that when an exception occurs and is caught by the engine, the connection is terminated. Let me step back and review the entire sequence of events so you can understand what behavior to expect from the application point of view:

1. The exception is handled and the stack dump is produced.

2. Any active transactions are rolled back.

3. Any other resources associated with the query or the connection are destroyed.

4. An error message is sent back to the client application.

5. The connection is closed.

The error message(s) returned to the application are the following:

```
Msg 0, Level 11, State 0, Line 0
A severe error occurred on the current command.  The results, if any, should
be discarded.
Msg 0, Level 20, State 0, Line 0
A severe error occurred on the current command.  The results, if any, should
be discarded.
```

The reason the connection is terminated is that all resources associated with the session and thread on the server side are discarded after rolling back any active transactions.

Exception Signatures

Based on my experience working with SQL Server and stack dumps due to exceptions, I've seen a few signatures that are worth showing so you will recognize them:

```
2005-04-30 03:19:25.46 spid150    SqlDumpExceptionHandler: Process 150
generated fatal exception c0000005 EXCEPTION_ACCESS_VIOLATION. SQL Server is
terminating this process..
*
******************************************************************************
*
* BEGIN STACK DUMP:
*    04/30/05 03:19:25 spid 150
*
*    Exception Address = 77F47931 (RtlAllocateHeap + 00000655 Line 0+00000000)
*    Exception Code    = c0000005 EXCEPTION_ACCESS_VIOLATION
*    Access Violation occurred reading address 00000031
*      S a v e D o c u   15 00 53 00 61 00 76 00 65 00 44 00 6f 00 63 00 75 00
*    m e n t F i n a l   6d 00 65 00 6e 00 74 00 46 00 69 00 6e 00 61 00 6c 00
*    _ p r c       & G   5f 00 70 00 72 00 63 00 00 00 00 00 26 04 04 47 c8 02
*      &       o  >+      00 00 00 26 01 01 02 00 00 6f 08 08 3e 2b 00 00 00 00
*        &      &     #M  00 00 00 26 01 01 01 00 00 26 01 01 00 00 00 23 4d
*             M   <?xml   16 00 00 09 04 00 01 88 4d 16 00 00 3c 3f 78 6d
6c 20
*    version="1.0" enco  76 65 72 73 69 6f 6e 3d 22 31 2e 30 22 20 65 6e 63 6f
*    ding="windows-1255  64 69 6e 67 3d 22 77 69 6e 64 6f 77 73 2d 31 32 35 35
*    "?><document Docum   22 3f 3e 3c 64 6f 63 75 6d 65 6e 74 20 44 6f 63 75 6d
*    entID="182343"> <p  65 6e 74 49 44 3d 22 31 38 32 33 34 33 22 3e 0a 3c 70
*    aragraph Paragraph  61 72 61 67 72 61 70 68 20 50 61 72 61 67 72 61 70 68
*    ID="18" ><savetype  49 44 3d 22 31 38 22 20 3e 3c 73 61 76 65 74 79 70 65
*     SaveType="7" ><ro  20 53 61 76 65 54 79 70 65 3d 22 37 22 20 3e 3c 72 6f
*    w  DocumentUserSig  77 20 20 44 6f 63 75 6d 65 6e 74 55 73 65 72 53 69 67
*    nName="ã&quot;ø øå  6e 4e 61 6d 65 3d 22 e3 26 71 75 6f 74 3b f8 20 f8 e5
*    ñìï àáãéàééá" Pati   f1 ec ef 20 e0 e1 e3 e9 e0 e9 e9 e1 22 20 50 61 74 69
*    e
....
* -------------------------------------------------------------------------
* Short Stack Dump
* 77F47931 Module(ntdll+00007931) (RtlAllocateHeap+00000655)
* 030E1D39 Module(ole32+00001D39) (CoTaskMemFree+0000003B)
* 062D1EAC Module(msxml2+00031EAC) (Ordinal10+00015B75)
* 0066CB25 Module(sqlservr+0026CB25) (CXMLRowset::PrepareDataValue+00000512)
* 0066DB24 Module(sqlservr+0026DB24) (CXMLRowset::PrepareData+0000009A)
* 0066DB98 Module(sqlservr+0026DB98) (CXMLRowset::GetData+00000027)
* 0040F621 Module(sqlservr+0000F621) (CQScanRowset::Prefetch+00000029)
* 00484F68 Module(sqlservr+00084F68) (CQScanRmtBase::RmtPrefetch+00000013)
* 00484E6D Module(sqlservr+00084E6D) (CQScanRmtScan::GetRow+000001BE)
* 0056D0EC Module(sqlservr+0016D0EC) (CQScanFilter::GetRow+00000019)
* 0040E19B Module(sqlservr+0000E19B) (CQScanTop::GetRow+000000BF)
* 006F85FC Module(sqlservr+002F85FC) (CQScanSpool::LoadSpool+00000048)
* 006F7C4B Module(sqlservr+002F7C4B) (CQScanSpool::Open+000000ED)
```

```
* 00425C9D Module(sqlservr+00025C9D) (CQScan::Open+0000001C)
* 0046D387 Module(sqlservr+0006D387) (CQScanUpdate::Open+000000D0)
* 006F85F2 Module(sqlservr+002F85F2) (CQScanSpool::LoadSpool+0000003E)
* 006F7C4B Module(sqlservr+002F7C4B) (CQScanSpool::Open+000000ED)
* 004FAABE Module(sqlservr+000FAABE) (CQScanSort::BuildSortTable+00000021)
* 004FAA94 Module(sqlservr+000FAA94) (CQScanSort::Open+00000032)
* 00425C9D Module(sqlservr+00025C9D) (CQScan::Open+0000001C)
* 0046D387 Module(sqlservr+0006D387) (CQScanUpdate::Open+000000D0)
* 006F9AF6 Module(sqlservr+002F9AF6) (CQScanSequence::Open+000000CA)
* 004214C4 Module(sqlservr+000214C4) (CQueryScan::Startup+0000010D)
* 0041D505 Module(sqlservr+0001D505) (CStmtQuery::ErsqExecuteQuery+0000026B)
* 0041E09C Module(sqlservr+0001E09C) (CStmtDML::XretExecuteNormal+000002AE)
* 0041DECA Module(sqlservr+0001DECA) (CStmtDML::XretExecute+0000001C)
* 0041B442 Module(sqlservr+0001B442) (CMsqlExecContext::ExecuteStmts+000003B9)
* 0041AA88 Module(sqlservr+0001AA88) (CMsqlExecContext::Execute+000001B6)
* 0041B9B6 Module(sqlservr+0001B9B6) (CSQLSource::Execute+00000357)
* 00498A8A Module(sqlservr+00098A8A) (CStmtExec::XretLocalExec+0000014D)
* 00498926 Module(sqlservr+00098926) (CStmtExec::XretExecute+0000031A)
* 0041B442 Module(sqlservr+0001B442) (CMsqlExecContext::ExecuteStmts+000003B9)
* 0041AA88 Module(sqlservr+0001AA88) (CMsqlExecContext::Execute+000001B6)
* 0041B9B6 Module(sqlservr+0001B9B6) (CSQLSource::Execute+00000357)
* 00498A8A Module(sqlservr+00098A8A) (CStmtExec::XretLocalExec+0000014D)
* 00498926 Module(sqlservr+00098926) (CStmtExec::XretExecute+0000031A)
* 0041B442 Module(sqlservr+0001B442) (CMsqlExecContext::ExecuteStmts+000003B9)
* 0041AA88 Module(sqlservr+0001AA88) (CMsqlExecContext::Execute+000001B6)
* 0041B9B6 Module(sqlservr+0001B9B6) (CSQLSource::Execute+00000357)
* 00438F0B Module(sqlservr+00038F0B) (execrpc+00000507)
* 0043816D Module(sqlservr+0003816D) (execute_rpc+00000019)
* 00427001 Module(sqlservr+00027001) (process_commands+00000232)
* 41075002 Module(UMS+00005002) (ProcessWorkRequests+00000272)
* 41074698 Module(UMS+00004698) (ThreadStartRoutine+00000098)
* 77BC90A2 Module(MSVCRT+000290A2) (endthread+000000A6)

* 77E4A990 Module(kernel32+0000A990) (FlsSetValue+00000779)


* - - - - - - - - - - - - - - - - - - - - - - - - - - - - - - - - - - - - - - - - - - - - - - -
```

This is an example of an access violation caused by heap corruption from SQL Server 2000 (I haven't run across one yet with SQL Server 2005). Remember, with 2005, you could symbolize the stack by using a debugger with public symbols with the associated .mdmp file. In this situation notice the module at the top of the stack is RtlAllocateHeap. Whenever I see this, I immediately think of some type of heap corruption problem. In other words, the AV is just a symptom that heap memory has been damaged by some previous event. Because SQL Server doesn't use much default Windows heap memory, I generally start looking immediately for other types of components that could have damaged the heap, including extended stored procedures and COM objects from sp_OA. You could resort to using gflags and pageheap (tools used to find heap problems), but be careful—you could run into memory problems very quickly.

```
***************************************************************************
*
* BEGIN STACK DUMP:
```

```
*    09/07/04 11:56:00 spid 219
*
*    Exception Address = 185D73C2 (nttini + 000063A2 Line 0+00000000)
*    Exception Code   = c0000005 EXCEPTION_ACCESS_VIOLATION
*    Access Violation occurred reading address 00000578
*    s p _ e x e c u   0a 00 73 00 70 00 5f 00 65 00 78 00 65 00 63 00 75 00
*    t e     &         74 00 65 00 02 00 00 00 26 04 04 01 00 00 00 00

* Short Stack Dump
* 185D73C2 Module(orantcp9+000073C2) (nttini+000063A2)
* 117AD200 Module(msafd+0000D200) (StartWsdpService+0000718C)
* 77F9FF3B Module(ntdll+0001FF3B) (KiUserApcDispatcher+00000007)
* 4107144D Module(UMS+0000144D) (UmsThreadScheduler::Switch+0000004C)
* 41071906 Module(UMS+00001906)
(UmsThreadScheduler::SwitchNonPremptive+0000003B)
* 00428648 Module(sqlservr+00028648) (write_data+0000029C)
* 0042876B Module(sqlservr+0002876B) (flush_buffer+000000DD)
* 006C78CE Module(sqlservr+002C78CE) (TSendRowClass<3,0>::TSendNVN+0000008F)
* 006C5A47 Module(sqlservr+002C5A47) (CValOdsRow::SetDataX+000001CB)
* 0040E5E7 Module(sqlservr+0000E5E7) (SetDataWithPop+0000001C)
* 0040EBFB Module(sqlservr+0000EBFB) (CEs::GeneralEval+00000088)
* 0041E13A Module(sqlservr+0001E13A) (CStmtQuery::ErsqExecuteQuery+000003D7)
* 0042CADB Module(sqlservr+0002CADB) (CStmtSelect::XretExecute+00000229)
* 0041B632 Module(sqlservr+0001B632) (CMsqlExecContext::ExecuteStmts+000003B9)
* 0041AC44 Module(sqlservr+0001AC44) (CMsqlExecContext::Execute+00000205)
* 0041BB0C Module(sqlservr+0001BB0C) (CSQLSource::Execute+00000357)
* 005F422A Module(sqlservr+001F422A) (SpExecute+00000227)
* 005F5F0E Module(sqlservr+001F5F0E) (CSpecProc::ExecuteSpecial+00000264)
* 005F59E3 Module(sqlservr+001F59E3) (CXProc::Execute+000000A3)
* 005F7BEB Module(sqlservr+001F7BEB) (CSQLSource::Execute+000003C0)
* 0043A57F Module(sqlservr+0003A57F) (execrpc+00000507)
* 004397E1 Module(sqlservr+000397E1) (execute_rpc+00000019)
* 00428B21 Module(sqlservr+00028B21) (process_commands+00000232)
* 41072838 Module(UMS+00002838) (ProcessWorkRequests+00000272)
* 410725B3 Module(UMS+000025B3) (ThreadStartRoutine+00000098)
* 78008454 Module(MSVCRT+00008454) (endthread+000000C1)
* 7C57438B Module(KERNEL32+0000438B) (TlsSetValue+000000F0)
```

This dump was taken from another SQL Server 2000 case. Note the top of the stack is not from SQL Server or even a Microsoft component. orantcp9.dll in this situation is a DLL shipped with ORACLE software. In this situation, I would immediately recommend my customer contact ORACLE technical support to resolve the problem.

Assertions

The most common scenario for the SQL Server engine to produce a stack dump is a Windows exception. The second most common scenario is an error condition called an *assertion*. An assertion is a technique for programmers to catch errors in their code during the development process. They are different from a standard error raised in the engine because they are not common expected error conditions. Most assertions are found only in a debug build of SQLSERVR.EXE and are used to catch error conditions during testing and beta builds. However, some *retail assertions* are still in the engine code. When a retail assertion is encountered in SQL Server 2005, the ERRORLOG stack dump looks like this (this time I have removed parts of the stack dump that are common to all dumps):

```
2006-02-19 20:53:23.08 spid51      Using 'dbghelp.dll' version '4.0.5'
2006-02-19 20:53:23.09 spid51      **Dump thread - spid = 51, PSS =
0x038272A0, EC = 0x038272A8
2006-02-19 20:53:23.09 spid51      ***Stack Dump being sent to C:\Program
Files\Microsoft SQL Server\MSSQL.1\MSSQL\LOG\SQLDump0119.txt
2006-02-19 20:53:23.09 spid51      *
*******************************************************************
2006-02-19 20:53:23.09 spid51      *
2006-02-19 20:53:23.09 spid51      * BEGIN STACK DUMP:
2006-02-19 20:53:23.09 spid51      *   02/19/06 20:53:23 spid 51
2006-02-19 20:53:23.09 spid51      *
2006-02-19 20:53:23.09 spid51      * Location:      dbmgr.cpp:6728
2006-02-19 20:53:23.09 spid51      * Expression:     !FindDB(dbid)
2006-02-19 20:53:23.09 spid51      * SPID:          51
2006-02-19 20:53:23.09 spid51      * Process ID:     3780
2006-02-19 20:53:23.09 spid51      *
2006-02-19 20:53:23.09 spid51      * Input Buffer 60 bytes -
2006-02-19 20:53:23.09 spid51      *          sp_detach_db 'msdb'
2006-02-19 20:53:23.09 spid51      *
<MODULE AND REGISTERS GO HERE >
2006-02-19 20:53:23.11 spid51
*******************************************************************
2006-02-19 20:53:23.11 spid51      *-----------------------------------------
-------------------------
2006-02-19 20:53:23.11 spid51      * Short Stack Dump
2006-02-19 20:53:23.12 spid51      7C81EB33 Module(kernel32+0001EB33)
2006-02-19 20:53:23.12 spid51      02172CE4 Module(sqlservr+01172CE4)
2006-02-19 20:53:23.12 spid51      02176BA0 Module(sqlservr+01176BA0)
2006-02-19 20:53:23.12 spid51      02019506 Module(sqlservr+01019506)
2006-02-19 20:53:23.12 spid51      020BFE04 Module(sqlservr+010BFE04)
2006-02-19 20:53:23.12 spid51      021D504B Module(sqlservr+011D504B)
2006-02-19 20:53:23.12 spid51      011E51D7 Module(sqlservr+001E51D7)
2006-02-19 20:53:23.12 spid51      011E463E Module(sqlservr+001E463E)
2006-02-19 20:53:23.12 spid51      013C6DB8 Module(sqlservr+003C6DB8)
2006-02-19 20:53:23.12 spid51      0102DB52 Module(sqlservr+0002DB52)
2006-02-19 20:53:23.12 spid51      0102E0D0 Module(sqlservr+0002E0D0)
2006-02-19 20:53:23.12 spid51      0102C5F8 Module(sqlservr+0002C5F8)
2006-02-19 20:53:23.12 spid51      01C09A39 Module(sqlservr+00C09A39)
2006-02-19 20:53:23.12 spid51      01C0813F Module(sqlservr+00C0813F)
2006-02-19 20:53:23.12 spid51      0102DB52 Module(sqlservr+0002DB52)
2006-02-19 20:53:23.12 spid51      0102E0D0 Module(sqlservr+0002E0D0)
2006-02-19 20:53:23.12 spid51      0102C5F8 Module(sqlservr+0002C5F8)
2006-02-19 20:53:23.12 spid51      011C1302 Module(sqlservr+001C1302)
2006-02-19 20:53:23.12 spid51      011C1179 Module(sqlservr+001C1179)
2006-02-19 20:53:23.12 spid51      011C100E Module(sqlservr+001C100E)
2006-02-19 20:53:23.12 spid51      0102DB52 Module(sqlservr+0002DB52)
2006-02-19 20:53:23.12 spid51      0102E0D0 Module(sqlservr+0002E0D0)
2006-02-19 20:53:23.12 spid51      0102C5F8 Module(sqlservr+0002C5F8)
2006-02-19 20:53:23.12 spid51      010438E5 Module(sqlservr+000438E5)
2006-02-19 20:53:23.12 spid51      01041C35 Module(sqlservr+00041C35)
2006-02-19 20:53:23.12 spid51      0100889F Module(sqlservr+0000889F)
```

```
2006-02-19 20:53:23.12 spid51          010089C5 Module(sqlservr+000089C5)
2006-02-19 20:53:23.12 spid51          010086E7 Module(sqlservr+000086E7)
2006-02-19 20:53:23.12 spid51          010D764A Module(sqlservr+000D764A)
2006-02-19 20:53:23.12 spid51          010D7B71 Module(sqlservr+000D7B71)
2006-02-19 20:53:23.12 spid51          010D746E Module(sqlservr+000D746E)
2006-02-19 20:53:23.15 spid51          010D83F0 Module(sqlservr+000D83F0)
2006-02-19 20:53:23.15 spid51          781329AA Module(MSVCR80+000029AA)
2006-02-19 20:53:23.17 spid51          78132A36 Module(MSVCR80+00002A36)
2006-02-19 20:53:23.17 spid51          Stack Signature for the dump is 0xA9D28AAB
2006-02-19 20:53:23.59 spid51          External dump process return code
0x20002001.
The error information has been submitted to Watson error reporting.

2006-02-19 20:53:23.59 spid51          Error: 17066, Severity: 16, State: 1.


2006-02-19 20:53:23.59 spid51          SQL Server Assertion: File: <dbmgr.cpp>,
line=6728 Failed Assertion = '!FindDB(dbid)'. This error may be timing-
related. If the error persists after rerunning the statement, use DBCC CHECKDB
to check the database for structural integrity, or restart the server to
ensure in-memory data structures are not corrupted.


2006-02-19 20:53:23.61 spid51          Error: 3624, Severity: 20, State: 1.
2006-02-19 20:53:23.61 spid51          A system assertion check has failed. Check
the SQL Server error log for details
```

In the stack dump header, notice that the Exception information has been replaced by

```
2006-02-19 20:53:23.09 spid51          * Location:      dbmgr.cpp:6728

2006-02-19 20:53:23.09 spid51          * Expression:     !FindDB(dbid)

2006-02-19 20:53:23.09 spid51          * SPID:          51

2006-02-19 20:53:23.09 spid51          * Process ID:     3780
```

This information is important. You can use it to search the Microsoft Knowledge Base for possible articles that describe this assertion. It is extremely rare for an assertion not to be a Microsoft SQL Server problem. I've seen a few instances where the assertion pointed to some other type of external error condition (like an I/O error), but in most cases, this is a logic problem in the SQL Server code.

All the other information in the stack dump as found with exceptions is there, including the name of the mini-dump file, the module listing, registers, and short stack dump.

Dump on Error

The third type of scenario for a stack dump is for an error number raised by the SQL Server engine. The SQL Engine is designed so that a stack dump can be produced when a specific error number is encountered. This behavior can be triggered by the –y command-line startup parameter or the undocumented DBCC DUMPTRIGGER command. These options should never be used by a customer without the specific guidance of Microsoft.

Remember that we talked about resource usage when dumping the stack and producing the mini-dump? If you set up the engine to produce a stack dump for a common error number (like Msg 208, which is simply Invalid object name '%.*ls'), you would be creating unnecessary resource consumption that can affect performance. PSS typically uses this feature only when trying to determine the exact place in the code a specific error number is being raised because other troubleshooting techniques will not work.

The engine will, however, produce a stack dump by default for some fatal errors. As of SQL Server 2005 SP1, these errors are

```
5242
Latch timeouts (844 and 846)
2006-02-18 19:33:09.40 spid51 ex_raise2: Exception raised, major=52, minor=42,
state=1, severity=22, attempting to create symptom dump
2006-02-18 19:33:09.58 spid51 Using 'dbghelp.dll' version '4.0.5'
2006-02-18 19:33:09.59 spid51 **Dump thread - spid = 51, PSS = 0x048B9278, EC
= 0x048B9280
2006-02-18 19:33:09.59 spid51 *
2006-02-18 19:33:09.59 spid51 * User initiated stack dump.  This is not a
server exception dump.
2006-02-18 19:33:09.59 spid51 *
2006-02-18 19:33:09.61 spid51 ***Stack Dump being sent to C:\Program
Files\Microsoft SQL Server\MSSQL.1\MSSQL\LOG\SQLDump0001.txt
2006-02-18 19:33:09.61 spid51
*********************************************************************
2006-02-18 19:33:09.61 spid51 *
2006-02-18 19:33:09.61 spid51 * BEGIN STACK DUMP:
2006-02-18 19:33:09.61 spid51 *   02/18/06 19:33:09 spid 51
2006-02-18 19:33:09.61 spid51 *
2006-02-18 19:33:09.61 spid51 * ex_raise2: Exception raised, major=52,
minor=42, state=1, severity=22
2006-02-18 19:33:09.61 spid51 *
2006-02-18 19:33:09.61 spid51 *   MODULE                           BASE
END       SIZE
< MODULE LIST WOULD BE HERE >
< REGISTER DUMP WOULD BE HERE >
2006-02-18 19:33:09.61 spid51
*********************************************************************
2006-02-18 19:33:09.61 spid51 *-------------------------------------------------
-----------------------
2006-02-18 19:33:09.61 spid51 * Short Stack Dump
2006-02-18 19:33:09.62 spid51 77E55DEA Module(kernel32+00015DEA)
2006-02-18 19:33:09.62 spid51 02172CE4 Module(sqlservr+01172CE4)
2006-02-18 19:33:09.62 spid51 02176BA0 Module(sqlservr+01176BA0)
2006-02-18 19:33:09.62 spid51 0217674D Module(sqlservr+0117674D)
2006-02-18 19:33:09.62 spid51 01597EA2 Module(sqlservr+00597EA2)
2006-02-18 19:33:09.62 spid51 01095FFE Module(sqlservr+00095FFE)
2006-02-18 19:33:09.62 spid51 02389FB0 Module(sqlservr+01389FB0)
2006-02-18 19:33:09.62 spid51 0158E526 Module(sqlservr+0058E526)
2006-02-18 19:33:09.62 spid51 0100C833 Module(sqlservr+0000C833)
2006-02-18 19:33:09.62 spid51 0100BF0F Module(sqlservr+0000BF0F)
2006-02-18 19:33:09.62 spid51 010106EB Module(sqlservr+000106EB)
2006-02-18 19:33:09.62 spid51 01010B3A Module(sqlservr+00010B3A)
2006-02-18 19:33:09.62 spid51 01010932 Module(sqlservr+00010932)
```

```
2006-02-18 19:33:09.62 spid51 010C0E2B Module(sqlservr+000C0E2B)
2006-02-18 19:33:09.62 spid51 01210454 Module(sqlservr+00210454)
2006-02-18 19:33:09.62 spid51 013F65A8 Module(sqlservr+003F65A8)
2006-02-18 19:33:09.62 spid51 013B3E42 Module(sqlservr+003B3E42)
2006-02-18 19:33:09.62 spid51 013B35EC Module(sqlservr+003B35EC)
2006-02-18 19:33:09.62 spid51 012101C2 Module(sqlservr+002101C2)
2006-02-18 19:33:09.62 spid51 01188FC9 Module(sqlservr+00188FC9)
2006-02-18 19:33:09.62 spid51 01189021 Module(sqlservr+00189021)
2006-02-18 19:33:09.62 spid51 01330A25 Module(sqlservr+00330A25)
2006-02-18 19:33:09.62 spid51 01330421 Module(sqlservr+00330421)
2006-02-18 19:33:09.62 spid51 01332C55 Module(sqlservr+00332C55)
2006-02-18 19:33:09.62 spid51 0100889F Module(sqlservr+0000889F)
2006-02-18 19:33:09.62 spid51 010089C5 Module(sqlservr+000089C5)
2006-02-18 19:33:09.62 spid51 010086E7 Module(sqlservr+000086E7)
2006-02-18 19:33:09.62 spid51 010D764A Module(sqlservr+000D764A)
2006-02-18 19:33:09.62 spid51 010D7B71 Module(sqlservr+000D7B71)
2006-02-18 19:33:09.62 spid51 010D746E Module(sqlservr+000D746E)
2006-02-18 19:33:09.62 spid51 010D83F0 Module(sqlservr+000D83F0)
2006-02-18 19:33:09.62 spid51 781329AA Module(MSVCR80+000029AA)
2006-02-18 19:33:09.64 spid51 78132A36 Module(MSVCR80+00002A36)
2006-02-18 19:33:09.65 spid51 * ---------------------------------------------
--------------------
2006-02-18 19:33:09.65 spid51 Stack Signature for the dump is 0xE09D5555
2006-02-18 19:33:10.48 spid51 External dump process return code 0x20000001.
External dump process returned no errors.
2006-02-18 19:33:10.58 spid51 Error: 5242, Severity: 22, State: 1.
2006-02-18 19:33:10.58 spid51 An inconsistency was detected during an internal
operation in database 'master'(ID:1) on page (1:306). Please contact technical
support. Reference number 3.
```

There are important differences between this stack dump and others, such as this exception to note:

```
2006-02-18 19:33:09.40 spid51 ex_raise2: Exception raised, major=52, minor=42,
state=1, severity=22, attempting to create symptom dump
```

The very first line indicates why the stack dump was created (note the legacy term *symptom dump* still in this message). If you see this as the first line before the dump, you know that either the error was a "default" error to dump or someone has enabled -y or used DBCC DUMPTRIGGER. In order to know the error number, simply take the value of major, multiply it by 100, and then add minor to it. So, in the preceding example, the error number is 5242 (52*100+42). If the dump occurs due to an error explicitly set with -y or DBCC DUMPTRIGGER, you either need to clear this if you don't need this dump, or you must already be working with Microsoft PSS to investigate an error. To clear the dump for a specific error, use one of the following methods:

- Use DBCC DUMPTRIGGER with the following syntax:

    ```
    dbcc dumptrigger('clear', <error number>)

    go
    ```

- Use the SQL Configuration Manager to remove the –y parameter.

DBCC DUMPTRIGGER sets or clears the dump-on-error functionality for the lifetime of the server until it is shut down. The -y parameter sets a dump on a particular error every time SQL Server starts (but you can use DUMPTRIGGER to disable/enable it dynamically after startup).

To see what errors are enabled for dump, you can run DBCC DUMPTRIGGER ('display').

The other interesting part of the stack dump for an error number is that the top of the function call stack is in the module kernel32:

```
2006-02-18 19:33:09.61 spid51 * Short Stack Dump
2006-02-18 19:33:09.62 spid51 77E55DEA Module(kernel32+00015DEA)
2006-02-18 19:33:09.62 spid51 02172CE4 Module(sqlservr+01172CE4)
```

This doesn't mean the error is not raised within SQL Server. If you used a debugger, you would find that the top of the stack looks something like this:

```
4db2dbbc 0244142e 000042ac 00000000 00000000 kernel32!RaiseException+0x53
4db2dc08 02194394 02a03564 4db28e9c 4db2dd68 sqlservr!CDmpDump::Dump+0x95
```

What this shows is that SQL Server produces a stack dump in this situation by using the Windows RaiseException API for its own user-defined exception (this is called the PRINTSTACK exception in the engine code, which is 17068 or 0x42ac). The server knows how to handle this exception and generate a dump when it is raised.

Troubleshooting Checklist

When I see a stack dump in an ERRORLOG, I ask myself the following questions:

1. What was the reason for the stack dump? Windows exception? Assertion?
2. For a Windows exception, is the top of the stack a Microsoft Module?
3. Can the problem be reproduced by running the query listed in the input buffer?
4. Do any known Knowledge Base articles describe the problem?

The last item is difficult because SQL Server 2005 doesn't symbolize the stack. You can use the debugger with public symbols to get that stack and try to match the conditions of the problem with known Knowledge Base article fixes. In general, service packs and major releases correct exceptions caused by SQL Server code. Microsoft may not create a hotfix for every exception encountered, depending on if a workaround exists or how often the problem might occur on customer systems.

SQL Server Crash Scenarios

You've learned quite a bit about stack dumps and the conditions that cause the server engine to generate them. In most of these situations, the effect of the exception, assertion, or error is the termination of a single user connection. That user can reconnect, and other users are not affected. What are scenarios where a stack dump or other error may result in the termination of the SQL Server engine affecting all users (affectionately known as a *crash*)?

I've attempted to list the various scenarios here so you can recognize them and understand what options you can take to recover and resolve them. But before I do that, let me point out one important feature of SQL Server 2005 (also available in SQL Server 7.0 and 2000): *auto restart* of SQL Server. The SQL Server Agent service, shown in Figure 6-7, is designed to monitor the SQL Server engine to detect if it has terminated abnormally or crashed (a good reason to use SQLAgent). You can enable/disable this option via the properties of SQL Server Agent in Management Studio.

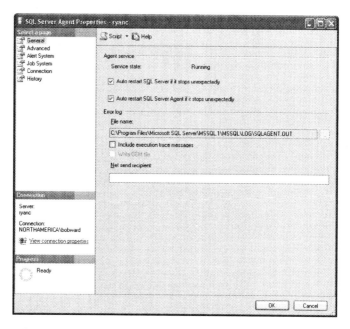

FIGURE 6-7   Sql Server Agent

The Auto Restart feature is on by default. I highly recommend you leave it on for production systems unless you have some specific troubleshooting you must perform before a restart should occur. I've had customers call in and say, "My SQL Server is restarting periodically, and I don't know why." What they usually are seeing is some type of crash occurring and then SQL Server Agent is restarting it. SQL Server Agent can detect a "stop unexpectedly" scenario versus a normal shutdown because there is a shared memory region each service knows about. When SQL Server normally shuts down, it writes a known signature into the shared memory region that is shutting down.

If SQL Server Agent restarts SQL Server, you will see EventID 17052 in the Application Event Log.

SQL Server Shutdown

When I use the term *SQL Server shutdown*, I mean a user-initiated action with the intent to shut down SQL Server. Therefore, I won't spend much time here talking about a normal SQL Server shutdown as a "crash," except to point out two important points about shutdown:

■ There is no method to track what program or what user initiated a shutdown request for the SQL Server service. The only exception is if the T-SQL SHUTDOWN command was used.

■ A shutdown of the SQL Server service due to a Windows shutdown could result in longer recovery times than you expect. This is because SQL Server has only a limited amount of time to shut down the service, which includes a checkpoint of all user databases.

Unhandled Windows Exception

Remember that we talked at length about how SQL Server is designed to catch Windows exceptions? Pardon this expression, but there are some exceptions to this design:

■ A thread created from a SQL worker thread that doesn't use SEH will, by design of Windows, result in an unhandled exception.

For example, if an extended stored procedure creates a new thread and has a bug that results in an AV in that new thread but doesn't use SEH in this new thread, an unhandled exception will occur in the SQL engine.

This applies to any child thread. SQL Server uses SEH for all its new threads, but any DLL, such as an extended stored procedure, COM object (sp_0A), or linked server OLE-DB provider, can cause this problem. I've seen this occur in all three of these situations.

■ Any thread not under the control of a SQL Server worker thread could cause an AV and not use SEH.

■ Some obscure exceptions are not handled by design.

For example, EXCEPTION_INVALID_HANDLE, would not be handled by the engine (though I've never seen this occur).

As I mentioned earlier in the chapter, by default, an unhandled exception results in the default debugger (Dr. Watson) being invoked and a dump signature. So even if SQL Server handles most exceptions, what about these unhandled scenarios? Well, up until SQL Server 7.0, the default debugger was the behavior. To make it worse, there was no signature or sign of any problem in the ERRORLOG. You didn't get any message about why the server engine was terminated.

When the design for SQL Server 7.0 was on the drawing board in 1997 and 1998, the SQL Server development team decided to use the Windows UnhandledExceptionFilter facility to trap these unhandled exceptions, report that an unhandled exception had occurred, and write a stack dump to the ERRORLOG. The engine process is still terminated, because applications should not do much in an unhandled exception filter routine, but the server could at least produce a short stack dump in the ERRORLOG before exiting. Here is a sample ERRORLOG entry from this exact type of scenario:

```
2006-05-30 22:23:17.14 Server  Error: 17311, Severity: 16, State: 1.
2006-05-30 22:23:17.14 Server  SQL Server is terminating because of fatal
exception c0000005. This error may be caused by an unhandled Win32 or C++
exception, or by an access violation encountered during exception handling.
Check the SQL error log for any related stack dumps or messages. This
exception forces SQL Server to shutdown. To recover from this error,
restart the server (unless SQLAgent is configured to auto restart).
2006-05-30 22:23:17.33 Server  Using 'dbghelp.dll' version '4.0.5'
2006-05-30 22:23:17.72 Server  **Dump thread - spid = 0, PSS = 0x00000000, EC
= 0x00000000
2006-05-30 22:23:17.72 Server  ***Stack Dump being sent to C:\Program
Files\Microsoft SQL Server\MSSQL.1\MSSQL\LOG\SQLDump0139.txt
2006-05-30 22:23:17.72 Server
************************************************************************
2006-05-30 22:23:17.72 Server  *
2006-05-30 22:23:17.72 Server  * BEGIN STACK DUMP:
2006-05-30 22:23:17.72 Server  *    05/30/06 22:23:17 spid 0
2006-05-30 22:23:17.72 Server  *
2006-05-30 22:23:17.72 Server  * ex_handle_except encountered exception
C0000005 - Server terminating
2006-05-30 22:23:17.72 Server  *
2006-05-30 22:23:17.72 Server  *
2006-05-30 22:23:17.72 Server  *   MODULE                         BASE
END       SIZE
<MODULE LIST GOES HERE >
<REGISTER DUMP GOES HERE >
2006-05-30 22:23:17.73 Server
************************************************************************
2006-05-30 22:23:17.73 Server  *------------------------------------------------
------------------------
2006-05-30 22:23:17.73 Server  * Short Stack Dump
2006-05-30 22:23:17.78 Server  7C81EB33 Module(kernel32+0001EB33)
2006-05-30 22:23:17.78 Server  02172CE4 Module(sqlservr+01172CE4)
2006-05-30 22:23:17.78 Server  02176BA0 Module(sqlservr+01176BA0)
2006-05-30 22:23:17.78 Server  0217674D Module(sqlservr+0117674D)
2006-05-30 22:23:17.78 Server  023D8B59 Module(sqlservr+013D8B59)
2006-05-30 22:23:18.12 Server  7C862CD3 Module(kernel32+00062CD3)
2006-05-30 22:23:18.12 Server  452A56C1 Module(xp_crash+000356C1)
2006-05-30 22:23:18.12 Server  4529DC3A Module(xp_crash+0002DC3A)
2006-05-30 22:23:18.12 Server  452B5B40 Module(xp_crash+00045B40)
2006-05-30 22:23:18.14 Server  452A59D7 Module(xp_crash+000359D7)
2006-05-30 22:23:18.14 Server  7C9037BF Module(ntdll+000037BF)
2006-05-30 22:23:18.14 Server  7C90378B Module(ntdll+0000378B)
2006-05-30 22:23:18.14 Server  7C90EAFA Module(ntdll+0000EAFA)
2006-05-30 22:23:18.14 Server  4529DC11 Module(xp_crash+0002DC11)
2006-05-30 22:23:18.14 Server  4529DB82 Module(xp_crash+0002DB82)
2006-05-30 22:23:18.14 Server  7C80B50B Module(kernel32+0000B50B)
2006-05-30 22:23:18.14 Server  Stack Signature for the dump is 0xAEF52CB8
2006-05-30 22:23:19.17 Server  External dump process return code 0x20002001.
The error information has been submitted to Watson error reporting.
```

You can see right away that Msg 17311 tells a lot about the situation. An exception (remember c0000005 is an Access Violation) has called the server to terminate. Below it is the stack dump that shows the cause.

In this case, the server doesn't show the Exception Address and other Exception record context. But from the short stack dump, you can see that the xp_crash is part of the problem. Because the server doesn't symbolize the call stack here, you can't tell exactly the sequence of events. But the top of the stack up until xp_crash would look like the following if you were to use a debugger with the provided mini-dump file and public symbols from Microsoft:

```
4538e6c0  02424dde  kernel32!RaiseException+0x53
4538e70c  0217f4e8  sqlservr!CDmpDump::Dump+0x95
4538e7cc  02176e82  sqlservr!CImageHelper::DoMiniDump+0x3d2
4538f584  0217674d  sqlservr!stackTrace+0x6c8
4538f5a4  023d8b59  sqlservr!stackTraceCallBack+0x40
4538f7c4  7c862cd3  sqlservr!ex_handle_except+0xf8
4538fa34  452a56c1  kernel32!UnhandledExceptionFilter+0x149
```

ex_handle_except is the function SQL Server registers with Windows to be called when an unhandled Windows exception occurs. You can see from this call stack that ex_handle_except calls the necessary code to produce the stack dump. As with dump on error, the engine raises a PRINTSTACK exception to trigger the dump.

Look at the exercises at the end of this chapter on how to use symbols for xp_crash and public symbols from Microsoft to see the exact cause of the crash.

Unhandled C++ Exception

Another crash scenario is an unhandled C++ exception. Much of the SQL Server engine is developed using C++, and the engine uses C++ exceptions (throw) to process and handle many errors. In some cases, usually due to a bug, a C++ exception doesn't have a proper "catch" handler. The default behavior of Windows applications for unhandled C++ exceptions thrown but not caught is for the default termination handler, *terminate*, to be called. Terminate, by default, simply calls the runtime routine *abort*, which results in the termination of SQL Server with no signature in the ERRORLOG (and no DefaultDebugger called). But just as you can trap a Windows unhandled exception, a Windows programmer can install his or her own unhandled C++ termination handler using the set_terminate routine. The SQL Server engine does just that by calling set_terminate with the function pointer for ex_terminator. Like the unhandled exception filter routine, ex_handle_except, ex_terminator calls the necessary code to produce a stack dump before the SQLSERVR.EXE process is terminated.

I don't have a specific ERRORLOG example to show you for this situation, but it looks identical to the preceding one for an unhandled Windows exception. Instead of seeing ex_handle_except in the header, you see ex_terminator. This is how you can distinguish between an unhandled Windows exception and an unhandled C++ exception. In my experience, most unhandled C++ exceptions are due to a problem with the SQL Server code. However, just like poorly written xprocs causing an unhandled AV, you could just as easily write an xproc that throws a C++ exception that is not handled. I have never seen this situation, but it is possible, and now you will know how to recognize it. Like in the Windows unhandled exception case, if you see a DLL not shipped by Microsoft in the call stack sequence, you should be prepared to work with the developer of the DLL to resolve the issue.

Server Protection

The developers who created SQL OS implemented two features that protect the server from intrusion and damaging exceptions:

1. Server thread stack protection

   They implemented protection for SQL Server worker thread stacks to detect possible stack corruption. If this type of problem is encountered, the ERRORLOG contains the following signature:

```
2005-09-09 10:18:40.42 spid51        Hit Fatal Error: Stack corruption
2005-09-09 10:18:40.44 spid51        Using 'dbghelp.dll' version '4.0.5'
2005-09-09 10:18:40.44 spid51        **Dump thread - spid = 51, PSS =
0x05E40A50, EC = 0x05E40A60
2005-09-09 10:18:40.44 spid51        ***Stack Dump being sent to C:\Program
Files\Microsoft SQL Server\MSSQL.1\MSSQL\LOG\SQLDump0011.txt
2005-09-09 10:18:40.44 spid51
*********************************************************************
2005-09-09 10:18:40.44 spid51        *
2005-09-09 10:18:40.44 spid51        * BEGIN STACK DUMP:

2005-09-09 10:18:40.44 spid51        *   09/09/05 10:18:40 spid 51
2005-09-09 10:18:40.44 spid51        *

2005-09-09 10:18:40.44 spid51        * ex_terminator - Last chance exception
handling
2005-09-09 10:18:40.44 spid51        *
```

   The first line of this ERRORLOG entry is produced when the stack corruption is detected. In order to get a dump file to analyze the problem, the engine explicitly calls the unhandled C++ exception handler ex_terminator. I can't go into the details of how the server implements this detection, but it is a very important feature. The signature for a problem without this detection is fairly unpredictable.

2. NX exception

Runtime Library Error

The C runtime library is the DLL that contains all the famous functions experienced C programmers have abused—I mean used—over the years. Functions like printf, strcpy, and so on. Some code within the runtime library is designed to abort the process if a fatal error is encountered. Unfortunately in these cases, there is no signature in the SQL Server ERRORLOG that it has happened. The design of the runtime library is usually to display an error to the std output, but for the SQL Server service, you can't see that output. Fortunately, the runtime library uses one of its own routines, exit, which uses the

Windows API ExitProcess. This is fortunate, because later in this section, I'll describe how you can trap the caller of ExitProcess that causes the SQL Server engine to terminate. Who can cause the runtime library problems? The SQL Server engine code can certainly be a candidate, because it uses the runtime library, but just as likely are the usual suspects like xprocs (Can you tell now how much I don't like xprocs?), COM objects, and linked server providers.

CLR Fatal Error

CLR is a great new feature for programmers for SQL Server. It allows you to create .NET assemblies and run them as user-defined functions and stored procedures. However, in order to support this functionality, SQL Server must *host* the CLR runtime environment within its process space. Although a tremendous amount of thought and testing were put into this feature, it still represents another dimension to server stability. Another DLL (mscorwks.dll) loaded in the SQL Server process space could encounter a problem. (This is why CLR is not enabled by default for SQL Server. You need to use the Surface Area Configuration tool to enable the execution of CLR-based functions and procedures.) Fortunately, CLR is designed to work well with the SQL Engine in the management of resources and execution. Errors encountered by CLR assemblies are coordinated to work with the SQL Server error-handling mechanisms.

However, one error scenario can result in a crash of SQL Server. If the CLR DLL itself encounters a fatal error, it reports this to the SQL Server engine, because it cannot continue to execute safely. The server has to be conservative here and shut down its process, because it may not be safe to execute any further. The signature for this problem is a stack dump and a shutdown of SQL Server:

```
**Dump thread - spid = 55, PSS = 0x0D232F80, EC = 0x0D232F90
***Stack Dump being sent to
d:\stressexec\SQLOfficeStress\MSSQL\LOG\SQLDump0001.txt
*
*************************************************************************
*
*  BEGIN STACK DUMP:
*     05/30/05 01:08:58 spid 55
*  Private server build.
*
*  A fatal error occurred in .NET Framework runtime.
*
*  Input Buffer 100 bytes -
*              exec SqlClrStressDb_OOM003_30..p_OOM003
*
*
<MODULE LIST GOES HERE >
<REGISTER DUMP GOES HERE >
*
*************************************************************************
*  ----------------------------------------------------------------------
--
*  Short Stack Dump
77E55DEA Module(kernel32+00015DEA)
023E17ED Module(sqlservr+01FE17ED)
```

```
023E54DD Module(sqlservr+01FE54DD)
00DF8E1B Module(sqlservr+009F8E1B)
79827375 Module(mscorwks+00167375)
7982C5A2 Module(mscorwks+0016C5A2)
7982DF91 Module(mscorwks+0016DF91)
79765A15 Module(mscorwks+000A5A15)
79765BB4 Module(mscorwks+000A5BB4)


79764305 Module(mscorwks+000A4305)


7C82EEB2 Module(ntdll+0002EEB2)
7C82EE84 Module(ntdll+0002EE84)

7C82ECC6 Module(ntdll+0002ECC6)
```

This problem is typically an issue that needs to be resolved with Microsoft technical support. You can help expedite the resolution to the problem by having the ERRORLOG and mini-dump files associated with the stack dump. Also, be prepared to provide the CLR assemblies behind the query that is listed in the input buffer. This is similar to the reproductions we talked about in this section. Anything you can do to reproduce the problem or assist PSS to reproduce the problem almost always results in a quicker resolution.

ExitProcess() or TerminateProcess()

SQL Server uses the ExitProcess Windows API routine when shutting down the SQL Server engine. This is based on a user-initiated request to shut down the engine. However, just like unhandled exceptions or runtime library errors, a DLL loaded in the process space for SQLSERVR.EXE could simply call ExitProcess, TerminateProcess, or even the runtime routines *abort* or *exit* (which end up calling ExitProcess—and technically ExitProcess eventually calls TerminateProcess).

So someone could develop an extended stored procedure and call ExitProcess based on some error condition. The only problem is that this results in a crash of SQL Server with no signature or symptoms of why SQL Server terminated.

So what choices do you have to find the cause of a termination of SQL Server with no apparent reason for the cause of the crash?

- **Attach a debugger to SQL Server.** This is what we traditionally have had to do for many years to find a mysterious problem like this.

- **Start SQL Server with trace flag 8029.** This was designed into the engine by the SQL OS development team for SQL Server 2005. The trace flag is not documented, and I do not encourage you to use this unless you specifically have a SQL Server crash you cannot explain.

Let's say you have this situation and you decide to start the server using trace flag 8029. If the conditions occurred to cause the server to crash, the ERRORLOG should contain a signature similar to the following:

```
2006-05-31 18:04:21.79 spid51   Using 'dbghelp.dll' version '4.0.5'
2006-05-31 18:04:24.29 spid51   **Stack Dump being sent to C:\Program
Files\Microsoft SQL Server\MSSQL.1\MSSQL\LOG\SQLDump0141.txt
2006-05-31 18:04:24.29 spid51   SqlDumpExceptionHandler: Process 51 generated
fatal exception 80000003 EXCEPTION_BREAKPOINT. SQL Server is terminating this
process.
2006-05-31 18:04:24.29 spid51
2006-05-31 18:04:24.29 spid51
*************************************************************************
2006-05-31 18:04:24.29 spid51   *
2006-05-31 18:04:24.29 spid51   * BEGIN STACK DUMP:
2006-05-31 18:04:24.29 spid51   *   05/31/06 18:04:24 spid 51
2006-05-31 18:04:24.29 spid51   *
2006-05-31 18:04:24.29 spid51   *
2006-05-31 18:04:24.29 spid51   * Exception Address = 7C81CAA2 Module
(kernel32+0001CAA2)
2006-05-31 18:04:24.29 spid51   * Exception Code    = 80000003
EXCEPTION_BREAKPOINT
2006-05-31 18:04:24.29 spid51   * Exception Information Array:
2006-05-31 18:04:24.29 spid51   * [1] 00000000:
2006-05-31 18:04:24.29 spid51   * [2] 441AF5FD: 32441AF6 C0010B20 010496E0
44000000 010496E5 04000000
2006-05-31 18:04:24.29 spid51   * [3] 00000000:
2006-05-31 18:04:24.29 spid51   * Input Buffer 56 bytes -
2006-05-31 18:04:24.32 spid51   *            exec xp_crash 1
2006-05-31 18:04:24.32 spid51   *
2006-05-31 18:04:24.32 spid51   *
2006-05-31 18:04:24.32 spid51   *  MODULE                          BASE
END        SIZE
< MODULE LIST GOES HERE >
< REGISTER DUMP GOES HERE >
2006-05-31 18:04:24.34 spid51
*************************************************************************
2006-05-31 18:04:24.34 spid51 *----------------------------------------------
-----------------------
2006-05-31 18:04:24.34 spid51 * Short Stack Dump
2006-05-31 18:04:24.38 spid51 7C81CAA2 Module(kernel32+0001CAA2)
2006-05-31 18:04:24.38 spid51 01635A24 Module(sqlservr+00635A24)
2006-05-31 18:04:24.38 spid51 01637B25 Module(sqlservr+00637B25)
2006-05-31 18:04:24.38 spid51 016373F9 Module(sqlservr+006373F9)
2006-05-31 18:04:24.38 spid51 01636360 Module(sqlservr+00636360)
2006-05-31 18:04:24.38 spid51 0163686E Module(sqlservr+0063686E)
2006-05-31 18:04:24.38 spid51 01BF269C Module(sqlservr+00BF269C)
2006-05-31 18:04:24.38 spid51 01497CA1 Module(sqlservr+00497CA1)
2006-05-31 18:04:24.38 spid51 011C1302 Module(sqlservr+001C1302)
2006-05-31 18:04:24.38 spid51 011C1179 Module(sqlservr+001C1179)
2006-05-31 18:04:24.38 spid51 011C100E Module(sqlservr+001C100E)
2006-05-31 18:04:24.38 spid51 0102DB52 Module(sqlservr+0002DB52)
2006-05-31 18:04:24.38 spid51 0102E0D0 Module(sqlservr+0002E0D0)
2006-05-31 18:04:24.38 spid51 0102C5F8 Module(sqlservr+0002C5F8)
2006-05-31 18:04:24.38 spid51 010438E5 Module(sqlservr+000438E5)
```

```
2006-05-31 18:04:24.38 spid51 01041C35 Module(sqlservr+00041C35)
2006-05-31 18:04:24.38 spid51 0100889F Module(sqlservr+0000889F)
2006-05-31 18:04:24.38 spid51 010089C5 Module(sqlservr+000089C5)
2006-05-31 18:04:24.38 spid51 010086E7 Module(sqlservr+000086E7)
2006-05-31 18:04:24.38 spid51 010D764A Module(sqlservr+000D764A)
2006-05-31 18:04:24.38 spid51 010D7B71 Module(sqlservr+000D7B71)
2006-05-31 18:04:24.38 spid51 010D746E Module(sqlservr+000D746E)
2006-05-31 18:04:24.42 spid51 010D83F0 Module(sqlservr+000D83F0)
2006-05-31 18:04:24.42 spid51 781329AA Module(MSVCR80+000029AA)
2006-05-31 18:04:24.45 spid51 78132A36 Module(MSVCR80+00002A36)
2006-05-31 18:04:24.48 spid51 Stack Signature for the dump is 0x018C4DBC
2006-05-31 18:04:26.84 spid51 External dump process return code 0x20002001.
The error information has been submitted to Watson error reporting.
2006-05-31 18:04:26.84 spid51 Error: 18002, Severity: 20, State: 1.
2006-05-31 18:04:26.84 spid51 Exception happened when running extended stored
procedure 'xp_crash' in the library 'xp_crash.dll'. SQL Server is terminating
process 51. Exception type: Win32 exception; Exception code: 0x80000003.
```

In this situation, you can see from the input buffer that an extended stored procedure was called that triggered the exit of the process. If you were to get the code for this extended procedure, you would find that it had a bug and called ExitProcess().

External Process Terminate

I've covered some interesting crash scenarios that typically involve a stack dump. In these cases, the SQL Server engine has logic to detect the crash and produce a stack dump. Even though in some of these cases you may have to involve Microsoft technical support to resolve the issue, the engine has done some work to leave a signature for a possible cause of the crash. This information can be very helpful in determining a quick resolution to the problem.

With all this great work, there is one scenario the server cannot detect and provide a signature via a stack dump: if an external program terminates the SQL Server process via the TerminateProcess API. This includes an administrator with the right privileges using a program like the KILL.EXE command from the resource kit or the End Process option for a program using Task Manager in Windows.

So what are your choices here to capture what program and/or user caused the termination of SQL Server? How do you even know an external program caused the crash?

The only thing I have found to be successful is to run SQL Server under the debugger and trace other pieces of information such as Performance Monitor and Security Audit logging to see which users might have logged on to the machine and what programs might have run that could have killed the server engine.

Other Server Critical Errors

Server critical errors other than a stack dump could occur that affect overall server execution of many user connections. I don't have a list of common critical errors, because there is no common trend for ones you might encounter. I do have some tips should you encounter an error that is fatal (causes a connection to terminate):

1. Search for any known Knowledge Base article that discusses the error and provides possible causes or fixes.

2. You can use SQLTrace to capture the events that led up to the critical error, including what queries and user.

3. You could use –y or DBCC DUMPTRIGGER to find the input buffer and stack trace. However, the stack trace might be meaningful to Microsoft PSS only when using a debugger.

4. You might already have the stack trace available via the SQL OS "ring buffer" DMV, sys.dm_os_ring_buffers.

The following query returns the most recent errors raised by the engine and nonsymbolized stack traces for where the error occurred:

```
select * from sys.dm_os_ring_buffers where ring_buffer_type =
'RING_BUFFER_EXCEPTION'
```

Depending on what errors have occurred recently (on my system I created a deadlock), you could see entries like this:

```
ring_buffer_address ring_buffer_type
timestamp           record


-------------------- ----------------------------------------------------------
- -------------------- ----------------------------------------------------------
-----------------------------------------------------------------------------
-----------------------------------------------------------------------------
-----------------------------------------------------------------------------
-----------------------------------------------------------------------------
-----------------------------------------------------------------------------
-----------------------------------------------------------------------------
-----------------------------------------------------------------------------
-----------------------------------------------------------------------------
-----------------------------------------------------------------------------
-----------------------------------------------------------------------------
-----------------------------------------------------------------------------
-----------------------------------------------------------------------------
-----------------------------------------------------------------------------
-----------------------------------------------------------------------------
-----------------------------------------------------------------------------
-----------------------------------------------------------------------------
-----------------------------------------------------------------------------
-----------------------------------------------------------------------------
```

```
-----------------------------------------------------------------------------
-----------------------------------------------------------------------------
-----------------------------------------------------------------------------
-----------------------------------------------------------------------------
-----------------------------------------------------------------------------
-----------------------------------------------------------------------------
-----------------
0x006B7388          RING_BUFFER_EXCEPTION
3070778                  <Record id = "12" type ="RING_BUFFER_EXCEPTION" time
="3070778"><Exception><Task
address="0x006B9798"></Task><Error>1205</Error><Severity>13</Severity><State>51
</State><UserDefined>0</UserDefined></Exception><Stack><frame id =
"0">0X010AC763</frame><frame id = "1">0X010AC89F</frame><frame id =
"2">0X010B105B</frame><frame id = "3">0X0102C5F8</frame><frame id =
"4">0X010438E5</frame><frame id = "5">0X01041C35</frame><frame id =
"6">0X0100889F</frame><frame id = "7">0X010089C5</frame><frame id =
"8">0X010086E7</frame><frame id = "9">0X010D764A</frame><frame id =
"10">0X010D7B71</frame><frame id = "11">0X010D746E</frame><frame id =
"12">0X010D83F0</frame><frame id = "13">0X781329AA</frame><frame id =
"14">0X78132A36</frame></Stack></Record>

0x006B7388          RING_BUFFER_EXCEPTION
3070778                  <Record id = "11" type ="RING_BUFFER_EXCEPTION" time
="3070778"><Exception><Task
address="0x006B9798"></Task><Error>1205</Error><Severity>13</Severity><State>51
</State><UserDefined>0</UserDefined></Exception><Stack><frame id =
"0">0X010AC763</frame><frame id = "1">0X010AC89F</frame><frame id =
"2">0X010B0A68</frame><frame id = "3">0X01079027</frame><frame id =
"4">0X01078D9D</frame><frame id = "5">0X0102DB52</frame><frame id =
"6">0X0102E0D0</frame><frame id = "7">0X0102C5F8</frame><frame id =
"8">0X010438E5</frame><frame id = "9">0X01041C35</frame><frame id =
"10">0X0100889F</frame><frame id = "11">0X010089C5</frame><frame id =
"12">0X010086E7</frame><frame id = "13">0X010D764A</frame><frame id =
"14">0X010D7B71</frame><frame id = "15">0X010D746E</frame></Stack></Record>
0x006B7388          RING_BUFFER_EXCEPTION
3070762                  <Record id = "10" type ="RING_BUFFER_EXCEPTION" time
="3070762"><Exception><Task
address="0x006B9798"></Task><Error>1205</Error><Severity>13</Severity><State>51
</State><UserDefined>0</UserDefined></Exception><Stack><frame id =
"0">0X010AC67E</frame><frame id = "1">0X01095FFE</frame><frame id =
"2">0X010AF449</frame><frame id = "3">0X010B47D0</frame><frame id =
"4">0X01557F9F</frame><frame id = "5">0X01088549</frame><frame id =
"6">0X0108870A</frame><frame id = "7">0X010886DC</frame><frame id =
"8">0X01E28C82</frame><frame id = "9">0X010473A7</frame><frame id =
"10">0X0103D32C</frame><frame id = "11">0X0103D23D</frame><frame id =
"12">0X01079027</frame><frame id = "13">0X01078D9D</frame><frame id =
"14">0X0102DB52</frame><frame id = "15">0X0102E0D0</frame></Stack></Record>
```

Using public symbols and a debugger, you could actually reconstruct the stack that caused these errors. You don't have the input buffer, but this information could be useful when working with PSS to avoid having to use -y or DBCC DUMPTRIGGER.

Troubleshooting a Server Hang

In the "Fundamentals" section of this chapter, I discussed a new feature in SQL Server 2005 called the Dedicated Admin Connection (DAC). I'll talk later about some scenarios where you can use DAC on a truly hung SQL Server. But before I do that, let me talk about some practical steps you should take anytime you suspect the SQL Server engine is hung and not processing logins or queries. I call this the *SQL Server health check*.

Why use a checklist or health check? Why not just use DAC and go right to the advanced debugging technique for a hang? It is because I've seen so many situations where what appears to be a hang is some other type of problem, like a SQL blocking problem.

Using the SQL Server Health Check to Solve a Hang

Let's say that you are an administrator and a colleague comes to you for advice. She says, "SQL Server is hung. Can you help?" Consider the following decision tree and checklist to determine if the engine is truly hung or there's some other problem:

1. Get a clear description of the problem.

2. Is Windows responsive?

3. Is SQLSERVR.EXE running?

4. Can you make a local sqlcmd.exe connection?

5. Can you run a query against sys.dm_exec_requests?

6. Check "health" perfmon counters.

7. Are there any errors or stack dumps in the SQL ERRORLOG?

8. Can you connect with DAC?

Let's look at each of these items in the health check:

Get a clear description of the problem.

Having a clear description of a problem is vital for any troubleshooting exercise, but it becomes very important for a hang. My first question in this situation is, "What do you mean by hang? What symptoms do you observe that lead you to believe SQL Server is hung?" You might get some of the items on your checklist answered by asking these questions. Typically, though, the answer is something like, "My application is getting time-outs" or "My users say the application that uses SQL Server is hung."

Is Windows responsive?

Okay, this seems pretty basic, but you would be surprised how many customers I've encountered who don't check this. If you can't log in to Windows, copy files, or run programs on the Windows machine, this problem is not likely a SQL Server issue. Even if it possibly is some type of resource usage issue with SQL Server, if you can't log in and run programs for diagnostics, there is not much from a SQL perspective for you to troubleshoot. If this type of situation occurs and you need to contact Microsoft technical support, start with Windows technical support.

Is `SQLSERVR.EXE` running?

At this point, you may be yawning and thinking, "Why am I going through the most basic of checklists here?" But these first two steps are very easy to do, and without them, going forward with anything else may lead you down the wrong path. Just do a quick check in Task Manager to make sure the `SQLSERVR.EXE` process is running. Of course, if you have multiple instances of SQL Server running, you can check the state of the services with the `net start` command or Services applet in Control Panel. Named instances have a Service Name indicating the name of the instance.

Can you make a local `sqlcmd.exe` connection?

This is a key decision point for your health check. `sqlcmd.exe` is the replacement for `osql.exe` from the previous version and uses the OLE-DB provider to connect to SQL Server. Make sure to do this on the actual computer where SQL Server is running. Why? Because if `sqlcmd.exe` can connect locally but not from a remote machine, there likely is some network issue to resolve. Let's say a local and remote `sqlcmd.exe` connection can work. Now you know a basic connection to the server can work. You now need to go back and consider the original problem description. You now know you can connect with `sql-cmd`, but for some reason the application cannot connect (perhaps it is a web application). If a remote `sqlcmd.exe` connection worked, you need to focus on why the application is having problems. We will cover later in the checklist what to do if a local `sqlcmd.exe` connection cannot work.

Can you run a query against `sys.dm_exec_requests`?

You now know you can make a local and remote connection with `sqlcmd.exe`. If you can connect locally but not remotely, you should work with your network administrators to find out the cause of possible network issues. Using your `sqlcmd.exe` connection (you may also be able to use the Management Studio Query window at this point), run the following query:

```
select * from sys.dm_exec_requests
```

If this query works, you know basic query functionality works within the engine (technically, if `sqlcmd.exe` works, a query was executed by the provider, but it is only a T-SQL `SET` command). Running this query gives you great data to start with.

The first thing I would do is look for blocking problems. Look for `blocking_sesion_id` values > 0 and `wait_time` > 0. I've seen so many issues that are described as a server hang that are really application-blocking problems.

Check "health" perfmon counters.

Another thing to check is the following perfmon counters:

- **Processor/% Processor Time.** What is the overall CPU usage on the machine? If all CPUs are hitting 100%, it may not be that SQL Server is technically hung. It might make sense that no one can connect or run queries because no CPU resources are available. If this value is very low or almost nothing, it could mean that SQL Server is hung (or it could just mean the machine is fairly idle).

- **Process/% Processor Time (SQLSERVR.EXE instance).** If CPU usage is very high, but this value is low, the problem is not with SQL Server. Use Performance Monitor to find out which process(es) are the ones consuming the CPU usage, and troubleshoot the problem with those programs. But if this value matches the high CPU usage of the overall machine, the problem could be with threads within SQL Server.

- **SQL Server:SQL Statistics/Batch Requests/Sec.** This measures how many query requests are coming into the SQL Server engine. If the server is idle, this counter shows up with 0. But if the server "should be" busy, this value should be at a constant rate. If it has dropped to 0, it could mean that SQL Server cannot process any requests (because it may be truly hung).

- **SQL Server:General Statistics/Processes Blocked.** This is a handy new perfmon counter for SQL Server 2005. This value counts the number of SQL Server sessions that are blocked every time a perfmon snapshot is collected. If the value is > 0: this is not a historical value. In other words, if blocking occurs, the value is > 0. After the blocking stops, the value goes back to 0. If this value is even 1, some SQL Server session is waiting on a resource. If the problem is prevalent across all users and it is a major blocking problem, I would expect this value to be much greater than 1. But don't ignore low values. Perhaps your application uses very few SQL sessions, they are blocked, and other threads from the middle-tier application are waiting on these small numbers of SQL sessions.

- **SQL Server:Wait Statistics.** This value provides more details if the Processes Blocked value is > 0. It provides more information about what "type" of wait is causing the resource wait problem. One in particular that could be interesting for "true" SQL hang problems is "Wait for the worker." If all worker threads are blocked, causing SQL Server to stop processing requests (because there are not worker threads available to do so), I would expect this value to go up significantly.

Are there any errors or stack dumps in the SQL ERRORLOG?

If you cannot connect locally or can't run a query against sys.dm_exec_requests, check your ERRORLOG. Check specifically for any errors like 17883, 17844, or 17888. If you see errors like this, you likely have an immediate explanation for the problem. Even if you don't see any errors but a local sqlcmd.exe connection cannot work, it is time to use the Dedicated Admin Connection (DAC).

Can you connect with DAC?

Notice this checklist doesn't have you go right to DAC up front. This is because it is only intended for situations where a normal connection will not work. It is possible you are very savvy with SQL Server and can easily run down this list quickly, but DAC is something you do after recognizing the true hang.

Let's say you can connect with DAC. What now? The first thing I would do is run a query against sys.dm_exec_requests just as you would if you could make a standard connection. Do the same steps as before. Look for blocking and sessions that are waiting. Before you do anything else, be sure to save the information from this DMV for future analysis.

It is conceivable that you could even find the "lead blocker" in a blocking problem and use the T-SQL KILL command to kill the session and free up the server. You should note that for SQL Server 2005 RTM, this is possible. But for RTM, you can kill the lead blocker only if it is actively running a query. With SQL Server 2005 SP1, you can kill a lead blocker that is idle. Before you try to kill any session, think carefully about gathering more information from other DMVs, such as

- sys.dm_exec_sessions

- sys.dm_os_wait_stats

- sys.dm_os_ring_buffers

- sys.dm_os_schedulers

- sys.dm_os_waiting_tasks

- sys.dm_os_workers

- sys.dm_tran_locks

- sys.dm_io_pending_io_requests

You may also choose to look at some of the requests from sys.dm_exec_requests and use sys.dm_exec_sql_text to grab the actual queries from specific requests that are running or waiting.

So what if you can't connect with DAC, or when using DAC, that connection becomes hung? You are now faced with a restart of SQL Server. I've seen in some situations where a standard shutdown of the SQL Server service will not work. Depending on how long it takes you to reboot your machine and the speed at which you need to get SQL Server back up and running, you could attempt to force a termination of the process through Task Manager. If SQL Server can't shut down as a service, doing this shouldn't cause any more harm than just ending the process. However, if you can afford the reboot of the computer, I recommend this. You never know if some transient issue with Windows is part of your issue, and rebooting the machine could clear this up.

But, before you reboot, if you want to pursue possible root causes as to why SQL Server hung and you can't use DAC to analyze DMVs, consider using the SQLDUMPER.EXE program I mentioned earlier in the chapter to capture a dump of the SQLSERVR.EXE program.

A full or filtered dump would be preferable, but it could take a long time, depending on how much memory SQL Server has consumed. At a minimum, get a mini-dump so PSS can look at the state of all thread call stacks in the process.

Service Broker Issues

By August Hill

The purpose of this chapter is to help you diagnose and troubleshoot database applications that are Service Broker-enabled. From the outset, this is a good way to think about the application that is using the Service Broker features in SQL Server 2005. The application is "just" another database application, and, to that extent, much of what you know about diagnosing other database applications applies.

Before we get started, let me describe how this chapter is arranged so that you can make the most of it. It has five parts:

- Because the Service Broker is new in SQL Server 2005, I wanted to lead off with a section describing the architecture of the Service Broker. In addition, I cover some of the key concepts and ideas behind the Service Broker so that when you are diagnosing a problem, you will have better understanding of why things are happening.

- The next section covers the bulk of the diagnostics. I show you where to look to uncover the inner workings of the Service Broker. As complex as the system is, it really comes down to just a couple of places to look to see what is going wrong.

- In the third section, we actually walk through a troubleshooting session, where you get to do some "hands-on" diagnostics with the tools covered in the preceding section. We all learn by doing, so this enables you to go step by step through the configuration of two separate services on two separate Service Brokers. You will see the views and trace events in action so that when you are actually troubleshooting a live system, it will all seem quite familiar.

- The fourth section is a compendium of all the other places to find Service Broker information. This includes things such as all the Service Broker-related views, Perfmon counters, DBCC CHECKDB, and the like.

- Finally, we wrap up with some pointers to online resources that are available to help in Service Broker troubleshooting.

So let's get started!

Broker Overview

Why Service Broker?

First, the purpose of this chapter is to help you diagnose problems in the Service Broker, not to try to sell you on the feature itself. However, if you are like many administrators, you might not even be familiar with the problem that the Service Broker solves. If nothing else, I want you to understand what this component is doing—it will give you the ability to reason about the problems you are seeing!

The Service Broker was designed to give the typical database developer the ability to create a distributed, loosely coupled application that scales to very high levels.

Let's think about this for a while. Writing a scalable application can be a pretty daunting task, even for a very experienced developer. How do you architect the system? How do you allow for scaling across a number of machines? (I call this decentralized scale-out.) How do you ensure that two different parts of the application are properly maintaining the state of your application? Distributed transactions? And so on.

What we really need is a framework to develop applications that does not demand so much of the database developer. All of our application data is in a database right now. Doesn't it make sense that if we could put the "smarts" into the database to allow for scaling out our applications, we could take our existing database applications, make a few changes to them (nothing is for free), and let the database do the "heavy lifting"?

The Service Broker does this. This is why we wrote the feature, to allow the typical database developer access to the decentralized scale-out world—and doing so without making his or her head hurt. We had to add a few key concepts to SQL Server to make this all work.

Okay, end of sales pitch!

What is interesting is that some of these concepts can actually be used without using all the full features of the Service Broker. For example, "activation" is a feature that allows a stored procedure to be started on a separate task when a message is placed in a queue. We are seeing a number of customers use just this part of the Service Broker, without using the distributed nature of the product. Why mention this? When you are trying to do problem determination, realize that only parts of the Service Broker might be in use. This will help you quickly rule out parts of the problem.

Service Broker Objects and Terms

The Service Broker-enabled applications make use of several new objects in SQL Server. Here is a brief description of each of these objects. (The details are in the fourth section of this chapter.)

- **Services.** A service is the Service Broker-enabled database application. All the communication happens between services.

- **Contracts.** Services support one or more contracts. Contracts describe the message flow between services.

- **Message Types.** A Message Type names a particular kind of message that can flow between services.

- **Queues.** Queues hold messages that the service is waiting to receive.

- **Routes.** A route specifies the location of a remote service.

- **Remote Service Binding.** A remote service binding specifies the identity to be used to authenticate with the remote service.

- **Connection Endpoint.** A connection endpoint specifies the network port used by the Service Broker.

- **Conversation Endpoint.** A conversation endpoint represents one side of a conversation between two services.

- **Conversation Group.** A conversation group is a collection of related conversations.

- **Conversation.** A conversation is a stream of messages between two services. This is the basic unit of work that occurs between two services. All messages within the conversation are delivered exactly one time and in the precise order they were sent.

Internal Architecture

Basically, the Service Broker runs on a number of background threads internal to the SQL Server process. (You can view these by looking at the sys.sysprocesses view, discussed later in this chapter.)

- **Service Broker Manager.** Responsible for the overall Service Broker operations. Starts and stops Active Service Brokers as needed.

- **Active Service Broker.** Responsible for one Service Broker's operation. One Active Service Broker per database has the Service Broker enabled. With a few notable exceptions, any database can be a Service Broker. As such, Service Brokers can be moved between SQL Server instances just by detaching and attaching the database.

- **Transport.** Responsible for maintaining the connections between remote Service Brokers.

- **Message Dispatcher.** Responsible for dispatching messages either locally or remotely.

- **Transmitter.** Responsible for sending messages to the network.

- **Classifier.** Responsible for routing messages either locally or remotely.

- **Internal Activation Manager.** Responsible for controlling the queue monitors and handling overall internal activation.

Primary Diagnostic Tools and Methods

There are a number of ways to look inside the Service Broker. A part of learning the diagnostic process is gaining an understanding of what tools to turn to first. This section describes the following:

- **The Transmission Queue view.** This one view is the single best place to start looking for problems.

- **SQL Profiler.** Trace events allow us to track the system's operation. Armed with these, we can see exactly what the Service Broker is doing in response to our commands.

- **SQL error log/NT event log.** These logs can contain errors that were encountered during background operations in the Service Broker.

Armed with these three items, you can solve 80 percent if not more of the Service Broker problems. There are a number of ways to connect into the SQL Server and gather this information, but one very handy tool is SQLDiag.exe. This program not only simplifies gathering Service Broker diagnostic information, but also gathers additional information about the SQL Server as a whole. SQLDiag ships with SQL Server and is located in the Tools\Binn folder. See Books Online for more information.

The Transmission Queue View

The Transmission Queue (sys.transmission_queue) is probably the most used diagnostic view in the Service Broker. There is one transmission queue per Service Broker. Table 7-1 are all about service-to-service communication.

TABLE 7-1   **Service-to-service communication transmission queues**

Column Name	Description
conversation_handle	The unique identifier used to programmatically access this conversation. Remember that all messages are part of a conversation.
to_service_name	The name of the service that will receive this message.
to_broker_instance	The unique identifier of the Service Broker that hosts the to_service.
from_service_name	The name of the service that sent this message.
from_broker_instance	The unique identifier of the Service Broker that hosts the from_service.
service_contract_name	The name of the contract that contains this message.
enqueue_time	The time that the Service Broker enqueued this message into the queue.
message_sequence_number	This number represents the current sequence number of the message in the dialog.
message_type_name	The name of the message type of this message.
is_conversation_error	If the value of this field is 1, this is a dialog error message.
is_end_of_dialog	If the value of this field is 1, this is an end of dialog message.
message_body	The contents of the message.
transmission_status	If there is an error transmitting the message, the reason for the error is found here.

Of all these columns, the transmission_status is the most critical. When the Service Broker encounters any kind of transmission problem, the information is recorded in this column. This should be the first place to look for reasons why messages are not flowing between services. In short, look here for the error message and fix what it says to.

Another thing to remember is that much of the work of the Service Broker occurs in the background. When you select from this view, you see the state of the system at that point in time. The Service Broker automatically retries transmission operations. Therefore, repeated selection from the view will potentially show changes in the state of the conversation.

The SQL Profiler—Service Broker Trace Events

Trying to diagnose Service Broker systems can seem a bit daunting at first. Unlike most SQL processes, almost all the work goes on asynchronously. Therefore, we turn to the SQL Profiler (or SQLDiag.exe) to be able to monitor in real time the actions of the Service Broker.

It is beyond the scope of this book to describe all the capabilities of the SQL Profiler or SQLDiag, so it is a good idea to familiarize yourself with their operation. However, we will touch on SQL Profiler use a bit here. SQL Profiler groups the traceable events in the system into event categories. To diagnose Service Broker problems we need to concern ourselves with two of these event categories: the Broker event category and the Security Audit event category.

One caveat applies when looking at the output of the SQL Profiler. The column headings are shared between all the trace events in SQL Server. This means that sometimes to provide the information in the trace event, we were forced to use a named column that does not really mean anything within the context of the Service Broker. So, when looking at the trace events for the Service Broker, keep your Books Online open to the "SQL Server Event Class Reference" so that you can understand the data you are seeing.

Broker Event Category
The majority of Service Booker events are found in this category. When starting the SQL Profiler, I normally just select this whole category. The following subsections go through each event and describe what information is given and when to use that event.

Broker:Activation Event Class
This event class shows the life cycle of an activated stored procedure. In addition to a number of common columns, the data included in this trace event is the database ID, the queue, the number of currently activated tasks on this queue, and the action of the event: start, stop, or abnormally terminated.

This class should be the first place you go to see whether your stored procedures are being activated.

Broker:Connection Event Class
This event class shows the status of the "transport" that is the SQL Server instance–to–SQL Server instance connections. This includes data such as the connection endpoint name and ID, the number of times the connection has been closed, whether an error has been detected with the connection (the error code will be filled in), whether the connection is closed, and the reason for the close.

This is the trace event to use when two Service Brokers cannot "talk" to each other.

Broker:Conversation Event Class
The Conversation event class shows the life cycle of the dialog conversation. The conversation ID, conversation handle, conversation group, from and to service, and from and to broker instance are shown so that you have an easy way to identify the conversation in the SQL Profiler. All the state changes in the conversation are reflected here, so it is easy to monitor the progress of the conversation between two services.

This is the event to look at when diagnosing service-to-service application issues.

Broker:Conversation Group Event Class

The events in this class fire any time a conversation group is created or dropped. The main piece of information included in the event is the conversation group ID.

Typically, this event gives some additional context when troubleshooting a problem. However, if your application makes extensive use of the MOVE CONVERSATION TSQL command, this event can really help determine that the application is operating correctly.

Broker:Corrupted Message Event Class

This event is fired only when a corrupted message has been received and detected by the Service Broker. The data included is the type of corruption that has been found.

Under normal circumstances, you should never see this event fire. If you do see it occur, this implies that a message has been received that the Service Broker cannot successfully understand. This could be due to a number of reasons:

- A hardware problem somewhere in the network. If this is the case, I would expect to see other non-Service Broker network errors occurring, too.

- Perhaps some type of hacking attempt going on, where a program is trying to send invalid data to the Service Broker

- A bug!

Broker:Forwarded Message Dropped Event Class

The Service Broker can be configured to act as a conversation forwarder. In this configuration, neither endpoint of the conversation exists within the forwarding Service Broker. Forwarded messages can be dropped from the forwarding Service Broker for a number of reasons, and in many situations this is not indicative of a problem. It is important to note that the Service Broker(s) that contain the initiating or target service are responsible for retransmission of messages, so dropping a message from a forwarding Service Broker does not harm the conversation.

The information contained in this event includes the typical things needed to identify the conversation: the conversation ID, the initiator flag, to and from service names, to and from broker instance IDs, and, most important, the reason for dropping the message.

The thing to remember here is that a few dropped messages are fine, but lots of dropped messages could indicate a problem.

Broker:Forwarded Message Sent Event Class

This is a companion trace event to the Forwarded Message Dropped event. However, this event is fired when the forwarded message is successfully sent. The information contained in this event includes the typical things needed to identify the conversation—the conversation ID, the initiator flag, to and from service names, and to and from broker instance IDs.

This event can be used to verify your forwarding configuration. However, on a heavily loaded system, I would not run this trace event for long periods (because of the volume of data it could produce).

Broker:Message Classify Event Class

This event shows the results of the message classification process in the Service Broker. The data included here is the to and from service name and the type of classification: local, remote, or delayed.

This is the number one trace event to use for troubleshooting routing problems.

Broker:Message Drop Event Class

This trace event is fired when the Service Broker drops a message that should have been delivered to a service in this instance. The data included is the reason for dropping the message, the conversation ID, the initiator flag, to and from service names, and to and from broker instance IDs.

The primary usage of this trace event is to diagnose conversation problems. Again, it is useful to note that dropping a message does not harm the conversation. The message is automatically retransmitted by the originating Service Broker.

Broker:Remote Message Ack Event Class

This event is generated when the Service Broker sends or receives a message acknowledgment. Message acknowledgments are used to guarantee the successful delivery of a message from Service Broker to Service Broker. The information included is the conversation ID, the initiator flag, and other acknowledgment information.

This event class is primarily used in diagnosing conversation and routing issues. This is especially useful when the return path from target service to initiating service is not configured properly.

Security Audit Event Category

Two more Service Broker event classes appear under the Security Audit event category. These events are primarily used to diagnose security configuration problems.

Audit Broker Conversation Event Class

This event reports on the current security state of the conversation. Data reported includes the conversation ID and reason for the failure.

The primary use of this event is to troubleshoot service-to-service security issues.

Audit Broker Login Event Class

This event reports on the current state of the Service Broker connection. The data included is the authentication method, connect string, far and local authentication support levels, and the state of the connection.

`Broker Login` processing is all about SQL Server instance-to-instance connections, not service-to-service.

Error Log and NT Event Log

Much of the Service Broker's processing occurs in the background, and, unlike other database tasks, often there is no "connection" to a client. Normally, the client connection is the correct place to send error messages; however, in this model of background processing, the SQL error log and the NT event log are locations where errors in the Service Broker system itself will appear.

The Service Broker tasks attempt to catch, report, and recover from errors that occur while processing. It is important to note that often the error messages reported by the Service Broker are reported on behalf of some other component. The key to successfully troubleshooting these problems is diagnosing and fixing the underlying problem.

One exception I do want to point out is error number 9724. This is *not* an error in the Service Broker. It is a feature of the activated stored procedure processing that allows customers to copy diagnostic text to the error log. The format of the message is as follows:

```
9724 The activated proc <name-of-the-activated-procedure> running on queue <queue
name> output the following: '<text>'
```

Broker Troubleshooting Walkthrough

The best way to learn troubleshooting is to just practice. To that end, this next section is meant to be a practice session. We configure two SQL Servers to communicate securely. However, instead of just setting up everything correctly, we purposely make a few mistakes along the way. During the process, you will see how the tools previously discussed really work. So, with that, let's get started!

Walkthrough of a Simple/Secure Broker Application

For the purposes of this walkthrough, I am using two machines, each with a copy of SQL Server already installed on it. I have also started SQL Profiler on each machine, and each instance has all the Service Broker trace events enabled.

Now let's set up the first of our machines by creating a fresh database:

```
CREATE DATABASE ssbdiag
```

For the purposes of the demonstration, we disable the broker in this database:

```
alter database ssbdiag set DISABLE_BROKER
```

Now we switch to the new database and begin creating our simple application:

```
use ssbdiag
```

This is the initiating side of our Broker service, so we create a queue for our responses:

```
create queue initiator_queue
```

We create the service, attach it to the queue, and, for this example, use the built-in "default" contract and message type:

```
create service get_sql_version on queue initiator_queue ([DEFAULT])
```

Now we try to send a message to the sql_version service on the other machine:

```
begin tran
declare @conv uniqueidentifier;
BEGIN DIALOG @conv FROM SERVICE get_sql_version
     TO SERVICE 'sql_version';
SEND ON CONVERSATION @conv;
commit
```

Now take a look at the output of the SQL Profiler. There will be an event from the classifier, which says the following:

```
Broker:Message Classify - Delayed - The broker is disabled in the sender's
database.
```

So, the classifier says the Service Broker is disabled in this database. Let's verify that:

```
select name, service_broker_guid, is_broker_enabled
     from sys.databases where name = 'ssbdiag'
```

And indeed, the Service Broker is disabled, because we purposely disabled it just a few moments ago. So, let's enable the Service Broker:

```
alter database ssbdiag set ENABLE_BROKER
```

Now we're getting a new event in the Profiler:

```
Broker:Message Classify - Delayed - The target service name could not be found.
```

Normally, we would ensure that the service name was specified correctly, and in this case it is. The next thing to check is that the routing information has been supplied:

```
select * from sys.routes
```

There is our next problem; we have no route to our target service. So, let's add that route:

```
CREATE ROUTE sql_version_route_1
     WITH SERVICE_NAME = N'sql_version',
     ADDRESS = 'TCP://machine2.somewhere.com:4022'
```

After the preceding change, the SQL Profiler event now reads as follows:

```
Broker:Message Classify - Remote
```

However, things still do not appear to be flowing, so let's look at the transmission queue:

```
select * from sys.transmission_queue
```

Specifically, the transmission_status column reads as follows:

Dialog security is not available for this conversation because there is no remote
service binding for the target service. Create a remote service binding, or specify
ENCRYPTION = OFF in the BEGIN DIALOG statement.

Well, we want this to be a secure dialog, so we create a remote service binding. However, we need a user to associate to the target (or far) service:

```
CREATE USER sql_ap_far_user WITHOUT LOGIN
CREATE REMOTE SERVICE BINDING sql_version_binding_1
   TO SERVICE 'sql_version'
   WITH USER = sql_ap_far_user;
```

However, things still do not appear to be flowing, so let's look at the transmission queue:

```
select * from sys.transmission_queue
```

Specifically, the transmission_status column reads as follows:

The session keys for this conversation could not be created or accessed. The
database master key is required for this operation.

So, let's create the database master key:

```
CREATE MASTER KEY ENCRYPTION BY PASSWORD = '23987hxJ#KL95234nl0zBe';
```

However, things still do not appear to be flowing, so let's look at the transmission queue:

```
select * from sys.transmission_queue
```

Specifically, the transmission_status column reads as follows:

Dialog security is unavailable for this conversation because there is no security
certificate bound to the database principal (Id: 1). Either create a certificate
for the principal, or specify ENCRYPTION = OFF when beginning the conversation.

So who is principal 1?

```
select * from sys.database_principals where principal_id = 1
```

Well, that's dbo. Why is dbo involved in this conversation? Let's look at the conversation:

```
select * from sys.conversation_endpoints
select principal_id, far_principal_id from sys.conversation_endpoints
```

Aha! This conversation was begun with my (dbo) ID so that I could create a certificate for my ID, but it would be better to create a user specifically for this service. (Do not use CREATE USER FOR CERTIFICATE; that works only for assemblies.)

```
CREATE USER sql_ap_user WITHOUT LOGIN
```

And create the certificate:

```
CREATE CERTIFICATE sql_ap_certificate
WITH SUBJECT = 'SQL Applications',
     EXPIRY_DATE = '11/11/2011';
```

Let's look at that certificate:

```
select * from sys.certificates
```

The principal ID is 1 (dbo), and we need to be associated with our newly created user:

```
ALTER AUTHORIZATION ON Certificate::sql_ap_certificate TO sql_ap_user
```

Let's look at that certificate again:

```
select * from sys.certificates
select * from sys.database_principals where name = 'sql_ap_user'
```

Yes, it is showing our new principal ID, so now we need to associate this user to the service:

```
ALTER AUTHORIZATION ON Service::get_sql_version TO sql_ap_user
```

Looking at the service definition now:

```
select * from sys.services where name = 'get_sql_version'
```

But things still don't appear to be working.

```
select * from sys.transmission_queue
```

What about the conversation?

```
select * from sys.conversation_endpoints
select principal_id, far_principal_id from sys.conversation_endpoints
```

The principal ID is still 1. This conversation, alas, is doomed, and we need to get rid of it and start over now that we have a new configuration:

```
select conversation_handle from sys.conversation_endpoints
end conversation 'B5F0ED4D-9D50-DA11-B165-00065BBD0A16' with cleanup
```

And now let's try this again:

```
begin tran
declare @conv uniqueidentifier;
BEGIN DIALOG @conv FROM SERVICE get_sql_version
     TO SERVICE 'sql_version';
SEND ON CONVERSATION @conv;
commit
```

Well, everything in the profiler looks okay. What does `transmission_status` tell us?

```
select * from sys.transmission_queue
```

```
Dialog security is unavailable for this conversation because there is no
security certificate bound to the database principal (Id: 5). Either create
a certificate for the principal, or specify ENCRYPTION = OFF when beginning
the conversation.
```

And principal 5 is as follows:

```
select * from sys.database_principals where principal_id = 5
```

Ack! We never set up the certificate for our far-end user! So now we need to do a little work on the second machine:

```
CREATE DATABASE ssbdiag
GO

use ssbdiag
GO

CREATE MASTER KEY ENCRYPTION BY
PASSWORD = 'we8%rwr$#97we987##%';
CREATE USER sql_ap_user2 WITHOUT LOGIN
CREATE CERTIFICATE sql_ap_certificate2
WITH SUBJECT = 'SQL Applications2',
     EXPIRY_DATE = '11/11/2011';
ALTER AUTHORIZATION ON Certificate::sql_ap_certificate2 TO sql_ap_user2

BACKUP CERTIFICATE sql_ap_certificate2
TO FILE = 'c:\storedcerts\sql_ap_certificate2';
```

We copy that file back to our first machine, and then on the first machine, we import the certificate from the far end:

```
CREATE CERTIFICATE sql_ap_certificate2
FROM FILE = 'c:\storedcerts\sql_ap_certificate2'
ALTER AUTHORIZATION ON Certificate::sql_ap_certificate2
TO sql_ap_far_user
```

Well, everything in the profiler looks okay. What does `transmission_status` tell us?

```
select * from sys.transmission_queue
```

`transmission_status` says:

```
The Service Broker protocol transport is disabled or not configured.
```

Verifying this:

```
select * from sys.endpoints
```

Okay, so let's create an endpoint:

```
create endpoint ep1 state = started as tcp (listener_port = 4022)
FOR SERVICE_BROKER ()
```

Verifying this:

```
select * from sys.endpoints
select * from sys.service_broker_endpoints
```

Now we jump-start this process and send another message so that the transport wakes up:

```
begin tran
declare @conv uniqueidentifier;
BEGIN DIALOG @conv FROM SERVICE get_sql_version
     TO SERVICE 'sql_version';
SEND ON CONVERSATION @conv;
commit
```

And in SQL Profiler, we see a `Broker:Connection` event:

```
Connection attempt failed with error: '10061(No connection could be made because
the  target machine actively refused it.)'.
```

Note the `transmission_status` reflects this, too! And this is true because we've not set up the far-end server. Before we do that, however, let's export the certificate we created on this machine:

```
BACKUP CERTIFICATE sql_ap_certificate
TO FILE = 'c:\storedcerts\sql_ap_certificate';
```

Now let's copy this file to the second machine that we're configuring. We need to set things up just like we're in the process of doing on the first machine. However, we'll be more straightforward the second time around:

```
-- This certificate is the one we copied from the first machine...
CREATE CERTIFICATE sql_ap_certificate
FROM FILE = 'c:\storedcerts\sql_ap_certificate'
CREATE USER sql_ap_far_user2 WITHOUT LOGIN
```

```
ALTER AUTHORIZATION ON Certificate::sql_ap_certificate
TO sql_ap_far_user2


create queue target_queue
create service sql_version on queue target_queue ([DEFAULT])
ALTER AUTHORIZATION ON Service::sql_version TO sql_ap_user2


create endpoint ep2 state = started as tcp (listener_port = 4022)
FOR SERVICE_BROKER ()
```

After a few moments, we see the following event in the Profiler:

Connection handshake failed. The login 'SOMEWHERE\MACHINE1$' does not have CONNECT permission on the endpoint. State 84.

When we created the endpoint, the default was to use Windows Authentication. We could drop the endpoints and configure them with certificates (like we did with the services), but for now we'll just continue with Windows Authentication. We need to add the far machine as a login and grant the connect privilege:

```
use master
create login [somewhere\machine1$] from windows
grant connect on endpoint::ep2 to [somewhere\machine1$]
use ssbdiag
```

Now we see this in the Profiler:

An error occurred while receiving data: '10054(An existing connection was forcibly closed by the remote host.)'.

Time to go look at the first machine! Now that we have the far end configured, the Profiler here is showing this:

Connection handshake failed. The login 'SOMEWHERE\MACHINE2$' does not have CONNECT permission on the endpoint. State 84.

Yes, this is the same as what we saw on the second machine, so we will fix it:

```
use master
create login [somewhere\machine2$] from windows
grant connect on endpoint::ep1 to [somewhere\machine2$]
use ssbdiag
```

Things still are not quite right. We see this message in the SQL Profiler:

An error occurred while receiving data: '64(The specified network name is no longer available.)'.

Let's go look at the second machine again. Now that we have the permissions granted on the first machine, we now get this error:

```
This message could not be delivered because the user with ID 6 in database ID 5
does not have permission to send to the service. Service name: 'sql_version'.
```

If we check this principal:

```
select * from sys.database_principals where principal_id = 6
```

We need to allow the far user access to this service:

```
GRANT SEND ON SERVICE::sql_version TO sql_ap_far_user2
```

We have make a bit more progress, but Profiler says this:

```
The target service name could not be found. Ensure that the service name is
specified correctly and/or the routing information has been supplied.
```

Note the name in the `FileName` column: get_sql_version. The Broker is trying to respond (acknowledge) back to the initiating service, and we have no route to do so. Let's add one:

```
CREATE ROUTE get_sql_version_route_1
    WITH SERVICE_NAME = N'get_sql_version',
    ADDRESS = 'TCP://machine1.somewhere.com:4022'
```

So, the Profiler is quiet. How about `transmission_status`?

```
select * from sys.transmission_queue
```

Hey! How about the service queue?

```
select * from target_queue
```

Be still my foolish heart! The message is in the queue! Okay, so let's reply to the message:

```
begin tran
declare @message varbinary(4000);
declare @conv uniqueidentifier;
declare @mtid integer;
RECEIVE TOP (1) @conv=conversation_handle, @message=message_body,
    @mtid=message_type_id
    FROM target_queue;
if @conv is NOT NULL
begin
    if @mtid = 2       -- END DIALOG
    begin
        end conversation @conv;
        print 'ending'
    end
    else if @mtid = 1        -- END DIALOG WITH ERROR
```

```
begin
        end conversation @conv;
        print 'ending with error'
    end
    else
    begin
        SEND ON CONVERSATION @conv (@@version);
    end
end
commit
```

Things look okay in the Profiler and transmission_queue. Let's check the first machine. If all has gone well, we should have our reply to our message in our queue:

```
select * from initiator_queue
```

In fact, we can see the text of the message_body:

```
select convert(nvarchar(4000),message_body) from initiator_queue
```

So, now our client will receive the message and end the dialog:

```
begin tran
declare @message varbinary(4000);
declare @conv uniqueidentifier;
RECEIVE TOP (1) @conv=conversation_handle, @message=message_body
    FROM initiator_queue;
if @conv is not null
begin
    declare @text nvarchar(4000);
    set @text = @message
    print @text; -- Just for fun...
    end conversation @conv;
end
commit
```

And back to the target machine. Let's check the queue for the end dialog message:

```
select * from target_queue
```

And let's run the service code again:

```
begin tran
declare @message varbinary(4000);
declare @conv uniqueidentifier;
declare @mtid integer;
RECEIVE TOP (1) @conv=conversation_handle, @message=message_body,
    @mtid=message_type_id
    FROM target_queue;
if @conv is NOT NULL
begin
    if @mtid = 2      -- END DIALOG
    begin
        end conversation @conv;
```

```
            print 'ending'
      end
      else if @mtid = 1        -- END DIALOG WITH ERROR
      begin
            end conversation @conv;
            print 'ending with error'
      end
      else
      begin
            SEND ON CONVERSATION @conv (@@version);
      end
end
commit
```

This concludes the walkthrough.

Other Service Broker Diagnostic Tools

There are a number of other ways to look inside the Service Broker. A part of learning the diagnostic process is gaining the understanding of what tools to turn to first. This section describes the following:

- **Views.** Views enable us to look at the configuration and state of the system "right now."

- **Perfmon.** Gives a high-level look at the operation of the Service Broker.

- **DBCC CHECKDB.** Although CHECKDB is not a Service Broker-exclusive command, the Service Broker's data is checked for constancy during a database check. We describe what's being checked and how to recover a suspect database.

Views

The Service Broker truly provides SQL Server with asynchronous operation. As such, with so much going on the background, I think it is helpful to think of the views in four different groups:

- **Static views.** Static views are really just like most of the SQL Service views you are used to using. These views do not change over time unless you as the administrator of the server issue a command to change your configuration. For example, if you were to use CREATE MESSAGE TYPE to create a new message type for your service, you could look up that that message type with the sys.service_message_types view. The data returned by the view won't change unless you issue an ALTER MESSAGE TYPE or DROP MESSAGE TYPE. It's that simple.

- **Semi-static views.** So what about things that happen in the background? Some data is created by T-SQL commands, but that information changes over time as events are processed in the background. For example, if we use the BEGIN DIALOG command to start a conversation between two services, we can see the result of that in the sys.conversation_endpoints view. But, as messages are transferred back and forth between the services, message counts and other data are updated in that end-point. If we repeatedly select against this view, we will be able to see the data chang-ing over time, even if we have not issued a T-SQL command on our side of the endpoint.

- **Dynamic management views.** These views contain runtime-only data. None of this information is hardened to disk, like the other views we have been discussing. For example, the sys.dm_broker_activated_tasks view shows the current status of the tasks that have been started via the activation system. This information is cur-rent as of the moment the SELECT is run, but restarting the SQL Server would reset all of this information.

- **Other views with Service Broker information.** Besides the views just men-tioned, other existing SQL Server views now contain Service Broker information. For example, if you need to know whether a particular database has the Service Broker enabled in it, the sys.databases view contains a column named is_broker_enabled that describes the current state of the Service Broker.

Static Views

Static views show data that is, as we like to call it, "hardened to disk." This means that the data is transactionally committed to disk. The data found here is created by using T-SQL data definition language (DDL) commands. The only way that this data changes is by use of other DDL to alter or drop it.

We'll talk in turn about each types of static Service Broker data that can be stored. We will also highlight some of the most important columns included in the views. However, it is not really within the scope of this book to describe all the columns and their data types. That's the purpose of Books Online, which is shipped with every copy of SQL Server. If you need more details, or are programming a script to help you in your diagnostics, be sure to look in Books Online for all the details.

Displaying Services

Services are the heart and soul of the Service Broker, and as such, we cover their view first.

TABLE 7-2   sys.services

Column Name	Description
name	The name of this service.
service_id	The object ID of the service.
principal_id	The ID of the principal that owns this contract.
service_queue_id	The object ID of the service queue.

This is the view that you turn to when you are asking yourself, "Does this service really exist in this Service Broker?" The other thing you find here is the ID of the service, which is used as a foreign key in a number of other views. Likewise, we have the ID of the ser-vice queue where this service will receive its incoming messages.

Displaying Service Contracts

Service contracts group the message types that the service can send. However, this view contains only part of that story.

TABLE 7-3   sys.service_contracts

Column Name	Description
name	The name of this contract.
service_contract_id	The object ID for this contract.
principal_id	The ID of the principal that owns this contract.

Here we just have the name and ID of the service contract. So, we are limited to being able to answer only one question: "Does this service contract exist?"

Displaying What Message Types Are Used by a Contract

And here is the view that finishes out the service contract description by linking the service contract IDs and the message type IDs so that we can tell what message types are used by what service contracts.

TABLE 7-4   sys.service_contract_message_usages

Column Name	Description
service_contract_id	The object ID of the service contract.
message_type_id	The object ID of the message type that is referenced by the above contract.
is_sent_by_initiator	If the value is 1, the message type is to be sent by the initiator.
is_sent_by_target	If the value is 1, the message type is to be sent by the target.

Displaying Message Types

Message types describe the type of messages being sent and received by the initiating and target services.

TABLE 7-5   sys.service_message_types

Column Name	Description
name	The name of this message type.
message_type_id	The object ID for this message type.
principal_id	The ID of the principal that owns this contract.
validation	The type of the validation requested for the message type. The values are as follows: N for none (that is, no validation) X for XML (the Service Broker validates the XML) E for empty (the message body is always empty)

Column Name	Description
validation_desc	A text version of the above column; the values can be NONE, XML, or EMPTY.
xml_collection_id	The object ID for this XML collection.

Again, we have the name and ID of the message type. We also have a number of columns that indicate what type of validation, if any, we want applied to the message when it is received by the Service Broker. A word of warning: Message type validation is a great tool when developing a service. It is an easy way to know that the XML you sent will be able to be properly interpreted by the target service. However, in a production environment, I would not expect to find validation, turned on. When the application is in production, turn off the validation and you will see a noticeable performance boost. Is this true *all* the time? Well, no; if you are not in control of the sending application, you might want to incur the overhead of validation (even in production) just as an extra measure of protection for the target service.

Displaying Service Queue Definitions

If messages are the equivalent of a letter, a service queue is the mailbox. How do you know what service queues are available in the Service Broker?

TABLE 7-6 sys.service_queues

Column Name	Description
All the sys.objects columns	
max_readers	The maximum number of queue readers the Service Broker should ever have running in parallel.
activation_procedure	The name of the activated stored procedure.
execute_as_principal_id	The activated stored procedure will run as this principal.
is_activation_enabled	If the value is 1, activation is enabled on this queue.
is_receive_enabled	If the value is 1, services may issue RECEIVE commands on this queue.
is_enqueue_enabled	If the value is 1, services may issue SEND commands on this queue.
is_retention_enabled	If the value is 1, retention is enabled for this queue.

Note that this just describes the service queue itself; it does not show the contents of the named queue. (See the section "Displaying Queue Contents.")

Displaying What Contracts Are Used by a Service

So we know that services implement contracts, but how do we tell what contracts are currently used by a particular service? The sys.service_contract_usages view contains the relationship between services and service contracts. Note that this is a normalized form of the metadata and hence contains only the service ID and the service contract ID, so using this view in a join with sys.services and sys.service_contracts is common. For example, to list all the service names and associated service contract names, you could issue the following T-SQL command:

```
select s.name, s.name from sys.services as s, sys.service_contract_usages as u,
sys.service_contracts as c where s.id = u.service_id and u.service_contract_id =
c.service_contract_id
```

Displaying What Services Are Using a Queue

The Service Broker allows any number of services to receive from the same queue. The only requirement is that all the services must be able to understand and process any message in the queue. But, given a queue name, what services are using that queue? The sys.service_queue_usages view joins the service and queue definitions so that it is easy to answer this question by joining the appropriate views.

TABLE 7-7   sys.service_queue_usages

Column Name	Description
service_id	The object ID of the service.
service_queue_id	The object ID of the queue.

Displaying Routes to Other Brokers

Routes are the communication linkage between Brokers. They describe the topology of your Broker network. Using this view, you can display that topology and see exactly, for a given service, what Broker is being sent those messages.

TABLE 7-8   sys.routes

Column Name	Description
name	The unique name of this route.
route_id	The object ID of the route.
principal_id	The ID of the principal that owns this route.
remote_service_name	The name of the remote service.
broker_instance	The unique instance identifier of the remote Service Broker that hosts the above remote service.
lifetime	The date and time that this route should expire (UTC time).

Column Name	Description
address	The network address of the remote Service Broker.
mirror_address	The network address of the mirror of the remote Service Broker. This is optional and is used only if database mirroring is enabled for this Service Broker.

Displaying Remote Service Bindings

The remote service binding enables us to specify the certificate to be used when communicating to a particular remote service. Thus, we "bind" that certificate to remote service.

TABLE 7-9   sys.remote_service_bindings

Column Name	Description
Name	The unique name of the remote service binding.
remote_service_binding_id	The object ID of the remote service binding.
principal_id	The ID of the principal that owns this remote service binding.
remote_service_name	The name of the remote service.
service_contract_id	The object ID of the service contract.
remote_principal_id	The object ID of the remote principal. The certificate that is associated with this principal will be used when communicating with this service.
is_anonymous_on	If the value is 1, conversations with this remote service are anonymous, meaning that the identity of the user who begins the conversation is not revealed.

Displaying Endpoints

SQL Server 2005 implements a number of different types of endpoints, one of which is the Service Broker endpoint. This view enables us to see exactly how the endpoint is configured.

TABLE 7-10   sys.service_broker_endpoints

Column Name	Description
All sys.endpoints columns	
is_message_forwarding_enabled	If the value is 1, this endpoint supports forwarding messages.
message_forwarding_size	The number of megabytes of space used in tempdb for forwarded messages.

TABLE 7-10   **continued**

Column Name	Description
All sys.endpoints columns	
connection_auth	The type of authentication required for connections to this endpoint. Valid values are as follows: 1 is NTLM. 2 is Kerberos. 3 is Negotiate. 4 is Certificate. 5 is NTLM, Certificate. 6 is Kerberos, Certificate. 7 is Negotiate, Certificate. 8 is Certificate, NTLM. 9 is Certificate, Kerberos. 10 is Certificate, Negotiate.
connection_auth_desc	The textual representation of the above field. Valid values are as follows: NTLM KERBEROS NEGOTIATE CERTIFICATE NTLM, CERTIFICATE KERBEROS, CERTIFICATE NEGOTIATE, CERTIFICATE CERTIFICATE, NTLM CERTIFICATE, KERBEROS CERTIFICATE, NEGOTIATE
certificate_id	The object ID of the certificate used for authentication.
encryption_algorithm	The encryption algorithm: 0 is None. 1 is RC4. 2 is AES. 3 is None, RC4. 4 is None, AES. 5 is RC4, AES. 6 is AES, RC4. 7 is None, RC4, AES. 8 is None, AES, RC4.

Column Name	Description
All sys.endpoints columns	
encryption_algorithm_desc	The textual representation of the above field. Valid values are as follows: NONE RC4 AES NONE, RC4 NONE, AES RC4, AES AES, RC4 NONE, RC4, AES NONE, AES, RC4

Semi-Static Views

Semi-static views change over time because of the background processing that occurs in the Service Broker.

Displaying Conversation Endpoints

The conversation endpoint is the heart and soul of the Service Broker. All services communicate via conversations. For every conversation that is initiated between two services, a conversation endpoint is created. This view enables us to check on the status of all the conversations in the system. Note that using this view gives you a look at the conversation endpoint at this particular point in time. For watching the endpoint go through its state changes over time, look at the SQL Profiler trace events.

TABLE 7-11   sys.conversation_endpoints

Column Name	Description
conversation_handle	The unique identifier used to programmatically access this conversation.
conversation_id	The unique identifier of the conversation.
is_initiator	If the value is 1, this endpoint is the initiator of the conversation. If the value is 0, this endpoint is the target of the conversation.
service_contract_id	The object ID of the service contract.
conversation_group_id	The unique identifier of the conversation group that contains this conversation.
service_id	The object ID of the service.
lifetime	The date and time this conversation is due to expire.

TABLE 7-11   continued

Column Name	Description
State	The current state of this conversation: SO is Started for an Outbound conversation. SI is Started for an Inbound conversation. CO is Conversing. DI is Disconnected Inbound. DO is Disconnected Outbound. ER is Error. CD is Closed.
state_desc	A textual description of the above state field. Valid values are as follows: STARTED_OUTBOUND STARTED_INBOUND CONVERSING DISCONNECTED_INBOUND DISCONNECTED_OUTBOUND ERROR CLOSED
far_service	The name of the far-end service.
far_broker_instance	The unique identifier of the far-end Service Broker.
principal_id	The object ID of the principal that owns the certificate used locally by this conversation.
far_principal_id	The object ID of the principal that owns the certificate used by the far end of this conversation.
outbound_session_key_identifier	The unique identifier used for outbound encryption.
inbound_session_key_identifier	The unique identifier used for inbound encryption.
security_timestamp	The time that the local session key was created.
dialog_timer	The time at which the Service Broker is to send a DialogTimer message.
send_sequence	This number represents the next number in the send sequence.
last_send_tran_id	The transaction identifier used for the last send operation.
end_dialog_sequence	The sequence number of the end dialog message.
receive_sequence	This number represents the next expected sequence number to be received.

Column Name	Description
`receive_sequence_frag`	This number represents the next expected message fragment sequence number to be received.
`system_sequence`	The last sequence number seen for a system message on this conversation.
`first_out_of_order_sequence`	The first out-of-order message's sequence number.
`last_out_of_order_sequence`	The last out-of-order message's sequence number.
`last_out_of_order_frag`	The last out-of-order message fragment's sequence number.
`is_system`	If the value is 1, this is a system dialog.

Displaying Conversation Groups

The conversation group enables us to bundle a number of conversations and work with them as a group.

TABLE 7-12 `sys.conversation_groups`

Column Name	Description
`conversation_group_id`	The unique identifier of the conversation group that contains this conversation.
`service_id`	The object ID of the service.
`is_system`	If the value is 1, this is a system-level conversation group and is not for use by the customer.

Displaying Queue Contents

Yes, it is possible (and handy) to be able to look at the contents of a service queue without actually removing messages from the queue. In T-SQL, we can just use the SELECT command to do this.

TABLE 7-13 `select * from <user_queue_name>`

Column Name	Description
`status`	The status of the message. Valid values are as follows: 0 is Received message. 1 is Ready. 2 is Not yet complete. 3 is Retained sent message.
`queuing_order`	The message order number within the queue.
`conversation_group_id`	The unique identifier of the conversation group that contains this conversation.
`conversation_handle`	The unique identifier used to programmatically access this conversation.

TABLE 7-13   continued

Column Name	Description
message_sequence_number	The relative position of this message within the conversation stream.
service_name	The name of the service this message was sent to.
service_id	The object ID of the service.
service_contract_name	The name of the service contract.
service_contract_id	The object ID of the service contract.
message_type_name	The name of the message type of this message.
message_type_id	The object ID of the message type.
validation	The type of the validation requested for the message type. The values are as follows: N for none (that is, no validation) X for XML (the Service Broker validates the XM) E for empty (the message body is always empty)
message_body	The binary payload of this message. Note this is completely dependent on the application as to the format of this data.
message_id	The unique identifier of this message.

Dynamic Views

Displaying Broker Connections

When communicating between SQL Server instances, the Service Broker opens one connection per pair of instances. By default, these connections are encrypted. This view shows the state of all connections in the SQL Server instance and shows what kind of encryption is currently being used.

TABLE 7-14   sys.dm_broker_connections

Column Name	Description
connection_id	The unique identifier of the connection.
transport_stream_id	The unique identifier of the transport stream.
state	The current state of this connection: 1 is a new connection. 2 is in the process of connecting. 3 is connected. 4 is successfully logged in. 5 is closed.

Column Name	Description
state_desc	A textual description of the above: NEW, CONNECTING, CONNECTED, LOGGED_IN, and CLOSED
connect_time	The date and time that this connection was opened.
login_time	The date and time that the login occurred.
authentication_method	The name of the authentication method that Windows used.
principal_name	The name of the login that was validated for connection permissions.
remote_user_name	The name of the remote user that was used by Windows Authentication.
last_activity_time	The last date and time this connection sent or received any data.
is_accept	If the value is 1, this connection was accepted from the remote side. If the value is 0, this connection was started locally.
login_state	This number represents the current state of the login process: 0 is Initial. 1 is Negotiate. 2 is SSPI. 3 is Public Key Login. 4 is Public Key Tentative. 5 is Logged In. 6 is Arbitration.
login_state_desc	A textual description of the above state. It can be one of the following: Initial Negotiate SSPI PublicKeyLogin PublicKeyTentative LoggedIn Arbitration
peer_certificate_id	The object ID of the peer certificate.
receives_posted	The number of asynchronous network receives that are currently posted.
is_receive_flow_controlled	If the value is 1, network receives have been postponed because of network flow control.

TABLE 7-14   continued

Column Name	Description
sends_posted	The number of asynchronous network sends that are currently posted.
is_send_flow_controlled	If the value is 1, network sends have been postponed because of network flow control.
total_bytes_sent	The total number of bytes sent on this connection.
total_bytes_received	The total number of bytes received on this connection.
total_fragments_sent	The total number of fragments sent on this connection.
total_fragments_received	The total number of fragments received on this connection.
total_sends	The total number of network sends on this connection.
total_receives	The total number of network receives on this connection.
encalg	The encryption algorithm used: 1 is No Encryption. 2 is RC4. 3 is AES.

Displaying Activated Tasks

When using Service Broker Internal Activation, it is often necessary to monitor which internal tasks are activated. This view lists the activated tasks that are currently running in the system. Note that it is simple to join this view with other system views to find out additional information about the task.

TABLE 7-15   sys.dm_broker_activated_tasks

Column Name	Description
spid	The ID of the session of the activated stored procedure.
database_id	The object ID of the database.
queue_id	The object ID of the service queue.
procedure_name	The name of the activated stored procedure.
execute_as	The object ID of the user that this procedure is executing as.

Displaying Queue Monitors

The Queue Monitor is used to track the status of activations on the service queue. This view shows the current state of all queue monitors in the system. Use this view if you suspect that activations are not occurring properly.

TABLE 7-16   sys.dm_broker_queue_monitors

Column Name	Description
database_id	The object ID of the database.
queue_id	The object ID of the service queue.
state	The current state of this queue monitor. Valid states are as follows: INACTIVE NOTIFIED RECEIVES_OCCURRING
last_empty_rowset_time	The date and time the last RECEIVE returned an empty rowset.
last_activated_time	The date and time the last stored procedure was activated.
tasks_waiting	The total number of RECEIVE statements waiting for a message to arrive.

Other Views with Broker Information

Besides the views that are dedicated to the Service Broker, a number of SQL Server 2005 views contain information about the Service Broker. We discuss some of these views now.

sys.databases

The sys.databases view contains two columns that are used by the Service Broker.

TABLE 7-17   sys.databases

Column Name	Description
service_broker_guid	The unique identifier of the Service Broker in this database.
is_broker_enabled	If this value is 1, the Service Broker is enabled in this database.

The Service Broker GUID uniquely identifies this broker. The is_broker_enabled column is a Boolean flag that indicates whether this particular broker is enabled.

sys.endpoints

SQL Server 2005 has available a number of types of endpoints. The current state of all SQL Server endpoints, including Service Broker endpoints, can be found in this view. For Service Broker endpoints, the columns should look like Table 7-18.

TABLE 7-18   Service Broker endpoints

Column Name	Description
Name	This should be a unique name for the endpoint. It is up to you how you want to name your endpoints, but you should come up with a method so that you do not run into duplicate names.
endpoint_id	This is a unique integer that also defines the endpoint. Because this is an integer, it is useful for JOINing with other tables that may have a foreign key reference to this view.
principal_id	This is the identifier number of the SQL Server principal that owns this endpoint.
Protocol	This is an integer that identifies what protocol is in use for this particular endpoint. Service Broker endpoints always use TCP/IP for the protocol, so the value here is 2.
protocol_desc	This field contains the textual description of the protocol setting for the endpoint. Service Broker endpoints always show TCP.
Type	This column describes the endpoint payload type. For all Service Broker endpoints, this is 3.
type_desc	This is the textual description of the Type column. For Service Broker endpoints, this is SERVICE_BROKER.
State	From a diagnostic standpoint, the next two columns are most important, because they describe the current state of the Service Broker endpoint. The allowable values are as follows: 0 means the endpoint is Started. 1 means the endpoint is Stopped. 2 means the endpoint is Disabled.
state_desc	This is the textual description of the state column. It is one of the following: STARTED, STOPPED, or DISABLED.
is_admin_endpoint	This is always 0 for Service Broker endpoints.

sys.certificates

When configuring the Service Broker to use Kerberos as an encryption method for secured dialogs, you store the public and private keys in certificates that are imported into the current database. In addition, to prevent configuration mistakes, the certificates allowed to be used for secured dialogs must be indicated as such. The `sys.certificates` view contains a column, `is_active_for_begin_dialog`, that is a bit field. If the value of this bit is 1, the certificate can be used by the Service Broker. If the value is 0, it cannot be used by the Service Broker.

Attempting to use a certificate that is not marked active for `BEGIN DIALOG` will result in an error that will show up in the `sys.transmission_queue/transmission_status`. To enable this flag on an existing certificate, you can use the `ALTER CERTIFICATE` command and then specify `WITH ACTIVE FOR BEGIN DIALOG = ON`.

sys.symmetric_keys

Service Broker needs to have available two important symmetric keys for the proper operation of secured communications. The Service Master Key and the Database Master Key are stored as rows in this view. You will get an error from the Service Broker if these keys are not found and needed. Creating them is easily done by using the `CREATE SYMMETRIC KEY` command.

sys.sysprocesses

A number of background tasks in the server are dedicated to Service Broker processing. The `cmd` column shows the name of the task. Listed here are the Service Broker-specific tasks and their responsibilities.

- `BRKR ASYNC CONN`. This task is responsible for connecting to the far-end Service Broker.

- `BRKR CMPLTN HDLR`. This task is responsible for handling IO completions.

- `BRKR MSG XMITTER`. This task is the message transmitter task. All messages sent over the network come through this task.

- `BRKR MSG DSPTCHR`. The message dispatcher is responsible for the sending of messages both locally and remotely.

- `BRKR EVENT HNDLR`. This task is responsible for the processing of internal events.

- `BRKR INITIALIZER`. SQL Server tries to initialize quickly after being asked to start so that users of the system can quickly begin using the system. However, suppose that you have a database containing a million active dialogs. The startup time could take longer than what we would be willing to wait. The Service Broker initialization task allows the server to continue startup and then asynchronously initializes the active Service Brokers in the background. Under normal circumstances, seeing this task in the background is no cause for alarm. However, if the system has been running for a long period of time or there are not tons of dialogs to initialize, this task should not be around.

- BRKR TASK. This is an internally activated stored procedure.

- DBCC SSB CHECK. This task checks the database consistency. You should see this task only if DBCC CHECKDB is running.

Perfmon

The information found in Perfmon for the Service Broker is really more global in nature and thus is more suited to monitoring the Service Broker as a whole, versus diagnosing problems at the service level. As with SQL Profiler, the info collected by Perfmon can also be collected by SQL Server's SQLDiag facility without requiring Perfmon itself. There are three groupings of Perfmon counters: Broker Activation, Broker Statistics, and Broker/DBM Transport. The following sections provide an overview of their use.

Broker Activation

These counters monitor the amount of activation going on from within a Service Broker. Note that these counters are for the Service Broker as a whole, not a particular service.

TABLE 7-19   Counters for monitoring the amount of activation going on from within a Service Broker

Counter Name	Description
Stored Procedures Invoked/sec	The number of activated stored procedures invoked in this Service Broker, expressed as a rate per second.
Task Limit Reached	The number of times that the activated task upper limit has been reached for all the queues in this Service Broker.
Task Limit Reached/sec	The above counter expressed as a rate per second.
Tasks Running	The number of activated tasks currently running in this Service Broker.
Tasks Started/sec	The number of activated tasks invoked in this Service Broker, expressed as a rate per second.

Broker Statistics

These counters monitor the overall operation of a particular Service Broker. They can give you an overall feel for the health of the Service Broker.

TABLE 7-20   Counters for monitoring the overall operation of a particular Service Broker

Counter Name	Description
Broker Transaction Rollbacks	The number of transaction rollbacks detected by this Service Broker.
Dialog timer event count	The number of dialog timers that are currently active in this Service Broker.
Enqueued Local Messages Total	The total number of messages delivered by this Service Broker. This counts only messages that were sent locally; it does not count messages that arrive via the network.
Enqueued Local Messages/sec	The above counter specified as a rate per second.
Enqueued Messages Total	The total number of messages enqueued to local queues.
Enqueued Messages/sec	The above counter specified as a rate per second.
Enqueued Transport Msg Frag Tot	The total number of message fragments that have been placed in a queue. Note that large messages are automatically split into a number of fragments for transmission.
Enqueued Transport Msg Frags/sec	The above counter specified as a rate per second.
Enqueued Transport Msgs Total	The total number of messages delivered by this Service Broker. This counts only messages that arrive via the network.
Enqueued Transport Msgs/sec	The above counter specified as a rate per second.
Forwarded Messages Total	The total number of messages that this Service Broker has forwarded.
Forwarded Messages/sec	The above counter specified as a rate per second.
Forwarded Msg Byte Total	The total number of bytes that have been forwarded by this Service Broker.
Forwarded Msg Bytes/sec	The above counter specified as a rate per second.
Forwarded Msg Discarded Total	The total number of forwarded messages that were dropped by this Service Broker.
Forwarded Msg Discarded/sec	The above counter specified as a rate per second.
Forwarded Pending Msg Bytes	The total number of bytes of all the forwarded messages that are waiting to be sent.

TABLE 7-20   continued

Counter Name	Description
Forwarded Pending Msg Count	The current count of forwarded messages that are waiting to be sent.
SQL RECEIVE Total	The total number of T-SQL RECEIVE commands that have been processed.
SQL RECEIVEs/sec	The above counter specified as a rate per second.
SQL SEND Total	The total number of T-SQL SEND commands that have been processed.
SQL SENDs/sec	The above counter specified as a rate per second.

Broker/DBM Transport

These counters are used by the transport layer that is shared by the Service Broker and database mirroring feature.

TABLE 7-21   Counters used by the transport layer that is shared by the Service Broker and database mirroring feature

Counter Name	Description
Current Bytes for Recv I/O	The current number of bytes to be read by the transport.
Current Bytes for Send I/O	The current number of bytes to be sent over the network by the transport.
Current Msg Frags for Send I/O	The current number of message fragments to be sent over the network.
Message Fragment Send Size Avg	The current average size in bytes of the message fragments sent over the network.
Message Fragment Send Total	The total number of message fragments sent over the network.
Message Fragment Sends/sec	The above counter specified as a rate per second.
Message Fragment Receive Total	The total number of message fragments received from the network.
Message Fragment Receives/sec	The above counter specified as a rate per second.
Message Fragment Recv Size Avg	The current average size of message fragments received from the network.
Open Connection Count	The current number of open connections.
Pending Bytes for Recv I/O	The number of bytes the Service Broker transport has received from the network but has yet to put in a queue or drop.

Counter Name	Description
Pending Bytes for Send I/O	The number of bytes in message fragments that are waiting to be sent over the network.
Pending Msg Frags for Recv I/O	The number of message fragments the Service Broker transport has received from the network but has yet to put in a queue or drop.
Pending Msg Frags for Send I/O	The number of bytes in message fragments that are waiting to be sent over the network.
Receive I/O Bytes Total	The total number of bytes received from the network.
Receive I/O Bytes/sec	The above counter specified as a rate per second.
Receive I/O Len Avg	The average number of bytes transferred per network receive.
Receive I/Os/sec	The number of network receives per second.
Send I/O Bytes Total	The total number of bytes sent over the network
Send I/O Bytes/sec	The above counter specified as a rate per second.
Send I/O Len Avg	The average number of bytes transferred per network send.
Send I/Os/sec	The number of network sends per second.

DBCC CHECKDB

The DBCC CHECKDB command enables you to detect and repair databases with corrupt data. Although this command is not a Service Broker-specific tool, it does analyze the database for a number of corruption types. These include things such as contracts that reference missing message types or services referencing missing queues. In the normal operation of the Service Broker, these types of errors cannot occur. For example, dropping of a message type that is in use is prevented. However, this command is provided should some failure occur that left the Service Broker metadata in a corrupted state.

Note that although DBCC CHECKDB has the option to repair corrupt Service Broker metadata, it is important to understand that it is limited to bringing the database as a whole back into a consistent state. In the above example, a contract was missing a message type. It is not possible for DBCC CHECKDB to create the missing message type, because it would not know any information about it. What it can do, however, is remove the contract that is missing the message type. Assuming that no other errors are found, after this is done the database would be in a consistent state. Of course, if this contract were referenced by a service, it would not be sufficient just to drop the contract. The service itself would have to be removed, too. This kind of cascading drop effect would continue until finally the database would be left in a consistent state.

More often than not, a better solution is to restore the corrupted database from a noncorrupt backup. However, sometimes that is not possible, so the repair option is available.

Further Reading

One of the best places to further your knowledge of Service Broker is the website maintained by some of the SQL Service Broker developers: www.sqlservicebroker.com. There you can find links to blogs, discussion boards, and newsgroups that focus on Service Broker application development and troubleshooting.

Another good source of info about Service Broker is Ken Henderson's forthcoming book, *The Guru's Guide to SQL Server Architecture and Internals, Second Edition*, due out in 2007 from Addison-Wesley.

SQLOS and Scheduling Issues

By Sameer Tejani

Today's computer architectures are increasingly diverse and difficult to exploit for maximum performance and scalability. What yesterday was research is now widely used in the industry. Just looking back to several years ago, computers with multiple CPUs were rare. Nowadays, multiple CPUs are no longer a privilege of large corporations. With multi-core CPUs available on the market, home computers already feature multiple CPUs in them. It is expected that tomorrow's market of computers with a high number of CPUs and large amount of memory will become the mainstream. Such computer architectures as Non-Uniform Memory Access (cc-NUMA) will continue gaining market share. Some processor manufacturers have built private memory bus for CPUs, thereby enabling cc-NUMA on even the low-end architectures.

Trends in the enterprise hardware design have become even more dramatic. Enterprise computers today look very similar to yesterday's supercomputers. Nowadays, computers with 64 CPUs and 512GB of memory are common. As current trends continue, soon configuration with 256 physical/logical CPUs and with more than 1TB of memory will dominate enterprise installations. As the number of CPUs grows, hardware manufacturers prefer more and more cc-NUMA architectures to SMP. In today's market, cc-NUMA computers have become the standard for manufacturers developing platforms with a number of CPUs higher than 16. Memory sizes and a number of CPUs is not the only trend present on the enterprise market. Hardware manufacturers are attempting to minimize system downtime and put more flexibility in their systems by introducing support for hot memory and CPU add-ons and removals. Hot add-ons and removals enable system administrators to automatically reconfigure hardware without rebooting systems.

As processing power and the amount of available memory have continued their growth at the speed of Moore's law, memory access latency hasn't kept up. Hardware manufacturers have been heavily investing resources in improving CPU memory behavior. They have built multiple-level caches and have added more support for instruction-level parallelism, weak consistency models, and prefetching.

Understanding and taking advantage of these features has become very important to software engineers designing performance-oriented, scalable applications with flexible administration support.

To make full use of this new paradigm, a new layer—SQLOS—was introduced to abstract the operating system (OS) from the rest of the SQL Server Engine and provide services that take maximum advantage of these architectures while at the same time preserving the current architectures. SQLOS provides user-level operating system services—hence the name "SQLOS"—to the rest of the server. Components in the SQL Server Engine make use of the services provided by SQLOS to schedule individual or multiple tasks, allocate memory, and so forth.

There were several major requirements for SQLOS. The SQLOS layer had to be highly configurable so that the SQL Server could run on low-end as well as on high-end hardware platforms. The SQLOS layer had to hide complexity from the high-level developers but give a broad range of flexibility to the low-level developers. In addition, it had to expand the operating system's services over the new hardware even when the actual underlying OS would have limited support for such services. SQLOS currently consists of the following components:

- Scheduling subsystem
- Memory management
- Error/exception handling
- Deadlock detection
- Hosting external components

SQLOS Architecture

Hardware trends show that locality exploration is the key in enabling application scalability, especially for different types of hardware. Locality can be explored by different means. A common way to achieve it is to create a hierarchical family of objects, in which each object provides locality-centric functionality and services that are meaningful for its level.

One of the major requirements of SQLOS design was the enabling of application scalability. SQLOS had to enable scalability both on the high-end and the low-end hardware. Since locality exploration is one of the ways to satisfy scalability requirements, and locality can be explored through hierarchy, SQLOS leverages hierarchical architecture. The major objects in SQLOS design are nodes, schedulers, and tasks. Each object at its level exposes functionality maximizing local state and minimizing global state. SQLOS attempts to minimize global state as much as possible. Figure 8-1 depicts SQLOS configurations on cc-NUMA hardware with two nodes and two CPUs per node.

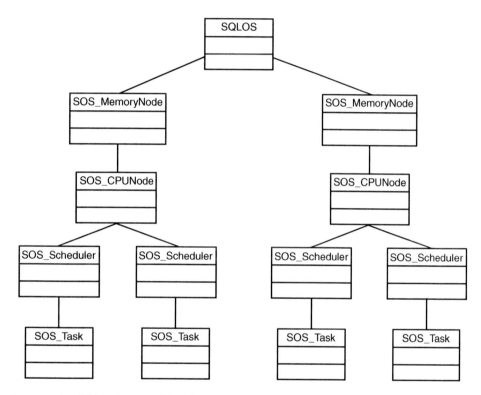

FIGURE 8-1   SQLOS on cc-NUMA hardware

Memory and CPU Nodes

The first objects in the SQLOS hierarchy are *memory nodes*. Think of a memory node as an abstraction primitive over memory attached to a CPU or a set of CPUs. Different hardware configurations have different relationships between CPU and memory. For example, the SMP architecture shares memory across all CPUs, whereas the cc-NUMA architecture shares memory across a set of CPUs. *Memory sharing* can be described as memory or residence affinity and represents memory locality. The memory node's goal is to provide locality of memory management on cc-NUMA or cc-NUMA-like hardware.

A *CPU node* is the next object in the SQLOS hierarchy. A CPU node provides a logical grouping of CPUs. On the SMP architecture, there is a single CPU node. The cc-NUMA architecture has as many CPU nodes as the hardware platform has, by default. CPU nodes provide locality of reference as well as scheduling affinity. They enable developers to dispatch related tasks on CPUs close to each other.

The relationship between a memory node and a CPU node is important. A CPU node is a proper subset of a memory node. As depicted in Figure 8-1, A CPU node can be associated with only one memory node but a memory node can be associated with multiple CPU nodes. This rule addresses two issues. First, it simplifies the software model and enables a well-defined relationship between nodes. Second, it enables SQLOS to model different node configurations on cc-NUMA as well as on the high-end SMP hardware platforms.

In addition to strict hardware configuration, SQLOS can be configured to use logical CPU nodes. Due to historical reasons, a configuration of the system that doesn't fully map to the real hardware configuration is called *Soft NUMA*. The Soft NUMA concept is extremely powerful. It enables application servers built on top of SQLOS to exploit different types of locality provided by the hardware as well as by the nature of the application domain. For example, an SMP system with two dual-core CPUs can be configured to have a single memory node containing two CPU nodes, in which case each node manages two cores. The configuration is shown in Figure 8-2. The benefits of Soft NUMA also include a way of testing SQLOS and SQL Server's cc-NUMA support without actually requiring costly hardware.

Each CPU node contains a set of schedulers. A scheduler is bound to the node's CPU. As shown in Figure 8-3, a CPU node, in addition to schedulers, has an I/O completion port associated with it. An I/O completion port can be bound to multiple I/O devices such as network cards and disks. Having an I/O completion port per node provides I/O locality so that all I/O requests can be scheduled and completed directly on the node's CPU in which they were initiated.

The CPU node's local storage can be used to store and associate data local to the node. Having local storage at the node level enables developers to have local state per node as well as to partition global state across nodes.

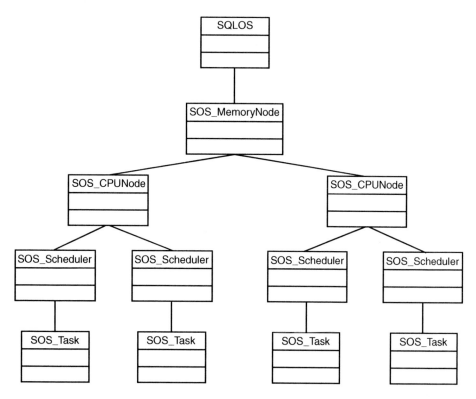

FIGURE 8-2   SQLOS on SMP hardware

A CPU node also provides functionality such as load balancing across its schedulers, I/O affinity, and local storage. Figure 8-3 depicts the high-level CPU node infrastructure.

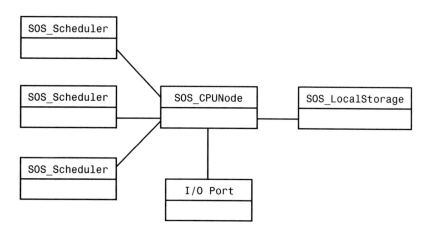

FIGURE 8-3   High-level CPU node infrastructure

Schedulers

The main goal of a scheduler is to schedule work requests like batches or parts of a parallel query on a given CPU. These work requests are driven by tasks. The scheduler is designed such that only one task is actively running or executing at a time (i.e., only one task is actively running on a CPU to which the scheduler is affinitized). This is similar to how only one thread is running at any given time on one CPU (or core) in the OS. To achieve this, the scheduler operates in a non-preemptive manner where the burden of yielding to other tasks is left to the author of the code that executes in the SQL Server Engine. Although this may put the burden on the code owners, it has been noted that database servers work best in non-preemptive mode due to the nature of database queries.[1] They tend to execute and block on synchronization at common points (e.g., when waiting for a lock). This allows tasks to yield at common points instead of being randomly context switched out by the OS.

Schedulers can be used to store local state per CPU as well as to partition global state across CPUs. SQL Server makes use of a lot of local state per scheduler—since there is a guarantee of only one task running, no synchronization is needed to access the local state information. Schedulers also provide support for non-preemptive I/Os. Asynchronous I/Os that are completed during a scheduler context switch are called *non-preemptive I/Os*. Their counterpart—asynchronous I/Os processed by the CPU node's I/O completion port—are called *preemptive I/Os*. The advantage of a non-preemptive I/O is that, upon completion, the completion routine is not invoked by the OS Kernel. That comes through an Asynchronous Procedure Call (APC) and generates an extra context switch. In some cases, it can take longer to complete an I/O. Hence, SQL Server uses non-preemptive I/Os to complete I/Os that complete within a definite timeframe such as Disk I/Os. Network I/Os make use of the preemptive I/O completion model.

Tasks and Workers

Tasks and workers complete the main SQLOS hierarchy. A *task* is an execution request. *Workers* are logical execution contexts (think threads) used to execute the tasks. Depending on the mode, a worker either maps to an OS thread or a fiber (logical thread). This is made easier by the fact that SQLOS employs a non-preemptive scheduling model. A task is dispatched by a scheduler on a CPU. Tasks, too, have local storage to enable storing per task data and finer data partitioning. To follow the non-preemptive model of SQLOS, a task will run as long as its quantum allows or until it gets suspended on a synchronization object. SQL Server (and SQLOS) code periodically check for quantum expiration and yield to other tasks waiting for a chance to run. Examples of places that check whether a yield is necessary include

- Fetching a database page

- Sorting through a resultset every 64KB rows

---

1   *Operating System Support for Database Management. Michael Stonebraker, Communications of the ACM 24(7), 1981, pp. 412-418.*

- After execution of each statement in a batch

- Common points when compiling a query

SQL Server and SQLOS

SQLOS enables SQL Server's scalability through its infrastructure and API design. SQL Server developers have an extremely configurable platform that enables them to exploit underlying hardware and write highly performing and scalable database server code. SQL Server developers have taken full advantage of SQLOS's exposed functionality. Moreover, starting with SQL Server 2005, a database administrator (DBA) has a choice of configuring and dynamically reconfiguring SQL Server according to either the hardware or the application requirements. For example, if a DBA has two applications sharing a SQL Server, SQL Server can be configured to run in two-node configuration so that every application will use its own node. This will make both work loads completely separate. Without SQLOS, this would be very hard to achieve.

Configuration and Troubleshooting

In the next section, we will examine how the scheduler and CPU node–related components are implemented and configured to give optimal performance on SQL Server. In order to understand why a particular option needs to be configured in a certain way, a brief explanation of the implementation is discussed. Some of the common issues discovered and steps to troubleshoot them to achieve a smooth-running SQL Server are also explained.

Node Configuration

As mentioned earlier, a CPU node encapsulates a set of CPUs that have a common resource (e.g., memory, cache). This grouping information can either be obtained from the OS, such as NUMA configuration information, or can be configured in the registry by the administrator of the SQL Box to mimic NUMA and is known as Soft NUMA. Soft NUMA is especially useful in cases where node information cannot be obtained from the OS. An example would be a machine that has a common L3/L4 cache shared among a group of processors. Soft NUMA allows the SQL Server to make the most use of this cache by scheduling tasks to run within the CPUs on that node and preserve locality. Soft NUMA configuration information is read from the registry and applies to all instances of SQL Server running on the machine. Soft NUMA can also be configured on a machine that is NUMA to gain the same advantages as above. In this case, a node that is specified in Soft NUMA cannot extend multiple nodes presented by the OS.

This is how a four-CPU SMP machine can be configured as a two-node, two-CPU machine:

```
[HKEY_LOCAL_MACHINE\SOFTWARE\Microsoft\Microsoft SQL
Server\90\NodeConfiguration]
[HKEY_LOCAL_MACHINE\SOFTWARE\Microsoft\Microsoft SQL
Server\90\NodeConfiguration\Node0]
```

```
"CPUMask"=dword:00000003
[HKEY_LOCAL_MACHINE\SOFTWARE\Microsoft\Microsoft SQL
Server\90\NodeConfiguration\Node1]
"CPUMask"=dword:0000000c
```

On startup, you will notice the following lines in the errorlog indicating that the server was able to successfully boot up in the configuration provided. This information is shown regardless of whether NUMA was detected by the OS or the server was configured in Soft NUMA:

```
2005-12-21 14:50:00.02 Server      Multinode configuration: node 0: CPU mask:
0x00000003 Active CPU mask: 0x00000003. This message provides a description of
the NUMA configuration for this computer. This is an informational message
only. No user action is required.
2005-12-21 14:50:00.04 Server      Multinode configuration: node 1: CPU mask:
0x0000000c Active CPU mask: 0x0000000c. This message provides a description of
the NUMA configuration for this computer. This is an informational message
only. No user action is required.
```

Information about all the nodes present in the system can be obtained at runtime from the dynamic management views (DMVs) to get information about how the server is configured:

```
select parent_node_id, scheduler_id
from sys.dm_os_schedulers
where scheduler_id < 255

parent_node_id scheduler_id
-------------- ------------
0              0
0              1
1              2
1              3

(4 row(s) affected)
```

Network Connection Affinity

Network connection affinity allows the administrator to create network end-points that are bound to a set of nodes. This allows an application to be configured in such a way that workloads can be partitioned across unique nodes. For example, an application that has unique workloads can be configured so that Workload A always connects to Node 0, while Workload B uses Nodes 1, 2, and 3. To configure a server in such a fashion, use the SQL Server Configuration Manager to assign IP ports and addresses to a set of nodes on which they can execute. By default, each port will allow execution on any node. The only network protocol that supports connection affinity is TCP/IP. Note that once a connection is made, that connection will only submit tasks (batches) on that particular node. If a port is associated with multiple nodes, a new connection established on that port will be associated with one of the nodes in the node mask. The decision is made at runtime by the SQL Networking Interface layer and takes into consideration multiple factors in choosing the right node.

To configure SQL Server to make use of Network Connection Affinity, start the SQL Server Configuration Manager, select SQL Server 2005 Network Configuration, and select the instance name that needs to be configured. Double-click on TCP/IP to configure it. Figure 8-4 illustrates Network Connection Affinity.

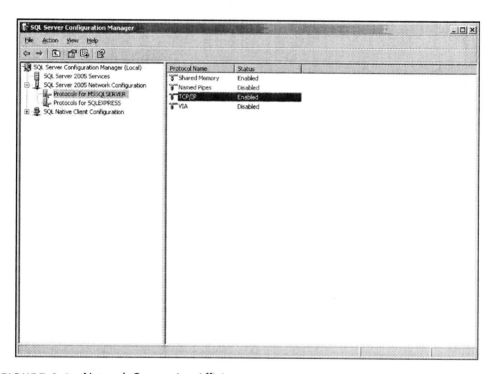

FIGURE 8-4 Network Connection Affinity

Next, configure the TCP/IP settings to control which ports will direct connections to which node. For each port, a node or a mask of nodes can be specified in square brackets ( ) to direct connections to a particular set of nodes. If you want to associate a particular port with all the nodes, which is the default case, you do not need to specify the mask of nodes or the square brackets.

Notice in the following example that two ports are created: 1433 and 1440. 1443 is assigned the mask 0x1, which includes only Node 0, and 1440 is assigned the mask 0x2, which only includes Node 1. If multiple nodes need to be assigned to one port, the mask needs to reflect that. For example, if 1433 should connect to both Node 0 and Node 1, the mask would be 0x3.

If, for example, an admin wants to create on a four-node machine two unique ports (1440 and 1441) for connection affinity to each of the two nodes (1440 connects to Nodes 0 and 1 and 1441 connects to Nodes 2 and 3) and leave the default port for all nodes (see Figure 8-5), the TCP port string would look as follows:

```
1433,1440[0x3],1441[0xc]
```

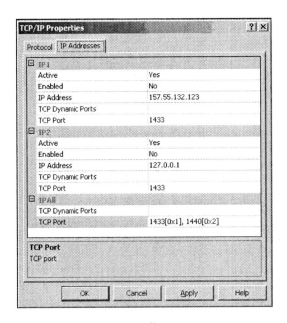

FIGURE 8-5   Another Network Connection Affinity scenario

On successful startup, the errorlog shows an entry similar to the following, indicating that the server is listening on multiple ports and also directing connections to the appropriate nodes:

```
2006-04-05 18:34:54.15 Server        Server is listening on [ 'any' <ipv4>
1433].
2006-04-05 18:34:54.15 Server        SQL Network Interfaces initialized
listeners on node 0 of a multi-node (NUMA) server configuration with node
affinity mask 0x00000001. This is an informational message only. No user
action is required.
2006-04-05 18:34:54.16 Server        Server is listening on [ 'any' <ipv4>
1440].
2006-04-05 18:34:54.16 Server        SQL Network Interfaces initialized
listeners on node 1 of a multi-node (NUMA) server configuration with node
affinity mask 0x00000002. This is an informational message only. No user
action is required.
```

If a machine has multiple Network Interface Cards (NICs), multiple IP addresses show up in the TCP/IP Properties dialog box (such IP1, IP2, ... IP*n*). Note that the IP with the IP address of 127.0.0.1 is the default loopback IP address used to connect locally on the machine. To achieve connection affinity using multiple NICs, associate the port with each NIC to a unique node or mask of nodes.

To verify that a connection is going to the right node, open a connection to SQL Server using the appropriate port (an alias can be created to connect to a port using the SQL Server Configuration Manager, SQL Native Client Configuration, Aliases) and then run the following query to see if the connection is on the right node:

```
select r.scheduler_id, s.parent_node_id
from sys.dm_exec_requests r, sys.dm_os_schedulers s
where r.session_id = @@spid
    and r.scheduler_id = s.scheduler_id
```

Network Connection Affinity is a powerful way of partitioning a workload across multiple nodes and can be used on any kind of machine—NUMA, by virtue of NUMA configuration obtained from the OS or SMP by configuring it using Soft NUMA—to create the appropriate nodes and run queries on them.

Scheduler

A scheduler is logically mapped and modeled to a CPU on the system. It is responsible for ensuring that only one task is currently running non-preemptively on the scheduler at any given time. A lot of its functionality mirrors what an OS scheduler would look like. In order for a task to be executed, it needs a worker to physically execute it to completion. During the duration of execution, the task will never give up possession of the worker until completion. Hence, it is common to see a task that is blocked on a resource while still holding on to a worker. The worker contains the execution state of the task at that point, including OS- and SQLOS-specific items. Runtime information about schedulers can be found in the DMV sys.dm_os_schedulers.

Schedulers have unique IDs (scheduler_id in sys.dm_os_schedulers). The schedulers that execute user requests have an ID between 0 and 255. This ID does not map to the Hardware CPU ID. By default, schedulers do not run on a particular CPU unless the Affinity Mask configuration option is specified. On a multi-node machine, the schedulers run on the set of CPUs that composes that node. When the Affinity Mask option is specified, a scheduler is then bound to run on the specified CPU. This can be found by looking at the cpu_id column in sys.dm_os_schedulers. Any changes in affinity mask are reflected at runtime without requiring a restart of SQL. At startup, all the schedulers that can be started on the system are started. Based on the affinity mask settings, the appropriate schedulers are made available for processing user requests. On an affinity mask change, schedulers that are not available are marked offline and no new tasks can be created on them. Existing tasks continue running on them until completion. Schedulers whose affinity masks have been specified are marked as online and new tasks can be created on them. Schedulers that have an ID > 255 are internal schedulers used for processing internal work. These are normally referred to as *hidden schedulers*. See the status column in sys.dm_os_schedulers to see if a scheduler is marked online or offline and if it is visible or hidden to user requests.

A scheduler contains the following state information to make it work:

- **Pending Queue of Tasks.** This is a queue of tasks that are waiting for a worker so that they can run on the Scheduler. (See work_queue_count in sys.dm_os_schedulers.)

- **Worker Pool.** This is a pool of idle workers that wait for new tasks to be enqueued to the scheduler. The worker pool works in conjunction with the pending queue to form the work dispatcher. (See current_workers_count and active_workers_count in sys.dm_os_schedulers. The difference between current_workers_count and active_workers_count is the number of idle workers available in the worker pool.)

- **Current Worker.** This is the worker that is currently executing a task on the Scheduler. It is the worker that is responsible to yielding when its quantum has completed or if it needs to block. This can be derived from the active_worker_address field in sys.dm_os_schedulers.

- **Idle Worker.** This is the worker that is used to initialize the scheduler during startup. It also controls the scheduler when there are no active tasks executing on the scheduler.

- **Runnable Queue.** This contains a list of tasks that already have workers and are waiting for a chance to run on the scheduler. The task that is currently running on the scheduler will voluntarily yield once its quantum is up or if it gets blocked on a resource and passes control to a task that is waiting on the runnable queue. (See runnable_queue_count in sys.dm_os_schedulers.)

- **Timer Queue.** Occasionally, a task will wait for a timeout to occur before proceeding to execute. For example, it could wait on a resource for up to a certain time upon which it may give up or execute something else. The scheduler provides a mechanism for a task to be alerted and woken up when the timeout is fired. In this case, the task would be put in the runnable queue and eventually be awakened.

- **I/O Queue.** As explained earlier, this contains a list of pending non-preemptive I/Os that have been posted and are waiting for completion. On a scheduler context switch, the status of these I/Os is checked and those that have been completed are processed and removed from the queue. Only Disk I/Os make use of the non-preemptive I/Os and use this queue. See sys.dm_io_pending_ios for a list of I/Os waiting to be processed or the pending_disk_io_count in sys.dm_os_schedulers to see if there are any pending I/Os.

- **Abort Queue.** This is an internal queue that is used to abort a currently running task. A task can be aborted due to several reasons such as cancellation by the user, internal error in a parallel query, and so on. SQLOS provides a way for another task to abort it by putting it on the Scheduler Abort queue. During a scheduler context switch, an attempt will be made to abort any tasks that are in this queue. There are some exceptions where a task cannot be aborted.

- **Load Factor.** The current perceived load on the scheduler based on the number and classification of tasks that are running at the current time. This is used by the CPU node when trying to figure out where to enqueue a new task.

Occasionally, a request may need to run in code that is not in the SQL Server domain (e.g., when executing a distributed query, an extended stored procedure call, or calling a Windows API). In these cases, it is possible for the call to take an indefinite time where the code will not be able to yield the scheduler to let other workers run. The worker is switched to what is known as preemptive mode—during this time, it is not governed by the scheduler and is treated like a free-running thread. Before moving to preemptive mode, it gives control of the scheduler to the next worker in the runnable queue or the idle thread. Upon completing the external call, it returns to non-preemptive mode where it then continues to be governed by the scheduler.

When a task transitions from running to suspended or preemptive, it goes through a scheduler context switch running any state transitions that are required (context_switches_count in sys.dm_os_schedulers). Usually, this involves completing any non-preemptive I/Os and calling their respective completion routines, expiring timers on the timer queue, and processing abort requests. After this, the next task on the runnable queue is woken up and given control of the scheduler. If there are no workers on the runnable queue, the scheduler transitions to an idle state (is_idle in sys.dm_os_schedulers). During idle state, the worker that is in idle state (or the idle worker) continues processing the context switch to check for any completions and brings the scheduler back to active (idle_context_switches_count in sys.dm_os_schedulers).

Figure 8-6 is a state diagram or flowchart that shows the flow of execution starting from when a new task is enqueued to the scheduler until it completes execution.

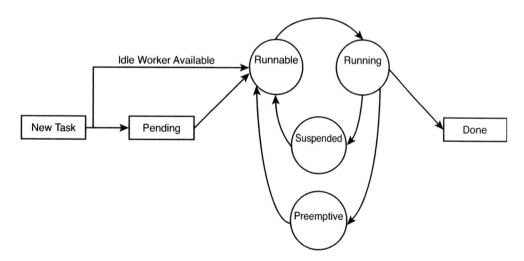

FIGURE 8-6   Flow of execution

Tasks and Workers

Tasks are work requests that are executed on schedulers using a worker. A task is created when a work request needs to be executed (e.g., a new batch request from a client) and is enqueued onto the appropriate scheduler to execute. Each scheduler has a pool of workers that are used to process tasks. A task will hold on to a worker until it completes.

Many tasks are short-lived and will complete execution after the batch request or parallel query request completes. There are some tasks that hold on to a worker forever—these are known as *permanent system tasks*, such as the Deadlock Monitor or the Lazy Writer.

A worker can be considered a logical thread that contains the execution context used to run. It runs on top of a system thread, which is the real physical thread that is created by the OS. Usually, SQL Server runs in thread mode (where the advanced configuration option Lightweight Pooling is off). In this mode, each worker is associated with a system thread during all points of execution (i.e., suspended, runnable, running). When Lightweight Pooling is turned on, the server runs in what is called fiber mode. In this case, the worker contains execution information that is made active on the system thread only when the worker is running. The advantage of running with lightweight pooling is that the cost of switching between two workers (one worker giving up its quantum to the next worker) is very low, because no kernel cost is involved. The system thread gets the execution information from the next worker, activates it, and starts running it. Execution starts from the point it gives up its quantum. For example, Worker A is running and has to block on a lock. At this point, it gives up its quantum and yields to the next worker, say Worker B. After a period of time, it acquires the lock and is put on the scheduler runnable queue. When the system thread finally picks up Worker A, it will start running from the point where it was waiting on the lock.

This optimization comes at a cost because not all information of a system thread can be stored on a worker. Similarly, some other components that run in the SQL Server process that are not part of SQL Server may not be aware of the concept of a worker (or a logical thread) and may store component-specific information on the system thread through thread local storage or other API calls such as floating-point precision. So, as workers switch between Active and Suspended on a system thread, this information may not get updated and end up causing instability problems while executing. At the same time, lightweight pooling should only be used when CPU usage is approaching 90%–100%. A lot of SQL Server users do not hit this kind of CPU utilization and many prefer to partition the workload to multiple servers when this kind of utilization is hit.

Workers are created in an on-demand fashion until the maximum number of workers is reached. The maximum is configured through the advanced configuration option Max Worker Threads. In SQL 2000, each scheduler was restricted to a certain number of workers and could not exceed that limit. The limit was calculated by dividing max worker threads by the number of schedulers. With SQL 2005, this limit is changed to an ideal limit, but if a scheduler needs more workers and workers can be created, it will exceed its ideal limit. In case all the worker threads have been used up and a scheduler with less than the ideal worker limit needs more workers, it will notify the Scheduler Monitor, which will then trim workers on those schedulers with more than the ideal limit. This works out well in multi-node configurations where some nodes may be busier than other nodes, especially if connection affinity is being used to partition the workload.

Schedulers with workers that have remained idle for more than 15 minutes will trim the worker pool to a minimum size. Similarly, if there is memory pressure on the system or within SQL Server, the Resource Monitor will notify the schedulers to trim the idle workers in order to free up memory.

Load-Balancing Tasks Between Schedulers

Each scheduler, depending on the number and kinds of tasks it is running, has an associated load factor. When a new task is enqueued to a node, the node has to figure out the best scheduler to put this task on—usually the one with the least load. Doing this every time can cause a bottleneck in the enqueuing procedure. Note that after a task starts running on a scheduler, it does not move away from that scheduler until it completes.

To improve on this, existing sessions remember the last scheduler they ran their task on and pass it down to the node as a hint to try and reuse the same scheduler, both from a performance point of view (in that the CPU cache may still contain some of its data on it) and to skip the least-loaded scheduler check. To achieve this, the node maintains an average scheduler load factor that is updated every so often, which it uses to compare the scheduler load to the average scheduler load. If the scheduler load is < 1.2 * average scheduler load, the node will allow the task to run on the scheduler (i.e., if it is within 20% of the average scheduler load).

Now, this does not work out well at times, especially when there are long-running tasks. In these cases, some imbalance may be observed between schedulers where some schedulers (and CPUs) are busier than others. This has been noted in some cases where parallel bulk inserts are run to insert data into a table. Running two or more similar bulk insert tasks on the same scheduler reduces the statement's performance throughput.

To work around this issue, a new global traceflag, 8008, was introduced. The effect of this traceflag is that it will always ignore the hint passed in to the node and enqueue on the least-loaded scheduler. You can turn on this traceflag just before starting the parallel long-running tasks (DBCC TRACEON (8008, -1)) and turn it off after completion. It also helps if the parallel tasks are started in a staggered fashion as opposed to starting them all at the same time.

Max Worker Threads Configuration

By default, SQL 2005 sets the advanced configuration option of Max Worker Threads to 0. This means that at startup time, SQL Server determines the ideal number for this configuration option. The ideal number is generated based on the number of processors on the system as well as the hardware that it is running on. The formula to determine the maximum number of worker threads is as follows:

For x86 systems: If the total number of processors (logical) <=4, then

```
# max worker threads = 256
```

Otherwise,

> # max worker threads = 256 + ((# Procs – 4) * 8)

For x64 systems: If the total number of processors <= 4, then

> # max worker threads = 512

Otherwise,

> # max worker threads = 512 + ((#Procs – 4) * 16)

So, on an eight-processor x86 machine (it could a four-processor hyperthreaded or dual-core machine, and therefore show eight logical processors, or a regular eight-processor single-core machine), max worker threads will be configured to 288 (256 + (4 * 8)).

On a 16-processor x64 machine, max worker threads will be configured to 704 (512 + (12 * 16)).

The default max worker thread count can be obtained by looking at the max_workers_count column in the sys.dm_os_sys_info DMV.

Since x86 machines are limited to 2GB of virtual address space (or 3GB when the /3GB option is specified in the Windows OS boot.ini), SQL Server prefers to limit the number of max worker threads to a smaller value relative to x64 machines. Each thread stack, which occupies 512KB, of memory, is committed in memory.

Ideally, you do not need to play around with these values, and most configurations work fine with the default settings. By changing the settings, the amount of memory available for other items, such as the Buffer Pool map, loaded DLLs, and so on, get affected.

If a workload on a SQL Server is well known and tuned such that it does not exceed using a certain number of threads, the max worker thread limit can be changed (especially if it is lower than the default value). This will give more memory to other components that can make better use of it.

At the same time, if the application is written in such a way that it holds on to a worker thread or another SQL Server resource for a long period of time, you may want to increase the limit of max worker threads to avoid 17884 (potential deadlocked scheduler) errors or thread deadlock problems. However, the best solution for these kinds of errors is to change the application to improve the user experience of running it on top of SQL Server.

To determine the number of workers being used at any given time, add the number of active_worker_count from sys.dm_os_schedulers and that will give you a good idea of how many workers are currently in use on the system. By tracing this value over a period of time, you can find out how many workers were used and what the maximum value was and use this to configure the max worker thread count if necessary. Similarly, by tracing the work_queue_count, you can figure out how many tasks are waiting for a worker to pick them up. If this count is pretty large, it may indicate that some workers are taking a really long time to execute or that the max worker thread count is too low.

Lightweight Pooling Configuration

Lightweight pooling is an option that was introduced in SQL Server 7.0 along with the User Mode Scheduler (UMS). Lightweight Pooling makes use of Windows fibers. A *fiber* is considered a lightweight thread that contains necessary information for a physical thread to run a context. Usually, a fiber contains a stack and register context information that a physical thread points to, to start running the fiber. The main advantage of using fibers in a multi-threaded application is the cost of switching contexts between two threads (workers), which is cheaper than switching contexts between two real OS threads since the switch does not incur an OS kernel call. Usually, you will see a performance advantage using lightweight pooling when a server is hitting maximum CPU usage or where there is a lot of context switching between threads. You can see this by observing the appropriate performance counters. Since fibers contain only the minimal context information for them to run, they have limitations that may make them unsuitable for certain types of applications. SQL Server works around some of these limitations, but for some use cases, fibers are not recommended.

Many components make use of Thread Local Storage (TLS) to store execution-specific data in a well-known location in a thread. This is a service that is exposed by the OS. Windows 2003 introduced Fiber Local Storage (FLS) that exposes similar functionality for fibers. SQL Server has had custom logic since SQL 7.0 that deals with SQL Server–related TLS entries and ensures that the correct TLS entries are populated on a context switch. Other external components running in SQL Server did not have similar logic and hence could run into errors when accessing their TLS entries since they could potentially contain incorrect data. Therefore, historically, lightweight pooling has not been recommended in a deployment that made use of some external components, such as extended stored procedures (XPs) or the Distributed Transaction Coordinator (DTC).

The memory occupied by a fiber is similar in size to a physical thread that is used to run the fiber. This memory is used to store the context information about the fiber. The maximum number of fibers is governed by the Maximum Worker Threads configuration option. Since a physical thread is still needed to run a fiber, and there can be multiple physical threads active in the system, running with lightweight pooling may consume more memory than running without it.

Before turning on lightweight pooling, test the application well before deploying it in production and ensure that you see a performance improvement by turning it on. Verify this improvement by analyzing the performance data (mentioned above).

There have been some cases where a server cannot start after turning on lightweight pooling due to some conflict with an external component that gets loaded into the SQL Server process space or with the way the machine has been configured. In that case, the lightweight pooling option can be overridden by passing in the traceflag 1615 that will cause the server to use threads instead of fibers.

To sum up, lightweight pooling is an option that should be used with caution. It can give gains in some unique scenarios, but consider the following before turning it on:

- Is the server approaching maximum CPU or showing high kernel times, possibly related to thread context switches?

- Are there any external components running in SQL Server that may not work well when run on fibers?

- Is there enough memory to support the extra overhead that lightweight pooling may require?

- Ensure that you test your applications thoroughly before deploying lightweight pooling in production and that there is a significant gain from turning this option on.

Affinity Mask Configuration

The advanced configuration options *Affinity Mask* and *Affinity64 Mask* have been used to specify what processors SQL Server can use. These settings cause SQL Server to only allow the schedulers to run on those particular processors. Since configuration options are stored as 32-bit integers in `sys.sysconfigures`, two rows are needed to store the affinity mask settings for up to 64 processors. That is why the configuration options for affinity mask are split into two fields.

In the past, any change to this configuration option would require a restart. With SQL Server 2005, this has become a dynamic option and any changes are applied right away. This is quite useful when trying to limit or increase the number of processors you want to assign to SQL Server. For example, if there are two instances of SQL Server running on a single machine, and one of them needs more processing time than the other, an admin can modify the affinity mask settings for both the instances and assign more processors to the processor-hungry instance. Similarly, another application may need more processing power at a certain time, and so SQL can be configured to use fewer processors when that application starts to run.

- Affinity Mask is used to configure the first 32 CPUs on the system (CPU ID 0 – 31).

- Affinity64 Mask is used to configure the next 32 CPUs on the system (CPU ID 32 – 63).

Usually, you should try to avoid overlapped affinity mask settings with the affinity I/O mask settings. `sp_configure/reconfigure` prevent this from happening, but can be overridden by calling `reconfigure` with `override`.

On startup, SQL Server will create as many schedulers as there are processors or as many as that edition of SQL Server can use, whichever is fewer. After the schedulers have been started up, if an affinity mask is specified, all those that are not in the affinity mask will be marked offline. When a scheduler is marked offline, any tasks that are running on it will run to completion, but no new tasks can be scheduled on it. Also, it is prevented from running on the CPU it was originally running on. By default, SQL Server does not have an affinity mask specified, and all the schedulers that are available can run on any CPU on the system. Note that on a multi-node system (like NUMA), the schedulers can run on any CPU that is on that particular node to preserve locality of reference. In the default case where no affinity mask is specified, the OS will schedule the threads running on the scheduler to any available CPU. It is best to leave this setting as-is, especially in a mixed environment where multiple applications are running on the host machine.

By turning on the affinity mask, you are instructing SQL Server to run each scheduler on a specific CPU. In that case, the OS respects the affinity setting and will not try to reschedule a thread to a different CPU in case the current CPU gets overloaded. So, it is possible to see some CPUs overloaded with respect to other CPUs when the affinity mask option is specified.

SQL Server 2000 SP3 and SQL Server 2005 introduced traceflag 8002 that models the default behavior of allowing a scheduler to use any CPU, but at the same time instructs the server to use only those CPUs that are specified in the affinity mask. For example, consider a scenario where SQL Server is running on a 32-way machine, and the admin wants SQL to only use the last four processors on the system. However, she does not want each scheduler bound to an individual CPU, but wants the option of them moving between any of the last four CPUs. In this case, she would configure the affinity mask to use the last four processors (sp_configure 'affinity mask', 0xf0000000) and also turn on Trace 8002.

As stated previously, SQL Server will start up as many schedulers as there are processors or the maximum number of processors that the edition of SQL Server can support. Each scheduler has an assigned minimum number of resources (e.g., threads, see the "Max Worker Threads Configuration" section earlier in this chapter) that it has. In some cases, an admin may not want to use all the processors and may never want to make use of dynamically changing the affinity mask setting. This is especially true in a case where multiple instances of SQL Server are running on a machine and each has been partitioned to use only a certain mask of CPUs such that they do not overlap with each other. Furthermore, the admin may want to have all the resources assigned to just those schedulers. In this case, the server can be started with Trace 8017, which will only start those schedulers that are specified in the affinity mask setting. All these schedulers will be online and there will be no offline schedulers. Any changes to the affinity mask in sp_configure will require a SQL Server restart. This can be used in conjunction with Trace 8002 to ensure that the load is spread amongst all the CPUs specified. Note that by default in the SQL Server Express editions, dynamic affinity is disabled and any changes require a server restart. This is because of the low resource consumption requirements on these editions of SQL Server.

When a scheduler is taken offline, no new tasks can be scheduled on it. Any existing tasks will run to completion. The scheduler will then be mapped to a set of CPUs that are currently in the affinity mask. It is possible that a system task was running on a scheduler that has been taken offline. In this case, the system task will continue running on that scheduler with little impact to the rest of the system.

If a group of schedulers that comprise a node are taken offline, the node is also considered offline. In this case, the I/O completion port that is associated with this node will also stop accepting new connections to be associated with this node (see "Network Connection Affinity" earlier in this chapter). It is important to remember that existing connections that are associated with this node will not be terminated and can still continue making use of this node. Because the threads running on this node will be mapped to other CPUs, there could be a performance impact when running queries on these existing connections.

sys.dm_os_schedulers shows the state of the schedulers that are currently running whether they are online or offline and the CPU mask that they are running on. The following explains more with respect to the affinity mask:

- **is_online.** A bit column that indicates if the scheduler is available to run new queries. If a group of schedulers that comprise a node are all offline, the node is considered offline too.

- **cpu_id.** The ID of the CPU that this scheduler is associated with. By default, with no affinity, it will show 255. This will only show a valid ID when a scheduler is mapped to only one CPU. An offline scheduler, or when the system is running with the preceding traceflags, cpu_id will always be 255.

The dynamic affinity mask allows greater control for an administrator to control her SQL Server instance. This can be used in multiple scenarios, including

- **Limiting or increasing the number of processors available to SQL Server.** This is useful when resources need to be allocated in a dynamic fashion between applications. For example, a backup application may need more processors when running its nightly backup job to complete in time. SQL Server can be configured to use fewer processors at that time and have it configured back to its original value after it is done.

- **Multiple instances can be shielded from each other by assigning each instance a unique mask of processors.** This is especially useful in consolidation scenarios where multiple instances of SQL may run on one machine.

Disk I/O Completion Processing

The scheduler provides a mechanism to complete pending asynchronous disk I/Os. These I/Os are completed whenever there is a scheduler context switch. During a scheduler context switch, all the pending disk I/Os are traversed and checked if they have been completed. If they are completed, the appropriate I/O completion routine associated with that I/O is called, which does the necessary work like release a latch associated with that buffer or wake up any worker threads waiting for the I/O to complete. An optimization at I/O time prevents a kernel call from being made so that they can be completed during context switches.

Occasionally, you may notice that a worker thread is blocked for a long time behind an I/O. You can recognize this directly by seeing it as a wait type in sys.dm_os_ waiting_tasks or indirectly by associating that wait type with a possible disk I/O wait type such as Buffer Latch wait type. If any pending I/Os are taking a long time to complete, it may be an indication of a disk or disk driver problem. Refer to the Windows Event Log for more information or use the manufacturer's disk diagnostics to see if there is a problem.

To figure out if there are long pending disk I/Os, look at the following DMVs:

- **sys.dm_os_schedulers.** There is a column called pending_disk_io. If the count is greater than 0 for a while, there may be pending disk I/O.

- **sys.dm_io_pending_ios.** This lists all the pending disk I/Os from all the schedulers. You have to join it with sys.dm_os_schedulers to get the correct scheduler ids. It will list each I/O that is waiting for completion and the amount of time it has been waiting. For those that have been waiting for longer than a certain threshold, you can query sys.dm_io_file_stats with the file handle from sys.dm_io_pending_ios to get the actual file on which the I/O is taking longer than normal. You can then examine the file or disk to see if there are any I/O problems.

- **SQL errorlog.** The errorlog may have entries indicating if a disk I/O has taken longer than 15 seconds to complete. This may give you a clue if there were any events in the past where a disk I/O took longer to complete. If there are more than a couple of these messages, it may be wise to run some diagnostic tests on your system.

For more information on troubleshooting disk I/O problems, refer to the I/O Troubleshooting guide.

Preemptive I/O Completion Processing

Each CPU node contains an I/O completion port and a listener. This is used to allow I/Os to bind to the completion port and complete them locally on the node. The I/O completion port listener is a task that runs continuously, monitoring for new completions coming through the I/O completion port and calling the appropriate (supplied) I/O completion routine.

Network I/O makes the most use of this model, and each client network connection is bound to its appropriate node. When a client connects to SQL Server, the SQL Networking Interface will bind the connection to an I/O completion port of a node that it selects (unless it had been preconfigured to connect to a particular node; see "Network Connection Affinity" earlier in this chapter). Thereafter, all requests from that connection will be processed by schedulers on that node. Each request will be executed on the least-loaded scheduler as determined by the CPU node. To preserve locality, each connection also remembers the last scheduler it executed a task on. The CPU node will then try to schedule new tasks from that connection on the same scheduler if possible.

When processing preemptive I/O completions, the I/O completion routine may run into a problem and potentially stall somewhere in the routine. This can be caused by resource issues such as low memory, synchronization hotspots, and other factors. This causes other pending I/Os to not get processed and may show up as the SQL Server being stuck. In this case, an error may be raised in the errorlog (17887). See the next section, "Scheduler Monitor," on how to troubleshoot this.

Scheduler Monitor

Each CPU node also has a Scheduler Monitor. The Scheduler Monitor is a task that runs continuously and is used to monitor the health of all the schedulers that include the following:

- Schedulers yield at regular intervals. All tasks running on the CPU node schedulers are supposed to yield at regular intervals. It is possible that, due to conditions on the machine such as the machine being overloaded, memory pressure, or a bug in SQL Server, some tasks may not be able to yield in a timely fashion. This will starve the other tasks from getting a quantum to run and cause performance problems. In this case, the Scheduler Monitor may try to correct this error or may raise an error—17883—in the errorlog and produce a diagnostic dump when such a condition is detected for the admin and Microsoft to investigate. The Scheduler Monitor tries to correct the condition if possible by calling components that could be causing the non-yielding situation. The only component that currently reacts to these messages is the SQLCLR interface that runs CLR modules in the SQL Server process space. If a badly written CLR app runs in a tight loop without making any API calls, it could conceivably get into a situation where it doesn't yield. The SQLCLR interface will detect this condition when called upon and cause the thread to yield by issuing a garbage collection event in the CLR. At the same time, it will penalize that thread from taking up a lot of time.

- New tasks that have been waiting for a long time get picked up by a scheduler. This usually happens when there aren't enough workers available in the system or if the application written on top of SQL Server has been written in a poor fashion, holding critical resources for a long time. In this case, an error—17884—is raised in the errorlog for the administrator to investigate further.

- Preemptive I/O completions get processed in a definite time. Because there is one IO completion port listener task per I/O completion port, the call to the completion routine needs to finish quickly so that it can process other pending I/O completions. If the completion routine takes a long time to complete, a diagnostic stack dump is produced along with an error message—17887.

These errors raised by the Scheduler Monitor are explained in detail in the following sections:

- Workers are balanced equally among all the schedulers and the system in general. It is possible that in some cases a scheduler or a group of schedulers may require more workers to process an intensive query, in which case it will create more workers than its ideal limit by borrowing workers from others. When other schedulers need their workers back, the Scheduler Monitor will put pressure on the schedulers to release workers so that other schedulers can make use of them.

- The Scheduler Monitor also ensures that schedulers are handling the appropriate load and that under-loaded schedulers pick up newer tasks coming in at the CPU node. Therefore, when making passes on each of the schedulers to do a health check, it will update the appropriate information regarding the state of the node to allow new tasks to be routed to the appropriate schedulers.

- Finally, the Scheduler Monitor maintains a health record on the node it is running on. This health record contains information about the system load and the process and memory utilization in a circular buffer. It contains approximately four hours worth of information that is quite useful when trying to debug scheduler-related issues.

Troubleshooting the Scheduler Monitor

Here, we will explore more about the common errors raised by the Scheduler Monitor and how to correctly diagnose the root cause. It is important to note that, by default, each of these errors will only produce one diagnostic userdump during the lifetime of a SQL Server process. Nevertheless, by using some traceflags, you can enable them to be produced every time they are encountered, but it is not necessary unless you need to further debug an issue. Experience shows that the same error may get raised multiple times and unnecessarily clogs the log directory.

These errors are also considered diagnostic errors that indicate a problem with another part of SQL Server or the environment SQL Server is running in. They do not necessarily mean that there is an issue with the scheduler. The userdump that is produced by this error allows Microsoft Customer Support Services to further troubleshoot the issue and provide guidance on how to resolve it.

Non-yielding Scheduler

Non-yielding scheduler error messages—17883—usually include a diagnostic stack dump on the first occurrence of a non-yielding situation. This stack dump is uploaded to Microsoft in case Automatic Upload of Watson Data was selected at startup. Other than the stack dump, a lot of information about the state of the server when the dump was produced can be gleaned from the error message in the errorlog and by querying DMVs.

The error message in the errorlog will look like this:

```
2005-12-21 15:27:15.04 Server      ***Unable to get thread context - no pss
2005-12-21 15:27:15.04 Server      *
*********************************************
***********************************
2005-12-21 15:27:15.04 Server      *
2005-12-21 15:27:15.04 Server      * BEGIN STACK DUMP:
2005-12-21 15:27:15.04 Server      *   12/21/05 15:27:15 spid 0
2005-12-21 15:27:15.04 Server      *
2005-12-21 15:27:15.04 Server      * Non-yielding Scheduler
2005-12-21 15:27:15.04 Server      *
2005-12-21 15:27:15.04 Server      *
*********************************************
***********************************
2005-12-21 15:27:15.04 Server      Stack Signature for the dump is 0x00000255
2005-12-21 15:27:16.35 Server      External dump process return code
0x20000001.

External dump process returned no errors.
2005-12-21 15:27:16.35 Server      Process 52:0:0 (0xba0) Worker 0x05E4E0E8
appears to be non-yielding on Scheduler 3. Thread creation time:
12779679003243. Approx Thread CPU Used: kernel 0 ms, user 74750 ms. Process
Utilization 25%. System Idle 74%. Interval: 74999 ms.
```

To try and figure out the problem, consider the following:

- **Approx Thread CPU Used.** This gives an idea as to whether the task was executing or possibly blocked. The amount of CPU used is further split into user and kernel times. If it was executing longer than 4000ms (4 seconds) in user time, this may indicate a bug in SQL Server where a portion of code could be running in an unbounded loop. If the kernel time is high while the user time low, it may be an issue with a call to the OS, which will require some kernel debugging to figure out the root cause. Contact Microsoft Customer Service Support to resolve this issue.

- **Process Utilization.** This shows the amount of CPU that SQL was consuming when this dump was produced. If SQL Server is using a lot of CPU, this could indicate a problem with SQL Server itself. This should be used in conjunction with the System Idle metric to get a good idea of how the system was behaving at a particular point in time. If the Approx Thread CPU Used is pretty low, it could indicate that another thread, potentially a thread running in preemptive mode, is driving the process utilization high and starving this thread from running. Check sys.dm_os_threads for threads with high CPU times (user_time and kernel_time) to figure out which thread is causing this issue. Taking a few snapshots of sys.dm_os_threads when this behavior is observed may give you a good idea which thread is consuming a lot of CPU and narrow down what it is doing at that point in time.

```
SELECT kernel_time + usermode_time as TotalTime, *
FROM sys.dm_os threads
ORDER BY kernel_time + usermode_time desc
```

■ **System Idle.** This shows the amount of CPU that was available on the system. If this is 0 or close to 0, it means that the machine was very busy—using nearly 100% CPU—and it may be that SQL Server was not getting enough CPU cycles from the OS. In this case, the administrator needs to look at the machine to figure out what process is using the majority of the CPU. Note that there are cases where the system may be paging or waiting on asynchronous I/Os to complete and would show a lot of System Idle time. In these cases, you would need to get Microsoft CSS involved to figure out the issue. It would be helpful to also have some performance data to figure out the root cause. In the preceding example, on a four-CPU machine, 25% of CPU was being used by SQL, and System Idle was close to 75%. Given that this was taken in a snapshot of about 60 seconds, it is possible that the non-yielding task was using all of the 25%.

Further information can be obtained from the Scheduler Monitor health records ring buffer. In these cases, you filter out the unnecessary schedulers and get to the pertinent information that is stored as an XML record.

The DMV `sys.dm_os_ring_buffers` has a binary column record that stores data in XML format. The first step to getting the information from this column is to get only those ring buffer records that are pertinent to the Scheduler Monitor. (The DMV has other ring buffer types related to error handling, memory management, and so on.) While doing this step, it is also better to cast the record type to an XML type so that you can XQuery expressions to get the appropriate data:

```
select *, convert(XML, record) as xml_record
into ring_buffer_scheduler_monitor_xml
from sys.dm_os_ring_buffers
where ring_buffer_type = 'RING_BUFFER_SCHEDULER_MONITOR'
```

The next step involves getting the appropriate information from the XML record:

```
declare @node int
declare @scheduler int
declare @beginyields int
declare @endyields int

SELECT
    @node = n.value ('(Node)[1]', 'int'),
    @scheduler = n.value ('(Scheduler)[1]', 'int'),
    @beginyields = n.value ('(Yields)[1]', 'int')
FROM
    ring_buffer_scheduler_monitor_xml
cross apply
xml_record.nodes('/Record/SchedluerMonitorEvent/NonYieldBegin') non_yield(n)
WHERE
    xml_record.exist ('(/Record/SchedluerMonitorEvent/NonYieldBegin)') = 1

SELECT
    @endyields = n.value ('(Yields)[1]', 'int')
FROM
    ring_buffer_scheduler_monitor_xml
```

```
cross apply
xml_record.nodes('/Record/SchedluerMonitorEvent/NonYieldEnd') non_yield(n)
WHERE
    xml_record.exist ('(/Record/SchedluerMonitorEvent/NonYieldEnd)') = 1
    AND n.exist ('Node[(text()[1] cast as xs:int?)=sql:variable("@node")]') = 1
    AND n.exist ('Scheduler[(text()[1] cast as xs:int?) =
sql:variable("@scheduler")]') = 1
    AND n.exist ('Yields[(text()[1] cast as xs:int?) >=
     sql:variable("@beginyields")]') = 1

SELECT
    'BEGIN' as State,
    @node as NodeId,
    @scheduler as SchedulerId,
    @beginyields as NumYields,
    n.value ('(Worker)[1]', 'varbinary (20)') as Worker,
    n.value ('(WorkerUtilization)[1]', 'int') as WorkerUtil,
    n.value ('(ProcessUtilization)[1]', 'int') as ProcessUtil,
    n.value (''(SystemIdle)[1]', 'int') as SystemIdle,
    n.value ('(UserModeTime)[1]', 'int')/10000.0 as UserModeTime,
    n.value ('(KernelModeTime)[1]', 'int')/10000.0 as KernelModeTime,
    n.value ('(PageFaults)[1]', 'int') as PageFaults,
    n.value ('(WorkingSetDelta)[1]', 'int') as WorkingSetDelta,
    n.value ('(MemoryUtilization)[1]', 'int') as MemoryUtilPct
FROM
    ring_buffer_scheduler_monitor_xml
cross apply
xml_record.nodes('/Record/SchedluerMonitorEvent/NonYieldBegin') non_yield(n)
WHERE
    n.exist ('Node[(text()[1] cast as xs:int?)=sql:variable("@node")]') = 1
    AND n.exist ('Scheduler[(text()[1] cast as xs:int?) =
        sql:variable("@scheduler")]') = 1
    AND n.exist ('Yields[(text()[1] cast as
xs:int?)=sql:variable("@beginyields")]')=1

UNION

SELECT
    'END' as State,
    @node as NodeId,
    @scheduler as SchedulerId,
    @endyields as NumYields,
    n.value ('(Worker)[1]', 'varbinary (20)') as Worker,
    n.value ('(WorkerUtilization)[1]', 'int') as WorkerUtil,
    n.value ('(ProcessUtilization)[1]', 'int') as ProcessUtil,
    n.value ('(SystemIdle)[1]', 'int') as SystemIdle,
    n.value ('(UserModeTime)[1]', 'int')/10000.0 as UserModeTime,
    n.value ('(KernelModeTime)[1]', 'int')/10000.0 as KernelModeTime,
    n.value ('(PageFaults)[1]', 'int') as PageFaults,
    n.value ('(WorkingSetDelta)[1]', 'int') as WorkingSetDelta,
    n.value ('(MemoryUtilization)[1]', 'int') as MemoryUtilPct
```

```
FROM
    ring_buffer_scheduler_monitor_xml
cross apply
xml_record.nodes('/Record/SchedulerMonitorEvent/NonYieldEnd') non_yield(n)
WHERE
    n.exist ('Node[(text()[1] cast as xs:int?)=sql:variable("@node")]') = 1
    AND n.exist ('Scheduler[(text()[1] cast as xs:int?) =
        sql:variable("@scheduler")]') = 1
    AND n.exist ('Yields[(text()[1] cast as
xs:int?)=sql:variable("@endyields")]') = 1
```

This returns information that shows the system health snapshots that are taken between the beginning and the end of the non-yielding scheduler. This helps to figure out what may have caused this error. For each of the columns, you can get an idea of what may have been happening to cause this event to occur:

- **WorkerUtilization.** Indicates the amount of time the worker thread spent on the scheduler without yielding.

- **ProcessUtilization.** Indicates the amount of CPU SQL Server was using when that snapshot was taken. A low amount indicates SQL Server was not using a lot of CPU. Combined with SystemIdle, it can show you if SQL Server was being starved of CPU or if it was stuck.

- **SystemIdle.** Indicates the amount of idle CPU on the system. It should be used in conjunction with ProcessUtilization.

- **UserModeTime.** Indicates the amount of user-mode CPU the worker thread used during the period it didn't yield. A higher number may indicate it was executing code in SQL Server (or one of the components it loads), which runs in user mode. Note that the UserModeTime and KernelModeTime columns are divided by 10000.0 to get the time in milliseconds. They are normally output in units of 100ns.

- **KernelModeTime.** Indicates the amount of kernel-mode CPU the worker thread used during the period it didn't yield. A higher number indicates that it spent a lot of time in the Windows kernel.

- **PageFaults.** The number of page faults that were seen at that instance. Too many may indicate that the system was paging (this can be used in conjunction with Performance Monitor).

- **WorkingSetDelta.** The difference between the last snapshot and the current SQL Server process working set (this can also be used in conjunction with Performance Monitor).

- **MemoryUtilization.** The percentage amount of memory that SQL Server is using. This is based on the amount it would ideally use on a stable system (based on max server memory settings, startup options, etc.). If it is using less than 100%, it indicates that SQL Server had to reduce its memory usage because of external factors, such as another process needing more memory on the same system.

You can examine the scheduler health records to see what the state of the server was when this problem happened. This can also be applied to the other problems that the Scheduler Monitor diagnoses, such as potentially deadlocked schedulers and non-yielding I/O completion processing:

```
select convert(XML, record) as xml_record
into scheduler_ring_buffer_xml
from sys.dm_os_ring_buffers
where ring_buffer_type = 'RING_BUFFER_SCHEDULER_MONITOR'
```

To check the state of the system, you need to extract some key values from the XML record. The columns returned have the same interpretation as the preceding query dealing with non-yielding schedulers:

```
select
    xml_record.value ('(/Record/@id)[1]', 'int') as RecordId,
    sh.value ('(ProcessUtilization)[1]', 'int') as ProcessUtil,
    sh.value ('(SystemIdle)[1]', 'int') as SystemIdle,
    sh.value ('(PageFaults)[1]', 'int') as PageFaults,
    sh.value ('(WorkingSetDelta)[1]', 'int') as WorkingSetDelta,
    sh.value ('(MemoryUtilization)[1]', 'int') as MemoryUtilPct
from
    scheduler_ring_buffer_xml
cross apply
xml_record.nodes('/Record/SchedulerMonitorEvent/SystemHealth')
Scheduler_health(sh)
where
    sh.exist ('(/Record/SchedulerMonitorEvent/SystemHealth)') = 1
order by
    RecordId desc
```

Following are some samples that have been encountered in real SQL Server deployment scenarios:

Scenario 1: In this case, a worker thread was not getting any CPU even though SQL Server was using a high percentage of CPU. For this particular case, it helped looking at the overall scheduler health, which led to the conclusion that slow I/Os on the disk subsystem were causing a worker thread to get stuck in an I/O call.

Errorlog output:

```
2006-03-24 15:07:42.94 Server    Using 'dbghelp.dll' version '4.0.5'
2006-03-24 15:07:50.94 Server    ***Unable to get thread context - no pss
2006-03-24 15:07:50.94 Server    *
*******************************************************************************
2006-03-24 15:07:50.94 Server    *
2006-03-24 15:07:50.94 Server    * BEGIN STACK DUMP:
2006-03-24 15:07:50.94 Server    *    03/24/06 15:07:50 spid 0
2006-03-24 15:07:50.94 Server    *
2006-03-24 15:07:50.94 Server    * Non-yielding Scheduler
2006-03-24 15:07:50.94 Server    *
2006-03-24 15:07:50.94 Server    *
*******************************************************************************
```

```
2006-03-24 15:07:50.94 Server        Stack Signature for the dump is 0x000001A1
2006-03-24 15:09:53.77 Server        Process 58:0:0 (0x108) Worker 0x0503E3C0
appears to be non-yielding on Scheduler 3. Thread creation time:
12787715045104. Approx Thread CPU Used: kernel 0 ms, user 0 ms. Process
Utilization 9%. System Idle 87%. Interval: 74999 ms.
```

This shows that the worker thread didn't use any CPU time, so it was most probably stuck somewhere, given that there was ample CPU left for SQL Server to process. It could have also been caused by an external factor such as memory paging on the machine (in this case, it wasn't since SQL Server was using all the memory it could and there were very few page faults; see the MemoryUtilPct and PageFaults columns below). Looking further into sys.dm_os_schedulers, four stuck I/Os were found that could be traced further by looking at sys.dm_io_pending_io_requests. This shows that you have to look at a variety of information to pinpoint the exact problem.

Output:

Scheduler Monitor Health Output:

RecordId	ProcessUtil	SystemIdle	PageFaults	WorkingSetDelta	MemoryUtilPct
3	9	86	58	32768	100
2	9	87	4	16384	100
1	29	63	2430	-1581056	100

Other scripts that were run:

```
SELECT
scheduler_address, scheduler_id, is_idle, current_workers_count,
current_tasks_count, runnable_tasks_count, pending_disk_io_count
FROM
    sys.dm_os_schedulers
WHERE
    scheduler_id < 255
```

scheduler_address	scheduler_id	is_idle	current_workers_count	current_tasks_count	runnable_tasks_count	pending_disk_io_count
0x006EC068	0		1	29		28
		0				
0x009E0068	1		1	30		28
		0				
0x00AF4068	2		1	29		26
		0				
0x00B88068	3		1	28		27
		1				
0x00D1C068	4		1	27		26
		0				
0x00F40068	5		1	30		29
		2				
0x00FD4068	6		1	29		26
		1				

| 0x00FE8068 | 7 | | 1 | 31 | 28 |
| 22 | | 0 | | | |

```
SELECT scheduler_address, io_handle, io_pending, io_pending_ms_ticks
FROM sys.dm_io_pending_io_requests
```

scheduler_address	io_handle	io_pending	io_pending_ms_ticks
0x00B88068	0x3f6	1	112812
0x00F40068	0x3f8	1	84640
0x00F40068	0x3f8	1	84641
0x00FD4068	0x3f8	1	84671

Scenario 2: Here, we found that SQL Server was not getting enough CPU by looking at the ProcessUtil and SystemIdle columns.

Errorlog output:

```
2006-03-04 09:15:11.76 Server      Process 854:0:0 (0x2058) Worker 0x1DD883C0
appears to be non-yielding on Scheduler 1. Thread creation time: 12785964184465.
Approx Thread CPU Used: kernel 0 ms, user 31 ms. Process Utilization 36%. System
Idle 0%. Interval: 74999 ms.
```

Output from non-yielding script from above:

State	NodeId	SchedulerId	NumYields	Worker		
WorkerUtil	ProcessUtil	SystemIdle	UserModeTime			
KernelModeTime				PageFaults	WorkingSetDelta	
MemoryUtilPct						
BEGIN 0		1		706	0x1DD883C0	
0	37		0	0.0		
31.0000000			2	8		100
END 0		1		707	0x1DD883C0	
0	37		0	0.0		
31.0000000			2	8		100

Output from the Scheduler Monitor health scripts:

RecordId	ProcessUtil	SystemIdle	PageFaults	WorkingSetDelta	MemoryUtilPct
70	36	0	6	0	100
66	37	0	47	-148	100
65	52	0	153	304	100
60	54	0	1486	764	100
58	43	0	131	-144	100
57	39	0	436	44	100
56	56	0	484	-96	100
55	53	0	842	-44	100
53	38	0	131	60	100

Scenario 3: Here, the worker thread was using a lot of CPU. Upon closer examination of the errorlog and the Scheduler Monitor ring buffer records, it looked like a bug in SQL Server. This should be a rare occurrence and you would need to follow up with Microsoft Support to get to the root cause of this issue.

Errorlog output:

```
2006-05-23 12:58:01.23 Server      Process 0:0:0 (0x1780) Worker 0x050200E8 appears
to be non-yielding on Scheduler 0. Thread creation time: 12792887707219. Approx
Thread CPU Used: kernel 0 ms, user 69859 ms. Process Utilization 24%. System Idle
74%. Interval: 70000 ms.
```

Output from the non-yielding script from above:

```
State NodeId       SchedulerId NumYields   Worker
WorkerUtil  ProcessUtil SystemIdle  UserModeTime
KernelModeTime                      PageFaults  WorkingSetDelta
MemoryUtilPct
----- ----------- ----------- ----------- ------------------------------------
----- ----------- ----------- ----------- ------------------------------------
----- --------------------------------------- ----------- ----------------
-------------
BEGIN 0           0           408         NULL
99          24          74          0.0000000
9953.1250000                        1           4096            100
END   0           0           410         NULL
99          24          74          0.0000000
80187.5000000                       742         368640          100
```

Using Trace 8022, you can obtain more information about a non-yielding worker. It displays more information in the errorlog about the point in time when the worker was determined to be non-yielding. For example, the following output shows one case:

```
2006-04-05 09:18:56.58 Server      Scheduler monitor trace: Scheduler 3 is
STALLED
2006-04-05 09:19:01.58 Server      Scheduler monitor trace:
   Worker         : 026BA0E8 (pass: 273)
   Wall           : 319765518
   System Use     : 639527562, User 371593, Kernel 639155968, Idle: 38835593
   System idle    : 99
   Thread Use     : 140
   Worker util    : 0
   Process util   : 0
   Page Faults    : 0
   WS delta       : 0
   Starved?       : N
   Verdict        : NON-YIELD
```

This gives more information about the conditions when the non-yielding situation was detected. It also gives more information on whether this is treated as a valid non-yielding worker by the Scheduler Monitor. Note that this traceflag produces a lot of information in the errorlog and should be used with caution.

Because the reporting gets done at 60-second intervals, it is possible that some non-yielding issues do not get caught if they run without yielding for less than 60 seconds. If an admin suspects this is happening, he can turn on Trace 1262 to dump at the first instance the Scheduler Monitor suspects a non-yielding situation. This is usually within 15 seconds of non-yielding. This traceflag will also continue dumping at every 60-second interval until the non-yielding worker finally yields. It will also dump on every occurrence of a non-yielding situation detected by the Scheduler Monitor. Therefore, this traceflag should be used with caution and should only be turned on when advised by Microsoft Customer Support Services.

You can also query the Scheduler Monitor ring buffer records (see the non-yielding scheduler examples previously) to see if there are any NonYieldBegin and NonYieldEnd records indicating any non-yielding that lasts less than 60 seconds where a dump would not be generated.

The following query can be used to determine if a worker thread on a scheduler is running long periods without yielding. This will give you a good idea about whether it is necessary to turn on Trace 1262 to debug this situation further:

```
SELECT
    yield_count,
    last_timer_activity,
    (SELECT ms_ticks from sys.dm_os_sys_info) - last_timer_activity AS
MSSinceYield,
    *
FROM
    sys.dm_os_schedulers
WHERE
    is_online = 1
     and is_idle <> 1
    and scheduler_id < 255
```

Non-yielding I/O Completion

Network I/O is done through an I/O completion Port to allow having multiple network I/Os pending that can be completed asynchronously. Each node has an I/O completion Port and a thread dedicated to listening to the I/O completion listener. The job of this thread is to get the I/O completions and call the appropriate completion routine. For network I/O, the normal completion routine either establishes the connection, or for established connections, enqueues a new task to process the new batch/query that came in with the network I/O request from the client.

Since there is only one I/O completion listener thread per node, if it gets stuck, no new network I/Os can be completed on that node. The I/O completion listener thread can get stuck when calling the user completion routine due to multiple reasons. The most common reason is the call getting stuck in the OS kernel, running low on memory and, in a few cases, a bug in the user completion routine.

The Scheduler Monitor keeps track of the I/O completion listener thread and if it notices that it hasn't made progress in two passes (~10 seconds), it will log an error message to the errorlog (17887) and generate a diagnostic userdump to allow Microsoft to debug the issue. This dump is produced only once per lifetime of the SQL instance, unless certain traceflags are enabled. The error message is written to the errorlog for all occurrences of the non-yielding scenario. This error message includes pertinent information about the amount of CPU used by the thread and memory paging.

The following sample shows output from the errorlog and corresponding output from the scheduler monitor ring buffer records showing that SQL Server was not getting enough CPU cycles to process the I/O completion:

```
2005-08-22 20:13:09.73 Server      *
*******************************************************************************
2005-08-22 20:13:09.73 Server      *
2005-08-22 20:13:09.73 Server      * BEGIN STACK DUMP:
2005-08-22 20:13:09.73 Server      *   08/22/05 20:13:09 spid 0
2005-08-22 20:13:09.73 Server      *
2005-08-22 20:13:09.73 Server      * Non-yielding IOCP Listener
2005-08-22 20:13:09.73 Server      *
2005-08-22 20:13:09.73 Server      *
*******************************************************************************
2005-08-22 20:13:49.28 Server      IO Completion Listener (0x874) Worker
0x03EFE3C8 appears to be non-yielding on Node 0. Approx CPU Used: kernel 0 ms,
user 0 ms, Interval: 15328.
```

RecordId	ProcessUtil	SystemIdle	PageFaults	WorkingSetDelta	MemoryUtilPct
490	45	0	10448	116	100
487	48	0	3815	96	100
485	60	0	792	536	100
482	55	0	618	624	100
479	57	0	1123	-372	100

Potential Scheduler Deadlock

The Scheduler Monitor checks to see that all schedulers are executing their tasks in an orderly fashion. Because of thread pooling, it is possible to have more tasks than threads/workers in the system at a given time. Those tasks that are not associated with a worker will wait until a worker becomes available (finishes processing its last task).

The Scheduler Monitor keeps track of the number of tasks that have been executed on a scheduler and if it notices that no new pending task got picked up in the last minute, it will mark the scheduler in a potentially deadlocked state. If all the schedulers belonging to a node are in this state, the Scheduler Monitor will log a message in the errorlog and also produce a diagnostic userdump for the first occurrence of this error.

A variant of this error message is if the same condition is detected, but a majority of the tasks that are executing (running) are blocked behind a common resource (Error 17888). In this case, the error message is a bit different in that it points out the resource wait type that a majority of the tasks are blocked behind. A diagnostic userdump is not produced in this case.

This can happen if the application written on top of SQL doesn't take into consideration some blocking scenarios. For example, if a session holds multiple locks for a long period of time and all the other sessions are trying to acquire it, they will be blocked until the original session releases it. Previous errors could also have caused the server to get into this situation. For example, non-yielding errors (like 17883) on all schedulers could cause the server to become unresponsive and produce this error.

Another infrequent scenario that can cause this is if SQL Server is starved of CPU resources (similar to the non-yielding scheduler) and isn't getting enough time to run. The Scheduler Monitor detects this case and does not generate a userdump, but still logs the same message (17884) in the errorlog with diagnostic information that can help an administrator diagnose this issue and figure out the cause of CPU starvation. Lastly, this can also be caused by a bug in SQL Server, and the diagnostic userdump can help Microsoft figure out the issue.

Based on what is detected from the error message and the userdump, this error can be fixed in multiple ways:

- Ensure that no other errors like 17883 have caused this to happen.

- Fix the application written on top of SQL if it is holding resources for a long time.

- Based on the waittype, it could be a configuration issue (e.g., a majority of tasks waiting on NETWORK_IO indicates that either there is a problem with the network taking a long time to complete an I/O, or the SQL clients are not processing the network I/O fast enough).

- Increase the number of worker threads that are used to process tasks. This is a tricky situation, because an increase of worker threads impacts the amount of memory available to the SQL server buffer pool. See the "Max Worker Threads Configuration" section earlier in this chapter for more information.

- It is possible that the server is hitting its peak load and either the workload needs to be partitioned, distributed, or reduced, or new hardware with faster (or more) processors or disks are needed.

To automatically detect the condition where some worker threads are blocked on certain resources for a certain threshold, use the Blocked Process Reporting configuration option. This allows you to configure a certain timeout after which it fires an event and/or a message to the errorlog if a worker thread has spent more than the threshold waiting for that resource. Resources that are currently monitored include all those that can be detected by the Deadlock Monitor. They include locks, memory grants, extended stored procedure waits, distributed queries, and network I/O.

For example, to be notified if a worker thread blocks for more than 30 seconds, configure it as follows:

```
sp_configure 'blocked process reporting', 30
reconfigure
go
```

In the following example, the errorlog shows a potential deadlocked scheduler problem:

```
2006-04-26 23:06:12.15 Server      Using 'dbghelp.dll' version '4.0.5'
2006-04-26 23:06:13.47 Server      **Dump thread - spid = 0, PSS =
0x00000000, EC = 0x00000000
2006-04-26 23:06:13.47 Server      ***Stack Dump being sent to
E:\MSSQL\MSSQL.1\MSSQL\LOG\SQLDump0001.txt
2006-04-26 23:06:13.47 Server      *
*******************************************************************************
2006-04-26 23:06:13.47 Server      *
2006-04-26 23:06:13.47 Server      * BEGIN STACK DUMP:
2006-04-26 23:06:13.47 Server      *   04/26/06 23:06:13 spid 0
2006-04-26 23:06:13.47 Server      *
2006-04-26 23:06:13.47 Server      * Deadlocked Schedulers
2006-04-26 23:06:13.47 Server      *
2006-04-26 23:06:13.47 Server      *
*******************************************************************************
2006-04-26 23:06:13.47 Server      * -----------------------------------------
-----------------------------------------
2006-04-26 23:06:13.47 Server      * Short Stack Dump
2006-04-26 23:06:20.03 Server      Stack Signature for the dump is 0x000002E4
2006-04-26 23:29:21.24 Server      External dump process return code
0x20000001.
```

In this query, a history of system health events are produced so that you can analyze if there was anything wrong with this system. Some of the rows from this query showed the following:

```
RecordId    ProcessUtil SystemIdle  PageFaults  WorkingSetDelta MemoryUtilPct
----------- ----------- ----------- ----------- --------------- -------------
90          4           7           1608        380928          3
82          4           7           2327        -4616192        3
75          6           0           2598        3772416         4
69          5           2           2156        -5660672        3
63          5           1           2828        1802240         4
60          4           0           2988        -1343488        4
55          4           1           2803        -8556544        4
54          5           0           3488        -9084928        5
53          6           3           4890        -9551872        7
51          7           0           5084        6975488         9
49          5           0           5731        -16297984       8
48          6           0           7435        -10698752       11
47          4           0           6638        -23576576       13
```

The first clue you get from these results is that the process utilization by SQL Server is very low (4%–6%) and the time spent in idle is also low (0%–7%). This indicates that another process on this system is using a lot of CPU. Furthermore, this process may also be using a lot of memory since the Memory Utilization by SQL is not at 100%. The WorkingSetDelta between records also indicates that the working set of SQL Server fluctuates a lot, most probably due to the external process. An admin would have to look at the system to find the process and why it is behaving this way.

Here is an example of errorlog output where a large number of worker threads are stuck behind a common resource (Error 17888):

```
2006-03-20 19:07:50.35 Server      All schedulers on Node 0 appear deadlocked
due to a large number of worker threads waiting on LCK_M_SCH_S. Process
Utilization 1%.
2006-03-20 19:08:50.34 Server      All schedulers on Node 0 appear deadlocked
due to a large number of worker threads waiting on LCK_M_SCH_S. Process
Utilization 1%.
2006-03-20 19:09:50.34 Server      All schedulers on Node 0 appear deadlocked
due to a large number of worker threads waiting on LCK_M_SCH_S. Process
Utilization 1%.
```

Hardware Configuration

Here, I'll talk about how hardware configuration relates to SQLOS operation and the types of hardware-related issues you can encounter.

Multi-node Machines

A lot of the new machines (especially the 64-bit machines) being introduced are employing some sort of the NUMA architecture so as to scale. It is important to understand how SQL Server makes use of this architecture in creating a server that can take full advantage of the benefits it offers.

On startup, SQL Server will query the OS to find out whether the host machine has NUMA enabled. (On some machines, it is possible to disable NUMA in the BIOS. In this case, the machine looks like an SMP machine, and memory access to different nodes is interleaved at the BIOS.) SQL Server will then map out the nodes and the CPUs associated with each node, and create the appropriate nodes and schedulers for them. In some circumstances, you may not want SQL Server to boot up in a multi-node configuration. In this case, Trace Flag 8015 can be specified in the startup trace flags to have SQL Server behave as though it is running on an SMP machine.

Some earlier machines that started making use of NUMA architecture had configurations where each node had only one CPU. For SQL Server, this was not an optimal configuration to start up in, especially when it came to executing workloads in parallel. SQL Server therefore ignores NUMA architectures and starts as if on an SMP machine, where each node has only one processor for machines that have fewer than or equal to four processors. This can be overridden by specifying Trace Flag 8021 in the startup trace flags. Newer machines sometimes have dual or multiple cores per CPU and, in this case, the OS treats each core as a CPU. Since each node appears to have multiple CPUs, SQL Server creates a node for each of these and functions correctly.

Empirical evidence shows that on a NUMA machine, a lot of resources are consumed on the default node (Node 0). Because SQL Server allocates a lot of memory on startup for data structures like the buffer pool, locks, and so on, SQL Server will normally start up on a node other than Node 0. This is to allow SQL to make the most use of resources on a normally untapped node and achieve the best locality of reference. To override this behavior in circumstances where this is not achieving its purpose, Trace Flag 8025 can be specified on startup to ensure that SQL Server starts on the default node.

Soft NUMA was also introduced to create configurations where SQL Server can best make use of the locality of reference. This was also in response to older systems that do not make use of NUMA architecture, but make heavy use of caching information at Level-3 or Level-4 caches. One example is the 32-bit Unisys ES-7000 that is identified as a Cellular Multiprocessor Machine (CMP). In this case, an admin can specify the node boundaries around a group of CPUs, and SQL Server will start up as if the machine is a NUMA machine. This can also be used on NUMA machines if further boundaries need to be created within each NUMA node. Note that a Soft NUMA node has to be within a single NUMA node and cannot traverse multiple NUMA nodes.

Since each node has an I/O completion listener, SQL Server can be configured to have unique end-points associated with a set of nodes. This allows your applications to be partitioned to make use of sets of nodes for different workloads. This is known as connection affinity, where connections are affinitized to a set a nodes. For example, a business application may have Human Resources work processing on one node, while Accounts Receivable and Accounts Payable are processing on another node. At the same time, batch jobs can be running on another node. Not only does this partition the resources between multiple nodes, it preserves locality of reference because the queries from the unique components will be making use of the same memory or code on their respective nodes. Similarly, multiple applications working against a single SQL Server can be partitioned in this fashion, too.

Hyperthreaded (HT) Machines

Intel introduced Hyperthreading technology where a single processor appears to have two processors. It does this by being able to run two threads simultaneously at the hardware level. Hyperthreading can be enabled in the BIOS of the machine.

In order to determine whether you should use Hyperthreading in your SQL Server deployment, test it to see if you see any gain with it turned on. Some benchmarks have shown up to a 20%–25% gain with Hyperthreading turned on. These applications are written in such a way that the individual worker threads or queries do not interfere with each other when running. However, some applications may see a performance loss with Hyperthreading turned on due to two threads on the same physical processor overwriting each other's local cache.

According to the Microsoft Knowledge Base, you may also want to consider configuring the Max DOP (Degree of Parallelism) to be equal to the number of physical processors on a HT machine. The idea behind this is that a parallel query plan may be limited to only as many worker threads as there are physical processors, and the chance that they might be scheduled on unique physical processors is high. You also may see a gain from it. As always, test this out before applying it in production.

If you suspect that Hyperthreading may be causing a performance slowdown on SQL Server 2005, you can try to disable one logical processor on each physical processor to see if it makes a difference. This can be achieved by setting the SQL Server Affinity Mask configuration option to only one logical processor on each physical processor. You will need to find out the correct configuration of logical-to-physical processor mapping (Intel has a tool available for download that shows this; see Intel.com for details). Two observations have been seen so far regarding the mapping of logical-to-physical processor. One is where adjacent logical CPU Ids are mapped to one physical CPU Id. For example, logical CPU Ids 0 and 1 are mapped to physical CPU Id 0. The other more common case is where the first N logical processors (logical CPU Id 0...N-1) are mapped to N physical processors. The next N logical processors (logical CPU Id N...$2N$-1) are mapped to N physical processors.

If we take an example of the second type of mapping on a four-processor physical (eight-processor logical) machine, where Physical Processor 0 contains Logical Processors 0 and 4, Physical Processor 1 contains Logical Processors 1 and 5 and so on, you could turn off Hyperthreading on SQL by configuring the Affinity Mask option as follows:

```
sp_configure 'affinity mask', 0xF
reconfigure
go
```

Multicore Machines

The newer processors coming out from Intel and AMD contain multiple cores in each physical processor. In all respects, they can be considered as unique CPUs and, depending on the architecture, may have their own unique caches or may share them between the cores.

A majority of multicore machines exhibit some sort of NUMA behavior where each processor has its own memory region from which it will always try to allocate. This architecture works well with the way SQL Server has been implemented on top of NUMA with no known issues at this time.

Given the flexibility of Soft NUMA and traceflags to configure different NUMA configurations, you can conceivably apply the same to these kinds of machines.

Dedicated Admin Connection

In the past, SQL Server could get into a situation where nothing was making progress on the server, and there was no way to find out why it got into that situation and how to resolve it. Usually, this required a reboot of SQL Server. With SQL Server 2005, a new connection called the Dedicated Admin Connection was introduced as a way for an admin to connect to SQL Server in cases where regular connections fail. Regular connections normally fail due to the system running on low resources, such as low memory or no worker threads available (possibly due to a misconfigured system or a bad application causing havoc). SQL Server achieves this by reserving necessary resources up front when it starts up.

On startup, SQL Server creates a DAC node with one scheduler in it. This scheduler has one dedicated worker thread to process admin queries. The DAC node and the DAC scheduler associated with it can be viewed in `sys.dm_os_schedulers` with the DAC node Id as 32 on a 32-bit system or 64 on a 64-bit system, and the DAC scheduler Id as 255. At the same time, the Memory Manager allocates 1MB of reserved memory for processing these queries. The SQL Networking Interface (SNI) creates a dynamic TCP/IP port to listen on and associates that port with the I/O completion listener of the DAC node. Therefore, all connection requests to this node will be processed by this I/O completion listener. Note that to connect through DAC, you can only use TCP/IP as the network protocol.

All in all, DAC uses about 2.5MB of memory for threads and memory. By default, this is disabled on the Express editions of SQL Server but can be enabled using an undocumented traceflag on the SQL Server command line.

On startup, the SQL Server errorlog will contain a message indicating whether the DAC connection listener was established and on what port. You can then connect directly to this port or, if SQL Browser is running, specify the option `-A` in `sqlcmd` to connect to it. To use SQL Server Management Studio (SSMS), prefix the server name with `admin:` to connect via the admin connection.

Examples:

With SQL Browser running:

- Connect to a local server using `sqlcmd`: `sqlcmd -E -A -S.`
- Connect to instance `FARHAT` using `SSMS:`. In the server name, specify `admin:.\FARHAT`.
- Connect to a remote server `GEEX` using `osql`: `osql -E -Sadmin:GEEX`.

If SQL Browser is not running, check the errorlog for a message indicating this.

Then, connect to SQL Server as follows:

- Connect to a remote server `GEEX` using `sqlcmd`: `sqlcmd -E -Stcp:GEEX,1450`.
- `SSMS:` Specify the server name as follows: `tcp:GEEX,1450`.

By default, you can connect to DAC only from the local machine. To enable a remote connection to the server using DAC, configure the Remote Admin Connections option to 1 to allow remote connections. This is a dynamic option and will allow remote connections without requiring a restart of SQL Server. Because there is no way to connect to a SQL cluster locally, it is always recommended to have this option turned on when running as a cluster.

To verify if your connection has indeed connected using DAC, run the following query from your connection:

```
select scheduler_id from sys.dm_exec_requests where session_id == @@spid
```

The `scheduler_id` returned should be 255, which is the scheduler id for the DAC scheduler.

Once a DAC connection is accepted, future connections to the DAC node will fail without a specific error message sent to the client. The DAC node will not accept a connection and it will appear as if the connection was broken on the client side. The errorlog will contain a message to that effect. If login auditing is enabled, you will be able to see the last connected session using DAC in the errorlog. The following example illustrates this:

```
2006-05-23 18:33:13.10 Logon      The dedicated administrator connection is
in use by "ARUSHA\farhat" on "GEEX". [CLIENT: 157.55.132.184]
2006-05-23 18:33:36.02 Logon      Error: 17810, Severity: 20, State: 2.
2006-05-23 18:33:36.02 Logon      Could not connect because the maximum
number of '1' dedicated administrator connections already exists. Before a new
connection can be made, the existing dedicated administrator connection must
be dropped, either by logging off or ending the process. [CLIENT: 127.0.0.1]
2006-05-23 18:33:36.04 Logon      Error: 17810, Severity: 20, State: 2.
2006-05-23 18:33:36.04 Logon      Could not connect because the maximum
number of '1' dedicated administrator connections already exists. Before a new
connection can be made, the existing dedicated administrator connection must
be dropped, either by logging off or ending the process. [CLIENT: 127.0.0.1]
```

A DAC connection is like a regular connection and runs the same way as a regular connection. There are only some caveats as to how it runs. There is only one worker thread available to run, it so it cannot run any queries that require parallel work to be done, such as Backup or a parallel query plan. It will use the regular system memory and, in case of failure, will use its reserved memory. Any queries that it compiles are not cached in the procedure cache (as they could have been compiled using the reserved memory). Neither is any memory cached that it allocates. Queries running on the DAC node do not have any raised priority compared to other queries—their only advantage is having reserved resources to run on. Therefore, they can block on other resources held by other sessions like locks or latches. Similarly, they can be killed by a regular connection.

Because there is only one thread and a limited amount of memory, an admin has to be careful what kind of queries she runs. This connection should be used exclusively for diagnostic purposes to resolve a condition that cannot normally be resolved through a regular connection. This would usually involve querying some DMVs to find out the state of the server and try to issue some commands to resolve the condition to let the server continue running.

The most common case where this is observed is when multiple queries end up blocking behind a common resource whose owner may have become orphaned or disappeared. In this case, an admin would usually query sys.dm_exec_requests or sys.dm_os_waiting_tasks to figure out that all of them are blocked behind a common session. The admin would then kill that session and all the other queries would be able to make progress.

Recommended queries and commands:

- DMV/Basic Single table queries

- `KILL` command

- `DBCC TRACEON/TRACEOFF`

- `SET` options

- `Sp_configure/RECONFIGURE` (for dynamic options that do not require a SQL restart, such as memory settings, affinity mask settings, etc.)

- Avoid taking too many locks (consider setting lock timeout to a small value)

Queries and commands to avoid:

- Queries that require multiple threads, such as Backup/Restore, DBCC Check, and so on

- Multiple table joins (they would require more memory)

- Statements that generate a lot of I/O

- DDL statements such as `CREATE/ALTER INDEX`

Note that DAC is not a panacea and can also lead to getting blocked or stuck, similar to regular connections. Therefore, you should only make use of it for diagnostic purposes and log off after they are done.

Further Reading

The following resources have more information about this subject:

- *Windows Internals, Fourth Edition* by Mark Russinovich and David Solomon

- *Inside SQL Server 2005* by Kalen Delaney

- *The Guru's Guide to SQL Architecture and Internals* by Ken Henderson

- *Operating System Support for Database Management*, Michael Stonebraker, Communications of the ACM 24(7), 1981, pp. 412-418

Tempdb Issues

By Wei Xiao

The basic concept of tempdb is simple: It is a system database. This means it is always present as long as SQL Server is working. It stores temporary data. This means if SQL Server is restarted, you lose all data stored in tempdb.

What kind of data can you store in tempdb? Just about anything. To the user, it is just like a regular database. You can use transactions and all the other SQL Server features, so long as you do not care about saving the data after stopping the SQL Server service.

If you store a small amount of data in tempdb, the data might not actually need to be written to disk. The SQL Server buffer manager tries to store the data primarily in memory when possible. The data gets written to disk only when there is not enough memory to cache it. SQL Server automatically decides which memory pages to write to disk based on how "hot" each page is—that is, how often the page is accessed. The more frequently a page is accessed, the hotter the page gets.

Because you can use transactions in tempdb, there is also a log file for tempdb. SQL Server transaction logs must always be written to disk. For example, if you do the following, about 1MB is written to tempdb:

```
Declare @i int
Set @i = 0
Create table #myTempTable (myBigCharColumn char (1000))
While (@i <1000) begin
Insert into #myTempTable values ('x')
        Set @i = @i +1
end
```

If your system has plenty of memory, there might not be any physical IO in the tempdb data file. However, you will see 1MB of physical IO in the tempdb log file.

What if you have an initial set of tables or stored procedures that you want to have in tempdb right after SQL Server restarts? You can create those in the model database. Each time SQL Server restarts, it copies tempdb from the model database. If you have set any database options in the model database, tempdb also inherits those.

For simplicity's sake, tempdb allows only one file group for data. By default, tempdb grows automatically based on the space required to complete database operations that involve it. This means that the tempdb file group grows until its host disk is full. Why is this the default behavior? The reason is to avoid out-of-space errors. SQL Server internally uses tempdb to store temporary data for query processing and other system tasks. Applications use tempdb to store temporary results. If you run out of space in tempdb, the server or end-user application gets an out-of-space error. By automatically using all available disk space, tempdb meets the space needs of the server and end-user applications as long as practically possible.

When SQL server restarts, the tempdb file size is reset to the configured value. (The default is 8MB.) The reason for this design is so that extra space consumed by tempdb is automatically returned to the operating system for other uses when SQL Server is cycled.

The best practice regarding file size is to configure it to 80 percent of what you believe your usage will be, and let auto-grow take care of the remaining 20 percent. If you're concerned about too much space being used, set a maximum size for tempdb files. Consider this scenario, for example:

- Disk volume D: has 5,000GB free space at the moment. You plan to put tempdb there. This disk volume is also used for other purposes.

- Estimated space usage is 200GB most of the time for tempdb. But you do not want tempdb to ever consume more than 1,000GB of space. If tempdb ever grows to be more than 1,000GB, you would rather fail the application than consume more space.

- You should set the tempdb size to 200GB with a maximum size of 1,000GB and auto-grow enabled.

Tempdb does not allow auto-shrink, and its database and file-shrink capabilities are limited. In a production system, file shrink on tempdb rarely succeeds because many hidden objects stored in tempdb by SQL Server cannot be moved by the file-shrink command.

So what should you do? My advice is to rarely shrink tempdb. You should not shrink it just because its size has grown. You should ask yourself, Is the larger size I am seeing now a normal occurrence because of my workload? If so, it does not make a lot of sense to shrink tempdb, because your normal workload will cause it to automatically grow back to its former size (or, worse, run out of space if you have disabled auto-grow).

If you do have to shrink the size of tempdb, I recommend that you do it offline with the -f SQL Server startup flags:

1. Stop the SQL Server service.

2. Find out where sqlservr.exe is on your hard drive. The default location is something like c:\Program Files\Microsoft SQL Server\MSSQL$instance name\instance folder\Binn for SQL Server 2000 and SQL Server 2005.

3. CD to that directory. Type the command sqlservr -c -f. This starts SQL server with a minimum tempdb size.

4. Use the TSQL command ALTER DATABASE TEMPDB MODIFY FILE () to change the size of the tempdb files.

5. Restart the SQL Server service.

What Has Improved in SQL Server 2005?

SQL Server 2005 did not make many external changes to tempdb. However, there are several important internal improvements:

1. Less IO activity in the tempdb log file

    For example:

    ```
    Create table #myTempTable (myBigCharColumn char (1000))
    Insert into #myTempTable values ('ABC')
    Update #myTempTable set myBigCharColumn = 'XYZ'
    ```

    Previously, 2,000 bytes of log data (both 'ABC' and 'XYZ') were written to the log. Now, only 1,000 bytes ('ABC') are written to the tempdb log file.

    This is great, but does it work for all data stored in tempdb? Unfortunately, it works only for data stored in heaps (tables without a clustered index) or LOBs. You will not see this improvement for data stored in a clustered index. Does it benefit all DML operations in tempdb? Only INSERT and UPDATE benefit. DELETE does not benefit.

2. Much faster auto-grow of tempdb data files

In SQL Server 2000, it works like this: You run out of space in tempdb's data file. SQL Server decides to grow the file by 10 percent. If your file is 10GB in size, SQL Server formats the new region of the file by writing 1GB of data (most of it is zeros) to disk. This can take awhile.

SQL Server 2005 takes advantage of the Windows API that expands the size of a file without doing IO on the new sections of the file. Because of this, growing a file occurs almost instantaneously.

This helps tempdb auto-grow significantly. There is, however, a bit of a security concern with this if the SQL Server service is not running under machine administrator credentials. It is possible for the SQL Server service to see data left by a previous process on disk. For example:

- One instance of SQL Server (we'll call it Instance A) is used to handle public information. It runs as User A on a machine. User A has normal user privileges on the machine.

- The machine has another instance of SQL Server (Instance B) that handles sensitive data. It runs as User B.

- Instance B shrinks its database file. Some sensitive data is left on disk.

- Instance A grows a file and picks up this data. Now User A can look at this data via a page-dump command (DBCC PAGE).

That is why this optimization is not always on. It requires Windows XP or 2003, and it requires special volume permissions for the SQL Server service account. If the service is running as the machine administrator, it already has these permissions.

You should take advantage of this important optimization, especially when the whole machine is used exclusively for a single SQL Server instance.

3. Improved scalability for concurrent access in tempdb

SQL Server does a good job of handling concurrent accesses to data. SQL Server also sports a full-featured, rich data store. Some features, if not used carefully, can cause performance issues when many users are trying to perform the same operation. Consider this scenario, for example:

```
Create Proc myProc As Begin
Create table #myTempTable (myBigCharColumn char (1000))
Insert into #myTempTable values ('ABC')
Drop table #myTempTable
End
```

If a large number of users are simultaneously trying to execute this procedure, they may encounter a bottleneck, because SQL Server needs to do several things to execute the procedure:

- Create metadata for table #myTempTable by inserting rows into the database system tables. These rows are visible through system views such as sys.objects in SQL Server 2005.

- Allocate two pages for the table even though the table needs only 1,000 bytes. These two pages are called the data page and the IAM page. PFS, GAM, and SGAM pages need to be scanned and updated to find and allocate these pages.

- Free the two pages as part of drop the table.

- Remove the rows from the system metadata for #myTempTable.

The tempdb metadata tables do not have many rows. Inserting and deleting a lot of rows inside tempdb can cause B-tree page-level read/write contention. These are known as page latch contentions.

Each PFS page covers a 64MB range of data. Each SGAM and GAM page covers a 4GB range of data. A lot of page allocation and free activity causes page-level latch contentions on these pages, too.

In SQL Server 2005, we did two things to reduce contention and improve the scalability in this scenario:

- We changed the page allocation algorithm so that read/write contention is not as severe as before.

- We cache metadata entries for tempory tables in tempdb so that we do not have to do many inserts and deletes in the B-tree. We track these activities in an in-memory cache instead.

4. Improved scalability for multiple files in tempdb

In SQL Server 2000, we recommend that people have the same number of files as CPUs in their system. The primary reason for this is to avoid page-level latch contention on PFS, GAM, and SGAM pages.

In SQL Server 2005, it is less important to do so because of improved scalability in our page-accessing algorithms. However, a highly concurrent workload might still encounter page latch contention. In these cases, we still recommend using the multiple-file approach.

There is another reason for using multiple files in tempdb: to achieve better IO bandwidth by file-level striping. Consider this scenario, for example:

- You have 25 physical disks in your server machine.

- You use operating system or hardware striping to group them into five volumes. Each volume has five disks.

- If you use only one tempdb file, you get only five disks working for you.

- If you use five tempdb files, one on each volume, you get all 25 disks working for you.

However, having multiple files also has its downside. SQL Server uses a proportional fill algorithm to choose the file on which to allocate the next page. The algorithm attempts to ensure that SQL Server fills each file in proportion to the free space left in that file so that they reach their maximum capacity at about the same time. In SQL Server 2000, this algorithm did not scale well when there were a huge number of page allocations. The improved algorithm in SQL Server 2005 removed these scalability limitations.

How Is Tempdb Space Consumed?

Three types of objects occupy space in tempdb—user objects, internal objects, and version store objects.

What Is a User Object?

The best way to find out what user objects are in tempdb is to do the following:

```
Select * from sys.all_objects
```

If you want to find out how much space they take as a whole, you can do this:

```
Exec Sp_spaceused
```

Perhaps a better name for user object is visible object. Some objects in tempdb that are created and managed by the server are not visible to the end user.

You might find it interesting that user-defined local temp tables also appear in the view sys.all_objects. These tables have names such as the following:

```
#myTempTable_____NNN
```

The reason for this naming convention is that different connections can have the same name for local temp tables. So, the *NNN* portion (a number) represents the connection that owns the table.

Even table variables such as @t tables also appear here. You will notice names that consist of a string of hex numbers:

F0ABCDE

This is the way table variables are named. We use an internal ID for each of them that is actually just a number.

What Is an Internal Object?

Contrary to common belief, sp_spaceused does not show all the spaces occupied in tempdb. A vast amount of space is occupied by "invisible" objects. These include internal objects and version store objects.

Most internal objects are created by queries. For example:

```
Declare @i int
Set @i = 0
Create table #myTempTable (keyColumn int, myBigCharColumn char (1000))
While (@i <1000000) begin
Insert into #myTempTable values (@i, 'x')
Set @i = @i +1
End

Select * from #myTempTable
order by keyColumn
```

The last select query has an order by. Because we have no index on 'keyColumn', it can be serviced only by sorting the result set. This particular query requires up to 1GB of internal tempdb space for sorting.

The space required for sorting in the preceding query is managed internally by a SQL Server sort work table object. This object is visible in the catalog view sys.all_objects.

Internal objects are used for lots of other purposes:

- Hash joins and hash aggregates
- Query spool to store data as part of a multistep query processing
- Keyset cursors to store the keys
- Static cursors to store the query result
- Service Broker to store messages in transit
- XML variables
- LOB variables, including TEXT, IMAGE, NTEXT, VARCHAR(MAX), and VARBINARY(MAX)
- DBCC CHECK
- Query and event notification

So how do you find out about the space occupied by these "invisible" internal objects?

SQL Server 2005 provides these three DMVs that help you determine this:

```
Sys.dm_db_file_space_usage

Sys.dm_db_task_space_usage

Sys.dm_db_session_space_usage
```

These DMVs give you a snapshot of current system activity. They can tell you how much invisible space internal objects occupy.

You may use these tools as you study each feature previously mentioned. This will give you some idea of how much space each feature requires.

What Is a Version Store Object?

Another type of invisible object is the version store object. The system creates version store objects on demand. The system can create up to one version store object every minute.

Any SQL Server 2005 feature that generates row version information may cause a version store to be created. These features include the following:

- Snapshot isolation

- Triggers

- MARS (multiple active result sets)

- Online index build

Consider this query, for example:

```
Declare @i int
Set @i = 0
Use master
Create table myBigTable (keyColumn int, myBigCharColumn char (1000))
While (@i <1000000) begin
Insert into myBigTable values (@i, 'x')
Set @i = @i +1
End
Update myBigTable set myBigCharColumn = 'y'
```

The master database always generates row versions for any update performed there. In this example, 1GB of row version information is generated by the last update statement. The version store will take 1GB of space in tempdb.

So how do you find out how much space is being occupied by the version store in tempdb?

The best way is to use the performance counter Transactions: Version store size. You can view this in Perfmon/Sysmon or using the SQL Server 2005 SQLDiag facility. It collects this counter by default.

Most internal objects are automatically freed at the end of the query in which they were created. In contrast, version store objects do not go away after the update statement that created them.

Instead, a version store is kept until the versions are no longer needed by the SQL Server instance as a whole. This is because most versions are generated for other users who might need to access them. Version stores are not needed only by the user who originally generated them.

Consider this scenario, for example:

- Assume we only have two users, A and B.

- User A starts a transaction that requires a version store. This is a snapshot isolation transaction.

- User B generates a 1GB version store. User B logs off.

- User A's transaction is open for five hours because it is doing a long and complex query. Then User A logs off.

- The 1GB row version store is removed from tempdb when User A finally logs off.

Practical Troubleshooting

Many SQL Server users never need to worry about tempdb. As mentioned previously, SQL Server uses it as a scratch space for internal data processing, but this is mostly invisible to the user. By default, the size of tempdb auto-grows based on the system's needs. As long as you have enough disk space for the work you want to perform, you can usually just let SQL Server take care of tempdb for you.

There are mainly two areas of troubleshooting for tempdb. One relates to the sizing of tempdb. The other is tempdb performance.

What to Do If You Run Out of Space in Tempdb

Many people want to know just how much tempdb space they should have. This question is difficult to answer. Space-usage estimation in tempdb is so complex that an accurate estimation is often not worth the effort. I am not even sure if it is practical to have an accurate estimate in an environment of any complexity.

The practical solution is to do some rough planning and run the system through some trial and error. You must balance several factors: hardware budget, performance, development, and testing time.

How much tempdb space can you afford to have? Most people have a finite hardware budget. You should give a reasonable amount of budget to tempdb. How much you should set aside for tempdb storage depends on your application. If you find out that you cannot afford the amount of space the application needs, you might be forced to change the application.

For example, if the application has a query that uses a hash join and a lot of tempdb space as a result, maybe you should consider changing that to a nested loop join by adding appropriate indexes or using query hints. Even if it takes longer to run, you will not need as much tempdb space.

Another example of a performance trade-off is the use of the snapshot isolation level. Without snapshot isolation, some applications experience reader-writer blocking, and throughput is low. With snapshot isolation, the application throughput is much higher, but tempdb use is bigger, too. As with many things related to performance, there are always trade-offs. What you can afford to trade for performance and how much you can afford to trade depends on your specific circumstances.

It is worth mentioning that tweaking an application has other costs besides the raw application performance cost or savings it yields. Modifying an application takes time and resources, as does testing your changes and redeploying them.

Here are some questions I recommend you ask yourself to develop a rough estimate of tempdb space usage:

- What are the main features in your application that use tempdb? You can refer to the earlier list in this chapter for the SQL Server features that use tempdb.

- For each feature, how much space will it roughly take if queries are performed in a serial way? This estimate does not have to be very accurate. You need to look at both the maximum space requirement and the most common requirement.

- Now consider which features will be used concurrently by your application. Sum the maximum space requirements of the largest set of features that will be used concurrently. This is your rough maximum tempdb space estimate.

After you have a rough estimate, you need to set up a test environment and create a workload that simulates your worst-case scenario. The closer your simulation workload mimics the real workload, the better.

If your real-world data set is too large for the test environment, you might consider a scaled-down test and multiply the scaling factor. You also need to watch out for cases where space usage is not linear to the amount of data you have.

To configure tempdb size properly, you should observe the free space in tempdb and tempdb size over a period of time.

The key point here is "over a period of time." Why is this important? Let's look at an example. Suppose SQL Server uses 10GB of tempdb space during weekdays, but on weekends it needs 30GB of tempdb to run a batch reporting job. In this case, it makes no sense to constantly shrink the tempdb file to 10GB during the week just to have it grow back to 30GB on the weekends. You should let the system keep 30GB of tempdb space. This advice applies to both the tempdb data file and tempdb log file.

No matter how accurate the planning or estimate is, you might still run out of space in production. Now what do you do?

The best practice here is to set up the SQLDiag service to constantly monitor the production system and take action before you run out of space.

A sampling method is recommended for this type of monitoring. For example, you could have SQLDiag run a query like the following at five-minute intervals:

```
Select * from sys.dm_db_session_space_usage
Select * from sys.dm_db_file_space_usage
Dbcc inputbuffer (51)
Dbcc inputbuffer (52)
Dbcc inputbuffer (53)
```

This script tells you the following:

- How free is tempdb at that moment? How is the occupied space divided among the user objects, internal objects, and version store objects?

- What is the tempdb space consumed by each session at that moment?

- What is the current batch executed by session 51 to 53?

Trapping these query outputs in a table allows you to monitor the system while it runs.

I offer this script only to illustrate a technique for monitoring tempdb. This method works well for large queries that consume a lot of space. I have seen queries that take upward of 10GB of tempdb space. These kinds of queries are not likely to finish in five minutes, so you should be able to catch them with a query like this one.

Polling the system state at five-minute intervals should not cause performance issues itself. Sometimes you will want a more-frequent collection interval. You must decide what the maximum impact your monitoring should have on the system. You can configure SQLDiag to collect data at any interval you want.

After your monitoring is set up, if you run out of space, you need to examine logged diagnostic data and determine what query is responsible. You might find that the version store is responsible for most of the space consumption. In that case, you must decide whether the versioning features should be disabled, or whether you should just add some disk space.

If a single query is consuming most of the space, and the version store is not the problem, you might not have many other options than simply increasing the disk space available to tempdb. Modifying your application to use less tempdb space might turn out to be too time-consuming to be worth the effort.

Tweaking your tempdb space usage is really just another variety of performance tuning. You find the place where you can achieve the maximum result with the minimum effort.

What Is Tempdb Page Latch Contention?

Another common issue in tempdb performance relates to latch contention. I have seen customer cases where the CPU is only 20 percent used, and the disk is only 10 percent used, but the throughput cannot improve regardless of the number of requests sent to the server.

This is a typical blocking scenario. In tempdb, a common source of blocking is the latch contention on metadata pages and on PFS, GAM, and SGAM pages.

Recall my earlier mention of SQL Server 2005's improvements in these two areas. You should see much less latch contention on SQL Server 2005; however, you might still see some contention if your application is not designed properly.

How do you identify such issues? My recommendation is still to use a sampling technique. Querying DMVs on a time interval obviously has higher overhead than querying them just one time, but latch contention is also a pretty rare issue. For example, you can execute the following pseudo-script every 100 mini-seconds:

```
Select * from sys.sysprocesses
Loop through all the processes
If blocked !=0 and lastwaittpe like 'PAGE%LATCH_%' and waitresource like '2%'
DBCC PAGE (…)
```

This script will tell you the following:

- What the waiting resource is at the moment of the snapshot
- If the process is blocked by a page latch, what type of page that is

If you collect enough data points during the time when you suspect the contention is occurring, you should be able to determine whether it is related to tempdb page latches.

Here is a scenario I have seen in the past. It was a heavily blocked system:

1. I have about 100 processes in the system.

2. I collected 1,000 data points.

3. I collected 100,000 rows from sys.processes.

4. Twenty percent of the rows have blocked != 0.

5. Among the 20 percent rows, 40 percent have a lastwaittype of PAGELATCH_UP, and page is in tempdb.

6. The output of DBCC PAGE reveals contention on data pages. The object ID of the data page shows that it is a system table.

In this case, it turns out that the stored procedure used by the application had an additional create index on a temp table, like this:

```
CREATE PROC myProc AS
create table #myTemp(k int)
insert into #myTemp values (1)
create clustered index .. on #myTemp()
```

The create index statement disabled the temp table caching functionality of SQL Server 2005.

The fix in this case is to create the clustered index in the same statement as the create table:

```
CREATE PROC myProc AS
create table #myTemp (k int primary key)
insert into #myTemp values (1)
END
```

In another case, I found out that most of the waiting a connection was doing was on PFS pages. The application was doing something like this:

```
Create table ##myGlobal (int k, myBigCharColumn varchar (4000))
Create non clustered index idx-k on ##myGlobal (k)
Insert ##myGlobal values (1, replicate ('x', 4000))
CREATE PROC myProc AS
Update ##myGlobal set myBigCharColumn = null
```

The change of row size in this heap caused lots of free-space state updates in the corresponding PFS pages.

The fix is to turn that nonclustered index into a clustered index. We do not need to update free-space information on PFS pages for B-tree pages.

Conclusion

Because it is a common resource used throughout the system, tempdb is an extremely important component in system performance and stability. By following a few common-sense rules and using tools such as SQLDiag and the server's DMVs, you can stay on top of your tempdb usage and help ensure that it supports optimal concurrency and performance.

Clustering Issues

By Cindy Gross

You're sitting at home, just about to log in to a long-anticipated XBox Live Halo tournament. The phone rings, and the operations manager informs you of a power outage that burned out several servers. One of the dead servers is a node in a SQL Server cluster—a mission-critical cluster you just inherited. You have never worked with clusters before; you were planning to dig into some documentation and experimentation next week after you got caught up. Management is nervous, because now the databases for four of the company's most critical applications are sitting on only three servers. Two of those databases are competing for scarce resources, and performance is less than optimal. Another storm is on the way, and they want full performance and full redundancy as soon as possible. What do you do? How do you get the system back up and management off your back in the shortest amount of time? That is what I am here to help you with.

The first thing you need is to be able to understand what the operations people are saying about the cluster. Lots of names are being thrown about, and you are not sure what everything means. I give you just enough information here to let you get through the situation, not so much that you spend all your time reading and no time fixing the problem. The first thing to know is that a node is a physical server. Depending on the version and edition of both Windows and SQL Server, you might have one to eight nodes (physical servers) in the cluster. The cluster name (aka cluster virtual name) is a logical (virtual) name that applications use so that they do not have to know which node (physical server) they are actually connecting to. The cluster has a name that is unique in the domain, just as the physical servers do. Each of the nodes and the logical cluster have or more IP addresses, too. Any clustered application, including SQL Server, also has a unique name and IP address. (I show you what I mean with an example. I refer to this example throughout the chapter.)

Example

This example has four nodes called Server1 through Server4. There are five instances of SQL Server; each has only one shared disk.

Cluster Virtual Name = MyCluster and the quorum drive is on the shared disk Q:

SQL Server 2005 Instance 1 Virtual Name = SQL1\SQLInst1:

data files, log files, and error log on R:, IP xxx.xxx.x.09

SQL Server 2000 Instance 2 Virtual Name = SQL2\SQLInst2:

data files, log files, and error log on S:, IP xxx.xxx.x.10

SQL Server 2005 Instance 3 Virtual Name = SQL3\SQLInst3:

data files, log files, and error log on T:, IP xxx.xxx.x.11

SQL Server 2000 Instance 4 Virtual Name = SQL4\SQLInst4:

data files, log files, and error log on U:, IP xxx.xxx.x.12

SQL Server 2005 Instance 5 Virtual Name = SQL5\SQLInst5:

data files, log files, and error log on V:, IP xxx.xxx.x.13

Each server has two network cards, each with its own IP address. One is for private communication within the cluster. The other is for public network communication. Some of the other clusters in your environment have multiple public networks on each server, but this particular cluster does not. (See Figure 10-1.)

Your coworkers tell you that normally SQL1\SQLInst1 is owned by Server1, SQL2\SQLInst2 is owned by Server2, SQL3\SQLInst3 is owned by Server3, and the quorum, SQL4\SQLInst4, and SQL5\SQLInst5 are owned by Server4. You lost Server1 today, and SQL1\SQLInst1 has failed over to Server2. All nodes are possible owners for all SQL Server instances, so potentially any instance could reside on any node. Although it would probably be bad for performance, any single node could host all five instances of SQL Server (assuming it had enough resources available for all of them to start).

So you're probably wondering what all the terms I have used here really mean.

Example   427

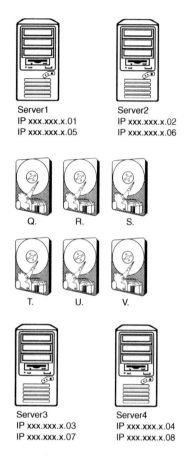

FIGURE 10-1   A sample cluster configuration

A *cluster resource* is anything that you want clustered or virtualized. SQL Server cluster resources include one or more shared disks, the SQL Server virtual name, one or more SQL Server IP addresses, the SQL Server service, the SQL Server Agent service, and the Full Text resource. (It is a pointer to the single MSSearch service with SQL Server 2000, a service that is also used by Sharepoint and so on; it is an actual separate service per SQL Server instance in 2005.) Individual resources cannot be failed over; they are part of a group, and failover is performed for the entire group. Each resource can belong to only one group.

A *cluster group* is a group of related cluster resources. When one of the resources fails, you generally want the entire group to fail. (You can choose to configure an individual resource to not cause the group to fail, but this is not the default.) You can only fail over the entire group; you cannot fail over individual resources. Therefore, for maximum high availability and flexibility, you do not want to add resources to a group if they can exist independently on a different node than the other resources.

In the context of a cluster, a *shared disk* is a disk that can be owned over time by any con-figured node in the cluster, but it can be owned only by one node at a time. The disk is connected by a controller to each node in the cluster, and at failover time one of the nodes takes ownership of the shared disk and handles all IO to that disk. This is not the same as sharing a drive (aka mapping a drive).

The point of having a cluster is that a cluster group can *fail over* to other nodes in the cluster. You can configure which nodes a group can fail over to, so you could have, for instance, a four-node cluster, but for a given group its possible owners are only node1 and node2. A failover means that all resources in the group are taken offline on the currently owning node and are "moved" to another node. That node takes ownership. (For any resource, it starts handling all IO, memory, and CPU requests; for a service, it starts the service on the owning node and services it just like a local service.) As an administrator, you may request a failover via cluster.exe or the Cluster Administrator GUI. More com-monly in a troubleshooting scenario, a failover happens because some predefined thresh-old was met that caused the cluster service to request a failover of the cluster group.

In a cluster, a *dependency* indicates that one resource cannot be brought online until another starts. For instance, the SQL Server service is dependent on at least one shared disk. If any of the disks do not come online, the SQL Server service cannot come online. (The service cannot start.) Dependencies are defined by SQL Server setup and can be mod-ified in the Cluster Administrator. Generally, you do not want to modify dependencies in the SQL Server group except for adding dependencies on additional shared disks. SQL Server cannot use a disk for data or log files or for "local" backups unless it is dependent on that disk.

Troubleshooting steps often involve taking either resources or entire groups *online* or *offline*. If a resource is online, it is available for use; under its virtual name, it looks just like it would as a standalone resource on the network. If a resource is offline, it is unavail-able. When you fail over a group, any online resource is brought offline and then brought online on the new node. However, any offline resource stays offline even after a failover; there is no attempt to start it on the new node. You can use this as a workaround if a less-important resource is affecting the group.

Each resource has a *LooksAlive* lightweight check to see whether it appears to be working. For the SQL Server service resource, this is a query to the operating system to see whether it looks like the service is up. Each resource also has an *IsAlive* check that is a bit more thorough. For the SQL Server resource, the IsAlive check is a simple query against the master database. This actually verifies that the cluster service can connect to SQL Server and retrieve a small result set within the configured time limit. There are times when the LooksAlive check succeeds but an IsAlive check fails. When the IsAlive check fails the configured number of times, it causes the group to fail (assuming it is set to affect the group).

You will hear people throwing around the word *quorum*. The quorum is the agreed-upon place for storing information common to the Windows cluster. Microsoft Windows clus-tering stores this information on a shared disk called the quorum disk. The quorum disk is a disk resource in the same resource group that also has the Windows cluster virtual name and the Windows cluster IP address. This group can reside on any node (server) in the cluster and can be failed between nodes without disrupting the activity of the other clustered groups. The group is often called the *Windows cluster group* or the *quorum group*.

Along with the data stored on the quorum, registry keys exist that need to be kept in sync. The quorum stores information about *what "checkpointed" registry keys* have changed. A checkpointed key can be identified by its existence in the cluster registry key hive. SQL Server setup adds several of its keys to the checkpoint list, including the keys that store the location of the master database data and log and the location of the SQL Server error log. The propagation of changes to these keys to other nodes in the cluster is called *registry cloning*.

Tools

Now that you can understand what everyone is saying, I'll walk you through some of the tools you can use to troubleshoot. Some of them will be familiar to you from troubleshooting problems on nonclustered SQL Server instances.

SQLDiag.exe is a valuable troubleshooting tool for any SQL Server instance. It gathers all the SQL Server error logs and configuration settings. In SQL Server 2005, you can configure SQLDiag to gather other information such as the event logs, a Profiler trace, and a Performance Monitor log. In SQL Server 2005, you can configure SQLDing to gather other information, such as the event logs, a Profiler trace, and a Performance Monitor log for SQL Server. For SQL Server 2000, you would use the PSSDiag utility available from Microsoft Customer Support Services and at http://www.microsoft.com.

The *cluster log* is not specific to SQL Server; it contains information about when any resource fails the LooksAlive or IsAlive check and tracks when resources are brought online and offline. All times in the cluster.log are in GMT in Windows 2000 and Windows 2003. You can find the cluster.log in the cluster directory under the systems folder.

The *event logs* can be a good source of information. Look for any error around the same time as whatever problem you are troubleshooting. Often, you will find that your problem is due to a disk failure or a network issue of some sort. Or perhaps some problem first occurred after a security policy or other domain policy was pushed to the computer. Make sure your event logs are set to keep an appropriate amount of information; on some systems, the default settings mean the logs are overwritten too frequently, and you can lose valuable troubleshooting information. If you are working on a machine in a different time zone than your local machine and are saving logs for later use, you might find it useful to save copies of the logs in text format, because that will preserve the machine's local time. The event logs are collected by SQLDiag in SQL Server 2005 and by PSSDiag in SQL Server 2000.

If you're getting some sort of "file not found" error, it could indicate that a file or registry key no longer exists or the process does not have sufficient permissions for the file or key. You can download tools such as *FileMon* and *RegMon* from http://www.sysinternals.com to help troubleshoot these types of issues.

Sometimes you need to check the settings for various registry keys, such as the location of the master data and log files. *Regedit.exe* is a useful tool in these situations. However, keep in mind that, in a cluster, extra steps are necessary to change the checkpointed keys.

Cluster Administrator is used for operations such as manually failing over to another node, reviewing and changing configuration settings, taking resources or resource groups offline or bringing them online, and changing cluster resource dependencies. There is also the command-line cluster.exe to perform these operations.

Sometimes the *SQL Server error logs* give you a clue as to why you are seeing problems. Always check the SQL Server error logs for messages that might indicate the problem or just to see what was happening around the time of your problem. They are collected by SQLDiag in both SQL Server 2005 and SQL Server 2000.

SQL Server *Profiler* is a great tool for seeing exactly what queries are being sent to SQL Server and how long they take to execute. Use Profiler on a cluster just like you would use it on a standalone instance. SQLDiag can also be configured to collect Profiler traces (it does not require or use the Profiler tool.)

System Monitor (also called Performance Monitor, PerfMon, or SysMon) is often used to monitor general performance as well as SQL Server-specific components. The impact to the system depends on which counters you choose and the sampling interval you use. These counters can be collected by SQLDiag in SQL Server 2005 and by PSSDiag in SQL Server 2000.

SQL Server 2005 has a new feature called *DAC* (Dedicated Administrator Connection). If it is enabled, you can use DAC to connect over TCP/IP to a SQL Server instance that is otherwise unavailable. By default, it is enabled only for local connections; you have to use the SAC utility or sp_configure to enable it for remote connections. Because all connections are remote in a cluster, you always have to manually enable this setting to be able to use DAC on a cluster. The SQL Server error log tells you which TCP/IP port is being used for the DAC connection; you might need to specify the port number in some situations where you have a loss of connectivity. DAC is for emergency situations only, and there are some limits on what you can do under that connection, mostly related to memory. See Books Online for more details.

Get Performance to an Acceptable Level

Let's get back to the problem at hand. Your users report that performance is fine on most applications, but two of the applications are much slower than normal. For simplicity in this chapter, I assume that each application uses a single database, and no two applications share a database. No changes occur to any middle-tier servers. So, application and database performance are the same for our purposes. If this is not the case in your environment, you will have to do extra troubleshooting steps to verify where the performance bottleneck actually resides.

The first thing to do is see whether you can improve performance while you order or reassign hardware. To do that, you must determine why performance is bad to begin with. Most likely it is because you have one physical server handling more activity than it was designed to handle. Most commonly the scarce resource is memory, although it could be IO or CPU. I do not get into the details of how to manage memory, but I do explore some of the things you need to check. From there, you can treat the problem just as you would a problem on a standalone system. See Chapter 3, "Memory Issues," for more info on troubleshooting memory-related problems.

For this example, I assume you used the troubleshooting techniques from Chapter 3 to determine that the problem in this case is insufficient memory. I'm using this as an example because memory is often misunderstood and often not well planned on a cluster.

The first thing to check regarding memory is whether you have enabled any of the SQL Server instances to use AWE, to have a set maximum memory limit, or to lock pages in memory. You should also check whether you have /3GB, /PAE, or /NOPAE in your boot.ini. These settings impact how much memory each SQL Server instance has and how well they play together. Depending on your settings, the first instance to reside on the node might "hog" all the memory, or it might eventually share equally with all other SQL Server instances. The specifics of how these settings impact your SQL Server instance depend on the version and edition of both Windows and SQL Server and also depend on whether you are using 32-bit or 64-bit. See Chapter 3 for more information.

Let's say that your instances are not using AWE or /3GB and you have not chosen to lock pages in memory. Therefore, the SQL2\SQLInst2 instance is configured to share memory. At the time of failover, the SQL Server instance SQL2\SQLInst2 was already running on Server2 and had been allocated almost 2GB of physical memory. Because it has periods of time when it is not actively using all the memory allocated to it, over time the SQL Server instance releases memory to the operating system, because the operating system is receiving requests from SQL1\SQLInst1 for more memory. As that memory is released, SQL1\SQLInst1 takes the memory if it needs it. Therefore, it is possible that eventually, depending on your configuration and the load on each instance, the two instances could balance out the memory in such a way that performance is acceptable for both instances. Unfortunately for you, in this particular scenario, that is not the case. The original owner of the cluster did not account for a doubling in the number of users/queries against both instances over the past year, and the server hardware is not sufficient to handle the needs of both SQL1\SQLInst1 and SQL2\SQLInst2 at the same time. Long term, you need to address this lack of resources. For now, however, you just need to get performance back to an acceptable level.

Here are some things you can consider doing, depending on your environment:

- It is likely that each instance needs a different number of resources to meet its needs. Depending on your environment, it might be possible to redistribute the SQL Server instances so that each server in the cluster has enough resources to meet the needs of the instances it is servicing.

- Although your managers will say that all the applications are equally important and that they all have to be operating at maximum capacity, we both know that is not really the case. Make your management choose what is most mission-critical. Redistribute the SQL Server instances so that the most important applications have sufficient resources and the other applications (databases) fight for resources on a single server (isolating slow performance to less-important applications/databases).

- Add memory, disks, or CPUs to one or more servers (temporarily or permanently) to address whatever bottleneck you have identified.

- Change the memory settings.

- Live with the slower performance temporarily.

- Longer term, you might be able to tune the application(s) so that it uses fewer resources.

Add a Node

Your hardware people tell you they've found a server you can add to the cluster. Maybe they got a new one, or maybe they pulled one from a test system or a less-important production system; but as long as the hardware and Windows version, edition, and 32/64-bitness are identical to the other nodes in the cluster, you do not care. The network administrators add the node to the Windows cluster, verify that they can fail over the quorum group to the new node, and hand it off to you. They have given the new server the same physical server name and IP addresses as the lost server. What next?

Get Prepared

You will save yourself a lot of trouble by preparing properly before you try to add the node. You can use these same basic steps to avoid problems during a new install of a clustered instance, too. If you get an error during setup—whether it's the initial install, adding or removing a node, upgrading, or anything else—revisit these steps to make sure you followed them all exactly.

- Determine the version, edition, service pack, and hotfix level of each instance:

```
SELECT SERVERPROPERTY('productversion'), SERVERPROPERTY ('productlevel'),
SERVERPROPERTY ('edition')
```

- Make sure you have the correct installation files for each version and edition (and 32/64-bit) of RTM. This is generally available on a CD or on a corporate network share. Then make sure you have the correct installation files, again per version and edition (and 32/64-bit), for whatever service packs or hotfixes are installed on each instance. Copy them to a location every node can see (has permissions to), either a commonly available share or one of the local drives on the cluster itself (as long as it is shared). Do not copy the files to the shared drive, because the other nodes (the ones that do not currently own the shared drive) will not be able to see the files, and setup will fail. The service packs for both SQL Server 2000 and SQL Server 2005 are cumulative. So, you only have to install the most recent service pack for your version of SQL Server.

- Review the ReadMe file that comes with each setup program for any issues specific to that build. Also search http://support.microsoft.com for known issues with each setup program.

- Add whatever account you will be using for executing the setup process (the account you use to log on to Windows) to the local administrator group on the newly added node (to all nodes for a new install). For SQL Server 2000, add the SQL Server startup account to the local administrators group or at least give it the minimum list of permissions as listed in the updated Books Online. For SQL Server 2005, create a group and add the SQL Server startup account to it.

- If at all possible, do all the setup directly (physically) from the node itself. There can be complications with permissions (leading to various errors) and temporary directories (leading to "file not found" errors) if you connect to the server using any sort of remote-control software such as the Terminal Services client.

- Verify that each network name has no spaces or special characters (anything other than a letter or number). Make sure there is no space at the end of the name. You should do this even if prior installs have succeeded; someone might have changed the network name since the last successful install. Special characters in the network name can cause SQL Server 2000 setup to fail.

- If this is a named instance of SQL Server 2000 and you are using Windows 2003, you need to create a named pipes alias for each node involved in setup. The name of the alias is the virtual server\instance name. This is necessary because until you apply SP3 of SQL Server 2000, TCP/IP connectivity is blocked, which will cause setup to fail.

- Stop all nonessential applications and services. They might have locks on files that SQL Server setup needs to replace. The most common culprits for locking files are antivirus software, IIS, backup software, WMI, and monitoring software such as MOM. However, many other services could cause problems, so it is best to stop all nonessential services and applications.

- Verify that the Task Scheduler service and Remote Registry service are both started on all nodes.

- Set the Windows local policies Unsigned driver installation behavior and Driver Signing security levels to Warn or lower. In general, all Windows policies should be identical on all nodes.

- For a service pack installation, make sure none of your existing SQL Server or MDAC files are configured to be read-only.

- Make sure the terminal services component is not installed if this is a Windows 2003 server. This refers only to the server component; it is acceptable to have the machine configured to accept Remote Desktop (MSTSC) connections.

- Verify that the registry key `HKEY_LOCAL_MACHINE\SYSTEM\CurrentControlSet\Control\FileSystem\NtfsDisable8dot3NameCreation` is set to 0.

- Verify these settings at the Windows level:

  - The network adapters for each node should be set to identical, manual speeds.

  - In Network and Dial-up Connections and in the Cluster Administrator priorities, the external public network should be listed first.

  - The heartbeat/private adapter should only have TCP/IP enabled. (If you have a Majority Node Set cluster, see your vendor recommendations about additional protocols.)

  - Disable NetBIOS over TCP/IP should be set on for the WINS tab of your network settings.

  - You should also review Microsoft Knowledge Base article 258750, *Recommended Private "Heartbeat" Configuration on a Cluster Server.*

SQL Server 2005 Setup

For SQL Server 2005, all the cluster-aware components except the client tools and SSIS are upgraded per instance. The tools and SSIS are upgraded per node. This means you install the instance one time no matter how many nodes are involved. However, you have to install or upgrade the tools and SSIS one time on each node, regardless of how many instances exist. The setup logs are the same as for standalone setup for the most part, although you will have multiple copies of each log file, one for each node in the cluster. All the setup files from each node are collected locally on the node where setup was launched, except for C:\Windows\Tasks\SchedLgU.Txt. This file must be gathered from each node. For the most part, the troubleshooting is the same as for a standalone instance.

SQL Server 2000 Setup

For SQL Server 2000, everything is upgraded per instance. In other words, you run setup one time per instance, and everything (including the client tools) is installed on every node. (Note that this does not apply to any Analysis Services, Notification Services, or Reporting Services instances; those have to be separately installed and manually clustered in SQL Server 2000.) So, you run setup on the node that owns the first instance. This adds the newly added node as a possible owner of that instance. You can do this while the instance is online, and there will not be any downtime. However, it does not have any service packs or hotfixes, so you cannot failover the instance to this node yet. Now you can apply whatever service pack you need to for this instance. If you run the service pack setup for Service Pack 3 or later from the newly added node, there will not be any downtime for the instance. However, if you need to apply a hotfix after the service pack, there will be downtime for the instance. Repeat the installation for each instance that needs to be able to fail over to the newly added node.

There are several SQL Server 2000 RTM setup logs. If the setup failed with the "Setup failed to perform required operations on the cluster nodes" error, the first log to look at is sqlstp.log in the Windows directory on the node where you ran setup. This is the master log for setup and tracks what is done on the node that is running setup. It tracks common things such as configuring the single copy of the system databases and the launching of other processes.

One of the things setup does is launch a remote unattended install (yes, even for the local node) for each node involved in setup. Therefore, for each node involved in the installation, setup creates a sqlstp$X$.log, where X is an incremental number one greater than the largest sqlstp$X$.log currently on that node. This log is written to each node. In the case of adding a node, you would have sqlstp.log on the node that owns the group and sqlstp$X$.log on the node being added. In the case of a full setup, you would have the main sqlstp.log on the node that owns the group (the node where you launched setup) and a sqlstp$X$.log on each node, and the X could theoretically be a different number on each node. The sqlstp$X$.log has information on the file copies and registry key changes as well as the MDAC setup on that particular node. Review these logs for any errors and search on http://support.microsoft.com for any errors you find. Look for any unexplained gaps in time. Something that takes longer than expected is a potential source of your problem. If there are no specific errors, check for what happened just before the generic error.

If setup failed with the message "An error occurred while creating virtual server resources for clustering. The system cannot find the file specified," start your troubleshooting by looking at the sqlclstr.log in the %systemroot%\Winnt\Cluster folder. This log tracks changes to the Windows cluster such as updating the resource and resource group information. It also tracks updates to Full Text Search related to the cluster.

General (SQL Server 2000 and 2005)

Repeat the installation steps (RTM, service pack, and hotfix) for each instance on the cluster. If you do not run setup for any one of the instances, that instance might not be able to fail over to this node. (The node will not be a possible owner for that instance.) Even if SQL Server could successfully start with mismatched files, there is a good chance that incompatibilities would exist between the code in the databases and the code in the binaries.

If you have any problems during setup, first make sure that you followed all the steps in the "Get Prepared" section. Then, verify that the Windows cluster is working and that you can failover the quorum group to the newly added node. If you cannot fail over the quorum group, the problem is outside SQL Server. If you still cannot install after that point, you must look at the setup logs.

In our particular scenario, your goal is to get one instance back to its preferred node as soon as possible and to have four nodes available so that the other instances have another node to fail over to in case of failure. Therefore, it is likely that in a 24/7 shop with more than two nodes, you would only run setup (RTM + SP + hotfix) for the instance that needs to run on the newly added node. You would likely wait and arrange a time later when it would be best to add this newly added node as a possible owner of the other instances. However, if you have only a two-node cluster, you would want to add back all instances as soon as possible so that all the instances have a place to fail over to. I recommend that you carefully evaluate your business needs and your specific environment before you make your decision on this.

Okay, so now your new node is installed. You can now move everything back to its preferred node. You move SQL1\SQLInst1 back to Server1. Everything is great, and you can go back home and enjoy what remains of the weekend and the XBox tournament! Great job!

After the Crisis

Now it is Monday. Your boss was impressed with how you handled the crisis over the weekend. Management can see that you are an expert at clustering, and they have assigned you to handle all future SQL Server clustering issues. I want to congratulate you on this exciting opportunity!

The first and most important thing to realize is that just because something happens on a cluster, that does not mean the problem is at all related to the clustering. So, do not panic. Your existing SQL Server knowledge and troubleshooting experience will still be valuable assets. There are some minor differences in some troubleshooting steps due to the virtualization, but for the most part, "cluster" problems have little to do with clustering. Take, for example, my favorite "cluster" problem: Why did the clustered SQL Server instance fail over?

Why Did My Clustered SQL Server Instance Fail Over?

What is a failover? An unplanned failover occurs when some resource in the cluster resource group meets a failure threshold. When a resource in the group fails, all resources are closed on the current physical server. For services, this means they are stopped. For disks, ownership is relinquished. Then the entire group, never an individual resource, is "moved" to another node. This means that the cluster service tells another server to take ownership of the resources and start them up. For services, this means the cluster service stops the service on the original node and starts the service on the new node.

If your SQL Server instance fails over, the first assumption is that the SQL Server service caused the failure. That is not always true. By default, all resources in the group are set to cause the group to fail over if the resource fails. If all resources are essential, this is the correct setting. However, sometimes the failure can be caused by a resource that you are not even using or that could be handled another way. You have to fail over the group as a whole (move all resources in the group to be hosted by another instance in the cluster);

you cannot fail over individual resources. But you can set individual resources to not cause the group to fail over by changing the "affect the group" setting for the resource in Cluster Administrator. If you aren't using a resource, you could even just take it offline. (Set it to never try to start and therefore never cause a failure.) If you are actively using a resource but temporary outages of that resource are not a big deal, you can set it to not "affect the group" but still stay online. You could even choose to send a notification of some sort or an automated response via custom code. This might be something you would do with SQL Agent or the Full Text Search resource, for instance.

If it is actually the SQL Server service resource that caused the failover, it is because SQL Server did not respond to an IsAlive request within the configured time. If you know this might happen periodically for some reason, you can change the IsAlive settings so that the service resource waits longer before causing a failover. In most cases, however, you need to find the underlying problem. The IsAlive check is just a connection to SQL Server followed by a simple, short-running query. If this fails, you might have a network problem, or SQL Server might be too busy to respond to either the connection request or the query. If you are paying close attention, you will notice that the underlying problem has nothing to do with clustering. You have a connectivity or performance problem to troubleshoot. Treat it like a standalone server and find out first whether you can connect to the SQL Server instance from the server that owns the quorum, from any node in the cluster, or from any clients in the domain. If you cannot connect from any particular location, troubleshoot it like a standalone connectivity problem. If you can connect, the problem is almost certainly related to performance. So, troubleshoot it like any other performance issue. See Chapter 5, "Query Processor Issues," for more info.

As you can see, other than understanding the terminology and knowing how the IsAlive functionality works, you do not need any special cluster knowledge to troubleshoot this scenario.

Why Does It Take So Long to Fail Over?

The time to fail over is how long it takes to shut everything down on the previously owning node and then start everything on the newly owning server. Occasionally, a slow failover could be due to a problem with a disk or controller; in my experience, however, generally either the shutdown or startup of the SQL Server service takes a long time. If there are long-running queries on the SQL Server, it waits for them to complete before shutting down and attempts to checkpoint each database. After a while, the cluster service stops waiting for a shutdown and forces the service to stop by killing the process. Then, the cluster service starts SQL Server on another node. If there are many transactions or one or more large transactions to undo/redo, this could take a while. So, in this scenario, you need to take a look at your application design. For instance, see whether you can reduce transaction size. Or you might need to do general performance tuning.

Neither of these are problems specific to clustering, so you troubleshoot them just as you would on a standalone system. Again, when you understand the terminology, successfully troubleshooting an issue on a cluster amounts to narrowing it down to a problem you are familiar with.

After Failover No One Can Connect

A common cause is that your instance is configured to use a static port and the port is in use by some other application on the new node. Check the SQL Server error log to see whether there are any errors, especially errors about not being able to open a TCP/IP port. Also check to see whether you can connect with named pipes (np:ServerName). You can resolve this issue by changing the instance to use dynamic ports. If you use a dynamic port, SQL Server tries the start with the last port it used; but if it cannot do so, it chooses another port. This is fine unless you have clients who have hard-coded the port number in their connection string or ODBC DSN. Another workaround is to track down what is using the static port and either change which port SQL Server uses or change which port the other application uses. This is no different than on a standalone instance.

Another potential cause of not being able to connect after SQL Server restarts (remember, a failover is just a stop and then a start on a different node) is that the server itself is not available on the network. Try to ping the node and the Windows virtual name and IP and connect to a network share on the node. Check for errors in the event logs and SQL Server error log. If that particular node is not available, either troubleshoot it as you would a standalone server or, at least temporarily, move that SQL Server cluster group to another node in the cluster.

Both named pipes and TCP/IP protocols must be enabled for a clustered instance of SQL Server. Verify this through the SQL Server Configuration Manager.

Verify that the SQL Server service is actually online. If not, troubleshoot why. Remember, being online means that the service is started. If the service will not start, check that SQL Server error log to see why it will not start. The service must be set to manual, not automatic. Again, troubleshoot it just like a standalone instance. For starters, try starting the service outside of the Service Control Manager by starting if from the command line with the -m parameter.

Add Disks

You have just added a new shared disk to your cluster. You want to put your SQL Server backups or maybe even some data or log files on this shared disk, but you cannot seem to do so. Why not? To read from or write to a disk, the disk must be in the SQL Server instance's group, and the SQL Server instance has to depend on the disk. This implies that each shared disk can be used by only one instance. To add the disk to a group and add the dependency, use the Cluster Administrator.

Replace a Disk

You have a disk that is misbehaving or just too slow. You want to replace it. At the Windows cluster level, you have to add the disk with the same drive letter as the old disk. You also have to update the Windows signature. But at the SQL Server level, as long as the disk has the same drive letter, all you have to do is put the files from the old disk on the new disk in the exact same location.

Move a Database

You need to move one or more files for a database to a different drive. This is pretty much the same as it would be on a standalone instance. The only difference is that the new drive must be in the SQL Server instance's resource group, and the SQL Server service must depend on the drive.

Conclusion

I hope you have enjoyed the journey through SQL Server clustering. As you can see, when you get over the initial terminology hurdles, it is really not that complicated. You need to troubleshoot most problems just as you would on a standalone SQL Server instance.

The Aging Champion

by Ken Henderson

About two weeks into his new job, Joe's boss asked if he'd like to meet Tom. Tom was the senior-most guy on the team. The boss, realizing Joe had a comparable amount of industry experience to Tom, thought they should get to know one another. Sounded good to Joe.

The boss walked Joe to Tom's office and casually asked, "Hey, Tom, you got time to meet Joe?" Tom was sitting at his desk reading a book. He looked up and replied dismissively, "No, as a matter of fact I don't," and returned to his book without ever looking at Joe.

Joe looked sheepishly at his boss. His boss looked back at him and shook his head. They both shrugged and left.

Joe later came to understand that this type of behavior wasn't unusual for Tom. From what he learned, Tom had gone to great lengths to wall himself off from the "little people" in the organization—to the point of sometimes reacting quite negatively if they emailed or spoke to him directly. He was, in fact, known for flaming people, along with their manager (and sometimes their manager's manager), whenever he felt like it. His own manager had neglected ever to raise the possibility with him that this might not be the best way to mentor people or bring along new hires. He had a few select buddies with whom he was generally cordial, but as for most everyone else, he appeared to believe he was above even speaking to them.

Over the years, Tom had come into possession of quite a treasure trove of valuable information about how the organization's business ran. He was good at his job—no one disputed that. Because he was in sole possession of so much of this crucial domain knowledge, and because so much of it existed nowhere but in his head, he was able to exert a fair amount of control over the organization even though he wasn't part of its management team. He carefully peddled his prized knowledge to his friends and held out on those whose careers he wanted to impede. Little by little, he fashioned his own clique within the team by sharing what he knew only with those whom he could trust not to share it with people he didn't like. Over time, he and his cronies built quite an exclusive little club for themselves. It was widely known in the organization that being Tom's friend was a prerequisite for career advancement.

Tom was so out of touch with the industry in which he worked that he was unaware of Joe's many accomplishments in it before joining the company. Even though Tom was a senior member of the staff, he was uninterested in maximizing Joe's value to the company. He didn't care whether the company got its money's worth out of Joe or not, and would just as soon Joe had never been hired. By doing things like refusing to greet Joe, he went out of his way to let Joe know that he didn't want him around and didn't care what talents he might have to offer the company.

Years passed, and Joe continued to be cordial with Tom when he saw him. Joe's career advanced within the company despite Tom, and eventually Joe was offered a position he knew Tom himself would like to have had.

Taking a cue from Jack Nicholson's character in *Wolf*, Joe asked management if they would let him tell Tom he had accepted the new position, and they agreed. Joe walked into Tom's office early the next morning and told him about his new position. Tom was visibly stunned, not even having been aware that the position was open. It was one he clearly wished he had been offered, but realized he'd been passed over for. All his scheming and snobbery had ultimately failed. The stranglehold he had on the organization was broken.

Tom moped around for a few days thereafter. Joe would see him at the water cooler from time to time. Tom kept muttering something about people not listening to him anymore. Evidently, he believed he should have at least been consulted before Joe was offered his new job and was miffed that hadn't been the case. He even briefly considered quitting his job "just to show them." Joe would just smile and go on his way.

There's a lesson to be learned here, and it has to do with the value of humility. Becoming arrogant and walling yourself off from the "little people" in the world is a fast ticket to stagnation. It's a good way to stop growing professionally. There are no little people. The world moves too quickly not to learn all you can from whomever you can whenever you can. No matter how long I work in this business, I continue to learn from practically everyone around me—new people and old alike, experienced and inexperienced as well. I have always considered myself lucky to have worked with so many great people over the years.

No matter who you are, you are never above exchanging a warm greeting or lending a helping hand when you can. People frequently write me or contact me for help, sometimes with the most esoteric of questions, and I do the best I can to assist them. I've been where they are, and their requests keep me moving—they keep me on my toes. I'm keenly aware that I owe much of what I've learned over the years to the many fine people I've had the privilege of coming in contact with, and exchanging a cordial greeting with them or helping them in some small way is the least I can do.

And you have to remember that there is always someone out there who's bigger and better. When you work harder at trying to hold other people back than at helping them realize their potential, you make what should be teamwork into a zero-sum game where only one party can win—everyone else, by definition, must lose. Even if you prevail for a time, this sets you up for what I call *the aging champion syndrome*. Eventually someone will come along that you can't stop. He'll be quicker or smarter or more determined than you in some way, and you'll soon find yourself lying flat on your back, knocked out of the match, staring up at the ref while he shouts out the 10-count, wondering why no one listens to you anymore.

Index

A

M

N

S